SITUATION THEORY
AND ITS
APPLICATIONS

CSLI
Lecture Notes
No. 26

SITUATION THEORY

AND ITS

APPLICATIONS

Volume 2

edited by
Jon Barwise, Jean Mark Gawron,
Gordon Plotkin, and Syun Tutiya

 CENTER FOR THE STUDY
OF LANGUAGE
AND INFORMATION

CSLI was founded early in 1983 by researchers from Stanford University, SRI International, and Xerox PARC to further research and development of integrated theories of language, information, and computation. CSLI headquarters and the publication offices are located at the Stanford site.

CSLI/SRI International **CSLI/Stanford** **CSLI/Xerox PARC**
333 Ravenswood Avenue   Ventura Hall   3333 Coyote Hill Road
Menlo Park, CA 94025   Stanford, CA 94305   Palo Alto, CA 94304

Printed in the United States

98 97 96 95 94 93 92 91   5 4 3 2 1

Library of Congress Cataloging-in-Publication Data

Situation theory and its applications.

(CSLI lecture notes ; nos. 22, 26,)
Vol. 2 edited by Jon Barwise, Jean Mark Gawron, Gordon Plotkin, and Syun Tutiya.
Proceedings of the Second Conference on Situation Theory and Its Applications at Loch Rannoch, Scotland, September 1991.
Includes bibliographical references and index.
1. Logic—Congresses. 2. Language and logic—Congresses. I. Cooper, Robin, 1947-   . II. Mukai, Kuniaki, 1946-   . III. Perry, John, 1943-   . IV. Center for the Study of Language and Information (U.S.) V. Conference on Situation Theory and Its Applications (1st : 1989 : Asilomar, Calif.) VI. Series: CSLI lecture notes ; no. 22, etc.

BC5.S57 1990   160   90-82189
                                                    CIP

ISBN 0-937073-55-5 (v. 1)
ISBN 0-937073-54-7 (pbk. : v. 1)
ISBN 0-937073-71-7 (cloth : v. 2)
ISBN 0-937073-70-9 (pbk. : v. 2)

Contents

Contributors   ix

Preface   xiii

Part I Situation Theory   1

1 **Universes and Parameters**   3
PETER ACZEL AND RACHEL LUNNON

2 **Situations as Mathematical Abstractions**   25
KEITH J. DEVLIN

3 **Oracles in Situation Semantics**   41
KEITH J. DEVLIN

4 **Many Sorted Universes, SRDs, and Injective Sums**   51
RACHEL LUNNON

5 **A Theory of Situations**   81
EDWARD N. ZALTA

Part II Logical Applications   113

6 **Peirce on Truth and Partiality**   115
TOM BURKE

7 **Information and Architecture**   147
DAVID ISRAEL AND JOHN PERRY

8 **Doxic Paradox: A Situational Solution**   161
ROBERT C. KOONS

9 **CLP(AFA): Coinductive Semantics of Horn Clauses with Compact Constraints**   179
KUNIAKI MUKAI

10 **Inferring *in* a Situation *about* Situations**   215
HIDEYUKI NAKASHIMA AND SYUN TUTIYA

11 Situation-Theoretic Aspects of Databases   229
BILL ROUNDS

12 Physical Situations and Information Flow   257
JERRY SELIGMAN

Part III Linguistic Applications   293

13 Persistence and Structural Determination   295
RICHARD P. COOPER

14 Negation in Situation Semantics and Discourse
Representation Theory   311
ROBIN COOPER AND HANS KAMP

15 The Absorption Principle and E-Type Anaphora   335
JEAN MARK GAWRON, JOHN NERBONNE, AND STANLEY
PETERS

16 Questions without Answers, Wh-Phrases without Scope:
A Semantics for Direct Wh-Questions and their
Responses   363
JONATHAN GINZBURG

17 Reducing Complexity of Constraint-Based
Grammars   405
KÔITI HASIDA

18 Perspectivity and the Japanese Reflexive 'zibun'   425
YASUHIRO KATAGIRI

19 A Formalization of Metaphor Understanding in Situation
Semantics   449
TATSUNORI MORI AND HIROSHI NAKAGAWA

20 Relational Semantics and Scope Ambiguity   469
MASSIMO POESIO

21 Parameters: Dependence and Absorption   499
HELLE FRISAK SEM, KJELL JOHAN SÆBØ,
GURI B. VERNE, AND ESPEN J. VESTRE

22 A Strictly Incremental Approach to Japanese
Grammar   517
HIROYUKI SUZUKI AND SYUN TUTIYA

23 Probing the Iroquoian Perspective: Towards a Situated
Inquiry of Linguistic Relativity   533
DIETMAR ZAEFFERER

Part IV Visual Information   551

24 **Visualization and Situations**   553
C. MICHAEL LEWIS

25 **A Situation-Theoretic Account of Valid Reasoning with
Venn Diagrams   581**
SUN-JOO SHIN

26 **Reasoning with Words, Pictures, and Calculi:
Computation Versus Justification   607**
KEITH STENNING AND JON OBERLANDER

Name Index   623
Subject Index   627

Contributors

PETER ACZEL is currently interested in mathematical logic and the development of mathematical tools for the semantics of natural and formal languages. He is professor of mathematical logic and computer science at Manchester Uniuversity.

TOM BURKE is a Ph.D. student in philosophy at Stanford University. He is interested in philosophical issues pertaining to mind, language, and logic. He is currently investigating contributions of classical American pragmatism to contemporary discussions of these topics.

RICHARD P. COOPER has recently completed his Ph.D. at the Centre for Cognitive Science, University of Edinburgh. He is now working on the computational modelling of cognitive architectures in the Department of Psychology at University College London.

ROBIN COOPER is reader in artificial intelligence and cognitive science and a principal investigator of the Human Communication Research Centre at the University of Edinburgh. His research interests include natural language semantics, computational linguistics, and topics in cognitive science having to do with information processing.

KEITH J. DEVLIN, is Carter Professor of Mathematics and chairman of the department of mathematics at Colby College in Maine.

JEAN MARK GAWRON is a researcher at CSLI and a consultant at Hewlett-Packard Laboratories.

JONATHAN GINZBURG is a Ph.D. student in the Department of Linguistics at Stanford University. His interests focus on semantics and pragmatics of natural language.

KÔITI HASIDA is a senior researcher at Institute for New Generation Computer Technology (ICOT). He received a doctoral degree from Tokyo University in 1986. He has been affiliated with Electrotechnical Laboratory since 1986, and with ICOT since 1988. His present research concerns constraint-based models of cognition, particularly of language use.

DAVID ISRAEL is a Senior Computer Scientist in the Artificial Intelligence Center at SRI International and a consulting professor in the Philosophy Department at Stanford University. His current work involves developing a unified theory of intelligent behavior and of the contents of cognitive states.

HANS KAMP is professor of logic and philosophy at the University of Stuttgart.

YASUHIRO KATAGIRI is a research scientist in the Information Science Research Laboratory of NTT Basic Research Laboratories. He received his Doctor of Engineering degree in 1981 from the University of Tokyo. He is currently interested in natural language discourse and situated reasoning.

ROBERT C. KOONS is an assistant professor in the Department of Philosophy and the Center for Cognitive Science at the University of Texas at Austin. His interests include semantical paradox; formal theories of belief, rationality, and action; game theory; and nonmonotonic reasoning.

C. MICHAEL LEWIS is an assistant professor in the department of information science at the University of Pittsburgh. His cuurrent research involves ecological design for graphical interfaces and distributed expertise in group problem solving.

RACHEL LUNNON has recently finished her Ph.D. in mathematical logic at Manchester University under the supervision of Peter Aczel. She is now affiliated with the Department of Mathematics at Indiana University where she hopes to continue research into abstraction and mixed foundedness.

TATSUNORI MORI is a research associate of computer engineering at Yokohama University, Japan. His current research focus is on the semantics and pragmatics of natural language, especially metaphor understanding.

KUNIAKI MUKAI is senior researcher at the Institute for New Generation Computer Technology, Tokyo. He has worked on introducing record structures into Prolog. His research interests include common logical foundations for natural and programming languages inspired by situation semantics and situation theory.

HIROSHI NAKAGAWA is associate professor in computer engineering at Yokohama University, Japan. He was a visiting scholar at CSLI from January 1990 to January 1991. His current interests include pragmatics of Japanese discourse and discourse oriented machine translation.

HIDEYUKI NAKASHIMA is a researcher at Electrotechnical Laboratories, Japan. He received his Dr.Eng. in information engineering at the University of Tokyo. His research interests include knowledge representation and reasoning.

JOHN NERBONNE is a computational linguist who has worked on computational lexicons, syntax, semantics and pragmatics. He is now at the German Research Center for Artificial Intelligence in Saarbrücken, where his current research focuses on speech and natural language processing.

JON OBERLANDER is a research fellow at the Human Communication Research Centre, University of Edinburgh. His main interests include temporal issues in computational linguistics, integrated semantics for graphics and natural language, and the philosophy of mind.

JOHN PERRY is professor of philosophy at Stanford University and a researcher at CSLI. He works on philosophical issues connected with mind and language.

STANLEY PETERS is professor of linguistics and symbolic systems at Stanford University. His research interests include situation semantics and computing based on situation theory.

MASSIMO POESIO is a Ph.D. student in computer science at the University of Rochester. He is interested in discourse inference, the representation of ambiguity, and temporal reasoning.

BILL ROUNDS is professor of computer science at the University of Michigan. He has worked in the mathematics of natural language, computational complexity, and concurrency, with occasional forays into software engineering and computer security. He is currently working on a book on the feature systems commonly used in computational linguistics, and exploring connections between these systems, the frame systems of artificial intelligence, and the complex objects in database programming, using situation theory as a motivation.

KJELL JOHAN SÆBØ is currently affiliated with the Department of Germanistics at the University of Oslo. His research interests include semantics and discourse reopresentation theory, particularly work on modals, discourse particles, cooperative response, and the generation of definite descriptions.

JERRY SELIGMAN received his Ph.D. in cognitive science from the University of Edinburgh. He subsequently worked in the Human Communication Research Centre, Edinburgh, and on the DYANA project. He is now a SERC post-doctoral fellow visiting Indiana University. His main research interests are situation theory, logic and proof theory, and the philosophy of cognitive science.

HELLE FRISAK SEM is currently affiliated with the Department of Mathematics at the University of Oslo. His research interests include the representation and semantics of discourse, particularly with respect to quantification, anaphora, and tense; dynamic and partial semantics, and update semantics.

SUN-JOO SHIN is assistant professor at the University of Notre Dame. Her research interests include the logic of graphical representations.

KEITH STENNING is a Professorial Fellow of Edinburgh University and Director of the Human Communications Research Centre. His research interests are in the implications of human working memory architecture for reasoning and communication with both linguistic and graphical information.

HIROYUKI SUSUKI is a research scientist at Tokyo Information and Communications Research Laboratory at Matsushita Electric Industrial Co., Ltd and research manager of Eighth Research Laboratory Research Center of Japan Electronic Dictionary Research Institute. His current interests include parallel logic programming, processing and producing documents in Japanese.

SYUN TUTIYA is associate professor of philosophy, Chiba University, Japan. His current research interests include action theory, speech acts and spoken communication, as well as text encoding, computer ethics, and history of Japanese technology.

GURI B. VERNE is currently affiliated with the Department of Mathematics at the University of Oslo. His research interests include semantics and pragmatics, particularly with respect to their interaction, and with respect to the influence of context and background on sentence meaning.

ESPEN J. VESTRE is currently affiliated with the Department of Computerlinguistik at the University of Saarbrücken. His research interests include the semantics and pragmatics of questions, dynamic semantics, belief revision, conditionals, and the syntax/semantics interface.

DIETMAR ZAEFFERER is associate professor of theoretical and German linguistics at the University of Munich. His research is focused on the semantics and pragmatics of natural language. He is curently developing, together with Bernard Comrie, Bill Croft, and Christian Lehmann, a universal framework for descriptive grammars.

EDWARD N. ZALTA is acting assistant professor of philosophy at Stanford University, and a researcher at CSLI. His main interests are in metaphysics, philosophy of language, and intensional logic.

Preface

This volume represents the proceedings of the Second Conference on Situation Theory and its Applications, held at Loch Rannoch, Scotland, in September of 1990. The Program Committee of the Conference consisted of the editors of this volume. Many people helped make the conference and this volume a success, too many to name here. Three deserve special mention, though: Nick Braisby (Convenor), Robin Cooper, and Margaret Rennex (secretary), who made up the organizing committee.

The conference was supported by contributions from the Center for the Study of Language and Information at Stanford University; the Human Communication Research Centre at Edinburgh University; the Logic for IT Initiative and the Systems Architecture Committee, Science and Engineering Research Council of the United Kingdom; the British Academy; ESPRIT Basic Research Action 3175 DYANA (Dynamic Interpretation of Natural Language); and Sun Microsystems.

As usual with such proceedings, the volume does not coincide exactly with the presentations at the meeting. Some papers appear here that were not given in Loch Rannoch, and, conversely, some papers given there do not appear here for one reason or another.

This volume is organized along the same lines as its predecessor, *Situation Theory and Its Applications*, Vol. 1 (CSLI Lecture Notes, No. 22, 1990), with one difference. Part I contains papers dealing with issues in situation theory itself. Part II is devoted to applications of the theory (or parts of the theory) to logic, computer science, philosophy, and so forth. Part III contains applications to natural language. A fourth section contains papers from a special session on visual information.

We feel that this volume is a worthy successor to the proceedings of the first conference on situation theory and its applications. We hope that all readers of this volume will profit from its existence and that some will feel inspired to contribute to the further development of the subject.

Jon Barwise, Bloomington *Mark Gawron, Palo Alto*
Gordon Plotkin, Edinburgh *Syun Tutiya, Chiba*

Part I

Situation Theory

Universes and Parameters

PETER ACZEL AND RACHEL LUNNON

1 Introduction

This paper continues the work initiated in Aczel 1990. The general aim is
to develop a mathematical framework for situation theory. A preliminary
stage in achieving that aim is to formulate a sufficiently general theory of
universes of structured objects. In the earlier paper the notion of a replacement system was formulated that was intended to capture the notion
of a single sorted universe of structured objects, where there are no explicit notions of parameter or parameter binding operation. In this paper
replacement systems will be called (*elementary*) *universes*. Also defined in
the earlier paper was the notion of an ontology. This is a generalization of
the notion of a signature that can be used to represent the possible forms of
object of an elementary universe. These definitions of elementary universe
and ontology are repeated in section 2.

The notions of parameter and parameter binding operation form central notions used in situation theory and need to be treated in our theory
of structured objects. Below we formulate the notion of a universe with
parameters, which consists of a universe together with a distinguished subclass of parameters for which there is a suitable notion of substitution.
The objects of such a universe may be parametric; i.e., have parameters
as constituents, or may be non-parametric; i.e., have no parameter constituents. The non-parametric objects form the *non-parametric core*, a
subuniverse of the whole universe with parameters. As with the notion of
a universe there are two extreme kinds of universe with parameters. At one
extreme are those that are well-founded and at the other extreme are those
that are anti-founded; i.e., those that satisfy a condition generalizing the
anti-foundation axiom of set theory. Examples of such universes at both
extremes are easily obtained using theorem 4.2 of Aczel 1990. Another pos-

This work was supported by a grant from SERC and sponsored by British Petroleum.

Situation Theory and Its Applications, vol. 2.
Jon Barwise, Jean Mark Gawron, Gordon Plotkin, and Syun Tutiya, eds.
Copyright © 1991, Stanford University.

sibility is to use the injective sum construction of Lunnon 1991b to embed any universe as the non-parametric core of a universe with parameters.

Another notion we formulate is that of a λ-universe. This also has parameters with a suitable notion of substitution and has objects with components which can be replaced, as in a universe with parameters. But in addition it has objects obtained by a lambda abstraction operation. These objects have the form $\lambda(\overline{x}, a)$, where $\overline{x} = \{x_i\}_{i \in I}$ is a non-repeating family of parameters x_i and a is an object which may have parameters x_i as constituents. These objects might be more familiarly written as $\lambda \overline{x}.a$. The criterion of equality for such lambda abstractions is taken over from the syntax of the lambda calculus where the α-convertible terms of the lambda calculus are identified. So it does not make sense to talk about bound parameters in an object of a λ-universe. The terms of the lambda calculus up to α-convertibility will form a λ-universe, of course, provided that a proper class of variables are supplied. The proviso is because we have built in to the definition of the notion of a λ-universe the requirement that the parameters form a proper class. This is to ensure that there are enough new parameters available to be used as needed. It seems that a proper class will be needed for the situation theoretic applications. Of course for the lambda calculus only an infinite set of variables are really needed. A λ-universe has three kinds of objects: parameters, lambda abstractions and objects having one of the forms of some specified ontology. In the case of the lambda calculus the specified ontology is that determined by a signature with one binary function symbol for the application operation of the lambda calculus. When the ontology is $\mathcal{U}$ we call the λ-universe a $\mathcal{U}, \lambda$-universe. The main aim of this paper is the statement and outline of a proof of a result concerning the existence and uniqueness up to isomorphism of an anti-founded $\mathcal{U}, \lambda$-universe, for any ontology $\mathcal{U}$. The corresponding result for well-founded $\mathcal{U}, \lambda$-universes also holds and has an easier proof which will not be discussed here.

After reviewing the definitions of ontology and elementary universe in section 2 we formulate the notion of a standard substitution operation in section 3. This last notion is involved in the definitions of the notions of universe with parameters and lambda universe. It is closely related to the notion of an instantiation system formulated in Williams 1990 and it should prove promising to investigate common generalizations of the two notions. A start on this has been made in Aczel 1991. After discussing universes with parameters in section 4 the notion of a lambda universe is defined in section 5 and the main result stated in section 6. The remainder of the paper is taken up with the proof of the main result. While the main stages of the proof are presented there are a number of details that have been left to the reader. A more complete proof will appear in Lunnon 1991a.

The metatheory for this paper can, for the most part, be taken to be ZFC. We work informally, using class notation, as in Aczel 1988 and

Aczel 1990. In some places there are uses of a global form of AC that is not available in ZFC alone.

2   Ontologies and Elementary Universes

This section contains some definitions and results from Aczel 1990. The main notions here are those of universe and ontology, which are special cases of the notion of an *X-form system*. The intuition behind the latter notion can be understood from the following example. Assume given a finitary (for simplicity) signature of function symbols. Let A be the set of X-forms

$$f(x_1, \ldots, x_n),$$

where f is an n-place function symbol of the signature and $x_1, \ldots, x_n$ is a possibly repeating list of n elements of X. If a is the above X-form then its set Ca of *components* is the set $\{x_1, \ldots, x_n\}$ and if $\sigma : Ca \to X$ then $\sigma \cdot a$ is the X-form

$$f(\sigma x_1, \ldots, \sigma x_n)$$

obtained from a by replacing the components of a by their values under the map σ. We have now defined an X-form system from the signature and, provided that X is large enough the signature can be recaptured from the X-form system. So for large enough X the notion of X-form system generalizes the notion of signature. It turns out to be convenient to work with the notion when X is taken to be the class V of all objects of our metatheory, when we get the notion of an *ontology*. The notion of a *universe* is intended to include the examples of terms or trees relative to some signature. In the case of a finitary signature each object of the universe can be viewed as a form

$$f(a_1, \ldots, a_n),$$

where the components $a_1, \ldots, a_n$ are themselves elements of the universe. More discussion and further examples may be found in Aczel 1990.

Let V throughout this paper be the universal class of objects of our metatheory.

Definition 1 $(A, C, \cdot)$ is a *X-form system* if A is a class, $C : A \to pow\, X$ and for each $a \in A$, if $\sigma : Ca \to X$ then $\sigma \cdot a \in A$ such that

- $C(\sigma \cdot a) = \{\sigma x \mid x \in Ca\}$,
- $\sigma \cdot a = a$ if $\sigma x = x$ for $x \in Ca$,
- $\sigma' \cdot (\sigma \cdot a) = (\sigma' \circ \sigma) \cdot a$ if $\sigma' : C(\sigma \cdot a) \to X$

Definition 2 $(A, C, \cdot)$ is a *(elementary) universe* if it is an A-form system.

Definition 3 An *ontology* is a V-form system.

Given an ontology $\mathcal{U} = (U, C_\mathcal{U}, \cdot_\mathcal{U})$ let $\mathcal{U}[\,]$ be the class operator given by

$$\mathcal{U}[X] = \{u \in U \mid Cu \subseteq X\}$$

for each class X. Given classes X and A and a bijection $\alpha : \mathcal{U}[X] \cong A$ we get a form system $\mathcal{U}(X, \alpha) = (A, C, \cdot)$ where, for each $a \in A$, $Ca = C_{\mathcal{U}}(\alpha^{-1}a)$ and if $\sigma : Ca \to A$ then $\sigma \cdot a = \alpha(\sigma \cdot_{\mathcal{U}} (\alpha^{-1}a))$. Such an X-form system will be called a $\mathcal{U}$-X-form system. The next result states that every X-form system arises in this way and that, provided that a size bound is place on the ontology, the ontology is unique up to isomorphism. The size bound is formulated as follows. For any class B a form system $(A, C, \cdot)$ is B-bounded if $Ca \preceq B$ (there is an injective map from Ca to B) for any $a \in A$.

Theorem 1 (Representation Theorem for Form Systems) *Every X-form system $(A, C, \cdot)$ is a $\mathcal{U}$-X-form system for some X-bounded ontology $\mathcal{U}$. Moreover $\mathcal{U}$ is unique up to isomorphism.*

If we have $\alpha : \mathcal{U}[A] \cong A$ then we call (A, α) a full algebra for $\mathcal{U}$ and $\mathcal{U}(A, \alpha)$ is a universe. We call such universes $\mathcal{U}$-*universes*. By putting $X = A$ in the previous theorem we get a representation theorem for universes as $\mathcal{U}$-universes.

Theorem 2 *Every universe $\mathcal{A} = (A, C, \cdot)$ is a $\mathcal{U}$-universe for some A-bounded ontology $\mathcal{U}$. Moreover $\mathcal{U}$ is unique up to isomorphism.*

We call $\mathcal{U}$, as in this theorem, a *representative ontology for the universe* $\mathcal{A}$.

Next we define the notions of well-founded and anti-founded universes.

Definition 4 A universe $(A, C, \cdot)$ is *well-founded* (*wf*) if for every non-empty set $x \subseteq A$ there is $a \in x$ such that Ca is disjoint from x.

This definition is a generalization of the foundation axiom, FA, of ZFC. It is equivalent to the non-existence of an infinite sequence $a_0, a_1, \ldots$ with $a_{n+1} \in Ca_n$ for $n = 0, 1, \ldots$.. The notion of an anti-founded universe is intended to generalize, in a similar way, the anti-foundation axiom, AFA, of Aczel 1988. Rather than give a direct generalization of the graph formulation of AFA we will use a solution lemma property analogous to the statement of the solution lemma given on page 13 of Aczel 1988. The general form of a solution lemma property is that every system of equation of a certain kind has a unique solution. We need to specify the kind of system of equations we have in mind and what a solution for it should be.

Definition 5 Let $\mathcal{U} = (U, C_{\mathcal{U}}, \cdot_{\mathcal{U}})$ be an ontology. A $\mathcal{U}$-*system of equations* has the form

$$y = u_y \quad (y \in Y)$$

where Y is a set and $u_y \in \mathcal{U}[Y]$ for all $y \in Y$.

If $\mathcal{A} = \mathcal{U}(A, \alpha)$ is a $\mathcal{U}$-universe, where (A, α) is a full algebra for $\mathcal{U}$ then a *solution* to such a system of equations in $\mathcal{A}$ is a map $\pi : Y \to A$ such that

$$\pi y = \alpha((\pi | C_{\mathcal{U}} u_y) \cdot_{\mathcal{U}} u_y) \text{ for all } y \in Y$$

We can now define the notion of an anti-founded universe.

Definition 6 Let $\mathcal{A} = (A, C, \cdot)$ be a universe. $\mathcal{A}$ is *anti-founded* if every $\mathcal{U}$-system of equations has a unique solution in $\mathcal{A}$, where $\mathcal{U}$ is a representative ontology for $\mathcal{A}$.

This definition differs slightly from the definition in Aczel 1990. See the discussion after definition 2.6 of Lunnon 1991b, where the following result is stated which should be compared with theorem 3.8 of Aczel 1990.

Theorem 3 *For every ontology $\mathcal{U}$ there is a wf (af) $\mathcal{U}$-universe. Moreover it is unique up to isomorphism.*

We end this section with a definition of the notion of a *subuniverse* of an elementary universe. Let $\mathcal{A} = (A, C, \cdot)$ be a universe. A class $B \subseteq A$ is *transitive* if $Cb \subseteq B$ for all $b \in B$ and is *closed* if $\sigma \cdot b \in B$ for all $b \in B$ and all $\sigma : Cb \rightarrow B$. If a class B is both transitive and closed then it determines the *subuniverse* $\mathcal{A}|B = (B, C_B, \cdot_B)$ of $\mathcal{A}$, where C_B and $\cdot_B$ are the obvious restrictions of C and $\cdot$ to B.

For any class $B \subseteq A$ let $TC(B)$ be the smallest transitive class including B. Also let $cl(B)$ be the smallest closed class including B. Observe that if B is transitive then so is $cl(B)$.

3   Substitution

We will be concerned with setups where we have classes X and A with $X \subseteq A$. To avoid the discussion of some special cases we will assume that X has at least two elements. A *substitution operation* on (A, X) is an assignment of a function $\hat{f} : A \rightarrow A$ to each $f : X \rightarrow A$ such that $\hat{f}$ extends f. The elements of X will be called *parameters* and the functions $\hat{f}$ will be called *substitutions*.

Given a substitution operation the following notation can be useful. For any set I we let A^I be the class of all the functions $I \rightarrow A$. Such functions may be written as families $\overline{a} = \{a_i\}_{i \in I}$ with $a_i \in A$ the result of applying $\overline{a}$ to $i \in I$. We also let $X^{\cdot I}$ be the class of injective functions $I \rightarrow X$. If $\overline{x} \in X^{\cdot I}$ and $\overline{a} \in A^I$ then we let $[\overline{a}/\overline{x}]$ be the substitution $\hat{f}$ where $f : X \rightarrow A$ is given by

$$
\begin{aligned}
fx_i &= a_i \quad (i \in I), \\
fx &= x \quad (x \in X - ran(\overline{x})).
\end{aligned}
$$

In the case when $I = \{1, \ldots, n\}$ we shall write $[a_1, \ldots, a_n / x_1, \ldots, x_n]$ for $[\overline{a}/\overline{x}]$. The following notion will be useful in the next definition. If $Y \subseteq X$ and $a \in A$ then Y *supports* a if for all substitutions s_1, s_2

$$
s_1|Y = s_2|Y \Rightarrow s_1 a = s_2 a.
$$

Note that X supports every element of A.

Definition 7 A substitution operation on (A, X) is *standard* if

1. The identity function on A is a substitution and the composition of two substitutions is a substitution.

2. There is a function $par : A \to pow X$ such that for all $x \in X$ $par(x) = \{x\}$ and for all $a \in A$

   a. $par(a)$ supports a,

   b. $par(sa) = \bigcup \{par(sx) \mid x \in par(a)\}$ for all substitutions s.

Note: par satisfying 2 above is uniquely determined. In fact $par(a)$ is the least set that supports a. For suppose that Y supports a, $x \in par(a)$ but $x \notin Y$. As we have assumed that X has at least two elements we may choose $x' \in X - \{x\}$. As x is not in Y, which supports a, $[x'/x]a = a$. Applying 2(b) with $s = [x'/x]$, we get that $x \notin par([x'/x]a)$, contradicting that $x \in par(a)$. We will call par the *parameters map* for the standard substitution operation.

4 Universes with Parameters

In this section we will formulate the notion of a *universe with parameters*. Let $\mathcal{A} = (A, C, \cdot)$ be an elementary universe and let $X \subseteq \{a \in A \mid Ca = \emptyset\}$. Again we will assume, for simplicity, that X has at least two elements. Define $par : A \to pow X$ by

$$par(a) = X \cap TC(\{a\})$$

for $a \in A$. $par(a)$ is the set of parameters that *occur* in a. Let $A_{np} = \{a \in A \mid par(a) = \emptyset\}$. It is the class of *non-parametric* elements of A. Note that it is a closed, transitive class and hence determines a subuniverse $\mathcal{A}_{np} = \mathcal{A}|A_{np}$ of $\mathcal{A}$ which we call the *non-parametric core* of $(\mathcal{A}, X)$.

Definition 8 $(\mathcal{A}, X)$ is a *universe with parameters* if

1. Every $f : X \to A$ has a unique extension to $\hat{f} : A \to A$ such that

   a. $\hat{f}a = a$ for $a \in A_{np}$,

   b. $\hat{f}a = (\hat{f}|Ca) \cdot a$ for $a \in A - X$.

2. For all $a \in A$ $par(a)$ supports a.

Note that 1 gives a substitution operation on $(\mathcal{A}, X)$ and it is easy to check that it is standard, with parameters map par. The next theorem follows from results in Aczel 1990.

Theorem 4 *If $\mathcal{A}$ is wf or af then $(\mathcal{A}, X)$ is a universe with parameters.*

The following notion can give rise to other examples of universes with parameters.

Definition 9 $(\mathcal{A}, X)$ is *generated* if $cl(A_{np} \cup X) = A$.

Theorem 5 *If $(\mathcal{A}, X)$ is generated then it is a universe with parameters.*

Note that if $(\mathcal{A}, X)$ is generated then $\mathcal{A}$ is A_{np}-bounded. Also if $\mathcal{A}$ is well-founded and A_{np}-bounded then $(\mathcal{A}, X)$ is generated. But the converse need not be true. In fact any universe can be embedded, in a canonical way, in a generated universe with parameters.

Definition 10 Let $\mathcal{A}_0$ be a universe and X_0 any class. Then $(\mathcal{A}, X)$ is an X_0-generated extension of $\mathcal{A}_0$ if $(\mathcal{A}, X)$ is generated, $X \cong X_0$ and $\mathcal{A}_{np} \cong \mathcal{A}_0$.

Theorem 6 *For any class X_0, every universe $\mathcal{A}_0$ has an X_0-generated extension. Moreover it is unique up to isomorphism.*

This result gives a natural canonical approach to adding parameters to a universe of non-parametric objects[1]. The proof of the result is a simple application of the injective sum construction of Lunnon 1991b. $\mathcal{A}$ can be defined to be the injective sum of the universe $\mathcal{A}_0$ and the universe $(X_0, C_{X_0}, \cdot x_0)$, where $C_{X_0} x = \emptyset$ for all $x \in X_0$. X_0-generated extensions are a special case of the following more general notion.

Definition 11 $(\mathcal{A}, X)$ is an X_0-parametric extension of $\mathcal{A}_0$ if $(\mathcal{A}, X)$ is a universe with parameters such that $\mathcal{A}$ is $\mathcal{A}_0$-bounded, $X \cong X_0$ and $\mathcal{A}_{np} \cong \mathcal{A}_0$.

Besides the X_0-generated extensions there are other examples of X_0-parametric extensions. For example if $\mathcal{A}$ is anti-founded and $\mathcal{A}_{np}$-bounded then $(\mathcal{A}, X)$ is an X-parametric extension of $\mathcal{A}_{np}$, which will usually not be an X-generated extension. It would be nice to have a canonical construction of *maximal* X_0-parametric extensions that is dual to the X_0-generated extensions, which are *minimal*.

5 Lambda Universes

We now assume that X is a proper class of *parameters*. We also assume given a class IND of sets, called *index* sets and let

$$X^{\cdot} = \bigcup_{I \in IND} X^{\cdot I}$$

If A is a class, $\mathcal{A}' = (A', C, \cdot)$ is an A-form system with $A' \subseteq A, X \subseteq A'$ with $Cx = \emptyset$ for $x \in X$ and $\lambda : (X^{\cdot} \times A) \overset{onto}{\to} (A - A')$ then we call $\mathcal{A} = (A, \mathcal{A}', X, \lambda)$ a *pre λ-universe*. We think of $\lambda(\overline{x}, a)$ as an abstraction object obtained from the object a by abstracting on the parameters x_i of $\overline{x}$ and A' is the class of those objects of the pre λ-universe that are not abstractions. We call *par* $: A \to powX$ a *parameters function for $\mathcal{A}$* if

1. $par(x) = \{x\}$ for $x \in X$,
2. $par(a) = \bigcup\{par(a') \mid a' \in Ca\}$ for $a \in A' - X$,
3. $par(\lambda(\overline{x}, a)) = par(a) - ran(\overline{x})$ for $(\overline{x}, a) \in X^{\cdot} \times A$.

Definition 12 A pre λ-universe $\mathcal{A}$ is a *λ-universe* if the following axioms hold.

---

[1]The possibility and interest of such a result was pointed out by Dag Westerståhl. In fact a result along these lines was one of the original motivations of Jon Barwise and the first author when we started to think about parameters and substitution, but this motivation got submerged in other problems.

Axiom 1 There is a least parameters function *par* for $\mathcal{A}$; i.e., *par* is a parameters function for $\mathcal{A}$ and

$$par(a) \subseteq par'(a) \text{ for } a \in A$$

for any other parameters function *par'* for $\mathcal{A}$.

Axiom 2 There is a unique standard substitution operation on (A, X), with parameters map the same function *par* given by axiom 1, such that for each $f : X \to A$

(a) $\hat{f}a = (\hat{f}|Ca) \cdot a$ for $a \in A' - X$,

(b) $\hat{f}(\lambda(\overline{x}, a)) = \lambda(\overline{x}, \hat{f}a)$ for $(\overline{x}, a) \in X^{\cdot} \times A$ such that $ran(\overline{x}) \cap par(f) = \emptyset$,

where

$$par(f) = \{x \in X \mid fx \neq x\} \cup \bigcup \{par(fx) \mid x \in X \ \& \ fx \neq x\}.$$

Axiom 3 For all $(\overline{x}, a), (\overline{y}, b) \in X^{\cdot} \times A$

$$\lambda(\overline{x}, a) = \lambda(\overline{y}, b) \ \Leftrightarrow \ (\overline{x}, a) \sim^I (\overline{y}, b) \text{ for some } I \in IND,$$

where $\sim^I$ is the equivalence relation on $X^{\cdot I} \times A$ given by

$$(\overline{x}, a) \sim^I (\overline{y}, b) \ \Leftrightarrow \ [\overline{c}/\overline{x}]a = [\overline{c}/\overline{y}]b \text{ for all } \overline{c} \in A^I.$$

6 The Main Result

Let $\mathcal{U}$ be an ontology and let X be a proper class with $X \subseteq \mathcal{U}[\emptyset]$. A $\mathcal{U}, \lambda$-*universe* is a λ-universe of the form $\mathcal{A} = (A, \mathcal{U}(A, \alpha), X, \lambda)$ where $\alpha : \mathcal{U}[A] \cong A'$ such that $\alpha x = x$ for $x \in X$.

We call

$$y = a_y \quad (y \in Y)$$

a $(\mathcal{U}, X)$-*system of equations* (*soe*) if Y is a set and for each $y \in Y$

$$a_y \in (\{0\} \times \mathcal{U}[Y]) \cup (\{1\} \times (X^{\cdot} \times Y)).$$

We say that $\pi : Y \to A$ is a *solution* of this soe in a $\mathcal{U}, \lambda$-universe $\mathcal{A}$ if for all $y \in Y$

$$
\begin{array}{lll}
\pi y & = & \alpha((\pi | C_{\mathcal{U}} u) \cdot_{\mathcal{U}} u) \quad \text{if } a_y = (0, u) \\
\pi y & = & \lambda(\overline{x}, \pi y') \quad\quad\quad \text{if } a_y = (1, (\overline{x}, y'))
\end{array}
$$

A $\mathcal{U}, \lambda$-universe $\mathcal{A}$ is *anti-founded* (*af*) if every $(\mathcal{U}, X)$-soe has a unique solution in $\mathcal{A}$.

Our aim is to outline a proof of the following result, which is the main new result of the paper.

Theorem 7 *For every ontology $\mathcal{U}$ with proper class $X \subseteq \mathcal{U}[\emptyset]$ there is an af $\mathcal{U}, \lambda$-universe $\mathcal{A} = (A, \mathcal{U}(A, \alpha), X, \lambda)$, which is unique up to isomorphism.*

The rest of the paper is taken up with a proof of this result. The proof is sketchy in parts. The details will appear in Lunnon 1991a.

Note: There is a companion result to the theorem obtained by replacing 'af' by 'wf', where a λ-universe $\mathcal{A}$ is *well-founded* (*wf*) if there is no infinite sequence $a_0, a_1, \ldots$ such that for $n = 0, 1, \ldots$ either $a_n \in A'$ and $a_{n+1} \in Ca_n$ or $a_n \in A-A'$ and $a_n = \lambda(\overline{x}, a_{n+1})$ for some $\overline{x} \in X$. This companion result is easier to prove than the stated theorem, and can either be proved along the same lines or else by obtaining a wf $\mathcal{U}, \lambda$-universe from an af one by forming the 'well-founded part' of the af $\mathcal{U}, \lambda$-universe.

7 The Construction of an Anti-Founded $\mathcal{U}, \lambda$-Universe

Let $\mathcal{U}$ be an ontology and X a proper class with $X \subseteq \mathcal{U}[\emptyset]$. We wish to construct an af $\mathcal{U}, \lambda$-universe $\mathcal{U} = (A, \mathcal{U}(A, \alpha), X, \lambda)$. We will obtain the class A as a quotient of a class D with respect to an equivalence relation $\equiv_\alpha$ on D. The class D will be analogous to the set of concrete terms of the λ-calculus and $\equiv_\alpha$ will be analogous to the α-convertibility relation on that set.

In order to simplify the treatment of "substitution up to α-convertibility" the parameters in X will not be used as *bound* parameters in the elements of D. Instead we will use a proper class Y of new parameters to be used as the bound parameters of the elements of D. We assume that Y is disjoint from U and hence from X. If the ontology $\mathcal{U}$ is too large we must replace it by a copy of $\mathcal{U}$ so that Y can be found.

We will need to use a superclass D' of D whose elements are allowed to have free occurrences of parameters from Y. The class D' will be obtained as the class of objects of an af $\mathcal{U}'$-algebra for an ontology $\mathcal{U}'$ suitably defined from $\mathcal{U}$ and Y. A substitution operation will be defined on (D', X') where $X' = X \cup Y$, although we will only be interested in substitutions given by functions $f : X' \to D'$ which are equal to the identity either on X or on Y. The construction of the af $\mathcal{U}, \lambda$-universe $\mathcal{A}$ will take the following stages.

Stage 1: The definition of the ontology $\mathcal{U}'$. Use $\mathcal{U}$ to define an ontology $\mathcal{U}'$ which will have forms corresponding to the forms of $\mathcal{U}$ but also forms corresponding to a class of 'parameters' Y, disjoint from U, which may be bound and forms corresponding to the desired abstractions $\lambda(\overline{x}, a)$.

Stage 2: The $\mathcal{U}'$-algebra (D', δ') and substitution on (D', X').
Apply theorem 3 to get a full $\mathcal{U}'$-algebra (D', δ') so that $\mathcal{U}'(D', \delta')$ is af, D' is a class and $\delta' : \mathcal{U}'[D'] \cong D'$. Let $\delta_\lambda : Y \times D' \to D'$ be given by $\delta_\lambda(\overline{y}, d) = \delta'(1, (\overline{y}, d))$
Define a substitution operation on (D', X'), which is substitution for free occurrences of parameters only, but allows free parameters from Y to be captured by parameter binding in a substitution.

Stage 3: The definition of D and substitution on (D, X). Take D to be those elements of D' which have no free parameters from Y. Partition

D into classes $D_\mathcal{U}$ and D_λ and define a bijection

$$\delta : \mathcal{U}[D] \ \cong \ D_\mathcal{U}$$

Identify each $x \in X$ with $\delta x \in D_\mathcal{U}$.

Stage 4: The definition of α-equivalence, $\equiv_\alpha$, on D. Define the α-equivalence relation $\equiv_\alpha$ on D. This is analogous to the equivalence relation of α-convertibility on the set of terms of the lambda calculus. But here the elements of D are not necessarily well-founded. So instead of inductively generating α-convertible pairs of terms it is necessary to use a coinductive definition. A notion of α-congruence relation on D is defined and the maximal one is taken to be the α-equivalence relation.

Stage 5: The formation of the quotient of D with respect to $\equiv_\alpha$. By global AC form a quotient $[[-]] : D \overset{onto}{\to} A$ of D with respect to α-equivalence. So for $d_1, d_2 \in D$

$$[[d_1]] = [[d_2]] \ \Leftrightarrow \ d_1 \equiv_\alpha d_2.$$

A can be partitioned into the classes $A_\mathcal{U} = \{[[d]] \mid d \in D_\mathcal{U}\}$, $A_\lambda = \{[[d]] \mid d \in D_\lambda\}$ and maps

$$\begin{aligned} \alpha : \mathcal{U}[A] \quad &\to \quad A_\mathcal{U} \\ \lambda : X^{\cdot} \times A \quad &\to \quad A_\lambda \end{aligned}$$

can be defined using δ and δ_λ so that α is a bijection, $\alpha : \mathcal{U}[A] \cong A_\mathcal{U}$, such that $\alpha x = [[x]]$ for $x \in X$ and λ is a surjection. By identifying $x \in X$ with $[[x]] \in A_\mathcal{U}$ we get the pre $\mathcal{U}, \lambda$-universe

$$\mathcal{A} = (A, \mathcal{U}(A, \alpha), X, \lambda).$$

Stage 6: The proof that $\mathcal{A}$ is a λ-universe.

Stage 7: The proof that $\mathcal{A}$ is anti-founded.

Stage 1: The Definition of the Ontology $\mathcal{U}'$

Let $\mathcal{U} = (U, C_\mathcal{U}, \cdot_\mathcal{U})$ be an ontology and X, Y proper classes with $X \subset \mathcal{U}[\emptyset]$, $Y \cap U = \emptyset$ and $X \cong Y$. For $I \in IND$ let $Y^{\cdot I}$ be the class of those families of elements of Y indexed by I, and let $Y^{\cdot} = \bigcup_{I \in IND} Y^{\cdot I}$. The ontology $\mathcal{U}' = (U', C_{\mathcal{U}'}, \cdot_{\mathcal{U}'})$ is defined as follows.

$$U' = (\{0\} \times (U \cup Y)) \cup (\{1\} \times (Y^{\cdot} \times V))$$

If $u \in U \cup Y$ then let

$$C_{\mathcal{U}'}(0, u) = \begin{cases} C_\mathcal{U} u & u \in U \\ \emptyset & \text{otherwise} \end{cases}$$

and if $\sigma : C_{\mathcal{U}'}(0, u) \to V$ then let

$$\sigma \cdot_{\mathcal{U}'} (0, u) = \begin{cases} (0, \sigma \cdot_\mathcal{U} u) & u \in U \\ (0, u) & \text{otherwise} \end{cases}$$

If $(\overline{y}, v) \in Y^{\cdot} \times V$ then let

$$C_{\mathcal{U}'}(1, (\overline{y}, v)) = \{v\}$$

and if $\sigma : \{v\} \to V$ let

$$\sigma \cdot_{\mathcal{U}'} (1, (\overline{y}, v)) = (1, (\overline{y}, \sigma v)).$$

It is easy to check that $\mathcal{U}'$ is an ontology.

Stage 2: The $\mathcal{U}'$-Algebra (D', δ') and Substitution on (D', X')

Let (D', δ') be a full $\mathcal{U}'$-algebra so that $\mathcal{U}'(D', \delta') = (D', C', \cdot)$ is af. This exists by theorem 3 So D' is a class and

$$\delta' : (\{0\} \times (\mathcal{U}[D'] \cup Y)) \cup (\{1\} \times (Y^{\cdot} \times D')) \cong D'.$$

Define $\delta_\lambda : Y^{\cdot} \times D' \to D'$ by

$$\delta_\lambda(\overline{y}, d) = \delta'(1, (\overline{y}, d)) \quad \text{for} \quad (\overline{y}, d) \in Y^{\cdot} \times D'.$$

Let $D'_\lambda = ran(\delta_\lambda)$ and $D_{\mathcal{U}'} = D' - D'_\lambda$. Then

$$\delta_\lambda : Y^{\cdot} \times D' \cong D'_\lambda.$$

Recall that $X' = X \cup Y$ and identify each $z \in X'$ with $\delta'(0, z) \in D'_\mathcal{U}$.

The substitution operation on (D', X') is given by the following result.

Lemma 8 *There is a unique substitution operation on (D', X') such that for each $f : X' \to D'$*

$$\begin{aligned} \hat{f}d &= (\hat{f}|C'd) \cdot' d &\text{if} \quad d \in D'_\mathcal{U} - X', \\ \hat{f}(\delta'_\lambda(\overline{y}, d)) &= \delta_\lambda(\overline{y}, \hat{f}'d) &\text{if} \quad (\overline{y}, d) \in Y^{\cdot} \times D', \end{aligned}$$

where

$$f'z = \begin{cases} fz & \text{if} \quad z \in X' - ran(\overline{y}) \\ z & \text{if} \quad z \in ran(\overline{y}) \end{cases}$$

We complete this stage by giving some of the properties of substitution that we will be using. Before we do this we need functions fv and bv which return the free and bound parameters occurring within elements of D'.

Lemma 9

- *There is a least function $fv : D' \to pow\, X'$ such that*

$$\begin{aligned} fv(z) &= \{z\} &\text{if } z \in X', \\ fv(d) &= \textstyle\bigcup\{fv(d') \mid d' \in Cd\} &\text{if } d \in D'_\mathcal{U} - X', \\ fv(\delta_\lambda(\overline{y}, d)) &= fv(d) - ran(\overline{y}) &\text{if } (\overline{y}, d) \in Y^{\cdot} \times D'. \end{aligned}$$

- *There is a least function $bv : D' \to pow\, Y$ such that*

$$\begin{aligned} bv(z) &= \emptyset &\text{if } z \in X', \\ bv(d) &= \textstyle\bigcup\{bv(d') \mid d' \in C'd\} &\text{if } d \in D'_\mathcal{U} - X', \\ bv(\delta_\lambda(\overline{y}, d)) &= bv(d) \cup ran(\overline{y}) &\text{if } (\overline{y}, d) \in Y^{\cdot} \times D'. \end{aligned}$$

Proof. We show there is such a function fv, the proof for the existence of bv being similar. We first define functions $fv_n : D' \to pow\, X'$ by recursion on $n \in \mathbb{N}$. Let $fv_0(d) = \emptyset$ for all $d \in D'$. Given fv_n let

$$
\begin{aligned}
fv_{n+1}(z) &= \{z\} && \text{if } z \in X', \\
fv_{n+1}(d) &= \bigcup\{fv_n(d') \mid d' \in C'd\} && \text{if } d \in D'_{\mathcal{U}} - X', \\
fv_{n+1}(\delta_\lambda(\overline{y}, d)) &= fv_n(d) - ran(\overline{y}) && \text{if } (\overline{y}, d) \in Y^{\cdot} \times D.
\end{aligned}
$$

We now let

$$
fv(d) = \bigcup_{n \in \mathbb{N}} fv_n(d)
$$

for all $d \in D$. It is easy to check that fv is the least function satisfying the required equations. $\qquad\square$

The substitution operation given by lemma 8 is not a standard substitution operation (standard in the sense of definition 7), since complications arise when previously free parameters get bound by a substitution. However, providing we are careful with free and bound parameters we get that the substitution operation is 'almost' standard, i.e.,

Lemma 10 (Properties of the substitution operation on (D', X'))
Let $d \in D$ and $f, g : X' \to D'$ with

(1) $$ bv(d) \cap \bigcup\{fv(fx) \mid x \in fv(d)\} = \emptyset. $$

Then

1. $fv(d)$ *supports d for all $d \in D'$,*
2. $fv(\hat{f}d) = \bigcup\{fv(fx) \mid x \in fv(d)\}$,
3. *if $gx = x$ for all $x \in X'$ then $\hat{g}d = d$,*
4. $(\hat{g} \circ \hat{f})d = \hat{h}d$, *where $h : X' \to D'$ is given by $h = \hat{g} \circ f$.*

Stage 3: The Definition of D and Substitution on (D, X)

We are interested in those elements of D' which only have free parameters from X. So let

$$ D = \{d \in D' \mid fv(d) \subseteq X\}. $$

We write $D_{\mathcal{U}}$ for $D \cap D'_{\mathcal{U}}$ and D_λ for $D \cap D'_\lambda$. Let $\delta : \mathcal{U}[D] \to D_{\mathcal{U}}$ be given by $\delta u = \delta'(0, u)$ and notice that $\delta : \mathcal{U}[D] \cong D_{\mathcal{U}}$ so let $(D_{\mathcal{U}}, C, \cdot)$ be the D-form system $\mathcal{U}(D, \delta)$. In fact C and $\cdot$ are simply the restrictions of C' and $\cdot'$ to $D_{\mathcal{U}}$.

If $f : X \to D$ we shall write $\hat{f}$ for the substitution which extends the function equal to f on X and equal to the identity on Y, it is easy to see that, for such an f, for all $d \in D$ $\hat{f}d \in D$. This means we have a substitution operation on (D, X).

Lemma 11 *The substitution operation on (D, X) is a standard substitution operation*

Proof. It is obvious that if $f : X \to D$ then taking $f' : X' \to D'$ to be the function equal to f on X and equal to the identity on Y that f'

satisfies equation (1) in lemma 10. From the properties of the substitution operation on (D', X') given in that lemma it follows that the substitution operation on (D, X) is standard. □

Stage 4: The Definition of α-Equivalence, $\equiv_\alpha$, on D

We shall need to use the following general construction.

If $\mathcal{A} = (A, C, \cdot)$ is a B-form system and R is a relation on B then let $R^{\mathcal{A}}$ be the equivalence relation on A defined as follows:

First let R^e be the equivalence relation on B generated by R. Then use global AC to choose $q : B \to B$ so that $R^e = \{(b_1, b_2) \in B \times B \mid qb_1 = qb_2\}$. Now let

$$R^{\mathcal{A}} = \{(a_1, a_2) \in A \times A \mid (q|Ca_1) \cdot a_1 = (q|Ca_2) \cdot a_2\}$$

By the lemma, below, $R^{\mathcal{A}}$ does not depend on the choice of q.

Lemma 12 *Let $(A, C, \cdot)$ be a B-form system. Let $q, q' : B \to B$ such that for all $b_1, b_2 \in B$*

$$qb_1 = qb_2 \Leftrightarrow q'b_1 = q'b_2.$$

Then for all $a_1, a_2 \in A$

$$(q|Ca_1) \cdot a_1 = (q|Ca_2) \cdot a_2 \Leftrightarrow (q'|Ca_1) \cdot a_1 = (q'|Ca_2) \cdot a_2$$

Proof. Given q, q' as stated there is a bijection $s : ran(q) \cong ran(q')$ such that $q' = s \circ q$. Now if $a = (q|Ca_1) \cdot a_1$ then

$$
\begin{aligned}
a = (q|Ca_2) \cdot a_2 &\Rightarrow (s|Ca) \cdot ((q|Ca_1) \cdot a_1) = (s|Ca) \cdot ((q|Ca_2) \cdot a_2) \\
&\Rightarrow ((s \circ q)|Ca_1) \cdot a_1 = ((s \circ q)|Ca_2) \cdot a_2 \\
&\Rightarrow (q'|Ca_1) \cdot a_1 = (q'|Ca_2) \cdot a_2.
\end{aligned}
$$

Using $q = s^{-1} \circ q'$ we get the converse implication. □

Given a relation R on D we shall define relations $R_\mathcal{U}$ on $D_\mathcal{U}$ and R_λ on D_λ. Let $R_\mathcal{U} = R^{\mathcal{A}}$, where $\mathcal{A} = \mathcal{U}(D, C, \cdot)$, using the previous construction. To define R_λ, if $I \in IND$ and $d \in D'$ let $Q^I(d)$ be the class of $\overline{y} \in Y^{\cdot I}$ such that $ran(\overline{y})$ is disjoint from $bv(d)$. Note that this is always non-empty and in fact is a proper class as Y is a proper class. Also, if $\overline{x} \in X^{\cdot I}$ and $\overline{y} \in Q^I(d)$ let

$$\lambda_D(\overline{y}, \overline{x}, d) = \delta_\lambda(\overline{y}, [\overline{y}/\overline{x}]d).$$

Now define

$$R_\lambda = \bigcup_{I \in IND} \{(\lambda_D(\overline{y}_1, \overline{x}, d_1), \lambda_D(\overline{y}_2, \overline{x}, d_2)) \mid \overline{x} \in X^{\cdot I} \ \& \ d_1 R d_2 \ \&$$
$$\overline{y}_i \in Q^I(d_i) \text{ for } i = 1, 2\}.$$

By the next lemma we get that R_λ is a relation on D and therefore it is a relation on D_λ.

Lemma 13 *For all $I \in IND$ and $d \in D'$, if $\overline{y} \in Y^{\cdot I}$ and $\overline{x} \in X^{\cdot I}$ then*

$$\lambda_D(\overline{y}, \overline{x}, d) \in D \Leftrightarrow d \in D$$

Proof. Using property 2 of substitution and the definition of fv

$$fv(\lambda_D(\overline{y}, \overline{x}, d)) = fv(d)$$

It follows from the definition of D that $\lambda_D(\overline{y}, \overline{x}, d) \in D$ if and only if $d \in D$. □

Definition 13 A relation R on D is an α-*bisimulation* if $R \subseteq R_\mathcal{U} \cup R_\lambda$.

Proposition 14 *There is a maximal α-bisimulation on D which is an equivalence relation*

The proof of this proposition is similar to the proof that there is a maximal congruence on a coalgebra in Aczel and Mendler 1990. However the proof in this case is made more complicated by the 'abstracts'. The proposition is proved by taking $\equiv_\alpha$ to be the union of all the small α-bisimulations. This relation is easily shown to be an α-bisimulation and can then be shown to be a maximal α-bisimulation by showing that given any α-bisimulation R with $d_1 R d_2$ there is a small α-bisimulation R' with $d_1 R' d_2$. The relation is shown to be an equivalence relation by showing that $\equiv_\alpha^e$ is an α-bisimulation, from which, by maximality, $\equiv_\alpha$ is an equivalence relation.

We will call $\equiv_\alpha$ α-*equivalence*. Let us write $\equiv_\mathcal{U}$ for $(\equiv_\alpha)_\mathcal{U}$ and $\equiv_\lambda$ for $(\equiv_\alpha)_\lambda$. Then $\equiv_\mathcal{U}$ and $\equiv_\lambda$ are equivalence relations on $D_\mathcal{U}$ and D_λ respectively and we can show that

$$d_1 \equiv_\alpha d_2 \iff [d_1 \equiv_\mathcal{U} d_2 \text{ or } d_1 \equiv_\lambda d_2].$$

Stage 5: Formation of the Quotient of D With Respect to $\equiv_\alpha$

We will form the af $\mathcal{U}, \lambda$-universe by taking a quotient of D with respect to α-equivalence. So let $[[-]] : D \overset{onto}{\to} A$ be such that for $d_1, d_2 \in D$

$$d_1 \equiv_\alpha d_2 \iff [[d_1]] = [[d_2]].$$

Let $A_\mathcal{U} = \{[[d]] \mid d \in D_\mathcal{U}\}$. As $x_1 \equiv_\alpha x_2 \iff x_1 = x_2$ for $x_1, x_2 \in X$ we can identify each $x \in X$ with $[[x]] \in A_\mathcal{U}$, so that $X \subseteq A_\mathcal{U}$. Use global AC to choose $q_0 : A \to D$ so that $[[q_0 a]] = a$ for $a \in A$. Let $q_1 : D \to A$ be given by $q_1 d = [[d]]$ for $d \in D$. Let $q = q_0 \circ q_1 : D \to D$. Note that $q \circ q_0 = q_0$ so that $q \circ q = q$ and for $d_1, d_2 \in D$

$$d_1 \equiv_\alpha d_2 \iff q d_1 = q d_2.$$

The following abbreviation will be convenient whenever $u \in \mathcal{U}[B]$ and $f : B \to V$. We shall let

$$f_\mathcal{U} u = (f|C_\mathcal{U} u) \cdot_\mathcal{U} u.$$

Lemma 15 *For all $u_1, u_2 \in \mathcal{U}[D]$*

$$[[\delta u_1]] = [[\delta u_2]] \iff [q_\mathcal{U} u_1 = q_\mathcal{U} u_2].$$

We define $\alpha : \mathcal{U}[A] \to A_\mathcal{U}$ by

$$\alpha u = [[\delta((q_0)_\mathcal{U} u)]] \text{ for } u \in \mathcal{U}[A].$$

Lemma 16 α *is a bijection,* $\alpha : \mathcal{U}[A] \cong A\mathcal{U}$.

Proof. To show that α is injective let $u_1, u_2 \in \mathcal{U}[A]$ such that $\alpha u_1 = \alpha u_2$. By the definition of α and lemma 15

$$q_{\mathcal{U}}((q_0)_{\mathcal{U}} u_1) = q_{\mathcal{U}}((q_0)_{\mathcal{U}} u_2)$$

so that

$$(q \circ q_0)_{\mathcal{U}} u_1 = (q \circ q_0)_{\mathcal{U}} u_2.$$

As $q \circ q_0 = q_0$ and q_0 is injective it follows that $u_1 = u_2$.

To show that α is surjective let $a \in A\mathcal{U}$. Then $a = [[\delta u_0]]$ for some $u_0 \in \mathcal{U}[D]$. Let $u = (q_1)_{\mathcal{U}} u_0$. As $q \circ q = q$,

$$q_{\mathcal{U}}(q_{\mathcal{U}} u_0) = q_{\mathcal{U}} u_0$$

so that, by lemma 15, $[[\delta(q_{\mathcal{U}} u_0)]] = [[\delta u_0]]$ and hence

$$
\begin{aligned}
\alpha u &= [[\delta((q_0)_{\mathcal{U}} u)]] \\
&= [[\delta((q_0 \circ q_1)_{\mathcal{U}} u_0)]] \\
&= [[\delta u_0]] \\
&= a \qquad\qquad\qquad \square
\end{aligned}
$$

As $\alpha : \mathcal{U}[A] \cong A\mathcal{U}$ we have the $\mathcal{U}$-A-form system $A\mathcal{U} = (A\mathcal{U}, C_A, \cdot_A) = \mathcal{U}(A, \alpha)$. The following result will be useful. Recall that $\mathcal{U}(D, \delta) = (D, C, \cdot)$.

Lemma 17 *Let* $d \in D$. *Then*

1. $C_A[[d]] = \{[[d']] \mid d' \in Cd\}$,
2. *If* $\sigma : C_A[[d]] \rightarrow A$ *and* $\sigma' : Cd \rightarrow D$ *such that* $\sigma[[d']] = [[\sigma' d']]$ *for all* $d' \in Cd$ *then*

$$\sigma \cdot_A [[d]] = [[\sigma' \cdot d]].$$

Let $A_\lambda = \{[[d]] \mid d \in D_\lambda\}$. We wish to define $\lambda_A : X \cdot \times A \rightarrow A_\lambda$ using the equation

$$\lambda_A(\overline{x}, [[d]]) = [[\lambda_D(\overline{y}, \overline{x}, d)]],$$

where if $I = dom(\overline{x})$ then $\overline{y}$ is chosen in $Q^I(d)$. We can do this because by lemma 13 $\lambda_D(\overline{y}, \overline{x}, d) \in D$ and by the next lemma the right hand side of the above equation is independent of the choices made.

Lemma 18 *Let* $I \in IND, \overline{x} \in X^{\cdot I}$ *and, for* $i = 1, 2$, *let* $d_i \in D$ *and* $\overline{y}_i \in Q^I(d_i)$. *Then*

$$d_1 \equiv_\alpha d_2 \implies \lambda_D(\overline{y}_1, \overline{x}, d_1) \equiv_\alpha \lambda_D(\overline{y}_2, \overline{x}, d_2).$$

Proof. From the properties of substitution we get that $[\overline{x}/\overline{y}_i][\overline{y}_i/\overline{x}]d_i = d_i$ from which the result follows. $\qquad\qquad \square$

Lemma 19 $\lambda_A : X^{\cdot I} \times A \rightarrow A_\lambda$ *is surjective.*

Proof. We show that if $\delta_\lambda(\overline{y}, d') \in D$ then there is some $\overline{x} \in X^{\cdot}, d \in D$ with

$$[[\delta_\lambda(\overline{y}, d')]] = \lambda_A(\overline{x}, [[d]])$$

Suppose that $I = dom(\overline{y})$ and take any $\overline{x} \in X^{\cdot I}$ with $ran(\overline{x}) \cap fv(d) = \emptyset$. From the properties of substitution $[\overline{y}/\overline{x}][\overline{x}/\overline{y}]d' = d'$ and $d = [\overline{x}/\overline{y}]d' \in D$. It follows that

$$[[\delta_\lambda(\overline{y}, d')]] = \lambda_A(\overline{x}, [[d]])$$

as required. □

Note that $A_\lambda = A - A_\mathcal{U}$ so that

$$\mathcal{A} = (A, A_\mathcal{U}, X, \lambda_A)$$

is a pre λ-universe.

Stage 6: The Proof that $\mathcal{A}$ is a λ-Universe

We show that the pre λ-universe $\mathcal{A}$ satisfies the three axioms for a λ-universe.

Axiom 1: We must define $par : A \to powX$ and show that it is the least parameters function for $\mathcal{A}$. We define it in terms of the function fv on D given by lemma 9. Recall that fv associates with each $d \in D$ the parameters occurring free in it. Using the next result we can define par to be the unique function $A \to powX$ such that

$$par([[d]]) = fv(d)$$

for all $d \in D$. This is independent of the choice of d since

Lemma 20 $d_1 \equiv_\alpha d_2 \;\Rightarrow\; fv(d_1) = fv(d_2)$.

Proof. It can be shown that if $\delta_\lambda(\overline{y}, d) \in D$ then $fv_n([\overline{y}/\overline{x}]d) = \{[\overline{y}/\overline{x}]z \mid z \in fv_n(d)\}$ where fv_n is as defined in lemma 9. Using this result it is easy to prove, by induction, that if $d_1 \equiv_\alpha d_2$ then $fv_n(d_1) = fv_n(d_2)$. □

It is easy to check that par is a parameters function. To see that it is the least one let par' be any parameters function. Then by induction on $n \in \mathbb{N}$ we can check that for all $d \in D$

$$fv_n(d) \subseteq par'([[d]])$$

and hence that

$$par([[d]]) = \bigcup_{n \in \mathbb{N}} fv_n(d) \subseteq par'([[d]]).$$

Axiom 2: We must associate with each function $f : X \to A$ a suitable extension $\hat{f} : A \to A$. We may use AC to define a function $g : X \to D$ such that

$$fx = [[gx]]$$

for all $x \in X$. We may then define the substitution $\hat{f} : A \to A$ in terms of the substitution $\hat{g} : D \to D$ as follows.

$$\hat{f}[[d]] = [[\hat{g}d]]$$

for all $d \in D$. For this to be well-defined we need

Lemma 21 *Let $a \in A$ and let $f : X \to A$. For all $d_1, d_2 \in D$ and all $g_1, g_2 : X \to D$ if*

    1. $a = [[d_1]] = [[d_2]]$,

    2. $fx = [[g_1 x]] = [[g_2 x]]$ *for all $x \in X$,*

then

$$[[\hat{g}_1 d_1]] = [[\hat{g}_2 d_2]].$$

Proof. Let

$$R = \{(\hat{g}_1 d_1, \hat{g}_2 d_2) \mid d_1 \equiv_\alpha d_2\} \cup \equiv_\alpha .$$

Then it suffices to show that R is an α-bisimulation. □

In fact we have a standard substitution operation on (A, X). This follows easily from lemma 7.4.

It is now easy to show, using lemma 17, that $\hat{f}$ satisfies the conditions (a) and (b) of axiom 2, so we have shown the existence of substitutions extending functions $X \to A$. We also need to show the uniqueness of the substitutions, i.e., that $\hat{f}$ is the unique function extending f and satisfying those conditions. This follows from the next lemma.

Lemma 22 *If $g_1, g_2 : A \to A$ satisfy conditions 2(a) and 2(b) of axiom 2 and $g_1|X = g_2|X$ then letting R be the relation on D given by*

$$R = \{(d_1, d_2) \mid \exists a \in A \cdot [[d_i]] = g_i a , i = 1, 2\} \cup \equiv_\alpha$$

R is an α-bisimulation.

Axiom 3: We want to show that for all $(\overline{x}_1, a_1), (\overline{x}_2, a_2) \in X^{\cdot} \times A$

$$\lambda_A(\overline{x}_1, a_1) = \lambda_A(\overline{x}_2, a_2) \Leftrightarrow (\overline{x}_1, a_1) \sim^I (\overline{x}_2, a_2) \text{ for some } I \in IND.$$

Recall that

$$(\overline{x}_1, a_1) \sim^I (\overline{x}_2, a_2) \Leftrightarrow [\overline{c}/\overline{x}_1]a_1 = [\overline{c}/\overline{x}_2]a_2 \text{ for all } \overline{c} \in A^I.$$

So first suppose that $\lambda_A(\overline{x}_1, a_1) = \lambda_A(\overline{x}_2, a_2)$ and, for $i = 1, 2$, let $d_i \in D$, with $[[d_i]] = a_i$, and $\overline{y}_i \in Q^I(d_i)$, where $I = dom(\overline{x}_1) = dom(\overline{x}_2)$. Then $\lambda_D(\overline{y}_1, \overline{x}_1, d_1) \equiv_\alpha \lambda_D(\overline{y}_2, \overline{x}_2, d_2)$ so that for some $\overline{x} \in X^{\cdot I}$, with $ran(\overline{x})$ disjoint from $fv(d_1) \cup fv(d_2)$,

$$[\overline{x}/\overline{x}_1]d_1 \equiv_\alpha [\overline{x}/\overline{x}_2]d_2.$$

From the definition of the substitution operation on $\mathcal{A}$ we get that

$$[\overline{x}/\overline{x}_1]a_1 = [\overline{x}/\overline{x}_2]a_2.$$

It follows that for any $\overline{c} \in A^I$

$$[\overline{c}/\overline{x}_1]a_1 = [\overline{c}/\overline{x}][\overline{x}/\overline{x}_1]a_1 = [\overline{c}/\overline{x}][\overline{x}/\overline{x}_2]a_2 = [\overline{c}/\overline{x}_2]a_2,$$

so that $(\overline{x}_1, a_1) \sim^I (\overline{x}_2, a_2)$.

For the converse implication suppose that $I \in IND$ and $(\overline{x}_1, a_1) \sim^I (\overline{x}_2, a_2)$. For $i = 1, 2$ choose $d_i \in D$ so that $[[d_i]] = a_i$. Let $\overline{x} \in X^{\cdot I}$ so that $ran(\overline{x})$ is disjoint from $fv(d_1) \cup fv(d_2)$. Then, as $[\overline{x}/\overline{x}_1]a_1 = [\overline{x}/\overline{x}_2]a_2$,

$$[\overline{x}/\overline{x}_1]d_1 \equiv_\alpha [\overline{x}/\overline{x}_2]d_2$$

and hence, by lemma 7.12, if $\overline{y}_i \in Q^I(d_i)$ for $i = 1, 2$ then

$$\lambda_D(\overline{y}_1, \overline{x}, [\overline{x}/\overline{x}_1]d)1 \equiv_\alpha \lambda_D(\overline{y}_2, \overline{x}, [\overline{x}/\overline{x}_2]d_2).$$

It easily follows that $\lambda_A(\overline{x}_1, a_1) = \lambda_A(\overline{x}_2, a_2)$.

This completes the proof that we have a λ-universe.

Stage 7: $\mathcal{A}$ is Anti-Founded

We have already shown that $\mathcal{A}$ is a $\mathcal{U}, \lambda$-universe. To show that $\mathcal{A}$ is af we need to show the existence of a unique solution to any $(\mathcal{U}, X)$-soe in $\mathcal{A}$. The existence of a solution comes from the existence of a solution to any $\mathcal{U}'$-soe in $\mathcal{U}'(D', \delta')$. The uniqueness comes from the fact that we have taken a quotient with respect to α-equivalence.

We first show there is a solution to any $(\mathcal{U}, X)$-soe in $\mathcal{A}$. Let

$$z = u_z \quad (z \in Z)$$

be a $(\mathcal{U}, X)$-soe. To get a solution we construct a $\mathcal{U}'$-soe from the above system. So let $\rho : X \cong Y$ be a bijection. If $z_0, \ldots, z_n \in Z$ write $\langle z_0, \ldots, z_n \rangle$ for the list containing these elements and call $\langle z_0, \cdots, z_n \rangle$ an *occurrence* if for all $i < n$

$$u_{z_i} = (0, u) \qquad \text{and } z_{i+1} \in C_{\mathcal{U}} u \text{ or}$$
$$u_{z_i} = (1, (\overline{x}, z_{i+1}))$$

If $\langle z_0, \ldots, z_n \rangle$ is an occurrence and $u_{z_n} = (0, x)$ for some $x \in X$ then we call $\langle z_0, \ldots, z_n \rangle$ a *bound occurrence* if there is some $i < n$ with $z_i = (1, (\overline{x}, z_{i+1}))$ and $x \in ran(\overline{x})$, otherwise we call $\langle z_0, \ldots, z_n \rangle$ a *free occurrence*.

Let $Z^* = \{\overline{z} \mid \overline{z} \text{ is an occurrence}\}$ and form the system of equations

$$\overline{z} = v_{\overline{z}} \quad (\overline{z} \in Z^*)$$

where, if $\overline{z} = \langle z_0, \ldots, z_n \rangle$ and writing $\overline{z}'$ for $\langle z_0, \ldots, z_n, z' \rangle$

$$v_{\overline{z}} = \begin{cases} (1, (\rho \circ \overline{x}, \overline{z}')) & \text{if } u_{z_n} = (1, (\overline{x}, z')) \\ (0, \sigma \cdot_{\mathcal{U}} u) & \text{if } u_{z_n} = (0, u), u \notin X \text{ where } \sigma z' = \overline{z}' \text{ for } z' \in C_{\mathcal{U}} u \\ (0, \rho u) & \text{if } u_{z_n} = (0, u), u \in X \text{ and } \overline{z} \text{ is a bound occurrence} \\ (0, u) & \text{if } u_{z_n} = (0, u), u \in X \text{ and } \overline{z} \text{ is a free occurrence} \end{cases}$$

This is a $\mathcal{U}'$-soe so since $\mathcal{U}'(D', \delta')$ is an af $\mathcal{U}'$-universe there is a unique solution to this system of equations in $\mathcal{U}'(D', \delta')$. Let this solution be π.

Lemma 23 $\pi\langle z \rangle \in D$ for $z \in Z$.

Lemma 24 *Let* $\tau : Z \to A$ *be given by*

$$\tau z = [[\pi\langle z \rangle]]$$

Then $\tau : Z \to A$ *is a solution to the* $(\mathcal{U}, X)$-*soe in* $\mathcal{A}$.

This gives us a solution to the system of equations. That the solution is unique follows from the next lemma.

Lemma 25 *If* $\pi_1, \pi_2 : Z \to A$ *are solutions in* $\mathcal{A}$ *to the above* $(\mathcal{U}, X)$*-soe then*

$$\{(d_1, d_2) \mid \exists z \in Z \cdot \pi_i z = [[d_i]], \, i = 1, 2\}$$

is an α*-bisimulation on* D.

Now if we have two solutions to a $(\mathcal{U}, X)$-soe it follows that they must be the same and so $\mathcal{A}$ is af. This completes the proof of the existence of an af $\mathcal{U}, \lambda$-universe. To finish the proof of the theorem it remains to show that if there is an af $\mathcal{U}, \lambda$-universe then it is unique up to isomorphism.

8 The Isomorphism of Any Two Anti-Founded $\mathcal{U}, \lambda$-Universes

That an af $\mathcal{U}, \lambda$-universe is unique up to isomorphism is shown in two parts. Firstly it is shown that α-equivalence on an af λ-universe is the equality relation on it. This result is then used to show that there is a structure preserving bijection between any two af $\mathcal{U}, \lambda$-universes.

8.1 Alpha Equivalence on a λ-Universe

We first need to define α-equivalence on a λ-universe. Let $\mathcal{A} = (A, \mathcal{A}', X, \lambda)$ be a λ-universe. Given a relation R on A, if $I \in IND$ then we define a relation R^I on $X^{\cdot I} \times A$ as follows. Let R^I be the class of all pairs $((\overline{x}, a), (\overline{y}, b))$ such that $([\overline{z}/\overline{x}]a) \, R \, ([\overline{z}/\overline{y}]b)$ for some $\overline{z} \in X^{\cdot I}$ such that $ran(\overline{z})$ is disjoint from $((par(a) - ran(\overline{x})) \cup (par(b) - ran(\overline{y})))$. Notice that if $\overline{x}_i, \overline{y}_i \in X^{\cdot I}$ and $a_i, b_i \in A$ for $i = 1, 2$ such that $\lambda(\overline{x}_1, a_1) = \lambda(\overline{x}_2, a_2)$ and $\lambda(\overline{y}_1, b_1) = \lambda(\overline{y}_2, b_2)$ then

$$(\overline{x}_1, a_1) R^I (\overline{y}_1, b_1) \Leftrightarrow (\overline{x}_2, a_2) R^I (\overline{y}_2, b_2).$$

Write R_λ for the relation

$$R_\lambda = \bigcup_{I \in IND} \{(\lambda(\overline{x}, a), \lambda(\overline{y}, b)) \mid (\overline{x}, a) R^I (\overline{y}, b)\}$$

We will say that R is an α*-bisimulation* on $\mathcal{A}$ if $R \subseteq R^{\mathcal{A}'} \cup R_\lambda$ where $R^{\mathcal{A}'}$ is the relation defined in stage four of section 7.

Lemma 26 *There is a maximal α-bisimulation on $\mathcal{A}$ which is also an equivalence relation.*

The proof of this result is essentially the same as the proof of the analogous result for D given in lemma 14. Take the union of all the small α-bisimulations, which is an α-bisimulation. This can then be shown to be maximal and an equivalence relation. We will call this maximal α-bisimulation α-equivalence and denote it by $\equiv_\alpha$.

Proposition 27 *α-equivalence on a wf/af $\mathcal{U}, \lambda$-universe is the equality relation on it.*

Proof. In the wf case this is proved by induction. In the af case let our $\mathcal{U},\lambda$-universe be $\mathcal{A} = (A, \mathcal{U}(A, \gamma), X, \lambda)$ and let *par* be the least parameters map. We will take a quotient of α-equivalence on A, this quotient will then be treated as a large $(\mathcal{U}, X)$-soe. The solution to such a large $(\mathcal{U}, X)$-soe will then be shown to be a bijection. A *large* $(\mathcal{U}, X)$-*soe* is of the form

$$y = a_y \quad (y \in Y)$$

where Y is a class and $a_y \in (\{0\} \times \mathcal{U}[Y]) \cup (\{1\} \times (X \times Y))$. A solution for a large $(\mathcal{U}, X)$-soe is as for a solution for a $(\mathcal{U}, X)$-soe.

Lemma 28 *Every large $(\mathcal{U}, X)$-soe has a unique solution in an af $\mathcal{U},\lambda$-universe.*

The solution to a large soe is obtained from piecing together the solutions to subequations of the large soe.

Lemma 29 *For any $a, b \in A$, if $a \equiv_\alpha b$ then $par(a) = par(b)$.*

The proof of this lemma is similar to the proof of 9, which states that alpha equivalent terms in D have the same free parameters. Now let $q : A \rightarrow B$ be a quotient of $\equiv_\alpha$. By the above lemma we can, for $b \in B$, let $par(b) = par(a)$ for some $a \in A$ with $qa = b$. For $I \in IND$ let $B_I = \{q(\lambda(\overline{x}, a)) \mid a \in A, \overline{x} \in X^{\cdot I}\}$ and for each $b \in B_I$ choose some $\overline{x}_b \in X^{\cdot I}$ with $ran(\overline{x}) \cap par(b) = \emptyset$. Notice that if $a \in A - A'$ then there is some $a' \in A$ with $a = \lambda(\overline{x}_{qa}, a')$. For $a \in A$ let u_a be given by

$$u_a = \begin{cases} (0, \gamma^{-1}a) & \text{if} \quad a \in A' \\ (1, (\overline{x}_{qa}, a')) & \text{if} \quad a = \lambda(\overline{x}_{qa}, a') \end{cases}$$

and for $b \in B$, letting $a \in A$ be such that $qa = b$ let v_b be given by

$$v_b = \begin{cases} (0, q_{\mathcal{U}}(\gamma^{-1}a)) & \text{if} \quad a \in A' \\ (1, (\overline{x}_b, qa')) & \text{if} \quad a = \lambda(\overline{x}_b, a') \end{cases}$$

Using the next lemma it is easy to show that v_b is independent of the choice of a.

Lemma 30 *If $a_1 \equiv_\alpha a_2$ and $s : X \rightarrow A$ then*

$$\hat{s}a_1 \equiv_\alpha \hat{s}a_2$$

This is proved by showing that $\{(\hat{s}a_1, \hat{s}a_2) \mid a_1 \equiv_\alpha a_2\} \cup \{(a, a) \mid a \in A\}$ is a α-bisimulation.

Now consider the two large $(\mathcal{U}, X)$-soes.

$$\begin{aligned} a &= u_a \quad (a \in A) \\ b &= v_b \quad (b \in B) \end{aligned}$$

Let $\pi : B \rightarrow A$ be a solution to the second soe in $\mathcal{A}$. Then $\pi \circ q : A \rightarrow A$ is a solution to the first soe in $\mathcal{A}$. However the identity is a solution to the first and so, by the uniqueness of solution, $\pi \circ q$ must be the identity on A. It follows that q and π are bijections and so α-equivalence must give equality. $\qquad\Box$

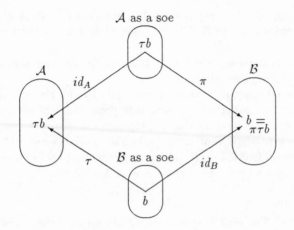

8.2 The Isomorphism

We now show that any two af $\mathcal{U},\lambda$-universes are isomorphic. Let $\mathcal{A} = (A, \mathcal{U}(A', \alpha), X, \lambda_A)$, $\mathcal{B} = (B, \mathcal{U}(B', \beta), X, \lambda_B)$ be af $\mathcal{U},\lambda$-universes. We assume without loss of generality that A and B are disjoint.

Lemma 31 *Let*

$$y = u_y \qquad (y \in Y)$$
$$z = v_z \qquad (z \in Z)$$

be two large $(\mathcal{U}, X)$-soe with π_A, π_B solutions to ihe first in $\mathcal{A}, \mathcal{B}$ respectively and τ_A, τ_B solutions to the second.

- *if $\pi_A y = \tau_A z$ in $\mathcal{A}$ for some $y \in Y, z \in Z$ then $\pi_B y = \tau_B z$ in $\mathcal{B}$.*
- *if $\pi_B y = \tau_B z$ in $\mathcal{B}$ for some $y \in Y, z \in Z$ then $\pi_A y = \tau_A z$ in $\mathcal{A}$.*

This lemma is proved by showing that if $\pi_A y = \tau_A z$ then $\pi_B y \equiv_\alpha \tau_B z$ from which, by proposition 27, we get $\pi_B y = \tau_B z$.

We will now consider $\mathcal{A}$ and $\mathcal{B}$ as large $(\mathcal{U}, X)$-soe. For each $a \in A - A'$ choose some $\overline{x}_a \in X^\cdot$ with $a = \lambda_A(\overline{x}_a, a')$ for some $a' \in A$. Similarly for each $b \in B - B'$ choose some $\overline{x}_b$. Now consider the large $(\mathcal{U}, X)$-soe

$$a = u_a \qquad (a \in A)$$
$$b = v_b \qquad (b \in B)$$

Where for $a \in A$ let u_a be given by

$$u_a = \begin{cases} (0, \alpha^{-1}a) & \text{if} \quad a \in A' \\ (1, (\overline{x}_a, a')) & \text{if} \quad a = \lambda_A(\overline{x}_a, a') \end{cases}$$

and for $b \in B$ let v_b be given by

$$v_b = \begin{cases} (0, \beta^{-1}a) & \text{if} \quad a \in A' \\ (1, (\overline{x}_b, b')) & \text{if} \quad b = \lambda_B(\overline{x}_b, b') \end{cases}$$

Let $\pi : A \to B$ be the solution to the first in $\mathcal{B}$ and let $\tau : B \to A$ be the solution to the second in $\mathcal{A}$. Notice that, if id_A, id_B are the identities on A

and B respectively then id_A is the solution to the first in $\mathcal{A}$ and id_B is the solution to the second in $\mathcal{B}$. We will show that π is a structure preserving bijection.

Firstly π is onto since if $b \in B$ then by the above lemma $b = \pi(\tau b)$, since $\tau b = id_A(\tau b)$ (see picture).

And π is 1-1 since if $\pi a = \pi a'$ then, again by the above lemma, $a = a'$.

It remains to show that π is structure preserving. Since π is a solution to the first soe it is obvious that π preserves components and abstraction and it is easy to show that it also preserves replacement. Therefore π is an isomorphism from $\mathcal{A} \rightarrow \mathcal{B}$. This completes the proof of theorem 7 that there is a, unique up to isomorphism, af $\mathcal{U}, \lambda$-universe.

References

Aczel, P. 1988. *Non-Well-Founded Sets*. CSLI Lecture Notes Number 14. Stanford: CSLI Publications.

Aczel, P. 1990. Replacement Systems and the Axiomatization of Situation Theory. In Cooper et al. 1990.

Aczel, P. 1991. Term Declaration Logic and Generalised Composita. In *Proceedings of the Sixth IEEE Symposium on Logic in Computer Science*.

Aczel, P., and N. Mendler. 1990. A Final Coalgebra Theorem. In *Proceedings of LNCS 384: Category Theory in Computer Science*.

Cooper, R., K. Mukai, and J. Perry (ed.). 1990. *Situation Theory and Its Applications*, vol. 1. CSLI Lecture Notes Number 22. Stanford: CSLI Publications.

Lunnon, R. 1991a. *Generalised Universes*. PhD thesis, Manchester University, Manchester, UK.

Lunnon, R. 1991b. Many Sorted Universes, SRDs and Injective Sums. This volume.

Williams, J. G. 1990. Instantiation Theory. Technical report, Mitre.

2

Situations as Mathematical Abstractions

KEITH J. DEVLIN

I present an answer to the oft-repeated question "What are situations?" I argue that situations, as required both for Situation Semantics and for a mathematical theory of information of the kind described in Barwise and Perry 1983 and Devlin 1991, constitute a class of abstract mathematical objects that are (a) quite distinct from anything else in mathematics, and (b) not reducible to anything else in the ontology of Situation Theory.

This paper continues the argument begun in Devlin 1990. The motivation for both papers was an electronic mail exchange with Pat Hayes of Xerox PARC. In the previous paper, I compared infons and numbers. Here I draw a parallel between situations and numbers.

1 Abstract Objects in Mathematics

Most present day mathematicians, myself included, have learned our mathematics in a mathematical environment in which abstraction, formal definition, and proof are not only pre-eminent, but almost taken to be synonymous with the word 'mathematics'. And for the most part, this is the tradition we pass on to our students in our lectures and our books. The "official" philosophy generally claimed to underpin this approach is essentially a Formalist one, but in truth, on a day-to-day basis, practically all contemporary mathematicians work in an out-and-out Platonistic fashion. Abstract mathematical entities such as numbers (natural, integer, rational, real, complex, infinite cardinal and ordinal) and spaces (geometric, metric, topological, linear, normed, etc.) are regarded as 'real objects' in a world that the mathematician sets out to *discover*. They are part of a mental world the mathematician learns to live in and become familiar with. Indeed, it is this intimate familiarity with an idealized, highly-ordered, ab-

---

I wish to thank David Israel for comments on an earlier draft of this paper.

Situation Theory and Its Applications, vol. 2.
Jon Barwise, Jean Mark Gawron, Gordon Plotkin, and Syun Tutiya, eds.
Copyright © 1991, Stanford University.

stract world of great simplicity that makes mathematics such an incredibly powerful tool with which to study certain aspects of the world.

So why then is there such a pretense of a Formalistic philosophy, if such it is? Well, it certainly gets the mathematician off a thorny philosophical hook with very little effort. As Cohen (1971) says:

> To the average mathematician, who merely wants to know that his work is securely based, the most appealing choice is to avoid difficulties by means of [Formalism].

Moschovakis (1980, pp. 605-6) is even more blunt about the situation:

> ...most attempts to turn [their] strong [Platonistic] feelings into a coherent foundation for mathematics invariably lead to vague discussions of 'existence of abstract notions' which are quite repugnant to a mathematician. Contrast with this the relative ease with which formalism can be explained in a precise, elegant and self-consistent manner and you will have the main reason why most mathematicians claim to be formalists (when pressed) while they spend their working hours behaving as if they were completely unabashed realists.

For the mathematician whose primary (indeed for most the sole) concern is to solve mathematical problems and prove mathematical theorems, this kind of "Sunday-best Formalism" is all well and good. The vast majority of mathematicians have enough to do without becoming embroiled in questions of philosophy, so any means of getting those persistent philosophers off their backs is worth adopting.

But as soon as the mathematician starts to investigate matters that arise in real life, the situation changes dramatically. For instance, as Putnam points out (1979b, p. 74):

> ...mathematics and physics are integrated in such a way that it is not possible to be a realist with respect to physical theory and a nominalist[1] with respect to mathematical theory.

And again in Putnam 1979a (p. 347):

> ...[talk about] mathematical entities is indispensable for science ...therefore we should accept such [talk]; but this commits us to accepting the existence of the mathematical entities in question. This type of argument stems, of course, from Quine, who has for years stressed both the indispensability of [talk about] mathematical entities and the intellectual dishonesty of denying the existence of what one daily presupposes.

Of course, the issue of intellectual dishonesty aside, a strict adherence to a Formalist philosophy leaves the mathematician unable to explain just why it is that his "formal game" invariably turns out to be extremely useful in everyday life, in a manner that other formal games (such as chess) do not.

---

[1] One who holds that abstract entities simply do not exist.

For instance, Steen (1988) writes:

> ...theoretical physics has continued to adopt (and occasionally invent) increasingly abstract mathematical models as the logical foundation for current theories: Lie groups and gauge theories, exotic expressions of symmetry, have joined fermions and baryons as fundamental tools in the physicist's search for a unified theory of both microscopic and macroscopic forces of nature.

As with physics, so too with any attempt to develop a mathematical theory of information. In Devlin 1990 and elsewhere, I have suggested that the search for a mathematical theory of information should be carried out in an empirical fashion, in much the same spirit as contemporary physics.[2] I believe that such an approach likewise leads to, in Putnam's words an "indispensable need" for mathematical entities, in this case the infons (among other objects).

The argument for infons presented in Devlin 1990 runs roughly as follows. Information of the kind we study arises by way of intentional representations in cognitive devices such as the brain. A particular cognitive state represents a certain piece of information by means of what situation-theorists refer to as a constraint.[3] Effective communication between cognitive agents requires that there be an empirical equivalence relation between two representations, an equivalence that can best be described as "representing the same item of information." If you factor out the set of all representations by this equivalence relation, the equivalence classes you obtain are what I call the infons—the 'fundamental items of information' of the theory.

In the same article (Devlin 1990), I point out the similarities between this process and the standard mathematical constructions of the various number systems of mathematics, from the natural numbers (equivalence classes of finite collections under equipollence) through to to the imaginary and complex numbers. In particular, this analogy indicates how the process avoids being circular, even though the most natural description using ordinary language involves the apparent circularity of using the phrase "represent the same item of information" in order to define the equivalence relation that produces those *items* of information, just as the standard definition of natural numbers involves reference to the equivalence relation of two sets having the same *number* of elements.

Now, the representations and the equivalences are surely *there* in the world, for otherwise how could we ourselves function and communicate in our society? So why not work directly with them? Why go to the additional step of introducing a realm of abstract objects?

---

[2]Indeed, the very word "infon" used to denote a basic 'item' of information, was chosen in order to draw a parallel with the electrons, protons, neutrons, photons, gravitons, fermions, baryons, etc., of physics.

[3]See Devlin 1991.

The answer seems as obvious to me as it appears to be baffling to others. Because it is far, far easier to reason using such entities. Certainly this is true in my own case. And I can only understand and appreciate the mathematics produced by other mathematicians under the assumption that this is how they too operate.

The axioms that we (mathematicians) develop for our Sunday-best formalism thus amount to the product of a carefully reasoned analysis of the most basic properties of those abstract objects that we 'create'. The fact that we appear to end up with just one common 'mathematics' about one particular collection of shared 'mathematical objects', follows from the common experience upon which we draw in order to make the various abstractions.

To anyone who objects to such an anthropological description of the mathematical enterprise, and I know there are such objectors, let me pose the following question: How else was it that many generations of mathematicians were able to develop some very sophisticated, and ultimately useful, mathematics, prior to the formulation of the axioms for that mathematics? Indeed, how is it that in practically all useful branches of mathematics, the axiomatization invariably came some time *after* the main ideas of the theory were worked out?

2   A Mathematical Theory of Information

It is one of the aims of this paper to convince you that a potentially useful mathematical theory of information (including the ability to handle the role played by language in the communication of information) is greatly facilitated by the introduction of certain abstract objects, in particular (but not exclusively) infons and situations.[4] Indeed, given the belief I expressed above that the human mind is only capable of mathematical reasoning in terms of the mental 'manipulation' of abstract *objects*, I claim that a useful theory of information *necessitates* the introduction of such mathematical objects. The complexity that would result were such a study attempted using only what is (in a sense) actually *there* (namely the various representations) would, I maintain, prevent any significant progress.

In trying to make my case for this view, there are in fact two issues I must address. First of all, the requirement for abstract objects at all in the intellectual activity of mathematicians. And secondly, the necessity of some *new* abstract objects in the case of a theory of information.

The first issue has already been addressed in the opening section. To those who maintain that strict Formalism is all that is required for mathe-

---

[4]David Israel has questioned whether situations should be classified as "abstract." After all, some of them are pretty concrete. He has a point, but since our theory will make use of abstract mathematical objectifications of situations, the word is not entirely inappropriate.

matics, there is little more I can say. I simply cannot imagine what they are *doing* (mentally) when they perform an arithmetic computation in their heads or seek a new theorem of number theory, field theory, algebraic topology, or whatever. Certainly, in performing positive whole number arithmetic for instance, they cannot surely be formally deriving some consequences of the Peano axioms?

What seems to single out the truly great mathematicians of any age, is the incredible 'familiarity' they develop with the 'domain of objects' they generally work with. They might indeed have little else other than this familiarity. Such was the case with the Indian mathematician Ramanujan, who was able to make wonderful *discoveries* about numbers, but lacked the knowledge or training required to 'deduce' those results from 'axioms'. Likewise Fermat, Gauss, and Euler appeared to have a deep understanding of the natural numbers *qua* objects, rather than as some formal system determined by axioms.

From now on, I shall assume that the reader either agrees with me that mathematical thought requires a realm of abstract objects, or at least grants me this assumption for the sake of argument. The question then is, why does a mathematically based study of information and natural language communication require a *new* collection of abstract objects?

3   Situations

A great deal of the basic, situation-theoretic ontology for the study of information and cognition has a fairly traditional look to it: individuals, relations, spatial and temporal locations, even types. One thing that is novel to the situation-theoretic approach, and what gives rise to the name of this theory, is the inclusion in the ontology of what we call *situations*.

In *Situation* Theory, we take note of the fact that an agent's world divides up into a collection (or succession) of situations: situations encountered, situations referred to, situations about which information is received, and so on. That is to say, our theory reflects the fact that agent's discriminate (by their behavior) situations.

Thus, the behavior of people varies systematically according to the kind of situation they are faced with: threatening situations, spooky situations, pleasant situations, challenging situations, conversations, and what have you, all evoke quite different responses. And likewise at the other end of the cognitive spectrum, the behavior of mechanical devices can depend quite dramatically on the situation in which the device is located: a computer will generally function quite differently in my office than it will when placed in a tub of water, and a moon buggy that moves smoothly on the surface of the Moon may not move at all when placed on Earth.

Again, natural language discourse relies heavily on context in many ways: to prevent ambiguities of meaning, to supply the referents to proper nouns and pronouns, to provide temporal and location referents for verbs, and so on. Thus, an utterance of the sentence

The boy in the red hat bought it from him

only makes a definite claim when linked to one or more situations that serve to determine who it is that the phrase "the boy in the red hat" refers to, and who is the referent of the pronoun "him".

In situation theory, we account for this kind of situation dependency when we take *propositions* (i.e., the *claims* made by utterances of declarative sentences) to be of the form

$$s \models \sigma$$

where σ is a compound infon (the *descriptive content* of the sentence uttered) and s is a situation.

But what exactly is the *object* denoted by the letter s is such an expression? In many of the examples that are given in accounts of situation theory and situation semantics, the situations that occur are determined by (what goes on in) simply-connected[5] regions of space-time. But this is purely because these provide a natural class of examples that are easily understood. Space-time regions certainly do provide examples of situations, but they by no means exhaust all possibilities.

A slightly more complex case arises in the semantic analysis of a telephone conversation between someone in (say) New York and someone in San Francisco. The physical extent of the "telephone-call situation" then comprises two connected regions of space over the same time interval, and possibly also the communication link between them (be it a landline, a satellite link, or whatever).

Again, the constraints that allow one situation to provide information about another, and which serve as the link between representations and the information they represent, are generally dependent on a whole range of "background conditions" that our theory takes in the form of *background situations*.

For example, take the familiar constraint that if an egg is dropped it will fall and break. At first glance this seems reasonable enough. But upon closer analysis, we see that it does not obtain universally. Rather it is subject to a whole host of background assumptions. For a start it only applies to eggs dropped within the Earth's gravitational field (or some similar gravitational field). And then only for eggs dropped more than some minimal distance. And then only for eggs that are not hard boiled (though even then if the distance is great enough there will be a breakage). And then there is the question of the surface onto which the egg is dropped. And then.... In fact, this one simple example illustrates that it is in general extremely difficult, if not impossible, to specify with any degree of certainty

---

[5]In the topologist's sense of this phrase.

or exactitude just what are the background conditions under which a given constraint obtains.

Now that does not render the constraint unreliable. Indeed, I am sure we are all aware of it and take account of it whenever we handle eggs. In practice, all that matters is that the background conditions, *whatever they may be*, are met at the time and place the constraint is utilized.

In general, the only occasions when it becomes necessary to take cognizance of background conditions and investigate what they are, are when a previously reliable constraint suddenly leads to error, or it is anticipated that a change in circumstances would result in a previously reliable constraint leading to error. Thus, for example, the background conditions pertaining to gravity are of no concern to the vast majority of mankind, who never experience anything other than the 'normal' effects of the Earth's gravity, but to the astronaut or to the team designing the space-ship and its equipment, these background conditions are important, and need to be specified as accurately as possible.

Now, this issue of the background conditions is one that has plagued workers in artificial intelligence ever since the discipline began a quarter of a century ago. If it is generally not possible to specify all the background conditions that govern the applicability of a constraint, how can we hope to design effective artificial agents that make use of such a constraint? The situation-theoretic approach of always taking constraints to be conditional on a background situation does not, in itself, solve that problem for AI, but it does keep our theoretical development in line with what happens in our everyday experience. Namely, we carry along the background situation to a constraint as an extra 'parameter', only to be examined when the constraint proves unreliable. Which sounds like little more than a linguistic cop-out, but in fact dovetails nicely with the manner in which we regard the acquisition of information about a situation, discussed presently. (So there is hope for AI applications—which is about par for the AI course.)

The inclusion of *situations* in our ontology then, serves to take account of the critical role played by context in practically all forms of behavior and communication, and by the background that governs the reliability of constraints.

But what kind of entities are these situations? The above examples, though simple to describe, should indicate that situations are in fact very hard to pin down. They include, but are not equal to any of, simply-connected regions of space-time, highly-disconnected space-time regions, contexts of utterance (whatever that turns out to mean in precise terms), collections of background conditions for a constraint, and so on.

So just what is and what is not a situation? This question is a natural one for us humans to raise, since it arises from the desire always to understand, and if possible *define*, the new in terms of the old and familiar. But it is simply not possible to give a precise definition of situations in terms of familiar mathematical concepts. Situations are a quite new kind of object.

They can be *modeled* using standard techniques, say as sets of infons, along the lines outlined in Barwise and Etchemendy 1987. But this is just a modeling process. As such it can provide *some aid to the intuition*, but not a *definition* of what a situation *is*. Situations are just that: situations. They are abstract objects introduced so that we can handle issues of context, background, and so on.

As abstract objects in their own right, distinct from all the other entities in the ontology of situation theory (or indeed the rest of mathematics for that matter), some questions that are meaningful when asked of, say, individuals, locations, or sets, are simply not appropriate for situations (in general), any more than it is appropriate to ask what color the number 7 is, or how hot a given Banach space is. In particular, it is in general not appropriate to ask for an "extensional definition" of a situation—even in the case of a situation determined by (what goes on in) a connected region of space-time.

For example, suppose John and David are having a conversation about a particular football game (say one they have both seen). Then they are both referring to a very definite *situation*—namely that particular game. This is a situation that they both individuate (as a *situation*). A long, informative, and confusion-free discussion can take place. And yet neither John nor David would be able to list every single event that formed a part of that game, or every item of information that related to it in some essential way. Indeed, it is highly likely that what makes their conversation about the game of interest to both parties is the fact that each one acquires from the other, *new* items of information about the game, information that the one picked up but the other did not. The fact that each person left the game with some information that the other did not, does not mean that their subsequent conversation is about two different games. The situation is the same for both individuals, a highly structured part of the world, having a fixed duration in time. What differs is what each knows about that situation.

But if it is not possible to get a complete definition of situations in terms of more familiar notions, how then are we to deal with them? How can we develop our intuitions and our understanding of situations? Well, that is something for situation theory itself to answer. But the answer will of necessity be an *internal* one, one within the framework of situation theory.

Exactly what does and what does not constitute a situation is largely a matter of what agent is under discussion. It may or may not be the case that the agent itself can *individuate* situations (i.e., regard and treat them as single, identifiable entities). Simple agents probably do not individuate any situations, though (if they are to be the kind of agent of interest to us here) they do discriminate them. In the case of sophisticated agents such as Man, it seems that we do often *individuate* situations (for example, we can individuate the situation that we *see*), but in many cases our behavior too simply discriminates situations, without there being any act of *individuation* going on.

Then too there are the situations that are required by the internal mechanics of the theory. These generally consist of finite sets of infons.[6] For details, I refer the reader to my account in Devlin 1991 (chap. 7).

Regardless of their status regarding individuation or discrimination by agents, within our theory situations are regarded as first class members of the ontology, alongside the individuals, relations, locations, and all the rest of the ontology. In particular, we allow situations to fill (appropriate) argument roles of relations, and thus to appear as constituents of infons.

Notice however, that (even in the case of agent-individuated situations) their status alongside individuals does not mean that situations are at all the same as individuals. An important feature of situations that our theory reflects, is that the structure of a situation is significant to the agent, in a way that the internal structure of an individual need not be.

The status of situations in our theory is, then, clear cut. They are first-class citizens alongside the rest of the theorist's ontology. But in what sense does an agent *individuate* a situation (when it does)? Not, in general, as an individual. Rather, the agent individuates a situation *as a situation*, that is to say, as a structured part of Reality that it (the agent) somehow manages to pick out. There are a number of ways that an agent such as Man is able to 'pick out' (that is, individuate) a situation. The most obvious examples are direct perception of a situation, perhaps the immediate environment, or thinking about a particular situation, say last night's dinner party.

In any event, it should be pointed out that the individuation of a situation by an agent does not (necessarily) entail the agent being able to provide an *exact* description of everything that is and is not going on in that situation. In particular, individuation of a situation s neither entails nor requires an extensional specification of the set

$$\{\sigma \mid s \models \sigma\}$$

What is the case is that an agent may obtain more and more information about a particular situation. The more conjuncts that can be added to a compound infon, σ, to produce a valid proposition

$$s \models \sigma$$

the more we know about the situation s. Indeed, our entire theory can be viewed as a study of how agents can acquire more information about particular situations. Without the situations to refer to, we would be forced to make theorist's assertions of the form "The agent acquires additional

---

[6] One instance involves the manner in which I treat causality.

information about whatever in the world it is that the agent acquires that additional information about." By putting *situations* into our theorist's ontology, we avoid such awkward circumlocutions, but we must accept that these new abstract objects might not behave as do the ones more familiar to us. The agent will in general only have partial information about a given situation, and our theory reflects that partiality.

The above state of affairs is not unlike the step from the rational numbers to the real numbers, when viewed from a finitist position. The normal means of specifying rational numbers by giving their decimal expansion does not prevent us from constructing the *completion* of the rational number system, namely the real numbers, a process that consists of *introducing* a new realm of abstract objects that, from the original (finitist) standpoint, may only be *partially* specified, by giving the decimal expansion to a certain finite number of places.

In fact, a better analogy is the step from the rational numbers to the *algebraic* irrational numbers.[7] Just as the irrational algebraic numbers are those idealized entities that require an infinite amount of decimal information to be completely specified, but admit of an alternative, 'higher-order,' finite definition, so too the situations are those idealized entities that cannot be completely specified by extensional, infonic means, but which find their way into the ontology because the agent somehow picks them out, either by cognitive individuation of some higher-order fashion (such as the football game example above) or else by behavioral discrimination.[8]

Given the uneasy feeling that the above discussion will likely produce in anyone meeting these notions for the first time, it is perhaps not unnatural to ask the question "Do we really need situations?"

I believe the answer is an emphatic "Yes." It simply *is* the case that informational constraints depend upon a whole host of background conditions that defy precise enumeration, and it *is* the case that natural language utterances are highly dependent on one or more contexts that cannot be extensionally specified. Thus if we are to be at all serious about investigating the nature of information and communication, then we have, it seems to me, no alternative than to take the bull by the horns and introduce something along the lines of situations: entities which, like the (algebraic) irrational numbers, defy precise specification in terms of the system they extend (though they allow for partial specification in those terms), but can be specified by other, what might be called 'higher-order' means, that have to do with the purpose for which the extension is made, rather than the framework upon which it is built.

---

[7]Those real numbers that are the roots of polynomial equations having rational coefficients.

[8]I am ignoring here those situations that are introduced for technical reasons connected with the theory. However, these are all avoidable steps that are made simply to take advantage of a framework that is already there.

Just as the step from the rational numbers to the real numbers involves a definite commitment to the 'uncertainty' (when viewed 'from below') of the completed infinite, so too the step from the individuals, locations, relations, and infons that form the familiar part of our ontology,[9] to the situations, requires a definite commitment to dealing with entities that can only be understood *in terms of the system that thereby results*.

4 Learning to Live with Abstraction

There is a natural tendency in humans to resist change. In mathematics (and in other areas of life), when something new comes along, we try to explain, or understand it in terms of, or even reduce it to, concepts with which we are familiar.

Thus there was for a long time, a considerable reluctance to accept the concept of negative (whole) numbers. Indeed, these were only accepted as genuine 'numbers' by the mathematical community as recently as the Eighteenth Century, despite mathematicians as long ago as the time of the Ancient Greeks having had a considerable facility with the algebraic manipulation of expressions involving minus signs. Such acceptance only came with a *geometric* picture of a number line, whereby negative whole numbers can be thought of as counting to the left from zero (i.e., counting in the *negative direction*), with the more familiar positive whole numbers being counted to the right (i.e., in the *positive direction*).

The discovery by the Greeks that not all lengths were expressible in terms of rational numbers[10] led to an unease concerning the real number system that lasted until the Nineteenth Century, when Weierstrass, Dedekind, Cauchy, and others developed the modern theory of the real number continuum.

Again, complex numbers[11] were regarded with considerable skepticism until the Norwegian mathematician Argand proposed the now familiar picture of the complex plane, whereby complex numbers are represented by the points of the two-dimensional Euclidean plane.

In each case, what happened was that something new was *modeled* in terms of something more familiar: geometric (and also algebraic) models in the case of negative and complex numbers, set-theoretic models (Cauchy sequences, Dedekind cuts) in the case of the real numbers. The process of modeling something new in terms of established notions is a powerful device on two counts. First of all it removes all worries about any formal inconsistency in the new notion. (Or rather, it throws any such worries back to a concern for the consistency of the previous notion.) Secondly, by

---

[9]Of course, the infons are not exactly 'familiar' to most people, but as argued in Devlin 1990, they are just a new twist on a very familiar theme.

[10]Numbers that are expressible as the quotient of two whole numbers.

[11]Numbers involving the square root of -1.

providing a bridge from the familiar to the new, it usually assists in the process of understanding the new concept.

The two potential dangers that accompany the modeling process are firstly that it can obscure the fact that a genuinely new collection of abstract objects is involved. Modeling something is just that: *modeling*. The real numbers are neither Dedekind cuts nor equivalence classes of Cauchy sequences of rationals; they are *real numbers*, abstract mathematical objects in their own right. The complex numbers are *not* points in the complex plane—numbers and points are not at all the same kind of object.

The second danger is that any model invariably brings with it features not only of the thing being modeled, but also the structure in which the modeling is done, and it is often quite difficult to decide if a particular aspect of the model says something about the thing being modeled or the theory providing the model.[12]

As with the various number systems of mathematics (and other examples that I could have given), so too with situations. But this does not mean that situations *are* certain sets. Rather they are *situations*, abstract objects in their own right.

The reason for any unease the reader might have about the status of (infons and) situations is, I suggest, entirely one of novelty. Human beings do not, it appears, have an innate ability to handle abstract concepts. Rather, as is suggested by some contemporary work in anthropology and linguistics, a facility with abstraction seems to be something we acquire (often with great difficulty) as part of our intellectual development.

For instance, the work of the cognitive psychologist Jean Piaget suggests that the abstract concept of volume is not innate, but is learned at a quite early age. Young children are not able to recognize that a tall, thin glass and a short, stout one can contain the same 'volume' of liquid, even if they see the one poured into the other. For a considerable time they will maintain that the quantity of liquid changes, that the tall glass contains *more* than the short one.

Likewise with the abstract concept of number. The ability to count appears to precede the formulation of the number concept. When asked to count the pencils in a pile of red and blue pencils, young children will readily report the number of blue or red pencils, but must be coaxed into reporting the total. The level of abstraction involved in the latter seems to be just beyond their capabilities.

Further evidence that even such basic (to us!) abstract concepts as

---

[12] A particular example of this within Situation Theory itself is provided by the original attempts of Barwise and Perry (1983) to model situations in classical set theory. The well-foundedness axiom of set theory, in particular, led to a number of difficulties in trying to understand situations, that turned out to be not issues concerning situations at all, but rather were a feature of that particular means of modeling.

natural numbers are not innate comes from the study of cultures that have evolved in isolation from modern society.[13]

Anthropologists have found that when a member of the Vedda tribe of Sri Lanka wants to count coconuts, he collects a heap of sticks and assigns one to each coconut. Each time he adds a new stick, he says "That is one." But if asked to say how many coconuts he possesses, he simply points to the pile of sticks and says "That many." The tribesman thus has a form of number system, but far from consisting of abstract *numbers*, his numbering is in terms of entirely concrete sticks.

In our Western culture, children typically form the concept of abstract numbers at around the age of six. But this appears to be not an innate development; rather it is a result of childhood conditioning.

It is only recently that evidence has been uncovered concerning the actual origins of our abstract number concept.

The earliest middle East artifacts connected with counting that have been discovered are notched bones found in caves in present-day Israel and Jordan, dating from the Paleolithic period (15,000 to 10,00 B.C.). The bones seem to have been used as Lunar calendars, with each notch representing one sighting of the moon. Similar instances of counting by means of a one-to-one correspondence appear again and again in preliterate societies: pebbles and shells were used in the census in early African kingdoms, and in the New World, cacao beans and kernels of maize, wheat, and rice were used as counters.

Any such system suffers from an obvious lack of specificity. A collection of notches, pebbles, or shells indicates a quantity but not the items being quantified, and hence cannot serve as a means of storing information for long periods. The first known enumeration system that solved this problem was devised in the Fertile Crescent, the rich lowland area stretching from Syria to Iran. Clay tokens an inch or less across, were used to represent specific commodities according to their shape. For example, a cylinder stood for an animal, cones and spheres referred to two common measures of grain (approximately a peck and a bushel). This still did not amount to a system of abstract numbers, of course, but it did ensure an enduring method of counting.

By 6,000 B.C., clay tokens had spread throughout the Middle East. Their use persisted largely unchanged until around 3,000 B.C., when the increasingly more complex societal structure of the Sumerians led to the development of more complex forms of token, involving both a greater

---

[13]The following discussion is based on the fascinating article by Denise Schmandt-Besserat (1989), of the Middle-Eastern Studies Department of the University of Texas at Austin. I am grateful to Adrienne Diehr, the Administrative Associate at the Center for Cognitive Science at the University of Texas at Austin, for bringing this article to my attention.

variety of shapes (ovoids, rhomboids, bent coils, parabolas, etc.) as well as markings on the tokens.

This development set the stage for the evolution of abstract numbers. It became common to store clay tokens in clay envelopes, each one imprinted with a mark indicating the owner or government agency whose account the envelope contained. Sealed clay envelopes thus served as accounts or contracts. Of course, one obvious drawback of a clay envelope is that the seal has to be broken open in order to examine the contents. So the Sumerian accountants began to impress the tokens on the soft exteriors of the envelopes before enclosing them, thereby leaving a visible exterior record of the contents of the envelope. But then, of course, the contents become largely superfluous. All the requisite information is stored on the envelope's outer markings. And in this way the clay tablet was (after some time) born, with marks on a single tablet used to denote numbers of items. The intermediate clay tokens were discarded. In present-day terminology we would say that they had been replaced by the abstract numbers that were left when the tokens were taken away.

Now, the above does not in itself prove the 'existence' of abstract numbers *qua* abstract objects. But the interesting thing is that the step from using physical tokens set in a one-to-one correspondence to whatever was being counted, to using markings on a single tablet, did not take place immediately. For some time the marked clay envelopes redundantly contained the actual tokens the outer markings depicted. This would suggest that going from physical tokens to an abstract, two-dimensional representation was a considerable cognitive development.

In modern terminology, it amounts to the *implicit* introduction of abstract numbers. [The abstract numbers themselves appeared when a later generation regarded the conceptual 'holes' left by the discarded tokens as abstract *objects*, namely the (positive whole) *numbers*.]

So what do the above discussions tell us about the future status of situations within the realm of mathematical abstract objects?

Certainly nothing I have said will guarantee that situations (or infons) will eventually take their place alongside the various number systems and spaces that are already an established part of mathematics. That will depend partly upon the way these putative new objects come to be regarded in the light of greater familiarity and use. Partly too upon how effective they prove to be in the study of information and communication.

But if the arguments presented in this paper in support of situations prove to carry sway, and if their adoption proves of use, then I see no reason why situations should not achieve a mathematical status equivalent to, say, the real or the complex numbers. I do not believe there are any 'absolutes' in mathematics; just intuition (an intuition that is subject to development and evolution) and utility. Had Abraham Robinson been alive a century earlier and developed his 'non-standard analysis' prior to the invention of the familiar ϵ, δ -theory of the real line, I am sure that infinitesimals would now rank alongside the real numbers as abstract objects of equal ontological status. Indeed, so strong is the human tendency to think in terms of 'infinitesimals', I suspect that the ϵ, δ-method would never have been developed as a means of defining continuity.[14]

The introduction and acceptance of abstract objects does not, I believe, follow some pre-ordained sequence of discoveries of an abstract world that awaits our investigation, but rather is a pragmatic matter of cognitive development, motivated and spurred on by necessity, utility, and intuition, guided by logic.

In the meantime, it is our task as mathematicians simply to investigate the issues of the age we live in, and leave it to future generations to judge if we are successful in the long run.

References

Barwise, J., and J. Etchemendy. 1987. *The Liar: An Essay on Truth and Circularity.* New York: Oxford University Press.

Barwise, J., and J. Perry. 1983. *Situations and Attitudes.* Cambridge, MA: MIT Press.

Cohen, P. J. 1971. Comments on the Foundation of Set Theory. In *Axiomatic Set Theory: Proceedings of Symposia in Pure Mathematics 13, Part 1*, ed. D. Scott. Providence, RI. American Mathematics Society.

Devlin, K. J. 1990. The Role of Infons in a Mathematical Theory of Information. In *Theories of Partial Information: Proceedings of the Conference held at the University of Texas at Austin.* January. To appear.

Devlin, K. J. 1991. *Logic and Information.* Cambridge: Cambridge University Press.

Moschovakis, Y. 1980. *Descriptive Set Theory.* North Holland.

Putnam, H. 1979a. Philosophy of Logic. In *Mathematics, Matter and Method: Philosophical Papers, Volume 1.* Cambridge: Cambridge University Press.

Putnam, H. 1979b. What is Mathematical Truth? In *Mathematics, Matter and Method: Philosophical Papers, Volume 1.* Cambridge: Cambridge University Press.

Schmandt-Besserat, D. 1989. Oneness, Twoness, Threeness. In *The Sciences*, 44–48. New York Academy of Sciences.

Steen, L. A. 1988. The Science of Patterns. *Science* 240:611–616.

---

[14]If you doubt this claim, just take a look at the fumbling attempts of most college freshmen to analyze the notions of functional continuity and Riemann integration. Infinitesimals abound, albeit lacking the rigor that Robinson finally supplied. The 'classical' approach to analysis, on the other hand, causes those same students no end of trouble, because of its extremely non-intuitive nature.

3

Oracles in Situation Semantics

KEITH J. DEVLIN

I introduce the notion of an *oracle* and illustrate its use in the semantic analysis of discourse. Oracles are somewhat analogous to the notion of Σ_n-skolem hulls in the theory of constructible sets, both in their definition and their use. This paper is a sequel to Devlin 1991. It assumes familiarity with Devlin 1991 and provides an example of the issues discussed in Devlin 1991.

1 Skolem Hulls in Set Theory

The motivation for the notion of an 'oracle' comes from set theory, and in particular the theory of constructible sets. (See Devlin 1984.)

A particularly powerful tool in model-theoretic set theory is the notion of the Σ_n-*skolem hull*, the smallest Σ_n-elementary submodel of a given set-theoretic structure containing certain sets. A 'typical' Σ_n-skolem hull argument goes as follows.

You are interested in the properties of some mathematical structure, $\mathcal{S}$. The properties of interest all have logical complexity Σ_n or less. That is to say, they can all be expressed in first-order fashion by means of a formula that is Σ_n, a Σ_n formula being one that consists of a quantifier-free formula preceded by n alternating blocks of quantifiers, starting with a block of existential quantifiers, then a block of universal quantifiers, then a block of existential quantifiers, etc.

The key step now is to define a new structure, $\mathcal{M}$, the smallest Σ_n-elementary submodel of V, the set-theoretic universe, that contains $\mathcal{S}$. That is to say, $\mathcal{M}$ is the smallest set such that $\mathcal{S} \in \mathcal{M}$ and for all Σ_n-

---

My talk at Kinnloch Rannoch broke into two parts. The first part took a broad view of situation theory and confined itself to the 'core' of the subject. The second part consisted of a proposal for a new class of situations: the oracles. Given the distinct, though closely connected, nature of these two topics, it seemed appropriate to write up the talk as two short papers, rather than one long one. I would like to thank David Israel for comments on an earlier draft of this paper.

Situation Theory and Its Applications, vol. 2.
Jon Barwise, Jean Mark Gawron, Gordon Plotkin, and Syun Tutiya, eds.
Copyright © 1991, Stanford University.

formulas $\phi(v_1, \ldots, v_n)$ and all elements $a_1, \ldots, a_n$ of $\mathcal{M}$,

$$\mathcal{M} \models \phi[a_1, \ldots, a_n] \quad \text{if and only if} \quad V \models \phi[a_1, \ldots, a_n]$$

(This construction is only possible when there is a global choice function available, as is the case in the theory of constructible sets. In the absence of such a function, there may be no minimal such $\mathcal{M}$. I return to this point again later.)

The model $\mathcal{M}$ is then a canonical 'mini-universe' as far as Σ_n-describable properties are concerned, that tells you everything there is to know in terms of Σ_n descriptions about S *from the inside of* $\mathcal{M}$ (that is to say, anything that does not explicitly refer, in a Σ_n fashion, to sets not in $\mathcal{M}$).

By manipulating the structures $\mathcal{M}$, it is possible to carry out highly intricate arguments without becoming bogged down in a mire of complex first-order formulas. The manipulation of mathematical structures replaces intricate linguistic arguments. The structure $\mathcal{M}$ provides you with a kind of 'oracle' for S.

The reason for the restriction to Σ_n formulas for some fixed (though arbitrary) n is that it is not in general possible to construct a complete *skolem hull* of the universe, where no such restriction on the complexity of the formulas is imposed. The descriptive power of full first-order predicate logic is simply too great to allow for such a construction.

2 Oracles

The analog to the above notion of Σ_n-formulas is provided by what I propose to call a *set of issues*. Intuitively, a set of issues provides a descriptive framework for saying certain kinds of things about certain parts of the world.

Formally, by a *set of issues* I shall mean a collection of parametric infons. The idea behind this definition is that a set of issues provides us with an information-theoretic framework for discussing the world or some part thereof. By anchoring the parameters in an infon in the set, we obtain an item of information. Clearly, different sets of issues will enable us to talk about, and obtain information about, different aspects of the world.

I fix some particular set of issues Γ. By a Γ-*infon* I mean any infon that results from anchoring the parameters in an infon in Γ.

Given an individual (animate or inanimate) or a situation a, the Γ-*oracle* of a, $Oracle_\Gamma(a)$, is the situation comprising that part of the world and the entire 'body of knowledge' that, within the framework provided by Γ, concerns a. That is to say, $Oracle_\Gamma(a)$ is the 'minimal' situation, s, such that

$$s \models \sigma$$

for any factual, parameter-free Γ-infon, σ, that 'genuinely' involves a.

Thus, if the only kind of information available is in the form of infons in the set of issues Γ, then starting with the object a, there is no way to distinguish $Oracle_\Gamma(a)$ from w, the world. For any infon σ that arises from Γ, in which only objects that are constituents of $Oracle_\Gamma(a)$ occur,

$$Oracle_\Gamma(a) \models \sigma \text{ if and only if } w \models \sigma$$

The previous discussion of Σ_n-skolem hulls notwithstanding, this is of course, very vague. For one thing, what do all those enquoted terms in the definition mean? The problem is that this notion is both new and highly intensional, and can really only be understood in terms of the situation theory we are currently developing.

For instance, I have used the phrase 'genuinely involves a' in order to help explain the notion. In the case where a is a person, for example, we do not want $Oracle_\Gamma(a)$ to include every person who lives or has ever lived on Earth, which would occur if we regarded as relevant information about a every infon of the form

$$\langle\!\langle \text{married-to}, a, b, 0 \rangle\!\rangle$$

for every such person b. This would in general be an instance of 'non-genuine' involvement. But how exactly do we define what I mean by 'genuine involvement' (or relevance)?

An analogy might help explain my answer. When mathematicians first introduce students to general topology, we tell them that the highly abstract notion of a topological space they are about to encounter captures the notion of two points being 'near to each other'. Now, of course, nearness is not at all a precisely defined notion. Nearness could mean 100 miles apart or a millionth of a micron apart. It all depends on the circumstances. The important point is that the student's vague idea as to what 'nearness' means is enough to motivate and explain the formal mathematical definition of a neighborhood system and a topological space, and once understood that formal notion itself provides a formal definition of 'nearness'.

Likewise in the case of oracles. I imagine that an axiomatic mathematical development of situation theory would most likely use the notion of an oracle to provide a *definition* of 'relevance': a *relevant* property being one that is decided by the oracle. This would be precisely the opposite way round to the original motivatory analysis.

3 Some Examples

In the examples that follow, I do not specify just what set of issues Γ is involved. That would be determined by the actual context on any one occasion. What I do assume is that each use of Γ will refer to a set of issues having sufficient expressive power to support the example concerned.

If a were a rock, then $Oracle_\Gamma(a)$ would involve a time-span stretching backwards to the origins of the rock and forwards at least to the moment (if such a moment exists) the rock ceases to exist (as such), and would support all the facts that pertain to that rock: its composition, color, mass, volume, shape, melting point, any names it has, the various locations it has occupied, who or what has touched it, etc. Clearly this is a long and varied list, that involves a great many properties and relations and a great many other objects. But note that by no means all properties and relations will be involved, nor all other objects. For instance, the property 'happy' is unlikely to figure in any infon supported by $Oracle_\Gamma(a)$, and since I am assuming a is a rock I myself have not encountered, nor ever will encounter, neither will I figure in $Oracle_\Gamma(a)$. [Of course, having now discussed the rock, a, in this paper, a now figures in *my* oracle, $Oracle_\Gamma(\text{Keith\_Devlin})$, as an object I have thought about and discussed in print. But this does not necessarily put me into $Oracle_\Gamma(a)$.]

Again, what about that oracle

$$s = Oracle_\Gamma(\text{Keith\_Devlin})$$

just mentioned? What kinds of objects will be constituents of s and what infons will be supported by s ?

Well, s will stretch back in time far enough to include all my ancestors and forward in time to include my descendants; it will contain my birthplace, my parents, grandparents, etc., my wife, my children, any grandchildren, etc., several dogs, even more cats, and various apartments, houses, and automobiles (associated with different times, I should add); it will support the infons that provide the information that I am human, male, a mathematician, married, a father, of British nationality, named KEITH DEVLIN, and so on.

Clearly, s has a considerably larger reach, both in time and in space, than the individual Keith Devlin. (Unless one wanted to take an extreme philosophical stance concerning the 'extent' of individuated objects, and identify $Oracle_\Gamma(a)$ with a for every object a.) But again, there are far more things *not* in $Oracle_\Gamma(\text{Keith\_Devlin})$ than are included, so for all that $Oracle_\Gamma(\text{Keith\_Devlin})$ seems unmanageably large, it has far less extent than the world, w.

4 Oracles in Situation Semantics

It is the thesis of this paper that given the basic assumptions that lie behind situation semantics, oracles arise naturally, indeed unavoidably, in the situation semantic analysis of everyday discourse. Let's look at another example in more detail, and see how oracles figure in the 'obvious' situation-theoretic analysis of an information transfer using a simple natural language utterance.

Suppose I say to you

Jon Barwise was the first director of CSLI.

First of all, how do I know this? Well, over the years I have acquired more and more information about Jon Barwise. But what does this mean in terms of our theory?

Well, situation theory takes information to be in the propositional form

$$s \models \sigma$$

where s is a situation and σ is a parameter-free infon. In the case of the above item of information, the infon concerned is obvious:

$$\langle\!\langle \text{first-director-of, Jon\_Barwise, CSLI, 1} \rangle\!\rangle$$

But which situation supports this infon? Or to put it another way, where (in the situation-theoretic world) do we find the facticity of this infon?

The answer is, I claim, the situation

$$s = Oracle_\Gamma(\text{Jon\_Barwise})$$

for an appropriate set of issues Γ.

As I see it, the situation-theorist looks at the above utterance as producing a transmission of information about the situation s. (There is an alternative possibility. Had a previous utterance set up the institute CSLI as the topic under discussion, then my utterance above would more likely be about the situation $Oracle_\Gamma(\text{CSLI})$. But uttered in isolation, it seems more likely to be intended to supply information about this character Jon Barwise. In any event, I shall analyze the utterance under this assumption.)

Now, among my current stock of information about Jon Barwise when I make my utterance, is the information, supported by s, that Jon Barwise was the first director of CSLI. I acquired this particular item of information some time in 1985. By then I knew Barwise moderately well, and my information concerning him was already quite extensive, though it did not at that time include any information about his family, as it does today.

Prior to 1971, however, when I met Barwise for the first time, my knowledge of s was very minimal, amounting to little more than that this character Jon Barwise was an American, male mathematician at the University of Wisconsin, who had proved a famous result called the *Barwise Compactness Theorem*. The point to note is that it was the same situation, s, throughout this twenty year time span. What changed over time was the information I have concerning s. (I take this point to be fundamental given the theoretical framework of situation theory.)

So much for me, the speaker of the above sentence. What about you, the listener? You may, of course, already have considerable knowledge about the situation s. Maybe you are a close friend of Barwise of many years standing. Or maybe just an acquaintance. Or perhaps you have never met the guy, but have long been an avid follower of his exploits. In any event, let us suppose that you already know that Jon Barwise was the first director of CSLI. Then of course my utterance does not provide you with any new information. Nevertheless, upon hearing the name JON BARWISE, your mind immediately conjures up a host of facts and/or images you associate with this name—facts and/or images that are part of the situation s. Having brought the situation s into focus, I could go on to provide you with new information about it.

Alternatively, it could be that although you have considerable knowledge about s, you were not previously aware that the person Jon Barwise was the first director of CSLI. So you now add this to your stock of information about s. You now know *more* about s. (Though unless you know what 'CSLI' refers to, your new information amounts only to the fact that Jon Barwise was the first director of *something*.)

At the other end of the spectrum, suppose you have never before heard of Jon Barwise. Then my utterance nevertheless still serves to convey information to you. From now on, you know that there is someone called JON BARWISE, and moreover you have some information about the associated situation $s = Oracle_\Gamma(\text{Jon\_Barwise})$, namely you know that:

$$s \models \langle\!\langle \text{named}, a, \text{JON BARWISE}, t_{JB}, 1 \rangle\!\rangle$$
$$\wedge \langle\!\langle \text{human}, a, t_{JB}, 1 \rangle\!\rangle \wedge \langle\!\langle \text{male}, a, t_{JB}, 1 \rangle\!\rangle$$
$$\wedge \langle\!\langle \text{first-director-of}, a, \text{CSLI}, 1 \rangle\!\rangle$$

You know this because of what you hear me say, coupled with your prior knowledge of the world: the kinds of objects that can be directors of things, and the way the English language operates, in particular its conventions concerning proper names. This would not, of course, enable you to recognize this guy Barwise if you saw him in the street. Nor do you know exactly what sort of an institution CSLI is, though you have also just learned of another situation, $Oracle_\Gamma(\text{CSLI})$, about which you know it is some form of human organization, whose first director was called JON BARWISE.

Though the amounts of information that are known and/or learned about the Jon Barwise situation, s, can vary enormously from case to case, the situation is *one and the same*: it is $Oracle_\Gamma(\text{Jon\_Barwise})$. Different people at different times have access to vastly different information about s. Barwise's friends will likely know more about s than strangers who have never met him but have simply read *Situations and Attitudes*. Barwise himself will know considerably more about s, though not everything. His physician will have access to information about s quite different from that known to his friends, or even to Barwise himself. Various government agencies will have files of information about s. Future biographers of mathematics may spend several months investigating the situation s.

5   Oracles are Not Files

Communication, in particular linguistic communication, can be regarded as the transmission of information about various situations. Indeed, we may regard the enormous efficiency of natural language as a carrier of information as stemming in large part from the fact that a single word or phrase can bring into focus an entire oracle situation. The more information about that oracle that the speaker and listener share, the more efficient can be the communication between them.

It should be emphasized that $Oracle_\Gamma(a)$ is *not* some kind of file or database of information concerning the object a, through which speakers and listeners search when discussing a. Rather, oracles are *situations*, objects about which it is possible to acquire and/or pass on information. It is highly unlikely that an agent ever has more than *partial* information about a particular oracle, $Oracle_\Gamma(a)$. And that information might not have a as its main focus. (For instance, my knowledge about Benjamin Franklin is almost exclusively concerned with those scientific facts supported by his oracle situation; about the man himself I know very little.)

6 The Nature of Oracles

At this stage it might be helpful to draw an analogy between oracle situations and numbers. For convenience, I restrict my attention to positive numbers.

Rooted as they are in our intuitions, the natural numbers have a certain *concreteness*. They are, in a sense, *individuals*, each of which we can completely identify (as the *first*, the *second*, the *third*, and so on).

Consider now the problem of specifying other numbers—that is to say, providing information that determines other numbers. Starting with the natural numbers, *decimal representations* provide us with a means of specifying (in principle) all rational numbers. And given the finite nature of the world, the rational numbers clearly suffice for all counting and measurement purposes. The one thing they do not provide is a number system that allows the development of powerful and elegant *mathematical theories* such as the differential and integral calculus. The problem is, as the Greeks discovered, that there are 'infinitesimal gaps' in the rational number system. 'Filling in' these gaps by the introduction of the irrational real numbers requires some significant mathematical effort.

Viewed from the informational standpoint of decimal representations, it seems impossible to specify even a single irrational number. The specification of an irrational number would require an infinitely long string of decimals—an infinite amount of information in our present sense—and thus the irrationals seem to be nothing more than conceptual idealizations that are postulated to exist. An irrational can only be approximated, albeit with as much finite accuracy as we desire.

The oracle situations are a situation-theoretic analogue of the irrational real numbers: idealized objects about which we can acquire arbitrarily large finite amounts of information (infons), but which cannot in general be uniquely specified in such a fashion. The only way to identify a particular oracle is in terms of a higher-order (i.e., higher than infonic) description, namely *as Oracle*$_\Gamma(a)$ for some object a and some set of issues Γ, a definition that has no meaning at the level of infons.

Analogously, it is of course possible to specify certain irrational real numbers in higher-order terms than at the level of decimal representations. For example, the algebraic irrational numbers (such as $\sqrt{2}$) can be specified as the solutions to rational polynomial equations, the irrational number π can be specified in geometric terms as the ratio of the circumference of any circle to its diameter, and the irrational constant e can be defined by analytic means. Indeed, given that oracle situations are, by virtue of *being* oracles, definable in situation-theoretic terms, the closest analogy would seem to be between the oracles and (say) the algebraic numbers, with arbitrary situations being the situation-theoretic analogue of arbitrary real numbers.

7 Do Oracles Exist?

This is clearly a loaded question, as is any question to do with existence. As a mathematician trying to develop a mathematical theory of information, I am content with a mathematical answer. Just as various kinds of number (e.g., complex numbers) 'exist' because we postulate their existence (in the mathematical realm), so too with oracles. As with the different kinds of number system, oracles are intended to provide a theoretical construct that corresponds to a certain feature in the world being studied. In this case, the 'feature' concerned is the situation comprising precisely those objects and facts of relevance to a given individual or situation.

Now, at an intuitive level, the notion of 'relevance' seems reasonable enough. But of course, it is notoriously difficult to pin down such concepts. How then can we be sure that the notion of an oracle is neither vacuous nor contradictory?

Well, as indicated earlier, in the long run the only solution would seem to be a formal mathematical development of situation theory, including the oracles, thereby providing a formal *definition* of the notion of 'relevance.' In the meantime we need to investigate the notion sufficiently to give rise to such a formal development, in much the same way that a study of 'nearness' eventually gave rise to the definition of a topological space (actually, to several alternative definitions of topological space).

The analogy with skolem hulls provides some aid to the intuition, it seems to me. The same analogy also suggests an alternative strategy. One possible objection to oracles as we have defined them concerns their 'uniqueness'. We took an oracle to be a *minimal* situation with a certain property. Is this reasonable? Maybe we run less risk of running into problems if we allow for a whole family of oracles for a given individual or situation, some sort of 'filter' of oracles. This is, after all, what happens in set theory when there is no global choice function available. Associated with a given set there is no single, minimal skolem hull but a whole non-principal filter-base of skolem hulls.

This is certainly a possibility to be entertained, though it seems to me to have a less strong intuitive base than that of a single oracle.

Certainly, what is the case is that oracles make no sense if you try to pin them down in terms of which infons they support. Just as irrational numbers make no sense if you try to specify them using decimal representations. Only in terms of the appropriate higher-order theory do oracles and irrational numbers make sense. The higher-order theory appropriate for the irrational numbers was fully worked out over a century ago (still a short time in the history of mathematics). We are still working on the theory appropriate for situations.

References

Devlin, K. J. 1984. *Constructibility*. Springer-Verlag.

Devlin, K. J. 1991. Situations as Mathematical Abstractions. This volume.

4

Many Sorted Universes, SRDs, and Injective Sums

Some work has been done towards developing a formal approach to situation theory by Fernando, Westerståhl and Aczel. In this paper we look at the relationship between Aczel's and Fernando's work and continue the development of Aczel's work to include many sortedness as well as considering parameterization.

1 Introduction

Aczel (1990) develops the notions of elementary universes (which are called replacement systems in his paper) and ontologies via form systems. Ontologies are a generalization of the notion of signature and elementary universes are a generalization of the notion of algebra. An elementary universe is given by a class of structured objects, which have components, along with a replacement operation on the elementary universe, which allows the components of an object to be replaced by other objects. In Section 2 we give a review of the definitions and results on ontologies, elementary universes and form systems which will be used in the rest of this paper.

Fernando's approach (1990) is through substitutional recursive definitions (srds), which are a generalization of production rules for context free grammars, and in Section 3 the relationship between simplified unsorted srds and form systems is explored, and the question of the representation of a form system in the set theoretic form system is looked at.

Westerståhl 1990 provides a mathematical theory. In his introduction he gives an informal account of how Aczel's elementary universes can be

_Thanks to Peter Aczel for his help and guidance and to SERC and British Petroleum for their financial support. The title of this paper was originally 'Many Sorted Universes, srds and Separated Sums'. Due to one of the referees comments the notion of separateness is no longer needed in the sum construction in Section 5 and so the title has been changed accordingly.

Situation Theory and Its Applications, vol. 2.
Jon Barwise, Jean Mark Gawron, Gordon Plotkin, and Syun Tutiya, eds.
Copyright © 1991, Stanford University.

expanded to give the mathematical tools for modeling his theory: Starting with an elementary universe with domain M_0 and a class of parameters X, form an elementary universe with domain $M_0[X]$ from the old elementary universe together with objects obtained by replacing occurrences of objects within objects from M_0 by elements of X. This 'parameterized' elementary universe should be closed under substitution. We could also consider certain abstraction operations on parametric objects, so now close $M_0[X]$ under abstraction to get the required universe. (Westerståhl then goes on to give a well-founded model for the theory he presents, however due to the way he models abstraction, his method does not generalize to give an anti-founded model.) In Section 4 we look at the notion of a many sorted universe and show the existence of well-founded, anti-founded and mixed founded sorted universes for a sorted ontology. Section 5 looks at the injective sum of two elementary universes which is a generalization of taking the initial parametric extension of an elementary universe. This paper does not deal with abstraction, Aczel and Lunnon 1991 looks at an unsorted universe with abstraction[1] and Lunnon 1991 will give an account of a many sorted universe with an abstraction operation.

Throughout most of this paper we will work informally in the metatheory of ZFC^- with atoms. Where ZFC^- is Zermelo-Frankel set theory with the axiom of choice and without the axiom of foundation. We sometimes assume a strengthening of the axiom of choice to a global axiom of choice which gives a well-ordering on the universe. This is not used explicitly in the paper but is used in the formation of a representative ontology for a form-system, i.e., in theorems 1 and 7. AFA which is mentioned in Section 3.1 is the anti-foundation axiom from Aczel 1988. This axiom can be used to replace the axiom of foundation and gives the existence of non-well-founded-sets.

Not all the proofs are given in full. The details will be appearing in my Ph.D. thesis sometime in 1991.

2 Preliminary Definitions

This section contains definitions and results from Aczel 1990, along with a generalization of his result for set continuous operators from Aczel 1988, which will be used in the rest of this paper.

2.1 Form Systems, Ontologies and Elementary Universes

The main notions here are those of elementary universe and ontology. We first give an informal description of the notions of elementary universe and ontology. An elementary universe is a universe of structured objects. Each object may have components, which are themselves objects of the system. From an object we may get a new object in the system by replacing

---

[1] This differs from the way the papers were presented at the conference.

the components of an object by other objects. So an elementary universe consists of a class of the objects of the system, an assignment of a set of components to each object and a replacement operation. Examples of elementary universes are set theoretic universes where the components of a set are the elements of the set. Other examples are given by purely syntactic universes of expressions where the components of an expression are its immediate subexpressions.

The notion of ontology is intended to generalize the notion of a signature. We call the elements of an ontology its forms. The forms of an ontology can be thought of as representing a template for the formation of the objects of some elementary universe. Each form is a structured thing which may have markers within it representing argument positions and the markers may be replaced by other markers to give another form.

We will now give the definitions for elementary universes and ontologies but first, to do this, we give the definition of the more general notion of a form system, of which ontologies and elementary universes are special cases. Let V throughout this paper be the universal class of objects of our metatheory.

Definition 1 $(A, C, \cdot)$ is an X-*form system* if A and X are classes, $C : A \rightarrow pow\, X$ and for each $a \in A$, if $\sigma : Ca \rightarrow X$ then $\sigma \cdot a \in A$ such that

- $C(\sigma \cdot a) = \{\sigma x \mid x \in Ca\}$,
- $\sigma \cdot a = a$ if $\sigma x = x$ for $x \in Ca$,
- $\sigma' \cdot (\sigma \cdot a) = (\sigma' \circ \sigma) \cdot a$ if $\sigma' : C(\sigma \cdot a) \rightarrow X$

Definition 2 $(A, C, \cdot)$ is an *elementary universe* if it is an A-form system.

Definition 3 An *ontology* is a V-form system where V is the universal class.

The next result ties up the notions of ontology and form system by showing that every X-form system $(A, C, \cdot)$ can be represented by an ontology $\mathcal{U}$ together with a bijection from the elements of the ontology which have components in X to A. With each ontology $\mathcal{U} = (U, C_{\mathcal{U}}, \cdot u)$ a class operator $\mathcal{U}[\,]$ can be associated, where $\mathcal{U}[X] = \{u \in U \mid Cu \subseteq X\}$. Given classes X and A and a bijection $\alpha : \mathcal{U}[X] \cong A$ for an ontology $\mathcal{U}$, we get a form system $\mathcal{U}(X, \alpha) = (A, C, \cdot)$ where $Ca = C_{\mathcal{U}}(\alpha^{-1}a)$ and $\sigma \cdot a = \alpha(\sigma \cdot u(\alpha^{-1}a))$. Such an X-form system will be called a $\mathcal{U}, X$-form system. For any class B a form system $(A, C, \cdot)$ is B-bounded if $Ca \preceq B$ (there is an injective map from Ca to B) for any $a \in A$.

Theorem 1 (The Representation Theorem for Form Systems) *Every X-form system $(A, C, \cdot)$ is a $\mathcal{U}, X$-form system for some X-bounded ontology $\mathcal{U}$. Moreover $\mathcal{U}$ is unique up to isomorphism.*

If we have $\alpha : \mathcal{U}[A] \cong A$ then we call (A, α) a full algebra for $\mathcal{U}$ and $\mathcal{U}(A, \alpha)$ is an elementary universe. We call such elementary universes $\mathcal{U}$-*universes*.

By putting $X = A$ in the previous theorem we get a representation theorem for elementary universes as $\mathcal{U}$-universes.

Before we give the definitions of well-founded and anti-founded elementary universes we will give the definition of a system of equations for an ontology and also the definition of a solution to such a system of equations. These are needed for the definition of anti-founded.

Definition 4 Let $\mathcal{U} = (U, C_\mathcal{U}, \cdot_\mathcal{U})$ be an ontology, a $\mathcal{U}$-*system of equations* is a system of equations of the form

$$y = u_y \quad (y \in Y)$$

where Y is a set and $u_y \in \mathcal{U}[Y]$ for each $y \in Y$. If (A, α) is a full algebra for $\mathcal{U}$ then a *solution* to such a system of equations in $\mathcal{U}(A, \alpha)$ is a map $\pi : Y \to A$ such that

$$\pi y = \alpha(\pi \restriction C_\mathcal{U} u_y) \cdot u_y \text{ for all } y \in Y$$

We now give the definitions for well-founded and anti-founded elementary universes.

Definition 5 Let $\mathcal{A} = (A, C, \cdot)$ be an elementary universe.

- $\mathcal{A}$ is *well-founded* if there is no infinite descending component sequence, i.e., there is no sequence $a_0, a_1, \ldots \in A$ with for every $n \in \mathbb{N}$ (the set of natural numbers), $a_{n+1} \in Ca_n$.
- $\mathcal{A}$ is *anti-founded* if there is a unique solution to any $\mathcal{U}$-system of equations where $\mathcal{U}$ is a representative ontology for $\mathcal{A}$.

The well-founded property is analogous to the foundation axiom for sets in *ZFC* set theory.

The anti-founded property is analogous to a simplified version of the solution lemma given in Aczel 1988. In fact the solution lemma is equivalent to AFA and so the anti-founded property is generalizing AFA. This definition of anti-founded differs from the definition in Aczel 1990 but from the results in that paper it follows that the definitions are equivalent for elementary universes whose representative ontology is normal. An ontology $\mathcal{U}$ is normal if it is I-bounded where I is the least fixed point of the operator $\mathcal{U}[\ ]$. We work with this definition of anti-founded for several reasons. Firstly it is simpler than the definition of anti-founded given in Aczel 1990 and is an obvious generalization of the solution lemma. It gives the result that every ontology has a, unique up to isomorphism, anti-founded universe. Lastly this definition is easily generalized to give a definition of an anti-founded λ-universe, see Aczel and Lunnon 1991.

Proposition 2 *Every ontology has a well-founded (anti-founded) elementary universe moreover such an elementary universe is unique up to isomorphism.*

Proof. In the well-founded case the proof is as in Aczel 1990, in the anti-founded case the proof comes from the final coalgebra theorem from Aczel and Mendler 1990 and Aczel 1988. □

2.2 Least and Greatest Fixed Points of K Set-continuous Operators

This section is a generalization of the section of Aczel 1988 on least and greatest fixed points of set continuous operators. In Aczel 1988 the operators are class operators, so they take a subclass of V and return a subclass of V. In this paper we consider operators which are defined on subclasses of some class K and return a subclass of K. We will call such operators K class operators. The proofs of the results are as in Aczel 1988 and only the results that are to be used in this paper are given here. So let K be a class:

Definition 6 A K class operator Φ is K *set-continuous* if it is monotone, i.e., for $X \subseteq Y \subseteq K$, $\Phi X \subseteq \Phi Y$ and set based i.e., if $x \in \Phi X$ for $X \subseteq K$ then $x \in \Phi X_0$ for some set $X_0 \subseteq X$.

Proposition 3 *If Φ is K set-continuous then*

1. *There is a class $I_\Phi \subseteq K$ such that*
   - *I_Φ is the least fixed point of Φ.*
   - *For $X \subseteq K$ if $\Phi X \subseteq X$ then $I_\Phi \subseteq X$.*
   - *$I_\Phi = \bigcup_{\beta \in On} I^\beta$ where $I^\beta = \Phi(\bigcup_{\beta' < \beta} I^{\beta'})$ and On is the class of ordinals.*
2. *There is a class $J_\Phi \subseteq K$ such that*
   - *J_Φ is the greatest fixed point of Φ.*
   - *For $X \subseteq K$ if $X \subseteq \Phi X$ then $X \subseteq J_\Phi$.*

3 Form Systems and SRDs

Substitutional recursive definitions (srds) are developed in Fernando 1989. We will now look at the relationship between a simplified version of Fernando's srds and form systems, where, for the rest of this section, a form system will be understood to be a form system over Z. We will need some more definitions to do this. srds are a generalization of the production rules for context free grammars where the right hand sides of the 'production rules' are well-founded sets (which possibly contain atoms in Fernando's definition, however here we will assume there are no atoms). Since form systems are unsorted we will consider only unsorted srds. In this section let Y be a class of objects, which we will call variables, and let Z be a class of objects which we will call indeterminates.

Definition 7 An *srd* is a subset of $WF[Y]$, the class of well-founded sets containing atoms from Y.

The definition given by Fernando is more complicated than this, but since the examples given in Fernando 1990 don't make any use of the extra complication we will, for the purposes of this paper, ignore it. An example of an srd from Fernando 1989 is

$$D_{full} = \{\{y_\alpha \mid \alpha < \kappa\} \mid \kappa \text{ is a cardinal }\}$$

where the y_α are distinct elements of Y.

Fernando (1989) considers fixed points of srds which are obtained by associating a class operator Γ_D with each srd D. $\Gamma_D X$ returns all those elements of V obtained by substituting elements of X for the occurrences of variables in elements of D. To give a formal definition of this operator let $\rho_Y a = Y \cap TC(a)$ where $TC(a)$ is the smallest transitive superset containing a, i.e., the smallest $b \supseteq a$ with $b' \in b - (Y \cup Z) \Rightarrow b' \subseteq b$. If $\sigma : \rho_Y a \to V$ let $\sigma \cdot_Y a = \hat{f}a$ where $f : Y \to V$ is such that $fy = \sigma y$ for $y \in \rho_Y a$ otherwise $fy = y$ and $\hat{f} : WF[Y] \to V$ is the unique extension of f to $WF[Y]$ with

$$\hat{f}a = \{\hat{f}a' \mid a' \in a \cap WF[Y]\} \cup \{fy \mid y \in Y \cap a\}$$

so $\hat{f}$ is the extension of f which replaces all occurrences of variables within a set by f applied to the variable. Now with each of our simplified srds, D, a class operator

$$\Gamma_D A = \{\sigma \cdot_Y a \mid a \in D, \sigma : \rho_Y a \to A\}$$

can be associated. The *fixed points of an* srd D are the fixed points of the class operator Γ_D. This notation is different to that used in Fernando 1990, however it illustrates the similarities between srds and the set theoretic form systems which is defined below.

Returning to our example srd D_{full} we get that the fixed points of D_{full} are those classes A with $A = pow\,A$, where pow is the power set operation which, given a class, returns the class of subsets of that class.

Before looking at the relationship between form systems and srds we define the set theoretic form system, $\mathcal{W}$, which will be used in the rest of this section. We take as our class of objects $WF[Z]$. The components of an object, given by ρ, are those elements of Z which occur in the object. So let

$$\rho a = Z \cap TC(a)$$

Let $f : Z \to WF[Z]$ then there is a unique function $\hat{f} : WF[Z] \to WF[Z]$ extending f where for $a \in WF[Z]$

$$\hat{f}a = \{\hat{f}a' \mid a' \in a \cap WF[Z]\} \cup \{fz \mid z \in Z \cap a\}$$

So $\hat{f}$ is the extension of f which replaces all occurrences of indeterminates within a set by f applied to the indeterminate. We use this to define replacement on objects: let $\sigma \cdot a = \hat{f}a$ with $fz = \sigma z$ if $z \in \rho a$ and $fz = z$ otherwise. Then $\mathcal{W} = (WF[Z], \rho, \cdot)$ is a form system.

3.1 From SRDs to Ontologies

We can obtain a form system and thus an ontology from an srd in the following way. An srd D determines a closed subclass D^* of $WF[Z]$ where D^* is the class of elements of $WF[Z]$ obtained from elements, a, of D by substituting atoms from Z for all the occurrences of variables from Y in a. This gives a subsystem of the form system W which can, by the representation theorem for form systems, be extended to an ontology, call this ontology U_D. Any full algebra for this ontology will give us an elementary universe. Notice that by proposition 2 there are well-founded and anti-founded universes for this ontology.

So what is the relationship between the fixed points of the srds and the elementary universes for the ontology? If we have an srd D then the elements of Y which occur in elements of D are acting like the components in our form system. Call an srd D *uniform* if it is such that

$$\sigma_1 \cdot_Y u_1 = \sigma_2 \cdot_Y u_2 \Rightarrow ran\, \sigma_1 = ran\, \sigma_2 \wedge (\sigma \circ \sigma_1) \cdot_Y u_1 = (\sigma \circ \sigma_2) \cdot_Y u_2$$

for any $u_1, u_2 \in D$, $\sigma_i : \rho_Y u_i \to V$ for any $\sigma : ran\, \sigma_1 \to V$.

Proposition 4 *If D is a uniform srd then U_D is such that*

1. *The fixed points of D give U_D-universes.*
2. *The least fixed point of D gives a well-founded U_D-universe.*
3. *Assuming* AFA *(the anti-foundation axiom) the greatest fixed point of D gives an anti-founded U_D-universe.*

Proof. For the second and third parts of this proposition we just give a sketch proof, quoting the results from which these results follow without giving the full definitions.

1. If D is uniform we can get an ontology $U = (U, C_U, \cdot_U)$ by letting

$$U = \{\sigma \cdot_Y (u) \mid u \in D, \sigma : \rho_Y u \to V\}$$

   Since D is uniform, for $u \in D$ and $\sigma : \rho_Y u \to V$ we can define $C_U(\sigma \cdot_Y u) = ran\, \sigma$ and if $\tau : ran\, \sigma \to V$, $\tau \cdot_U (\sigma \cdot_Y u) = (\tau \circ \sigma) \cdot_Y u$. This ontology can be shown to be a representative ontology for D^*. By the uniqueness of the representative ontology for a form system this ontology is isomorphic to U_D. It is easy to show that the class operator $U[\,]$ is in fact the class operator Γ_D and so each fixed point of the srd, A, will give a full algebra (A, id_A) for the ontology. This gives an elementary universe for U which will also be an elementary universe for U_D since U is isomorphic to U_D.

2. By the initial algebra theorem from Aczel 1988 the least fixed point of $U[\,]$ gives an initial full algebra for U. From the proof of the existence of a well-founded U-universe we get that an initial full algebra for U gives a well-founded universe for U. It follows that the least-fixed point of the class operator $U[\,]$ gives a well-founded U-universe.

3. The operator $\mathcal{U}[\ ]$ is 'uniform on maps'[2] and so, from the special final coalgebra theorem in Aczel 1988, the greatest fixed point of $\mathcal{U}[\ ]$ gives a final full algebra for $\mathcal{U}$. From the proof of the existence of an anti-founded $\mathcal{U}$-universe we get that a final full algebra gives an anti-founded $\mathcal{U}$-universe. It follows that the greatest fixed point of $\mathcal{U}[\ ]$ is an anti-founded $\mathcal{U}$-universe. $\qquad\square$

If we have an srd which isn't uniform then we can't define components and replacement for an ontology $\mathcal{U}$ in the above way. An example of an srd which isn't uniform is given by $D = \{\{\{y_0\}\}, \{y_1\}\}$. The problem here being that if we take an element, a, from the fixed point of this srd with $a = \{\{a'\}\}$ then we don't know whether we got it from $\hat{f}_0\{\{y_0\}\}$, or from $\hat{f}_1\{y_1\}$. So we don't know whether to take the components as being $\{\{a'\}\}$ or $\{a'\}$. We have therefore lost information, and the fixed points of the srd do not give $\mathcal{U}_D$-universes.

Returning to our example D_{full}, it is easy to show that D_{full} is uniform. The ontology we get from D_{full} is the power set ontology $\mathcal{U}_{pow} = (pow\, V, C_{pow}, \cdot_{pow})$ where the components of a set are the elements of that set, so $C_{pow}u = u$ for $u \in pow\, V$, and if $\sigma : Cu \to V$ then $\sigma \cdot_{pow} u = \{\sigma v \mid v \in u\}$. This is called the power set ontology since for any class X we get $\mathcal{U}_{pow}[X] = pow\, X$. Now given a fixed point of D_{full}, A, we get that $\mathcal{U}_{pow}(A, id_A)$ is an elementary universe. To summarize, we can get an ontology from each one sorted srd, moreover if the ontology is uniform then the fixed points of the srd will give elementary universes for the ontology.

We now give a slightly more complicated example of an srd and the ontology we get from the srd. Consider an example where we have types and propositions, this example is a subset of the situation theory example given in Section 4. It is not supposed to be realistic but is supposed to illustrate what is going on here. Let X_{prop}, X_{typ}, the classes of parameters of 'sorts' proposition and type, and T, the class of primitive types, be given. Let $X^{\cdot}$ be the non-repeating families from $X_{prop} \cup X_{typ}$ indexed by elements of $\mathbb{N}$. We shall assume suitable set theoretic coding of the forms that we use, so for example $(a_i)_{i<n} : t = (1, (a_0, \ldots, a_n, t))$, $\bigwedge \Theta = (2, \Theta)$, $[\bar{x} : \Theta] = (3, (\bar{x}, \Theta))$ and $X_{prop}, X_{typ}, T, \{1\} \times V, \{2\} \times V, \{3\} \times V$ are pairwise disjoint. We want a universe $A = A_{prop} \cup A_{typ}$ where A_{prop} are the parametric propositions and A_{typ} are the parametric types. A parametric proposition is either:

- A parameter, i.e., an element of X_{prop}.
- Of the form $(a_i)_{i<n} : t$. (This represents a proposition which is true if the n-tuple $(a_i)_{i<n}$ is of type t).

---

[2] The definition of uniform on maps is technical and does not give any intuition as to what is going on. However the proof that $\mathcal{U}[\ ]$ is uniform on maps is straightforward, so this is left to the interested reader to look up.

- Of the form $\bigwedge \Theta$. (This represents the conjunction of the set of propositions Θ).

A parametric type is either

- A parameter, i.e., an element of X_{typ}.
- A primitive type, i.e., an element of T.
- Of the form $[\bar{x} : \theta]$ where $\bar{x} \in X^{\cdot}$. (This represents the type obtained by 'abstracting' a proposition).

Since we are only looking at unsorted srds and form systems we will get a lot of extra things in our universe, for example $\bigwedge A'$ where A' is a set containing types. This example will be returned to in Section 4 where a sorted ontology will be given in which we will ensure that we only get the conjunction of propositions. An srd for this is $D = D_{prop} \cup D_{typ}$ where

$$D_{prop} = X_{prop} \cup \bigcup_{n \in \mathbb{N}} \{(y_i)_{i<n} : y\} \cup \{\bigwedge Y' \mid Y' \in pow\, Y\}$$

$$D_{typ} = X_{typ} \cup T \cup \{[\bar{x} : y] \mid \bar{x} \in X^{\cdot}\}$$

and $y, y_i \in Y$ are all distinct. Once again it is easy to show that D is uniform. We get an ontology from D by replacing all the elements of Y occurring within elements of D by elements of V to get $\mathcal{U} = (U, C_{\mathcal{U}}, \cdot_{\mathcal{U}})$ with $U = U_{prop} \cup U_{typ}$ where

$$U_{prop} = X_{prop} \cup \bigcup_{n \in \mathbb{N}} \{(v_i)_{i<n} : t \mid v_i, t \in V\} \cup \{\bigwedge \Theta \mid \Theta \in pow\, V\}$$

$$U_{typ} = X_{typ} \cup T \cup \{[\bar{x} : v] \mid \bar{x} \in X^{\cdot}, v \in V\}$$

and if $u \in U$ then the components and replacement are given by:

- If $u \in X_{prop} \cup X_{typ} \cup T$ then $C_{\mathcal{U}} u = \emptyset$ and if $\sigma : C_{\mathcal{U}} u \to V$ then $\sigma \cdot_{\mathcal{U}} u = u$.
- If $u = (v_i)_{i<n} : t$ then $C_{\mathcal{U}} u = \{v_i \mid i < n\} \cup \{t\}$ and if $\sigma : C_{\mathcal{U}} u \to V$ then $\sigma \cdot_{\mathcal{U}} u = (\sigma v_i)_{i<n} : (\sigma t)$.
- If $u = \bigwedge \Theta$ then $C_{\mathcal{U}} u = \Theta$ and if $\sigma : C_{\mathcal{U}} u \to V$ then $\sigma \cdot_{\mathcal{U}} u = \bigwedge \{\sigma \theta \mid \theta \in \Theta\}$.
- If $u = [\bar{x} : v]$ then $C_{\mathcal{U}} u = \{v\}$ and if $\sigma : C_{\mathcal{U}} u \to V$ then $\sigma \cdot_{\mathcal{U}} u = [\bar{x} : \sigma v]$.

Fixed points of D give elementary universes for $\mathcal{U}$. In the AFA universe the least fixed point gives a well-founded $\mathcal{U}$-universe and the greatest fixed point gives an anti-founded $\mathcal{U}$-universe.

3.2 The Representation of Form Systems

What about the relationship the other way round? Can we get from form systems to srds? Assuming that the class Y is large enough it is obvious we can go from a subsystem of $\mathcal{W}$ to an srd. So the question becomes one of whether the set theoretic form system is general enough to represent all other form systems or in other words, is every form system isomorphic to a subsystem of $\mathcal{W}$? Two form system $\mathcal{A}_1 = (A_1, C_1, \cdot_1)$, $\mathcal{A}_2 = (A_2, C_2, \cdot_2)$ are *isomorphic* if there is a bijection $\pi : A_1 \to A_2$ such that $C_2(\pi a) = C_1 a$ and if $\sigma : C_1 a \to Z$ then $\sigma \cdot_2 (\pi a) = \pi(\sigma \cdot_1 a)$. We will now look at the relationship between subsystems of $\mathcal{W}$ and other form systems. Call a form system $(A, C, \cdot)$ *large* if A is a proper class, otherwise call it *small*. Aczel has shown that, assuming X is a set, there are some large form systems which are not isomorphic to a subsystem of $\mathcal{W}$ (Details of this proof will appear in Lunnon 1991). We could instead consider the question for small form systems:

Problem 1 *Is every small form system isomorphic to a subsystem of $\mathcal{W}$?*

In fact in this section we will be considering a simpler question, that of whether every subsystem of a form system generated by a form of that system is isomorphic to a subsystem of $\mathcal{W}$. We will define the notion of shape and show that if every shape has a set theoretic form then this gives a positive answer to the simpler problem. In fact it has been shown by Larry Moss that if Z has two elements then the answer to problem 1 is yes (once again details of this proof will appear in Lunnon 1991). This result may generalize but it would seem to require the concept of shape and it is possible that a positive answer to the simpler problem would give a positive answer to problem 1. We don't answer the question here but we simplify it when Z is finite and show it is true when Z has three elements.

Definition 8 T is a *shape* on a subset U of Z if T is an equivalence relation on the unary maps on U such that for any maps $\sigma_1, \sigma_2 : U \to U$

- If $\sigma_1 T \sigma_2$ then $\forall \sigma : Z \to Z$. $(\sigma \circ \sigma_1)T(\sigma \circ \sigma_2)$
- If $\sigma_1 T \sigma_2$ then $ran\, \sigma_1 = ran\, \sigma_2$.

An element a of a form system $\mathcal{A} = (A, C, \cdot)$ has a shape S if for any $\sigma_1, \sigma_2 : Ca \to Ca$

$$\sigma_1 S \sigma_2 \Leftrightarrow \sigma_1 \cdot a = \sigma_2 \cdot a$$

Notice that every element of a form system has a shape. We now give the shapes on the set $\{1, 2\}$ along with an example of a form for each shape. There are two shapes on the set $\{1, 2\}$ and these are S_{max} where $\sigma_1 S_{max} \sigma_2$ if and only if $ran\, \sigma_1 = ran\, \sigma_2$, so the two maps with range $\{1, 2\}$ are equivalent, and S_{min} where $\sigma_1 S_{min} \sigma_2 \Leftrightarrow \sigma_1 = \sigma_2$. The form $\{1, 2\}$ has shape S_{max} and the form $(1, 2)$ has shape S_{min}. In fact given any set Z let S_{max} be the shape where all maps with the same range are equivalent and let S_{min} be the shape where each map is only equivalent to itself then Z is an element of $\mathcal{W}$ and has shape S_{max} and if $I \cong Z$ is a pure set, for any $f : I \cong Z$ (f is a bijection from I to Z) f is an element of $\mathcal{W}$ and has shape S_{min}.

Given an element a of a form system, $\mathcal{A} = (A, C, \cdot)$, the subsystem of $\mathcal{A}$ generated by a, $\mathcal{A} \!\restriction\! a$, contains those forms which can be obtained from a by replacing the components of a with other components of a. Replacement and components on $\mathcal{A} \restriction a$ are inherited from $\mathcal{A}$. So $\mathcal{A} \restriction a = (A', C', \cdot')$ where $A' = \{\tau \cdot a \mid \tau : Ca \to Ca\}$ and C' and $\cdot'$ are the obvious restrictions of C and $\cdot$.

Lemma 5 *If a_1, a_2 are elements of form systems $\mathcal{A}_1 = (A_1, C_1, \cdot_1)$, $\mathcal{A}_2 = (A_2, C_2, \cdot_2)$ and have shapes T_1, T_2 respectively and $C_1 a_1 = C_2 a_2$ then, there is an isomorphism $\pi : \mathcal{A}_1 | a_1 \to \mathcal{A}_2 | a_2$ with $\pi a_1 = a_2$ if and only if $T_1 = T_2$.*

The proof of this lemma is straightforward. It follows from this lemma that if we can show that every shape is the shape of an element of $\mathcal{W}$ then we have shown that for any form system $\mathcal{A}$ and any element of that form system a, $\mathcal{A} \restriction a$ is isomorphic to a subsystem of $\mathcal{W}$. We could try to solve a simpler problem than the first, i.e., whether the subsystem generated by an element of a form system is isomorphic to some subsystem of $\mathcal{W}$, or in other words,

Problem 2 *Is every shape the shape of some element of $\mathcal{W}$?*

We now simplify this problem when Z is finite and then give the classifications of the isomorphism classes of shapes when Z has three elements, along with set theoretic examples of forms with those shapes.

We will write Σ_n for the nth symmetric group, i.e., the group of permutations on $\{1, \ldots, n\}$. Notice that given a shape S on a finite set, which we will assume is a shape on $\{1, \ldots, n\}$ for some $n \in \mathbb{N}$ there is a subgroup of Σ_n which gives those maps which are equivalent to the identity under S. Write $G(S)$ for this subgroup. We will say that the shape is invariant under this subgroup.

3.2.1 The Simplification of a Problem

Let a finite shape be a shape on a finite set. We will now consider problem 2 for finite shapes, i.e., whether every finite shape is set theoretical. Since for every finite set there is a natural number n such that there is a bijection from that set to $\{1, \ldots, n\}$ we need only consider shapes on sets of the form $\{1, \ldots, n\}$ for some natural number n. For a finite shape T on $\{1, \ldots, n\}$ there is a subgroup of Σ_n under which the shape is invariant which we are denoting by $G(T)$. It is easy to show, using basic group theory, that the equivalence classes of permutations are the left cosets of this subgroup.

Let e be the identity map on U. Using the next proposition the above question can be simplified to the question—is every finite shape T with $G(T) = \{e\}$ the shape of some element of $\mathcal{W}$? This is done by showing that for any shape S on $\{1, \ldots, n\}$ there is a shape T on $\{1, \ldots, n\}$ with $G(T) = \{e\}$ and such that for any object $f \in \mathcal{W}$ with shape T, $\{\sigma \cdot f \mid \sigma \in G(S)\}$ has shape S.

Proposition 6 *Given shapes T and S on $\{1 \ldots n\}$ if*

- *$G(T) = \{e\}$ and*
- *for all maps σ_1, σ_2 either they are permutations or $\sigma_1 T \sigma_2 \iff \sigma_1 S \sigma_2$,*

then for every $f \in W$ with shape T, $\{\sigma \cdot f \mid \sigma \in G(S)\}$ has shape S.

Proof. Notice that, since $G(S)$ is a group and S is a shape,

1. $\sigma S(\sigma \circ \tau)$ for $\tau \in G(S)$
2. $\sigma_1 S \sigma_2 \Rightarrow (\sigma_1 \circ \tau) S (\sigma_2 \circ \tau)$ for $\tau \in G(S)$.

Let $f_S = \{\sigma \cdot f \mid \sigma \in G(S)\}$. to show that f_S has shape S it must be shown that

$$\sigma_1 S \sigma_2 \Leftrightarrow \sigma_1 \cdot f_S = \sigma_2 \cdot f_S$$

So first suppose that $\sigma_1 S \sigma_2$. If σ_1 and σ_2 are permutations then by elementary group theory $\sigma_1 \cdot f_S = \sigma_2 \cdot f_S$. If σ_1 and σ_2 aren't permutations then by 1, for $\sigma \in G(S)$, $(\sigma_1 \circ \sigma) S (\sigma_2 \circ \sigma)$. Since σ_1, σ_2 aren't permutation then neither are $\sigma_1 \circ \sigma$, $\sigma_2 \circ \sigma$ and so $(\sigma_1 \circ \sigma) T (\sigma_2 \circ \sigma)$. from which $(\sigma_1 \circ \sigma) \cdot f = (\sigma_2 \circ \sigma) \cdot f$ and so $\sigma_1 \cdot f_S = \sigma_2 \cdot f_S$

Now suppose that $\sigma_1 \cdot f_S = \sigma_2 \cdot f_S$. If σ_1, σ_2 are permutations then it follows from group theory that $\sigma_1 S \sigma_2$. If σ_1, σ_2 aren't permutations then, by the definition of f_S, for each $\tau \in G(S)$ there is a $\sigma \in G(S)$ such that $(\sigma_1 \circ \tau) T (\sigma_2 \circ \sigma)$, but by 2 $(\sigma_1 \circ \tau) T \sigma_1$ and $(\sigma_2 \circ \sigma) T \sigma_2$ so $\sigma_1 T \sigma_2$ which gives $\sigma_1 S \sigma_2$. $\square$

We will now give an example of this where $Z = \{1, 2, 3\}$ but first some notation. We will write [112] to represents the map $\{1 \to 1, 2 \to 1, 3 \to 2\}$. We will also use the permutation notation for the permutations so (12) is the map $\{1 \to 2, 2 \to 1, 3 \to 3\}$. Now take T to be the shape on $\{1, 2, 3\}$ with $G(T) = \{e, (12)\}$ and with $[aba] T [baa]$ for $a, b \in \{1, 2, 3\}$ and S to be the shape with $G(S) = \{e\}$ and $[aba] S [baa]$ then $\{(1, 2, 3), (2, 3, 3), (3, 1, 3)\}$ has shape S and so by the above proposition

$$\{ \{(1, 2, 3), (2, 3, 3), (3, 1, 3)\}, \{(2, 1, 3), (1, 3, 3), (3, 2, 3)\} \}$$

has shape T. Notice that this proposition does not give the simplest example of a form with a shape. Consider the shape T on $\{1, 2, 3\}$ in which all maps which can be made equivalent are, so $\sigma T \tau$ if $ran\, \sigma = ran\, \tau$, and the shape S with $G(S) = \{e\}$ and for all maps which aren't permutations $\sigma S \tau$ if $ran\, \sigma = ran\, \tau$. Then an example of a form with shape T is $\{1, 2, 3\}$ and an example of a form with shape S is $\{(1, 2, 3) \cup \{$all triples with components a strict subset of $\{1, 2, 3\}\}$. Using the above proposition on this example gives a more complicated form than $\{1, 2, 3\}$ with shape T.

This result does not extend to infinite sets. To see this consider the set $U = \{1, 2, \ldots\}$. There is a group of permutations on U but it contains only those maps from $U \to U$ which have an inverse so the mapping which takes a number to the integer part of half that number is not in this group, but from the axioms of a shape this may be equivalent to elements of the group so the equivalences on the maps with range U are not governed solely by the sub-groups of this group.

3.2.2 All Shapes on $Z = \{1, 2, 3\}$ are Set Theoretical

By proposition 6 we only need to consider shapes T with $G(T) = \{e\}$. The shapes, T, on the set $\{1, 2, 3\}$ with $G(T) = \{e\}$ are now classified up to isomorphism and an example from $\mathcal{W}$ is given for each such isomorphism class.

A shape on $\{1, 2, 3\}$ can be classified by two things. Firstly the equivalence classes on the permutations and secondly the equivalences on the maps with range $\{a, b\}$ for $a, b \in \{1, 2, 3\}$, $a \neq b$. The equivalences between maps with range 2 elements are determined by the equivalences between the maps $[112]$, $[121]$, $[211]$, $[221]$, $[212]$ and $[122]$.

A shape T on $\{1,2,3\}$ will be determined by:

- the subgroup of Σ_3 under which it is invariant. This is denoted $G(T)$.
- the equivalences between the maps with range $\{1,2\}$. These equivalences will be represented diagrammatically where two maps are equivalent if they are joined by a line.

So $G(T) = \{e\}$ and

$$
\begin{array}{ccc}
[112] & [121] & [211] \\
\bullet & \bullet & \bullet \\
| & & \\
\bullet & \bullet & \bullet \\
[221] & [212] & [122]
\end{array}
$$

represents a shape T where $[aab]T[bba]$ for $a, b \in \{1, 2, 3\}$. Notice that the bottom row must mirror the top row. The labels are left out from now on since up to isomorphism the order from left to right is unimportant as long as all maps on the bottom row can be obtained from the map above them by replacing one by two and two by one.

Definition 9 Two shapes T_1 and T_2 on a set U are *isomorphic* if there exists a permutation $\sigma : U \to U$ such that for all maps $\tau_1, \tau_2 : U \to U$,

$$\tau_1 T_1 \tau_2 \iff (\tau_1 \circ \sigma) T_2 (\tau_2 \circ \sigma)$$

Notice that if two shapes are isomorphic and one of them is the shape of some element of $\mathcal{W}$ then the other is the shape of an element of $\mathcal{W}$.

There are 56 shapes on $\{1, 2, 3\}$ in 24 isomorphism classes. There are two non-isomorphic shapes with $G(S) = \Sigma_3$, there are two non-isomorphic shapes with $G(S) = A_3$ (where $A_3 = \{e, (123), (132)\}$ is the alternating group), there are seven non-isomorphic shapes with $G(S) = \{e, (12)\}$ each of which is isomorphic to one of the seven shapes with $G(S) = \{e, (13)\}$, and to one of the seven shapes with $G(S) = \{e, (23)\}$. There are 31 shapes with $G(S) = \{e\}$ in 13 isomorphism classes.

The classifications of one shape from each isomorphism class with $G(T) = 3$ is now given along with an example of a form from $\mathcal{W}$ for that shape.

1. e.g., $(1, 2, 3)$

2. e.g., $\{(1, 2, 3), (3, 3, 1)\}$

3. e.g., $\{(1, 2, 3), (2, 1, 2), (3, 3, 1), (2, 2, 2), (3, 3, 3)\}$

4. e.g., $\{(1, 2, 3), (3, 3, 1), (3, 3, 3), (2, 1, 2), (2, 1, 1),$
   $(2, 2, 2), (1, 2, 2), (1, 1, 3), (1, 2, 1), (1, 1, 1)\}$

5. e.g., $\{(1, 2, 3), (1, 2, 1), (1, 2, 2)\}$

6. e.g., $\{(1, 2, 3), (1, 2, 1), (1, 2, 2), (3, 3, 3), (2, 2, 2),$
   $(1, 1, 1), (3, 3, 1), (2, 2, 1)\}$

7. e.g., $\{(1, 2, 3), (2, 3, 3), (3, 1, 3)\}$

8. e.g., $\{(1, 2, 3), (1, 3, 1), (1, 1, 2), (2, 1, 1), (3, 1, 1),$
   $(2, 1, 2), (3, 1, 3), (2, 2, 1), (3, 3, 1)\}$

9. e.g., $\{(1, 2, 3), (1, 2, 1), (1, 2, 2), (1, 1, 3), (1, 3, 3),$
   $(1, 3, 1), (1, 1, 2), (1, 1, 1)\}$

10. e.g., $\{(1, 2, 3), (3, 3, 2), (2, 2, 3), (3, 2, 2), (2, 3, 3),$
    $(2, 2, 2), (3, 3, 3)\}$

11. e.g., $\{(1, 2, 3), (3, 3, 1), (3, 3, 3), (2, 1, 2), (2, 1, 1),$
    $(2, 2, 2), (1, 2, 2), (1, 1, 3), (1, 2, 1), (1, 1, 1),$
    $(1, 1, 2), (2, 2, 1)\}$

12. e.g., $\{(1, 2, 3), (1, 3, 1), (3, 1, 1), (1, 1, 2), (2, 1, 1),$
    $(2, 1, 2), (3, 1, 3), (1, 2, 2), (1, 3, 3)\}$

13. e.g., $\{(1, 2, 3)\} \cup \{$all triples a with $\rho a \subset \{1, 2, 3\}\}$

To recap this section, we have shown that from a srd we can get an ontology and, providing the srd is uniform, the fixed points of the srd give us elementary universes for the ontology. We then investigated getting an srd from a given form system. We obviously get an srd from every subsystem of $\mathcal{W}$ so the question we want to answer is whether every small form system is isomorphic to a subsystem of $\mathcal{W}$. Rather than try and answer this question we have looked at the simpler problem of whether a subsystem of a form system $\mathcal{A}$ generated by an element of $\mathcal{A}$ is isomorphic to a a subsystem of $\mathcal{W}$. To put this another way, is every shape the shape of an element of $\mathcal{W}$. By proposition 6 the answer to this is yes if every shape T with $G(T) = \{e\}$ is the shape of an element of $\mathcal{W}$. This is then used in showing that every shape on a three element set is the shape of an element of $\mathcal{W}$, which is done by giving a form in $\mathcal{W}$ for every shape T on the set $\{1, 2, 3\}$ with $G(T) = \{e\}$.

4 Many Sorted Universes

In this section we generalize the notion of an elementary universe to that of a many sorted universe. Corresponding results are given for representation and the existence of well-founded and anti-founded many sorted universes and also the existence of a 'mixed-founded' sorted universe is shown. We also develop further the example of a universe containing propositions and types given in the previous section, and we give a more complicated 'situation theory' example.

A sorted universe has:

- A class of objects, each object having a sort.
- A components function which, for each object gives its components which are a subset of the objects.
- A restricted components function, which for each object gives a subset of the components.
- A replacement operation which may only replace the restricted components of an object by other objects which have the same sort.

This definition of a sorted universe has been influenced by the definitions of srds given in Fernando 1990.

Definition 10 Let T be a set, A *T-sorted class*, or *T-class*, is a class A along with a sorting function $\eta : A \to T$. A *T-sorted set* or *T-set* is a T-class which is a set.

Given a T-class A we will write A_t for $\{a \in A \mid \eta_A a = t\}$ if $t \in T$. We will consider a T-class, X, to be a sorted subclass of another T-class, Y, written $X \subseteq_T Y$, if they are subclasses of each other when considered as classes, so $X \subseteq Y$, and the sorting function on X is the same as the sorting function on Y restricted to X, so for each $x \in X$, $\eta_X x = \eta_Y x$. We also want a notion of mapping between T-classes which will preserve the sorting function.

Definition 11 A mapping f between T-classes, X and Y, written $f :$ $X \to^T Y$, is a mapping $f : X \to Y$ which preserves sorts, so $\eta_X x = \eta_Y f x$.

We will have a class of sorts S along with some $* \in S$ where objects of sort $*$ will always be unrestricted components.

Definition 12 Given S-classes X, X', Y with $X' \subseteq_S X$ write $\sigma : X, X' \to$ Y if $\sigma : X \to Y$ is such that $\sigma{\restriction}X' : X' \to^S Y$. So σ preserves sorts on X'.

We will use this notion for the replacement operation where we will require that the restricted components are replaced by objects which have the same sort.

Definition 13 $\mathcal{A} = (A, C, C_0, \cdot)$ is an S-sorted X-form system if X and A are S-classes, $C, C_0 : A \to powX$ with for each $a \in A$, $C_0 a \subseteq \{x \in Ca \mid \eta x \neq *\}$ and if $\sigma : Ca, C_0 a \to X$ then $\sigma \cdot a \in A$ with $\eta a = \eta(\sigma \cdot a)$ and

- $C\sigma \cdot a = \{\sigma x \mid x \in Ca\}$
  $C_0 \sigma \cdot a = \{\sigma x \mid x \in C_0 a\}$
- $\sigma \cdot a = a$ if $\sigma x = x$ for all $x \in Ca$.
- $\sigma' \cdot (\sigma \cdot a) = (\sigma' \circ \sigma) \cdot a$ if $\sigma' : C\sigma a, C_0 \sigma a \to X$.

As for the unsorted case C is a components function and $\cdot$ is a replacement operation. C_0 is a restricted components operation and we will only allow restricted components to be replaced by elements of X of the same sort. We now give the definition of S-sorted universes and ontologies.

Definition 14 $\mathcal{A} = (A, C, \cdot)$ is an S-sorted universe if it is an S-sorted A-form system.

To give the definition of an S-sorted ontology we need a sorted universe, so let $V_S = S \times V$ and $\eta_{V_S}(s, v) = s$.

Definition 15 An S-sorted ontology is a S-sorted V_S-form system.

Given an S-sorted ontology $\mathcal{U} = (U, C\mathcal{U}, C_0\mathcal{U}, \cdot_\mathcal{U})$ we can define an operator which takes a subclass of V_S and returns a subclass of V_S by

$$\mathcal{U}[X] = \{u \in U \mid (C\mathcal{U}u \subseteq X\}$$

So $\mathcal{U}[X]$ returns the class of elements of U which have components from X. This operator is only defined for subclasses of V_S, so to get an operator which is defined on any S-class we associate a subclass of V_S with each S-class. Given an S-class X we define a subclass $\overline{X}$ of V_S by $\overline{X} = \{(\eta_X x, x) \mid x \in X\}$. If A is a S-class and $\alpha : \mathcal{U}[\overline{A}] \to^S A$ is a bijection, then $\mathcal{U}(A, \alpha) = (A, C, C_0, \cdot)$ is an S-sorted universe, where for $a \in A$,

$$\begin{aligned} Ca &= \{a' \mid (\eta_A a', a') \in C\mathcal{U}\alpha^{-1}a\} \\ C_0 a &= \{a \mid (\eta_A a', a') \in C_0\mathcal{U}\alpha^{-1}a\} \end{aligned}$$

and if $\sigma : Ca, C_0 a \to A$ then

$$\sigma \cdot a = \alpha \sigma' \cdot_\mathcal{U} \alpha^{-1} a$$

where $\sigma'(\eta_A a', a') = (\eta_A(\sigma a'), \sigma a')$. We will say that $\mathcal{U}(A, \alpha)$ is an S-sorted $\mathcal{U}$-universe.

Write $X, X' \preceq B$ if there is an injective function $f : X \to B$ such that $f : X, X' \to B$. Let an S-sorted X-form system, $(A, C, \cdot)$ be B-bounded if for each $a \in A$, $Ca, C_0 a \preceq B$. We can now give the sorted version of the representation theorem.

Theorem 7 The Sorted Representation Theorem

Every S-sorted universe $\mathcal{A} = (A, C, C_0, \cdot)$ is a S-sorted $\mathcal{U}$-universe for some A-bounded S-sorted ontology $\mathcal{U}$. Moreover $\mathcal{U}$ is unique up to isomorphism.

The proof of this theorem is similar to the proof of the unsorted representation theorem. Once again call $\mathcal{U}$ a representative S-sorted ontology for $\mathcal{A}$.

Before we give the definitions of well-founded and anti-founded S-sorted universes we will give the definition of a system of equations for an ontology and the definition of a solution to such a system of equations. These definitions are similar to the definitions in the unsorted case.

Definition 16 A *system of equations* for an S-sorted ontology $\mathcal{U} = (U, C_{\mathcal{U}}, C_{0\mathcal{U}}, \cdot_{\mathcal{U}})$ is of the form

$$y = a_y \quad (y \in Y)$$

where Y is an S-class and for $y \in Y$, $a_y \in \mathcal{U}[\overline{Y}]$ with $\eta_Y y = \eta_U a_y$. A solution to such a system of equations in an S-sorted $\mathcal{U}$-universe $\mathcal{U}(A, \alpha)$ is a map $\pi : Y \to^S A$ such that $\pi y = \alpha \pi' \cdot_{\mathcal{U}} a_y$ where $\pi'(\eta_Y y', y') = (\eta_A(\pi y'), \pi y')$.

Definition 17 Let $\mathcal{A} = (A, C, C_0, \cdot)$ be an S-sorted $\mathcal{U}$-universe,

- $\mathcal{A}$ is *well-founded* if there is no infinite descending component sequence in A, i.e., there is no sequence $a_0, a_1, \ldots \in A$ with, for $i \in \mathbb{N}$, $a_{i+1} \in Ca_i$.
- $\mathcal{A}$ is *anti-founded* if there is a unique solution to every $\mathcal{U}$-system of equations in $\mathcal{A}$.

Proposition 8 *For every S-sorted ontology, $\mathcal{U}$, there is a well-founded and anti-founded S-sorted $\mathcal{U}$-universe, moreover these are unique up to isomorphism.*

Proof. The proof of this is a generalization of the proof in the unsorted case which is rather technical. Sorted versions of the initial algebra and final coalgebra theorems are required, these go through as for the unsorted case as in Aczel 1988, 1990. For each S-sorted ontology we can then define a sorted functor whose initial algebra and final coalgebra can be shown to give well-founded and anti-founded universes as in the unsorted case in Aczel 1990. These can then be shown to be unique up to isomorphism. $\square$

In Section 3 the relationship between unsorted srds and form systems was investigated. The relationship between (sorted) srds and sorted form systems is not so straightforward. srds may have overlapping sorts while form systems do not, and even if attention is restricted to the non-overlapping srds it is not obvious what should be taken as restricted components.

We now give an example of an S-sorted ontology. In Section 3 we wanted to consider universes which contained propositions and types and an unsorted ontology was given. However this meant there were extra objects in the universe which had no meaning, this can be rectified by using a sorted ontology. Let $S = \{prop, typ, *\}$ and let X_{prop}, X_{typ}, X_*, the parameters of sort proposition, type and $*$, and T, the primitive types, be given. Let X be the non-repeating families from $X_{prop} \cup X_{typ} \cup X_*$ indexed by elements of $\mathbb{N}$. We want a universe $A = A_{prop} \cup A_{typ}$ where A_{prop} are the parametric propositions and A_{typ} are the parametric types and a parametric proposition is either:

- A parameter, i.e., an element of X_{prop}.
- Of the form $(a_i)_{i<n} : t$ with components $\{a_i \mid i < n\} \cup \{t\}$ and restricted components $\{t\}$ with sort typ. So the a_i may have any sort but t must be a type.
- Of the form $\bigwedge \Theta$ with restricted components the set Θ of sort $prop$. So the elements of Θ are all propositions.

A parametric type is either

- A parameter, i.e., an element of X_{typ}.
- A primitive type, i.e., an element of T.
- Of the form $[\overline{x} : \theta]$ where $\overline{x} \in X$ with restricted components $\{\theta\}$ of sort $prop$. So θ is a proposition.

Let $\mathcal{U} = (U, C_{\mathcal{U}}, C_{0\mathcal{U}}, \cdot_{\mathcal{U}})$ with $U = U_{prop} \cup U_{typ} \cup U_*$ where

$$U_{prop} = X_{prop} \cup \bigcup_{n \in \mathbb{N}} \{(v_i)_{i<n} : t \mid v_i \in V_S, t \in V_{typ}\} \cup \{\bigwedge \Theta \mid \Theta \in pow\, V_{prop}\}$$

$$U_{typ} = X_{typ} \cup T \cup \{[\overline{x} : \theta] \mid \overline{x} \in X, \theta \in V_{prop}\}$$

$$U_* = X_*$$

and for $u \in U$

- If $u \in X_{prop} \cup X_{typ} \cup X_* \cup T$ then $C_{\mathcal{U}}x = C_{0\mathcal{U}}x = \emptyset$.
- If $u = (v_i)_{i<n} : t$ then $C_{\mathcal{U}}u = \{v_i \mid i < n\} \cup \{t\}$, $C_{0\mathcal{U}}u = \{t\}$ and if $\sigma : C_{\mathcal{U}}u, C_{0\mathcal{U}}u \to V_S$ then $\sigma \cdot_{\mathcal{U}} u = (\sigma v_i)_{i<n} : \sigma t$.
- If $u = \bigwedge \Theta$ then $C_{\mathcal{U}}u = C_{0\mathcal{U}}u = \Theta$ and if $\sigma : C_{\mathcal{U}}u, C_{0\mathcal{U}}u \to V_S$ then $\sigma \cdot_{\mathcal{U}} u = \bigwedge \{\sigma\theta \mid \theta \in \Theta\}$.
- If $u = [\overline{x} : \theta]$ then $C_{\mathcal{U}}u = C_{0\mathcal{U}}u = \{\theta\}$ and if $\sigma : C_{\mathcal{U}}u, C_{0\mathcal{U}}u \to V_S$ then $\sigma \cdot_{\mathcal{U}} u = [\overline{x} : \sigma\theta]$.

Then $\mathcal{U}$ is an S-sorted ontology. And from the above results there is a well-founded and anti-founded S-sorted $\mathcal{U}$-universe.

We have shown the existence of well-founded and anti-founded S-sorted universes, however the universe required may fall somewhere in between. In situation theory non-well-founded objects are wanted, for example to model common knowledge, (see Barwise 1989b) or to model liar like propositions such as 'This proposition is false', (see Barwise and Etchemendy 1987). There is, however, no interest in being able to form a proposition $\theta = \bigwedge\{\theta\}$. If we simply take an anti-founded universe to work in then propositions like this may be formed. Fernando (in 1989 and 1990) considers fixed points of his srds which allow non-well-foundedness through some 'components' but not through other 'restricted components'. We will now give the definition and construction of a mixed-founded universe which only allows non-well-foundedness through those components which aren't restricted. The construction given here differs from that given in Barwise 1989a which is referred to in Fernando 1989.

A mixed founded universe is one in which any system of equations, which is well-founded with respect to restricted components, has a unique solution. To give a formal definition of this we first give the definition of a coalgebra for an ontology and say what it means for that coalgebra to be well-founded with respect to restricted components.

Definition 18 A *coalgebra* for an S-sorted ontology $\mathcal{U} = (U, C_\mathcal{U}, C_{O\mathcal{U}}, \cdot_\mathcal{U})$ is a pair (U, β) where Y is an S-class and $\beta : Y \to^S U[\overline{Y}]$.

Given a coalgebra (Y, β) for an S-sorted ontology $\mathcal{U}$ write $C_Y(y)$ for $\{y' \mid (\eta_Y y', y') \in C_\mathcal{U} \beta y\}$ and write $C_{OY}(y)$ for $\{y' \mid (\eta_Y y', y') \in C_{O\mathcal{U}} \beta y\}$. A coalgebra (Y, β) for $\mathcal{U}$ is *well-founded with respect to the restricted components* if there is no infinite descending restricted component sequence in Y i.e., there is no sequence $y_o, y_1 \ldots \in Y$ with for each $i \in \mathbb{N}$, $y_{i+1} \in C_{OY} y_i$.

Notice that a system of equations for an S-sorted ontology gives a coalgebra for that S-sorted ontology and an S-sorted universe gives a coalgebra for its representative S-sorted ontology.

Definition 19 An S-sorted $\mathcal{U}$-universe $\mathcal{A}$ is *mixed-founded* if it is well-founded with respect to the restricted components and there is a unique solution to every $\mathcal{U}$-system of equations which is well-founded with respect to the restricted components.

Having given the definitions for a mixed-founded universe we now show that for any S-sorted ontology such a universe exists and is unique up to isomorphism.

Proposition 9 *For every S-sorted ontology there is a mixed-founded S-sorted $\mathcal{U}$-universe which is unique up to isomorphism.*

Proof. This proposition is proved by taking an anti-founded S-sorted $\mathcal{U}$-universe and then constructing a mixed founded S-sorted $\mathcal{U}$-universe as a subuniverse of the anti-founded one. The mixed founded universe is constructed by taking the greatest fixed point of an operator on the anti-founded universe, derived from the ontology operator, which is well-founded with respect to the restricted components.

So let $\mathcal{U}$ be an S-sorted ontology and let $\mathcal{U}(J, \gamma)$ be an anti-founded S-sorted $\mathcal{U}$-universe. Let

$$\mathcal{U}[X, Y] = \{u \in U \mid C_{\mathcal{U}}u - C_{0\mathcal{U}}u \subseteq X, C_{0\mathcal{U}}u \subseteq Y\}$$

So $\mathcal{U}[X, Y]$ returns those elements of U which have unrestricted components from X and restricted components from Y. Notice that $\gamma(\mathcal{U}[\overline{X} \cup \overline{Y}, \overline{X}])$ is J set continuous as a function of X and so has a least fixed point, let

$$\Phi Y = \mu X.(X = \gamma(\mathcal{U}[\overline{X} \cup \overline{Y}, \overline{X}]))$$

Where μ gives the least fixed point. Φ is also J set continuous and so has a greatest fixed point which we shall take to be K and $\mathcal{U}(K, \gamma \restriction K)$ gives a mixed founded universe.

To see that $\mathcal{U}(K, \gamma \restriction K)$ gives a mixed founded universe we first show that it is well-founded with respect to restricted components. First call an element of J well-founded with respect to restricted components if for every infinite descending component sequence $a_0, a_1, \ldots$ starting with $a_0 = a$ there is a strictly increasing sequence of natural numbers $n_0, n_1, \ldots$ with $a_{n_i+1} \in (Ca_{n_i} - C_0 a_{n_i})$ and let L be the class which contains all well-founded with respect to the restricted components elements of J. Notice that L is closed under components.

Lemma 10 $x \in \Phi X$ *if and only if every infinite descending component sequence* $a_0, a_1, \ldots$ *with* $a_0 = x$ *has an* $a_{i+1} \in (Ca_i - C_0 a_i) \cap X$ *for some* $i \in \mathbb{N}$.

Now $K = \Phi K = \mathcal{U}[\overline{\Phi K}, \overline{\Phi K}]$ and so K is closed under components, from which, since $K \subseteq \Phi K$ and using the above lemma, it is obvious that every element of K is well-founded with respect to restricted components, so $K \subseteq L$. But, using the lemma the other way round, we get $L \subseteq \Phi L$ and so $L \subseteq K$ since K is the greatest post-fixed point of Φ, giving us $L = K$. From the definition of K we get that $(K, \gamma \restriction K)$ is a full algebra for $\mathcal{U}$, and from the definition of L we get that it is well-founded with respect to the restricted components. To show that $\mathcal{U}(K, \gamma \restriction K)$ is mixed founded it remains to be shown there is a unique solution to every well-founded with respect to the restricted components system of equations. This is easily shown since if we have a system of equations

$$y = u_y \quad (y \in Y)$$

with solution $\pi : Y \to^S J$ then if $(\eta_Y y', y') \in C_{0\mathcal{U}} u_y$ then $\pi y' \in C_0 \pi y$. From which the image of a solution to a well founded with respect to restricted components system of equations in $\mathcal{U}(J, \gamma)$ must be a subset of K.

The proof of uniqueness up to isomorphism of the mixed founded S-sorted $\mathcal{U}$-universe is similar to the proof of the uniqueness up to isomorphism of the anti-founded S-sorted $\mathcal{U}$-universe. $\qquad\qquad\square$

A Situation Theory Example

We now look at how the apparatus we have presented here may be used to construct a universe for modeling an example situation theory. We will ignore the complications introduced by modeling abstraction. Let $S = \{*, ind, inf, rel, prop, sit, \{\}\}$ be the set of sorts. These are the sorts of objects, individuals, infons, propositions situations and sets. Let I,T,R be given, these are the primitive objects of sort ind, typ and rel respectively. Let X, an S-class of parameters, be given. Let $Index$, the set of indexes, be given and let $X^\cdot$ be the class on non repeating families from X, indexed by elements of $Index$. We now give an ontology for our example. Once again we will assume that we have suitable set theoretic coding.

In our example individuals will be either parameters or primitive individuals, so let

$$U_{ind} = X_{ind} \ \cup \ I$$

Propositions are either parameters or compound propositions with the following forms:

- $\overline{v} : t$ where t is a type (this represents a propositions which will be true if $\overline{v}$ is of type t).
- $s \models \theta$ where s is a situation and θ is an infon (this represents a proposition which is true if the situation supports the infon).
- $\neg\theta$ or $\theta_1 \supset \theta_2$ where $\theta, \theta_1, \theta_2$ are propositions (negation and implication).
- $\bigwedge \Theta$ or $\bigvee \Theta$ where Θ is a set of propositions (the disjunction and conjunction of propositions).
- $\exists(\overline{x} : \theta)$ or $\forall(\overline{x} : \theta)$ (existential and universal quantification).

So let

$$
\begin{aligned}
U_{prop} = \ & X_{prop} \ \cup \ \bigcup_{i \in Index}\{\overline{v} : t \mid \overline{v} \in V_S{}^i, t \in V_{typ}, n \in \mathbb{N}\} \\
& \cup \ \{s \models \theta \mid s \in V_{sit}, \theta \in V_{inf}\} \ \cup \ \{\neg\theta \mid \theta \in V_{prop}\} \\
& \cup \ \{\theta_1 \supset \theta_2 \mid \theta_1, \theta_2 \in V_{prop}\} \ \cup \ \{\textstyle\bigwedge \Theta, \bigvee \Theta \mid \Theta \in pow V_{prop}\} \\
& \cup \ \{\exists(\overline{x} : \theta), \forall(\overline{x} : \theta) \mid \overline{x} \in X^\cdot, \theta \in V_{prop}\}
\end{aligned}
$$

An infon is either a parameter, of the form $\langle\langle r, \overline{v} : \epsilon \rangle\rangle$ where r is a relation and ϵ is the polarity or an implication, conjunction, disjunction or quantification of infons so let

$$
\begin{aligned}
U_{inf} = \ & X_{inf} \ \cup \\
& \bigcup_{i \in Index}\{\langle\langle r, \overline{v}; \epsilon \rangle\rangle \mid n \in \mathbb{N}, r \in V_{rel}, \overline{v} \in V_S{}^i \\
& \qquad\qquad\qquad \text{for } i \in Index, \epsilon \in \{0, 1\}\} \ \cup \\
& \{\theta_1 \supset \theta_2 \mid \theta_1, \theta_2 \in V_{inf}\} \ \cup \ \{\textstyle\bigwedge \Theta, \bigvee \Theta \mid \Theta \in pow V_{inf}\} \ \cup \\
& \{\exists(\overline{x} : \theta), \forall(\overline{x} : \theta) \mid \overline{x} \in X^\cdot, \theta \in V_{inf}\}
\end{aligned}
$$

A type is either a parameter, a primitive type or of the form $[\overline{x} : \theta]$ where θ is a proposition (this represents the type given by 'abstracting' over a proposition), so let

$$U_{typ} = X_{typ} \ \cup \ T \ \cup \ \{[\overline{x} : \theta] \mid \overline{x} \in X^{\cdot}, \theta \in V_{prop}\}$$

A relation is either a parameter, a primitive relation or of the form $[\overline{x} : \theta]$ where θ is an infon, so let

$$U_{rel} = X_{rel} \ \cup \ R \ \cup \ \{[\overline{x} : \theta] \mid \overline{x} \in X^{\cdot}\theta \in V_{inf}\}$$

A set is either a parameter or a set where the elements are of any sort, so let

$$U_{set} = X_{set} \cup \{\{[\}Y] \mid Y \in pow\, V_S\}$$

A situation is either a parameter or a set of infons, so let

$$U_{sit} = X_{sit} \cup \{sit[\Theta] \mid \Theta \in pow\, U_{inf}\}$$

And let

$$U_* = X_*$$

Let $U = \bigcup_{s \in S} U_s$. A sorting function $\eta_U : U \to S$ is given by $\eta_U u = s$ for $u \in U_s$. We can define the components C_U and the restricted components C_{OU} of an object in the following way, parameters and primitives have no components, for a form $sit[\Theta]$ $C_U sit[\Theta] = \bigcup\{C_U\theta \mid \theta \in \Theta\}$ and $C_{OU} sit[\Theta] = \bigcup\{C_{OU}\theta \mid \theta \in \Theta\}$ and for all other forms the unrestricted components of a form are those taken from V_S, the restricted components are those taken from V_s for some given $s \in S$. So the restricted components and components of elements of U_{prop} are

$$
\begin{array}{lll}
u = \overline{v} : t & C_{OU}u = \{t\} & C_U u = C_{OU}u \ \cup \ ran\, \overline{v} \\
u = s \models \theta & C_{OU}u = \{s, \theta\} & C_U u = C_{OU}u \\
u = \neg\theta & C_{OU}u = \{\theta\} & C_U u = C_{OU}u \\
u = \theta_1 \supset \theta_2 & C_{OU}u = \{\theta_1, \theta_2\} & C_U u = C_{OU}u \\
u = \bigwedge\Theta & C_{OU}u = \Theta & C_U u = C_{OU}u \\
u = \bigvee\Theta & C_{OU}u = \Theta & C_U u = C_{OU}u \\
u = \exists(\overline{x}, \theta) & C_{OU}u = \{\theta\} & C_U u = C_{OU}u \\
u = \forall(\overline{x}, \theta) & C_{OU}u = \{\theta\} & C_U u = C_{OU}u
\end{array}
$$

Replacement is the obvious operation, and we have an S-sorted ontology $\mathcal{U} = (U, C_U, C_{OU}, u)$. Now given any S-sorted $\mathcal{U}$-universe $\mathcal{A} = \mathcal{U}(A, \alpha)$ we have a sorted universe in which we have individuals, propositions, infons, types, relations, sets and situations. Furthermore by proposition 8 there is a well-founded and anti-founded S-sorted $\mathcal{U}$-universe. By proposition 9 there is also a mixed-founded S-sorted $\mathcal{U}$-universe which is well-founded with respect to the restricted components and in which there is a unique solution to every $\mathcal{U}$-system of equations which is well-founded with respect to the restricted components.

5   The Injective Sum of Two Elementary Universes

Given an elementary universe $\mathcal{A}$ we may want to create a new elementary universe by parameterizing the elements of $\mathcal{A}$. This parameterization should contain a copy of $\mathcal{A}$, along with a class of parameters, and all objects obtained from objects of $\mathcal{A}$ by replacing some occurrences of objects within an object of $\mathcal{A}$, by parameters. The new elementary universe should not contain any extra objects, and also there should be a notion of substitution of parameters in the new elementary universe.

If the class of parameters is viewed as a trivial elementary universe, then the problem becomes one of adding two elementary universes together, so that the new elementary universe contains disjoint copies of each of the original elementary universes and also does not contain too many objects. We now look at such a sum of two elementary universes.

5.1   The Injective Sum of Two Elementary Universes

To define an injective sum of two universes we must first define a 'universe map'. This is a map between universes which preserves the structure of the universe. Once we have defined this an injective sum, $\mathcal{A}$, of elementary universes $\mathcal{A}_1, \mathcal{A}_2$, can be taken to be the universe which contains copies of $\mathcal{A}_1, \mathcal{A}_2$ and for which, given any other universe, $\mathcal{B}$, containing copies of $\mathcal{A}_1, \mathcal{A}_2$, there is a unique universe map from $\mathcal{A}$ to $\mathcal{B}$. The following definition of compatible is required in the definition of universe map to formalize the notion of preserving replacement. Let $\mathcal{A}_0 = (A_0, C_0, \cdot_0)$, $\mathcal{A} = (A, C, \cdot)$ be elementary universes and $\pi : A' \to A$ for some transitive subclass A' of A (where $X \subseteq A_0$ is *transitive* in $\mathcal{A}_0$ if X is closed under components, i.e., for every $a \in X$, $C_0 a \subseteq X$). If $a \in A'$ and $\sigma : Ca \to A'$ then we will say that σ is *compatible* with π if $\pi a_1 = \pi a_2 \Rightarrow \pi(\sigma a_1) = \pi(\sigma a_2)$ for $a \in A_0$, $a_1, a_2 \in Ca$. In which case we will write σ^π for the map with $\sigma^\pi(\pi a') = \pi(\sigma a')$. So if π preserves components we get that $\sigma^\pi : C(\pi a) \to A$ and so we get $\sigma^\pi \cdot (\pi a) \in A$. Notice that if π is injective then we get any $\sigma : Ca \to A'$ is compatible with π.

Definition 20 A *universe map* $\pi : \mathcal{A}_0 \to \mathcal{A}$ from an elementary universe $\mathcal{A}_0 = (A_0, C_0, \cdot_0)$ to an elementary universe $\mathcal{A} = (A, C, \cdot)$ is a function $\pi : A_0 \to A$ which preserves components and replacement, i.e.,

- $C(\pi a) = \{\pi a' \mid a' \in C_0 a\}$ for $a \in A_0$.
- If $\sigma : C_0 a \to A_0$ is compatible with π then $\pi(\sigma \cdot_0 a) = \sigma^\pi \cdot \pi a$.

Definition 21 If $\mathcal{A}_1$, $\mathcal{A}_2$ are elementary universes then $(\mathcal{A}, \pi_1, \pi_2)$ is a *cover* of $\mathcal{A}_1$ and $\mathcal{A}_2$ if $\pi_i : \mathcal{A}_i \to \mathcal{A}$ is a universe map for $i = 1, 2$. We will call $(\mathcal{A}, \pi_1, \pi_2)$ an *injective cover* if π_1, π_2 are injective.

$(\mathcal{A}, \pi_1, \pi_2)$ is an *injective sum* of elementary universes $\mathcal{A}_1, \mathcal{A}_2$ if it is a cover of $\mathcal{A}_1, \mathcal{A}_2$ and for any injective cover $(\mathcal{B}, \tau_1, \tau_2)$ of $\mathcal{A}_1, \mathcal{A}_2$ there is a unique universe map $\tau : \mathcal{A} \to \mathcal{B}$ such that for any $a \in A_i$, $(\tau \circ \pi_i) a = \tau_i a$ i.e., the following diagram commutes.

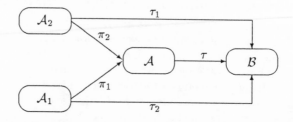

So the injective sum of two universes is the initial universe which gives an injective cover of the two universes.

Proposition 11 *Any two elementary universes have an injective sum which is unique up to isomorphism.*

Proof. Let our two elementary universes be $\mathcal{A}_1, \mathcal{A}_2$. This result is proved by taking the union ontology of the representative ontologies for $\mathcal{A}_1, \mathcal{A}_2$ and then taking 'the smallest' elementary universe for this which contains our original elementary universes, let this be $\mathcal{A}$. It is easy to show that $\mathcal{A}$ is a cover of $\mathcal{A}_1, \mathcal{A}_2$. Now given any other injective cover $(\mathcal{B}, \tau_1, \tau_2)$ we then extend the τ_1, τ_2, by recursion, to a universe map from $\mathcal{A}$ to $\mathcal{B}$.

Let $\mathcal{A}_1 = (A_1, C_1, \cdot_1)$, $\mathcal{A}_2 = (A_2, C_2, \cdot_2)$ be elementary universes. By the representation theorem there are unique, up to isomorphism, ontologies $\mathcal{U}_1, \mathcal{U}_2$ bounded by A_1 and A_2 respectively, and functions $\alpha_i : \mathcal{U}_i[A_i] \to A_i$ with $\mathcal{A}_i = \mathcal{U}_i(A_i, \alpha_i)$. Without loss of generality, we may assume that $A_1, A_2, \mathcal{U}_1[V], \mathcal{U}_2[V]$ are pairwise disjoint. We can form a union ontology $\mathcal{U} = \mathcal{U}_1 \cup \mathcal{U}_2$ in the obvious way. Let

$$\Phi Y = (\mathcal{U}[Y] - (\mathcal{U}_1[A_1] \cup \mathcal{U}_2[A_2])) \cup A_1 \cup A_2$$

Φ is set continuous and so, from proposition 3, has a least fixed point. Let A be the least fixed point of Φ, and let

$$\alpha u = \alpha_i u \text{ if } u \in \mathcal{U}_i[A_i]$$
$$\alpha u = u \text{ otherwise}$$

Then (A, α) is a full algebra for $\mathcal{U}$ and so $\mathcal{A} = \mathcal{U}(A, \alpha)$ is an elementary universe, let $\mathcal{A} = (A, C, \cdot)$. For $i = 1, 2$ let $\pi_i : A_i \to A$ be the inclusion map, we will now show that $(\mathcal{A}, \pi_1, \pi_2)$ is an injective sum of $\mathcal{A}_1$ and $\mathcal{A}_2$, i.e., $(\mathcal{A}, \pi_1, \pi_2)$ is a cover of $\mathcal{A}_1$ and $\mathcal{A}_2$ and for any other injective cover $(\mathcal{B}, \tau_1, \tau_2)$ of $\mathcal{A}_1$ and $\mathcal{A}_2$ there is a unique universe map $\tau : \mathcal{A} \to \mathcal{B}$ which extends τ_1 and τ_2. It is easy to show that we have a cover, so now suppose $(\mathcal{B}, \tau_1, \tau_2)$ is an injective cover of $\mathcal{A}_1, \mathcal{A}_2$ where $\mathcal{B} = (B, C_\mathcal{B}, \cdot_\mathcal{B})$. We will now extend the universe maps τ_1, τ_2 to a universe map $\tau : \mathcal{A} \to \mathcal{B}$. Let $\mathcal{A} = (A, C, \cdot)$, we will use the following notion of a good function to define τ:

Definition 22 Let A' be a transitive subclass of A and let $f : X \to B$. Call f *good on* X if

- f preserves components,
- if $a \in A_i \cap X$ then $fa = \tau_i a$,
- if $a \in (\mathcal{U}_i[A] - \mathcal{U}_i[A_i]) \cap X$ then for any $\sigma : Ca \to A_i$ which is injective

$$fa = (\sigma^{-1})^f \cdot_{\mathcal{B}} \tau_i(\sigma \cdot a)$$

Notice that in the above formula, since f is an extension of τ_i and τ_i is injective then σ^{-1} is compatible with f and so $(\sigma^{-1})^f$ is defined.

Lemma 12 *If $A' \subseteq A$ is transitive and there is a unique good function f on A' then there is a unique extension of f to $\Phi A'$ which is the unique good function on A'*

Proof. We define the extension of f, f^+, to be

$$f^+ a = \begin{cases} \tau_i a & a \in A_i \\ ((\sigma^{-1})^f \cdot_{\mathcal{B}} (\tau_i(\sigma \cdot a))) & a \in \mathcal{U}_i[A'] - \mathcal{U}_i[A_i] \end{cases}$$

where $\sigma : Ca \to A_i$ is injective. For any $a \in \mathcal{U}_i[A] - \mathcal{U}_i[A_i]$ there is some injective $\sigma : Ca \to A_i$ since $\mathcal{U}_i$ is bounded by A_i, use the axiom of choice to get an injective $\sigma_a : Ca \to A_i$ for each $a \in \mathcal{U}_i([A'] - \mathcal{U}_i[A_i])$. In fact the definition of f^+ is independent of the choice of σ. To see this suppose $a \in \mathcal{U}_i([A] - \mathcal{U}_i[A_i]) \cap A'$ and let $\sigma_1, \sigma_2 : Ca \to A_i$ be injective and write $\rho = \sigma_1 \circ \sigma_2^{-1}$, so $\rho : ran\,\sigma_2 \to A_i$ is compatible with τ_i since τ_i is injective.

$$((\sigma_1^{-1})^f \cdot_{\mathcal{B}} (\tau_i(\sigma_1 \cdot a))) = ((\sigma_2^{-1})^f \cdot_{\mathcal{B}} (\rho^{-1})^{\tau_i} \cdot_{\mathcal{B}} (\tau_i(\rho \circ \sigma_2 \cdot a)))$$

and since τ_i preserves replacement

$$((\sigma_2^{-1})^f \cdot_{\mathcal{B}} (\rho^{-1})^{\tau_i} \cdot_{\mathcal{B}} (\tau_i(\rho \circ \sigma_2 \cdot a))) = ((\sigma_2^{-1})^f \cdot_{\mathcal{B}} (\tau_i(\sigma_2 \cdot a)))$$

as required. f^+ is obviously an extension of f since f is good. To show that f^+ is a good function it remains to show that f^+ preserves components but this follows since for $a \in \mathcal{U}_i[A] - \mathcal{U}_i[A_i]$, $C_{\mathcal{B}}(f^+ a) = ran(\sigma^{-1})^f$ for some injective $\sigma : Ca \to A_i$. So $C_{\mathcal{B}}(f^+ a) = \{fa \mid a \in Ca\} = \{f^+ a \mid a \in Ca\}$. It follows that f^+ is the unique good extension of f to $\Phi A'$. That f^+ is the unique good function on $\Phi A'$ follows from the fact that f is the unique good function on f. $\qquad\square$

We can, by proposition 3, take

$$A \quad = \quad \bigcup_{\beta \in On} A^\beta$$

$$\text{where} \quad A^{\beta+1} \quad = \quad \Phi A^\beta \qquad \beta \in On$$
$$A^\lambda \quad = \quad \bigcup_{\beta' < \lambda} A^{\beta'} \qquad \lambda \text{ a limit}$$

By transfinite recursion, using the previous lemma, we can define $\tau : A \to B$ to be $\tau = \bigcup_{\beta \in On} \tau^\beta$ where $\tau^\beta : A^\beta \to B$ is the unique good function on A^β given by

$$\tau^{\beta+1} \quad = \quad (\tau^\beta)^+ \qquad \beta \in On$$
$$\tau^\lambda \quad = \quad \bigcup_{\beta < \lambda} \tau^\beta \qquad \lambda \text{ a limit}$$

where $\bigcup_{\beta < \lambda} \tau^\beta$ is a good function since each of the τ^β is a good function and if $\beta' < \beta$ then τ^β is an extension of $\tau^{\beta'}$. We want to show that τ is a universe map. It is easy to show that τ is a good map, so τ preserves components. It remains to show that τ preserves replacement.

Lemma 13 *If $\rho : Ca \to A$ is compatible with τ then*

$$(\rho^\tau) \cdot_{\mathcal{B}} \tau a = \tau(\rho \cdot a)$$

Proof. Suppose $a \in \mathcal{U}_i[A] - \mathcal{U}_i[A_i] \cup A_i$

$$(\rho^\tau) \cdot_{\mathcal{B}} \tau a = (\rho \circ \sigma^{-1})^\tau \cdot_{\mathcal{B}} \tau_i(\sigma \cdot a)$$

for some injective $\sigma : Ca \to A_i$ and

$$\tau(\rho \cdot a) = (\sigma_\rho^{-1})^\tau \cdot_{\mathcal{B}} \tau_i((\sigma_\rho \circ \rho) \cdot a)$$

for some injective $\sigma_\rho : ran\,\rho \to A_i$. Since σ is injective we can let $\rho' : ran\,\sigma \to A_i$ with $(\rho' \circ \sigma)a' = (\sigma_\rho \circ \rho)a'$ for $a' \in Ca$. It follows from the fact that τ_i is injective that ρ' is compatible with τ_i and since τ_i preserves replacement we get

$$\tau(\rho \cdot a) = (\sigma_\rho^{-1} \circ \rho')^\tau \cdot_{\mathcal{B}} \tau_i(\sigma \cdot a)$$

It is easy to show that $(\sigma_\rho^{-1} \circ \rho')^\tau = (\rho \circ \sigma^{-1})^\tau$ from which the required result follows. □

It remains to show that τ is the unique universe map extending τ_1, τ_2. Any universe map extending τ_1 and τ_2 must be a good function on A but we have already shown that τ is the unique good function on A. This completes the proof of the existence of an injective sum of two universes. We have in this proof used transfinite recursion on classes. To do this proof in ZFC^- it can be shown that any transitive set has a unique good function on it. τ can then be taken to be the union of these good functions, and from this the τ_α can be defined for $\alpha \in On$. We have shown that $\mathcal{A}$ is an injective sum of $\mathcal{A}_1, \mathcal{A}_2$.

Notice that any injective sum $\mathcal{B}$ of $\mathcal{A}_1, \mathcal{A}_2$ must be an injective cover of $\mathcal{A}_1, \mathcal{A}_2$, since otherwise there wouldn't be a universe map from $\mathcal{B}$ to $\mathcal{A}$ satisfying the conditions in the definition of universe map. It then follows from the definition of injective sum that an injective sum is unique up to isomorphism. □

For those familiar with a little category theory, a word or two could be said about the connection between the injective sum of two universes and their categorical sum, in the category where objects are universes and arrows are universe maps. First notice that if there is a categorical sum of universes $\mathcal{A}_1, \mathcal{A}_2$ then it must be the injective sum since a categorical sum would be an injective cover of $\mathcal{A}_1$ and $\mathcal{A}_2$. If the need for the maps τ_1, τ_2 to be injective in the above proposition was removed then we would get that the injective sum is indeed the categorical sum (that τ_1, τ_2 are injective is used in the definition of a good function, in the proof of lemma

12 to show that f^+ is independent of σ, and in the proof of 13 to show that τ preserves replacement. In each case injectivity is used to get the compatibility of other functions). Alternatively if it could be shown that for some cover $(\mathcal{B}, \tau_1, \tau_2)$ of $\mathcal{A}_1, \mathcal{A}_2$ with τ_1, τ_2 not injective there is no universe map from $\mathcal{A}$ to $\mathcal{B}$ which extends τ_1 and τ_2 then the categorical sum does not exist in general.

The generalization of the definition of an injective sum to the injective sum of two sorted universes and the existence and uniqueness of such a sum should be straightforward. There should also be a straightforward generalization of the notion injective sum to the notion of an injective sum of any family of universes.

An Example of an Injective Sum

Let us consider the injective sum of a well-founded set universe with a well-founded term-universe. Let $\mathcal{A}_1 = (A_1, C_1, \cdot_1)$ where A_1 is the class of pure well-founded sets (the least fixed point of the power set operator). Given a set a the components of a, $C_1 a$ is given by the set a itself. If $\sigma : a \to V$ then $\sigma \cdot_1 a = \{\sigma a' \mid a' \in a\}$. Let $\mathcal{A}_2 = (A_2, C_2 \cdot_2)$ where A_2 is a term algebra for a signature with two function symbols, f with arity two and c with arity zero. The components of a term are its subterms, so $C_2 c = \emptyset$ and $C_2 f(t_1, t_2) = \{t_1, t_2\}$ and if $\sigma : C_2 f(t_1, t_2) \to A_2$ then $\sigma \cdot f(t_1, t_2) = f(\sigma t_1, \sigma t_2)$. Assume that A_1 and A_2 are disjoint (If we were doing this formally in ZF^- then we could build the term algebra by taking some set coding of the function symbols and taking the terms to be tuples, we would need to take a coding of the pure well-founded sets and a coding of the terms to ensure that we had disjointness). Then an injective sum of $\mathcal{A}_1$ and $\mathcal{A}_2$ is given by the least class A with

$$pow\, A \cup \{f(a_1, a_2) \mid a_1, a_2 \in A\} \cup \{c\} \subseteq A$$

where the component and replacement operations are the obvious things. So A contains the pure well-founded sets, the term algebra and hybrid terms and sets which may have either terms or sets as their components such as $f(\{\{c\}\}, f(\emptyset, c))$ which has components $\{\ \{\{c\}\}\ ,\ f(\emptyset, c)\ \}$.

If $\mathcal{A}_1$ and $\mathcal{A}_2$ are well-founded elementary universes then the injective sum of $\mathcal{A}_1$ and $\mathcal{A}_2$ is well-founded. If $\mathcal{A}_1$ and $\mathcal{A}_2$ are anti-founded elementary universes then the injective sum of $\mathcal{A}_1$ and $\mathcal{A}_2$ is not anti-founded. For an example of this consider the injective sum of the anti-founded elementary universe of pure sets, where the objects are sets and their components are the elements of the set and the tree algebra for a signature with two functions, f and c as above, so the objects are the (possibly infinite) terms and the components of a term are it's direct subterms. The injective sum of these two elementary universes will contain objects like $f(\{c\}, \{\emptyset, \{f(c, c)\}\})$ and also things like $f(\Omega, c)$ where $\Omega = \{\Omega\}$ but it will not contain objects like Ω' where $\Omega' = \{f(\Omega', \emptyset)\}$.

5.2 From Injective Sum to Parameterization

In Aczel and Lunnon 1991 an elementary universe $\mathcal{A} = (A, C, \cdot)$ is, by definition, an X_0 *generated parametric extension* of an elementary universe $\mathcal{A}_0$ if $(\mathcal{A}, X)$ is generated, $X \cong X_0$ and $\mathcal{A}_0$ is isomorphic to the non-parametric core of $\mathcal{A}$. Where $(\mathcal{A}, X)$ is *generated* if A is the smallest class B which contains the non parametric core of $\mathcal{A}$, which is closed under components and with $\{\sigma \cdot a \mid a \in B \ \& \ \sigma : Ca \rightarrow B\} \subseteq B$.

Let $[X]$ be the trivial elementary universe with objects elements of X where every object has no components, then $\mathcal{A}$ is an X generated parametric extension of $\mathcal{A}_0$ if and only if there are universe maps $\pi_0 : \mathcal{A}_0 \rightarrow \mathcal{A}$ and $\pi_X : [X] \rightarrow \mathcal{A}$ such that $(\mathcal{A}, \pi_0, \pi_X)$ is an injective sum of $\mathcal{A}_0$ and $[X]$. Therefore for each elementary universe $\mathcal{A}_0$ and class of parameters X there is an X generated parametric extension of $\mathcal{A}_0$ which is unique up to isomorphism. Substitution can be defined on such a generated parametric extension by transfinite recursion.

Westerståhl (1989) has given an alternative construction of an X-parametric extension of an elementary universe. His construction is similar to the construction of a representative ontology for a form system given in Aczel 1990.

References

Aczel, P. 1988. *Non-Well-Founded Sets*. CSLI Lecture Notes Number 14. Stanford: CSLI Publications.

Aczel, P. 1990. Replacement Systems and the Axiomatization of Situation Theory. In Cooper et al. 1990.

Aczel, P., and R. Lunnon. 1991. Universes and Parameters. This volume.

Aczel, P., and N. Mendler. 1990. A Final Coalgebra Theorem. In *Proceedings of LNCS 384: Category Theory in Computer Science*.

Barwise, J. 1989a. Mixed Fixed Points. In *The Situation in Logic*, 285–287. CSLI Lecture Notes Number 17. Stanford: CSLI Publications.

Barwise, J. 1989b. On the Model Theory of Common Knowledge. In *The Situation in Logic*. CSLI Lecture Notes Number 17. Stanford: CSLI Publications.

Barwise, J., and J. Etchemendy. 1987. *The Liar: An Essay on Truth and Circularity*. New York: Oxford University Press.

Cooper, R., K. Mukai, and J. Perry (ed.). 1990. *Situation Theory and Its Applications*, vol. 1. CSLI Lecture Notes Number 22. Stanford: CSLI Publications.

Fernando, T. 1989. On Substitutional Recursion Over Non-Well-Founded Sets. In *Proceedings of the Fourth IEEE Symposium on Logic in Computer Science*. Washington. IEEE Computer Society Press.

Fernando, T. 1990. On the Logic of Situation Theory. In Cooper et al. 1990.

Lunnon, R. 1991. *Generalised Universes*. PhD thesis, Manchester University, Manchester, UK.

Westerståhl, D. 1989. A Note on Parameterization. In *Cum Grano Salis: Essays Dedicated to Dick A. R. Haglund*, ed. C. Adberg, 221–233. Acta Philosophica Gothoburgiensia no. 3. Goteborg.

Westerståhl, D. 1990. Parametric Types and Propositions in First-Order Situation Theory. In Cooper et al. 1990.

5

A Theory of Situations

EDWARD N. ZALTA

In this paper, I produce a *theory* (as opposed to a model) of situations. The theory is embodied in some definitions and theorems, all of which are cast in a precise logical framework. However, none of the theorems are *stipulated* to be true; rather they fall out as consequences of a formal, axiomatic theory of objects and relations for which the logical framework was originally developed. Thus, the theory of situations described in what follows is a derived one.

The plan for the paper is as follows. In Section 1, I make some observations on the present state of situation theory and isolate a fundamental, but undeveloped, intuition that underlies the conception of a situation. I then show how distinctions developed in my axiomatic theory of objects and relations (Zalta 1983, 1988) explicitly represent this intuition. In Section 2, I sketch the basic logical and non-logical features of the system in which the results will be cast. In Section 3, I articulate twenty-five basic theorems, thereby forging the theory of situations. Finally, in Section 4, I demonstrate that the results do indeed constitute a theory of *situations* by showing not only that it defines a path through the branch points described in Barwise 1989, but also that it realizes other important pretheoretic ideas of situation theory. Thus, I hope to show that the theory constitutes a kind of *model* of those ideas.

1   Ideas Underlying the Theory

Though there is a consensus regarding the basic outline of situation theory, there is disagreement about the details. In particular, there are conflicting intuitions about some of the fundamental properties of situations. This conflict of intuitions is the subject of Barwise 1989. After positing a partial

This research was conducted at the Center for the Study of Language and Information (CSLI). I would like to thank John Perry for generously supporting my research both at CSLI and in the Philosophy Department at Stanford.

Situation Theory and Its Applications, vol. 2.
Jon Barwise, Jean Mark Gawron, Gordon Plotkin, and Syun Tutiya, eds.

ordering of situations under the *part-of* relation, and assuming that there is at least one maximal element (i.e., world), Barwise presents a list of 19 questions, each of which constitutes a "branch point" in situation theory. The various answers to these questions lead to different sets of first principles for situation theory. Though I shall presuppose some familiarity with Barwise's paper, here are some of the more important questions that he raises: whether there is more than one world, whether every part of a situation is a situation, whether every world is a situation, whether there are nonactual situations, whether situations are well-founded, whether every state of affairs has a dual, and whether a rich algebra should be imposed on the domain states of affairs. These are obviously fundamental questions, and different answers to these questions lead to rather different theories of situations.

The theory presented in this paper makes a decision at almost all of the branch points that Barwise identifies. These decisions are derived from a more general background theory of objects and relations. It turns out that this background theory axiomatizes a distinction which is implicit in the very conception of a situation. This distinction has directed the development of situation theory from its inception, but has never been made explicit at the level of theory. From the beginning, situation theorists have appealed to a distinction between the internal properties of a situation and its external properties. Barwise and Perry (1981) assert:

> Situations have properties of two sorts, internal and external. The cat's walking on the piano distressed Henry. Its doing so is what we call an external property of the event. The event consists of a certain cat performing a certain activity on a certain piano; these are its internal properties.

This distinction between internal and external properties appears throughout the course of publications on situation theory. Barwise (1986) writes:

> If $s \models \sigma$, then the fact σ is called a fact of s, or more explicitly, a fact about the internal structure of s. There are also other kinds of facts about s, facts external to s, so the difference between being a fact that holds in s and a fact about s more generally must be borne in mind. (p. 185)

And Barwise (1989) writes:

> The facts determined by a particular situation are, at least intuitively, intrinsic to that situation. By contrast, the information a situation carries depends not just on the facts determined by that situation but is relative to constraints linking those facts to other facts, facts that obtain in virtue of other situations. Thus, information carried is not usually (if ever) intrinsic to the situation.
>
> The objects which actual situations make factual thus play a key role in the theory. They serve to characterize the intrinsic nature of a situation. (pp. 263–4)

The main point here is that the conception of an object having intrinsic, internal properties as well as extrinsic, external properties is crucial to the very idea of situations. But, oddly enough, situation theory has not developed *per se* the conception of an object that can have internal as well as external properties.

However, this is just the conception underlying the theory of objects developed in Zalta 1983 and Zalta 1988. The theory begins with two primitive domains: objects $(x, y, \ldots)$ and relations $(F^n, G^n, \ldots)$. The domain of objects is partitioned into two mutually exclusive subdomains. One consists of the ordinary, real objects such as electrons, tables, planets, people, etc. These objects have all of their properties *externally*. The other subdomain consists of objects having a special nature—they have both internal and external properties. The distinction between the internal and external properties of such objects is represented in terms of the distinction between two ways (modes) of predicating properties. To indicate that a special object x has property F internally, we say that x *encodes* F. To indicate that object x (special or ordinary) has F externally, we say that x *exemplifies* F. Formally, the distinction between encoding and exemplifying a property is captured by having two kinds of atomic sentences: 'xF' ('x encodes F') and 'Fx' ('x exemplifies F'). Our special objects may both exemplify and encode the very same properties, or may encode properties that are distinct from the ones they exemplify. Though encoding is restricted to 1-place properties, exemplification can be generalized to n-place relations in the usual way. Thus the theory allows us to (externally) predicate relations among objects (of any kind) in the usual way, using sentences of the form '$F^n x_1 \ldots x_n$'.[1]

Before we discuss our special objects further, let us return briefly to the discussion of ordinary objects. It is an axiom of the theory that ordinary objects fail to encode properties. Where '$O!$' denotes a property exemplified by all and only the ordinary objects, this axiom can be stated as follows: $\forall x(O!x \rightarrow \neg \exists F \, xF)$. The theory doesn't say much more about these ordinary objects (an *a priori* metaphysical theory shouldn't say much about contingent objects). But it can be applied in the usual way to analyze typical statements about such objects. Thus, one may represent 'George is happy' and 'George loves Barbara' in the standard way, as 'Hg' and 'Lgb'. So the usual sorts of intuitions we have regarding the use of predicate logic are preserved, though we have to understand standard predicate logic as the logic of exemplification, or as the logic of external predication. Modal intuitions are also preserved. An ordinary object x may exemplify (exter-

---

[1] The distinction between exemplifying and encoding a property can be traced to the work of Ernst Mally (1912), who distinguished a class of objects that were 'determined' by properties without necessarily 'satisfying' the properties that determined them. Recently, this distinction has resurfaced in the work of Castañeda (1974) and Rapaport (1978).

nally) a property F *necessarily* ($\Box Fx$), but this is not to say that x encodes F. The theory does tell us one other fact about ordinary objects, namely, that two ordinary objects are identical iff necessarily, they exemplify the same properties.

The special objects in the other subdomain have a fundamentally different nature. Their individuality resides in having a fixed, internal group of properties that are even more crucial to their identity than properties they may exemplify either contingently or necessarily. These are the properties they encode. Consider, for example, mathematical objects such as the numbers of Peano number theory. The number 1, if treated as an object, contingently exemplifies having been thought about by Peano and being denoted by the numeral '1', whereas it necessarily exemplifies such properties as having no location, having no shape, having no texture, etc. On the other hand, the theoretical properties of the number 1, such as being greater than 0, being odd, being prime, etc., are even more crucial to its identity than any of the properties previously mentioned. The present theory treats these theoretical properties of the number 1 as the properties it encodes. These are the properties internal to its nature.

Consider next an object of fiction, such as Sherlock Holmes. The present theory treats the properties attributed to Holmes in the Conan Doyle novels as the properties he encodes. These include: being a person, being a detective, living at 221B Baker Street in London, having a prodigious talent for solving crimes, etc.[2] These are regarded as more crucial to the identity of Holmes than such properties as being fictional, being the main character of the Conan Doyle novels, being an inspiration to modern criminologists, etc., which are properties that are externally exemplified by Holmes (note that many of these properties are relational, based on the external relations Holmes bears to ordinary objects). These exemplified properties are contingent ones; had circumstances been different, the internally constituted object we have identified as Holmes might not have had these properties. On the other hand, given that we have identified him as a certain theoretical object, we could say that Holmes necessarily exemplifies such properties as not being a person, not being a detective, not living in London, not being a spoon, etc.[3]

Let us assume, as an intuitive comprehension principle, that for every group of properties, there is a special object that encodes just the properties in the group and no others. As an identity principle, let us assume that two such objects are identical iff necessarily, they encode the same properties. So this populates the subdomain of special objects with a wide variety of objects. Many of these objects will be partial in the sense that for any

---

[2] Many of these properties are not explicitly attributed to Holmes in the novels, but are reasonably inferred from a common sense based understanding of the novels.

[3] The reader may consult Zalta 1983 and 1988 for further details on the treatment of mathematical and fictional objects.

given property F, they encode neither F nor the negation of F ('$\bar{F}$'). But each special object is complete with respect to the properties it exemplifies. Indeed, for any object x whatsoever, ordinary or special, either Fx or $\bar{F}x$.

We can now begin to see how this conception of an object having internal and external properties can be applied to our intuitive understanding of situations. Situations are supposed to be internally characterized by states of affairs. Note that a state of affairs is not a property, and so, strictly speaking, doesn't characterize anything. States of affairs either obtain or they don't. However, there are properties that are intimately linked to states of affairs. These are properties that objects exemplify in virtue of a state of affairs obtaining. Consider, for example, the following two properties: being such that George loves Barbara, and being such that Barbara doesn't love George. These are properties that are constructed out of states of affairs—the former is constructed out of the state *George's loving Barbara*, whereas the latter is constructed out of the state *Barbara's not loving George*. If we let the formula 'Lgb' denote the first state of affairs and '$\neg Lgb$' the second, then we could use the λ-predicates '$[\lambda y\, Lgb]$' and '$[\lambda y\, \neg Lgb]$' to denote, respectively, the properties being such that George loves Barbara and being such that Barbara doesn't love George. In the complex λ-predicates, the variable 'y' is vacuously bound by the λ. Nevertheless, these are perfectly good predicates, and the properties they denote are perfectly well-behaved. An object x *exemplifies* being such that George loves Barbara iff George loves Barbara ($[\lambda y\, Lgb]x \leftrightarrow Lgb$), and x exemplifies being such that Barbara doesn't love George iff Barbara doesn't love George ($[\lambda y\, \neg Lgb]x \leftrightarrow \neg Lgb$). If we follow recent practice and call states of affairs 'SOAs' for short, then we may call the properties constructed out of states of affairs 'SOA-properties'.

Now suppose that every state of affairs p has a corresponding SOA-property $[\lambda y\, p]$. Note that the corresponding SOA-property provides a means by which a state of affairs can characterize an object. A situation can be characterized by a SOA-property, for example, when we say that the situation *is such that p*. We might have said: the situation of unrequited love between George and Barbara is such that George loves Barbara, but such that Barbara doesn't love George. Unfortunately, as far as the logic of external predication goes, no object is distinguished by the SOA-properties that it exemplifies. If a state of affairs p obtains, then everything whatsoever exemplifies $[\lambda y\, p]$. If p fails to obtain, then nothing whatsoever exemplifies $[\lambda y\, p]$. But this standard feature of the logic of exemplification does not hold for the logic of encoding. Whether or not an object encodes $[\lambda y\, p]$ is independent of whether or not p obtains. In particular, if p obtains, it does not follow from the fact that every object exemplifies $[\lambda y\, p]$ that every special object encodes $[\lambda y\, p]$. Formally, whether or not a special object x encodes $[\lambda y\, p]$ depends on the whether this property satisfies the defining condition of the relevant instance of abstraction. Metaphysically, though, these are just the brute facts. Thus, as internally encoded properties, soa-properties may serve to distinguish all sorts of special objects.

We now have a way to capture the intuition that situations are "intrinsically characterized by states of affairs." We just think of a situation as a special object that encodes (only) soa-properties. This gives us a clear sense in which a state of affairs can be an internal property of a situation—the property that corresponds to the state of affairs is encoded by the situation. Given the intuitive comprehension principle for special objects described above, it follows that for every group of soa-properties, there is a situation that encodes just the soa-properties in the group. This guarantees, for example, that there is an object that 'is' such that George loves Barbara and 'is' such that Barbara doesn't love George.[4] This is the object that encodes $[\lambda y\, Lgb]$, $[\lambda y\, \neg Lbg]$, and no other properties. This constitutes a situation of unrequited love between George and Barbara. It will be a 'part' of any situation that encodes these properties and others as well. The principle of identity for special objects ensures that the identity of this situation is completely determined by its internal properties. Thus, the situation just described is 'partial' in nature, for its identity is linked just to the two states of affairs Lgb and $\neg Lbg$. Note that this conception of situations leaves us free to treat the external properties of a situation as ones that it exemplifies. Properties such as being distressing to Henry, being seen by Mary, carrying information (of a certain kind), etc., are all properties that situations exemplify. These happen to be examples of contingent properties that situations may exemplify, though some properties that situations exemplify will be necessary. Properties such as not being a number, not being a person, not being a building, being such that p-or-not-p, etc., are all properties that situations exemplify necessarily.

2   The Background Theory

These ideas may be formalized as follows.[5] Recall that we have variables $x, y, \ldots$ ranging over a domain of objects, and variables $F^n, G^n, \ldots$ ranging over a domain of n-place relations. And we have atomic statements of the form $F_1^x \ldots x_n$ to express external, exemplification predications and statements of the form xF^1 to express internal, encoding predications. Now build up a (syntactically) second order modal predicate calculus (without identity) based on these atomic formulas. Associate with this language your favorite *classical* axioms of propositional, predicate, and *S5* modal logic. Don't worry about the interaction between the quantifiers and the modal operators, because the Barcan formulas are included as logical axioms.

---

[4] In my previously cited work, I have gathered evidence for thinking that there is a lexical and structural ambiguity underlying the the copula 'is', namely, the ambiguity between exemplifying and encoding a property.

[5] Readers who are familiar with Zalta 1983 or 1988 may skip most of this section.

Here is an informal semantic picture for this language.[6] The quantifier $\forall x$ ranges over a fixed domain of objects, the quantifier $\forall F^n$ ranges over a fixed domain of primitive n-place relations, and $\Box$ is a universal quantifier ranging over a fixed domain of worlds. Intuitively, each relation receives an exemplification extension at each world, and moreover, each property (i.e., one-place relation) receives, in addition, an encoding extension (which is independent of the worlds). In terms of this picture, we can sketch the truth conditions of our atomic formulas. '$F^n x_1 \ldots x_n$' is true at a world $\mathbf{w}$ (relative to a model $\mathbf{M}$ and assignment $\mathbf{f}$ to the variables) just in case the n-tuple consisting of the objects denoted by the variables $x_1, \ldots, x_n$ (relative to $\mathbf{M}$ and $\mathbf{f}$) is a member of the exemplification extension at $\mathbf{w}$ of the relation denoted by F^n (relative to $\mathbf{M}$ and $\mathbf{f}$). The formula 'xF' is true at $\mathbf{w}$ (relative to $\mathbf{M}$ and $\mathbf{f}$) just in case the object denoted by x (relative to $\mathbf{M}$ and $\mathbf{f}$) is an element of the encoding extension of the property denoted by F (relative to $\mathbf{M}$ and $\mathbf{f}$).

Notice that the encoding extension of a property does not vary with the worlds. Consequently, if an encoding formula is true at some world, it is true at all worlds. So the modal logic of encoding is captured by the following principle:

Logical Axiom: $\Diamond xF \rightarrow \Box xF$

This captures the intuition that the properties encoded by a special object are internal to its nature, and so do not change with the changing circumstances from world to world. From the usual rules and axioms of $S5$, it follows that:

Lemma: $xF \leftrightarrow \Diamond xF \leftrightarrow \Box xF$

This *Lemma* plays a very important role in what follows.

The rest of the theory is outline in the following two subsections, one describing the logical axioms (and definitions) governing relations, and one describing the proper axioms (and definitions) governing objects.

The Logic of Relations and States of Affairs

The most important features of our logic are the comprehension and identity principles governing n-place relations. The following comprehension schema, which forces the domain of relations to contain a wide variety of complex relations, asserts that for any (complex) *exemplification* condition

---

[6]The reader is cautioned not to take this picture too seriously. In particular, the fact that possible worlds appear as primitive entities in the semantics does not imply that the metaphysical theory expressed in the object language is committed to primitive possible worlds. It is not. It is committed only to two domains, objects and relations, and takes the modal operator as primitive. Worlds will be defined within the theory, and it is this definition, coupled with the object-theoretic theorems about worlds, that grounds and justifies our use of worlds as primitive in the semantics.

ϕ having no quantifiers binding relation variables, there is a relation F^n which is such that necessarily, objects $x_1, \ldots, x_n$ exemplify F^n iff ϕ:

> *Relations*: $\exists F^n \Box \forall x_1 \ldots \forall x_n (F^n x_1 \ldots x_n \leftrightarrow \phi)$, where ϕ has no free Fs, no encoding subformulas, and no quantifiers binding relation variables.

Note that the theory doesn't guarantee that there are any new relations definable in terms of encoding formulas. In other words, the theory sanctions only *familiar*, first-order definable, complex relations. For example, the following formulas all constitute acceptable ϕs: $\neg Gx$, $Gx \,\&\, Hx$, $\Box(Gx \rightarrow Hx)$, $\exists y Gyx$, $\exists y Gxy$.[7] Each of these can be used to form an instance of the schema, and each resulting instance asserts that there is a 1-place property of a certain kind. Thus every property G will have a negation, every two properties G and H will have a conjunction, etc. Of course, complex n-place relations for $n > 1$ are formulable as well. I shall assume some familiarity with this kind of comprehension schema.

Let us define a 'state of affairs' or 'SOA' to be a 0-place relation.[8] Let the variables p, q, and r range over states of affairs. In the present theory, the notion of a state of affairs *being factual* or *obtaining* is a basic notion (i.e., not defined). To assert that a state of affairs p is factual (or obtains), one just *uses* the expression 'p'. To assert that p isn't factual, or that both p and q obtain, or that p's factuality is necessary, one uses the expressions '$\neg p$', '$p \,\&\, q$', or '$\Box p$', respectively.

Now if we let $n = 0$, the following 'degenerate' case of the *Relations* principle asserts that for any complex exemplification statement ϕ, there is a state of affairs p such that, necessarily, p is factual (obtains) iff ϕ:

> *States of Affairs*: $\exists p \Box (p \leftrightarrow \phi)$, where ϕ has no free ps, no encoding subformulas, and no quantifiers binding relation variables.

This requires that the domain of states of affairs be a rich algebra. There are basic exemplification SOAs for any $R, a_1, \ldots, a_n$; in addition, every SOA has a negation and a necessitation, every two SOAs has a conjunction, there

---

[7] We include the restriction that there be no conditions ϕ in which there appear quantifiers binding relation variables (such as $\exists G\, Gx$) only because there is no simple way to extend the semantic picture to account for them. As it stands, the semantics includes a set of logical functions derived from Quine's predicate functors (1960), which harness the simple relations into complex ones. The exemplification extensions of any complex relation that results must mesh in the natural way with the exemplification extensions of the relations it may have as parts. One of these logical functions can generate relations defined in terms of quantifiers binding object variables, but there is no natural way to develop a logical function that can generate relations defined by quantifiers binding relation variables. See Zalta 1983 (pp. 20–27) and 1988 (pp. 46–51).

[8] In earlier work, I called these entities 'propositions', but in the context of situation theory, it is best to identify them as states of affairs.

are general SOAs such as $\forall x \forall y Rxy$, and there are complex conditional and modal SOAs.[9]

Let us now introduce λ-expressions so that we may form names of the n-place relations posited by *Relations* and *States of Affairs*. Where ϕ is any (complex) exemplification formula (with no quantifiers binding relation variables), and $y_1, \ldots y_n$ $(n \geq 0)$ are variables that may or may not be free in ϕ, $[\lambda y_1 \ldots y_n \, \phi]$ shall be an n-place relation term subject to the following principle:

λ-*Equivalence*: $\forall x_1 \ldots \forall x_n ([\lambda y_1 \ldots y_n \, \phi] x_1 \ldots x_n \leftrightarrow \phi^{x_1, \ldots, x_n}_{y_1, \ldots, y_n})$, where x_i is substitutable for y_i in ϕ $(1 \leq i \leq n)$.[10]

Note that λ-expression may have 0 variables bound by the λ; such expressions denote states of affairs. Here are some examples of λ-expressions, the first four of which denote properties, the last four of which denote SOAs: $[\lambda y \, \neg Gy]$, $[\lambda y \, Gy \, \& \, Hy]$, $[\lambda y \, \Box(E!y \rightarrow Py)]$, $[\lambda y \, \exists z Rzy]$, $[\lambda \, Ra_1 \ldots a_n]$, $[\lambda \, \neg Ra_1 \ldots a_n]$, $[\lambda \, Pa \, \& \, Qb]$, $[\lambda \, \Box(Pa \rightarrow Qb)]$. In what follows, we shall abbreviate the 0-place λ-expressions $[\lambda \, \phi]$ simply as 'ϕ'.[11]

Note that both *Relations* and *States of Affairs* are derivable from λ-*Equivalence* (apply necessitation and existential generalization). So we shall officially designate λ-*Equivalence* to be a logical axiom of the system. This axiom is complemented by a definition of identity for relations. Identity for relations is defined in terms of identity for properties, which in turn is defined in terms of the notion of encoding. We stipulate that two properties are identical just in case, necessarily, they are encoded by the same objects:

$$F = G =_{df} \Box \forall x (xF \leftrightarrow xG)$$

In terms of this definition, we may say that two relations F^n and G^n are identical just in case no matter which order you plug $n - 1$ objects into both F^n and G^n (plugging F^n and G^n up in the same order), the resulting properties are identical.[12] Note that our definition of property

---

[9] These results already resolve Choices 14–17 in Barwise 1989. We can freely form states of affairs out of any objects and relations (Choice 14); not every SOA is basic (Alternative 15.2, Choice 15); there is a rich algebraic structure on the space of SOAS (Choice 16); and every SOA has a dual (Choice 17).

[10] The notation $\phi^{x_1, \ldots, x_n}_{y_1, \ldots, y_n}$ stands for the result of replacing, respectively, each x_i for y_i in ϕ, and the requirement that x_i be substitutable for y_i guarantees that x_i will not be 'captured' by a quantifier when the substitution is carried out.

[11] Thus, instead of designating the *basic* state of affairs in which $a_1, \ldots, a_n$ stand in the relation R as '$\langle\langle R, a_1, \ldots a_n; 1\rangle\rangle$', as in many works in situation theory, we shall designate it as '$Ra_1 \ldots a_n$'. By abbreviating $[\lambda y \, \phi]$ as ϕ, (complex) exemplification *formulas* (without relation variables) serve also as *terms* denoting SOAs.

[12] Formally, this can be stated as follows: For $n > 1$,
$$F^n = G^n \equiv_{df} (\forall x_1) \ldots (\forall x_{n-1})([\lambda y \, F^n y x_1 \ldots x_{n-1}] = [\lambda y \, G^n y x_1 \ldots x_{n-1}] \, \&$$
$$[\lambda y \, F^n x_1 y x_2 \ldots x_{n-1}] = [\lambda y \, G^n x_1 y x_2 \ldots x_{n-1}] \, \& \ldots \&$$
$$[\lambda y \, F^n x_1 \ldots x_{n-1} y] = [\lambda y \, G^n x_1 \ldots x_{n-1} y])$$

and relation identity is compatible with the idea that necessarily equivalent relations may be distinct. From the fact that two properties (relations) are necessarily exemplified by the same objects, it does not follow that they are necessarily encoded by the same objects. One may consistently assert that $F \neq G$ even though $\Box \forall x(Fx \leftrightarrow Gx)$.

To complete the theory of relations, we offer a definition of identity for states of affairs. To state this definition, however, we shall have to make use of some of the machinery we have developed so far. Notice that the instances of *Relations* can be constructed which assert that there are 1-place properties definable in terms of conditions containing no free xs. E.g.,

$$\exists F \Box(Fx \leftrightarrow Ra_1 \dots a_n)$$
$$\exists F \Box(Fx \leftrightarrow \neg Ra_1 \dots a_n)$$

The first of these asserts that there is a property which is necessarily such that an object x exemplifies it iff the objects $a_1, \dots, a_n$ stand in the relation R. The second asserts that there is a property objects exemplify iff $a_1, \dots, a_n$ fail to stand in R. These properties should be familiar—they are the SOA-properties that we discussed in the previous section. These SOA-properties can be constructed out of states of affairs of any complexity. It is a simple consequence of *Relations* that for any state of affairs p, there is a property F which is such that, necessarily, an object x exemplifies F iff p (obtains):

$$\forall p \exists F \Box \forall x(Fx \leftrightarrow p)$$

So for every state of affairs p, there is a property of *being such that p*, i.e., $[\lambda y\, p]$, which everything either exemplifies or fails to exemplify, depending on whether or not p obtains. If $F = [\lambda y\, p]$, we say that F is *constructed out of p*.[13]

This discussion of SOA-properties serves to make the following definition of identity for states of affairs understandable: p and q are identical just in case the property of *being such that p* and the property of *being such that q* are identical.

$$p = q =_{df} [\lambda y\, p] = [\lambda y\, q]$$

This defines the identity of states of affairs in terms of the defined notion of property identity.[14] It allows necessarily equivalent states of affairs to be distinct.

---

[13] In earlier work, I have called these 'propositional properties' or 'vacuous properties'.

[14] This definition yields certain theorems that decide Choice 13 in Barwise [1989] in favor of Alternative 13.2. Our semantic picture of basic SOAS treats them as structured complexes, in which the objects are 'plugged' into places of the relation. But there are so many abstract objects generated by the abstraction schema that the theory entails, for some abstract objects a and b, that $Pa = Pb$ even though $a \neq b$. When a and b are ordinary, however, then $Pa \neq Pb$ follows from $a \neq b$. See Zalta 1983, p. 75, footnote 8, and the discussion in Zalta 1988, pp. 31-2.

Finally, since we have now defined '$F^n = G^n$' for $n \geq 0$, we may assert that identical relations are substitutable for one another. Consequently, the following axiom shall govern our defined notions of relation identity ($n \geq 0$):

Axiom: $F^n = G^n \rightarrow [\phi(F^n, F^n) \leftrightarrow \phi(F^n, G^n)]$, provided G^n is substitutable for F^n in ϕ.[15]

This principle of substitution is entirely unrestricted. It completes the presentation of the theory of relations and states of affairs.

The Theory of Objects

The proper part of the theory can be stated with just a few basic principles and definitions. In the previous section, we asserted that ordinary objects don't encode properties. In fact, let us say that ordinary objects couldn't possibly encode properties:

$$O!x \rightarrow \neg\Diamond\exists F\, xF$$

Ordinary objects are just not the kind of thing that could encode a property. Let us call our special objects 'abstract', using the predicate '$A!$' to pick them out. We define '$A!$' as the negation of '$O!$'. Thus, $A! =_{df} [\lambda y \, \neg O!y]$. This partitions the domain of objects into two subdomains. The following principle offers a general identity condition for objects:

$$x = y =_{df}$$
$$[O!x \,\&\, O!y \,\&\, \Box\forall F(Fx \leftrightarrow Fy)] \lor [A!x \,\&\, A!y \,\&\, \Box\forall F(xF \leftrightarrow yF)]$$

This simply says that two objects x and y are identical iff either x and y are both ordinary objects and necessarily exemplify the same properties or they are both abstract objects and necessarily encode the same properties. The following principle governs this defined notion of identity:

Proper Axiom: $x = y \rightarrow [\phi(x, x) \leftrightarrow \phi(x, y)]$, provided y is substitutable for x in ϕ.[16]

Now the main principle comprehending the domain of abstract objects asserts that for any expressible condition ϕ on properties F, there is an abstract object that encodes all and only the properties satisfying the condition:

A-Objects: $\exists x[A!x \,\&\, \forall F(xF \leftrightarrow \phi)]$, where ϕ has no free xs

Intuitively, this guarantees that for every set of properties expressible in the language of the theory in terms of a condition ϕ, there is an abstract object that encodes just the properties in the set. Since there

---

[15]The notation $\phi(F^n, G^n)$ stands for the result of substituting G^n for F^n at some, but not necessarily all, free occurrences of F^n in $\phi(F^n, F^n)$.

[16]The notation $\phi(x, y)$ stands for the result of substituting y for x at some, but not necessarily all, free occurrences of x in $\phi(x, x)$.

is a wide variety of conditions on properties, this axiom ensures that there is a wide variety of abstract objects. Examples of this schema may be found in Zalta 1983 and 1988. In Zalta 1983 I tried to show that various objects in the resulting subdomain are suitable for analyzing Platonic Forms, Leibnizian Monads, Possible Worlds, fictional characters, Fregean Senses, and mathematical objects. In Zalta 1988 I tried to show how they help us to analyze the problems of intensional logic. In the next section, I show how these objects provide an analysis of situations.

3 Twenty-Five Basic Theorems

Recall that in Section 1 we suggested that a situation is a special object (one that can both encode and exemplify properties) which is such that every property it encodes is a SOA-property. Formally, this suggestion can be represented in terms of the following definition:

$$Situation(x) =_{df} A!x \ \& \ \forall F(xF \rightarrow \exists p(F = [\lambda y \ p]))$$

This definition sets the stage for the following series of definitions and theorems. In what follows, we shall use the variable 's' to range over the situations. The proofs of the theorems are all presented in Appendix A.

The first and foremost theorem of situation theory is a comprehension theorem schema that falls directly out of the proper axiom schema *A-Objects*. The schema for situations asserts that for any condition on SOA-properties, there is a situation that encodes all and only the SOA-properties satisfying the condition. To represent this theorem formally, let us say that a formula $\phi(F)$ is a condition on SOA-properties iff every property F that satisfies ϕ is a SOA-property. The following is then a theorem schema that comprehends the domain of situations:

> *Theorems 1*: $\exists s \forall F(sF \leftrightarrow \phi)$, where ϕ is any condition on SOA-properties having no free ss.

Let us call this theorem scheme '*Situations*'. It forces the domain of situations to be rather rich, and evidence of this richness will be presented as we proceed through the theorems. For the present, let us look just at the instance that yields the situation discussed previously, namely, the situation which is only such that George loves Barbara and such that Barbara doesn't love George:

$$\exists s \forall F(sF \leftrightarrow F = [\lambda y \ Lgb] \ \lor \ F = [\lambda y \ \neg Lbg])$$

In this example, $\phi = \ulcorner F = [\lambda y \ Lgb] \ \lor \ F = [\lambda y \ \neg Lbg] \urcorner$. Any property F satisfying this ϕ is a SOA-property, and so the object encoding just such properties will be a situation.[17] Other instances of *Situations* will be found frequently in what follows.

Each instance of our theorem scheme asserts that there is a situation that encodes just the SOA-properties meeting a certain condition ϕ. In fact, for each instance, a unique situation encodes just the SOA-properties satisfying ϕ. Where '$\exists!x\psi$' is defined in the usual way to assert that there is a unique x such that ψ, then the following is a lemma to *Situations*, for any condition ϕ, on SOA-properties with no free ss:

   Lemma 1: $\exists!s\forall F(sF \leftrightarrow \phi)$

To see why this is true, note that for any particular instance of *Situations*, there couldn't be two distinct situations encoding all and only the SOA-properties satisfying the condition ϕ in question, for distinct situations have to differ with respect to at least one of the properties they encode.

Now one of the principal notions of situation theory is that of a state of affairs p *being factual in* a situation s (sometimes it is said that s *makes p factual*). In most other developments of situation theory, the claim that p is factual in s is taken as basic (i.e., undefined) and it is formally represented as: $s \models p$. But we define this notion within the present theory. Given our basic theoretical understanding of situations, it should be apparent that the states of affairs encoded in a situation (via SOA-properties) are the ones *factual in* that situation. So we shall say: state of affairs p is *factual in* situation s (or, s *makes p factual*) iff s encodes the SOA-property of being such that p. Using the notation of situation theory, this can be formalized as:[18]

   $s \models p =_{df} s[\lambda y\, p]$

It is very important to note that '$s \models p$' is defined in terms of the variable 'p' that ranges over states of affairs of any complexity. Thus, any formula ϕ that contains no encoding subformulas and no quantifiers binding relation variables may be substituted for the variable p, for these constitute terms that denote (complex) states of affairs. For such ϕ, the expression '$s \models \phi$' is well-defined as $s[\lambda y\, \phi]$. Also, in order to disambiguate formulas containing '$\models$', we adopt the following convention: '$\models$' shall be dominated by all the other connectives in a formula. For example, a formula of the form '$s \models p \rightarrow p$' shall be short for '$(s \models p) \rightarrow p$.' We write '$s \models (p \rightarrow p)$' to assert that s makes the complex state of affairs $p \rightarrow p$ factual.

---

[17]Some readers may find it useful to recall that the set $\{x \mid x=1 \lor x=2\}$ is a set that contains just two numbers, and that the set $\{F \mid F=[\lambda y\, Lgb] \lor F=[\lambda y\, \neg Lbg]\}$ contains just two properties. Therefore, the condition ϕ in the above instance of *Situations* yields an object that encodes just two SOA-properties.

[18]The notation typically used in situation theory is: $s \models \langle\langle R^n, a_1, \ldots, a_n; 1\rangle\rangle$. This is used to indicate that situation s makes factual the state of affairs (with 'polarity' 1) that has R^n as the governing relation and the objects $a_1, \ldots, a_n$ filling the argument roles. In our notation, however, this is simply rendered as: $s \models R^n a_1 \ldots a_n$.

Given this definition, it now follows that two situations are identical just in case the same SOAs are factual in them.[19]

Theorem 2: $s = s' \leftrightarrow \forall p(s \models p \leftrightarrow s' \models p)$

In other applications of the theory of abstract objects, it has proven useful to define the following notion of part-whole: x is a *part-of* y iff y encodes every property x encodes. To capture this definition formally, let us use the symbol '$\unlhd$' to represent the notion *part-of*. We therefore have:

$x \unlhd y =_{df} \forall F(xF \rightarrow yF)$

Consequently, it follows that every part of a situation is a situation:[20]

Theorem 3: $\forall x[x \unlhd s \rightarrow Situation(x)]$

It is also an immediate consequence that a situation s is a part of situation s' iff every SOA factual in s is factual in s'.

Theorem 4: $s \unlhd s' \leftrightarrow \forall p(s \models p \rightarrow s' \models p)$

This simple theorem is significant because it shows that the theory predicts a natural situation-theoretic analysis of the notion of *part-of*. The theory also makes two other simple predictions, namely, that two situations are identical iff each is part of the other, and that two situations are identical iff they have the same parts:

Theorem 5: $s = s' \leftrightarrow s \unlhd s' \ \& \ s' \unlhd s$
Theorem 6: $s = s' \leftrightarrow \forall s''(s'' \unlhd s \leftrightarrow s'' \unlhd s')$

In light of these results, we shall say that a situation s is a *proper* part of s' just in case s is a part of s' and $s \neq s'$.

In addition to these facts about parts and wholes, it turns out that the entire domain of situations is partially ordered by the notion of *part-of*:[21]

Theorem 7: *Part-of* ($\unlhd$) *is reflexive, anti-symmetric, and transitive on the situations.*

Another important notion of situation theory is *persistency*. Following the situation theorists, we say that a state of affairs p is *persistent* iff whenever p is factual in a situation s, p is factual in every situation s' of which s is a part.[22]

---

[19]This determines another choice at one of the branch points of situation theory. In Barwise 1989, Choice 5 (p. 264) concerns the question of whether situations that support the same infons (or SOAs) are identical. The following theorem decides the issue in favor of Barwise's Alternative 5.1, namely, such SOAs are identical.

[20]This rather simple theorem decides another choice point in situation theory, namely, Choice 2, where Barwise (1989, p. 261) asks whether every part of a situation is a situation. Our theory asserts that it is.

[21]Note that whereas the partial ordering of situations is assumed in Barwise 1989 (p. 259), before the branch points of situation theory are even enumerated, this partial ordering turns out to be a consequence of our theory.

[22]This definition follows Barwise 1989, p. 265.

$Persistent(p) =_{df} \forall s[s \models p \rightarrow \forall s'(s \trianglelefteq s' \rightarrow s' \models p)]$

Clearly, persistency is built right into the theory, for given the above definition of *part-of*, it is an immediate consequence of the foregoing that all states of affairs are persistent:[23]

$Theorem\ 8$: $\forall p\ Persistent(p)$

In the next group of theorems, we consider what kinds of situations are to be found in our domain. One of the most important questions to ask about a situation is whether or not it is actual. In other versions of situation theory, philosophers have restricted themselves to the actual situations. For us, the actual situations constitute just a part of the domain of situations. Let us say that a situation s is *actual* iff every SOA factual in s is factual; i.e.,

$Actual(s) =_{df} \forall p(s \models p \rightarrow p)$

Given this definition, it follows that there are both actual and non-actual situations:[24]

$Theorem\ 9$: $\exists s\ Actual(s)\ \&\ \exists s\,\neg Actual(s)$

Moreover, it follows that no state of affairs and its negation both are factual in any actual situation,[25] and that some SOAs are not factual in any actual situations:

$Theorem\ 10$: $\forall s[Actual(s) \rightarrow \neg\exists p(s \models p\ \&\ s \models \neg p)]$

$Theorem\ 11$: $\exists p \forall s(Actual(s) \rightarrow s \not\models p)$.

Our comprehension principle also guarantees that for any two (actual) situations, there is an (actual) situation of which they are both a part.[26]

$Theorem\ 12$: $\forall s \forall s' \exists s''(s \trianglelefteq s''\ \&\ s' \trianglelefteq s'')$

On our theory of situations, there are two different notions of maximality, as well as two corresponding notions of partiality. Let us say that a situation s is *maximal$_1$* iff every SOA or its negation is factual in s. A situation s is *partial$_1$* iff some SOA and its negation are not factual in s. A situation s is *maximal$_2$* iff every SOA is factual in s. A situation s is *partial$_2$* iff some SOA is not factual in s. Formally:

$Maximal_1(s) =_{df} \forall p(s \models p\ \vee\ s \models \neg p)$

$Partial_1(s) =_{df} \exists p(s \not\models p\ \&\ s \not\models \neg p)$

$Maximal_2(s) =_{df} \forall p(s \models p)$

$Partial_2(s) =_{df} \exists p(s \not\models p)$

---

[23] Thus, the theory comes down in favor of Alternative 6.1 at Choice 6 (p. 265) in Barwise 1989.

[24] The theory here decides Choice 4 (p. 262) of Barwise 1989 in favor of Alternative 4.2.

[25] Compare the Coherency Principle in Barwise 1989, p. 235.

[26] Compare the Compatibility Principle in Barwise 1989, p. 235.

The reader should now be able to use *Situations* to demonstrate the following:

> *Theorem 13: There are maximal$_1$ and partial$_1$ situations.*
>
> *Theorem 14: There are maximal$_2$ and partial$_2$ situations.*

The discussion of maximality brings us naturally to the question of whether there are any maximal situations that could reasonably be called "possible worlds." Let us say that a situation s is a *world* iff it is possible that all and only factual SOAs are factual in s; i.e.,

$$World(s) =_{df} \Diamond\forall p(s \models p \leftrightarrow p)$$

In other words, those situations that *might* make factual all and only the facts are worlds.[27] Note that since the modal operator 'possibly' is defined in terms of the primitive modal operator 'necessarily', we are using a primitive notion of modality to define the notion of a world. Instead of taking possible worlds as primitive entities, as one does in "possible world semantics," we are taking the first step in developing a *theory* of worlds.

This theory has lots of interesting consequences, but before we describe them, it is important to make a few observations about the modal behavior of situations. First, note that *Situations* is a necessary truth! This necessary truth, or $\Box Situations$, is derived from a comprehension axiom (the one for abstract objects) that is (provably) necessarily true. The derivation makes no appeal to contingent truths. So the rule of necessitation applies, yielding $\Box Situations$. Second, recall that the logical axiom for encoding asserts that if an object possibly encodes a property, it necessarily does. This principle ensures that any SOA-property that a situation possibly encodes is one that it necessarily encodes, and *a fortiori*, one that it in fact encodes. In situation theoretic terms, this means that if it is possible that s makes p factual, it is necessary that s makes p factual. In fact, by the *Lemma* to the logical axiom for encoding (see Section 2), we have the following:

> *Lemma 2:* $s \models p \leftrightarrow \Diamond s \models p \leftrightarrow \Box s \models p$

Lemma 2 and $\Box Situations$ combine to produce the following effect: whenever we are describing a particular possibility, not only can we always appeal to $\Box Situations$ to tell us what situations s there are relative to this possibility (since $\Box Situations$ is necessary), but furthermore, any truth of the form $s \models p$ *relative* to this possibility that we discover when appealing to $\Box Situations$ turns out, by *Lemma 2*, to be true *simpliciter*, and a necessary truth at that. This effect proves to be crucial to the proofs of the theorems that follow. With this observation, we turn to the theorems of world theory.[28]

---

[27] This decides Choice 3 in Barwise 1989 in favor of Alternative 3.1: worlds are situations.
[28] A few of the theorems that follow were proved in the section on worlds in Zalta 1983. However, in that work, I formulated the world theory without developing any of the present results in situation theory that underly the theory of worlds.

The first, but not foremost, theorem of world theory is that every world is maximal:

Theorem 15: All worlds are maximal$_1$.

Let us say next that a situation s is *possible* iff it is possible that s is actual. Let us also say that a situation s is *consistent* iff s doesn't make incompatible states of affairs factual (i.e., iff no contradictory SOAs are factual in s). Formally, we have:

$Possible(s) =_{df} \Diamond Actual(s)$
$Consistent(s) =_{df} \neg\exists p\exists q[\neg\Diamond(p \mathbin{\&} q) \mathbin{\&} s \models p \mathbin{\&} s \models q].$

It now follows both that:

Theorem 16: All possible situations are consistent.

Theorem 17: All worlds are possible and consistent.

Now that we have derived some basic truths about worlds in general, it seems reasonable to ask whether there are worlds that are actual, and if so, how many there are. On the present theory, the answers to these questions are "yes" and "one", for there is a unique actual world:

Theorem 18: $\exists! w\, Actual(w)$

In what follows, let us rename the unique actual world with the more appropriately chosen symbol 'w_α'.

The next basic intuition concerning situations and worlds predicted by the theory is that all and only actual situations are part of the actual world:

Theorem 19: $\forall s(Actual(s) \leftrightarrow s \trianglelefteq w_\alpha)$

Let us take a moment to reflect on these results before we turn to the next group of theorems. In some versions of situation theory, only actual situations are tolerated. It is assumed that there is an actual world, and that it is a maximal element under the relation of *part-of*.[29] Thus, the actual world is not a proper part of anything, but is a "maximal element" in the sense that every (actual) situation is a part of it.

Contrast such versions of situation theory with the present one. *Theorem 19* tells us that w_α is a "maximal element" in the sense that every actual situation is a part of it. But note that w_α is nevertheless part of lots of nonactual situations (though no nonactual situation will be part of it). For example, take the situation in which all the SOAs factual in w_α are factual, and in addition, the negation of one of those SOAs is factual as well. Such a situation is non-actual (for it makes a contradiction factual). It is maximal$_1$, but not maximal$_2$. It is neither a possible nor a consistent

---

[29]For example, in Barwise 1989, on p. 259, it is *assumed* that there is an actual world and that it is a maximal element. On p. 261, the actual situations are *defined* to be the ones that are part of the actual world.

situation. But w_α is a part of it. And w_α is also a part of the "universal situation", the situation in which every SOA is factual. The universal situation is maximal$_1$, maximal$_2$, and is a genuine maximal element under *part-of* (every situation is a part of it, but it is not a proper part of any situation). But it is neither actual, possible, nor consistent. Consequently, though the actual world is part of lots of nonactual situations, it is not a part of any actual situation other than itself. So our subdomain of actual situations looks almost exactly like the domain of situations posited by the philosophers who believe that there are only actual situations. Thus, when restricted to the subdomain of actual situations, the theory still yields theorems that capture most of the intuitions held by the "actualist" situation theorists.

The next theorem gives us some basic information about the actual world. It follows from the definition of the actual world w_α that a state of affairs is factual (*simpliciter*) iff it is factual in w_α.

Theorem 20: $p \leftrightarrow w_\alpha \models p$

Recall that the notion of *being factual* is basic to the theory. But no new primitive notation was introduced to mark this notion. *Theorem 20* therefore shows that the theory offers an analysis of *being factual* (or *obtaining*) in terms of its other primitive notions.

Theorem 20 also points us toward some important results about the relationship between the internal and external properties of actual situations in general. We have been treating the internal properties of a situation s as encoded properties of the form $[\lambda y\ p]$. The external properties of a situation are the ones that it exemplifies. For example, all situations exemplify the property of *not being a spoon*. Some, but not others, exemplify the property of *being seen by Mary*. In general, however, situations, like all other objects, are *complete* with respect to the properties they exemplify, in the sense that: $\forall s \forall F(Fs \vee \bar{F}s)$, where $\bar{F} = [\lambda y\ \neg Fy]$. Consequently, situations will be complete with respect to the SOA-properties that they exemplify: $\forall s \forall p([\lambda y\ p]s \vee \neg[\lambda y\ p]s)$. If we now think about the relationship between the internal and external properties of an actual situation, it should be clear that actual situations exemplify (externally) every (internal) property they encode.

Theorem 21: $\forall s[Actual(s) \rightarrow \forall F(sF \rightarrow Fs)]$

We may express this theorem in situation theoretic terms as the follow lemma:

Lemma 3: $\forall s[Actual(s) \rightarrow \forall p(s \models p \rightarrow [\lambda y\ p]s)]$

Of course, there are lots of properties that actual situations exemplify that they won't necessarily encode, such as not being a spoon, being seen by Mary, being depressing, etc. But if we restrict ourselves to the SOA-properties, then the actual world w_α turns out to be a rather special actual situation that has exactly the same internal and external SOA-properties. In situation theoretic terms, a state of affairs p is factual in w_α iff w_α exemplifies being such that p:

Theorem 22: $w_\alpha \models p \leftrightarrow [\lambda y\, p]w_\alpha$

Theorems 20 and *22* have the following interesting consequence about the actual world, namely that a state of affairs p is factual iff the state of affairs, w_α's being such that p, is factual in w_α:

Theorem 23: $p \leftrightarrow w_\alpha \models [\lambda y\, p]w_\alpha$

What is noteworthy about this theorem is its logical form: if we think of the formula '$[\lambda y\, p]s$' as a formula of the form $\phi(s)$, then *Theorem 23* shows that w_α is a situation s such that $s \models \phi(s)$. Intuitively (indeed, semantically) this suggests that w_α is a constituent of the facts that it makes factual.[30]

Let us turn to the final group of theorems—ones which verify our deepest intuitions about the relationship between modality, situations, and possible worlds. The foremost principle of world theory is that a state of affairs (proposition) is necessary iff it is factual (true) in all worlds. Of course, this principle led Kripke (1959, 1963) to conceive of his semantics of modal logic, and set the stage for thirty years of fruitful research in modal logic. In Kripke's work, this principle was the guiding force by which the primitive notions of modality were interpreted by the primitive semantic notions of world theory. In the present theory, however, the primitive notions of modality are couched in our object language and the notions of world theory are defined in terms of them. We *derive* the equivalence of necessity and factuality in all worlds as a theorem:

Theorem 24: $\Box p \leftrightarrow \forall w(w \models p)$

---

[30] In situation theory, statements of the form $s \models \phi(s)$ constitute the defining characteristic of 'nonwellfounded' situations. So the actual world w_α seems to be nonwellfounded in the sense that it makes factual states of affairs p of which it is a constituent. These theorems decide Choices 8, 9, and 10 in Barwise 1989: situations can be constituents of facts; not every object is a situation; and at least some situations are non-well-founded.

There is other evidence for thinking that w_α, and actual situations in general, are nonwellfounded in some sense. And that has to do with what appears to be a "natural" model of the theory, but which cannot be developed within the theory of wellfounded sets. To see this, note that the actual world, and other actual situations all have the following feature: they are objects that, for certain properties F, encode and exemplify the very same F. Now suppose you tried to model, within ZF, 'x encodes (internally) F' as '$F \in x$' (modeling x as a set of properties) and model 'x exemplifies (externally) F' as '$x \in F$' (modeling F as the set of individuals that exemplify it). This seems to be a natural way to use $\in$ to model encodes. But, then, this picture turns out to be in violation of the wellfoundedness of ZF sets, since for certain actual situations s and properties F, the fact that sF & Fs would require, in the model, that both $F \in s$ and $s \in F$. This result seems to square with the intuitions of the situation theorists who believe that nonwellfounded sets provide the best picture of situations.

Of course, the dual of this claim is also a theorem, namely, that a state of affairs is possible iff it is factual in some world:[31]

Theorem 25: $\Diamond p \leftrightarrow \exists w(w \models p)$

This is an important consequence for world theory. Anytime we add to the system a statement that to the effect that $\neg q \ \& \ \Diamond q$ (i.e., that q doesn't obtain but might have), *Theorem 25* guarantees that there is a world other than the actual world in which q is factual. For example, let q be the state of affairs: *George Bush lost the 1988 presidential election*. Then q is not factual but might have been. So, by *Theorem 25*, there is a world w that makes q factual. The world w is not the actual world w_α, since the former makes q factual while the latter makes $\neg q$ factual. So there is a possible world other than the actual world.

Thus, the great variety of truths of the form $\neg q \ \& \ \Diamond q$ *theoretically implies* that there is a great variety of possible worlds. The principles of the theory therefore support an argument for the 'existence' of possible worlds other than the actual world, for the fact that there are such worlds is an immediate consequence of accepting, with respect to some state of affairs p, that p doesn't obtain but might have.[32]

This concludes the formal presentation of the theorems. From this base, the theory can be developed in numerous ways, for there are still lots of interesting notions that can be defined. For example, it seems useful to distinguish the modally closed and the physically closed situations. A situation is *modally closed* iff every necessary consequence of a SOA factual in s is also factual in s. Possible worlds are examples of modally closed situations. A situation is *physically closed* iff every physical consequence of a SOA factual in s is also factual in s. Even more interesting are the situations that are closed under constraints. We may think of the situation-theoretic notion of a *constraint* as follows: constraints are (physically) necessary truths about the exemplification relationships between properties and relations. Here are two examples of constraints, where 'S' denotes the property of sitting, 'B' the property of having bent knees, 'K' the property of kissing, 'T' the relation of touching, and '$\Box$' is an operator expressing some form of physical necessity:

$$\Box\forall x(Sx \rightarrow Bx)$$
$$\Box\forall x\forall y(Kxy \rightarrow Txy \ \& \ Tyx)$$

---

[31] This principle seems to be just stipulated by Lewis (1986). On p. 2, in the middle of a paragraph, we find the following remark, which Lewis doesn't distinguish in any way:

> There are so many other worlds, in fact, that absolutely *every* way a world could possibly be is a way that some world is.

He repeats this claim in several other places (for example, pp. 71, 86). I take this to mean that for each possible state of affairs, there is a world where that state of affairs obtains.

[32] So given at least one claim of the form $\neg p \ \& \ \Diamond p$, the theory decides Choice 1 in Barwise 1989 in favor of Alternative 1.2: there is more than one world.

Suppose the constraints have all been identified. Then we may say that a situation is *closed under constraints* iff every consequence under some constraint of a SOA factual in s is also factual in s. Here is an example. Suppose s is a situation such that $s \models Sa$. Then, if s is closed under constraints, we may conclude, given the above constraints, that $s \models Ba$.

4 Reflections on the Results

The foregoing set of theorems forms an effective foundation for the theory of situations. All twenty-five theorems seem to be basic, reasonable principles that structure the domains of properties, relations, states of affairs, situations, and worlds in true and philosophically interesting ways. There are two reasons one might give for thinking that our results in fact constitute a theory of *situations*, as opposed to some other entity. First, and foremost, they resolve 15 of the 19 choice points defined in Barwise 1989. These were the branch points, discussed in Section 1, through which any situation theory must travel. I have tracked many of these choices in the footnotes to the previous two sections. But the entire list of choices made by the theory are gathered together in Appendix B. This is convincing evidence that the foregoing constitutes a theory of situations. And it is a striking fact that the choices are derived rather than stipulated. Though each of the choices made by the present theory deserves some discussion, this task will be left for the reader. Instead, we turn to the second reason one might give for thinking that our results constitute a theory of situations, namely, the variety of other intuitions and informal ideas underlying situation theory (besides the idea that situations have internal and external properties) that find expression in the present work.

The following list was compiled by retracing some of the basic ideas of situation theory from its inception:

- *The denotation of a sentence is not a truth value.* This intuition motivated a lot of the ideas in Barwise and Perry 1980, 1981, 1983. In these works, Barwise and Perry go to some length to undermine "the slingshot", which was the argument frequently used to establish that the denotation of a sentence is a truth value. The present theory is immune to the slingshot, and moreover, rejects the idea that the denotation of a sentence is a truth value. Instead, it assumes that the denotation of an exemplification statement is a state of affairs (conceived as a structured complex having constituents).

- *Properties and relations are not functions from worlds to sets.* The early work in situation theory was in part motivated by the dissatisfaction with the reconstruction of properties and relations as functions. Such a reconstruction entailed that necessarily equivalent properties and relations are identical, contrary to intuition. The early papers on situation theory take properties and relations as primitive, and we have followed this procedure here.[33] However, we have taken the additional step of developing a full-fledged theory of properties and relations.

- *The denotation of a sentence does not shift when the sentence is embedded in intensional contexts.* This intuition, along with the idea that the denotation of a sentence is not a truth value, constitutes part of our pre-Fregean "semantic innocence". One loses this innocence when one adopts Frege's view, which is that the denotations of terms and sentences shift from their ordinary denotation to their ordinary sense when they appear inside intensional contexts. This view became part of the orthodox approach to the philosophy of language, for it was incorporated into the influential intensional logics developed by Church and Montague. Though we have not discussed intensional contexts here, the present theory offers a treatment of the attitudes that rejects Frege's view that terms and sentences inside these contexts *automatically* shift their denotation.[34] The theory offers readings of intensional contexts in which such shifts do not occur, as well as readings in which they do. It is therefore more flexible than Frege's theory, and accommodates, at least to some extent, a semantic innocence.

- *A theory of situations should be a realistic one.* Barwise and Perry wanted to avoid the mistake of thinking of situations merely as models, indices, or 'analytic tools', in the way some possible world theorists looked at worlds. In Barwise and Perry 1984, they criticize those philosophers who used worlds in their work without appreciating the nature of the ontological commitment that had to be made.[35] Barwise and Perry wanted to be explicit about their own ontological commitment to situations, by treating them as genuine entities in their own right and not merely as formal devices used in semantic models of language. The present theory adopts this view, for it is explicitly realistic. It asserts that *there are* objects, properties, relations, states of affairs, situations and worlds. These entities

---

[33] Recall especially the following passage from Barwise and Perry 1984:

> **B:** But if you need properties and to understand language and the world, and if, as it seems from a scientific point of view, there really are properties and relations between things in the world, independent of language, why not just admit that and stop trying to define them in terms of some other less plausible entities. (p.17)

[34] See Zalta 1983, Chapters V and VI, and Zalta 1988, Chapters 9–12.

[35] In Barwise and Perry 1984, we find:

> **P:** ...The Montague grammarian, or other possible world theorist, is committed to possible worlds and needs to tell us what they are if we are to take their theory seriously. (p. 14)

are not treated simply as formal devices that are useful for doing semantics.

- *Possible worlds are not ontologically fundamental.* It is one thing to reject the reconstruction of properties and relations as functions from worlds to sets, and quite another to reject the possible worlds semantic framework. Barwise and Perry took the extra step of rejecting possible world semantics, and they may have been guided by this intuition in doing so. This intuition may also have led them to reject David Lewis' conception of a world.[36] They deny Lewis' fundamental brute fact, namely, that reality consists of an infinite number of concrete, isolated, alternative worlds. The present theory comes out in favor of Barwise and Perry in this regard, but without abandoning worlds altogether. Possible worlds are not taken as primitive, or otherwise ontologically fundamental; rather, a theoretical account of them as situations of a certain kind is given. The definition of a world, and the resulting theorems governing worlds, *justify* the use of (primitive) possible worlds in semantics for the purposes of developing mathematical models of various (modal) systems when checking for consistency, completeness, etc. Notice that in asserting that there are worlds, the theory does not assert that there are objects that exemplify the property of *being a world*! For one thing, the theory doesn't guarantee that there is any such property (the notion of a world is defined in terms of encoding formulas, so the defining condition can't automatically be used in the comprehension principle *Relations*). Moreover, the claim that there are worlds is not an exemplification claim of the form '$\exists x W x$'; rather, it is a claim that there are certain objects which encode certain properties in a certain way. Thus, our commitment to worlds is not analogous to Lewis' commitment. It doesn't involve an appeal to Lewis' fundamental brute fact. Our work shows that situations are more fundamental than worlds, in the sense that the latter are defined in terms of and constitute a subset of the former.

- *Situations are in some sense partial ways the world is or might have been.* This intuition was the subject of Perry 1986. In that paper, Perry treated situations as partial functions from "issues" to "answers". The situations we've defined can also be correlated with partial functions mapping issues to answers. Here is how. Take the domain of issues to be the domain of states of affairs. Let p be an arbitrary SOA (issue). Now consider a given situation s. We may define a function f_s as follows: f_s maps p to the answer 'Yes' iff s encodes $[\lambda y\ p]$ and f_s maps p to the answer 'No' iff s encodes

---

$[\lambda y \; \neg p]$. Clearly, then, for each s, $\boldsymbol{f_s}$ is a function from issues to answers. Moreover, such functions are partial with respect to the domain of issues, for by *Theorem 13*, there are lots of partial$_1$ situations. If s is partial$_1$, then there are SOAs p such that $\boldsymbol{f_s}(p)$ is undefined. Note that worlds will be total functions from issues to answers. By *Theorem 15*, worlds are maximal$_1$, and a given world w is such that for each SOA p, $\boldsymbol{f_s}(p)$ is defined. This validates Perry's view (1986, p. 83) that worlds are just a special case of situations.

- *Modeling situations set-theoretically is not a substitute for axiomatizing situation theory directly.* In their early works, Barwise and Perry introduced lots of abstract, set-theoretic constructions into situation semantics. In particular, abstract situations were introduced as set-theoretic constructs in terms of which real situations could be classified. In addition to abstract situations, there were event types, roles, constraints, anchors, indeterminates, etc. This profusion of abstract objects led them to reconsider the extent to which their theory could be called 'realistic'. Reality supposedly consisted of situations and a few uniformities across them (such as objects and relations), but all of the work in the theory was being done by abstract situations and constructs thereof. In Barwise and Perry 1984, they shifted their focus and began the search for the axioms of situation theory. In comparison, the present theory is based on a direct axiomatization. The principles and definitions directly characterize situations. The latter are not classified by set-theoretic constructs of any kind, nor is set theory used in stating the first principles.

- *Situations, as pieces of reality, are not the kind of thing that can have negations.* In the early papers on situation semantics, negation was handled by introducing abstract situations to classify reality. The world, however, consists of the real situations, and the latter have no negations. Abstract situations, on the other hand, could have negations. However, these abstract situations were eventually replaced by states of affairs, which were either of positive or negative polarity. Part of the motivation underlying all of these developments is simply the idea that situations, as pieces of reality, are just the wrong kind of thing to have negations. The present theory preserves this intuition by treating situations as objects rather than as relations. Relations and states of affairs are the kinds of thing that can have negations; objects aren't.

These, then, are some of the less obvious pre-theoretic intuitions underlying situation theory which have been realized by the present approach.

Of course, there are intuitions that the present theory *fails* to preserve.

For example, there are the intuitions in favor of the rejected alternatives at the "branch points" that Barwise discusses. However, for now, we shall leave those aside, since the very fact that they are connected with a branch point indicates that they are less firm and more controversial. Are there intuitions to which all situation theorists subscribe but which are not preserved? One such intuition that appears to be abandoned is that situations are concrete. Most situation theorists pretheoretically describe situations not just as pieces of reality but as "concrete pieces of reality." Our *Theorem 19* is a manifestation only of the idea that the actual situations are "pieces of reality". But, in general, situations are regarded as more abstract, and as fundamentally different from ordinary, concrete objects.

Though this is not the place for a full discussion of the issue, it should be mentioned that we have used the words 'concrete' and 'abstract' to label a certain technical predicate and its negation. The sole purpose of this predicate is to partition the domain of objects into those that do and those that don't encode properties. But really, the way the theory is now formulated, it is the distinction between exemplification and encoding that is doing all of the work. What is crucial is to believe in a realm of objects (it doesn't matter what you call them) that encode properties, that have properties internal to their nature in a way which is distinct from having properties external to their nature. Given that the abstract/concrete distinction has come in for a lot of criticism lately, it may be best to avoid these notions altogether.[37] Less controversial labels could be employed, and the theory could be trivially reformulated so as to avoid the controversial notions altogether.

I suspect that once this obstacle is removed, there will still be some who are uncomfortable with the main distinction between exemplification and encoding a property. Let me end by saying that this distinction does seem to capture what it is for a situation to have a *nature* that is inextricably tied to the states of affairs that are factual in them. It is part of the very nature of situations that they make certain states of affairs factual. This divides the properties that characterize the nature of situations, from the other contingent and necessary properties that situations appear to have. Moreover, the distinction between exemplifying and encoding properties has proven to have other applications besides the theory of situations. Maybe by seeing more applications of the theory, one will become more comfortable with the distinction. It is a significant fact that the general metaphysical principles upon which the theory is based were not specifically designed with this particular application in mind. This is evidence that the present theory and the underlying distinction have

---

[37]See Lewis 1986 (Chapter 1, Section 7), and in addition, Hale 1988. I would like to thank Susan Hale for reminding me that the abstract/concrete distinction is not crucial to the theory.

explanatory power—they relate and systematize apparently unrelated phenomena. And after all, drawing distinctions is an important prelude to building theories and solving puzzles.

5 Appendix A: Proofs of the Theorems

Proof of T1: The comprehension principle for abstract objects is: $\exists x(A!x \ \& \ \forall F(xF \leftrightarrow \phi))$, where ϕ has no free xs. But the conditions ϕ on SOA-properties constitute a subset of the conditions that may be used in this comprehension schema for abstract objects. Moreover, any object 'generated' by such a condition on SOA-properties encodes only SOA-properties, and will therefore be a situation.

Proof of T2: ($\leftarrow$) Our hypothesis is that the same SOAs are factual in both s and s', and we want to show that these two situations are identical. Since both s and s' are situations, and hence abstract objects, to show that they are identical, we must show that necessarily, they encode the same properties. We reason by showing, for an arbitrary property Q, that $\Box(sQ \leftrightarrow s'Q)$, for then by universal generalization and the Barcan formulas we are done.

The first step is to show $sQ \leftrightarrow s'Q$, and then we'll show that this is necessary. ($\rightarrow$) Assume sQ. Then since s is a situation, Q must be a SOA-property, say $[\lambda y \ q]$ (for some state of affairs q). So s encodes $[\lambda y \ q]$, and by the definition of 'factual in', q is factual in s ($s \models q$). But our initial hypothesis is that the same SOAs are factual in s and s', and so $s' \models q$, i.e., $s'[\lambda y \ q]$. So s' encodes the property Q. ($\leftarrow$) Reverse reasoning. Thus we have $sQ \leftrightarrow s'Q$.

Now, for *reductio*, suppose that this biconditional is *not* necessary. Then, it must be possible that sQ and $s'Q$ differ in truth value. So, without loss of generality, let us say $\Diamond(sQ \ \& \ \neg s'Q)$. But if so, then (a) $\Diamond sQ$ and (b) $\Diamond \neg s'Q$. Now in virtue of the *Logical Axiom* $\Diamond xF \rightarrow \Box xF$, it follows from (a) that $\Box sQ$, and so in fact sQ. Now (b) is equivalent to $\neg \Box s'Q$, and so it also follows from the *Logical Axiom* (this time by *Modus Tollens*) that $\neg \Diamond s'Q$, i.e., $\Box \neg s'Q$. So in fact, $\neg s'Q$. But we have now proved both sQ and $\neg s'Q$, and this contradicts our first result that sQ and $s'Q$ in fact have the same truth value.

Thus, $\Box(sQ \leftrightarrow s'Q)$. And so by universal generalization and the Barcan formulas, $\Box \forall F(sF \leftrightarrow s'F)$. Thus, s and s' are identical. ⋈

Proof of T3: Suppose x is a part of situation s and that x encodes G (to show G is a SOA-property). Then, since s encodes every property x encodes, s encodes G. But since s is a situation, every property it encodes is a SOA-property. So G is a SOA-property.

Proof of T4: ($\rightarrow$) Assume s is a part of s' and that $s \models q$ (to show $s' \models q$). By definition of $s \models q$, we have $s[\lambda y \ q]$. Since every property encoded by s is encoded by s', $s'[\lambda y \ q]$, i.e., $s' \models q$. ($\leftarrow$) Assume $\forall p(s \models$

$p \to s' \models p$) and that s encodes G (to show s' encodes G). Since s is a situation, $G = [\lambda y \, q]$, for some SOA q, and so $s \models q$. By hypothesis, then, $s' \models q$, and so s' encodes G.

Proof of T5: ($\leftarrow$) If s and s' are both parts of each other, then they encode exactly the same properties. So by the definition of identity for abstract objects, they are identical.

Proof of T6: ($\leftarrow$) Suppose s and s' have the same parts. To show that s and s' are identical, we must show that they encode the same properties. For *reductio*, suppose they don't. Then (without loss of generality) s encodes a property G that s' fails to encode. Now by the lemma to *Situations*, there is a unique situation, call it 's_0', that encodes just the property G. Clearly, s_0 is a part of s, but since s_0 encodes a property s' doesn't encode, s_0 is not a part of s'. Thus, s and s' don't have the same parts, contrary to hypothesis.

Proof of T7: Reflexivity is straightforward. To see that *part-of* is anti-symmetric, assume $s \trianglelefteq s'$ and $s \neq s'$. Then, there is a property s' that is not encoded in s. So, $\neg(s' \trianglelefteq s)$. To see that *part-of* is transitive, assume $s \trianglelefteq s'$ and $s' \trianglelefteq s''$ and that s encodes property G (to show that s'' encodes G). Since s is a part of s', s' encodes G. Since s' is a part of s'', s'' encodes G.

Proof of T8: Assume $s \models p$ and that $s \trianglelefteq s'$. Then by *Theorem 4*, $s' \models p$.

Proof of T9: Consider the following two instances of *Situations*:

$$\exists s \forall F(sF \leftrightarrow F = [\lambda y \, q])$$
$$\exists s \forall F(sF \leftrightarrow F = [\lambda y \, \neg q])$$

Now if q obtains, then $\neg q$ doesn't. So the first instance gives us an actual situation (in which q and no other SOA is factual), while the second instance gives us a non-actual situation (in which $\neg q$ and no other SOA is factual). However, if $\neg q$ obtains, then q doesn't obtain. Then, the first instance gives us a non-actual situation whereas the second gives us an actual one. But either q or $\neg q$ obtains.

Proof of T10: Assume s is actual. Then $\forall p(s \models p \to p)$. For *reductio*, assume that there is a SOA q such that both $s \models q$ and $s \models \neg q$. Then, since s is actual, both q and $\neg q$ obtain, which is impossible.

Proof of T11: By *States of Affairs*, for an arbitrary SOA q, there is a complex SOA $q \& \neg q$. Assume for an arbitrary situation s that s is actual and that $s \models (q \& \neg q)$. Then by the actuality of s, $q \& \neg q$, which is impossible. So, for any actual situation s, if s is actual, $s \not\models (q \& \neg q)$. So there is a SOA p that is not made factual by any situation.

Proof of T12: By *Situations*, there is a situation that encodes all and only the SOA-properties F constructed out of SOAs factual in either s or s'; that is,

$$\exists s''\forall F[s''F \leftrightarrow \exists p((s \models p \lor s' \models p) \;\&\; F=[\lambda y\, p])]$$
Note that if s and s' are both actual, so is s''.

Proof of T13: Consider the following two instances of *Situations*:
$$\exists s\forall F[sF \leftrightarrow \exists p(F = [\lambda y\, p])]$$
$$\exists s\forall F(sF \leftrightarrow F = [\lambda y\, q])$$
The first instance yields a situation ('s_1') that makes every state of affairs factual. *A fortiori*, s_1 is maximal$_1$. The second instance yields a situation ('s_2') that makes just q factual. Then, for any SOA r such that $q \neq r$ and $q \neq \neg r$, s_2 makes neither r nor $\neg r$ factual. So s_2 is partial$_1$.

Proof of T14: Consider the same two instances of *Situations* utilized in the previous proof. Situation s_1 is maximal$_2$, and s_2 is partial$_2$.

Proof of T15: Suppose s is a world. Then $\Diamond\forall p(s \models p \leftrightarrow p)$. We first try to establish, for an arbitrary SOA q, that $\Diamond(s \models q \lor s \models \neg q)$, for then it will follow by *Lemma 2* that $s \models q \lor s \models \neg q$, and hence that $Maximal_1(s)$. Now if we momentarily assume $\forall p(s \models p \leftrightarrow p)$, we can use the fact that $\Box(q \lor \neg q)$ to establish that $s \models q \lor s \models \neg q$. So by conditional proof: $\forall p(s \models p \leftrightarrow p) \rightarrow (s \models q \lor s \models \neg q)$. Since this conditional was proved without appealing to any contingencies, the rule of necessitation applies and we get: $\Box[\forall p(s \models p \leftrightarrow p) \rightarrow (s \models q \lor s \models \neg q)]$. From this fact, and the original fact that $\Diamond\forall p(s \models p \leftrightarrow p)$, we may apply the following well known theorem of modal logic: $\Box(\phi \rightarrow \psi) \rightarrow (\Diamond\phi \rightarrow \Diamond\psi)$. Applying this theorem yields: $\Diamond(s \models q \lor s \models \neg q)$, which is our first objective.

From this fact, it follows that $\Diamond s \models q \lor \Diamond s \models \neg q$. But by *Lemma 2*, each disjunct gives us a nonmodal truth about s, and so it follows that $s \models q \lor s \models \neg q$. Since q was arbitrary, we have shown: $Maximal_1(s)$.

Proof of T16: Assume s is possible. Then, $\Diamond\forall p(s \models p \rightarrow p)$. For *reductio*, assume s is not consistent. Then, there are states of affairs q and r such that $\neg\Diamond(q \;\&\; r)$ and for which both $s \models q$ and $s \models r$. Note that by *Lemma 2*, these last two facts are necessary. Moreover, they are all that is needed to establish: $\forall p(s \models p \rightarrow p) \rightarrow (q \;\&\; r)$. Since this conditional is provable using only necessary truths, the rule of necessitation applies and yields: $\Box[\forall p(s \models p \rightarrow p) \rightarrow (q \;\&\; r)]$. But, by hypothesis, $\Diamond\forall p(s \models p \rightarrow p)$. So it follows by a previously mentioned principle of modal logic that $\Diamond(q \;\&\; r)$, which contradicts the fact (derived from our *reductio* hypothesis) that $\neg\Diamond(q \;\&\; r)$.

Proof of T17: Suppose s is a world. Then it follows immediately that s is possible. So by *Theorem 16*, it follows that s is consistent.

Proof of T18: Consider the situation that encodes all and only those properties F constructed out of SOAs that are factual; i.e,
$$\exists s\forall F[sF \leftrightarrow \exists p(p \;\&\; F=[\lambda y\, p])]$$
Call such a situation 's_0.' It is straightforward to show that s_0 has the following feature, for an arbitrary SOA q: $s_0 \models q \leftrightarrow q$. So, *a fortiori*, s_0 is

both a world and actual. Now to see that there couldn't be two distinct actual worlds, suppose for *reductio* that s' is a distinct actual world. Since s' and s_0 are distinct, there must be a SOA q factual in one but not in the other (by *Theorem 2*). Suppose, without loss of generality, that $s_0 \models q$ and $s' \not\models q$. Then since s' is a world, it is maximal$_1$. So $s' \models \neg q$. But since both s_0 and s' are actual, both q and $\neg q$ must obtain, which is a contradiction.

Proof of T19: ($\rightarrow$) Suppose s is actual and that q is a state of affairs factual in s. Then q must be factual. But since all and only the factual SOAs are factual in w_α (by definition of w_α), q is factual in w_α. So by *Theorem 4*, $s \trianglelefteq w_\alpha$. ($\leftarrow$) By reverse reasoning.

Proof of T20: By definition of w_α.

Proof of T21: Assume s is actual and encodes G (to show s exemplifies G). Then, for some p, $G = [\lambda y\ p]$. So s makes p factual, and since s is actual, p obtains. But, by λ-abstraction, necessarily, an object x exemplifies $[\lambda y\ p]$ iff p obtains (i.e., $[\lambda y\ p]x \leftrightarrow p$). So, in particular, s exemplifies $[\lambda y\ p]$, i.e., s exemplifies G.

Proof of T22: ($\rightarrow$) By *Lemma 3*. ($\leftarrow$) Suppose $[\lambda y\ p]w_\alpha$. Then, by λ-abstraction, p is factual. So, by *Theorem 20*, $w_\alpha \models p$.

Proof of T23: ($\rightarrow$) Suppose p. Then by *Theorems 20* and *22*, $[\lambda y\ p]w_\alpha$. But let $q = [\lambda y\ p]w_\alpha$. Then, by *Theorem 20*, $w_\alpha \models q$, i.e., $w_\alpha \models [\lambda y\ p]w_\alpha$. ($\leftarrow$) By reverse reasoning.

Proof of T24: ($\rightarrow$) Assume $\Box q$. We want to show, for an arbitrarily chosen world w, that $w \models q$. Since w is a world, $\Diamond \forall p(w \models p \leftrightarrow p)$. Moreover, by appealing to $\Box q$, it is easy to establish: $\Box[\forall p(w \models p \leftrightarrow p) \rightarrow w \models q]$. Since we know $\Diamond \forall p(w \models p \leftrightarrow p)$, it follows by now familiar reasoning that $\Diamond w \models q$, and by *Lemma 2*, $w \models q$. ($\leftarrow$) Assume that $\forall w(w \models q)$. By *Lemma 2*, we know that if $w \models q$ then $\Box w \models q$. So $\forall w \Box(w \models q)$, and by the Barcan formulas that $\Box \forall w(w \models q)$. Now if we can show $\Box[\forall w(w \models q) \rightarrow q]$, then by a familiar theorem of $S5$, namely, $\Box(\phi \rightarrow \psi) \rightarrow (\Box\phi \rightarrow \Box\psi)$, we are done. But recall that, by hypothesis, $\forall w(w \models q)$. So, in particular, $w_\alpha \models q$. So q. By conditional proof, $\forall w(w \models q) \rightarrow q$. Since no contingent information was used in the proof, $\Box[\forall w(w \models q) \rightarrow q]$.

Proof of T25: By contraposition and modal negation of *Theorem 24*.

6   Appendix B: Situation Theory Branch Path

Choice 1: There are many worlds (Alternative 1.2). Also, situations can be parts of more than one world (Alternative 1.2.2).

Choice 2: Every part of a situation is a situation.

Choice 3: Worlds are situations (Alternative 3.1).

Choice 4: There are non-actual situations (Alternative 4.2).

Choice 5: Two situations in which the same SOAs (infons) are factual are identical (Alternative 5.1).

Choice 6: Situations are persistent (Alternative 6.1).

Choice 7: Does not apply (sets are not part of the foundations).

Choice 8: Not all situation-theoretic notions are first class citizens! Given the restrictions on *Relations*, we cannot assume that $\models$ is a relation in the domain of ordinary relations. These restrictions are motivated in part by the paradoxes of encoding, and our solution suggests that we can not automatically assume that there are always *new* SOAs that derive from theoretical assertions of the form: $s \models p$. In some cases, it may be safe to assert that there are such relations and SOAs, but the resulting theory has to be proved consistent. So the evidence suggests something more than intuition is required if we are to assert that $\models$ is a relation.

Choice 9: Some objects are situations, and some are not (Alternative 9.2).

Choice 10: Though the question doesn't apply to the theory as developed, some situations appear to be nonwellfounded. Recall that the actual world w_α makes factual states of affairs of which it is a constituent.

Choice 11: No relations are perspectival (Alternative 11.1).

Choice 12: The question does not apply since there are no functions or assignment functions at the level of the object theory.

Choice 13: Basic SOAs are not necessarily determined by the relation and objects they have as constituents (Alternative 13.2).

Choice 14: We can't form SOAs too freely—we can't stick a relation into one of the argument places of a relation without violating the typed nature of the theory.[38] But given any relation R, and objects $x_1, \ldots, x_n$, there is a SOA that is factual iff $x_1, \ldots, x_n$ stand in R.

Choice 15: Not all SOAs are basic (Alternative 15.2).

Choice 16: There is a very rich structure of SOAs—there are SOAs that are the negations, conjunctions, conditionalizations, disjunctions, quantifications, necessitations, etc., of other SOAs.

Choice 17: Every SOA has a dual.

Choice 18: Does not apply.

Choice 19: This depends on how propositions, as distinct from states of affairs, are incorporated into the theory.

References

Barwise, J. 1986. Situations, Sets, and the Axiom of Foundation. Reprinted in Barwise 1989, 177–200.

Barwise, J. 1989. *The Situation in Logic*. CSLI Lecture Notes Number 17. Stanford: CSLI Publications.

---

[38] See Zalta 1983, Chapter 5, and Zalta 1988, Appendix, for the type-hierarchy version of the theory.

Barwise, J., and J. Perry. 1980. The Situation Underground. In *Stanford Working Papers in Semantics*, ed. J. Barwise and I. Sag. Stanford: CSLI Publications.

Barwise, J., and J. Perry. 1981. Semantic Innocence and Uncompromising Situations. In *Midwest Studies in Philosophy, Volume 6*, ed. French, Uehling, and Wettstein, 387–404. Minneapolis: University of Minnesota.

Barwise, J., and J. Perry. 1983. *Situations and Attitudes*. Cambridge, MA: MIT Press.

Barwise, J., and J. Perry. 1984. Shifting Situations and Shaken Attitudes. Report Number CSLI-84-13, CSLI. Reprinted in *Linguistics and Philosophy* 8(1):105–61, 1985 (all quotations cite page numbers in the 1984 publication).

Castañeda, H. N. 1974. Thinking and the Structure of the World. *Philosophia* 4:3–40.

Hale, S. 1988. Space-time and the Abstract/Concrete Distinction. *Philosophical Studies* 53:85–102.

Kripke, S. 1959. A Completeness Theorem in Modal Logic. *Journal of Symbolic Logic* 24:1–15.

Kripke, S. 1963. Semantical Considerations on Modal Logic. *Acta Philosophica Fennica* 16:83–94.

Lewis, D. 1986. *On the Plurality of Worlds*. Oxford: Blackwell.

Mally, E. 1912. *Gegenstandstheoretische Grundlagen der Logik und Logistik*. Leipzig: Barth.

Perry, J. 1986. From Worlds to Situations. *Journal of Philosophical Logic* 15:83–107. Also Report Number CSLI-87-73, CSLI Publications, Stanford.

Quine, W. V. O. 1960. Variables Explained Away. In *Selected Logic Papers*, 227–35. New York: Random House.

Rapaport, W. 1978. Meinongian Theories and a Russellian Paradox. *Noûs* 12:153–80.

Zalta, E. 1983. *Abstract Objects: An Introduction to Axiomatic Metaphysics*. Dordrecht: Reidel.

Zalta, E. 1988. *Intensional Logic and the Metaphysics of Intentionality*. Cambridge, MA: MIT Press.

Part II

Logical Applications

6

Peirce on Truth and Partiality

TOM BURKE

Situation theory can help to make sense out of Peirce's various definitions of truth. Reading some situation-theoretic ideas into Peirce's various definitions of truth does not substantially alter what he means to say, but rather it helps to dispell the apparent incoherence and otherwise enigmatic character of those definitions.

On the other hand, some of Peirce's ideas seem foreign to situation theory. In particular, Peirce's *operationalist* view of properties and relations (and hence of "individuation schemes") has to be acknowledged in coming to terms with his views on truth and reality. I will try to show how situation theory can accommodate this operationalist orientation. In so doing it would have to give up essentially nothing and yet would gain even more theoretical flexibility than it already has.[1]

Peirce's Definitions of Truth

I will begin by discussing two of Peirce's statements about truth and reality, namely:

(A) Thus we may define the real as that whose characters are independent of what anybody may think them to be.

But, however satisfactory such a definition may be found, it would be a great mistake to suppose that it makes the idea of reality perfectly clear. ...

On the other hand, all the followers of science are animated by a cheerful hope that the processes of investigation, if only pushed far enough, will give one certain solution to each question to which they apply it. ... Different minds may set out with the most antagonistic views, but the progress of investigation carries them by force outside of themselves to one and

---

I would like to thank Jon Barwise, John Perry, and also H. S. Thayer for helpful comments on earlier drafts of this paper.

[1] Various ways that situation theory already affords greater theoretical flexibility than standard model-theoretic and/or possible-worlds semantics are discussed by Perry 1986, 1989, Barwise 1989b, and Barwise & Etchemendy 1989.

Situation Theory and Its Applications, vol. 2.
Jon Barwise, Jean Mark Gawron, Gordon Plotkin, and Syun Tutiya, eds.

the same conclusion. This activity of thought by which we are carried, not where we wish, but to a fore-ordained goal, is like the operation of destiny.... *The opinion which is fated*[2] *to be ultimately agreed to by all who investigate is what we mean by the truth, and the object represented by this opinion is the real.* That is the way I would explain reality. (1878, *CP* 5.406–407[3])

(B) Truth is a character which attaches to an abstract proposition, such as a person might utter. It essentially depends upon that proposition's not professing to be exactly true.... *Truth is that concordance of an abstract statement with the ideal limit towards which endless investigation would tend to bring scientific belief, which concordance the abstract statement may possess by virtue of the confession of its inaccuracy and one-sidedness, and this confession is an essential ingredient of truth....* [On the other hand,] Reality is that mode of being by virtue of which the real thing is as it is, irrespectively of what any mind or any definite collection of minds may represent it to be....

Even with regard to ... the immediate judgments we make concerning our single percepts, the same distinction is plain. The percept is the reality. It is not in propositional form. But the most immediate judgment concerning it is abstract. It is therefore essentially unlike the reality, although it must be accepted as true to that reality. Its truth consists in the fact that it is impossible to correct it, and in the fact that it only professes to consider one aspect of the percept....

All of the above relates to *complex truth,* or the truth of propositions. This is divided into many varieties, among which may be mentioned ... *logical truth,* that is, the concordance of a proposition with reality, in such a way as is above defined. (1901, *CP* 5.565–570)

The two parts of these passages that have been italicized for emphasis have been often discussed and are commonly taken to be definitive expressions of Peirce's conception of truth. The present paper will not pursue a lengthy analysis of these passages, but will address just two questions: (1) what does Peirce mean by the "ideal limit" of investigation, and (2) how do we make sense of his saying that truths are inaccurate and one-sided?

Passages (A) and (B) are not entirely consistent with each other, though that is not surprising, given that they appeared twenty or so years apart. Passage (A), which is from "How to Make Our Ideas Clear," is an earlier and less careful statement, indicating that "the truth" is a fully articulated description of reality as would be uncovered through endless inquiry.[4]

On the other hand, (B) utilizes a number of terms and concepts which are absent in (A). For instance: truth is a character or property that *abstract statements* (or *propositions*) may have; hence there are potentially

---

[2] "Fate means merely that which is sure to come true, and can nohow be avoided...."

[3] I will follow the convention of referring to material from Peirce's *Collected Papers* by volume and paragraph numbers.

[4] Except for the emphasis on "processes of investigation," this is reminiscent of Frege's notion of "the True."

many instances of truths, rather than just one all-embracing description or opinion which happens to be "the truth." There is still an idea of inquiry *tending toward* an ideal limit, as in (A); but the truth of an abstract statement or proposition is rather a matter of its *concordance* with the ideal limit of investigation, whereas in (A) truth would appear to be *identified* with that ideal limit.

The various clauses on *confessions of inaccuracy* say in effect that any claim to complete and perfect comprehension of reality would be misguided. Peirce apparently means to say that a true proposition will constitute a less than complete description of reality. By the term 'concordance' Peirce would seem to mean a *partial fitting*—between, on one hand, an actual humanly-accessible abstract statement and, on the other, the ideal limit of investigation—whereby acknowledging that partiality is important to the truth of the abstract statement. Such partiality ought to somehow be built into an account of the truth-conditions of propositions.

Some objections. Almeder 1975 and Thayer 1980 discuss a number of objections to (A) and (B). Russell, for instance, questions Peirce's reference to "fate" and the "operation of destiny" as to the ultimate outcome of collective inquiry.[5] How can Peirce be sure there is anything like a "foreordained goal" of investigation? In the same vein, it is not clear what is meant by the "ideal limit" of "endless" investigation. Does Peirce have in mind a chronological limit of collective inquiry? It would seem in this case that truth would depend only on the opinions of the last inquirers alive. Or is it more like a notion of numerical convergence? In either case, how can Peirce be sure of the *existence* of such a limit? Not all numerical sequences converge, so why should all collective inquiries?

Putting aside the question of whether a numerical analogy makes sense, Quine further questions the assumption that such a limit will be *unique*. This echoes Russell's questioning whether we can justifiably assume that there will be an ultimate agreement among all who investigate a given question. Surely it happens some of the time that various investigators come to agree in their conclusions, but also some of the time not.

The remarks about "confessions of inaccuracy" are another feature of Peirce's definition (B) which Russell questions. It is as if a proposition is not true unless it explicitly claims not to be. Can Peirce's claim be so misguided as this makes it seem. He cites as an example (or rather as an analogy) statements about partial expansions of π. The bare claim that $\pi = 3.14159$ is just false, but a claim including the necessary "confession of inaccuracy," namely that $\pi = 3.14159$ *to six significant digits*, is true. This admittedly partial expansion of π will not be refuted by calculations of subsequent digits in the expansion, hence it is "in concordance with the ideal limit" of such calculation procedures, that is, with the actual infinite expansion.

---

[5] See Almeder 1975 and Thayer 1980 for references.

But then Quine questions the appropriateness of a numerical analogy in the first place, given that there is no workable notion of "nearness," and hence no notion of "convergence," that can be applied to inquiries, presumably thought of as sequences of theories.

Both Russell and Ayer also discuss a different kind of objection. Namely, what about uninvestigated facts (such as the number of grains of sand on a given beach, or prehistoric facts)? Peirce's definition doesn't seem to allow for either the truth or falsity of propositions that are not results of any kind of investigation (or if read in another way, it renders all uninvestigated propositions vacuously true, in the sense that they are agreed to by all who investigate since in fact no one investigates them). On the other hand, it is trivial to say that infinite inquiry in some abstract sense would eventually uncover all the facts. Peirce's view begins to sound either like a verificationist theory of truth, which is unacceptable, or else rather empty of any real insight.

A preliminary response. The following paragraphs in defense of Peirce are mostly a summary of some points discussed by Thayer and Almeder. First of all, as for the appropriateness of the numerical analogy and the question of the existence of an ideal limit of investigation of some given subject matter, the term 'limit' is being used too roughly. We could interpret Peirce's use of the phrase 'in the limit' in the perhaps unusual sense that *every* infinite sequence of real numbers has some sort of behavior in the limit—it's just that some sequences of reals are not convergent. By analogy, some inquiries, such as into an ill-posed question, will have unresolvable or uncertain conclusions: no matter how you proceed, nothing is settled for certain. But still, such inquiry has a kind of behavior "in the limit" though it may yield indeterminate nonsense. In such a case, a proposition that would claim otherwise would be false.[6]

Also, none of what Peirce writes requires or assumes that we think of inquiry in terms of a series of theories (or opinions, etc.). At the same time, something more needs to be said about how we *should* think about inquiry, in order to be able to invoke more than just analogies, numerical or otherwise.[7] I will pursue this in later sections where I discuss Peirce's operationalism.

---

[6] For Dewey, who basically endorsed the conception of truth expressed in (A) and (B), *convergence* of inquiry (as focused on the transformation of some given situation) is not a measure of truth but rather of warranted assertibility. Strictly speaking, neither the *convergence* of inquiry, nor the *stability* of the results of inquiry, are measures of *truth*, though they are among the best measures we have for determining how to orchestrate our actions in the world.

[7] Vickers 1989 and Barwise and Etchemendy 1990 discuss various topological notions that could help make sense of information gathering and handling in the course of inquiry and problem-solving. The fact that non-metrical approaches to the study of information are possible suggests that Quine's reservations about there being no "metric" for comparing theories, though understandable, are not entirely relevant.

Peirce's views may begin to sound like a verificationist theory of truth; but the subjunctive term *'would'* in definition (B) makes all the difference in deflecting that charge. If a proposition p is true, then it *would* be affirmed *if* it were subject to endless (ideal) inquiry. Hence, in reply to Ayer, lots of things can be true, and lots of things can be false, though never actually inquired into. Peirce's critics often fail to take into account the fact that definitions (A) and (B) do not state conditions to be satisfied by actual inquiries in order that a statement be true; truth is not *produced* by inquiry. Inquiry doesn't *make* anything true in the same sense that actually throwing dice doesn't make the probabilities of various outcomes be what they are. The probabilities exist whether or not the dice are ever tossed, though the results of repeated tossings tend to indicate what the probabilities are. Peirce explicitly says that reality isn't made or determined by inquiry, though it is partially revealed through actual inquiry.

It apparently needs to be stressed that one shouldn't confuse properties of ideal inquiry with those of actual inquiry. Actual inquiries only approximate the would-be results of ideal inquiry. Whether or not we ever come to an agreement on the results of our actual shared inquiries, reality would ultimately compel agreement if the inquiry were to be pursued with perfect scientific competence and without any limitations on resources or ingenuity. There are lots of truths that we will never know nor have reason to believe because actual inquiry is so often unable to reach as far as is otherwise ideally possible.

In this regard, Thayer argues at length that many objections to (A) and (B) are largely the result of a failure to distinguish why we might *believe* that p is true, how we might *know* that p is true, and what we might *mean* to say that p is true. Peirce was concerned with the latter of these three—not to delineate criteria for belief or knowledge but more simply to specify what it means to say that a proposition is true whether or not we can know so or have reason to believe so. Peirce's basic insight was to explain truth and reality by explaining non-trivially how they figure into our experience; but that does *not* make experience in any sense prior to what is true or what is real, i.e., that does not make truth or reality *dependent* on experience.[8]

Still, a number of questions remain unanswered. Given the various replies to Peirce's critics so far outlined, it is still not clear beyond a vague intuition what is meant by the "ideal limit" of inquiry. Might Peirce have supplied more than just *analogies*? If the analogy with numerical sequences is inadequate, what otherwise can be said to make sense of his strange

---

[8]Dewey (1916, 72) points out that Peirce thought of pragmatism as being primarily concerned with "the determination of the meanings of terms, or better, propositions," rather than with formulating a theory of truth. Later, after the term 'pragmatism' had been adopted by James, Schiller, and others to designate a theory of truth, Peirce concocted another name, 'pragmaticism', to label his original view (1905, *CP* 5.414).

remarks about the "inaccuracy and one-sidedness" of true propositions? And by appealing to ideas of "fate" and "as-if-by-destiny," did Peirce intend anything more than to advocate a realist view of probabilities as suggested by the analogy with rolling dice?

In an attempt to answer such questions, I want to suggest that, in passage (B) where Peirce uses terms like 'inaccuracy' and 'one-sidedness', it is possible to substitute situation-theoretic terms like 'partiality', 'context-dependence', and 'perspectival relativity' without significantly changing the intended content of the definition.

But first, where Peirce talks about the "ideal limit of endless inquiry," situation theory as it stands is less able to directly contribute to an understanding of what he is getting at. So before discussing connections with situation theory, I will propose in the next section a way to make concrete sense out of Peirce's notion of the "ideal limit" of an inquiry. Peirce's jargon about ideal limits of endless inquiries is just an unfortunate way of talking about purely abstract, formal properties of what I will term "investigation schemes" (where the latter, once properly defined, are related but theoretically prior to the situation-theoretic notion of "individuation schemes").

Salvaging Peirce's Operationalism

I will admit to a certain amount of difficulty in accepting much of what I find in Peirce's writings. But I want to highlight one aspect of his views that is worth pursuing. Namely, in trying to understand his views on logic and truth, it is important to square up to the fact that he was developing and working within an *operationalist* framework. By 'operationalist' I mean a conceptual framework where what are taken to be fundamental are the notions of *actions* and *consequences* (or operations and their outcomes). This is in direct contrast to standard model-theoretic semantics where *individuals* and *properties-&-relations* are fundamental.

An operationalist view of how to explicate any general predicate is formulated by Peirce in various writings. One of the earliest formulations occurs in "How to Make Our Ideas Clear" (1878), a few pages prior to the occurrence of passage (A):

(C) [T]he whole function of thought is to produce habits of action; ... If there be a unity among our sensations which has no reference to how we shall act on a given occasion, ... we do not call that thinking. To develop [a thing's] meaning, we have, therefore, simply to determine what habits it produces, for what a thing means is simply what habits it involves. Now the identity of a habit depends on how it might lead us to act ... What the habit is depends on *when* and *how* it causes us to act. As for the *when*, every stimulus to action is derived from perception; as for the *how*, every purpose of action is to produce some sensible result. Thus, we come down to what is tangible and conceivably practical, as the root of every real distinction of thought, no matter how subtle it may be; and there is no distinction of meaning so fine as to consist in anything but a possible difference of practice....

... The occasion of such action would be some sensible perception, the motive of it to produce some sensible result. Thus our action has exclusive reference to what effects the senses, our habit has the same bearing as our action, our belief the same as our habit, our conception the same as our belief; and we can consequently mean nothing by [a certain sort of thing] but what has certain effects, direct or indirect, upon our senses; and to talk of something as having all the sensible characters of [that sort of thing], yet being in reality [something else], is senseless jargon....

It appears, then, that the rule for attaining the third grade of clearness of apprehension is as follows: Consider what effects, that might conceivably have practical bearings, we conceive the object of our conception to have. Then, our conception of these effects is the whole of our conception of the object. (1878, *CP* 5.400–402)

The last paragraph in (C), by the way, is Peirce's earliest formulation of the so-called "pragmatic maxim," one of the passages which William James referred to when crediting Peirce with originating pragmatism as a philosophical "ism."

Peirce's operationalism is amply evidenced in later writings as well. One of the more explicit statements is the following:

(D) If you look into a textbook of chemistry for a definition of *lithium*, you may be told it is that element whose atomic weight is 7 very nearly. But if the author has a more logical mind he will tell you that if you search among minerals that are vitreous, translucent, grey or white, very hard, brittle, and unsoluble, [and then Peirce describes some expected results of half a dozen experimental procedures] ... *that* is a specimen of lithium. The peculiarity of this definition—or rather this precept that is more serviceable than a definition—is that it tells you what the word lithium denotes by prescribing what you are to *do* in order to gain a perceptual acquaintance with the object of the word. (c.1902, *CP* 2.330)

Similar ideas came to play an important part in the views of P. W. Bridgman and in scientific empiricism more generally, though Peirce cannot be fairly judged solely on the basis of these later renditions of operationalism. There is of course not a whole lot of support to be found anymore for a naive operationalist view of things. In the usual vulgarization of that view, realities are supposed to be specified purely in terms of "operational definitions." For instance, when asked what an electron is, the naive operationalist will specify some characteristic set of experimental procedures and the observable results one should expect, and say that that is all there is to electrons. One simply does not ask any further about what an electron "really is." It doesn't make sense to talk about electrons other than in terms of such operations and their results.

Notice that this is not what Peirce was saying in (C) and (D). He would say that our "conception" of electrons can only be specified operationally, but this leaves open the possibility that our conception of a thing may not get at everything that a given thing *really is*. So it is always meaningful to press the question of what a thing "really" is. Progress in science consists rather in honing our conceptions of things; hence it is our conception of electrons, not what electrons really are, that has changed in the past hundred years as a result of refining experimental procedures in physics and chemistry.

So what does it mean to say that it is *true* that something has a certain property or falls under a given concept (e.g., 'is wine', 'is wooden', 'is an electron') when properties or concepts are defined operationally? How is it possible within an operationalist framework to retain a robust notion of truth, independent of notions of belief, knowledge, or verification?[9]

Passages (A) and (B) are typical of Peirce's answer to such questions. In the remainder of this section, I want to propose a reconstruction of some of the ideas underlying Peirce's definition of truth. I want to claim, first, that his notion of an "ideal limit of inquiry," as what would be the upshot of inquiry if pursued endlessly, is at worst a cumbersome way of appealing to the notion of wholesale formal properties of *investigation schemes*; and second, that this does contribute to the formulation of a robust notion of truth.

---

[9] A Tarskian account of satisfaction and logical truth is not helpful in answering this question, since Peirce is essentially trying to answer a question that Tarski left up in the air. Namely, what does it mean to say that an object does in fact *satisfy* a sentential function? Tarski advanced a notion of logical truth based on the idea of sequences of objects *satisfying* sentential functions. A sentence of a given language, relative to a given domain of discourse D, is logically true if it is satisfied by all sequences of objects in D. Peirce rather is addressing the *base case* of Tarski's recursive notion of satisfaction. Namely, what does it mean to say that a given sequence (not to mention all such sequences) satisfies a given sentential function? Equivalently, what does it mean to say that a token sequence is in the extension of a relation? Of course, it just either is or isn't, and a lot can be done without addressing the question; but still, what are the criteria, if there are any, for determining such membership in some principled way?

Peirce answered this question by characterizing "concepts" (viz. properties and relations) in operationalist terms—in terms of *actions* and *expected consequences*. This may seem to be in opposition to the usual model-theoretic approach to semantics where individuals and properties-&-relations are taken as primitives. In working with a different set of philosophical primitives, the idea of a sequence of *objects* satisfying a *sentential function* would have to be a "derived" idea. This allows Peirce to say something non-trivial in answer to a question about basic, simple truth which Tarski leaves unanswered if not unasked.

Peirce's project may also be clarified by considering standard truth-table definitions of the sentential connectives. Given the truth-values of statements p and q, these tables supply the truth-values of $p * q$ for any binary sentential connective '$*$'. But Peirce is asking the more basic question, prior to addressing sentential truth-*functions*, of what it means in the first place to say that an atomic sentence p is true. (It might be thought that a treatment of sentential connectives remains unaffected by how this questioned is answered; but that isn't so clearly the case from a pragmatist standpoint.)

By an investigation scheme, I mean a structured system of exploratory actions.[10] A simple example would be all the different sorts of laboratory experiments that might be useful in an investigation of, say, electrons, or lithium, or some other physical phenomenon. Otherwise, think of an investigation scheme as an organized collection of procedures for identifying some range of even common everyday things.

Presumably we are to associate each such action in an investigation scheme with some characteristic set of possible outcomes or "immediate results," along the same lines of controlled experimental activities in a laboratory.

Each *concept* (each property or relation) that is relevant to a given inquiry, is determined not just by some subset of actions in a given investigation scheme but also by some space of possible immediate results to be expected from those characteristic actions. The following remarks stress the subjunctive character of Peirce's operationalist view of *concepts*:

(E) In order to ascertain the meaning of an intellectual conception one should consider what practical consequences might conceivably result by necessity from the truth of that conception; and the sum of these consequences will constitute the entire meaning of the conception. (c.1902 and 1905, *CP* 1.2–10)

(F) [Pragmatism] is, in itself, no doctrine of metaphysics [but] is merely a method of ascertaining the meanings of hard words and of abstract concepts. . . . [which] is no other than that experimental method by which all the successful sciences . . . have reached the degrees of certainty that are severally proper to them today; . . .

I understand pragmatism to be a method of ascertaining the meanings, not of all ideas, but only of what I call "intellectual concepts," that is to say, of those upon the structure of which, arguments concerning objective fact may hinge. . . . My pragmatism, having nothing to do with qualities of feeling, permits me to hold that the predication of such a quality [as *blue* or *red* or *hard* or *soft*] is just what it seems, and has nothing to do with anything else. . . . Those qualities have no intrinsic signification beyond themselves. Intellectual concepts, however—the only sign-burdens that are properly denominated "concepts"—essentially carry some implication concerning the general behaviour either of some conscious being or of some inanimate object, and so convey more, not merely than any feeling, but more, too, than any existential fact, namely, the "would-acts," "would-dos" of habitual behaviour; and no agglomeration of actual happenings can ever completely fill up the meaning of a "would-be." But . . . the *total* meaning of a predication of an intellectual concept is contained in an affirmation that under all conceivable circumstances of a given kind . . . the subject of the predication would behave in a certain general way—that is, it would

---

[10] See page 133 below for a more precise definition. The definition requires two things: an assembly 𝔄 of operations and a set ℭ of constraints defined on 𝔄, the latter being what makes an investigation scheme not just a *set* but rather an organized *system* of operations. For the present though, I will avoid mentioning such constraints.

be true under given experiential circumstances (... *taken as they would occur*, that is in the same order of succession, *in experience*). (c.1906, *CP* 5.464–467)

According to these statements, the meaning of an operationally defined concept is not determined solely by actual experiences but rather by the range of all *possible* experiences fitting the specifications of its definition in terms of various actions and the immediate results of those actions. Some of Peirce's terminology is unfortunate, but such a concept would be termed "intellectual" not because its definition involves operations of intellectual thought, but because the possible range of mutually constrained experiences characteristic of that concept, no matter what kind of operations are involved in its definition, is *formally* or *abstractly* (intellectually?) fathomable even if not practically so—in contrast to simple qualities of the sort that have no such range beyond immediate token experiences.

Given this operationalist view of concepts, consider how it ties into Peirce's view of the ideal limit of inquiry. First, the following passage describes Peirce's view of logic as a formal theory of "signs."

(G) Logic, in its general sense, is ... only another name for *semiotic* ... the quasi-necessary, or formal, doctrine of signs. By describing the doctrine as "quasi-necessary," or formal, I mean that we observe the characters of such signs as we know, and from such an observation, by a process which I will not object to calling Abstraction, we are led to statements, eminently fallible, and therefore in one sense by no means necessary, as to what *must be* the characters of all signs used by a "scientific" intelligence, that is to say, by an intelligence capable of learning by experience.... By such a process [of abstraction], which is at bottom very much like mathematical reasoning, we can reach conclusions as to what *would be* true of signs in all cases, so long as the intelligence using them was scientific. (1897, *CP* 2.227)

By a "sign" Peirce does not mean just a linguistic symbol or expression, nor just a "mental representation," though such things can be instances of signs. More generally, a sign is anything—in the head, in the world, on the page, etc.—that "stands for," "indicates," "refers to," "points to," or otherwise "compels the intelligence toward" something else. He gives such examples as words, weather-vanes, and tallies; and otherwise his meaning is no doubt very general (if not so general as to be useless). Passages (H) and (I) make this clear, and, in conjunction with (A) and (B), indicate how a theory of signs is built into his inquiry-based account of truth. I have italicized one sentence in (H) for particular emphasis in this regard.

(H) Truth belongs exclusively to propositions. A proposition has a subject (or set of subjects) and a predicate. The subject is a sign; the predicate is a sign; and the proposition is a sign that the predicate is a sign of that of which the subject is a sign. If it be so, it is true. But what does this correspondence or reference of the sign, to its object, consist in? ... [If] it be conceivable that [the answer to this question] should be disclosed to human intelligence, it will be something that thought can compass. Now thought is of the nature of a sign. In that case, then, *if we can find out the right method of thinking and can follow it out—the right method of transforming signs—then truth can be nothing more nor less than the last result to which the following out of this method would ultimately carry us.* In that case, that to which the representation should conform, is itself something in the nature of a representation, or sign—something noumenal, intelligible, conceivable, and utterly unlike a thing-in-itself. (1906, *CP* 5.553)

(I)   Truth is the conformity of a representamen [i.e., a sign] to its object, *its* object, ITS object, mind you.... There must be an action of the object upon the sign to render the latter true. Without that, the object is not the representamen's object....

So, then, a sign, in order to fulfill its office, to actualize its potency, must be compelled by its object. (1906, *CP* 5.554)

So the ideal limit to which true propositions presumably conform is a feature of some respective "method of transforming signs" and is itself a sign? This starts to sound rather baffling. But given his distinction between reality and the ideal limit of inquiry in (A) and (B), what he is saying here, I think, is that the ideal limit of inquiry (to which propositions must conform if they are true) "is itself in the nature of a sign" standing for or indicating its object, namely reality.

One might feel that Peirce is coming dangerously close to advocating a Russellian "correspondence" theory of truth. But that way of interpreting what he is saying is avoidable. Peirce's "concordance" theory of truth is based on the idea of a fitting or conformity between one sign, namely a proposition, and another sign, namely the ideal limit of inquiry—not between facts and representations of facts.[11]

Trying to avoid getting pulled any further into a discussion of Peirce's conception of "signs," I would like to focus on the picture that is beginning to emerge here of the ideal limit of inquiry as an abstract-yet-concrete feature of inquiry. Peirce seems to be saying, almost paradoxically, that the ideal limit of inquiry is, on one hand, an *abstract* feature of a system of signs but, on the other, only in regard to that system of signs being *concretely* employed in the world.

Consider first the description of the ideal limit of inquiry as an abstract feature of a system of signs. Relating such remarks as in (H) and (I) back to previous quotes where truth is characterized as concordance with the ideal limit of endless inquiry, the final remark in passage (H) could be rephrased to say that that with which a proposition is in concordance (if it is true) is at bottom an *abstract* feature of some system of signs— not necessarily some "language" or "theory" but a system including such things as concepts, names, propositions, even concrete objects like weather-

---

[11] See page 138 below for further elaboration of this point.

vanes. Then, to accommodate Peirce's operationalist view of concepts (and therefore subjects, predicates, propositions, etc.) as well as the general idea of inquiry as involving an employment of investigatory operations, such systems of signs as Peirce has in mind may at bottom be understood in terms of arrays of possible actions and their possible immediate results. That is, we could just as well think of the ideal limit of inquiry as an abstract feature of a system of possible actions and their possible immediate results.

Any actual inquiry into some given question will be based on some (possibly evolving) investigation scheme. The constitution of this scheme at any point in an inquiry will of course depend on the sorts of things being inquired into, according to the operational specifications of whatever concepts are determined to be relevant.[12] And in place of talking about "all who investigate" a given question (as in (A)), Peirce could rather have talked in terms of all possible manners or courses of investigation relative to some given collection of exploratory operations.[13]

Following this out in a bit more detail, a particular phase of an investigation will be pursued in terms of some structured collection $\mathfrak{A} = \{A_1, A_2 \ldots\}$ of exploratory actions, where each action A_i is associated with a characteristic collection $\{r_1, r_2, \ldots\}$ of possible registerable outcomes. There are two spaces of possibilities to consider: the field of all possible *courses of action* constructible from the elements of $\mathfrak{A}$, consisting of all ways of concatenating or otherwise deploying complexes of operations in $\mathfrak{A}$; and derivatively, the space of all possible strings or arrays of immediate results producible by these courses of actions. This twofold domain of possibilities is purely a formal feature of $\mathfrak{A}$, limited in practice only by agents' capacities to orchestrate and deploy operations in $\mathfrak{A}$.

In practice, one would presumably pursue courses of action that would permit the confirmation or refutation of various sorts of information, based on operational specifications of whatever concepts are determined to be relevant. From an operationalist standpoint, any given concept is determined by a set $\mathcal{A}$ of operations and a space Σ of possible arrays of outcomes, such as would be expected as results of performing operations in $\mathcal{A}$ toward an object that "falls under" that concept.[14] A given investigation scheme may be built out of exactly the sum of the sets of operations characteristic of a fixed set of concepts. For instance, particular research programs are

---

[12] Inquiring into questions about electrons will involve a collection of operations characteristic of our conception of electrons and probably not those of our conception of breakfast cereals (or whatever). More generally, it is normal in the actual course of scientific affairs that investigation schemes are continually modified—improved, refined, extended, economized—in accordance with ongoing alterations in our conceptions of things.

[13] But then this reconstruction of Peirce's definition appears to ignore the *social* nature of inquiry, which Peirce clearly found significant. See Thayer 1980 and Dewey 1916, 77.

[14] See pages 135ff for an alternative definition in terms of operations and constraints.

generally geared to investigating objects falling under only a limited range of concepts, such as electrons or temperatures but not elephants or homing instincts (or vice versa). Conversely, regardless of how a given investigation scheme is determined, such a scheme will permit the discrimination of a relatively limited collection of concepts, limited namely to what is constructible in terms of subsets A of $\mathfrak{A}$, and second, by the collections of distinct outcome-states definable on each of these subsets.

On the other hand, what is *not* determined by mapping out this twofold domain of possibilities (of possible courses of actions, and possible arrays of outcomes of those courses of actions) is how the world would react in any given instance to any of the courses of action in that domain, even though all possible ways it *might* react are determined once $\mathfrak{A}$ is fixed. The ideal limit of inquiry is going to involve more than just these abstract possibilities. It also has a kind of concreteness. Passage (I) asserts that, beyond the abstract properties of a given investigation scheme, certain aspects of the ideal limit of inquiry would be determined *by the part of the world* in which concrete instances of those respective activities would be carried out.

An investigation scheme by itself is hardly more than a "frame of reference" which determines a "geometry" of possibilities, saying little about the world until it is concretely oriented in and otherwise imposed on the world. We cannot say how the world will in fact react to actually employing such actions other than mapping out all the possibilities; but the sense of *realism* inherent in Peirce's views (and which is essentially all that lies behind his figurative references to "fate" and the "operation of destiny") asserts that certain concrete results would indeed be achieved from each token course of action from among those abstract possibilities.[15] We cannot necessarily fathom exactly *how* things would turn out but only *that they would* turn out. And the sum total of exactly how the world would react in a given inquiry to each and every possible course of action relative to $\mathfrak{A}$, whether we can fathom it or not, constitutes the ideal limit of that inquiry as geared to $\mathfrak{A}$.

So it is *not only* the abstract realm of possible actions and results associated with some given assembly of operations $\mathfrak{A}$ *but also* what would be the case in applying $\mathfrak{A}$ to the world that determines the ideal limit of a given inquiry. So far as I can see, this will yield as robust a notion of truth as is conceivably possible without begging the question. Relative to some given inquiry, a proposition—such as a claim about various objects falling under various concepts—will be true if it accords with the abstract and yet concrete ideal limit of that inquiry.

Robust or not, this definition supports the idea that there is no general guarantee that we can always *know* that a statement is true or not, though

---

[15] Cf. Dewey 1916 (75–78).

it just is or it isn't. What we can or can't know in this regard would depend on the nature of the given inquiry. In the case of partial expansions of π, not only the given "investigation scheme" but also the "part of the world" in which it is applied is very well-behaved. Hence we can actually fathom what is true and what is not for a very wide range of related propositions. But this isn't typical of everyday truths.[16]

If this reconstruction of Peirce is on track, then what is needed to substantiate Peirce's concept of truth is an extensive development of the idea of investigation schemes.[17] I would rather keep the present discussion as informal as possible, though the next section hints at some of the details of such a theory by outlining how to construct individuation schemes out of investigation schemes.

Situation Theory and Peirce

The previous discussion of Peirce's operationalism has been aimed primarily at clarifying his notion of the ideal limit of inquiry. The second question I want to address concerns how to make sense of his saying in (B) that truths are inaccurate and one-sided. I want to argue that this makes perfectly good sense and, when cast in the right light, seems like just an awkward way of pointing out the *partiality* of information, which is a familiar idea in situation theory.

There are several different ways to interpret Peirce's talking about "confessions of inaccuracy and one-sidedness." He might have meant that a

---

[16] Actually there are a couple of ways to understand the relativization of inquiry and hence truth to investigation schemes. Without complicating things too seriously, we could on purely formal grounds talk about at least *two* kinds of "ideal limits" of inquiry relative to a given investigation scheme: (a) by considering all possible ways of employing some fixed set $\mathfrak{A}$ of exploratory operations; and (b) by allowing maximal compatible extensions of $\mathfrak{A}$.

That is, (a) for a given assembly of operations $\mathfrak{A}$, let $\mathfrak{A}^{\#}$ denote the abstract domain of all possible "courses of action" constructible from the elements of $\mathfrak{A}$, consisting of all abstractly possible ways of concatenating or otherwise deploying *complexes* of operations in $\mathfrak{A}$. This could include courses of action that are endless in time or unbounded in spatial extent; and the topological idea of *dense* inquiry that is otherwise bounded in finite space-time seems like a potentially useful notion as well.

But, (b) we can also "idealize" a given $\mathfrak{A}$ in a different sense by considering extensions of $\mathfrak{A}$. One might want to hold that the truest truth, truth with a capital 'T'—with respect to a collection of operations $\mathfrak{A}$—is to be understood not in terms of $\mathfrak{A}^{\#}$ but rather in terms of a domain $\mathfrak{A}_{\infty}^{\#}$, where $\mathfrak{A}_{\infty}$ is one or another *maximal* extension of $\mathfrak{A}$—one that preserves $\mathfrak{A}$ as some sort of basic kernel of operations but which otherwise is extended to a non-extendable set of operations that are compatible with $\mathfrak{A}$. There is no reason offhand to think there is just one such $\mathfrak{A}_{\infty}$ for a given $\mathfrak{A}$, hence there may be a number of standards of "truest truth" relative to $\mathfrak{A}$.

[17] I won't pursue any such development here. For one thing, one should probably try to incorporate Dewey's refinements of Peirce's views before pursuing such a project. Some aspects of Dewey's theory of inquiry—including a more detailed discussion of an operationalist conception of "properties and relations"—have been discussed in Burke 1990, 1991.

given proposition is not true unless it confesses its own *falsity*. In this case, every true proposition is a variation on the liar proposition. But this is too coarse for what Peirce had in mind.

Or, he might have meant that a proposition is not true unless it admits some degree of *probability*. This is perhaps involved in what he meant, in some cases; but it isn't broad enough in scope, and he most likely would have talked about probabilities explicitly, rather than use terms like 'inaccuracy' and 'one-sidedness', if that is all he had in mind.

Or third, there are various situation-theoretic notions relevant to the emphasis on *partiality* which, though not necessarily an exhaustive account of what Peirce had in mind, are more to the point and come closer to accommodating what he was getting at. I would like to briefly discuss two such notions in light of Peirce's definitions of truth and reality. These are, respectively, the notion of *situations*, and the notion of *perspectival relativity*.

Situations. As discussed by Barwise 1989b and Perry 1986, situations are conceived of as entities encompassing less than the whole world, i.e., as parts of the world. And ways that *parts* of the world can be are similarly contrasted with possible worlds, that is, with ways that the total world can be.

Situations (and ways that situations can be) play an important role in a situation-theoretic story about what propositions are. Perry 1986 (92) considers a preliminary suggestion that, in place of total functions from possible worlds to truth-values, we consider "a more general class of propositions, as partial functions from ways to truth-values." A proposition in this view could presumably be modeled by, or otherwise closely associated with, a pair $\langle W^+, W^- \rangle$ where W^+ is the collection of ways that make the proposition true, W^- is the collection of ways that make the proposition false, and $W^+ \cup W^-$ may not exhaust all the ways that parts of the world can be.

And one doesn't have to reach too far to connect this up with Peirce. The fact that propositions are made true (or not) by ways that *parts* of the world can be (rather than insist on reference to total ways), and the related fact that $W^+ \cup W^-$ (for a given proposition) need not exhaust all the ways things can be, builds a "confession of inaccuracy and one-sidedness"—namely, two different kinds of partiality—into the constitution of propositions.

Perry 1986 (105) later suggests that propositions be modeled by partial functions mapping pairs of ways *and* situations, not just ways alone, to truth-values. This is motivated by consideration of the non-persistence of information, and seems to parallel Kaplan's distinction (1989) between circumstances (of evaluation) and contexts (of utterances). The point is that concrete utterances occur in, and are about, concrete situations; and we can't assume that the propositional contents of such utterances will not change their truth-values across situations that are the same way, or perhaps are of two different ways but such that one way is "part of" the second.[18]

This demonstrates the need to include, as part of any given proposition, reference not just to ways that parts of the world might be but also to actual parts of the world to which that proposition pertains. But this twofold relativization of propositions to both abstract ways and concrete situations is reminiscent of passages (H) and (I) where we saw that the "inaccuracy and one-sidedness" essential to the truth-value of a proposition is understood not just in terms of abstract possibilities but also with regard to concrete links to the world. It appears that Perry's discussion of "ways" versus "situations" at least runs parallel to Peirce's discussion of *abstract* and *concrete* aspects of truth.

On the other hand, Barwise 1989a, 1989c presents an analysis of propositional contents of utterances which includes for each proposition a parameter s for the concrete situation the proposition is about—thus determining a context for a descriptive-content asserting that some relation holds or doesn't hold of some given bunch of individuals. Such a proposition can be written in the form '$s \models \langle\!\langle R, \vec{a}; \delta \rangle\!\rangle$', where R is some relation, $\vec{a}$ is some bunch of individuals, and δ is a "polarity" ($+$ or $-$) corresponding to whether or not R holds of $\vec{a}$ in s.

And the connection with Peirce is clear: the situation parameter 's' yields a means for "confessing the inaccuracy and one-sidedness" of the propositional content of an utterance by explicitly indexing the part of the world in or to which it applies.

Barwise 1989a discusses a second sort of proposition, namely one of the form '$s \Vdash_{c} \langle\!\langle R, \vec{a}; \delta \rangle\!\rangle$', where the relation '$\Vdash$' applies when a situation

---

[18]Information that is supported by one situation, but not by a larger situation that in some sense contains the former, is referred to in situation theory as "non-persistent" information. For example, the descriptive content of an utterance of the sentence 'The sandwich was made with white bread' may be supported by a concrete situation limited to yesterday's lunch, but not by a situation that includes several other meals as well, where a use of the definite description 'the sandwich' is perhaps ambiguous or otherwise inappropriate. This may sound like the familiar idea that the truth-values of sentences may fluctuate in the absence of definite specifications of time, place, and so forth. The difference here is that the focus is not on sentences but on information and descriptive-contents of utterances; and the notion of non-persistence involves not truth per se but rather information that various situations may or may not support. Otherwise the intuition is basically a familiar one.

Besides definite descriptions, Perry 1986 discusses a number of examples of noun phrases ('only one person' (has false teeth), 'everyone' (was asleep during your talk)) whose uses easily permit failure of persistence. It is on this basis that Perry recommends modeling propositions as partial functions from ways *and* situations to truth-values, not just from ways. Concrete utterances are tied to (occur in, are about) concrete situations in such a manner that references to the latter play an essential role in constituting the propositions expressed by those utterances, precisely because we cannot assume they will not change their truth-values from one situation to the next.

"carries" the information that R holds of $\vec{a}$ (or not) relative to some set C of constraints.[19] The basic idea, as I understand it, is that the information that R holds (or not) of $\vec{a}$ may not be immediately given in s, though the information that *is* immediately given in s, coupled with some constraints linking that information with other possibilities, "compels" the information that R holds (or not) of $\vec{a}$. For example, cat hairs in the butter indicate (perhaps wrongly) that a cat was earlier present in the kitchen—the latter information is carried by the current situation in the kitchen, relative to certain general constraints linking the presence of cat hairs to the previous presence of a cat. Such a proposition will say something different about s than would the previous sort of proposition involving the "supports" relation '$\models$', but it nevertheless says something about s.

But now consider the following remarks by Peirce, where he discusses the structure of propositions:

(J)   [One] kind of reasoning which I employ in the analysis of assertion consists in deducing what the constitution of assertion must be from the theory, which I accept, that truth consists in the definitive compulsion of the investigating intelligence. ...

[An] assertion consists in the furnishing of evidence by the speaker to the listener that the speaker believes something, that is, finds a certain idea to be definitively compulsory on a given occasion. There ought, therefore, to be three parts in every assertion, a sign of the occasion of the compulsion, a sign of the enforced idea, and a sign evidential of the compulsion affecting the speaker in so far as he identifies himself with the scientific intelligence.

Because compulsion is essentially [here and now], the occasion of the compulsion can only be represented to the listener by compelling him to have experience of that same occasion. Hence it is requisite that there should be a kind of sign which shall act dynamically upon the hearer's attention and direct it to a special object or occasion. Such a sign I call an *Index*. It is true that there may, instead of a simple sign of this kind, be a precept describing how the listener is to act in order to gain the occasion of experience to which the assertion relates. But since this precept tells him how he is to act, and since acting and being acted upon are one and the same, and thus action is also [here and now], the precept must itself employ an Index or Indices. ... (c.1895, *CP* 2.333–336)

This is not the place to discuss this passage at length; but what is significant in this quote is the relatively sophisticated notion of propositions that it presents, which is at least roughly similar to what you find in situation theory, in definite contrast to the simple function-argument idea in the logic of Frege and Russell.

When Peirce says "there ought, therefore, to be three parts in every assertion," I take this to mean that the propositional content of a declarative utterance should be resolvable into three parts—not that all three will

[19] A different rendition of this idea of *constraints* is also discussed in Israel and Perry 1990.

be explicitly articulated but that each is present at least implicitly in the context of utterance.

There is a close correspondence to be seen (1) between Barwise's situation parameter s and Peirce's "index" of an "occasion of the compulsion"; (2) between Barwise's information (or descriptive-content) $\langle\!\langle R, \vec{a}; \delta \rangle\!\rangle$ and Peirce's "enforced idea"; and (3) between Barwise's set $\mathcal{C}$ of constraints and Peirce's "compulsion affecting the speaker in so far as he identifies himself with the scientific intelligence."

Though Peirce lacked a solid notion of situations, his idea of an "occasion of experience" comes close to serving the same purpose. And the situation-theoretic notion of constraints is apparently more general than Peirce's notion of "compulsion," the latter being tied somehow (and probably unnecessarily) to the functioning of "the scientific intelligence"; but the essential idea is the same in regard to the role of constraints in the constitution of propositions. There needs to be some reference to the constraints backing up an assertion in order to effect communication. Something, perhaps explicitly in the expression itself but otherwise present in the context of utterance, must indicate these constraints.

In this case, the requisite "confession of inaccuracy and one-sidedness" consists in relativizing propositional contents of utterances to a set of constraints as well as to some concrete situation.

Perspectival relativity. A related notion of "inaccuracy and one-sidedness" that might enter into the propositional contents of utterances consists in the relativization of information to what in some of the situation theoretic literature is called a *perspective*. Barwise (1989a, 1989c) and Jerry Seligman (1990) have initiated some preliminary discussions of such considerations.

The notion of perspectives is significant in situation theory insofar as the very same situation s can be viewed by an agent (or by different agents) from different perspectives, hence s may support different and perhaps conflicting kinds of information. In this regard, one does not capture all relevant "contextual" factors by relativizing propositions to situations. Barwise (1989c) appeals to this principle in his discussion of Kripke's puzzle about Pierre's conflicting beliefs about London.

Though the notion of perspectival relativity has not yet been developed extensively, it is related to the situation-theoretic notion of relativity to an individuation scheme.[20]

> [The notion of an individuation scheme] is an important notion in guiding our intuitions about the rest of [situation theory]. For it is only relative to one or another scheme of individuation that we have

---

[20]This is at least the case in Barwise's discussion of these notions, where the term 'related' could in this last sentence be replaced by the term 'identical'. This is not so clearly the case in Seligman's work.

situations being carved up into objects, properties, and relations. (Barwise 1989a, 260-1)

The idea that the information-content of an utterance is determined relative to an individuation scheme begins to accommodate the fact that situation theory is concerned with finite agents with limited information-handling capabilities. The objects, properties, and relations which a given agent is geared to—in terms of which it registers and otherwise handles information about the world—are a product of the unique evolutionary history of that agent's species as well as of that agent's individual development (physical, cultural, social, psychological) which give to it certain modes of behavior in the world. Due to differences in such capabilities, different agents will tend to cull different information from essentially the same part of the world. For example, we humans see flies in a very different light than frogs do. We "carve the world up differently" into objects, properties, and relations.

I want to argue that this fact that different agents bring to bear different schemes of individuation in their respective experiences is due to their operating in the world in terms of different investigation schemes. To explain this claim, I will briefly outline an operationalist account of perspectives and individuation schemes.

Investigation schemes. As before, let $\mathfrak{A}$ denote some fixed set of types of operations (modes of action, routines, programs, etc.). And let $\mathfrak{C}$ denote a fixed collection of "constraints" defined on $\mathfrak{A}$. The notion of constraints is left somewhat open to interpretation here, but think of $\mathfrak{C}$ as consisting of various kinds of conditional relations involving elements of $\mathfrak{A}$.

One possible line of development would be to use systems of equations to express constraints (equations in a broad sense of the term, perhaps to include things not unlike grammatical production rules). The basic idea would be to associate each operation-type A_i in $\mathfrak{A}$ with a variable ranging over A_i's respective set of possible outcomes (data-values, qualities, or some manner of registerable symbol), as opposed to ranging over individuals in some universe of discourse. Such equations could specify constraints on the outcomes of a given operation as a function of the outcomes of other operations. This seems straightforward especially if the outcomes are all numerical (or yes/no); otherwise it may not be the most general way to express constraints.

Such constraints are what make $\mathfrak{A}$ a "system" or "scheme" rather than just a "set" of operations. A pair $\langle \mathfrak{A}, \mathfrak{C} \rangle$ determines what I will call an *investigation scheme.*

One can proceed on this basis to construct a number of basic situation-theoretic notions. This construction will proceed more or less as pictured in Figure 2, where the arrows simply indicate the hierarchy of dependencies among various theoretic notions, though I will necessarily have to consider these things one at a time in linear sequence.

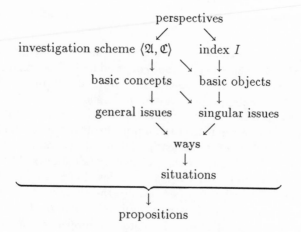

Figure 1 Perspectives, individuation schemes, etc.

Perspectives. The following construction of situation-theoretic notions is based on one other thing besides an investigation scheme, in line with Peirce's conjoining both abstract and concrete features of inquiry in his discussion of concepts and truth. Namely, we need to be able to think in terms of an investigation scheme being concretely employed somehow in the world. An investigation scheme by itself is hardly more than a frame of reference determining a "geometry" of possibilities, saying little about the world until it is actually oriented and employed in the world.

It would be pointless to launch at this point into a detached and detailed story about the structure of the world, independent of any investigation scheme. The following construction should apply as much to frogs and dogs as to humans, but it should be admitted up front that we do not have much of a grasp of what the world is like in its own right independent of ourselves, nor as it appears to beings other than beings like ourselves. All we need to say at this point is (a) that the world is out there (in here, out there, everywhere), (b) that we may think of it as being all of one piece and yet complexly variegated, and (c) that different agents, as particular parts of the world, come to grips with different aspects of it, depending on where they are in it and how they interact with the rest of it. The many things we make assertions about and otherwise take note of do not usually include pieces of the world in its bare independence but are rather the products and features of our actions in it. The present goal then is to give a general account of such features of agent/world interaction, whereas an account of what the world is like independent of the existence and activities of such finite agents could presumably be the concern of some other inquiry (such as *physics* perhaps, or metaphysics?).

So in talking about an investigation scheme being anchored and employed in the world, we need not presuppose an independent account of the world. We only have to be able to acknowledge *the fact of* an investigation scheme being thus anchored. As finite agents ourselves, such anchoring in the world is immediately given to us—we cannot *not* be positioned somewhere in the world as long as we are living agents. On the other hand, as theorists about finite agency, we should be able to refer to the actual positioning of agents—others as well as ourselves. A theory of propositions should include a parameter for such references. The symbol 'I' (together with subscripts or primes; and which is not presumed to have any connection so far as I can tell with the first person singular, but is simply a capitalization of the first letter of the word 'index') will be used here to *index* token occasions of such anchoring.

A triple $\langle \mathfrak{A}, \mathfrak{C}; I \rangle$ constitutes a *perspective* in or on the world. A perspective consists of a "frame of reference" $\langle \mathfrak{A}, \mathfrak{C} \rangle$, i.e., an investigation scheme, that is actually oriented in some place or manner I in the world. I is not unlike a token demonstrative act that directly refers to some "here and now" part of the world.

Basic concepts. We can next develop an account of properties and relations relative to a perspective. This account is intended to cover what Peirce calls "concepts," which make up the basic categories or kinds in terms of which one's experience is organized.

By itself, an investigation scheme generates a characteristic space $\mathfrak{K}$ of properties and relations, assuming of course an operationalist account of such things. That is, each property K relative to an investigation scheme $\langle \mathfrak{A}, \mathfrak{C} \rangle$ will correspond to a pair $\langle A, C \rangle$ where $A \subseteq \mathfrak{A}$ and $C \subseteq \mathfrak{C}{\restriction}A$. More generally, each n-ary relation K^n will correspond to a pair of the form $\langle A^n, C \rangle = \langle A_1 \times \cdots \times A_n, C \rangle$,[21] where each A_i is a subset of $\mathfrak{A}$ and where C will be a subset of the restriction of $\mathfrak{C}$ to $\bigcup_1^n A_i$.[22]

An agent will not necessarily be acquainted with every possible concept definable with respect to a given investigation scheme since, if for no other reason, the world is such that certain concepts are worth being familiar with while others are useless or unlikely possibilities. For instance, given a zoological investigation scheme for identifying animals, there are such concepts as of goats sporting lion's heads with peacock feathers sprouting out of their ears, but the world is such as to not encourage seriously bothering about whether there are things that fall under such concepts. In other

---

[21] One would want to distinguish this pair from a product of concepts, of the form $K_1 \times \cdots \times K_n = \langle A_1, C_1 \rangle \times \cdots \times \langle A_n, C_n \rangle$. For instance, not all binary relations are merely "products" of unary properties.

[22] This treatment of concepts is consistent with Dewey's 1938 treatment of *kinds*, and also with the operational treatment of object-types in the "empirical logic" of Randall and Foulis 1978, Foulis and Randall 1981, and Foulis, Piron, & Randall 1983. The latter works are aimed primarily at the foundations of quantum theory, but it is relevant to any formal framework that adopts "operations" as primitives.

words, the world encourages "attunement" to certain concepts (that is, to the respective constraints characteristic of certain concepts) and not others, where such attunement is contingent upon actually operating in the world and becoming habituated to those constraints which seem to best facilitate one's coming to workable terms with the world.

This analysis of concepts is to be distinguished from a "bundle theory" of names and nouns (as discussed, for instance, by Kripke 1972). By virtue of constraints $\mathcal{C}$, we would expect an object falling under a concept $K = \langle \mathcal{A}, \mathcal{C} \rangle$ to evidence certain qualitative traits, and not others, as results of performing $\mathcal{A}$-actions. This yields a sort of bundle theory of concepts— bundles not of linguistic "descriptions" per se but of qualitative features relative to specific feature-producing actions. It isn't clear how this takes care of the semantics of proper names, though it is claimed to easily handle common nouns, like 'lithium' or 'lemon' or other "hard words" that label more than just simple qualities of things. Kripke's major complaint against a bundle theory, of either names or common nouns, appears to be that it is not able to guarantee unique reference, to an individual or to some specific extension, respectively. But it is not clear why this should be required of a theory of concepts (kinds, etc.), in the sense that it may locate the problem of unique reference in the wrong place. In any case, we can read Kripke's lectures as an extended reductio against a naive and/or excessive extensionalism.

Basic objects. An investigation scheme that is anchored in the world will generate a dynamic domain, Θ, of basic objects, depending as much on the contingencies of the world at large as upon structural specifics of the investigation scheme. Simply put, as you act in the world (e.g., open your eyes and look, reach out and touch, etc.), under normal circumstances you will no doubt discern things falling under various concepts. Of course, you discern only such things as are discriminable by means of the investigation schemes you employ. Within any one perspective, the world will fall out into more or less distinct things, depending on how it is filtered through the given investigation scheme.

The basic objects in the world from a given perspective—the *this*es and *that*s that populate a given field of experience—are the distinguishable, singular, individual token things (not necessarily "discrete" nor "convex") that enjoy some kind of stability as distinct loci of qualitative features. Any such object θ will present itself by virtue of the execution of certain token actions $\mathcal{A}'$ that result in a stable (though perhaps dynamic) space Σ' of qualitative features. So for instance, that thing over there is now exhibiting to me various colors and sometimes tastes, due to specific actions now and then being performed, which are typical of things falling under the "apple" concept.

A singular object $\langle \mathcal{A}', \Sigma' \rangle$ "falls under" a given concept $K = \langle \mathcal{A}, \mathcal{C} \rangle$ just in case $\mathcal{A}' \subseteq \mathcal{A}$ (or is it the other way around?) and if its space

Σ' of qualitative features consists of allowable "solutions" of the set $\mathcal{C}$ of constraints characteristic of K.[23] This is easily generalizable to n-tuples of objects "standing in" various relations K^n. (See the discussion of "singular issues" below.)

Individuation schemes. With respect to a given perspective $\langle \mathfrak{A}, \mathfrak{C}; I \rangle$, we now have the basic building blocks for generating an individuation scheme: namely, a perhaps fleeting domain Θ of concrete ostensive objects and a space $\mathfrak{K}$ of properties and relations.

Is this construction incompatible with a realist view of properties, relations, and the world at large? The present treatment does not posit primary Lockean properties and relations as ontological primitives, as if they were attached to bare undisturbed objects out there in the world. Such an approach forces a problematic theoretical bifurcation between agent-independent *facts* out there in the world and *representations* of facts inside agents' heads. Without denying the reality of reality, the present approach instead treats properties and relations as *products* of the interactions going on between agents and environments. This is the basic idea behind specifying concepts in terms of modes of action and constraints.

This basic idea applies to token objects as well. Ostensive things are discriminable and otherwise function as objects in an agent's experience only as products of that agent's ongoing activities (e.g., perceptual activities). This is not to say that *reality* is created by such activities, but rather that reality carves up and falls out into distinguishable bits and pieces only as a result of such activities. How the world falls out into bits and pieces depends on the nature of these activities and the manner of their orchestration; that is, it depends on the perspective one takes in the world. Reality is reality, period; but "facts" are facts *from a perspective*.

This assumes a principle of realism which would guarantee that the world is going to fall out into various bits and pieces if acted on in the ways specific to a given perspective. This principle says that there will in fact be such a domain Θ of concrete *thises* and *thats* from a given perspective, whether or not we can specify ahead of time what Θ is going to consist of purely on the basis of knowing the details of the given investigation scheme. There is an element of contingency involved in the constitution of Θ, depending on the nature of the given investigation scheme, and on the part of the world in which the given investigation scheme is positioned, as well as

---

[23]Rather than the subset relation here, whichever way it might go, one could instead talk in more sophisticated terms of structure-preserving "morphisms" between the action/consequence pairs of token objects and those characteristic of various concepts. This could provide a treatment of metaphors ('The boxer had cauliflower ears and mush for brains') and pictures (of a "bird" named Tweety), as opposed to the stronger notion of actually being a token instantiation of a given concept—for instance, the thing on your plate actually being cauliflower, or your real pet parakeet being named after a cartoon character.

upon the actual courses that actions take in a given perspective. Certain actions performed now may preclude the *existence* of certain objects later; and conversely, certain objects may exist in a given instance only by virtue of certain token actions having been executed at some earlier point. We can only be sure that there *is* such a domain Θ even if we are not always able to enumerate it.

The upshot of this view of individuation schemes is that we need not have to be able to specify a domain of objects prior to or independent of a given perspective, as if a perspective must conform or otherwise comport with some independently given universe of discourse. Rather, each perspective *generates* a universe of discourse, contingent upon the peculiarities of the investigation scheme employed as well as upon the actual part of the world in which that investigation scheme is employed.

In any case, the concrete objects discernible from a given perspective as well as the properties and relations possible within that perspective are treated here as features of agent/world interactions, and only in that sense as features of the world. In questioning whether a given object falls under a given concept, there is no need to talk in terms of a "correspondence" between the world, on one hand, and representations of the world, on the other. Rather it is a matter of a "fitting" or not between the results of token actions going on (or that would have to go on) to experience that object and the action/constraint pair constitutive of the given concept to which the given agent is presumably attuned.

General issues. A fixed individuation scheme generates a domain $\mathfrak{I}$ of *issues*. Singular objects aside, there will be a subdomain of *general issues* having to do with relations among concepts. For instance, in an investigation scheme designed for investigating elementary particles in physics, there are numerous general issues such as whether or not electrons are leptons, whether or not they are hadrons, whether or not they are protons, whether or not they are meter-sticks, and so forth.

General issues can be represented in the form $\langle\!\langle R, K_1, K_2; \pm \rangle\!\rangle$, where K_1 and K_2 are concepts (properties, relations) and R is a (second-order) relation between K_1 and K_2. In languages like English, determiners such as 'all', 'some', 'many', 'the', and so forth, express such relations R.

The plus-or-minus indicates that issues can be settled positively or negatively, yes or no. In situation theory, a settled issue, one way or the other, is called an *infon*. A general infon—a settled general issue—constitutes a piece of general information about the world relative to (or as filtered through) the given perspective $\langle \mathfrak{A}, \mathfrak{C}; I \rangle$. Such information is said to be general in that, other than being relative to a token perspective, it does not directly refer to any particular object or another. That is, it involves various concepts constructible within the given perspective but is not specific to particular ostensive objects.

Singular issues. Given the field Θ of singular objects within a given perspective, there will also be a domain of *singular issues* having to do with concrete ostensive objects "falling under" this or that concept. Such issues can be represented in the form $\langle\!\langle K^n, \vec{\theta}; \pm\rangle\!\rangle$ where K^n is an n-ary concept and $\vec{\theta}$ is some n-tuple of concrete objects discriminable within the given perspective.

Settled singular issues, when settled, yield information that is referential. They are referential in the sense that they explicitly involve token objects in the world relative to a given perspective $\langle \mathfrak{A}, \mathfrak{C}; I \rangle$.

A singular object (from a given perspective) is going to be discerned by virtue of the registration of some sort of space Σ' of qualitative features, as the result of the ongoing execution of some number of operations $\mathcal{A}'$. Every such discerned object in the world from a given perspective will be associated with or otherwise determined by some such pair $\langle \mathcal{A}', \Sigma' \rangle$. On the other hand, a concept is determined by a pair $\langle \mathcal{A}, \mathcal{C} \rangle$, consisting of a set $\mathcal{A}$ of operations and a set $\mathcal{C}$ of constraints. We need to be able to explain how an object associated with the action/result pair $\langle \mathcal{A}', \Sigma' \rangle$ "falls under" a concept given by the action/constraint pair $\langle \mathcal{A}, \mathcal{C} \rangle$.

Intuitively, the idea is that the constraints in $\mathcal{C}$ will be such as to require that certain qualitative features will be registered given that other features are registered, determining therefore a space of possible feature-combinations and excluding others. The set of constraints $\mathcal{C}$ are meant to determine such a space of feature-bundles much in the mathematical sense that rules for functions determine sets of ordered pairs, or in the way that a system of equations determines a space of possible solutions. The idea then is that for the given object to fall under the given concept, the constraints in $\mathcal{C}$ should be applicable to the actions in $\mathcal{A}'$, and the space Σ' of registered features should be compatible with what the constraints $\mathcal{C}$ would allow.

The fact that such information about objects falling under various concepts is defeasible is a positive aspect of this account of properties and relations.

Ways. Following Perry 1986, ways can be thought of as coherent sets of settled issues, taken from the domain of issues $\mathfrak{I}$ fixed by a given perspective. It follows that *ways* are possible "ways that parts of the world can be," but only from a given perspective. Let $\mathfrak{W}$ denote the set of all abstractly possible ways parts of the world can be from a given perspective $\langle \mathfrak{A}, \mathfrak{C}; I \rangle$.

Definitions of "necessity" and "possibility" *relative to a perspective* suggest themselves here, in terms of ways rather than worlds. Namely, an infon is *necessary* (*possible*) relative to a given perspective just in case it is "made actual" by every (some) way $w \in \mathfrak{W}$. This distinction is useful—that is, the notion of relative necessity will not be vacuous—only if we impose stronger conditions on way-hood besides coherence. One would also want to impose some kind of closure conditions on ways (for instance: "deductive" closure, assuming some sort of infon logic; or closure by virtue of constraints in $\mathfrak{C}$.)

Situations. Ways are to situations what possible worlds are supposed to be to the actual world. Namely, *situations* are actual, concrete fields of agent/world interaction that fit the specifications of various ways, i.e., that *are* (of) various ways.

Situations, as fields of objects falling under various concepts, are not "absolute" parts of the world, any more than singular objects are; but they are concrete parts of the world as carved out by an agent's operating from or in terms of a given perspective. Situations may in this regard be discernible and hence "existent" from some perspectives but not others. For instance, various olfactory "hills and valleys" discernible to flies or dogs will be essentially "nonexistent" for humans (which is not to say they aren't real). Even if discernible from different perspectives, the very same part of the world may turn out to *be* different ways from different perspectives. We discern fields of flies and lily pads differently than frogs do, though it seems both we and frogs are able to experience the very same flies and lily pads.

At some point we will want to be able to talk about situations as "objects" in their own right. But this is not to say that we should collapse the distinction between situations and objects. Though both singular objects and situations may be the referents of demonstratives, situations do not always function as "objects" "falling under various concepts." They function primarily as concrete *contexts in which* objects are discerned as falling under various concepts.

Classifying objects in a given situation comes down to determining the concepts they fall under, whereas classifying situations qua situations comes down to determining the *ways* they are. This distinction is presumably a matter of perspective, literally, in the sense that it is a distinction that can always be made with respect to a fixed perspective but which, in particular instances, can be erased by an appropriate change of perspective.

Propositions. Is it then possible to reconcile Barwise's treatment of propositions in terms of the 'carries' relation with Perry's treatment, outlined earlier, in terms of partial functions from ways and situations to truth-values? It isn't clear on the surface how these two treatments are related; but the construction of situation-theoretic ideas sketched above, beginning with a notion of investigation schemes and ending with notions of ways and situations, could conceivably serve as a bridge between these two accounts.

These two accounts constitute two manners of juggling the same ideas— paralleling the difference between modeling possible worlds by sets of propositions (compare: modeling situations by the information they carry and/or support, i.e., by sets of infons) versus modeling propositions by sets of possible worlds (compare: modeling settled issues by sets of ways). Even if it isn't easy to reconcile the two accounts (I'm not claiming it can't be done but only that I am not in a position to do it here), the preceding discussion at least proposes a way to bridge the different theoretic machinery underlying the two accounts.

Holmesian propositions are resolvable into two things: (a) a *descriptive content*, consisting of some piece of information, and (b) the *contextual factors* relative to which that information is pertinent and factual, consisting in a concrete situation s plus a set C of constraints. An account of constraints has been presented above, as relations among modes of action, that is essential to an operationalist story about the constitution of investigation schemes as well as of individual concepts. This account accommodates intuitions motivating Barwise's treatment of propositions in the first place, though it is not apparently the same as Barwise's notion of constraints as (facts about) relations between situation-types. My only point here is that if we impose the present conception of constraints on Barwise's treatment of propositions, then we are able to generate an account of the various notions that are primitives in Perry's treatment of propositions.

Namely, the notion of a perspective, as presented above, is implicit in the idea of relativizing propositions to situations and a set of constraints. Specifying a set $\mathfrak{C}$ of constraints already presupposes some domain of constrained things, as it were, which in the present view would be some set $\mathfrak{A}$ of action-types. But this pair $\langle \mathfrak{A}, \mathfrak{C} \rangle$ determines an investigation scheme. And including a reference to a concrete situation s effectively indexes a concrete part of the world to which that investigation scheme is presumably applied. But $\mathfrak{A}$, $\mathfrak{C}$, and this concrete part of the world determine a perspective relative to which the descriptive content of the proposition is presumably factual. On this basis we are able to generate the concepts fundamental to Perry's discussion of propositions, namely, issues, answers, ways, and situations.

On the other hand, the treatment that starts with the idea of propositions as partial functions of ways and situations into truth-values assumes that ways be taken as primitives. Perhaps this is how to reconcile the present account of perspectives with Seligman's 1990 account in terms of sets T of situation-types (namely, ways, treated as primitives), but where his '$\Rightarrow$' and '$\perp$' relations could be understood not in the usual situation-theoretic sense of involvement and preclusion relations but rather as analogues or generalizations of accessibility and *in*accessibility relations in a possible-worlds framework (see Chellas 1980, Chapter 3, for a standard reference). Seligman does after all begin pretty much where the present treatment ends up, and ends up fairly close to where the present treatment begins.

But then there is the bothersome suspicion that an account of propositions as partial functions from ways and situations to truth-values may not work, for basically the same reason (with certain refinements) that the standard possible-worlds account doesn't work. Namely, the situation-theoretic treatment is a more fine-grained account of propositions, but it has a certain graininess nevertheless which may permit the conflation of distinct propositions because they happen to be true in or of exactly the same ways and situations. Admittedly, this is just a suspicion, in the absence of concrete examples; but notice for instance that infons that are "necessary" relative to a given perspective are "made factual" by exactly the same ways, namely all the ways there are, relative to that perspective. If they are moreover supported by the very same situations (and I can't see why that couldn't be the case), then we are back in the soup, having failed to satisfactorily individuate propositions by sets of ways and situations.

Notice though that Perry is not necessarily advocating this latter account of propositions so much as proposing that situation theory is able to accommodate this kind of account if one insists on pursuing it. Situation theory has all the machinery a possible-worlds enthusiast requires, and lots more as well. But he needn't claim that this extensionalist-inspired account is a correct account of propositions, even if it is a fascinating formal exercise. Meanwhile, Barwise's account of propositions more readily represents the "innocent" approach to semantics one is inclined to associate with situation theory.

Truth. We can glance back at Peirce's definition of truth to see how it is consistent with the development of situation-theoretic ideas outlined above. Truth is something attributable not to infons, concepts, objects, etc., but to propositions. The concern now is to be sure that the operationalist conception of propositions given above, which is more detailed than what Peirce was able to formulate, is consistent with Peirce's operationalist conception of the *truth* of propositions.

Following Barwise fairly closely but slightly amending his account of Holmesian propositions, let σ denote an infon (either general or singular) relative to a given perspective $\langle \mathfrak{A}, \mathfrak{C}; I \rangle$. Then a proposition will have the form '$s \Vdash_{\langle \mathfrak{A}, \mathfrak{C} \rangle} \sigma$' (or for greater typographical ease, '$\langle \mathfrak{A}, \mathfrak{C}; I_s \rangle \Vdash \sigma$'), where the 'carries' relation is relativized not just to a situation and a set of constraints but to a perspective indexed by a given situation. The perspective determines or reflects the context of some declarative utterance. Such references to a perspective in the propositional content of a declarative utterance is of course supposed to serve as the "confession of inaccuracy and one-sidedness" that Peirce requires of propositions.

So what does it mean to say that such a proposition is true? The situation s is a concrete and usually a complex part of the world. The information σ will be something to the effect that some array of n objects do or don't fall under a certain n-ary concept, for some n, or that some array of concepts are or aren't related in some fashion. Such information has to be confirmable or refutable by means of orchestrating the $\mathfrak{A}$-operations definitive of the given perspective.

Practically speaking, one will be interested in confirmations and refutations of such information in the course of actually making one's way through the world. But we can step back and ask about the truth of the proposition independent of actual confirmations and refutations. If a proposition is formulatable relative to a given perspective $\langle \mathfrak{A}, \mathfrak{C}, I \rangle$, then it is at least *ideally* testable by means of some one or more courses of action in $\mathfrak{A}^{\#}$.[24] If it were not refuted by any such course of action, and in fact confirmed by at least one, then the proposition is true. If it is refuted and not confirmed (ideally speaking), then it is false; and if it is both confirmed and refuted (by different ideal courses of action, presumably), then it indicates perhaps the use of a faulty conceptual scheme but otherwise is not true.

Notice that in this view it is not truth that is relative to a perspective but rather the propositional contents of utterances that are. Truth is an absolute notion, whereas propositional contents are relativized to perspectives on parts of the world.

The point is that a given proposition is true or not depending on how it stacks up against the ideal limit of inquiry relative to the perspective that is "confessed" in its formulation. In the absence of specifying such a perspective, no definite means for making sense of and testing the proposition (even if only ideally) would be possible, in which case nothing could be said about its truth or falsity. An utterance doesn't express a meaningful proposition if there is no indication of what would count as "truth-conditions" for that proposition, which is what a perspective supplies. One could just as well say that one doesn't *have* a proposition unless such relativity to a perspective is given.

Concluding remarks. The foregoing discussion is meant to show that a study of Peirce's writings could benefit by viewing them in light of ongoing developments in situation theory. Now eighty or more years after Peirce was working, situation theory may help to remedy problems inherent in Peirce's often obscure terminology. Peirce anticipated in his own way some of the concerns of situation theory (or rather, he happened to be working before it went out of fashion to wrestle with such concerns), to the point that using situation-theoretic terminology in place of Peirce's can help to clarify what he was trying to say. In particular, Peirce's definition of truth given in (B), in light of the previous discussion, could be re-worded as follows:

(B′) A proposition is true just in case it accords with results that would be obtained be deploying in the world some given investigation scheme with ideal proficiency; and a necessary part of the constitution of that proposition, if true, is its expressed reference to the investigation scheme that would be so deployed, and to the part of the world in which it would be deployed.

---

[24] This is essentially Putnam's notion of "ideal justifiability" (1983).

This is a rather general and perhaps unwieldy attempt at translating Peirce's definition into more familiar terms, but I think it does salvage the basic intuitions behind Peirce's views, including his operationalist orientation. In place of talking about "all who investigate," the reference here to "ideal proficiency" is meant to accommodate even investigation scenarios that are practically unlikely but nevertheless abstractly possible. Relativizing propositional contents of utterances to actual parts of the world (namely, situations) as well as to investigation schemes summarizes the discussion above of the "confession of partiality" which is necessary to their being true.

As for situation theory in its own right, is there any reason to adopt an operationalist viewpoint? Why make the theory more complicated by throwing all this extra pragmatist business about actions and consequences into the picture?

For one thing, an operationalist viewpoint constitutes one approach to developing a theory of individuation schemes, the need for which is recognized in situation theory. As reflected in his definition of truth, Peirce was essentially working with a different set of theoretical primitives than the usual "individuals" and "properties and relations." From an operationalist viewpoint, one should nevertheless be able to give a constructive account of properties and relations in terms of directly accessible actions and their directly accessible consequences, as outlined above.

In contrast with a Russellian metaphysics that simply posits a world full of objects having properties and standing in relations, a pragmatist wants to supply an account of properties and relations—in the individuation scheme of some given community of agents—in terms of agents' orientation to future results of ongoing activities as well as to past and present conditions of those activities. This allows for a refinement of the notion of individuation schemes by thinking of agents not primarily in terms of the properties and relations they are sensitive to but rather in terms of the activities of which they are capable and which are *the means* by which they register properties and relations of things. The notion of individuation schemes remains intact as a working notion, but it would be a derived notion based on the more fundamental ideas of actions and their immediate consequences.

References

Almeder, R. 1975. Fallibilism and the Ultimate Irreversible Opinion. In *American Philosophical Quarterly, Monograph No. 9: Studies in Epistemology*, 33–54. Oxford: Basil Blackwell.

Barwise, J. 1989a. Notes on Branch Points in Situation Theory. In *The Situation in Logic*, 255–276. CSLI Lecture Notes Number 17. Stanford: CSLI Publications.

Barwise, J. 1989b. Situations and Small Worlds. In *The Situation in Logic*, 79–92. CSLI Lecture Notes Number 17. Stanford: CSLI Publications.

Barwise, J. 1989c. Situations, Facts, and True Propositions. In *The Situation in Logic*, 221–54. CSLI Lecture Notes Number 17. Stanford: CSLI Publications.

Barwise, J., and J. Etchemendy. 1989. Model-Theoretic Semantics. In *Foundations of Cognitive Science*, ed. M. I. Posner, 207–43. Cambridge, MA: MIT Press.

Barwise, J., and J. Etchemendy. 1990. Information, Infons, and Inference. In Cooper et al. 1990.

Burke, T. 1990. Dewey on Defeasibility. In Cooper et al. 1990.

Burke, T. 1991. *Propositions and Judgments in Dewey's Logic*. PhD thesis, Stanford University.

Chellas, B. F. 1980. *Modal Logic: An Introduction*. Cambridge: Cambridge University Press.

Cooper, R., K. Mukai, and J. Perry (ed.). 1990. *Situation Theory and Its Applications*, vol. 1. CSLI Lecture Notes Number 22. Stanford: CSLI Publications.

Dewey, J. 1916. The Pragmatism of Peirce. *Journal of Philosophy, Psychology, and Scientific Methods* 13:709–15. Reprinted in J. A. Boydston, Ed., *John Dewey: The Middle Works, 1899–1924*, Vol. 10, 71–8 (Southern Illinois University Press, Carbondale, 1980).

Dewey, J. 1938. *Logic: The Theory of Inquiry*. New York: Henry Holt and Company.

Foulis, D., C. Piron, and C. Randall. 1983. Realism, Operationalism, and Quantum Mechanics. *Foundations of Physics* 13(8):813–41.

Foulis, D. J., and C. H. Randall. 1981. Empirical Logic and Tensor Products. In *Interpretations and Foundations of Quantum Theories*, ed. H. Neumann, 9–20. Mannaheim: Bibliographisches Institüt.

Israel, D., and J. Perry. 1990. What is Information? In *Information, Language, and Cognition*. Vancouver Studies in Cognitive Science, Volume 1, ed. P. P. Hanson, 1–19. Vancouver: University of British Columbia Press. Also available as Report No. CSLI-91-145, CSLI Publications, Stanford.

Kaplan, D. 1989. Demonstratives: An Essay on the Semantics, Logic, Metaphysics, and Epistemology of Demonstratives and Other Indexicals. In *Themes from Kaplan*, ed. J. Almog, J. Perry, and H. Wettstein, 481–614. New York: Oxford University Press.

Kripke, S. A. 1972. *Naming and Necessity*. Cambridge, MA: Harvard University Press.

Peirce, C. S. 1931–1958. *Collected Papers of Charles Sanders Peirce*. Cambridge, MA: Harvard University Press. Vols. 1–6 ed. C. Hartshorne and P. Weiss; vols. 7–8 ed. A. W. Burks.

Perry, J. 1986. From Worlds to Situations. *Journal of Philosophical Logic* 15:83–107. Also Report Number CSLI-87-73, CSLI Publications, Stanford.

Perry, J. 1989. Possible Worlds and Subject Matter. In *Possible Worlds in Humanities, Arts and Sciences*, ed. S. Allén, 124–37. Berlin: Walter de Gruyter.

Putnam, H. 1983. *Realism and Reason: Philosophical Papers, Volume 3*. Cambridge: Cambridge University Press.

Randall, C. H., and D. J. Foulis. 1978. The Operational Approach to Quantum Mechanics. In *Physical Theory as Logico-Operational Structure*, ed. C. A. Hooker, 167–201. Dordrecht: Reidel.

Seligman, J. 1990. Perspectives in Situation Theory. In Cooper et al. 1990.

Thayer, H. S. 1980. Peirce on Truth. In *Two Centuries of Philosophy in America*, ed. P. Caws, 63–76. Totowa, NJ: Rowman and Littlefield.

Vickers, S. 1989. *Topology via Logic*. Cambridge Tracts in Theoretical Computer Science 5. Cambridge: Cambridge University Press.

7

Information and Architecture

DAVID ISRAEL AND JOHN PERRY

1   Incremental and Reflexive Information

Elwood lies on a hospital bed, a thermometer—we'll call it **t**—in his mouth. Bad news about Elwood:

(1)   The fact that the mercury in **t** is above 98.6 carries the information that Elwood has a fever.

The fact referred to we call the *signal* or *indicating fact*. The thermometer is the *carrier* of the signal, the property of containing mercury that has risen past 98.6 is the *indicating property*. The proposition that Elwood has a fever is the *incremental informational content* of the signal. The property of having a fever is the *indicated property*; Elwood is the *subject matter* of the proposition that is the content, and derivatively, he is the subject matter of the signal. A signal has *incremental* content, given a *connecting fact* and relative to a *constraint*.[1] In this case, the connecting fact is that the thermometer is in Elwood's mouth, the *connecting relation* is that of one thing being in the mouth of another, and the constraint C_1 is:

(C_1)   Given that a thermometer is in a person's mouth, if the mercury goes above 98.6, that person has a fever.

Informational content is only information when the constraints and connecting facts are factual. If a signal carries the information that P, then P is true. But a signal can have the *informational* content that P relative to a constraint and a connecting fact, even though P is not true. This happens when the constraint or connecting "fact" or both are not factual. We shall

The research reported in this paper has been made possible by a gift from the System Development Foundation.

[1]This paper is a continuation of Israel and Perry 1990 and builds on both the theory and the terminology of that earlier work. However, our treatment of reflexive content is different.

often use "information" more casually than this suggests, however, noting the distinction only when it is relevant to a point we are making.

Incremental information contrasts with various sorts of *reflexive information*, which are relative to constraints, but not connecting facts. Suppose that in the physician's office thermometers are always shaken down after they are used and stored in a cool place until their next use. Then this somewhat stronger constraint is in force:

(C_2) If the mercury in a thermometer goes above 98.6, there is a person whose mouth it has been in, and that person has a fever.

Relative to C_2, setting the connecting fact to one side, our signal carries the *pure information*:

(2) The fact that the mercury in t is above 98.6 carries the information that there is a person whose mouth it has been in, and that person has a fever.

The information content of (2) quantifies over people and has the thermometer itself as a constituent; in these ways it differs from the information content of (1), which has Elwood as a constituent and does not involve any thermometers. It is the presence of the thermometer itself, the carrier of the information, in the information content that leads us to call the content *reflexive*. If we consider just our original constraint (C_1), setting the connecting fact aside, we have what we call the *conditional* information, which is similarly reflexive.

(3) The fact that the mercury in t is above 98.6 indicates that if there is a person in whose mouth it has been, that person has a fever.

In many cases, the most useful way to express reflexive information will be in the form of a statement in which the subject matter is identified by a description in terms of the carrier of the signal, thus reformulating (2) as :

(4) The fact that the mercury in t is above 98.6 indicates that the person in whose mouth t was, has a fever.[2]

In Israel and Perry 1990, we developed the notions of pure and incremental information, and stressed the importance of both in fully understanding the way we handle information. (See also Perry 1988, 1990). In this paper we will use the term *signal structure* for a signal together with a constraint, connecting facts, and the contents generated thereby. We introduce the notion of an *information system* for a system of signal structures, in which relations are established among the carriers of the signals in order to induce or reflect relations among the contents. We call these relations *architectural*. To analyze information systems, we need a further type of informational content, which we call *architectural content*. We shall consider

---

[2] (4) can also be understood as a reformulation of (3), with an implicit "if there is one", after the definite description.

three types of informational structures: *coincident architectures, combinative architectures* and *flow architectures*. We then show how the notion of architectural content is important to the analysis of information-using devices.

2 Coincident Architectures

Consider the familiar apparatus doctors use to check height and weight. Elwood stands on the platform of the scale; weights are moved on the weight bar and the height bar is lowered; we learn that Elwood needs to grow taller or lose weight. Given the concepts of Israel and Perry 1990, we can distinguish the reflexive and incremental contents:

(5)   The fact that the weights on the weight bar are at 100 and at 80 carries the information that the person affecting the weight bar weighs 180 pounds.

(6)   The fact that the weights on the weight bar are at 100 and at 80 carries the information that Elwood weighs 180 pounds.

(7)   The fact that the height bar is at the 5 foot mark carries the information that the person whose head it contacts is 5 feet tall.

(8)   The fact that the height bar is at the 5 foot mark carries the information that Elwood is 5 feet tall.

There is an intermediate kind of information (5)–(8) don't capture. The weight bar and the height bar are connected to each other independently of their connection to Elwood, in a way that assures that they will generate information about the same person. In this case, we can distinguish the following informational contents that are available to the physician, when he considers the two signals—that the weights are on 100 and 80, and that the height bar is at the 5 foot mark.

(9)   The fact that the height bar is at the 5 foot mark carries the information that the person affecting the weight bar is 5 feet tall.

(10)   The fact that the weights on the weight bar are at 100 and at 80 carries the information that the person whose head the height bar contacts weighs 180 pounds.

(5) and (7) are purely reflexive. The subject is identified only via the carrier of the signal. (9) and (10) are similar in that the subject is identified via the carrier of a signal. As between (9) and (7), however, the *mode of presentation* has been changed. It is not the relation to the height bar (the carrier of the signal) that is used to identify the subject matter, but the relation to the weight bar.

(9) and (10) are also similar to (6) and (8), in that the information is carried only relative to connecting facts. With (9) and (10) a new sort of connecting fact and a new sort of constraint is involved. The fact is just that the height bar and the weight bar are parts of an apparatus of

this sort. We shall call such facts *architectural connecting facts*, and the relations involved in them *architectural relations*. The weight bar is the *architecturally connected carrier* in (9); it is the height bar in (10). The constraint reflects the architecture of the apparatus and facts about the shapes and sizes of humans: if a weight bar and height bar are connected that way, the person whose head contacts the height bar is the person who is affecting the weight bar. We call the sort of constraint involved in (9) and (10) an *architectural constraint* and the relation between subject matters (in our case, identity), the *architecturally grounded relation*. Information relative to architectural connections and constraints, we call *architectural*.

Stereo vision provides another example of architectural content. There is a stable architectural relationship between the two eyes of a single person—the two eyes, that is, whose states directly affect a single brain. They are fixed in the head in such a way that in normal conditions the regions of space towards which they are directed and about which they carry information will overlap to a great degree.[3] That is, the region that the left retina carries information about will stand in a certain relationship to the region the right retina carries information about, because the eyes stand in a certain relationship. Imagine you are looking at a middle-sized object, say another person, standing in front of and not too far from you. The state of the retina of each eye will not only carry reflexive information about the person reflecting light onto *it*, but also architectural information about the person reflecting light onto the retina of the other eye in the same head. Because of this stable architectural relationship, one does not normally need to *keep track* of the relations between the things one sees with one eye and the things one sees with the other.

Contrast this with the case of two television cameras feeding information into the production booth at a football game. The architectural connection between the cameras is much looser. One camera may be pointing at the quarterback, while another points at the safety on the opposing team. Sometimes the cameras will feed information about a single player from different perspectives to the production booth. The director will have to be keeping track of the relation of the cameras to one another to realize when this is happening, however.[4] The director is still exploiting architectural information. She is able to assume that the cameras are providing information about players in the same game. The director of the "scores and highlights" show which comes on during commercials cannot even make this assumption, since signals are being fed from games all around the country.

We will discuss information structures in terms of four questions about how the architectures organize the informational content:

---

[3]A complete account of stereo vision would also be seen to involve a complex pattern of information flow.

[4]This isn't quite right, because the director may take advantage of converging information, in the sense explained below.

(i) What are the architectural relations—that is, how are the carriers related?

(ii) What is the architectural constraint?

(iii) What relationship among the contents is determined by this architecture? Is this relationship induced or reflected by the architecture?

(iv) How are the constraints and connecting facts in the signal structures related to one another and to the architectural constraints and connections?

Let's consider our example in terms of these four questions.

(i) The doctor's apparatus is constructed so that the height bar is directly above the platform, force upon which affects the weight bar.

(ii) This relation, in virtue of facts about the shapes and sizes of human beings, guarantees that the person whose head is in contact with the height bar is the very one whose feet are on the platform, and hence the one whose weight is registered by the position of the weights on the weight bar.

(iii) Thus, the subject matter of the two signal structures is the same; this is induced by the architecture, not merely reflected by it.

(iv) In this case, the original constraints are independent of one another, and of the architectural constraint. If the weight bar is broken, the apparatus can still be used to measure height, and vice versa.

This is the pattern we take to be characteristic of coincident architectures, with one exception. In our case, the relation between subject matters induced by the architecture is identity. Coincident architectures allow for relations other than identity. Thus in the case of stereo vision, the relevant relation between regions of space is that they (significantly) overlap. To take a simpler example, the fact that a given fuel gauge and temperature gauge are mounted in the same dashboard carries the information that the fuel tank and cooling system about which the gauges carry information are in the same car.

3 Combinative Architectures

In *combinative architectures*, the architectural relations reflect, rather than induce, the relations among contents. We begin by contrasting combinative architectures with two sorts of case in which the relations between the carriers of signals don't carry information.

(11) An x-ray has been taken of Elwood's chest. It exhibits property ϕ, which clearly shows that the person x-rayed had a cracked rib, but there is no indication of whom—there is no label on the x-ray. An unlabelled printout of Elwood's blood test lies next to the x-ray on the physician's desk. There is no way for the physician to tell that they carry information about the same patient.

This pair of carriers sitting beside each other on the desk is what we might call a (mere) pile. There is, of course, a relation between the x-ray sheet and the printout—they are on the same desk—but that fact does not itself indicate anything. That is, within the information-using system (the physician, the materials on her desk, the standard operating procedures in the office), there is no relevant constraint that generates the pertinent information from the relation between the carriers. Although the signals have the same subject matter, this is in no way determined (either reflected or induced) by the relation between the two carriers.

(12)   On the physician's desk are two x-rays, the one mentioned in (11) and another taken of Elwood a short time later, showing a recently mended rib. Again, there is nothing in the fact that the x-rays are both on the desk that indicates that they have the same subject matter. But in this case the physician can tell, by careful examination, that they are earlier and later x-rays of the same person.

In (12), unlike (11), there is something in the system of signals to indicate identity of subject matter: an *internal* indication of an external identity. But the internal indication is not architectural. We call this type of case one of *convergence*.

(13)   This is example (11) but with an important change. The printout has been stapled to the x-ray. In the physician's office the practice is to staple together only documents that concern the same patient.

This is an example of a combinative information system, in particular of what we call a *file*. As in (12), we have an internal indication of an external identity In the case of (13), however, the indication is architectural. A relationship has been established between the carriers that indicates that the signals have the same subject matter.[5]

In both files and convergences, it seems, the fact that a certain relation holds between two or more signals carries the information that they have the same subject matter. But in the case of a file, this will be a relation between the carriers; in the case of convergence, a relation between the indicating properties. This difference reflects a difference in the constraints relating signals that generate the relevant information. In the case of a convergence, the constraint meshes with the constraints involved in the original signal structures. In (12), these original constraints generated the information that the rib the first signal was of was cracked in a certain way, and that the rib the second signal was of had recently mended from a crack of that sort. There is then a third constraint, a nonarchitectural constraint, that generates the information that the ribs are the same. It is about ribs in both its antecedent and consequent: a rib that looks like this

---

[5]Of course, we can also say that a new carrier has been generated: a printout and an x-ray stapled together. See below.

when broken, and one that looks like that when recently mended, are the same rib. In (13), the constraint that generates the information that the signals are of the same person does not mesh with the original constraints. Its antecedent is about carriers being stapled together, and its consequent is to the effect that the contents of the signals involving those carriers have the same subject matter.

Let us look at one more case of a combinative architecture.

(14)   The x-ray and the printout have been put into a manila file-folder labeled "Elwood Fritchey". The physician's staff are very careful so that only data about the right person gets into such a file-folder.

We call this a *labeled file*. We can use the notion of architectural information to get at the usefulness of such file-folders.

That the file-folder contains the carriers it does is itself a signal that combines with the signals provided by the carriers in it. Such labeled files are likely to have many uses in our doctor's office, but let's simplify matters by supposing that the sort of label in question is reserved for patients. The relevant constraint is:

$(\mathcal{C}_{label})$ If a file-folder f is labeled α, there is a patient to whom α refers, and all of the signals provided by the carriers in f have that patient as subject-matter.

Relative to $\mathcal{C}_{label}$ and the fact that the x-ray is in a file-folder f, we have:

(15)   The fact that the x-ray exhibits ϕ indicates that the patient to whom the label of f refers had a cracked rib.

The value of a labeled file is that it provides a useful mode of presentation of the subject matter of the information in the file. If the nurse were just to find the x-ray by itself, he will know that it is of the person who is x-rayed, but this knowledge probably won't be of much use to him by itself. Unless the x-ray has just been taken, he won't know how to contact that person, or how to refer to him in a way that the doctor will find useful—or how to send him the bill. If he finds the x-ray in the file, he will get the architectural information that the patient the label refers to had a cracked rib. The mode of presentation provided by the label—perhaps the name "Elwood Fritchey" or a patient I.D. number that is connected in the office records with this name—will be useful. It will be connected in various ways to addresses, phone numbers and other modes of interaction with Elwood.

We now turn to our four questions.

(i)   In (13), the carriers are related by being stapled together; in (14), they are put into the same (labeled) file-folder.

(ii) In (13), the architectural constraint is that if documents are stapled together, then the relevant signals share a subject matter; in (14) it is $\mathcal{C}_{label}$.

(iii) In both cases, the relation among contents determined by the architecture is identity, and in both this relationship is reflected in the architecture, not induced. The apparatus involved in generating and carrying x-ray signals and that involved in generating and carrying blood-test signals are not related in such a way that the person who is the subject matter of signals generated and carried by the first is the same as that involved in the second. In combinative architectures, some relation must be established between the carriers that reflects the fact that a relation of interest holds among the subject matters of the signals.

(iv) Here, too, the constraints involved in the signal structures can be completely independent of one another, and of the architectural constraint.

4 Flow Architectures

Coincident and combinative architectures yield *architecturally coordinated* information; because of the architectural relations, the signals involved carry information about the same subject matter or, more generally, subject matters with a fixed relationship. We now consider information flow, which involves *architecturally mediated* information, in which signals contain information about a certain subject matter in virtue of carrying information about other signals to which they are architecturally connected.

In *Knowledge and the Flow of Information* (1981, p. 57), Fred Dretske states the following basic principle of the flow of information:

Xerox principle: If A carries the information that B, and B carries the information that C, then A carries the information that C.

Dretske says that this is "a regulative principle, something inherent in and essential to the ordinary idea of information, something that any *theory* of information should preserve." We'll try to explain why our theory preserves the Xerox principle, and say what we think this regulative principle regulates.

One of Dretske's examples of the flow of information involves a radio:

> The acoustic waves emanating from a radio speaker carry information about what is happening in the broadcasting studio *because* they carry accurate information about what is happening in the audio circuit of the receiver; these events in turn carry information about the modulation of the electromagnetic signal arriving at the antenna; and the latter carries information about the manner in which the microphone diaphragm (in the broadcasting studio) is vibrating. The microphone's behavior, in turn, carries information about what the announcer is saying. This whole chain of events constitutes a communication system, a system whose output carries

> information about its input, because of iterated applications of the
> Xerox principle. (Dretske 1981, p. 58)

This is an example of an information system. We'll make the example more concrete by supposing it is John Madden who is sitting in the sportscasters' booth, speaking into the microphone, announcing a 49ers game. We can take the first signal to be the pattern of sound waves that fill the booth. These carry information about what the occupant of the booth is saying; in our example the occupant is Madden, and they carry the incremental information that he said, "The 49ers score." The second signal is the pattern of vibration of the microphone's diaphragm; the architectural fact is that this is the microphone in the booth. The third signal is the modulation of the electromagnetic signal arriving at the antenna; this is of course the antenna that is connected by the circuitry to the microphone in the broadcasting booth. The next signal is what is happening in the audio circuit of the receiver. This receiver is within the range of the signal from the antenna, and is tuned to the relevant frequency. Finally, there are the waves emanating from the speaker of that radio. Of course, this system could be broken up into signals and connections in a variety of different ways, and this way of doing it is relatively crude.

According to Dretske, in a case of flow of information some information is to be carried along the signals, so that the last signal carries the information of interest that was carried by the first signal. We'll call that the *target* information. In this example the target information is the incremental information that Madden said, "The 49ers score." Each signal in the system, from the sound waves in the booth, to vibrations of the microphone, to the sound waves emanating from the speakers, carries this information, which is incremental information about Madden. But this is not the *only* information carried by the signals.

In the first place, it's not just the target information that flows. The reflexive information that the occupant of the booth said, "The 49ers score" also flows. In designing an information flow architecture, one would naturally focus on this sort of reflexive information.

More germane to the present point, the later signals also each carry architectural information about the earlier ones. As Dretske points out, it is only because they do this that they carry any information about Madden's activities.

The second signal in our chain is the fact that the diaphragm in the microphone is vibrating in a certain way. The first link in the architecture is the fact that the microphone is located in the booth. The architectural constraint associated with this fact is that the vibrations of the diaphragm of the microphone are correlated with a certain type of sound-wave in the booth. The second signal carries information about the first signal, in virtue of this architectural connection and constraint.

The second signal also carries the target information about Madden. It does so in virtue of the architectural connections and constraints just mentioned, together with the connections and constraints associated with the first signal. So, considering the first two signals, and using w for the sound wave, d for the diaphragm, and Φ_i for the indicating property involved in signal i, we have the following constraints, connecting facts, and contents.

First, the connecting fact and constraint involved in the first signal structure:

($\mathcal{C}_1$)   Given that an acoustic wave is produced by the vocal activities of an occupant of the booth, the wave will be of type Φ_1 only if the announcer said, "The 49ers score."

(C$_1$)   Madden is occupying the booth and producing acoustic wave w.

The incremental content of the first signal relative to $\mathcal{C}_1$, given C$_1$ is that Madden said, "The 49ers score." Next, the architectural fact and constraint that are relevant to the second signal:

($\mathcal{C}_2$)   If a diaphragm of a microphone is being bombarded by an acoustic wave, the diaphragm will exhibit Φ_2 only if the wave is of type Φ_1.

(C$_2$)   Acoustic wave w is bombarding d.

The architectural content of the second signal, relative to $\mathcal{C}_2$ and given C$_2$, is that the wave w is of type Φ_1.

Next, we have the combined constraints and connecting facts:

($\mathcal{C}_{1-2}$)   If the diaphragm of a microphone is vibrating because it is being bombarded by acoustic waves and the acoustic waves are produced by an announcer's vocal activities, the vibrations will be of type Φ_2 only if the announcer said, "The 49ers score."

(C$_{1-2}$)   Madden is in the booth and is producing w and w is bombarding d.

The incremental information content of the second signal, relative to $\mathcal{C}_{1-2}$ and given C$_{1-2}$, is just the same as the incremental content of the first signal, that Madden said, "The 49ers score."

Each signal further along the flow architecture repeats the same pattern; it carries architectural information about the previous signals, and, in virtue of that, it also carries the target information about Madden.

Let's turn to our four questions.

(i)-(ii)   The architectural connections in a case of information flow are causal connections, whereby the indicating properties of the earlier signals causally determine those of the later ones. In virtue of the architectural facts and constraints, the later signals carry information about the earlier ones.

(iii)   It is in virtue of this that the later signals can carry the same incremental information content as the first. The architecture does not reflect the relation between contents that the signals would have independent of it, but induces the identity among contents.

(iv) The constraints and connecting facts for the later signals are combinations of the connecting facts and constraints of the earlier signals, together with the architectural constraints relating the types of the earlier signals and architectural connections relating the carriers of those signals.

The hallmark of information flow systems, then, is that the relevant incremental information carried by the later signals in the system depends on the architectural information they carry about earlier signals. The state of the antenna carries information about Madden only because it carries information about the microphone. This wasn't the case with coincident and combinative systems.

Let's return to the Xerox principle. Although Dretske distinguishes the signal from the information it carries, he conflates them in his statement of the principle. Given our terminology, it should be stated as follows:

If s carries the information that b is F, and the fact that b is F carries the information that Q, then s carries the information that Q.

Given the relativity of information content to constraints and connecting facts, this principle is really a statement to the following effect:

If (i) there are architectural constraints C and architectural connections C such that s carries the architectural information that b is F, relative to C given C, and (ii) there are constraints C' and connecting facts C' such that the fact that b is F carries the information that Q relative to C' and C',

then there are constraints C'' and connecting facts C'' such that s carries the information that Q relative to C'' given C''.

On our theory, this conditional is true. The constraints and connecting facts called for in the consequent are simply the combinations of the constraints and connecting facts provided by the antecedent, as in the example above.[6]

We can now see one sense in which the Xerox principle is regulative. It regulates the way information flow architectures are constructed. The point of such systems is to insure that the signals at the terminus of the architecture will contain incremental information about objects connected

---

[6] We need to be careful here, though. We have stated the Xerox principle in terms of information, not informational content. We assume that reality is coherent, so that there are combined facts and constraints of the sort we relied on in the example. Attributions of informational content, however, are made relative to possible facts and constraints; the principle will only hold if the facts and constraints relevant to the antecedent and consequent don't interfere with one another.

to the initial signals. The way to get this relationship between the incremental contents is to design the architecture so that each signal carries the architectural information about the indicating properties of earlier signals.

5 Using Information

The architectures of information-using devices rely on both coordinated and flow architectures.

Consider a simple mousetrap. A small lever is attached to a rod which engages a cam on a spring, which is attached to a stiff wire blade. The rod prevents the spring from releasing. When the lever moves, the rod slips, the spring is released and the blade snaps down on the base of the trap.

This is a simple device that converts information into action. Cheese is placed on the lever. When a mouse eats the cheese, the lever moves, the rod slips, the spring is released and the mouse is crushed.

To analyze this, we need an additional concept, the *success conditions* of an action relative to a constraint and a chosen end-state or goal. In this case, the goal is the killing of mice. The action of the blade moving will succeed in bringing about this goal, only if the thing in its path is a mouse, not a toe or mere empty space. P is a success condition of act a relative to constraint and a goal, if P is a requirement, according to the constraint, for a to bring about the goal. Relative to the goal of killing mice and the constraint that a mouse in the path of this sort of blade will be crushed when it snaps shut, we have, as a success condition of the blade's moving:

(P)   The thing in the path of the blade is a mouse.

In a well-run household, in which mousetraps are located in an area in which dogs can't roam and children don't play, the lever of a mousetrap will move only if a mouse in standing on the platform nibbling on the cheese spread on the lever. Thus the reflexive information carried by the lever moving relative to this latter constraint is:

(Q)   The thing nibbling on the cheese on the lever is a mouse.

The gap between P and Q is bridged by a combination of coincident architectural content and information flow. The movement of the blade carries the architectural information that the lever is moving, which carries the reflexive information that the thing nibbling at the lever is a mouse. The relevant architectural connection is the rod and cam structure that insures that the blade will be released only when the lever moves. So the information that the thing nibbling on the cheese on the lever is a mouse, flows and is also carried by the movement of the blade. This doesn't get us from Q to P, though. Notice that this flow might take place, even if the architecture were defective—say because the platform is too long—and the blade will miss the mouse. If the trap is well-designed, however, the information that Q will not only flow, but be coordinated with the success condition. This is not due to the rod and cam connection, but to the fact that the distance between the blade and the lever is about the size of the average mouse. The constraint associated with this architectural feature is that the thing nibbling at the lever is the thing the blade will hit. This constraint justifies the shift in modes of presentation that gets us from Q to P.

6 Conclusion

As we pointed out in Israel and Perry 1990, ordinary information reports focus on incremental content. There we argued that to understand the way in which the information content of a signal is derived from the regularities that generate that content, one also needs to recognize reflexive information. Here, we have argued that to understand how devices generate, combine, and use information, we need to recognize architectural information of various sorts.

References

Dretske, F. I. 1981. *Knowledge and the Flow of Information*. Cambridge, MA: MIT Press.

Israel, D., and J. Perry. 1990. What is Information? In *Information, Language, and Cognition*. Vancouver Studies in Cognitive Science, Volume 1, ed. P. P. Hanson, 1–19. Vancouver: University of British Columbia Press. Also available as Report No. CSLI-91-145, CSLI Publications, Stanford.

Perry, J. 1988. Cognitive Significance and New Theories of Reference. *Noûs* 22(1):1–18.

Perry, J. 1990. Individuals in Informational and Intentional Content. In *Information, Semantics and Epistemology*, ed. E. Villenueva. Oxford: Basil Blackwell.

8

Doxic Paradox: A Situational Solution

ROBERT C. KOONS

1 Doxic Paradox

The following is adapted from an example of Haim Gaifman's (1983, 150–2): Rowena makes the following offer to Columna: Columna may have either box A (which is empty) or box B (which contains $100), but not both. Rowena also makes the following promise to Columna: if Columna makes an irrational choice in response to the first offer, Rowena will give her a bonus of $1000. Let's assume that they are both ideal reasoners and that Rowena always keeps her promises, and that both of these facts are common knowledge between Rowena and Columna.

How should Columna respond to this situation? If we suppose that taking box A would be irrational, then doing so would yield Columna $900 more than taking box B, which makes taking A the rational thing to do. If, alternatively, we suppose that taking box A would not be irrational, than taking box A would yield at least $100 less than taking box B, so taking box A would be irrational after all. Taking box A is irrational for Columna if and only if it is not irrational.

There is an obvious analogy between this situation and that of the liar paradox. In the liar paradox, we have a sentence which says of itself: 'I am not true'. Such a sentence is true if it is not true (since that is what is says), and it is false, and therefore not true, if it is true (since that is what it denies). Tarski demonstrated that this ancient puzzle constitutes a genuine antinomy by showing that any theory which implies every instance of an intuitively very plausible schema, Convention T, is logically inconsistent. Convention T is simply the requirement that for every sentence s of the language, our semantical theory should entail the claim that the sentence is true if and only if ϕ (where 's' is a name of the sentence ϕ). For example,

Situation Theory and Its Applications, vol. 2.
Jon Barwise, Jean Mark Gawron, Gordon Plotkin, and Syun Tutiya, eds.
Copyright © 1991, Stanford University.

where the sentence is 'snow is white', our semantical theory should imply that 'snow is white' is true if and only if snow is white.

In order to demonstrate that Gaifman's puzzle also constitutes an antinomy, I must produce intuitively plausible principles concerning the notion of rationality which force us into inconsistency, just as Tarski produced the intuitively plausible Convention T concerning truth. Moreover, these principles should be the ones we are implicitly appealing to in the informal reasoning which led to a contradiction above. In this paper, I will produce such principles, and I will sketch out one way of resolving the antinomy, applying to this case some work on the liar paradox by Charles Parsons (1974), Tyler Burge (1979), Haim Gaifman (1988), and Barwise and Etchemendy (1987). Like other antinomies, there is no ordinary, non-technical solution to this problem. My solution will involve a fairly radical re-construal of the semantics of the language of justification.

As ideal thinkers, we must assign to the various sources of purported information upon which we are relying some degree of apparent reliability, that is, a degree of cognitive tenacity in the face of conflicting data. This degree of reliability cannot be identified with degree of probability, since it does not in general satisfy anything like the axioms of the probability calculus, nor does it have anything much to do with betting ratios. Application of the probability calculus to an individual's judgments presupposes that the individual is "logically omniscient," i.e., that sum of the probabilities of two inconsistent propositions never exceeds one. Degrees of reliability of data have to do with an earlier, pre-deductive aspect of ratiocination. We want to consider cases in which two inconsistent sentences both have a very high initial plausibility or apparent reliability, which is possible if their mutual inconsistency is not immediately apparent.

When a data set is revealed through logical analysis to be inconsistent or otherwise dissonant, the rational reasoner rejects the elements of the set with the lowest degree of reliability until consistency and coherency are restored.

A reasoner's epistemic situation can simply be identified with the set of sentences which are found by the reasoner to be initially plausible, together with an assignment of a degree of apparent reliability or cognitive tenacity to each such sentence. Ideally, one should accept everything which follows (either logically or by means of some sort of non-monotonic inferences) from the epistemically strongest logically consistent subset of one's data (the "epistemically strongest" such subset is, roughly, the one which preserves the most sentences with the greatest degree of apparent reliability).

For the moment, let 'J' be a sentential operator representing *justifiable for me*. The paradoxical Columna-Rowena situation can be represented as a situation in which there is a proposition p, viz., *taking the $100 is optimal*, such that the following two propositions are true for Columna:

A1. $J(p \leftrightarrow \neg Jp)$

A2. $JJ(p \leftrightarrow \neg Jp)$

Given these two assumptions, we can derive a contradiction within an epistemic logic consisting of the following doxic[1] axiom schemata:

J1. $J\neg J\phi \rightarrow \neg J\phi$

J2. $J\phi$, where ϕ is a logical axiom

J3. $J(\phi \rightarrow \beta) \rightarrow (J\phi \rightarrow J\beta)$

J4. $J\phi$, where ϕ is an instance of J1–J3

The schemata J1 through J4 are modifications of some of the schemata discussed by Montague and Thomason. They are substantially weaker than Montague's in that schema J1 is a special case of the analogue of Montague's schema (i), '$J\phi \rightarrow \phi$'. This corresponds to that fact that these schemata are meant to capture the properties of justifiability of belief, as opposed to knowledge. At the same time, I suggest that J1–J4 are a substantial improvement over the schemata discussed by Thomason as characterizing ideal belief. In particular, schema J1 is much more plausible as a principle of ideal or rational belief than are the principles of Thomason's which I omit: '$J\phi \rightarrow JJ\phi$' and '$J(J\phi \rightarrow \phi)$'.

In an article on the surprise quiz paradox, Doris Olin (1983) discussed the principle I call J1. She argued:

> It can never be reasonable to believe a proposition of the form 'p and I am not now justified in believing p'. For if a person a is justified in believing a proposition, then he is not (epistemically) blameworthy for believing it. But if a is justified in believing that he is not justified in believing p, then he would be at fault in believing p. Hence, if a is justified in believing that he is not justified in believing p, then he is not justified in believing p.

If one has overwhelmingly good reason for believing that acceptance of p is not ultimately justifiable in one's present epistemic situation, then that fact must undermine any reasons one has for accepting p itself. To believe that p is not ultimately justifiable in one's present epistemic situation is to believe that it is inconsistent or otherwise not cotenable with data which is, by one's own lights, weightier than the data (if any) which supports or seems to support p. This realization should undermine one's confidence in any data supporting p.

The other axiom schemata are equally unexceptionable. J2 and J3 simply ensure that the property of being rationally justifiable in a situation is closed under logical entailment.[2]

Schema J4 guarantees that certain obviously true axioms of doxic logic

---

[1] From the Greek δοξα, for belief or opinion.

[2] If you are persuaded by what Henry Kyburg (1970) has said against "conjunctivitis," then read '$J\phi$' as saying that ϕ belongs to the corpus of subjectively certain propositions

are rationally justifiable in the situation under consideration. There can be little doubt that if schemata J1 through J3 are rationally defensible, there must be a large and variegated class of epistemic situations in which every instance of these schemata are rationally justifiable.

Another route to doxic paradox is the familiar one employing Gödelian self-reference. If we allow 'J' to be a predicate of sentences or structured propositions, then we can use Gödel theory to construct a self-referential sentence p which is provably equivalent to $\neg Jp$. Then, if we require that the theorems of arithmetic are justifiable, we can dispense with assumptions A1 and A2.

2 Construction of a Situation-Theoretic Solution

In this paper I will use a formal "language" of propositions, modeled after those used by Barwise and Etchemendy (1987), as modified by myself in "Three Indexical Solutions to the Liar" (1990). I will introduce two properties: 'I', for the interpretation of a token by a proposition, and 'J', for the rational justifiability of belief in a proposition by a person. '$\langle\!\langle I, i, k, p; 1\rangle\!\rangle$' shall express the atomic fact that sentence k in individual i's language of thought expresses the proposition p. '$\langle\!\langle J, i, p; 1\rangle\!\rangle$' shall express the atomic fact that belief in proposition p is rationally justifiable for individual i. '$\langle\!\langle Ep, i, e; 1\rangle\!\rangle$' shall express the fact that e is i's epistemic state.

Definition 1 Let X and Y be any two classes. The *closure* $\Delta(X, Y)$ *of X and Y* is the smallest collection containing X and closed under:

(1) If Z is a finite sequence of elements of $\Delta(X, Y)$, then $[\bigwedge Z]$ is in $\Delta(X, Y)$.

(2) If $p \in \Delta(X, Y)$, and $v \in Y$, then $[\forall v : p[v/d]] \in \Delta(X, Y)$.

(3) If $z \in \Delta(X, Y)$, then $[\neg z]$ is in $\Delta(X, Y)$.

I will assume, for simplicity's sake, that there is a single language of thought $\mathcal{L}$. I will further assume that the structure of the sentences in this language mirrors that of propositions sans parameters. A *situated sub-sentence* is simply a part of some sentence in , together with that part's location within that sentence. Formally, I will represent a sub-sentence as a finite sequence, the first of which is a sentence, and the rest of which are sentences, each of which is an immediate constituent of its predecessor. The last constituent, the *face* of the sub-sentence, represents the grammatical form of the sub-sentence proper. The first constituent, the *base* of the sub-sentence, represents the ultimate cognitive context of that sub-sentence.

For each set of concrete individuals, propositions, soas, situations and sentences, there shall be denumerably many arbitrary individuals. Each arbitrary individual has such a set as its unique range of significance. Ar-

---

in the relevant situation. Even Kyburg admits that the conjunction of two subjectively certain propositions is itself subjectively certain.

bitrary individuals shall be represented as ordered pairs, consisting of a set (the range of significance) and a natural number (distinguishing each arbitrary individual from others with the same range).

Definition 2 Let SOA, SIT, AtPROP, PROP, V, $\mathcal{L}$, and $\mathcal{L}+$ be the largest classes satisfying:

* Every $\sigma \in$ SOA is either of the form $\langle\langle H, a, b; t\rangle\rangle$ (a typical non-semantical atomic proposition), $\langle\langle J, a, p; t\rangle\rangle$ or $\langle\langle I, a, k, p; t\rangle\rangle$, where H, Ep, J and I are distinct atoms, a and b are concrete individuals or members of V, $k \in \mathcal{L}+$, $p \in$ PROP, and t is either 0 or 1.p

* Every $s \in$ SIT is a subset of SOA.

* Every $p \in$ PROP belongs to $\Delta($AtPROP$, V)$.

* Every $p \in$ AtPROP is of the form $\langle s, \sigma\rangle$, where $s \in$ SIT and $\sigma \in$ SOA.

* Every $v \in V$ is of the form $\langle n, A\rangle$, where n is a natural number and A is a subset of U (the set of concrete individuals), SIT, SOA, PROP, V, $\mathcal{L}$ or $\mathcal{L}+$.

* Every $\phi \epsilon \mathcal{L}$ belongs to $\Delta($SOA$, V)$.

* Every $k \in \mathcal{L}+$ is a finite sequence $\langle\phi_0, \ldots, \phi_n\rangle$ such that (1) each ϕ_i belongs to $\mathcal{L}$, and (2) for each i such that $0 \le i \le n - 1$, either

  (a) $\phi_i = \neg\phi_{i+1}$
  (b) $\phi_i = [\bigwedge Z]$ and ϕ_{i+1} is a constituent of Z, or
  (c) $\phi_i = [\forall v : \psi[v/d]], \phi_{i+1} = \psi[c/d], v = \langle n, A\rangle$, and $c \in A$.

I can now introduce the following truth-definition for these propositions.

Definition 3 *Truth Definition.* Let g be a function whose domain is a set of arbitrary individuals and whose range is a set of concrete individuals, propositions, soas, and situations such that for each $x \in \mathcal{D}(g)$, $g(x) = x^3$ or $g(x)$ is in the range of significance of x. Let σ/g be the result of replacing every occurrence of an individual d in the domain of g with $g(d)$.

1. The proposition $\langle s, \sigma\rangle$ is true relative to g if and only if $\sigma/g \in s$.
2. The proposition $[\neg p]$ is true relative to g if and only if p is not true relative to g.
3. The proposition $[\bigwedge Z]$ is true relative to g if and only if every member of Z is true relative to g.
4. The proposition $[\forall v : q[v/d]$ is true relative to g if and only if for every member c of the range of v, $q[c/d]$ is true relative to g.
5. p is true iff there is a g such that p is true relative to g.

Next, I define the relation of one set of propositions being a deductive consequence of another. This notion of deductive consequence is needed, in

---

[3]When $g(x) = x$, the proposition is interpreted as being about the variable x, as in $\langle\langle$Variable, $x\rangle, s\rangle$ (this corresponds to the mention of a variable in standard formal languages). When $g(x)$ is some member of the range of x's significance, the proposition is being interpreted as parametric, as about some unspecified member of this range (this corresponds to the use of a variable).

order to require that the rational agent's beliefs be deductively closed. Since each Austinian proposition is either necessarily true or necessarily false, it is not immediately obvious what a useful notion of deductive consequence would be like. We could stipulate that two propositions $\langle s, \sigma \rangle$ and $\langle s', \sigma \rangle$ are logically independent whenever $s \neq s'$. Instead, I have stipulated that $\langle s, \sigma \rangle$ entails $\langle s', \sigma \rangle$ whenever $s \subseteq s'$.

Definition 4 $\mathcal{A}$ is a *model* iff $\mathcal{A}$ is a class of soa's such that for every σ, either σ or its dual belongs to $\mathcal{A}$, but not both.

I will assume that for each soa σ, for each situation s in model $\mathcal{A}$ (i.e., s is a subset of $\mathcal{A}$) and for each model $\mathcal{A}'$, there is a counterpart $C(\mathcal{A}', s, \mathcal{A}, \sigma)$ of s in $\mathcal{A}'$. $C(\mathcal{A}', s, \mathcal{A}, \sigma)$ is always a subset of $\mathcal{A}'$. Moreover, the counterpart function is subset-preserving: if $s \subseteq s' \subseteq \mathcal{A}$, then $C(\mathcal{A}', s, \mathcal{A}, \sigma) \subseteq C(\mathcal{A}', s', \mathcal{A}, \sigma) \subseteq \mathcal{A}'$, for every model $\mathcal{A}'$.

Definition 5 Let g be a function whose domain is a subset of V such that, for every $v \in \mathcal{D}(g)$, if $v = \langle n, A \rangle$, then $g(v) \in A$. A proposition p is *true in $\mathcal{A}$ relative to $\mathcal{A}'$ and g* (given counterpart function C) iff:

1. if $p = \langle s, \sigma \rangle$, then $\sigma/g \in C(\mathcal{A}', s, \mathcal{A}, \sigma/g)$.
2. if $p = \neg q$, then q is not true in $\mathcal{A}$ relative to $\mathcal{A}'$ and g.
3. if $p = [\bigwedge Z]$, then every q in Z is true in $\mathcal{A}$ relative to $\mathcal{A}'$ and g.
4. if $p = [\forall v : q[v/d]]$ and $v = \langle n, A \rangle$, then for every $c \in A$, $q[c/d]$ is true in $\mathcal{A}$ relative to $\mathcal{A}'$ and g.

A *set P of propositions is true in $\mathcal{A}$ relative to $\mathcal{A}'$* iff there exists a g such that every member of P is true in $\mathcal{A}$ relative to $\mathcal{A}'$ and g.

Definition 6 $\Delta \models \Delta'$ iff Δ and Δ' are sets of propositions, and, for every $\mathcal{A}, \mathcal{A}'$ and C such that there is a g such that every member of Δ is true in $\mathcal{A}$ relative to $\mathcal{A}'$ and g given C, there is an h such that every member of Δ and of Δ' is true in $\mathcal{A}$ relative to $\mathcal{A}'$ and h given C.

An Ur-model shall be a situation which contains no doxic soa's (soa's involving 'I' or 'J') and which is maximal and consistent with respect to non-doxic soa's. I will assume that we have a fixed set of concrete individuals, U.

Definition 7 An *Ur-model M* is a situation which is such that

(1) it contains no doxic soa's,
(2) for every pair of individuals a and b in U, every cognitive individual i, and every epistemic situation e, exactly one of each of the following pair of soa's belongs to M : $\langle\!\langle H, a, b; 0 \rangle\!\rangle$ or $\langle\!\langle H, a, b; 1 \rangle\!\rangle$, $\langle\!\langle Ep, i, e; 0 \rangle\!\rangle$ or $\langle\!\langle Ep, i, e; 1 \rangle\!\rangle$,
(3) if $\langle\!\langle Ep, a, e; 1 \rangle\!\rangle \in s$ and $\langle\!\langle Ep, a, e'; 1 \rangle\!\rangle \in s$, then $e = e'$.

An *Ur-situation* is a situation which is a subset of some Ur-model.

Situation theory introduces situation-parameters for a variety of reasons; dealing with Liar-like paradoxes is only one of them. I will assume that initially every atomic sub-sentence in the thought-language of every cognitive individual has been assigned some ur-situation as a preliminary parameter. The task of this paper is to describe how to extend these preliminary parameters by adding appropriate doxic soa's. I will assume that there is a *preliminary parameter function* B such that, for every cognitive individual i, and every atomic situated sub-sentence k, $B(i,k)$ is an Ur-situation such that $B(i,k) \subseteq M$.

We can represent a *thought-token* by an ordered pair $\langle i, k \rangle$, where i is a cognitive individual and k is a situated sub-sentence. The process of interpreting such tokens begins with an Ur-model M and a preliminary parameter function B and produces a new situation in which the appropriate facts about the interpretation of tokens are registered. I will describe an operation which is monotonic in the sense that, when applied to a situation s and a function B, it always results in a situation which extends s.

Epistemic states can be defined as partial functions which assign epistemic weights of some kind to sentences in $\mathcal{L}$. The exact nature of these epistemic weights I will leave undefined. What is important is that such an epistemic state induces a weak preference ordering on the set of subsets of $\mathcal{L}$.

Now, I must define when a proposition p is justifiable for a cognitive individual i. If M is an Ur-model, let $E_M(i)$ be the epistemic situation e such that $\langle\!\langle Ep, i, e; 1 \rangle\!\rangle \in M$. A possible situation[4] s is a *total context* for individual i iff s extends M and, for every situated sub-sentence k in $\mathcal{L}*$, there is exactly one proposition p such that $\langle\!\langle I, i, k, p; 1 \rangle\!\rangle \in s$. As an epistemic situation, $E_s(i)$ is a partial function which assigns epistemic weights to sentences in $\mathcal{L}$. Let $D_s(i)$ be the set of data-sentences in $E_s(i)$, i.e., $D_s(i)$ is the range of $E_s(i)$.

Definition 8 The *privileged subset of $D_s(i)$ in total context s* is that subset $K(i,s)$ of $D_s(i)$ having the greatest epistemic weight which satisfies the following condition: the set $P = \{p : \exists\phi(\langle\!\langle I, i, \langle K(i,s), \phi\rangle, p; 1 \rangle\!\rangle \in s)\} \cup \{p : \exists Q(p = \langle s, \langle\!\langle J, i, Q; 1 \rangle\!\rangle\rangle \& p \text{ is true})\} \cup \{p : p \text{ is a doxic axiom and } p \text{ is expressible in } s\}$ is consistent. The set $\{p : \exists\phi(\langle\!\langle I, i, \langle K(i,s), \phi\rangle, p; 1 \rangle\!\rangle \in s)\} \cup \{p : p \text{ is a doxic axiom and } p \text{ is expressible in } s\}$ is called the *propositional basis* of $E(i)/s$.

Definition 9 A proposition p is *justifiable for i in such a total context s* iff p is a logical consequence of the propositional basis of $E(i)/s$.

A proposition p is *justifiable for cognitive individual i in situation s* iff p is justifiable for i in every total context extending s.

---

[4] See the Appendix for a formal definition of "possible situation", Def. 17.

A *sentence k is justifiable for i in s* iff for every s' which is a total context for a such that s' extends s, the proposition p such that $\langle\!\langle I, i, k, p; 1 \rangle\!\rangle \in s'$ is justifiable for i in s'.

A *sentence k is unjustifiable for i in s* iff for every s' which is a total context for a such that s' extends s, the proposition p such that $\langle\!\langle I, i, k, p; 1 \rangle\!\rangle \in s'$ is not justifiable for i in s'.

Now that we have introduced Austinian propositions, complete with situational parameters, we must modify the axioms of doxic logic developed above.

J1. $\langle s, \langle\!\langle J, x, \neg\langle s', \langle\!\langle J, x, p; 1 \rangle\!\rangle \rangle; 1 \rangle\!\rangle \rangle \rightarrow \neg\langle s', \langle\!\langle J, x, p; 1 \rangle\!\rangle \rangle$

J2. $\langle s, \langle\!\langle J, x, p; 1 \rangle\!\rangle \rangle$, where p is a logical axiom

J3. $\langle s, \langle\!\langle J, x, (p \rightarrow q); 1 \rangle\!\rangle \rangle \rightarrow (\langle s, \langle\!\langle J, x, p; 1 \rangle\!\rangle \rangle \rightarrow \langle s, \langle\!\langle J, x, q; 1 \rangle\!\rangle \rangle)$

J4. $\langle s, \langle\!\langle J, x, p; 1 \rangle\!\rangle \rangle$, where p is an instance of J1–J3

This logic resolves the self-referential, Liar-like version of the doxic paradoxes in the following way. Suppose we define the circular proposition p as follows:

$$p = \neg\langle s, \langle\!\langle J, i, p; 1 \rangle\!\rangle \rangle$$

Proposition p expresses the thought that the justifiability of p for cognitive individual i is not settled in situation s. We can show by a reductio that if s is actual, p must be true. Suppose s is actual, and p is false. Then $\langle\!\langle J, i, p; 1 \rangle\!\rangle \in s$. By the definition of p, $\langle\!\langle J, i, \neg\langle s, \langle\!\langle J, i, p; 1 \rangle\!\rangle \rangle; 1 \rangle\!\rangle \in s$. By axiom J1, $\langle\!\langle J, i, p; 1 \rangle\!\rangle \in s$. Contradiction. So, if s is actual, p is true. Individual i could also establish the truth of p by a similar argument, but the fact that p is justifiable for i must be incorporated in some distinct situation s' (presumably, $s \subseteq s'$), not in s itself.

In the Rowena-Columna case, we must supplement the doxic logic above with three special assumptions about the situation, which correspond to our old assumptions A1 and A2:

A1a. $\langle s, \langle\!\langle J, i, (p \rightarrow \neg\langle s, \langle\!\langle J, i, p; 1 \rangle\!\rangle \rangle); 1 \rangle\!\rangle \rangle$

A1b. $\langle s, \langle\!\langle J, i, (\neg\langle s, \langle\!\langle J, i, p; 1 \rangle\!\rangle \rangle \rightarrow p); 1 \rangle\!\rangle \rangle$

A2. $\langle s, \langle\!\langle J, i, \langle s, \langle\!\langle J, i, (p \rightarrow \neg\langle s, \langle\!\langle J, i, p; 1 \rangle\!\rangle \rangle); 1 \rangle\!\rangle \rangle; 1 \rangle\!\rangle \rangle$

Given these three assumptions, we can derive a contradiction as follows:

1. $\langle s, \langle\!\langle J, i, (p \rightarrow \neg\langle s, \langle\!\langle J, i, p; 1 \rangle\!\rangle \rangle); 1 \rangle\!\rangle \rangle$ A1a

2. $\langle s, \langle\!\langle J, i, p; 1 \rangle\!\rangle \rangle \rightarrow \langle s, \langle\!\langle J, i, \neg\langle s, \langle\!\langle J, i, p; 1 \rangle\!\rangle \rangle; 1 \rangle\!\rangle \rangle$ 1, J3

3. $\langle s, \langle\!\langle J, i, \neg\langle s, \langle\!\langle J, i, p; 1 \rangle\!\rangle \rangle; 1 \rangle\!\rangle \rangle \rightarrow \neg\langle s, \langle\!\langle J, i, p; 1 \rangle\!\rangle \rangle$ J1

4. $\neg\langle s, \langle\!\langle J, i, p; 1 \rangle\!\rangle \rangle$ 2,3

5. $\langle s, \langle\!\langle J, i, \neg\langle s, \langle\!\langle J, i, p; 1 \rangle\!\rangle \rangle; 1 \rangle\!\rangle \rangle$ A2, J4, J2, J3

6. $\langle s, \langle\!\langle J, i, (\neg\langle s, \langle\!\langle J, i, p; 1 \rangle\!\rangle \rangle \rightarrow p); 1 \rangle\!\rangle \rangle$ A1b

7. $\langle s, \langle\!\langle J, i, \neg\langle s, \langle\!\langle J, i, p; 1 \rangle\!\rangle \rangle; 1 \rangle\!\rangle \rangle \rightarrow \langle s, \langle\!\langle J, i, p; 1 \rangle\!\rangle \rangle$ 6, J3

8. $\langle s, \langle\!\langle J, i, p; 1 \rangle\!\rangle \rangle$ 6, 7

Therefore, it is impossible for all three of assumptions A1a, A1b and A2 to be true. In the Rowena-Columna case, it seems to be most natural to deny A2, on the grounds that the justifiability of A1a should be registered in a different, richer situation than the one to which A1a is itself relativized, namely, s. If we instead assume A2′,

A2′. $\langle s', \langle\!\langle J, i, \langle s, \langle\!\langle J, i, (p \rightarrow \neg\langle s, \langle\!\langle J, i, p; 1\rangle\!\rangle)\rangle); 1\rangle\!\rangle\rangle; 1\rangle\!\rangle\rangle$

then the above argument reaches the non-paradoxical conclusion:

$$\neg\langle s, \langle\!\langle J, i, p; 1\rangle\!\rangle\rangle \ \& \ \langle s', \langle\!\langle J, i, p; 1\rangle\!\rangle\rangle.$$

The problem that remains is that of explaining how it is that concrete thoughts and beliefs come to be relativized to appropriate situations, so that all potentially paradoxical situations are resolved in this way. I take up this challenge in the next section.

3   Correlating Tokens and Situations

In the construction to follow, I will detail how, given a network of concrete thought-tokens and basic, non-doxic parameters, the doxic situational parameters are to be assigned to each token. The first issue to be decided is: shall we include merely possible tokens in doxically accessible worlds in the network, or shall we limit the network to the actual world. If we take the first alternative, the interpretation of a cognitive individual's thoughts will be entirely independent of his actual environment and will depend only on features internal to the world-as-it-appears-to-him. On the second alternative, facts about the actual world will make an uneliminable contribution to the content of a cognitive individual's thoughts. Since the second alternative seems more consonant with the spirit of situation theory, I will pursue it here.

The interpretation of tokens will be guided by three principles: the Principles of Symmetry, of Charity, and of Interest, in that order.[5] My first priority will be to avoid arbitrary violations of various symmetries within the network. Secondly, I will try to interpret each maximal token (representing a separate thought or belief) so as to make it true, if possible. Thirdly, I will try to interpret each token so as to assign it as rich a content as possible (maximizing its interest, for us and the individual himself). In order to make sense of the Charity requirement, we must define the truth-value of a token in a situation.

Definition 10 The *truth-value of token* $\langle i, k \rangle$ *in situation* s *(given B)* is partially defined by recursion:

  1. If k is an atomic, non-doxic situated sub-sentence, then $\langle i, k \rangle$ has value 1 in s iff $k \in B(i, k)$. Otherwise, $\langle i, k \rangle$ has value 0 in s.

---

[5]See Burge (1979). His three principles were Symmetry, Charity and Minimality.

2. If k is an atomic, doxic situated sub-sentence, then $\langle i, k \rangle$ has value 1 in s iff there is a true proposition $\langle s', \sigma \rangle$ such that $\langle\!\langle I, i, k, \langle s', \sigma \rangle; 1 \rangle\!\rangle \in s$, and $\langle i, k \rangle$ has value 0 in s iff there is a false proposition $\langle s', \sigma \rangle$ such that $\langle\!\langle I, i, k, \langle s', \sigma \rangle; 1 \rangle\!\rangle \in s$.

3. If $k' = k^\frown\langle\phi\rangle$, and $\text{Face}(k) = \neg\phi$, then $\langle i, k \rangle$ has value 1 in s iff $\langle i, k' \rangle$ has value 0 in s, and $\langle i, k \rangle$ has value 0 in s iff $\langle i, k' \rangle$ has value 1 in s.

4. If $\text{Face}(k) = [\bigwedge Z]$, Z is an n-ary sequence $\langle\phi_0, \ldots, \phi_{n-1}\rangle$, and for all $m < n$, $\langle i, k^\frown\langle\phi_m\rangle\rangle$ has value 1 in s, then $\langle i, k \rangle$ has value 1 in s. If $\text{Face}(k) = [\bigwedge Z]$, Z is an n-ary sequence $\langle\phi_0, \ldots, \phi_{n-1}\rangle$, and for some $m < n$, $\langle i, k^\frown\langle\phi_m\rangle\rangle$ has value 0 in s, then $\langle i, k \rangle$ has value 0 in s.

5. If $\text{Face}(k) = [\forall v : \phi[v/a]]$, $v = \langle n, A\rangle$, and for all $c \in A$, $\langle i, k^\frown\langle\phi[c/a]\rangle\rangle$ has value 1 in s, then $\langle i, k \rangle$ has value 1 in s.

If $\text{Face}(k) = [\forall v : \phi[v/a]]$, $v = \langle n, A\rangle$, and for some $c \in A$, $\langle i, k^\frown\langle\phi[c/a]\rangle\rangle$ has value 0 in s then $\langle i, k \rangle$ has value 0 in s.

Definition 11 *Token* $\langle i, k \rangle$ *is open in situation* s *iff* $\langle i, k \rangle$ *does not have a value in* s, *and either:* (1) k *is a sentence (a 1-ary sequence), or* (2) k *is an immediate constituent of* k', *and* $\langle i, k' \rangle$ *is open in* s.

The calling relation will turn the set of concrete tokens into a directed network, by incorporating information about which tokens depend on which for their interpretation.

Definition 12 *The calling relation.* *Token* $\langle i, k \rangle$ *immediately calls token* $\langle j, k' \rangle$ *in situation* s *iff one of the following conditions holds:*

1. (a) $\langle i, k \rangle$ is open in situation s, (b) $\text{Face}(k) = \langle\!\langle J, j, p; t\rangle\!\rangle$, (c) there are total contexts c and c' extending s such that c and c' agree on all atomic sub-sentences except for k', and p is justifiable for j relative to c iff p is not justifiable for j relative to c'.

2. $\langle i, k \rangle$ is open in s, and $\text{Face}(k) = \langle\!\langle I, j, k', p; t\rangle\!\rangle$.

3. $i = j$, $\text{Face}(k')$ is an atomic doxic token, and k' is a sub-sentence of k.

A *token* $\langle i, k \rangle$ *calls token* $\langle j, k' \rangle$ iff there is a finite calling path from $\langle i, k \rangle$ to $\langle j, k' \rangle$.

Paradoxical tokens belong to loops or infinitely descending chains in the directed network associated with the calling relation. In order to interpret such tokens properly, the notion of a closed chain must be defined and several varieties of such chains distinguished.

Definition 13 A set of tokens is a *loop* iff $S \neq \emptyset$, and for all k, k' in S, there is a calling path from k to k'. A *maximal loop* is a loop which is not a proper subset of any loop. A set of tokens is an *infinitely descending chain* iff every token k in S immediately calls another token in S. A *proper chain* contains no loops. A *maximal proper chain* is a proper chain which is not a proper subset of any proper chain.

I present a formal definition of the interpretation construction in the appendix of this paper. Here, let me simply sketch how I envisage that construction's being guided by the three interpretive principles mentioned above. When the interpretation of a token is grounded, when that token does not belong to a loop or infinite descending chain, then its interpretation can be fixed by a combination of charity and interest. Where possible, the sub-tokens and instances of a token are interpreted so as to make the maximal token true, and, subject to that constraint, it is to be interpreted so as to maximize its content.

For example, suppose atomic sub-token k is affirmative or positive (i.e., it occurs within an even number of external negations in its syntactic location), and it affirms that proposition p is justifiable. Suppose that the interpretation process has to decide between assigning situation s_0 and assigning situation s_1 to k, where $s_0 \subseteq s_1$. If p is justifiable in s_0, then either assignment would be charitable, but assigning s_0 would maximize k's content and so would be preferred. If p is justifiable in s_1 but not in s_0, then only assigning s_1 would be charitable. If p is justifiable in neither, then neither would be charitable, so assigning s_0 would again be preferred, since it maximizes content. If we supposed instead that token k was negative, then each of these assignments would be reversed.

Once atomic sub-tokens are interpreted, the more complex tokens in which they figure can also be interpreted. In the case of sentential operations, the complex tokens simply inherit the situation-assignments made to their parts. In the case of generalizations, the interpretation must again be guided by the two principles of Charity and Interest. Suppose k is an affirmative or positive universal generalization (one occurring within an even number of negations in its syntactic location). Then k should be assigned a proposition which is the generalization of the greatest lower bound, in terms of content, of the propositions assigned to its instances.[6] This will ensure that the interpretation is charitable, since the assignment is a lower bound, while maximizing interest. Similarly, if k occurred in a negative syntactic context, it should be assigned the generalization of the least upper bound of the propositions assigned to its instances.

Since the interpretation process is monotonic, repeated application of these principles eventually reaches a fixed point. Thanks to the presence of closed loops and infinitely descending chains, however, this fixed point does not constitute a total interpretation of the network of tokens. Therefore, after the minimal fixed point is reached, the non-well-founded structures in the network must be systematically eliminated. It is here that the principle

---

[6]The construction defined in the appendix requires that at each stage, a choice be made between a finite number (in fact, only two) possible situation-parameters for each node in the token's structure. This guarantees the existence of the greatest lower and least upper bounds, in the relevant senses.

of Symmetry is paramount: non-arbitrary choices must be avoided.[7] By distinguishing as we have between positive and negative atomic sub-tokens, we can use the Principle of Charity to make some discriminations. In general, we should prefer breaking the chains and loops by fixing the interpretation of negative rather than positive atomic sub-tokens, since fixing their interpretation at this stage will mean assigning them smaller situations, an assignment which is charitable toward negative tokens but uncharitable toward positive ones. In the appendix, a systematic foundationalizing operation is defined which satisfies these desiderata.

Once the non-well-founded structures in the network have been eliminated, each token which remains uninterpreted at that stage can be interpreted by repeated application of the original principles used to reach the first fixed point. In the end, a total interpretation results, in which every atomic sub-token is assigned one of two situations: either the situation s_0, the situation obtained at the minimal fixed point, or situation s_1, the final situation obtained after all tokens have been interpreted. Thus, only two situation-parameters are needed to resolve any doxic paradox expressible in natural language.

4   Illustrations

The interpretation operation described in the last section handles circular propositions and tokens as one might expect. For instance, consider the circular token k:

$$k = \langle\!\langle I, i, k, \langle s, k \rangle; 0 \rangle\!\rangle$$

Token k is apt for asserting that token k is not to be interpreted by means of the situation-parameter s. Since k induces a closed loop, it is assigned the situation s_0 as its parameter. The resulting proposition $\langle s_0, k \rangle$ is false, and, if $s \neq s_0$, then $\langle\!\langle I, i, k, \langle s, k \rangle; 0 \rangle\!\rangle \in s_1$.

In the case of Columna and Rowena, the network of tokens is as shown in Figure 1.

Here I assume that assumption A2 involves quantifying over a set of situations, a set rich enough, I will assume, to include the fixed point s_0. There is, for each situation s in the range of quantification, a closed loop containing k_1 (a sub-component of A1a), k_2 (a sub-component of A2a), and A2s, an instance of A2. Since k_1 is negative, it is he function ϕ assigned the parameter s_0. There then remains a closed loop consisting of k_2 alone. Thus, s_0 is also assigned as k_2's parameter. The interpretations of A1a and A1b are now fixed. The relevant instance of A2, A2s_0, receives the final fixed point s_1 as its parameter. A2 inherits the parameter s_1 from its

---

[7] Jon Barwise suggested (in conversation) that instead of defining a deterministic, non-arbitrary process for eliminating loops and chains, one could stipulate that some random, non-deterministic process do the job.

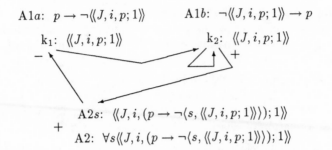

A1a: $p \to \neg \langle\!\langle J, i, p; 1 \rangle\!\rangle$ A1b: $\neg \langle\!\langle J, i, p; 1 \rangle\!\rangle \to p$

k_1: $\langle\!\langle J, i, p; 1 \rangle\!\rangle$ k_2: $\langle\!\langle J, i, p; 1 \rangle\!\rangle$

A2s: $\langle\!\langle J, i, (p \to \neg \langle s, \langle\!\langle J, i, p; 1 \rangle\!\rangle \rangle); 1 \rangle\!\rangle$

A2: $\forall s \langle\!\langle J, i, (p \to \neg \langle s, \langle\!\langle J, i, p; 1 \rangle\!\rangle \rangle); 1 \rangle\!\rangle$

Figure 1 Network of tokens for the Columna-Rowena case

instance $A2s_0$.[8] This confirms the expectation I expressed at the end of section 2.

Thus, it is possible to define a principled and total interpretation of any network of tokens which averts Liar-like paradoxes in this domain in a natural and plausible way.

5 Appendix: A Formal Definition of the Construction

The central task of this construction is to assign propositions to situated sub-sentences. If a proposition is to be a candidate for assignment to a given situated sentence, the structure of the proposition must mirror that of the sentence. Thus, we must define a relation of structural isomorphism between propositions and sentences.

Definition 14 Situated sub-sentence k and proposition p are *structurally isomorphic* iff

1. Face$(k) = \phi, \phi$ is atomic and $p = \langle s, \phi \rangle$ for some situation s;
2. Face$(k) = \neg \psi, p = \neg q$, and $k^\frown \langle \psi \rangle$ and q are isomorphic;
3. Face$(k) = [\bigwedge Z], p = [\bigwedge Q], Z$ and Q are finite sequences of the same length, and for each i, $k^\frown \langle Z_i \rangle$ and Q_i are isomorphic; or
4. Face$(k) = [\forall v : \psi[v/b]], p = [\forall v : q[v/b]]$, and $k^\frown \langle \psi \rangle$ and q are isomorphic.

The assignment of propositions to sub-sentences will be guided, at least in part, by a principle of Charity. If a situated atomic sentence affirms that a soa belongs to the as-yet-unspecified situation, then we will try to assign it as proposition containing as inclusive a situation as possible. In contrast, if the situated atomic situation is being used, in its logical context, to deny that a soa belongs to the situation, then Charity will lead us to assign a proposition containing a sufficiently circumscribed situation. Atomic sub-sentences occurring within an even number of negations will be thought of as affirmative or positive; the others will be classified as negative.

---

[8] See Def. 17.8 in the Appendix.

Definition 15 A situated sub-sentence k is *positive* iff its face occurs within the scope of an even number of external negations ($\neg$) in its base-sentence. k is *negative* iff its face occurs within an odd number of external negations.

Another principle which should guide the interpretation is the maximizing of interest. Other things being equal, we would like to interpret a given thought as having more rather than less content. The following definition introduces a relation of relative contentfulness.

Definition 16 The relation $\leq$ is defined on $\text{PROP} \times \text{PROP}$ by the following recursion:

1. $\langle s, \sigma \rangle \leq \langle s', \sigma \rangle$ iff $s' \subseteq s$.
2. $\neg p \leq \neg q$ iff $q \leq p$.
3. $[\bigwedge Z] \leq [\bigwedge Z']$ iff Z and Z' are of length n, for every $i < n, z_i \leq z'_i$.
4. $[\forall v : p[v/c]] \leq [\forall v' : q[v'/c]]$ iff $v = v'$ & $p \leq q$.

There are a variety of additional conditions which can be placed upon any interpretation of thought-tokens. Firstly, we can require that the interpretation of complex thoughts depend solely on the interpretation of their parts (Parts III–V of the following definition). Here, definitions 15 and 16 play a crucial role in defining how the interpretation of a generalization depends upon the interpretation of its instances (Part V). Secondly, we can require that only propositions which are structurally isomorphic to the sentence-type of the token be assigned to that token (part VI). Finally, we should require that only accessible propositions be assigned, that is, propositions whose situation-parameters are all sub-situations of the model so far constructed (part VII). The following definition imposes these requirements as conditions on the possibility of situations.

Definition 17 A situation s is *possible* iff

  I. Consistency

    1. There is no soa σ such that both σ and its dual belong to s.

  II. Uniqueness of functional outputs

    2. If $\langle\!\langle I, i, k, p; 1 \rangle\!\rangle \in s$ and $\langle\!\langle I, i, k, q; 1 \rangle\!\rangle \in s$, then $p = q$.

    3. If $\langle\!\langle Ep, i, e; 1 \rangle\!\rangle \in s$ and $\langle\!\langle Ep, i, e'; 1 \rangle\!\rangle \in s$, then $e = e'$.

  III. Interpretation of Negations

    4. If $k = k'^\frown\langle \phi \rangle$, $\text{Face}(k') = \neg\phi$, and $\langle\!\langle I, i, k, p; 1 \rangle\!\rangle \in s$, then $\langle\!\langle I, i, k', \neg p; 1 \rangle\!\rangle \in s$.

    5. If $k = k'^\frown\langle \phi \rangle$, $\text{Face}(k') = \neg\phi$, and $\langle\!\langle I, i, k, p; 0 \rangle\!\rangle \in s$, then $\langle\!\langle I, i, k', \neg p; 0 \rangle\!\rangle \in s$.

  IV. Interpretation of Conjunctions

    6. If $\text{Face}(k) = [\bigwedge Z]$, Z is an n-ary sequence $\langle \phi_0, \ldots, \phi_{n-1} \rangle$, and for every $m < n$, $\langle\!\langle I, i, k^\frown\langle\phi_m\rangle, p_m; 1 \rangle\!\rangle \in s$ for some p_m, then $\langle\!\langle I, i, k, q; 1 \rangle\!\rangle \in s$, where $q = [\bigwedge \langle p_0, \ldots, p_m \rangle]$.

7. If $\text{Face}(k) = [\bigwedge Z]$, Z is an n-ary sequence $\langle \phi_0, \ldots, \phi_{n-1} \rangle$, and for some $m < n$, $\langle\!\langle I, a, k^\frown \langle \phi_m \rangle, p_m; 0 \rangle\!\rangle \in s$ for some p_m, then $\langle\!\langle I, i, k, q; 0 \rangle\!\rangle \in s$, where $q = [\bigwedge Q]$ and p_m is the mth component of Q.

V. Interpretation of Generalizations

8. If $\text{Face}(k) = [\forall v : \phi[v/d]]$, k is positive, $v = \langle n, A \rangle$, and for every $c \in A$, $\langle\!\langle I, i, k^\frown \langle \phi[c/d] \rangle, pc; 1 \rangle\!\rangle \in s$ for some p_c, then $\langle\!\langle I, i, k, q; 1 \rangle\!\rangle \in s$ and $\langle\!\langle I, i, k, q'; 0 \rangle\!\rangle \in s$ for all $q' \neq q$, where $q = [\forall v : p[v/d]]$, and p is a $\leq$-maximal proposition such that for all $c \in A$, $p[c/a] \leq p_c$.

9. If $\text{Face}(k) = [\forall v : \phi[v/d]]$, k is negative, $v = \langle n, A \rangle$, and for every $c \in A$, $\langle\!\langle I, i, k^\frown \langle \phi[c/d] \rangle, pc; 1 \rangle\!\rangle \in s$ for some p_c, then $\langle\!\langle I, i, k, q; 1 \rangle\!\rangle \in s$ and $\langle\!\langle I, i, k, q'; 0 \rangle\!\rangle \in s$ for all $q' \neq q$, where $q = [\forall v : p[v/d]]$, and p is a $\leq$-minimal proposition such that for all $c \in A$, $p_c \leq p$.

10. If $\text{Face}(k) = [\forall v : \phi[v/d]]$, k is positive, $v = \langle n, A \rangle$, and for some $c \in A$, $\langle\!\langle I, i, k^\frown \langle \phi[c/d] \rangle, p; 0 \rangle\!\rangle \in s$ for every p such that $q[c/d] \leq p$, then $\langle\!\langle I, i, k, [\forall v : q[v/d]]; 0 \rangle\!\rangle \in s$.

11. If $\text{Face}(k) = [\forall v : \phi[v/d]]$, k is negative, $v = \langle n, A \rangle$, and for some $c \in A$, $\langle\!\langle I, i, k^\frown \langle \phi[c/d] \rangle, p; 0 \rangle\!\rangle \in s$ for every p such that $p \leq q[c/d]$, then $\langle\!\langle I, i, k, [\forall v : q[v/d]]; 0 \rangle\!\rangle \in s$.

VI. Structural Isomorphism

12. If k and p are not structurally isomorphic, then $\langle\!\langle I, i, k, p; 0 \rangle\!\rangle \in s$.

VII. Accessibility of Objects of Belief

13. If $\langle\!\langle J, i, p; t \rangle\!\rangle \in s$ and $\langle s', \sigma \rangle$ is a sub-proposition of p, then $s' \subseteq s$.

14. If $\langle\!\langle I, i, k, p; t \rangle\!\rangle \in s$ and $\langle s', \sigma \rangle$ is a sub-proposition of p, then $s' \subseteq s$

I now need to define two monotonic operations on doxic trees. The first operation, represented by τ, adds information to the model about the doxic facts which have been determined at a given stage in the construction.

Definition 18 The *doxic closure* $\tau(s)$ *of situation* s is the minimal possible situation s' extending s such that

1. If p is justifiable for i in s, then $\langle\!\langle J, i, p; 1 \rangle\!\rangle \in s'$.
   If p is unjustifiable for i in s, then $\langle\!\langle J, i, p; 0 \rangle\!\rangle \in s'$.

2. If (a) $\text{Face}(k) = \langle\!\langle J, j, p; t \rangle\!\rangle$, and (b) $\langle\!\langle J, j, p; t \pm 1 \rangle\!\rangle \in s$, then $\langle\!\langle I, i, k, \langle s', \langle\!\langle J, j, p; t \rangle\!\rangle \rangle; 1 \rangle\!\rangle \in s'$.

3. If (a) $\text{Face}(k) = \langle\!\langle I, j, k', p; t \rangle\!\rangle$, and (b) $\langle\!\langle I, j, k', p; t \pm 1 \rangle\!\rangle \in s$, then $\langle\!\langle I, i, k, \langle s', \langle\!\langle I, j, k', p; t \rangle\!\rangle \rangle; 1 \rangle\!\rangle \in s'$.

4. If (a) $\text{Face}(k)$ is an atomic, doxic sentence, and (b) $\langle i, k \rangle$ is not open in s, then $\langle\!\langle I, i, k, \langle s', \text{Face}(k) \rangle; 1 \rangle\!\rangle \in s'$.

5. If $\text{Face}(k)$ is an atomic, non-doxic situated sub-sentence, then $\langle\!\langle I, a, k, \langle B(i, k), \text{Face}(k) \rangle; 1 \rangle\!\rangle \in s'$.

Definition 19 An occurrence of 'J' or 'I' in a sentence is *negative* if the corresponding occurrence in the prenex-disjunctive normal form of the sentence is externally negated (by $\neg$). Otherwise, the occurrence of 'J' or 'I' in the sentence is *positive*.

An occurrence of 'J' or 'I' in a sub-sentence is positive if and only if the corresponding occurrence in the related sentence is positive, and similarly for negative occurrences. An atomic doxic token $\langle i, k \rangle$ is positive or negative as the occurrence of 'J' or 'I' in k is.

Definition 20 A *pure loop* contains only positive atomic tokens or only negative ones.

A *partly pure chain* S is a chain which can be divided into two sets S_1 and s_2 such that S_1 is an infinitely descending chain containing only positive or only negative atomic doxasitic tokens, and no token in S_1 calls any token in S_2. In this case, any maximal such S_1 is called a *pure part of S*.

Definition 21 The *foundationalization* $\phi(s)$ *of a situation* s relative to τ-fixed point s_0 is the minimal situation s' extending s which meets the following four conditions:

1. If S is a pure loop or chain, $\langle i, k \rangle$ belongs to a pure part of S, and $\mathrm{Face}(k) = \langle\!\langle J, j, p; t \rangle\!\rangle$, then $\langle\!\langle I, i, k, \langle s_0, \langle\!\langle J, j, p; t \rangle\!\rangle \rangle; 1 \rangle\!\rangle \in s'$.

2. If S is a pure chain containing no atomic J-tokens, $\langle i, k \rangle$ belongs to a pure part of S, and $\mathrm{Face}(k) = \langle\!\langle I, j, k', p; t \rangle\!\rangle$, then $\langle\!\langle I, i, k, \langle s_0, \langle\!\langle I, j, k', p; t \rangle\!\rangle \rangle; 1 \rangle\!\rangle \in s'$.

3. If S is an impure loop or chain, $\langle i, k \rangle$ is a negative token, $\langle i, k \rangle \in S$, and $\mathrm{Face}(k) = \langle\!\langle J, j, p; t \rangle\!\rangle$, then $\langle\!\langle I, i, k, \langle s_0, \langle\!\langle J, j, p; t \rangle\!\rangle \rangle; 1 \rangle\!\rangle \in s'$.

4. If S is an impure loop or chain and S contains no atomic J-tokens, $\langle i, k \rangle$ is a negative token, $\langle i, k \rangle \in S$, and $\mathrm{Face}(k) = \langle\!\langle I, j, k', p; t \rangle\!\rangle$, then $\langle\!\langle I, i, k, \langle s_0, \langle\!\langle I, c, k', p; t \rangle\!\rangle \rangle; 1 \rangle\!\rangle \in s'$.

The embellishment of a doxic network proceeds as follows. First, the monotonic operation τ is repeatedly applied (with limits taken at limit ordinals) until the minimal fixed point s_0 is reached. Then, the foundationalizing operation ϕ is repeatedly applied, resulting in a fixed point $s*$. Finally, a final closure operation $\tau*$ is again applied repeatedly, until a new fixed point s_1 is reached.

Definition 22 The *final doxic closure* $\tau * (s)$ *of situation* s (given τ-fixed point s_0) is the minimal situation s' extending s such that

1. If p is justifiable for i in s, then $\langle\!\langle J, i, p; 1 \rangle\!\rangle \in s'$. If p is unjustifiable for i in s, then $\langle\!\langle J, i, p; 0 \rangle\!\rangle \in s'$.

2a. If (a) $\mathrm{Face}(k) = \langle\!\langle J, j, p; t \rangle\!\rangle$, (b) there is no q such that $\langle\!\langle I, i, k, q; 1 \rangle\!\rangle \in s$, and (c) either $(i)k$ is positive and either $\langle\!\langle J, j, p; t \pm 1 \rangle\!\rangle \in s$ or $\langle\!\langle J, j, p; t \rangle\!\rangle \in s$, or $(ii)k$ is negative and $\langle\!\langle J, j, p; t \pm 1 \rangle\!\rangle \in s$, then $\langle\!\langle I, i, k, \langle s', \langle\!\langle J, j, p; t \rangle\!\rangle \rangle; 1 \rangle\!\rangle \in s'$.

2b. If (a) $\text{Face}(k) = \langle\!\langle J, j, p; t \rangle\!\rangle$, (b) there is no q such that $\langle\!\langle I, i, k, q; 1 \rangle\!\rangle \in s$, and (c) k is negative and $\langle\!\langle J, j, p; t \rangle\!\rangle \in s$, then $\langle\!\langle I, i, k, \langle s_0, \langle\!\langle J, j, p; t \rangle\!\rangle \rangle; 1 \rangle\!\rangle \in s'$.

3a. If (a) $\text{Face}(k) = \langle\!\langle I, j, k', p; t \rangle\!\rangle$, (b) there is no q such that $\langle\!\langle I, i, k, q; 1 \rangle\!\rangle \in s*$, and (c) either (i) k is positive and either $\langle\!\langle I, j, k', p; t \pm 1 \rangle\!\rangle \in s$ or $\langle\!\langle I, j, k', p; t \rangle\!\rangle \in s$, or (ii) k is negative and $\langle\!\langle I, j, k', p; t \pm 1 \rangle\!\rangle \in s$, then $\langle\!\langle I, i, k, \langle s', \langle\!\langle I, j, k', p; t \rangle\!\rangle \rangle; 1 \rangle\!\rangle \in s'$.

3b. If (a) $\text{Face}(k) = \langle\!\langle I, j, k', p; t \rangle\!\rangle$, (b) there is no q such that $\langle\!\langle I, i, k, q; 1 \rangle\!\rangle \in s*$, and (c) k is negative and $\langle\!\langle I, j, k', p; t \rangle\!\rangle \in s$, then $\langle\!\langle I, i, k, \langle s_0, \langle\!\langle I, j, k', p; t \rangle\!\rangle \rangle; 1 \rangle\!\rangle \in s'$.

4. If (a) $\text{Face}(k)$ is an atomic, doxic sentence, and (b) $\langle i, k \rangle$ is not open in s, and (c) there is no q such that $\langle\!\langle I, i, k, q; 1 \rangle\!\rangle \in s$, then: (i) if k is positive, $\langle\!\langle I, i, k, \langle s_0, \text{Face}(k) \rangle; 1 \rangle\!\rangle \in s'$, and (ii) if k is negative, $\langle\!\langle I, i, k \langle s', \text{Face}(k) \rangle; 1 \rangle\!\rangle \in s'$.

Some Results

Proposition 1 *If there is no q such that $\langle\!\langle I, i, k, q; 1 \rangle\!\rangle \in \tau(s)[\tau * (s)]$, then $\langle i, k \rangle$ calls some token (relative to s). And conversely, if $\langle i, k \rangle$ is an atomic doxic token.*

Proof. This follows immediately from the definitions of τ, τ^* and the calling relation. $\square$

Proposition 2 *If $\langle j, k' \rangle$ is called by $\langle i, k \rangle$ relative to s, then there is no q such that $\langle\!\langle I, j, k', q; 1 \rangle\!\rangle \in s$.*

Proof. Follows immediately from the definition of the calling relation. $\square$

Proposition 3 *If s is a fixed point with respect to ϕ, then s contains no loops or descending chains.*

Proof. The definition of the calling relation ensures that every loop or chain contains some uninterpreted atomic doxic tokens, and only uninterpreted atomic doxic tokens. The loop or chain must be either pure or impure, and in either case, an application of ϕ would result in the interpretation of some uninterpreted tokens. Hence, s cannot be a fixed point with respect to ϕ. $\square$

Proposition 4 *If $s*$ is a fixed point with respect to ϕ given s_0, and s_1 is a fixed point with respect to $\tau*$ which extends $s*$, then for every cognitive individual i and every sub-sentence k, there is a q such that $\langle\!\langle I, i, k, q; 1 \rangle\!\rangle \in s_1$.*

Proof. Since $s*$ is a ϕ-fixed point, by proposition 2, it contains no loops or chains. Suppose for contradiction that k is uninterpreted in s_1. By proposition 1, k calls some token k' relative to s_1. By proposition 2, token k' must be uninterpreted in s_1. By induction, there must be a closed loop or chain in s. But, since s_1 extends a ϕ-fixed point without introducing any new tokens, there can be no such closed loops or chains. $\qquad\Box$

The existence of these fixed points depends crucially on the fact that all quantification is bounded, since each variable contains a set as its range of significance. If absolutely unbounded quantification is permitted, then it is impossible to define an interpretation function for a network of tokens (which may itself be a proper class) which can be guaranteed to be total. Therefore, the believer in unbounded quantification must either suppose that all tokens are interpreted, but some receive their interpretation in a mysterious way beyond all formal definition, or she must suppose that some perfectly respectable tokens are not interpreted at all. The latter choice would be especially unfortunate, since it would cut out the ground beneath the context-sensitive approach to the Liar. One of the essential motivations for this approach is the avoidance of saying of perfectly respectable tokens, such as empirical liar paradoxes, that they do not express propositions at all.

References

Barwise, J., and J. Etchemendy. 1987. *The Liar: An Essay on Truth and Circularity.* New York: Oxford University Press.

Burge, T. 1979. Semantical Paradox. *Journal of Philosophy* 76:169–198.

Cooper, R., K. Mukai, and J. Perry (ed.). 1990. *Situation Theory and Its Applications,* vol. 1. CSLI Lecture Notes Number 22. Stanford: CSLI Publications.

Gaifman, H. 1983. Infinity and Self-Applications, I. *Erkenntnis* 20:131–155.

Gaifman, H. 1988. Operational Pointer Semantics: Solution to the Self-referential Puzzles, I. In *Proceedings of the Second Conference on Theoretical Aspects of Reasoning about Knowledge,* ed. M. Vardi. Los Altos, CA. Morgan Kaufman.

Koons, R. 1990. Three Indexical Solutions to the Liar. In Cooper et al. 1990.

Kyburg, H. 1970. Conjunctivitis. In *Induction, Acceptance and Rational Belief,* ed. M. Swain. Dordrecht: Reidel.

Olin, D. 1983. The Prediction Paradox Resolved. *Philosophical Studies* 44:225–233.

Parsons, C. 1974. The Liar Paradox. *Journal of Philosophical Logic* 3:381–412.

9

CLP(AFA): Coinductive Semantics of Horn Clauses with Compact Constraints

Kuniaki Mukai

A constraint language L_A over the class V_A of hypersets over A is proposed, where A is a class of atoms. L_A is a quantifier-free sublanguage of the first-order language with equality, subsumption, disjunction, and negation. For a natural sublanguage $L_{A\omega}$ of L_A and subclass $V_{A\omega}$ of V_A it is proved that $V_{A\omega}$ is solution compact with respect to $L_{A\omega}$. A subtheory of $L_{A\omega}$ is given that is satisfaction complete for positive constraints in the sense of the constraint logic programming (CLP) schema. In fact, $V_{A\omega}$ is the class of hereditarily finite hypersets in the universe V_A of Aczel's hyperset theory $ZFCA$[1] and $L_{A\omega}$ is the class of constraints in L_A that consists of finitary set terms. A characterization of the canonical programs in L_A is given in terms of extended bisimulation relations. Thus CLP(AFA) over the hypersets is obtained as a new instance of the CLP schema.

Furthermore, the CLP scheme is reconstructed and given a foundation based on the hyperset theory. First, a declarative semantics and an operational semantics of Horn clause programs over $L_{A\omega}$ and $V_{A\omega}$ are given based on coinductive definition. Then, soundness and completeness of the two semantics are proved by showing what we call a *simulation* relation between the two semantic domains.

I would like to thank Hideki Yasukawa, Kaoru Yoshida, Makoto Imamura, Satoshi Tojo, Hideyuki Nakashima, Koiti Hasida, S. Menju, William Rounds, Yōsuke Sato, Jon Barwise, and Hozumi Tanaka for giving useful comments and suggestions on an earlier version of this work on various occasions. Special thanks goes to the anonymous referee of the paper for pointing out many careless errors and giving useful suggestions. The term *ZFCA* and rational set were proposed by him. Also I am indebted to Mark Stickel for reading the final version and providing useful comments and help in improving the English.

[1] *ZFC* minus the axiom foundation plus Aczel's antifoundation axiom.

Situation Theory and Its Applications, vol. 2.
Jon Barwise, Jean Mark Gawron, Gordon Plotkin, and Syun Tutiya, eds.

Two applications are given by restricting $V_{A\omega}$ and $L_{A\omega}$ in a natural way. One application is an infinite tree unification in logic programming. The other is a feature structure unification as used in unification grammar formalisms. It is pointed out that not only can the UNION-FIND algorithm be applied to the restricted cases as usual, but a partition refinement algorithm on transition nets can also be applied straightforwardly to find the coarsest bisimulation relation that extends a given relation on hypersets.

1 Introduction

Aczel 1988 proposed the universe of hypersets (= non-well-founded sets) for modeling non-well-founded structured objects such as streams in Milnor's (1989) SCCS. He provided a powerful coinductive method like the inductive one in the standard universe of well-founded sets. Barwise and Etchemendy 1987 and Barwise 1989 apply Aczel's theory to circular situations and unification of feature structures, respectively. In the universe of hypersets, any collection called a system of equations has a unique solution. This lemma is called the solution lemma. For example, $x = \{x\}$ has a unique solution, which is obtained by unfolding the right side of the equation unboundedly to get, intuitively, $x = \{\{\{\cdots\}\}\}$.

Jaffar and Lassez 1987 proposes a scheme CLP(X) as a generalization of standard logic programming, where X is a parameter for constraint languages. A constraint language consists of a syntax of constraints, a notion of solutions, and a set of constraint solving rules. Pure Prolog is an instance of the scheme with X being the constraint language of the standard theory of equality over the Herbrand domain. The CLP scheme requires X to be *solution compact* and *satisfaction complete* to assure that SLD fair computation is sound and complete. Moreover, the scheme assures soundness and completeness of the negation-as-failure rule (NAFR) (Lloyd 1984) for *canonical* programs. The notions "solution compact," "satisfaction complete" and "canonical," among others, are explained informally below and will be defined formally in a later section. By soundness we mean that (2) ∨ (3) ⇒ (1) for every goal g, and by completeness we mean the converse, where

(1) g has a solution.
(2) There exists a finite success derivation for g.
(3) There exists an infinite derivation for g.

Also by soundness of NAFR we mean that (4) ⇒ (5) for every goal g and by completeness of NAFR we mean the converse, where

(4) g has no solution.
(5) Every SLD fair derivation for g fails in a finite number of steps.

A program is called *canonical* iff for every success derivation, the constraints appearing in the derivation have a solution. For example, it will be shown that a program in CLP(L_A) explained below is canonical if every parameter appearing in the negative part or on the right side of subsumption ($\sqsubseteq$) constraints in the derivation will be bound to non-parameter terms in a finite number of steps in the derivation.

A constraint language X is *constraint definable* if for every element x in the domain of X, there is a constraint c in X such that x is a unique solution of c. In other words, constraint definability means that every element is a limit of a sequence of finitarily representable elements. For example, as every real number is a limit of some sequence of rational numbers, the domain of real numbers is constraint definable with respect to the order $<$ and rational number constants. A constraint language X is called *compact* provided that for every set C of constraints, C has a solution iff every finite subset of C does.

The solution compactness condition is divided into two parts. One half is the same as constraint definability above. The other half is that for any given finite constraint c each element which does not satisfy c can be covered with a finite constraint c' that shares no solution with c. Clearly it follows from these definitions that if X is constraint definable and compact then X is solution compact. However, the converse is not always true.

Roughly speaking, the satisfaction completeness condition of the CLP scheme means that unifiability and solvability are equivalent. More precisely, it requires that the existence of solutions of given constraints is characterized by the syntactic rules of the constraint language. For example, standard unification language over the Herbrand domain, i.e., first-order term unification, is satisfaction complete because unifiability and solvability of constraints are equivalent. Recall that a given family of equations is unifiable iff there exists a congruence relation that extends the given family.

Based on these notions, the CLP scheme provides a foundation for logic programming to treat infinite objects such as irrational numbers through constraints (Jaffar and Michaylov 1987) and perpetual processes (Lloyd 1984). We are interested in nonterminating programs that process non-well-founded structures such as streams. These applications need maximum semantics because the standard minimum semantics is not able to give meanings to programs that treat streams, for example.

So far, the complete Herbrand domain, i.e., the domain of infinite trees, and the domain of real numbers with a certain appropriate class of constraints have been counted as two major instances of the CLP scheme. In recent years, logics of feature structures have been studied extensively. The reader is referred to Moss 1990 as one of the most up-to-date works on a logical foundation of feature structures. Several authors, Rounds (1988) for example, suggest that the domain of feature structures is a new and important instance of the scheme. Barwise 1989 shows that feature structures can be modeled as hypersets in V_A (the full universe of hypersets over A)

with the hereditary subset relation as subsumption relation. Accordingly, the domain of hypersets should be examined as a bridge that connects unification grammar formalisms and constraint logic programming.

Guided by the CLP schema, first we propose a constraint language L_A over the class V_A of hypersets over A, where A is a class of atoms. L_A is a quantifier-free sublanguage of the first-order language with equality, subsumption, disjunction, and negation intended for application to feature structure unification. We then propose a natural sublanguage $L_{A\omega}$ of L_A so that $L_{A\omega}$ is the class of constraints in L_A consisting of finitary terms. We will show that $V_{A\omega}$ is solution compact with respect to $L_{A\omega}$. As negative constraints are allowed, $L_{A\omega}$ is not satisfaction complete with respect to $V_{A\omega}$. However, we give a complete characterization of solvable positive constraints. Moreover, a subclass of $L_{A\omega}$ which consists of *canonical* constraints is proved to be satisfaction complete. The essential points here are that the solution lemma (Aczel 1988) is just constraint definability and that the class of positive constraints in $L_{A\omega}$ is compact. We give more details for these points.

In fact, there are clear reasons why $V_{A\omega}$ and $L_{A\omega}$ satisfy the CLP criteria. Constraint definability is clearly satisfied because of Aczel's solution lemma, i.e., every element of $V_{A\omega}$ can be represented as a unique solution of a system of equations in $L_{A\omega}$. As will be seen in the proof of solution compactness of $L_{A\omega}$, the second half of the solution compactness is obtained from constraint definability and compactness of the positive constraints. Barwise 1989 gives a characterization of solvability of *positive* constraints in terms of a certain kind of extensions of the given constraints. The extension is called a *simulation pair*. A simulation pair is a set c of equations and subsumptions such that c is closed under the rules for bisimulation and subsumption relations and that *every parameter in the constraint is bound to a set term*. We refer to this theorem as Barwise's unification theorem. We need to extend the theorem to the case in which constraints have unbound parameters. In fact, we will obtain Proposition 11 that asserts that every simulation pair with "unbound parameters" can be extended to a simulation pair without unbound parameters. This is a key lemma in this paper. We refer to this lemma as the *binding lemma*.

A complete characterization of solvable constraints is an open problem at this time; this paper gives only a partial characterization. Barwise's unification theorem is a complete characterization for the class of the solvable positive constraints over hypersets. We introduce a class of canonical constraints explained above. The notion of *canonical supports* is an extension of the notion of simulation pairs to the case in which negative constraints are allowed. Soundness and completeness of both the SLD fair computation rule and the NAFR (negation-as-failure-rule) are proved for the class of programs such that the accumulated constraints on the whole of unfailing derivation always form a canonical constraint.

In an earlier stage of logic programming, Colmerauer 1984 introduced the domain of infinite trees for modeling circularity. This paper tries to extend infinite trees to hypersets to see how well the CLP schema and unification grammar formalisms can be reconstructed. One technical advantage of hypersets over infinite trees is that the theory can be constructed in an abstract way which is highly independent of the concrete structure of objects. Remember that the mathematical formulation of the complete Herbrand domain needs auxiliary notions such as path, metrics and limit (Lloyd 1984), while in the universe of hypersets we can start immediately from the solution lemma.

We use Aczel's theory in two ways. One is to use it for defining semantics of a program coinductively and the other is to use it as a domain of logic programming as described above. In the former, two classes are defined coinductively. One is a class of non-well-founded triples for the declarative semantics of the program and the other is the class of non-well-founded pairs for SLD-like fair computation trees for queries (= goals). Soundness and completeness results are proved by showing a relation called *simulation* between them. Indeed, the simulation relates solutions to computations in a hereditary and coinductive way.

Here are a few remarks on algorithm complexity concerning hypersets. First, one of the partition refinement algorithms proposed in Paige and Tarjan 1987 can be applied to check the solvability of a given system of equations. Let n and m be the numbers of nodes and edges, respectively, appearing in the system, assuming that the system is represented suitably as a directed graph. Then there exists an $O(m \log n)$ time-complexity algorithm to compute the coarsest bisimulation for a given partition of the system. Second, the subdomain of records in $V_{A\omega}$ has an efficient implementation for a theory of $=$ and $\neq$. In fact, these constraints can be solved with UNION-FIND technique (Aho et al. 1974).

This paper is a progress report on foundations of a practical logic programming system CIL (Mukai 1990), which is based on records and lazy control. Also, the idea of CLP over hypersets and the results on unification over hypersets presented in this paper have been used as the kernel of the knowledge representation language called Quixote (Yasukawa and Yokota 1990).[2]

Here is a list of conventions which are used in throughout this paper. By $x \subseteq y$ we means that x is a subset of y, including the case of $x = y$. Also, by $x \sqsubseteq y$ we mean that x is a hereditary subset of y, including the case of $x = y$. V_A denotes the class of hypersets over a set A of atoms. $V_{A\omega}$ denotes the subclass of hypersets in V_A that are hereditarily finite. We use L for L_A where A is understood but never use it for $L_{A\omega}$.

---

[2]Quixote is under development at ICOT, Tokyo.

2 Unification over Hypersets

2.1 Preliminaries

We use Aczel's hyperset theory *ZFCA* (1988) as a metatheory throughout the paper. The following concepts are from Aczel 1988: coinductive definition, the substitution lemma, the solution lemma, the bisimulation relation (Park 1981). The definition of solution compactness and satisfaction completeness are from Stuckey 1987.

Let A be a possibly empty set of *atoms* and let X be an infinite set of *parameters* (= variables). V_A denotes the class of *hypersets* over A. $V_A[X]$ denotes the class of hypersets over $A \cup X$. Sets in $V_A[X]$ are called X-sets (over A). V_A is a subclass of $V_A[X]$. $V_{A\omega}$ denotes the class of hypersets in V_A that are hereditarily finite, i.e., finite at all levels. $V_{A\omega}[X]$ denotes the class of X-sets over A that are hereditarily finite. $V_{A\omega}$ is a subclass of $V_{A\omega}[X]$. An element of $V_A[X]$ is also called a *term*.

The *transitive closure* of a set $x \in V_A[X]$ is the least transitive set T in $V_A[X]$ such that $x \subseteq T$. The transitive closure of x is denoted as trans(x). For example

$$\text{trans}(\{a, \{b, c\}\}) = \{a, \{b, c\}, b, c\}$$

where a, b, c are atoms. In general, u *appears in* v when $u \in \text{trans}(\{v\})$.

Definition 1 A set is *rational* if it has the finite transitive closure.[3]

Clearly a rational set is hereditarily finite but the converse is not always true. To see this, let $\{A_i\}_{i \in N}$ be a family of finite sets of atoms such that A_i is a proper subset of A_j for $i < j$, where N is the set of nonpositive integers. It is clear that the solution for x_0 of the system $\{x_i = A_i \cup \{x_{i+1}\} \mid i \in N\}$ of equations is hereditarily finite but it has no finite transitive closure.

Definition 2 A *system of equations* is a collection of *equations* $x = b_x$ for $x \in X$, where X is a collection of parameters and $\{b_x\}_{x \in X}$ is a family of X-sets.

Theorem 1 (Substitution Lemma, Aczel 1988) *Let* $f: X \to V$. *There is a unique function* $\hat{f}$ *that satisfies the following for each X-set b:*

$$\hat{f}(b) = \{x \in b \mid x \text{ is an atom}\} \cup \{f(x) \mid x \in X \cap b\}$$
$$\cup \{\hat{f}(x) \mid x \in b, \ x \text{ is a set}\}.$$

The notion of a solution for a system of equations is defined by the substitution lemma as usual.

Theorem 2 (Solution Lemma, Aczel 1988) *Every system of equations has a unique solution in* V_A.

Definition 3 For any A and X, a set u in $V_A[X]$ is *finitary* if u is hereditarily finite and well-founded.

---

[3]This term was proposed by the referee of this paper.

Let N be the set of natural numbers. Then the set $\{N\}$ is finite but neither finitary nor rational. The set Ω such that $\Omega = \{\Omega\}$ is finite. Moreover, it is hereditarily finite and rational, but not finitary.

Definition 4 We assume a collection of *nodes*. A *system* M is a collection of ordered pairs of nodes such that for any node a in the system, the successors of a form a set (not a proper class) which is denoted by a_M.

Definition 5 A binary relation R on the system M is a *bisimulation* on M if $R \subseteq R^+$, where for $a, b \in M$

$$aR^+b \iff \forall x \in a_M \, \exists y \in b_M \; xRy \quad \& \quad \forall y \in b_M \, \exists x \in a_M \; xRy.$$

For the sake of convenience we represent a bisimulation relation R as the collection c_R of equations $a = b$ such that aRb. A collection c of equations is called a *bisimulation constraint* if $c = c_R$ for some bisimulation relation R, c can be a proper class. We make no distinction between the bisimulation relation and the bisimulation constraint.

2.2 Constraint Language L_A

In this subsection we introduce a constraint language L_A using the definition of Smolka 1989.

2.2.1 Constraint Language

Definition 6 A *constraint language* is a quadruple $(X, C, \mathcal{V}, \mathcal{I})$, where

1. X is a set of *parameters* (= variables[4]).
2. C is a set of *constraints*.
3. $\mathcal{V}$ is a function which assigns to each constraint, say ψ, a set $\mathcal{V}(\psi)$ of parameters.
4. $\mathcal{I}$ is a set of *interpretations*. An *interpretation* is given as a pair (D, S) of a *domain* D and a function S such that, for any constraint $\psi \in C$, S assigns a set $S(\psi)$ of partial functions from X into D. An element of $S(\psi)$ is called a *solution* of ψ. If the restriction of f to $\mathcal{V}(\psi)$ belongs to $S(\psi)$ then $f \in S(\psi)$.

Definition 7 A constraint language is *compact* if for any countable set c of constraints in the language, c is solvable iff every finite subset of c is solvable.

We fix the syntax of constraint languages $L = L_A$ and $L_{A\omega}$ by giving X and C. X is fixed to be an infinite set of parameters. A set u is *flat* if every element of u is either the empty set, an atom, or a parameter. A constraint is *flat* if ever set term in the constraint is flat. Without loss of generality for our purpose and for the sake of simplicity we use a convention that every term in the formal part of the paper is flat unless mentioned explicitly. A special constant symbol $\emptyset$ is reserved to denote the *empty* set: $\emptyset = \{\}$.

---

[4] We make no distinction between parameters and variables.

Definition 8 An *atomic constraint* is an *equation* $(=, u, v)$ or a *subsumption* $(\sqsubseteq, u, v)$, where $u, v \in V_A[X]$. The equation and subsumption are written as $u = v$ and $u \sqsubseteq v$, respectively, as usual.

Both u and v above are called *arguments* of the atomic constraint.

Definition 9 A *literal* is an atomic constraint or its negation $(\neg, u)$ written as $\neg u$, where u is an atomic constraint. A *clause* is a set of literals.

Definition 10 A *constraint* is an element of M, where M is the least subclass of $V_A[X]$ such that M has every literal and is closed under $\neg$, $\bigvee$, $\bigwedge$, i.e., if $t \in M$, $u \subseteq M$ then $(\neg, t), (\bigvee, u), (\bigwedge, u) \in M$.

The above three forms are written $\neg t$, $\bigvee u$, $\bigwedge u$ as usual, respectively.

Let c be a constraint in L_A. The *field* of c is the transitive closure of the set of arguments of atomic constraints appearing in c. The field of c is denoted as $\mathit{fld}(c)$. For example,

$$\mathit{fld}(\{x = a, y \neq \{b, c\}\}) = \{x, a, y, \{b, c\}, b, c\}$$

where x, y, a, b, and c are supposed to be not set terms. Clearly $\mathit{fld}(c)$ is finite whenever c is *finitary*.

For a constraint c in L_A a term t is called a *term of constraint* c if $t \in \mathit{fld}(c)$. We assume that constraints are elements of $V_{A \cup S}[X]$, where S is the set of logical connectives and relation symbols, i.e., $S = \{\bigvee, \bigwedge, \neg, \cdots, =, \sqsubseteq, \cdots\}$. We do not assume that A and S are disjoint. A *positive constraint* is a constraint in which no negation sign $\neg$ appears.

Definition 11 $L_{A\omega}$ is the sublanguage of L_A whose constraint consists of all *finitary* constraints in L_A.

As a convention, we write $u \neq v$ and $u \not\sqsubseteq v$ for $\neg(u = v)$ and $\neg(u \sqsubseteq v)$ respectively. We also write $u \vee v$ and $u \wedge v$ for $\bigvee\{u, v\}$ and $\bigwedge\{u, v\}$ respectively. We fix an interpretation $\mathcal{I}$ of L_A in the following way. The distinguished constant symbol $\emptyset$ denotes the empty set. Each constant symbol denotes itself. Let s be a set term and f be an assignment such that each parameter appearing in s is in $dom(f)$, i.e., $\mathcal{V}(s) \subseteq dom(f)$. The interpretation of s with respect to f is $\hat{f}(u)$. Note that we have assumed that every term in $L_{A\omega}$ is well-founded. The interpretation of the equality symbol '$=$' in L_A is the identity relation in the domain V_A.

Definition 12 The interpretation of the *subsumption relation symbol* '$\sqsubseteq$' is the largest relation R on V_A such that if xRy then one of the following holds:

1. $x = y \in A$, i.e., x and y are the same atom in A.
2. x and y are sets in V_A and for each $u \in x$ there is some $v \in y$ such that xRy.

Remark. The $\sqsubseteq$ relation is a preorder on V_A but not a partial order. In fact the following are true, which show a failure of the antisymmetric law for subsumption:
$$\{\emptyset, \{\emptyset\}\} \sqsubseteq \{\{\emptyset\}\}.$$
$$\{\{\emptyset\}\} \sqsubseteq \{\emptyset, \{\emptyset\}\}.$$

Remark. Even in the case of ordered pairs we cannot reduce subsumption to pairwise subsumption. For example, $(a, b) \sqsubseteq (b, a)$ is true by definition of subsumption, but also by definition neither $a \sqsubseteq b$ nor $b \sqsubseteq a$ are possible, where a and b are two distinct atoms.

Remark. There are "minimum" and "maximum" elements in V_A with respect to $\sqsubseteq$. In fact $\emptyset \sqsubseteq x$ and $x \sqsubseteq \Omega_A$ for any set x in V_A, where Ω_A is defined by the equation $\Omega_A = A \cup \{\Omega_A\}$ for a set A.

Proposition 3 $x \sqsubseteq \Omega_A$ *for any set x in V_A.*

Proof. Let $R = \{(x, \Omega_A) \mid x \in V_A\}$. R is a binary relation on V_A. Clearly R satisfies all clauses of definition of $\sqsubseteq$. As $\sqsubseteq$ is the largest such relations we get $R \subseteq \sqsubseteq$. $\qquad\square$

Definition 13 $\models$ is a binary relation between assignments f and constraints c such that $\mathcal{V}(c) \subseteq dom(f)$, which is defined inductively on the structure of c:

1. $\models_f u = v$ if $\hat{f}(u) = \hat{f}(v)$.
2. $\models_f u \sqsubseteq v$ if $\hat{f}(u) \sqsubseteq \hat{f}(v)$.
3. $\models_f \neg c$ if it is not the case that $\models_f c$.
4. $\models_f \bigvee u$ if $\models_f d$ for some $d \in u$.
5. $\models_f \bigwedge u$ if $\models_f d$ for all $d \in u$.

Definition 14 An assignment f is a *solution* of a constraint c in L_A iff $\models_f c$. We also say that c is *solvable* or *satisfiable* when c has a solution in the domain.

Now we have fixed the constraint language L_A. It is easy to see that a constraint c is solvable iff some disjunct of the disjunctive normal form of c is solvable. So it suffices to study the solvability of clauses.

2.2.2 Constraint Rules

We define a list of constraint rules for the constraint theory in L_A. We take constraint rules to be condition on clauses in L_A. It is straightforward to see that the logical reading of the following rules is sound with respect to the constraint language L_A. In the definition, c is a clause being conditioned. x, y, z are any terms and u, v are set terms. So u and v are neither atoms nor parameters.

Definition 15 *Constraint Rules*

1. If x is a term appearing in c then $x = x \in c$.
2. If $x = y \in c$ then $y = x \in c$.

3. If $x = y \in c$ and $y = z \in c$ then $x = z \in c$.
4. If $u = v \in c$ then for each $x \in u$ there is $y \in v$ such that $x = y \in c$ and for each $y \in v$ there is $x \in u$ such that $x = y \in c$.
5. If $x \neq y \in c$ then $y \neq x \in c$.
6. If $x = y \in c$ and $x \neq z \in c$ then $y \neq z \in c$.
7. If $u \neq v \in c$ then either there is some $x \in u$ such that $x \neq y \in c$ for all $y \in v$ or there is some $y \in v$ such that $x \neq y \in c$ for all $x \in u$.
8. If x is a term appearing in c then $x \sqsubseteq x \in c$.
9. If $x \sqsubseteq y \in c$ and $y \sqsubseteq z \in c$ then $x \sqsubseteq z \in c$.
10. If $x = y \in c$ and $x \sqsubseteq z \in c$ then $y \sqsubseteq z \in c$.
11. If $x = y \in c$ and $z \sqsubseteq x \in c$ then $z \sqsubseteq y \in c$.
12. If $x \sqsubseteq y \in c$ and either x or y is an atom (in A) then $x = y \in c$.
13. If $x \sqsubseteq \emptyset \in c$ then $x = \emptyset \in c$.
14. If $u \sqsubseteq v \in c$ then for each $x \in u$ there exists some $y \in v$ such that $x \sqsubseteq y \in c$.
15. If $x = y \in c$ and $x \not\sqsubseteq u \in c$ then $y \not\sqsubseteq u \in c$.
16. If $x = y \in c$ and $u \not\sqsubseteq x \in c$ then $u \not\sqsubseteq y \in c$.
17. If $u \not\sqsubseteq v \in c$ then there is some $x \in u$ such that $x \not\sqsubseteq y \in c$ for any $y \in v$.

In fact, these rules can be used as an effective method to solve finitary constraints as described later. However, they are intended only for theoretical exposition, not efficient computation. Record structures, for example, should be used for practical computation. The record structure will be discussed later in the paper as an implementation issue.

2.2.3 Support

Recall that by a clause, i.e., a possibly infinite clause in L_A, we mean the conjunction of literals in the set. For example the clause $\{p, q, r\}$ means $p \wedge q \wedge r$.

Definition 16 A parameter x is bound in a clause c if c has an equation $x = b$ where b is a set (not a proper class), atom, or $\emptyset$.

Definition 17 A clause c is normal if each parameter x appearing in c is bound in c.

Intuitively, a normal clause is a "grounded constraint," i.e., every parameter is fully instantiated.

Definition 18 A clause c is canonical if the following hold.

1. For each negative literal $l \in c$ there is a finite normal subset c' of c such that $l \in c'$.
2. For each positive literal $u \sqsubseteq x \in c$ x is bound in c, where x is a parameter.

Note that a normal clause is canonical but a canonical clause is not always normal. For example the clause

$$\{x \neq y, z \sqsubseteq x, y = \emptyset, x = \emptyset\}$$

is canonical but not normal because z is not bound in the clause.

Definition 19 A *presupport* is a consistent clause closed under the constraint rules. That is, it is a clause in L_A that has no complementary pair of literals and is closed under the above constraint rules (1)–(17) of the language L_A.

Every bisimulation constraint and subsumption constraint is a presupport. Also a "simulation pair" in Barwise's unification theorem (1989) is a presupport, which is, roughly speaking, the union of a bisimulation and a subsumption constraint.

Definition 20 A *support* s is a presupport in L_A such that there is no pair p and d that satisfies the following:

• p is a positive subset of s.
• $\neg d$ is a negative literal in s.
• $p \cup \{\neg d\}$ is canonical.
• There is a presupport s' in L_A such that $p \cup \{d\} \subseteq s'$.

Every positive presupport is a support by definition.

Example 1 Take a set s:

$$\{x \neq y, x = \{x\}, y = \{y\}, y \neq x, \{x\} = x, \{y\} = y,$$
$$x = x, y = y, \{x\} = \{x\}, \{y\} = \{y\}\}.$$

Clearly s is a presupport. However s is not a support. To see this, consider the canonical subset

$$\{x \neq y, x = \{x\}, y = \{y\}\}$$

of s. It suffices to show a presupport that extends the clause $\{x = y, x = \{x\}, y = \{y\}\}$. In fact the clause s':

$$\{x = y, x = \{x\}, y = \{y\}, y = x, \{x\} = x, \{y\} = y,$$
$$x = x, y = y, \{x\} = \{x\}, \{y\} = \{y\}\}$$

is immediately determined to be the presupport.

Presupports and supports will be used heavily to characterize the satisfiability (=solvability) of constraints. We say a clause p is a *presupport of clause* c if p is a presupport such that $c \subseteq p$. We also say a clause c *has a presupport* p when p is a presupport of c. We say that p is a *small presupport* of a clause c if $fld(p) \subseteq fld(c)$, i.e., only terms of c appear in p.

Proposition 4 *For every finitary constraint c the following hold.*

(1) *The set of small presupports of c is finite.*
(2) *The set of small supports of c is finite.*

(3) *If there exists a presupport of c then there exists also a small presupport of c.*

(4) *If there exists a support of c, then there exists also a small support of c.*

Proof. Let Q be the set of literals l such that $fld(l) \subseteq fld(c)$. As c is finitary $fld(c)$ is finite. So Q must be finite. As every small presupport of c is a subset of Q, we get (1). Similarly, we get (2).

Now we prove (3). Let p be a presupport of c. Clearly $c \subseteq p$. As Q is finite, $p \cap Q$ is finite. It is routine to check that the clause $p \cap Q$ satisfies the definition of presupport. As $c \subseteq Q$ we get $c \subseteq p \cap Q$. Therefore, $p \cap Q$ is a small presupport of c. Similarly, we get (4). □

Proposition 5 *For every finitary clause c the existence of a presupport and support of c are decidable, respectively.*

Proof. In general, for a given finite set B, the existence of a presupport p such that $fld(p) \subseteq B$ is decidable by an exhaustive search method.

Clearly p is a small presupport of c iff p is a support such that $fld(p) \subseteq fld(c)$. Since c is finitary, $fld(c)$ is finite. So it follows from the above general remark that the existence of a small presupport of c is decidable. Hence, from Proposition 5, the existence of a presupport of c is decidable. Similar we can prove the case of a support. □

2.2.4 Motivating Examples

Generally speaking, some infinite computations fail to have limit solutions even if there is no conflict found in the accumulated constraints of computation with respect to the built-in constraint rules. So it is necessary to find a subclass of possibly infinite computations that have a "limit." "Canonical" supports characterize such a subclass of computations. More precisely, every computation has a limit whenever the limit constraints on the computation has a canonical support. In fact, as will be shown later in detail, the constraint sublanguage $L_{A\omega}$ of L_A has the nice property that every canonical support is solvable in $V_{A\omega}$ (theorem 17). We use several motivating examples from some constraint languages which leads to the theorem.

First, the standard equality constraint language L_H over Herbrand universe H is not compact, where H is the set of all first-order ground terms generated by given constants and function symbols. To see this take a set c of atomic constraints

$$x_1 = f(x_2), x_2 = f(x_3), \cdots, x_n = f(x_{n+1}), \cdots$$

where f is a unary function symbol. Every finite subset of c is satisfiable but c itself is not satisfiable in H. This example shows that there is a consistent constraint in L_H which is unsolvable in H. However it should be noticed that the compactness of the language $L_{A\omega}$ over $V_{A\omega}$ holds only with respect to positive constraints. In fact because of negative constraints $L_{A\omega}$ is not compact. Consider the constraint (1) consisting of literals

(1) $\qquad x_1 \neq x_2, x_2 \neq x_3, \cdots, \ x_1 = \{x_2\}, x_2 = \{x_3\}, \cdots.$

Clearly every finite subset of (1) is satisfiable. However, by the solution lemma the global solution of the equations is uniquely determined as

$$x_1 = x_2 = x_3 = \cdots = \Omega \ (= \{\{\{\cdots\}\}\}),$$

which does not satisfy any unequation $x_i \neq x_j$ in the constraint. Note that constraint (1) is normal but not canonical. Moreover, it is not the case that every finite normal presupport is solvable. To see this let $c = \{x = \{x\}, y = \{y\}, x \neq y\}$. c has a finite normal presupport. However, c is unsolvable because the unique solution for the equations is $x = \Omega$ and $y = \Omega$, which does not satisfy the unequation in c.

2.3 The Constraint Logic Programming Scheme

The CLP(X) scheme of Jaffar and Lassez 1987 is a foundation for treating infinite objects, e.g., irrational numbers and infinite computations in logic programming. There are two well-known instances for the parameter X. One is the domain H^* of infinite trees. The other is the domain $\mathcal{R}$ of real numbers. The CLP scheme assures soundness and completeness of the semantics including the negation-as-failure rule. Also the CLP scheme gives a duality between maximum and minimum semantics for a large class of programs which we will call *canonical*) in a later section. That is, roughly speaking, the maximum model of the program can be reached by a countable monotone decreasing sequence of approximations as well as the minimum model by an increasing one. First of all, let us recall the definition of "solution compactness" and "satisfaction completeness."

Definition 21 (Jaffar and Lassez 1987, Stuckey 1987) A many sorted structure $\mathcal{R}$ is called *solution compact* if the following hold.

1. every element in $\mathcal{R}$ is the unique solution of a finite or infinite set of constraints.

2. for every *finite* constraint c and choice of n there exists a finite or infinite family of *finite* constraints c_i containing n parameters $x_1, \cdots, x_n$ such that:

$$\mathcal{R}^n - \{(f(x_1), \cdots, f(x_n)) \mid f \text{ is } \mathcal{R}\text{-solution of } c\}$$
$$= \bigcup_i \{(g(x_1), \cdots, g(x_n)) \mid g \text{ is } \mathcal{R}\text{-solution of } c_i\}.$$

Intuitively speaking, the second condition of solution compactness says that for any given finite constraint c each element in the complement of c can be separated from c by a "finite covering." We shall treat only the case of $n = 1$, since the general case in which parameters $x_1, \cdots, x_n$ in the given constraint c are chosen is reduced to this simple case by adding the equation $x = (x_1, \cdots, x_n)$ to c in which the new parameter x is the only parameter chosen, where x is a new parameter. In what follows, $\tilde{\exists}c$ means the closed formula obtained by existentially quantifying the parameters of c. Similarly $\tilde{\forall}c$ means the universal closure of c.

Definition 22 A theory T and structure $\mathcal{R}$ are said to *correspond* if
1. $\mathcal{R} \models T$ ($\mathcal{R}$ is a model of T) and
2. $\mathcal{R} \models \tilde{\exists}c$ implies $T \models \tilde{\exists}c$ for all constraints c.

In order to obtain negative information from a theory T we require a further condition.

Definition 23 (Jaffar and Lassez 1987, Stuckey 1987) A theory T is *satisfaction complete* if $T \models \tilde{\forall}\neg c$ whenever $T \not\models \tilde{\exists}c$.

In other words, a theory T is *satisfaction complete* if whenever there is a model M of T such that c is unsolvable in M, then c is unsolvable in every model of T. Satisfaction completeness roughly means that solvability is characterized within the theory on the domain. For example, standard unification theory over the Herbrand domain is satisfaction complete because, for any set c of equations, the solvability of c is equivalent to the syntactic condition that there exists a congruence relation that extends the given system of equations. Thus, the standard unification theory T is the set of clauses of first-order equations which represents a congruence relation over first-order terms with no clash between signatures.

2.4 Solvability of Hyperset Constraints

We relate *ZFCA* to the constraint logic programming scheme (Jaffar and Lassez 1987). We show that the constraint language $L_{A\omega}$ introduced above satisfies the criteria of the schema.

2.4.1 Normal Constraint

The following theorem is due to Barwise 1989. X and A are classes of parameters and atoms respectively. We repeat the proof given by Barwise using normal supports instead of "simulation pairs."

Theorem 6 (Unification Theorem (Barwise)) *Given any set p of equations and subsumptions over $V_A[X]$ the following are equivalent.*

(1) *p has a normal support.*

(2) *p has a solution in V_A.*

Proof. (1) $\Rightarrow$ (2): Let q be a normal support of p. Since q is normal for each x in $\mathcal{V}(q)$ there exists a set term b_x such that $x = b_x$ is in q. Let $S = \{x = b_x \mid x \in \mathcal{V}(q)\}$. S is a system of equations. Clearly S is a subset of q. By the solution lemma, there is a solution f for S. Let B be the set of ordered pairs $(\hat{f}(u), \hat{f}(v))$ such that $u = v$ is in q. Let D be the set of ordered pairs $(\hat{f}(u), \hat{f}(v))$ such that $u \sqsubseteq v$ is in q. B and D are binary relations on V_A. Since p is a support, B and D satisfy all defining clauses of the bisimulation and subsumption relation on V_A, respectively. Since the maximum bisimulation on V_A is the identity relation (Aczel 1988), we obtain $B \subseteq \{(x, x) \mid x \in V_A\}$. Similarly D is a subset of the hereditary subset relation on V_A. Hence we obtain (2).

(2) $\Rightarrow$ (1): Suppose f is a solution for p in V_A. Let P be the set of equations $u = v$ such that u and v are in $fld(p)$ and $\hat{f}(u)$ and $\hat{f}(v)$ are the same element of V_A. Let Q be the set of subsumptions $u \sqsubseteq v$ such that u and v are in $fld(p)$ and $\hat{f}(u)$ is a hereditary subset of $\hat{f}(v)$ in V_A. Let $q = P \cup Q \cup \{x = \hat{f}(x) \mid x \in \mathcal{V}(p)\}$. It is easily checked that $p \subseteq q$ and q has a normal support in L_A. □

Note that this theorem does not assure that any normal support in the language $L_{A\omega}$ has a solution in $V_{A\omega}$ even if every atomic constraint in the given support is finitary. We will discuss this later. By a *positive support* we mean a support without negative literals, i.e., consisting of only atomic constraints.

Lemma 7 (Binding Lemma) *Any positive support has a positive normal support.*

Proof. Let p be a positive support. Let x be any unbound parameter of p, i.e., we suppose that if $x = u$ in p then u is a parameter. Let L_x be the set of terms u such that $u \sqsubseteq x \in p$. Similarly, let U_x be the set of terms u such that $x \sqsubseteq u \in p$. As p is a positive support, if $x = y$ is in p for some parameter y, then $L_x = L_y$ and $U_x = U_y$. Let B_x be the union of sets in L_x and let

$$
\begin{aligned}
p' \;=\; & p \cup \{u \sqsubseteq B_x \mid u \in L_x\} \\
& \cup \{B_x \sqsubseteq u \mid u \in U_x\} \\
& \cup \{B_x = B_x\} \\
& \cup \{B_x \sqsubseteq B_x\}.
\end{aligned}
$$

As p is a positive support it is certain that p' satisfies all the constraint rules. For example, we can see that p' satisfies constraint rule (14) as follows. Let $y \in B_x$ and suppose that $B_x \sqsubseteq v \in p'$ for some set v. By definition of B_x $x \sqsubseteq v \in p$ and $y \in u$ and $u \sqsubseteq x \in p$ for some u. As p is a support $u \sqsubseteq v \in p$ and $y \sqsubseteq z \in p$ for some $z \in v$. Hence, p' satisfies constraint rule (14). Thus we can prove that p' is a support. Hence the reflexive closure p'' of $p' \cup \{x = B_x\}$ with respect to the equality $=$ is a support. Note that $\mathcal{V}(p) = \mathcal{V}(p'')$. By repeating this extension procedure for each free parameter in p we get a monotone increasing sequence of supports of p. It is easy to see that the union of supports in the sequence is a normal support of p. □

Example 2 Take the least support of $\{\{x\} \sqsubseteq x\}$. Then the above proof constructs the least normal support of $\{\{x\} \sqsubseteq x, x = \{x\}\}$ of the given support.

I do not know whether 'positive' in the lemma can be dropped or not. In this case at least, the above proof does not work. To see this, consider the least support of $\{\{x\} \sqsubseteq x, x \neq \{x\}\}$. The normal constraint constructed by the method in the proof is the reflective and symmetric closure of $\{\{x\} \sqsubseteq x, x = \{x\}, x \neq \{x\}\}$, which is not a support.

Theorem 8 *Every positive support in L_A is solvable in V_A.*

Proof. Let p be a positive support. p has a positive normal support p' by the binding lemma. As Barwise's unification theorem 6 can be applied to arbitrary positive supports p' has a solution in V_A. □

Theorem 8 together with Proposition 5 gives a decision procedure for subsumption problems. More precisely, given a set of positive equations and subsumptions, it is decidable whether the set has a solution or not.

Remark. The distinction between atom and parameter is important. Consider the constraint $a = \{x\}$. If a is an atom then, by definition, there is no support for this constraint. In fact there is no solution in this case. Otherwise, if a is a parameter, clearly $a = \{x\}$ has a support and is in fact solvable.

Remark. Applying this theorem, I found an elegant decision procedure for a class of extensional subsumption problems over feature structures (Mukai 1991). The procedure in Mukai 1991 is a hyperset-theoretical positive answer to the problem class, which was first solved by Dörre (April 1990). On the contrary, it was proved in Dörre and Rounds 1990 that the intensional version of subsumption problems is undecidable.

Lemma 9 *Given a countable clause c of finitary literals, the following are equivalent.*

(1) Every finite subset of c has a support.

(2) c has a support.

Proof. $(2) \Rightarrow (1)$: Obvious.

$(1) \Rightarrow (2)$: Suppose (1) is true. If c is finite, (2) is obviously true. So we assume c is infinite: $c = \{q_n \mid 0 \leq n\}$, where q_i are literals. Let S_n be the set of small supports of $\{q_0, \cdots, q_n\}$. It follows from the assumption that S_n is a nonempty finite set and that for any $n \geq 1$ and $p \in S_n$ there is a support $p' \in S_{n-1}$ such that $p' \subseteq p$. For each $n \geq 1$, let T_n be the set of all sequences $\{p_j\}_{0 \leq j \leq n}$ of supports such that $p_j \in S_j$ and $p_{j-1} \subseteq p_j$ $(j \neq 0)$. Clearly, every T_n is finite and nonempty. Also, T_n and T_m are disjoint from each other for $n \neq m$. Let T be the union of the family $\{T_n\}_{n \geq 0}$. Let R be a binary relation on T such that $R(p, p')$ is true just in case p is an initial segment of p', i.e., p' is an extension of p as a sequence. It is easy to see that (T, R) is a tree with finite branches at each node. Applying the standard argument of König's lemma to this tree, we can construct an infinite sequence $\{p_j\}_{0 \leq j}$ such that $p_j \in S_j$ and $p_{j-1} \subseteq p_j$ $(j \neq 0)$. Let p

be the union of the sequence: $p = \bigcup \{p_j \mid 0 \le j\}$. It is easily checked that p is a support of c. $\square$

Proposition 10 *The following are equivalent for any countable set p of finite atomic constraints:*

1. *Every finite subset of p has a support.*
2. *p has a normal support.*

Proof. This is a direct combination of the previous two lemmas. $\square$

The normal support p in condition (2) may have infinite terms.

Proposition 11 *For any normal support p the following are equivalent.*

(1) *p has a solution in V_A.*
(2) *For each negative literal $l \in p$, $p' \cup \{l\}$ has a solution in V_A, where p' is the set of positive literals in p.*

Proof. (1) $\Rightarrow$ (2): Obvious.

(2) $\Rightarrow$ (1): Suppose (2) is true. Let p' be the set of positive literals in p. As p is normal, p' is also normal and $\mathcal{V}(p) = \mathcal{V}(p')$. By the solution lemma, there is a unique solution f of p'. From the hypothesis, the uniqueness of f, and $\mathcal{V}(p) \subseteq dom(f)$, it follows that f is a solution of $p' \cup \{l\}$ for any negative literal l in p. Therefore, f is a solution of p. $\square$

Lemma 12 *For a positive normal support p and an atomic constraint d such that $\mathcal{V}(d) \subseteq \mathcal{V}(p)$, the following are equivalent.*

(1) *$p \cup \{\neg d\}$ has a solution in V_A.*
(2) *$p \cup \{d\}$ has no solution V_A.*

Proof. As p is a normal positive support, there is a unique solution f of p in V_A such that $dom(f) = \mathcal{V}(p)$ and $\mathcal{V}(d) \subseteq dom(f)$.

(2) $\Rightarrow$ (1): Suppose (2) is true. Then f does not satisfy d. Otherwise, f would be a solution of $p \cup \{d\}$ in $V_{A\omega}$, which contradicts (2). So f is a solution of $\neg d$. Hence, f is a solution of $p \cup \{\neg d\}$.

(1) $\Rightarrow$ (2): Suppose (1) is true but (2) is not, i.e., there is a solution g of $p \cup \{d\}$. So g must satisfy d. On the other hand, it follows from (1) that f must satisfy $\neg d$. As f and g are solutions of p and $\mathcal{V}(d) \subseteq \mathcal{V}(p)$, f and g must coincide on $\mathcal{V}(d)$, which is a contradiction. Hence (2) must be the case. $\square$

Lemma 12 and the binding lemma (Lemma 7) form the basis for a unification algorithm. To see this, let p and d be a finite normal support and an atomic constraint, respectively, such that $\mathcal{V}(d) \subseteq \mathcal{V}(p)$. Then it is decidable by a naive saturation method whether $p \cup \{\neg d\}$ has a solution or not by checking the solvability of $p \cup \{d\}$, which can be determined by Barwise's simulation pair theorem. This remark will be used in a later section for application to the usual term structures and record structures.

Lemma 13 (Compactness Lemma) *For a positive constraint* $c = \{d_n \mid 0 \leq n\}$ *the following are equivalent.*

(1) *Each finite subset of* c *has a solution in* V_A.

(2) c *has a solution in* V_A

Proof. (2) $\Rightarrow$ (1): Obvious.

(1) $\Rightarrow$ (2): Suppose (1) is true. By the binding lemma, since every finite subset of c has a support, c has a normal support p. Then, by Barwise's theorem, there is a solution of p in V_A. $\qquad\qquad\qquad\qquad$ $\square$

The following is a corollary of the compactness lemma (Lemma 13).

Lemma 14 *For a set* c *of atomic constraints in* L_A, *the following are equivalent.*

1. *There is no support of* c.

2. *There is some finite set* c' *of* c *such that there is no support of* c'.

Now we address the problem of compactness of $V_{A\omega}$ with respect to $L_{A\omega}$. Barwise's theorem is used again. Consider a countable family of subsumptions $\{a_i\} \sqsubseteq x$ for $i > 0$, where a_i are distinct atoms. Then every a_i must be an element of x. So x must be infinite. This means $V_{A\omega}$ is not compact in general with respect to subsumption. The theorem below gives more precise information about this problem. In the proof, we treat only positive constraint, which is a countable set of equations and subsumptions between *well-founded* elements of $V_{A\omega}[X]$. Note that each element of a constraint is finitely representable as a tree.

Theorem 15 *Let* A *be a set of atoms.* $V_{A\omega}$ *is compact with respect to the class of supports in* $L_{A\omega}$ *iff* $A = \emptyset$.

Proof. Unlike the other parts of the paper, set terms here may not be flat. The proof is divided into two cases, (1) and (2).

(1) Suppose $A \neq \emptyset$ and $a \in A$. Let Ω_a be the unique solution of $z = \{a, z\}$. Define a countable sequence b inductively as follows.

- $b_0 = \{\Omega_a\}$.
- $b_n = \{a, b_{n-1}\}$ $(n > 0)$.

Define a countable sequence d inductively as follows:

- $d_0 = \{a\}$.
- $d_n = \{d_{n-1}\}$ $(n > 0)$.

Let $e_n = \{d_n, b_n\}$ for $n \geq 0$. It is clear that if $d_n \sqsubseteq u$ then u must have the "path" d_n by definition of d_n. If $u \sqsubseteq e_n$ and u has the path d_n then u cannot have any path $d_{n'}$ for $n' \neq n$. Hence for $n \neq n'$ if $d_n \sqsubseteq u \sqsubseteq e_n$ and $d_{n'} \sqsubseteq u' \sqsubseteq e_{n'}$ then $u \neq u'$. Consider the positive support s as the closure of the constraint

$$\{d_n \sqsubseteq x \mid n \geq 0\} \cup \{x \sqsubseteq e_n \mid n \geq 0\}$$

where x is a parameter. By Theorem 8 the support s has a solution in V_A. It is clear that every subset of s has a solution in $V_{A\omega}$. But by the remark above, any solution for x must have an infinite number of elements. So it is impossible for s to have a solution in $V_{A\omega}$. Therefore, $V_{A\omega}$ is not compact with respect to $L_{A\omega}$.

(2) Suppose $A = \emptyset$. For $u, v \in V_{A\omega}$, use König's lemma to prove that $u \sqsubseteq v$ iff the "height" of u is less than or equal to that of v, where the height of non-well-founded sets is ∞ and the height of $\emptyset$ is 0. The height of other nonempty set is defined to be $1 +$ the maximum of the heights of members of the set.

Let s be a clause. Consider functions h that assign nonnegative integers including ∞ to each parameter x, y appearing in s in such a way that

- $h(y) < h(x)$ if $u \sqsubseteq x \in s$ and $y \in u$.
- $h(y) < h(x)$ if $u = x \in s$ and $y \in u$.
- $h(y) \leq h(x)$ if $y \sqsubseteq x \in s$.
- $h(y) = h(x)$ if $x = y \in s$.

where we use the conventions $\infty < \infty$ and $n < \infty$ for finite integers n. Intuitively, $h(x)$ is the "height" of a solution for x satisfying s. Let H be the set of such height functions on s and let h_s be the least function in H, which is defined so that $h_s(x)$ has the least integers in $\{h(x) \mid h \in H\}$. It is easy to see that $h_s \in H$. Define a sequence p inductively as follows.

- $p_\infty = \{p_\infty\}$, i.e., Ω.
- $p_0 = \emptyset$.
- $p_n = \{p_{n-1}\}$. $(n > 0)$

Consider $s' = s \cup \{x = p_{h_s(x)} \mid x$ is unbound in $s\}$. As s' is clearly a support, s' has a solution in $V_{A\omega}$, say f. It follows from the definition of f that the height of $\hat{f}(u)$ is $h_s(u)$, for u appearing in s. For $u \sqsubseteq v \in s$, it follows from the remark above on the relationship between the subsumption and the height that $h_s(u) \leq h_s(v)$ and therefore $\hat{f}(u) \sqsubseteq \hat{f}(v)$. Hence, s is solvable in $V_{A\omega}$. Therefore, $V_{A\omega}$ is compact with respect to $L_{A\omega}$. □

2.4.2 Canonical Constraints

We treat a more general case of compactness in which negative information is involved. Note that a canonical constraint does not always have a solution. For example the constraint consisting of the literals

$$x \neq y, x = \{x\}, y = \{y\}$$

is a canonical support but clearly has no solution.

Theorem 16 (Canonical Compactness) *For a canonical set c of literals in $L_{A\omega}$, the following are equivalent.*

1. *c has a solution in $V_{A\omega}$.*
2. *Every finite subset of c has a solution in $V_{A\omega}$.*

Proof. Let $c = p \cup p'$ where p and p' are the sets of positive and negative literals of c, respectively.

(2) $\Rightarrow$ (1): Suppose (2) is true, i.e., every subset of c has a solution in $V_{A\omega}$. So every subset of p has a solution in $V_{A\omega}$. It follows from the compactness of positive supports that there is a solution f in $V_{A\omega}$ of p. We show that f is also a solution of p' in $V_{A\omega}$. As c is canonical, then for each negative literal d in p' there is a finite subset q of c that is a normal constraint containing d. By condition (2) q has a solution in $V_{A\omega}$, say h. As the set of positive literals in q is normal and is a subset of p, it follows from the uniqueness of a solution that f and h must coincide on each parameter of q. Thus f satisfies every negative constraint in p'. Therefore f is a solution of c in $V_{A\omega}$.

(1) $\Rightarrow$ (2): Obvious. $\square$

Theorem 17 (Canonical Support) *Every canonical support c in $L_{A\omega}$ is solvable in $V_{A\omega}$.*

Proof. Let $c = p \cup p'$ be a canonical support where p and p' are the positive and negative parts respectively. By Theorem 8, p has a solution in $V_{A\omega}$, say f. As c is canonical, f is defined on every parameter appearing in p'. Suppose that f satisfies $d \in p'$. Then $\{d\} \cup p$ has a support. As c is canonical there is a normal finite subset p'' of p such that $\{d\} \cup p$ is also normal. Hence, $\{d\} \cup p''$ has a support, which contradicts that c is a support. So f is not a solution of d. Hence f is a solution of $\neg d$. Therefore f is a solution of c. $\square$

By saying that a constraint c has a solution $x = t$ we mean that there is a solution f of c such that $f(x) = t$. Let c be a constraint in $L_{A\omega}$, x the distinguished parameter of c, and t a hyperset of $V_{A\omega}$. Then a *separating cover of t from c* is a clause s in $L_{A\omega}$ such that s has a solution $x = t$, but no common solution with c.

Theorem 18 (Solution Compactness) *$V_{A\omega}$ is solution compact with respect to $L_{A\omega}$.*

Proof. Let c be a finite constraint in $L_{A\omega}$. By transforming c into disjunctive normal form we can assume without loss of generality that

$$c = c_1 \lor c_2 \lor \cdots \lor c_n$$

for some positive integer n. Let x be the distinguished parameter in c. Assume $t \in V_{A\omega}$ such that the constraint c has no solution for $x = t$.

Our goal is to find a finite separating cover s of t from c. If c is unsolvable in $V_{A\omega}$ we can take the constraint $\{\emptyset = \emptyset\}$, for example, as the finite separating cover of t from c. So we assume that c is solvable. Let E_t be a system of equations

$$x_0 = b_0, x_1 = b_1, \cdots, x_m = b_m, \cdots$$

that defines t as the unique solution for x_0. Note that, as $t \in V_{A\omega}$, clearly E_t can be constructed so that E_t is a constraint in $L_{A\omega}$. It suffices to show that for each $1 \leq i \leq n$, if c_i is solvable in $V_{A\omega}$, there is a finite subset s_i of E_t such that s_i is a separating cover of t from c_i because, if so, then it clearly follows that $s_1 \cup \cdots \cup s_n$ is a separating cover of t from c. So let i be any integer $1 \leq i \leq n$ such that c_i is solvable in $V_{A\omega}$. Let p and p' be the positive and negative parts of c_i respectively. We show that there is a subset of E_t that is a separating cover of t from $p \cup p'$. The proof is divided into two cases, (1) and (2).

(1) Suppose that the constraint $\{x = x_0\} \cup E_t \cup p$ has no solution. Then there is some finite subset E' of E_t such that $\{x = x_0\} \cup E' \cup p$ has no solution, for otherwise, by the compactness lemma (Lemma 13), there must be a solution of $\{x = x_0\} \cup E_t \cup p$. But this means that $x = t$ is a solution of p, which contradicts the assumption. Now we have obtained a separating cover $s = \{x = x_0\} \cup E'$ of t from $p \cup p'$.

(2) Suppose that the constraint $\{x = x_0\} \cup E_t \cup p$ has a solution. We divide this case into two parts.

(2a) Suppose that $E_t \cup p \cup \{d\}$ has a support for some negative literal $\neg d$ in p'. Then $p \cup \{d\}$ is a separating cover of t from $p \cup p'$.

(2b) Suppose that $E_t \cup p \cup \{d\}$ has no support for any literal $\neg d$ in p'. Let $\neg d$ be any literal in p'. Then no solution of $\{x = t\} \cup p$ can be extended to that of $\{d\}$. So any solution of $\{x = t\} \cup p$ satisfies $\neg d$. Hence any solution of $\{x = t\} \cup p$ satisfies p'. So $x = t$ is an solution of $p \cup p'$. This is a contradiction. Therefore, the last case is impossible. This concludes the proof. □

The solvability of canonical constraints in $L_{A\omega}$ is characterized using a syntactic notion of the support in the following theorem:

Theorem 19 *Let $c = q \cup q'$ be a canonical constraint in $L_{A\omega}$, with positive part q and negative part q'. Then the following are equivalent.*

(1) *c is solvable in $V_{A\omega}$.*

(2) *q has a normal support p such that $p \cup q'$ is a canonical support.*

Proof. Use Lemma 12. □

Now we establish the satisfaction completeness of unification theory as a direct consequence of the results obtained so far. Let $\mathcal{T}_{A\omega}$ be the theory of *ZFCA* plus the theory of the constraint language $L_{A\omega}$, taking the latter theory to be the set of $\tilde{\exists} p$, where p is a canonical support.

Theorem 20 (Satisfaction Completeness) *For any canonical constraint c in $L_{A\omega}$, $\mathcal{T}_{A\omega} \models \tilde{\forall} \neg c$ whenever $\mathcal{T}_{A\omega} \not\models \tilde{\exists} c$.*

Proof. We prove the contrapositive. Suppose that $\mathcal{T}_{A\omega} \models \tilde{\forall} \neg c$ is not the case. Then there must be a model of $\mathcal{T}_{A\omega}$ that satisfies c. Hence, by Theorem 19, c has a canonical support c'. Then, by the canonical support theorem (Theorem 17), c' must be solvable in any model of $T_{A\omega}$. Hence, so is c. Therefore, we get $T_{A\omega} \models \bar{\exists}c$. □

We have proved the necessary properties required by the constraint logic programming scheme. Thus we have CLP($L_{A\omega}$), for which also we write loosely CLP(AFA).

3 Coinductive Semantics of Horn Clauses

We turn to the constraint logic programming (CLP) over the hyperset domain $V_{A\omega}[X]$, where sets A and X are assumed to be large enough to include all necessary atoms and parameters respectively. We start by defining two semantic domains. One domain consists of *computation trees* for the operational semantics and the other one consists of *solution trees* for the declarative semantics. Intuitively speaking, a computation tree is obtained from some solution tree by "forgetting" information about solutions coded in the solution tree. Elements of the two domains are coded in hypersets in a more natural way than the usual representation by state transition nets.

For a given Horn clause program, the two semantic domains above are defined coinductively in the domain $V_{A\omega}$. Soundness and completeness are formalized as a relation between the computation trees and the solution trees. In fact, this relation is a "forgetful" projection from solution trees into computation trees. This simulation relation is defined coinductively in a straightforward way.

Throughout this section, A and X denote sets of atoms and parameters respectively. It follows from this assumption that various constructions given in this section form sets but never proper classes unless mentioned otherwise.

3.1 Horn Clause with Constraints

We introduce a class of Horn clauses with constraints in the constraint language $L_{A\omega}$. Let A and X be *sets* of atoms (= constants) and parameters, respectively, as before. Let Π be a set of *predicate symbols*. If $p \in \Pi$ and $x_1, \cdots, x_n$ are parameters, then $p(x_1, \ldots, x_n)$ is an *atomic goal*. A *goal* is a finite set of atomic goals. A *head* is a form $p(x_1, \ldots, x_n)$ where p is a predicate symbol and x_i $(i \neq j)$ are distinct parameters. A *constraint Horn clause* is a triple (h, c, g), where h is a head, c is a constraint, and g is a goal. We write

$$h :- c \mid b_1, \cdots, b_n$$

for $(h, c, \{b_1, \cdots, b_n\})$. A *program* is a *finite* set of constraint Horn clauses, each clause in it is called *a program clause*.

We use a simple running example to illustrate the idea of the coinductive semantics defined below. Let Ψ_0 be the program consisting of three constraint Horn clauses:

(C1) $bit(0)$.

(C2) $bit(1)$.

(C3) $stream(x) :\!- x = (b, y) \mid bit(b), stream(y)$.

Intuitively, the coinductive semantics of the program Ψ_0 is a function $\mathcal{I}_0$ such that $\mathcal{I}_0(bit) = \{0, 1\}$ and $\mathcal{I}_0(stream)$ is the set of streams over 0 and 1. Note that the standard least semantics of Ψ_0 is a function $\mathcal{I}_0'$ such that $\mathcal{I}_0'(bit) = \{0, 1\}$ but $\mathcal{I}_0'(stream) = \emptyset$.

3.2   Computation Trees

We introduce notions of a *state* and *computation tree* to give an operational semantics of the program. Computation trees have information only about steps of successful computations. In other words, they have no explicit information about failure branches.

Definition 24 A *computation state* (state for short) is a triple (c, g, ξ) of a constraint c, a goal g, and a set ξ of parameters such that c has a support and $\mathcal{V}(g) \cup \mathcal{V}(c) \subseteq \xi$.

A set of parameters that is the last component of a state may be omitted when the context is clear. Given a goal g, the *initial state* is the state $(\emptyset, g, \mathcal{V}(g))$, where the empty set $\emptyset$ means the 'true' constraint that always holds. As the program Ψ is finitary and X is finite, the collection of states for the program Ψ forms a set.

Example 3 The triple

$$(\{x = (z, y), x = y\}, \{bit(z), stream(x), stream(y)\}, \{x, y, z, u\})$$

is a state. Note that u is a parameter that does not appear in the first two components of the triple.

Definition 25 A *choice* γ *on* g is a function that assigns a program clause to each atomic goal in g. That is, $\gamma \colon g \to \Psi$, where Ψ is a program fixed in the context.

Example 4 Let g be the goal $\{bit(z), stream(x), stream(y)\}$. The mapping γ which assigns (C1), (C2), (C2) to the atomic goals $bit(z)$, $stream(x)$, $stream(y)$, respectively, is a choice on g, where (C1) and (C2) are clauses in Ψ_0.

Let S_g denote the set of choices on g. Then S_g is finite because both g and the program Ψ are finite.

Definition 26 Let $s = (c, g, \xi)$ and $s' = (c', g', \xi')$ be two states. Let γ be a choice on g. A triple (s, γ, s') is a *transition*, written as $s \xrightarrow{\gamma} s'$, if for each atomic goal $a \in g$ there is a "renamed version" $C_a \colon h_a :\!- c_a \mid g_a$ of the clause $\gamma(a) \in \Psi$ such that

    1. $\mathcal{V}(C_a) \cap \mathcal{V}(C_{a'}) = \emptyset$. $(a \neq a')$

    2. $\xi \cap \mathcal{V}(C_a) = \emptyset$.

3. $g' = \bigcup \{g_a \mid a \in g\}$.
4. $c' = c \wedge \bigwedge \{\{a = h_a\} \wedge c_a \mid a \in g\}$.
5. c' has a support.
6. $\xi' = \xi \cup \bigcup \{\mathcal{V}(C_a) \mid a \in dom(\gamma)\}$.

Example 5 $(\{x = y, x = (b, y)\}, \{stream(y)\}, \{x, y, b\}) \xrightarrow{\gamma_0}$
$(\{x = y, x = (b, y), u = y, u = (d, v)\}, \{bit(d), stream(v)\}, \{x, y, b, u, v, d\})$
where γ_0 is the choice that assigns the clause (C3) of Ψ_0 to the atomic goal
$stream(y)$. u, v, d are the new parameters generated for this transition.

We formalize the set of all possible "computations" for the program.

Definition 27 $\mathcal{C}_\Psi$ is the largest set M such that if $x \in M$ then $x = (s, b)$
for some state s and a partial function $b: S_g \to M$, where

1. g is the goal component of the state s.

2. $s \xrightarrow{\gamma} s'$ if $\gamma \in dom(b)$ and $b(\gamma) = (s', b')$ for some b'.

As the collection of states of the program is a set and the number of
branches is finite at each node, $\mathcal{C}_\Psi$ forms a set for any program Ψ.

Definition 28 A binary order $\prec$ is the largest relation on $\mathcal{C}_\Psi$ such that if
$x \prec y$ then the following hold for some s, b, b':

1. $x = (s, b)$ and $y = (s, b')$.
2. $dom(b) \subseteq dom(b')$.
3. If $\gamma \in dom(b)$ then $b(\gamma) \prec b'(\gamma)$.

Proposition 21 $(\mathcal{C}_\Psi, \prec)$ *is a partial order structure.*

Proof. Let R be a binary relation on $\mathcal{C}_\Psi$ such that $x R y$ iff $x \prec y$ and $y \prec x$.
It is easy to show that R extends to a bisimulation on $(\text{trans}(\mathcal{C}_\Psi), \in)$. Aczel
1988 showed that every bisimulation on the class of sets is a subclass of $=$.
So the preorder $\prec$ is a partial order. $\square$

Definition 29 A *computation tree* is a maximal element of $(\mathcal{C}_\Psi, \prec)$.

As will be shown later in Lemma 26, maximal computation tree in $(\mathcal{C}_\Psi, \prec)$
exists.

Definition 30 A minimal element of $(\mathcal{C}_\Psi, \prec)$ is called a *path*.

3.3 Coinductive Semantics

Definition 31 An *interpretation* of the program is a function $\mathcal{I}$ which
assigns a subset of $(V_{A\omega})^n$ to predicate symbols p, where n is the arity of
p. Interpretations are partially ordered by pointwise inclusion. That is,
$\mathcal{I} \leq \mathcal{I}'$ iff $\mathcal{I}(r) \subseteq \mathcal{I}'(r)$ for each predicate symbol of the program.

Definition 32 A *model* of the program Ψ is an interpretation $\mathcal{I}$ of Ψ such
that for any $(a_1, \cdots, a_n) \in \mathcal{I}(p)$ there exists a program clause

$$p(x_1, \ldots, x_n) :\!- c \mid g$$

and assignment f such that

1. $f(x_i) = a_i$ for $1 \leq i \leq n$.
2. $V_{A\omega} \models_f c$.
3. $(\hat{f}(z_1), \ldots, \hat{f}(z_m)) \in \mathcal{I}(q)$ for each atomic goal $q(z_1, \ldots, z_m) \in g$.

where m is the arity of the predicate symbol q.

The maximum model is denoted by $\mathcal{M}_\Psi$ and is also called the *coinductive semantics* of the program Ψ. As $V_{A\omega}$ is a set, it follows that the class of interpretations forms a set. It is a routine to define a monotone operator T_Ψ on interpretations so that $\mathcal{M}_\Psi$ is the maximum fixpoint of T_Ψ.

3.4 Solution Trees

Definition 33 An assignment f is a *solution* of (c, g) if $V_{A\omega} \models_f c$ and $\mathcal{M}_\Psi \models_f g$, where c and g are a constraint and a goal, respectively, such that $\mathcal{V}(c) \cup \mathcal{V}(g) \subseteq dom(f)$.

Definition 34 $\mathcal{A}_\Psi$ is the set of triples (f, c, g) such that f is a solution of (c, g).

Definition 35 A binary relation $\longrightarrow$ is the largest relation on $\mathcal{A}_\Psi$ such that, if $(f, c, g) \longrightarrow (f', c', g')$ is defined, there is a choice γ on g such that for any $a \in g$ there is a "renamed program clause" $C_a \colon h_a :- c_a \mid g_a$ of $\gamma(a)$ that satisfies the following.

1. f' is an extension of f.
2. $g' = \bigcup \{g_a \mid a \in g\}$.
3. $c' = c \wedge \bigwedge \{\{a = h_a\} \wedge c_a \mid a \in g\}$.
4. $\mathcal{V}(C_a) \cap \mathcal{V}(C_{a'}) = \emptyset$ $(a \neq a')$.
5. $dom(f) \cap \mathcal{V}(C_a) = \emptyset$ for any $a \in g$.

We write $(f, c, g) \xrightarrow{\gamma} (f', c', g')$ indicating γ explicitly.

Lemma 22 *If $s = (f, c, g)$ is in $\mathcal{A}_\Psi$ and g is not empty then $s \xrightarrow{\gamma} s'$ for some s' in $\mathcal{A}_\Psi$ and choice on g.*

Proof. Let $a = p(y_1, \cdots, y_n)$ be an atomic goal in g. f is a solution of a by the hypothesis. Then by the definition of a solution, there is a program clause γ_a, a fresh copy $h_a :- c_a \mid g_a$ of it, and some extension f_a of f such that f_a is a solution of both (c_a, g_a) and $a = h_a$. Let

$$s' = (f', c \wedge \bigwedge \{\{a = h_a\} \wedge c_a \mid a \in g\}, \bigcup \{g_a \mid a \in g\})$$

where f' is an extension of any f_a for $a \in g$. So, by definition, we get $s \xrightarrow{\gamma} s'$, where γ is a choice on g such that $\gamma(a) = \gamma_a$ for $a \in g$. $\square$

Definition 36 Given the program Ψ, $\mathcal{S}_\Psi$ is the largest collection $M \subset V_{A\omega}[X]$ such that if $x \in M$ then $x = (s, b)$ for some $s = (f, c, g) \in \mathcal{A}_\Psi$ and a function b such that the following hold.

1. $dom(b)$ consists of choices on g.
2. $ran(b) \subseteq M$.
3. $s \xrightarrow{\gamma} s'$ if $b(\gamma) = (s', b')$ for some b'.

$\mathcal{S}_\Psi$ is a set for a similar reason to $\mathcal{C}_\Psi$'s.

Definition 37 $\prec$ is the largest binary relation on $\mathcal{S}_\Psi$ such that if $x \prec y$ then the following hold.

1. $x = (s, b)$ and $y = (s, b')$ for some s, b, b'.
2. $dom(b) \subseteq dom(b')$.
3. If $\gamma \in dom(b)$ then $b(\gamma) \prec b'(\gamma)$.

$(\mathcal{S}_\Psi, \prec)$ is a partial order structure for a similar reason to $\mathcal{C}_\Psi$'s above.

Definition 38 A *solution tree* is a maximal element of $(\mathcal{S}_\Psi, \prec)$.

It will be shown in Lemma 26 that there exist maximal solution trees in $(\mathcal{S}_\Psi, \prec)$.

Definition 39 A minimal element in $(\mathcal{S}_\Psi, \prec)$ is called a *path*.

We illustrate a computation tree t for the goal $\{stream(x)\}$ of the program Ψ_0. t is an infinite binary tree. t has all the information about how each stream is generated by the program Ψ_0. The general form of states at nodes ν of t is a triple (c_ν, g_ν, X_ν), where

$$
\begin{aligned}
c_\nu &= \{x = (b_1, x_1), x_1 = (b_2, x_2), \cdots, x_{n-1} = (b_n, x_n), \\
&\quad b_1 = \beta_1, \cdots, b_{n-1} = \beta_{n-1}\} \\
g_\nu &= \{bit(b_n), stream(x_n)\} \\
X_\nu &= \{x, b_1, x_1, \cdots, b_n, x_n\}
\end{aligned}
$$

where β_i is either 0 or 1. The other symbols are parameters. The state means that a finite stream $\beta_1 \beta_2 \cdots \beta_{n-1}$ has been produced as an initial finite segment of some stream. The node ν has two successor nodes ν_0 and ν_1, whose states are $(c_{\nu_0}, g_{\nu_0}, X_{\nu_0})$, $(c_{\nu_1}, g_{\nu_1}, X_{\nu_1})$, respectively, where

$$
\begin{aligned}
c_{\nu_0} &= c_\nu \cup \{x_n = (b_{n+1}, x_{n+1}), b_n = 0\}, \\
g_{\nu_0} &= \{bit(b_{n+1}), stream(x_{n+1})\}, \\
X_{\nu_0} &= X_\nu \cup \{b_{n+1}, x_{n+1}\},
\end{aligned}
$$

and

$$
\begin{aligned}
c_{\nu_1} &= c_\nu \cup \{x_n = (b_{n+1}, x_{n+1}), b_n = 1\}, \\
g_{\nu_1} &= \{bit(b_{n+1}), stream(x_{n+1})\}, \\
X_{\nu_1} &= X_\nu \cup \{b_{n+1}, x_{n+1}\}.
\end{aligned}
$$

An example of a solution tree for the same goal $\{stream(x)\}$ is a tree t' with a single path. Take the union of constraints on the single path to obtain a system of equations:

$$\{x = (b_1, x_1), x_1 = (b_2, x_2), \cdots, x_{n-1} = (b_n, x_n), \cdots,$$
$$b_1 = \beta_1, \cdots, b_{n-1} = \beta_{n-1}, \cdots\}$$

Let f be the unique solution of the union. The solution tree has the following information at each node:

$$(f', c', \{bit(b_n), stream(x_n)\}, \{x, b_1, x_1, \cdots, b_n, x_n\}),$$

where f' is a restriction of f to the set $\{x, b_1, x_1, \cdots, b_n, x_n\}$, and c' is the set

$$\{x = (b_1, x_1), x_1 = (b_2, x_2), \cdots, x_{n-1} = (b_n, x_n),$$
$$b_1 = \beta_1, \cdots, b_{n-1} = \beta_{n-1}\}.$$

Lemma 23 *If $x = (s, b)$ is a path such that $dom(b) \neq \emptyset$, then there are some γ, s', and b' such that the following hold:*

1. $dom(b) = \{\gamma\}$.
2. $b(\gamma) = (s', b')$ *is a path.*
3. $s \xrightarrow{\gamma} s'$.

Proof. It is obvious by the definition of a path. $\qquad\square$

Lemma 24 *Let Ψ be a program and p be a predicate. Then the following are equivalent.*

(1) $(a_1, \cdots, a_n) \in \mathcal{M}_\Psi(p)$.
(2) *There is a path $((f, \emptyset, \{p(x_1, \cdots, x_n)\}), b) \in \mathcal{S}_\Psi$ for some b such that $\hat{f}(x_i) = a_i$ $(1 \leq i \leq n)$.*

Proof. (1)$\Rightarrow$ (2): Suppose (1) is true. Then by repeated application of Lemma 22 we can make a sequence of possibly countably infinite length in $\mathcal{A}_\Psi$

$$s_0 \xrightarrow{\gamma_0} s_1 \xrightarrow{\gamma_1} \cdots \xrightarrow{\gamma_{n-1}} s_n \xrightarrow{\gamma_n} \cdots$$

where $s_0 = (f, \emptyset, \{p(x_1, \cdots, x_n)\}) \in \mathcal{A}$ and $\hat{f}(x_i) = a_i$ $(1 \leq i \leq n)$. The path z_0 obtained by solving the following equations satisfies (2).

$$\begin{aligned}
z_0 &= (s_0, \{(\gamma_0, z_1)\}) \\
z_1 &= (s_1, \{(\gamma_1, z_2)\}) \\
&\vdots \\
z_n &= (s_n, \{(\gamma_n, z_{n+1})\}) \\
&\vdots
\end{aligned}$$

(2) $\Rightarrow$ (1): Suppose (2) is true. Then f is a solution of $p(x_1, \ldots, x_n)$ by definition. Hence, $(a_1, \cdots, a_n) = (\hat{f}(x_1), \cdots, \hat{f}(x_n)) \in \mathcal{M}_\Psi(p)$. $\qquad\square$

Lemma 25 $(\mathcal{S}_\Psi, \prec)$ *is chain complete.*

206 / Kuniaki Mukai

Proof. Suppose we are given the following sequence of elements of $\mathcal{S}_\Psi$:

$$x_0 \prec x_1 \prec \cdots \prec x_n \prec \cdots.$$

Let us define a sequence X_i ($i \geq 0$) inductively:

- $X_0 = \{x_i \mid i \geq 0\}$.
- $X_{i+1} = \{b(x) \mid \exists s \ (s,b) \in X_i, x \in dom(b)\}$.

Let $X = \bigcup \{X_i \mid i \geq 0\}$ and $\Lambda = \bigcup \{dom(b) \mid \exists s \ (s,b) \in X\}$. Let Λ^* be the set of finite sequences over Λ. Let us define a partial operation $\alpha \in \Lambda^*$ on $x = (s,b) \in X$ inductively:

- $x(\varepsilon) = x$.
- $x(\gamma\alpha) = b(\gamma)(\alpha)$

where ε is the empty sequence and $\gamma \in \Lambda$. Then consider the system of equations for $\alpha \in \Lambda^*$

$$y_\alpha = (a_\alpha, Y_\alpha)$$

such that

- there is some x_i in the given sequence such that $x_i(\alpha) = (a_\alpha, b)$ for some b.
- $(\gamma, y_{\alpha\gamma}) \in Y_\alpha$ iff there is some x_j such that $x_j(\alpha\gamma)$ is defined.

This system of equations is well defined though some $\alpha \in \Lambda$ may fail to have a corresponding equation. By the solution lemma, there is a unique solution of the system. Let y be the solution to y_ε. Now we show that y is the least upper bound of the family x_i ($0 \leq i$). Suppose that z is an upper bound of the family, i.e., $x_i \prec z$ for all $0 \leq i$. By comparing the defining system of equations for z with that for y it follows that $y \prec z$. $\square$

Lemma 26 *If x is an element of $\mathcal{S}_\Psi$ there is a maximal element x' in $\mathcal{S}_\Psi$ such that $x \prec x'$.*

Proof. Let $X = \{z \in \mathcal{S}_\Psi \mid x \prec z\}$. By Lemma 25, any monotone family of elements of X has a limit with respect $\prec$. Hence, by Zorn's lemma, there exists a maximal element x' in X. $\square$

3.5 Soundness and Completeness

Let $\mathcal{S}_\Psi$ and $\mathcal{C}_\Psi$ denote the sets of solution trees and computation trees, respectively. We have remarked above that they are sets when the program Ψ fixed. We formulate soundness and completeness of the semantics of programs in terms of a correspondence between $\mathcal{S}_\Psi$ and $\mathcal{C}_\Psi$. The correspondence will be called a *simulation*.

Before going into details, we introduce a notion of *hereditary projection* that will be used later. Let $\mathcal{T}(S, \Sigma)$ be the largest class T of sets such that if $x \in T$ then $x = (a, b)$, where $a \in S$ and b is a partial function from Σ to T. An element of T is called a *tree* over S and Σ. Let $X_i = \mathcal{T}(S_i, \Sigma)$ for

$i = 1, 2$ and let f be a function from S_1 to S_2. Then there is a function F from T_1 to T_2 such that

$$F((a, b)) = ((f(a), F\,{}^{\text{a}}b))$$

where $F\,{}^{\text{a}}b = \{(z, F(b(z))) \mid z \in dom(b)\}$. We write f^* for F. We call f^* a *hereditary projection* if f is a projection.

Definition 40 A *simulation between* $\mathcal{S}_\Psi$ *and* $\mathcal{C}_\Psi$ is a subset R of $\mathcal{S}_\Psi \times \mathcal{C}_\Psi$ such that if xRy then the following hold for some f, c, g, b, b':

(1) $x = ((f, c, g), b)$ and $y = ((c, g), b')$.

(2) If $dom(b) \neq \emptyset$ then $b(\gamma)Rb'(\gamma)$ for *some* $\gamma \in dom(b) \cap dom(b')$.

Lemma 27 *There is the largest simulation between* $\mathcal{S}_\Psi$ *and* $\mathcal{C}_\Psi$

Proof. Take the union of all simulations between $\mathcal{S}_\Psi$ and $\mathcal{C}_\Psi$. $\qquad\square$

We say that w *simulates* p if wRp, where R is the largest simulation.

Lemma 28 (Simulation) *The following are equivalent.*

(1) x *simulates* y.

(2) *There exist paths* $p \prec x$ *in* $\mathcal{S}_\Psi$ *and* $q \prec y$ *in* $\mathcal{C}_\Psi$ *such that* p *simulates* q.

Proof. Let R be the largest simulation between $\mathcal{S}_\Psi$ and $\mathcal{C}_\Psi$.

(2) $\Rightarrow$ (1): Let S be the largest subset of $\mathcal{S}_\Psi \times \mathcal{C}_\Psi$ such that if xSy then there exist paths $p \prec x$ in $\mathcal{S}_\Psi$ and $q \prec y$ in $\mathcal{C}_\Psi$ such that p simulates q. It suffices to show that S is a simulation between $\mathcal{S}_\Psi \times \mathcal{C}_\Psi$. Suppose xSy. Then by the definition of S, there are paths $p \prec x$ in $\mathcal{S}_\Psi$ and $q \prec y$ in $\mathcal{C}_\Psi$ such that p simulates q. As p simulates q and both p and q are paths, we get $p = ((f, c, g), \{(\gamma, p')\})$ and $q = ((c, g), \{(\gamma, p')\})$ such that p' simulates q' for some f, c, g, γ, p', q'. Furthermore, as $p \prec x$, we get $x = ((f, c, g), b)$ for some b such that $p' \prec b(\gamma)$. Similarly, as $q \prec y$, we get $y = ((c, g), b')$ for some b' such that $q' \prec b'(\gamma)$. As p' simulates q' we get $b(\gamma)Sb'(\gamma)$. Therefore, S is a simulation between $\mathcal{S}_\Psi \times \mathcal{C}_\Psi$.

(1) $\Rightarrow$ (2): For the converse suppose (1) is true. By the definition of xRy, there exists a sequence x_i, y_i ($i \geq 0$), where $x_0 = x$ and $y_0 = y$, such that

- $x_i R y_i$.
- $x_i = ((f_i, c_i, g_i), b_i)$.
- $b_i(\gamma_i) = x_{i+1}$.
- $y_i = ((c_i, g_i), d_i)$.
- $d_i(\gamma_i) = y_{i+1}$.

From this we get the following system of equations:

$$u_i = ((f_i, c_i, g_i), \{(\gamma_i, u_{i+1})\})$$
$$v_i = ((c_i, g_i), \{(\gamma_i, v_{i+1})\}).$$

By the solution lemma, we can let p and q be the solutions for u_0 and v_0 respectively. By definition of $\prec$ and R, it is easy to see that $p \prec x$, $q \prec y$, and pRq. $\qquad\qquad\qquad\qquad\qquad\qquad\qquad\qquad\qquad\qquad\qquad\qquad\quad$ □

Let π be a projection such that $\pi((x, y, z)) = (y, z)$.

Definition 41 Given a path p of a computation tree in $\mathcal{C}_\Psi$, let c_p be the conjunction of constraint components of states on the path. The path p *is canonical* if every disjunct component of c is canonical. A computation tree *is canonical* if all paths of the tree are canonical. A program *is canonical* if every computation tree of the program is canonical.

It is not difficult to show that if Ψ is a canonical program then $\mathcal{M}_\Psi = \bigcap \{(T_\Psi)^n (V_{A\omega}) \mid n \in N\}$, where N is the set of non-negative integers; the maximum semantics can be reached downward in at most countably infinite number of iterations of the transformation T_Ψ.

Theorem 29 (Soundness) *For any canonical computation tree $y \in \mathcal{C}_\Psi$ there is a solution tree $x \in \mathcal{S}_\Psi$ such that x simulates y.*

Proof. Let q be any path of a computation tree $y \in \mathcal{C}_\Psi$. We apply the canonical compactness theorem (Theorem 16) to select a global solution f to the path q. Make a family of solutions by restricting f to each step on the path of y. Write a system of equations

$$y_i = ((c_i, g_i), z_i)$$
$$z_i = \{(\gamma_i, y_{i+1})\}$$

for $i \geq 0$ such that $y_0 = q$, i.e., q is the solution to y_0. Then apply the solution lemma to the system of equations

$$x_i = ((f_i, c_i, g_i), w_i)$$
$$w_i = \{(\gamma_i, x_{i+1})\}$$

where f_i is the above-mentioned restriction of f to $\mathcal{V}(c_i) \cup \mathcal{V}(g_i)$ for $i \geq 0$. Let p be the solution to x_0. It is clear that $\pi^*(p) = q$. By Lemma 26, there is a solution tree x such that p is a path of x. Hence, by Lemma 28, x simulates y. $\qquad\qquad\qquad$ □

Theorem 30 (Completeness) *For any solution tree $x \in \mathcal{S}_\Psi$ there is a computation tree $y \in \mathcal{C}_\Psi$ such that x simulates y.*

Proof. Let R be the largest simulation. By definition of $\prec$, $xR\pi^*(x)$ is true. By Lemma 26 there exists a computation tree y in $\mathcal{C}_\Psi$ such that $\pi^*(x) \prec y$. Therefore, we get xRy. $\qquad\qquad\qquad\qquad\qquad\qquad\qquad\qquad\qquad\qquad\quad$ □

We turn to the soundness and completeness of the negation-as-failure rule (NAFR). Note that soundness and completeness are almost obvious because of the maximum semantics, provided only canonical programs are considered. An important point is that the formulation of NAFR needs ground goals, which may be infinite or irrational in the language $L_{A\omega}$, whereas actual computations require that constraints and goals in computation states be *finitary*. Thus a nontrivial aspect of the following Theorem 31 is that NAFR is given a meaning over a domain of infinite and irrational objects such as hypersets through implicit and finitary representations as approximations for those objects.

Theorem 31 (Negation As Failure) *Let g be a goal with $x_1, \cdots, x_n$ as parameters and which has the* canonical *computation tree $q = ((\emptyset, g), b)$ for some b. Let f be an assignment such that $\hat{f}(x_i) = \xi_i \in V_{A\omega}$ is not a solution of g. Then there is a finitary constraint c such that f is a solution of c and there is no computation tree for the goal $c \wedge g$.*

Proof. For any path $p \prec q$ such that

$$
\begin{aligned}
q_0 &= p = ((c_0, g_0), \{(\gamma_0, q_1)\}) \\
q_1 &= ((c_1, g_1), \{(\gamma_1, q_2)\}) \\
q_2 &= ((c_2, g_2), \{(\gamma_2, q_3)\}) \\
&\vdots
\end{aligned}
$$

where $c_0 = \emptyset$, $g_0 = g$, and $\gamma_0 \in dom(b)$, there is some q_j in the path such that no extension of f satisfies c_j, for otherwise f could be extended to the solution of q. As every computation tree is hereditarily finite, by applying the standard argument of König's lemma, the set d of such constraints c_j must be finite:

$$ d = \{c_1, \cdots, c_r\} $$

for some integer r. Then by the solution compactness theorem (Theorem 18) there exists a positive finite "covering" constraint c of $(\xi_1, \cdots, \xi_n)$ such that c has no common solution with c_j above. It follows from the construction of the constraint c in $L_{A\omega}$ that there is no computation tree for the goal $c \wedge g$. Otherwise, from the canonical computation tree q_0, we could also get a canonical computation tree that has the following path.

$$
\begin{aligned}
q_0' &= ((c \wedge c_0, g_0), \{(\gamma_0, q_1')\}) \\
q_1' &= ((c \wedge c_1, g_1), \{(\gamma_1, q_2')\}) \\
q_2' &= ((c \wedge c_2, g_2), \{(\gamma_2, q_3')\}) \\
&\vdots
\end{aligned}
$$

By the canonical support theorem (Theorem 17), this implies that c and $\bigwedge \{c_i \mid i \geq 0\}$ have a common solution, which is also a solution of g. This is a contradiction. □

4 Applications to Terms and Records

In this section, we make several more specific remarks about implementation issues. First of all, we point out that a partition refinement algorithm in Paige and Tarjan 1987 can be used to compute bisimulation relations over hypersets. Secondly we take the domains of trees and records as two special subclasses of $V_{A\omega}$, respectively, by making the following embedding of standard constraint theories into $L_{A\omega}$ in a natural way:

- Unification theory over (infinite) trees.
- Unification theory over (infinite) records.

4.1 Computing Bisimulations over Hypersets

Recall the definition of $V_{A\omega}[X]$ for a class X of parameters and a class A of atoms: $V_{A\omega}[X]$ is the largest class M such that $M \subseteq A \cup X \cup pow'(M)$, where $pow'(M)$ is the set of finite subsets of M. Let U be a transitive set of $V_{A\omega}[X]$, i.e., $U \in V_{A\omega}[X]$ and for all $x \in U$ if $y \in x$ then $y \in U$. We modify the notions of partition and bisimulation slightly for our purpose: a binary relation P on U is a *partition* of U if P is an equivalence relation on U such that the following hold:

- If aPx and $a \in U \cap A$ then $x = a$.
- For any parameter $x \in U$ there is a *set* $y \in U$ such that xPy.

A *bisimulation* R is a partition of U such that, for any sets $x, y \in U$, if xRy then the following hold:

- For any $u \in x$ there exists $v \in y$ such that uRv.
- For any $v \in y$ there exists $u \in x$ such that uRv.

Then the following two propositions are easy consequences of Paige and Tarjan 1987:

Proposition 32 *For a given partition P of U, there exists a coarsest bisimulation R that is a refinement of P.*

Let n, m be the numbers of nodes and edges, respectively, appearing in U, provided that U is represented suitably as a directed graph.

Proposition 33 *There exists an $O(m \log n)$ time-complexity algorithm to compute the coarsest bisimulation for a given partition P of U.*

4.2 Hyperterms

Let Σ and Δ be sets of *function symbols* and *argument places*, respectively. σ_0 is a distinguished function symbol in Σ. We assume that $N \subseteq \Delta$, where N is the set of positive integers. Each symbol $\sigma \in \Sigma$ is supposed to be assigned a *finite* subset $\arg(\sigma)$ of Δ. A function symbol σ such that $\arg(\sigma) = \emptyset$ is taken as a constant symbol as usual. A function b is a *partial assignment for* a symbol $\sigma \in \Sigma$ if $dom(b) \subseteq \arg(\sigma)$. A function b is a *full assignment for* a symbol $\sigma \in \Sigma$ if $dom(b) = \arg(\sigma)$.

Definition 42 $\mathcal{H}^*(\Sigma, \Delta, X)$ is the largest set $M \subseteq V_{(\Sigma \cup \Delta)\omega}[X]$ such that $M \subseteq X \cup \bigcup \{A_\sigma \mid \sigma \in \Sigma\}$, where $A_\sigma = \{(\sigma, b) \mid b: \arg(\sigma) \to M \quad \text{(partial)}\}$

Elements of $\mathcal{H}^*(\Sigma, \Delta, X)$ are called *hyperterms over* (Σ, Δ, X). A hyperterm u is called a *subterm* of a hyperterm v if u appears in v. A *fully specified hyperterm* is a hyperterm u such that for every subterm (σ, b) of u, b is a *full* assignment for the symbol σ.

Definition 43 $\mathcal{H}(\Sigma, \Delta, X)$ is the smallest set $M \subseteq \mathcal{H}^*(\Sigma, \Delta, X)$ such that $X \cup \bigcup \{A_\sigma \mid \sigma \in \Sigma\} \subseteq M$, where $A_\sigma = \{(\sigma, b) \mid b : \arg(\sigma) \to M \quad \text{(partial)}\}$

It is clear that every element of $\mathcal{H}(\Sigma, \Delta, X)$ is finitary and that $\mathcal{H}(\Sigma, \Delta, X)$ is the set of finitary hyperterms in $\mathcal{H}^*(\Sigma, \Delta, X)$.

We write $\sigma(b(1), b(2), \cdots, b(n))$ for hyperterms (σ, b) if $dom(b) = \arg(\sigma) = \{1, \cdots, n\}$. Also, we write record structures $\{(a_1, b(a_1)), \cdots, (a_n, b(a_n))\}$ for hyperterms (σ_0, b) if $\sigma_0 \in \Sigma$ is the distinguished function symbol and $dom(b) = \{a_1, \cdots, a_n\} \subset \arg(\sigma_0)$. Thus we can see that the usual first-order terms and record structures are special cases of hyperterms.

4.3 Hyperterm Subsumption

Let Σ, Δ, X be the same as above.

Definition 44 A binary relation $\sqsubseteq$ on $\mathcal{H}^*(\Sigma, \Delta, \emptyset)$ is defined to be the largest relation $\sqsubseteq$ such that $x \sqsubseteq y \Rightarrow x \sqsubseteq^+ y$ where $x \sqsubseteq^+ y$ iff there are some $\sigma \in \Sigma$ and partial assignments u, v for σ such that

- $x = (\sigma, u)$ and $y = (\sigma, v)$.
- $dom(u) \subseteq dom(v)$.
- For all $z \in dom(u)$ $u(z) \sqsubseteq v(z)$.

It is clear that the domain of hyperterms is ordered by $\sqsubseteq$. The relation $\sqsubseteq$ is called *hyperterm subsumption*. Recall that the set subsumption relation as a hereditary subset relation was not a partial order, but only a preorder on V_A. A decision procedure for hyperterm subsumption is given in Mukai 1991.

4.4 Unification over Hyperterms

A *hyperequation* is an expression of the form $u \bowtie v$, where u and v are parametric hyperterms. A set of hyperequations is called a *solved form* if every hyperequation in the set has a parameter on the left side and no two equations have the same parameter on the left hand side. A hyperequation $u \bowtie v$ is a *conflict* if $u = (\sigma, b)$ and $v = (\sigma', b')$ for distinct function symbols σ and σ'.

The following algorithm is an extension of the standard unification of records. The input of the unification algorithm is a finite set of hyperequations. The output is a set of hyperequations. The unification algorithm proceeds as follows: Repeat applying the steps below to the input set of hyperequations until no step is applicable. When this process terminates, check whether there is a *conflict* or not. In what follows, x, y are parameters, $\sigma \in \Sigma$, and u, v, w are partial assignments for σ.

(1) If $x \bowtie x$ is in the set, remove it.

(2) If $x \bowtie y$ is in the set, replace all occurrences of y with x.

(3) If $u \bowtie x$ is in the set for a non-parameter u, replace it with $x \bowtie u$.

(4) If $x \bowtie (\sigma, u)$ and $x \bowtie (\sigma, v)$ are in the set, remove it and add to the set all hyperequations in the set

$$\{x \bowtie (\sigma, w)\} \cup \{w(a) \bowtie u(a) \mid a \in dom(u)\}$$
$$\cup \{w(a) \bowtie v(a) \mid a \in dom(v)\}$$

where w is a *parametric* (partial) assignment satisfying the following:

(4a) $dom(w) = dom(u) \cup dom(v)$.

(4b) $w(a) \in X$ are distinct new parameters for $a \in dom(w)$.

Definition 45 A set E of hyperequations is *unifiable* if the unification process for E terminates with no conflict.

Definition 46 A hyperequation $u \bowtie v$ is *solvable* (in $H^*(\Sigma, \Delta, \emptyset)$) if the *equation* $\theta(u) = \theta(v)$ is solvable, where θ is the translation satisfying the following:

1. $\theta(x) = x$ if x is a parameter.

2. $\theta((\sigma, b)) = (\sigma, b')$, where $dom(b') = \arg(\sigma)$, $b'(a) = \theta(b(a))$ for $a \in dom(b)$ and $b'(a)$ are new parameters for $a \in dom(b') \backslash dom(b)$.

A set S of hyperequations is *solvable* if the set $\{\theta(u) = \theta(v) \mid u \bowtie v \in S\}$ of equations is solvable.

The following two propositions can be proved without much difficulty.

Proposition 34 *The unification algorithm over hyperterms always terminates.*

Proposition 35 *For a set E of hyperequations, the following statements are equivalent:*

1. *E is unifiable.*

2. *E is solvable.*

5 Concluding Remarks

Using hypersets and compact constraints, declarative and operational semantics have become essentially the same. In this respect, the present semantics seems to be closely related to constructive type theory (Martin-Löf 1984) in that the meaning of a given goal is a proof tree that is decorated by satisfiable constraints at each node. The goal can be viewed as a non-canonical constraint. Also, the solution compactness requirement of the CLP scheme is close to the intuitive notion of constructive approximation. A clearer relationship between these theories remains to be discovered.

The original purpose of the present work was to describe semantics of meta-predicates of logic programming languages using basic ideas in situation theory and situation semantics (STASS). Meta-predicates such as *var* or *cut* of Prolog are essentially defined operationally. So the clear structure of the proposed semantics in hypersets is expected to provide a good new setting for defining the semantics of these meta-predicates. For example, using the idea from STASS that the meaning of a sentence is a relation between situations, the meaning of commands will be formalized as relations between computation trees. Moreover, constraint logic programming certainly has aspects of *infon logic programming*, seeing constraints as infon or soa in the sense of the STASS literature. For instance, it can be seen that the infon $x = y$ is supported by a physical computation state s, i.e.,

$$s \models \langle\!\langle =, x, y \rangle\!\rangle.$$

The situation or state s has parameter cells for x and y with pointers from x to y. However, details are outside the scope of the present paper.

References

Aczel, P. 1988. *Non-Well-Founded Sets*. CSLI Lecture Notes Number 14. Stanford: CSLI Publications.

Aho, A. V., J. E. Hopcroft, and J. D. Ullman. 1974. *The Design and Analysis of Computer Algorithms*. Addison-Wesley.

Barwise, J. 1989. *The Situation in Logic*. CSLI Lecture Notes Number 17. Stanford: CSLI Publications.

Barwise, J., and J. Etchemendy. 1987. *The Liar: An Essay on Truth and Circularity*. New York: Oxford University Press.

Colmerauer, A. 1984. Equations and Unequations on Finite and Infinite Trees. In *Proceedings of the Second International Conference on Fifth Generation Computer Systems*. Tokyo.

Dörre, J., and W. Rounds. 1990. On Subsumption and Semiunification in Feature Algebra. In *Proceedings of IEEE Symposium on Logic in Computer Science*. Washington. IEEE Computer Society Press. Also in IWBS Report, IBM Deutschland, Stuttgard, Dec. 1989.

Jaffar, J., and J.-L. Lassez. 1987. Constraint Logic Programming. In *Proceedings of the 14th ACM Symposium on Principles of Programming Languages*.

Jaffar, J., and S. Michaylov. 1987. Methodology and Implementation of a CLP system. In *International Conference on Logic Programming*.

Kfoury, A. J., J. Tiuryn, and P. Urzyczyn. 1990. The Undecidability of the Semiunification Problem. In *Proceedings of the 22nd ACM Symposium on Theory of Computing*.

Lloyd, J. W. 1984. *Foundations of Logic Programming*. Springer-Verlag.

Martin-Löf, P. 1984. *Intuitionistic Type Theory*. Bibliopolis.

Milnor, R. 1989. *Communication and Concurrency*. Prentice-Hall.

Moss, L. S. 1990. Completeness Theorems for Logics of Feature Structure. In *Proceedings of the MSRI Workshop on Logic From Computer Science*, ed. Y. N. Moschovakis. Springer-Verlag. To appear.

Mukai, K. 1990. A System of Logic Programming for Linguistic Analysis. Technical Report TR-540, ICOT, Tokyo. To appear also from SRI Tokyo series.

Mukai, K. 1991. *On Synthesis of Feature Structures as Constraint Satisfaction Problems over Hypersets*. Densi-Jouhou-Tsushin-gakkai. (in Japanese).

Paige, R., and R. E. Tarjan. 1987. Three Partition Refinement Algorithms. *SIAM Journal of Computing* 16(6).

Park, D. 1981. Concurrency and Automata on Infinite Sequences. In *Proceedings of the 5th GI Conference*. Springer Lecture Notes in Computer Science Number 104. Springer-Verlag.

Rounds, W. 1988. Set Values for Unification-Based Grammar Formalisms and Logic Programming. Technical Report Number CSLI-88-129, CSLI, Stanford.

Sato, Y., K. Sakai, and S. Menju. n.d. SetCal: A Solver of Set Constraint in CAL. Technical report, ICOT, to appear.

Smolka, G. 1989. Feature Constraint Logics for Unification Grammars. IWBS Report 93, IBM Deutschland, Stuttgart, November.

Stuckey, P. J. 1987. On the Foundation of Constraint Logic Programming. Technical Report, Department of Computer Science, Monash University, Victoria, Australia, August.

Yasukawa, H., and K. Yokota. 1990. Labeled Graphs as Semantics of Objects. Technical Report, ICOT, November. SIGDBS & SIGAI OF IPSJ.

10

Inferring *in* a Situation *about* Situations

Hideyuki Nakashima and Syun Tutiya

This paper presents an AI application of situation theory. Deciding what inference mechanism to use provides a key to better and more efficient machine intelligence. The goal of this paper is to establish a set of basic ideas about inference which supports a new type of inference mechanism, based on ideas and insights of situation theory and situation semantics. Some of the ideas have already been realized in PROSIT, a knowledge representation and programming language based on situation theory.

Our proposal involves introducing situational parameters as necessary representational tools for dealing with the situatedness of actions and plans. We will test this idea by solving a version of the Frame Problem and showing that by representing situations in the representational system, i.e., the system within which inferences are made, the system can correctly predict the course of events it will undergo.

Although this idea has an obvious association with a formalization of situation theory, and a logical system based on the Austinian concept of propositions in particular, it has its own independent motivations. We explain some of the motivations which concern planning and reasoning. We call the type of inference which is conducted with aid of situational parameters *inference about situations* and distinguish it from *inference in a situation*, which makes use of multi-modal information accessible in situations in which the inferencing is being done. We discuss the difference and argue that the latter is a special case of the former.

We owe to Stanley Peters acknowledgment for suggesting some of the ideas presented in this paper. Without his suggestions, we could not have completed this paper in its present form.

Situation Theory and Its Applications, vol. 2.
Jon Barwise, Jean Mark Gawron, Gordon Plotkin, and Syun Tutiya, eds.

1 Introduction

Inference is an action by humans and machines. The representations machines use in inferring are the tools for inference just as language is a tool humans use in verbal communication. Inference is performed in situations. Being in a situation, humans can infer from premises and facts to conclusions in a way which might not be possible if they were not in the situation. They take advantage of the information they can extract by virtue of being in the situation. We call such inference "inference in a situation". Situation theory has supplied the conceptual equipment for analyzing how this kind of inference works making use of information made relevant by contexts and goals. The idea is that the agent can shift from the information carried by a fact in the world to another fact in the world supported by the facts in the situation she is in. This kind of inference is useful in inferring about the things you are visually presented given a linguistic fact about them.

Our proposal is that there are other cases in which we apply inference to "other" situations. By other situations, we mean situations, i.e., parts of the world, any of which is not exactly the same as the one in which the agent is inferring. What in AI has been called *hypothetical reasoning* or *reasoning about other person's reasoning* is the case in point. In such a case the inference mechanism must be equipped with representational tools which allow the system to plan, hypothesize, surmise beyond the information immediately available in the situation. We will call this type of inference as "inference about situations."

In this paper, we show that the framework of inference in a situation (IIS hereafter) and inference about situations (IAS hereafter) is powerful enough to attack several chronic problems in AI. As an example, we will discuss the Frame Problem which consists of two different types of problems (Shoham and McDermott 1988):

- the qualification problem
- the extended prediction problem.

We will show that IIS gives us a framework to solve the former problem and IAS, the latter.

2 Inference In a Situation

An agent takes advantage of the information he can extract by virtue of being in the situation. When the agent is in a situation to which its representation [1] is attuned, it can carry out inference efficiently. One example of the efficiency is gained by not explicitly representing, and therefore not using, the background condition (Barwise 1981).

---

[1] We assume that the information is represented as a set of infons about the situation.

If an agent is in the situations about which it is reasoning, it can forget about the situation and can make inference solely relying on infons and/or constraints holding among infons. However, as we will see in Section 3, the agent must select by itself the situation in which it makes inference. The agent needs a parameter to talk about the situation with.

We suppose that the representational tools with which we infer are basically set of unanchored parameters. By parameters we mean objects which get anchored and which, if they are not anchored, are used by an agent to keep track of identities of the objects to which they are anchored without really anchoring the parameters to those objects.

2.1 Abstract Situations

Although the situations considered here are actual ones, the reasoning agent must represent situations abstractly. When the representation correctly corresponds to the actual situation, we say the agent is attuned to the situation on which it is reasoning. We will first consider a case in which abstract representations of the actual situations are used in inference, in order to get a clue to formulate inference about situations.

The actual situation is conceived by the agent as a set of abstract situations. Let S be the actual situation. Then the agent's conception of S, called S_a, is defined as follows:

$$S_a = \{s \mid s \supseteq s' \text{ for some } s' \in S\}.$$

We differentiate two kinds of relations between situations: class inclusion (is-a), which is denoted by $\supseteq$, and physical inclusion (part-of), which is denoted by $\in$. When an agent sees a bird singing in a tree (S), it can divide the whole situation into subpieces like bird(s'_1), tree(s'_2), and so on. If each piece is small enough to correspond to its elementary concept (like bird and tree), it can also access the class hierarchy of the concept (s corresponds those upper-classes). So, it sees an actual situation as a combination of is-a and part-of hierarchies of situations.

Let us consider the proposition "birds fly" as an example of inference using an abstract situation. In the first order logic, it may be written as

$$\forall x\, fly(x) \subset bird(x).$$

We propose to write this as information about an abstract situation, bird[2]

$$bird \models \langle\!\langle fly \rangle\!\rangle$$

The latter expresses that the infon $\langle\!\langle fly \rangle\!\rangle$ holds in the situation *bird*. To understand the above expression, one should imagine an abstract situation

---

[2]Surely this may look like an unintelligible notation, but remember that situations are parts of the world and the "partition" is not spatio-temporal. There is no *a priori* discussion which precludes this notation. The difficulty is more in the difference in use of the same word, "bird", which is used on the left of $\models$ as a name of a situation and on the right as a name of a predicate.

in which only the properties of birds are in question. In those situations, since any infon is about birds, there is no need to explicitly state it. In this paper we assume that any n-ary relation on birds can be represented as an $n-1$-ary relation.

Here is more detailed explanation. In

$$\forall x\, fly(x) \subset bird(x),$$

the antecedent limits the range of x on which the consequent holds: Only those which are birds are validly said to fly.

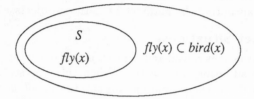

It is then possible to construct an abstract situation s which satisfies the following:

$$s \models \langle\!\langle \text{bird}, \tau \rangle\!\rangle$$

where τ stands for any individual in the situation. We will further call the situation simply as *bird*. Now, if we assume that

$$\text{bird} \models \langle\!\langle \text{bird}, \tau \rangle\!\rangle$$

is a background condition for the situation *bird*, then we can reduce the above logical formula to

$$\text{bird} \models \langle\!\langle \text{fly}, \tau \rangle\!\rangle.$$

If the above statement is always true, we don't have to mention τ and will be able to project this one-argument relation into a null-argument relation:

$$\text{bird} \models \langle\!\langle \text{fly} \rangle\!\rangle$$

As we project an n-ary relation into n-1-ary relation, the situation should be projected into a more specific one accordingly. In general, any argument role of a relation may be turned into background information of the situation. If we write such a new situation s' which has information in addition to the original one s, then the following transformation is allowed:

$$s \models \langle\!\langle R, x_1, ..., x_{i-1}, x_i, x_{i+1}, ..., x_n \rangle\!\rangle$$
$$\downarrow$$
$$s' \models \langle\!\langle R, x_1, ..., x_{i-1}, x_{i+1}, ..., x_n \rangle\!\rangle$$

The transformation falls within the descriptive power of PROSIT (Nakashima et al. 1988) which is a language based on Situation Theory.

We will write the relation between s and s' as

$$s \sqsubseteq s'$$

meaning that

1. s' is a projection of s.
2. s' is, therefore, a further specialization of s.
3. s' therefore contains all the information in s (s' is larger information-wise).

As we will see later, an infon may not be persistent through $\sqsubseteq$. For example, some birds do not fly. In that case, the projection is not a logical procedure. But we do not restrict ourselves to "logical" procedures here.

2.2 Efficiency of IIS

In projection, the same phenomena as efficiency of language (Barwise and Perry 1983) is observed. An infon $\langle\!\langle fly \rangle\!\rangle$ expresses a proposition "A bird flies" in a bird situation and "An airplane flies" in an airplane situation. And it becomes a false proposition in, say, a dog situation.

Let us consider the same principle under a different light. A clock whose hands read 4 P.M. has the information:

$$\langle\!\langle 4pm \rangle\!\rangle.$$

This information has an unarticulated constituent, which is that the time is, say, Pacific standard time (PST). Therefore, the information the clock actually carries is:

$$\langle\!\langle 4pm, PST \rangle\!\rangle.$$

We write both cases as follows:

theclock $\models \langle\!\langle 4pm \rangle\!\rangle$,
world $\models \langle\!\langle 4pm, PST \rangle\!\rangle$.

The constituent "PST" is implicit in the *theclock* situation while it is explicit in the *world* situation, just as birdness is implicit in the *bird* situation.

When an intelligent agent makes an inference, it uses the *theclock* rather than the *world* situation. By using the situated version of representation, the inference becomes simpler and faster. It is obvious in the clock example. We do not usually mention "PST". And by ignoring it, we can avoid extra processing on the time zone. It is also true in the bird example. Imagine a person observing a canary, say Tweety, in front of him. Now the question whether Tweety flies becomes whether

Tweety $\models \langle\!\langle fly \rangle\!\rangle$

holds. The situation part:

Tweety $\models$

is obvious to the reasoner, because he is in the situation, and is omitable. But we mention it to make the argument clear. The situation *Tweety* is a projection of *bird* and thus contains all the infons in bird. Therefore, it is obviously known that the *Tweety* situation contains ⟨⟨fly⟩⟩ without invoking any inference.

It is also true that we can see a canary as a singing object rather than as a bird. Every concept belongs to many concept hierarchies. The hierarchy to be used in reasoning among those many hierarchies is also situation dependent, that is whether we view a canary as a bird or as a pet (or both) depends on the situation (including our internal state). Inheritance itself can be managed by almost any knowledge representation systems: frame, semantic network, logical sentences, and so on. However, none of them can handle this meta-level context dependent nature of the hierarchy.

Once the hierarchy to be used is fixed (as the result of preceding problem solving), it is easy to conclude that the canary flies. Note that if the reasoner viewed the canary as a singing object, he might forget that it flies.

2.3 Projection and Persistence

We showed that when an infon is projected into a smaller (therefore, more specific) situation, the number of arguments decreases. In the projection hierarchy of situations, the smaller (in terms of arity) infon is supported in smaller situations.

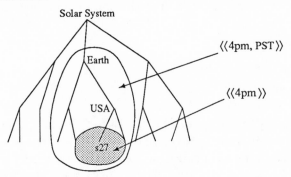

In the case of sets, we can observe another example of persistence. Suppose the following case:

$Set_1 \subset Set_0$
$Set_2 \subset Set_0$
$e \in S_1$

Assuming that every situation denoting a set has information about other sets, we can say that the following propositions hold:

$Set_0 \models$ ⟨⟨element-of, e, Set_0⟩⟩
$Set_1 \models$ ⟨⟨element-of, e, Set_0⟩⟩
$Set_2 \models$ ⟨⟨element-of, e, Set_0⟩⟩
$Set_0 \models$ ⟨⟨element-of, e, Set_1⟩⟩

$$Set_1 \models \langle\!\langle \text{element-of, e, } Set_1 \rangle\!\rangle$$
$$Set_2 \models \langle\!\langle \text{element-of, e, } Set_1 \rangle\!\rangle$$
$$Set_0 \not\models \langle\!\langle \text{element-of, e, } Set_2 \rangle\!\rangle$$
$$Set_1 \not\models \langle\!\langle \text{element-of, e, } Set_2 \rangle\!\rangle$$
$$Set_2 \not\models \langle\!\langle \text{element-of, e, } Set_2 \rangle\!\rangle$$

A projected (therefore, more situated) infon is supported by smaller number of situations:

$$Set_0 \models \langle\!\langle \text{element-of, e} \rangle\!\rangle$$
$$Set_1 \models \langle\!\langle \text{element-of, e} \rangle\!\rangle$$
$$Set_2 \not\models \langle\!\langle \text{element-of, e} \rangle\!\rangle$$

In general, a certain form of infon is supported by a certain group of situations as we see in the following diagram:

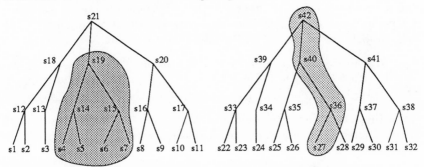

The region could be all subnodes of a node (s19) as shown in the left hand side, or could be part or all of a thread (from s42 to s27) as shown in the right hand side. In either cases, the marked region is the area for IIS and outside is the area for IAS. The most interesting case for IIS is at the boundary of the region where the infon is maximally efficient.

3   Inference About Situations

IAS is inference whose object contains situations, e.g., inference about situation change, or inference about other situations. It is known that infons supported by a situation and infons supported by another situation about the original situation may not be the same (Barwise and Etchemendy 1987). This suggests that we can conclude something different by talking about situations other than the one we are in.

An extreme case of IAS is that sets of rules[3] used in inference differ from one situation to another. An example involves a difference in driving rules in Japan and America:

$$\text{Japan} \models \langle\!\langle \text{lefthandside, } \dot{x} \rangle\!\rangle \;\Leftarrow\; \langle\!\langle \text{runs, } \dot{c}, \dot{x} \rangle\!\rangle \wedge \langle\!\langle \text{car, } \dot{c} \rangle\!\rangle$$
$$\text{America} \models \langle\!\langle \text{righthandside, } \dot{x} \rangle\!\rangle \;\Leftarrow\; \langle\!\langle \text{runs, } \dot{c}, \dot{x} \rangle\!\rangle \wedge \langle\!\langle \text{car, } \dot{c} \rangle\!\rangle$$

---

[3] Constraints are used as rules in PROSIT.

This means that we can change our mode of inference by shifting to another situation. Note that we do not have to actually travel between Japan and America to change the mode. We can just simulate other situations.

In a sense, IIS is inference on the right-hand side of $\models$, and IAS is inference on the left-hand side of $\models$. In other words, IAS is inference on setting the context for IAS, or inference whose objects are situations. For example, by moving information about temporal location from infon (right-hand-side) to situation (left-hand-side), we can formulate inference on situations which changes in a certain time sequence as IAS. Difficulties which arise in this type of reasoning, known as frame problems (McCarthy and Hayes 1969), can be overcome this way.

It is worthwhile to point out that the original idea of Minsky's frame[4] theory (McCarthy and Hayes 1969) depicts a frame network which consists of frames and pointers to other frames. The pointers are used to shift viewpoints when one frame does not match the situation any more. The idea parallels our framework in the following two points:

1. Any abstract situation is viewed as a frame whose slots correspond to infons holding in the situation.

2. Situational parameters match pointers to other frames.

Given these mappings, we could almost say that the frame theory is an informal version of the idea presented in this paper.

4 The Frame Problem

4.1 The Qualification Problem and IIS

The qualification problem is "the problem of making sound predictions about the future without taking into account everything about the past" (Shoham and McDermott 1988). In other words, it is impossible to take into account all possibly relevant factors which might affect the successful completion of an action. It is completely bypassed by using IIS: There is no need to specify every precondition of an action beforehand. We can refer to the situation whenever something goes wrong or new information is required. Even a human may sometimes fail to predict the future properly.

Backward chaining is associated with this type of inference, since requirement of new information is goal-driven. Whenever a goal is given, we check if we already have information to solve the goal. If not, we observe the situation to get it.

However, we do not go into details of extracting information from actual situations, since we have to build a robot to do so. In this paper, we limit ourselves to mechanical aspects of reasoning implementable on cur-

---

[4]Frame theory should not be confused with the frame problem. The former is a framework for knowledge representation while the latter is a problem in machine reasoning.

rent computers. Hyperproof (Barwise and Etchemendy 1990) employs an different approach and explores the issue more deeply.

4.2 The Extended Prediction Problem and IAS

We conjecture that the solution to the extended prediction problem requires the mode-change of inference, i.e., IAS. However, it must be made clear that IAS is not the solution to the problem. It is rather a framework with which the problem is attacked. The following example should be taken as an example to show that we can employ an arbitrary schema and inference on time-sequence.

Although the extended prediction problem occurs during inference, it is too late to try to solve the problem at the time of inference. Framework of inference, that is, the inference schema to be used to reason about a particular problem must be set up before initiating the inference. Selection of the schema corresponds selection of situation(s) for IAS. In the case of the Yale shooting problem (Hanks and McDermott 1986), the set-up should be done while the problem is presented to the inference engine. Before the problem is completed, the schema (for example, to use inference on time-sequence) should be chosen. Then, the rest of the task is simple: just invoke the schema.[5]

Our ultimate goal is to write a program which automatically selects an appropriate mode of inference to a given problem. This requires the ability of the program to handle inference modes as objects of manipulation. It is exactly what we mean by IAS. The advantages of our approach over others are as follows:

- We use situations as objects.
- Different situations may contain different inference rules.
- It is thus possible to set up an arbitrary framework for reasoning.

A meta-interpreter could do the work. It takes a program on how to reason and executes it on particular problems. However, it is not only too slow but it is also unlikely that humans are doing this. It is true that we do follow some written (or remembered) instructions occasionally. But it is not the normal mode. In everyday life we just shift our inference mode and do it unconsciously.

In other words, once the system is in a certain mode, the inference must be as efficient as other modes. We will present an example of inference along a time sequence. In the framework, although the inference acts as if the whole time-sequence is followed from past to future to yield the answer, it actually looks only at relevant facts, rules and time slices, resulting in an efficient computation.

---

[5]There are cases in which the schema itself must be changed dynamically. IAS is also capable of doing this. But we don't believe it necessary for simple cases like the Yale shooting problem.

5 An Example: YSP

We will use the Yale shooting problem to illustrate our approach. We will show two inference schemata for the program. The problem goes like this: Someone (A) is alive; Someone else (B) loads a gun; B waits; B shoots; Is A alive now?

5.1 A Simple Solution

Suppose we include the timing information in a infon and use $\langle\langle$alive, t0$\rangle\rangle$ to mean that someone is alive at t0, and represent the sequence as follows:

$$s \models \langle\langle\text{before, t0, t1}\rangle\rangle$$
$$s \models \langle\langle\text{before, t1, t2}\rangle\rangle$$
$$s \models \langle\langle\text{before, t2, t3}\rangle\rangle$$
$$s \models \langle\langle\text{before, t3, t4}\rangle\rangle$$
$$s \models \langle\langle\text{alive, t0}\rangle\rangle$$
$$s \models \langle\langle\text{load, t1}\rangle\rangle$$
$$s \models \langle\langle\text{wait, t2}\rangle\rangle$$
$$s \models \langle\langle\text{shoot, t3}\rangle\rangle$$
$$s \models \langle\langle\text{alive, } \dot{t}'; 0\rangle\rangle \Leftarrow \langle\langle\text{loaded, } \dot{t}\rangle\rangle \wedge \langle\langle\text{shoot, } \dot{t}\rangle\rangle \wedge f\langle\langle\text{before, } \dot{t}, \dot{t}'\rangle\rangle$$
$$s \models \langle\langle\text{loaded,} \dot{t}'\rangle\rangle \Leftarrow \langle\langle\text{load,} \dot{t}\rangle\rangle \wedge \langle\langle\text{before,} \dot{t}, \dot{t}'\rangle\rangle$$

How can we conclude whether $s \models \langle\langle\text{alive, t4}\rangle\rangle$ is true. We cannot, unless we have some rule connecting those time slices.

It is natural to assume inertia on states, that is, to assume that the state remains to be so unless something explicitly changes it. In logical formulation, it is expressed as a frame axiom:

$$\langle\langle\dot{p}, \dot{t}'\rangle\rangle \Leftarrow \langle\langle\dot{p}, \dot{t}\rangle\rangle \wedge\langle\langle\text{before,} \dot{t}, \dot{t}'\rangle\rangle\wedge\langle\langle\dot{a}, \dot{t}\rangle\rangle\wedge \texttt{unless } \langle\langle\text{ends, } \dot{a}, \dot{p}, \dot{t}\rangle\rangle$$

Although it is logical, introduction of the frame axiom makes inference slow and complicated (the original frame problem in McCarthy and Hayes 1969). Furthermore, it is unlikely that human is employing such inference rule. Instead, use of IAS makes it efficient and simple. The above problem is restated as follows: [6]

$$s \models \text{t0} \sqsubseteq \text{t1}$$
$$s \models \text{t1} \sqsubseteq \text{t2}$$
$$s \models \text{t2} \sqsubseteq \text{t3}$$
$$s \models \text{t3} \sqsubseteq \text{t4}$$
$$s \models (\text{t0} \models \langle\langle\text{alive}\rangle\rangle)$$
$$s \models (\text{t1} \models \langle\langle\text{load}\rangle\rangle)$$
$$s \models (\text{t2} \models \langle\langle\text{wait}\rangle\rangle)$$
$$s \models (\text{t3} \models \langle\langle\text{shoot}\rangle\rangle)$$
$$s \models \langle\langle\text{alive; 0}\rangle\rangle \Leftarrow \langle\langle\text{loaded}\rangle\rangle \wedge \langle\langle\text{shoot}\rangle\rangle$$
$$s \models \langle\langle\text{loaded}\rangle\rangle \Leftarrow \langle\langle\text{load}\rangle\rangle$$

---

[6]The situation s is the context of the reasoning. The agent itself may not be aware of the situation it is in.

There is no need for the frame axiom. The $\sqsubseteq$ relation takes care of it. Note that the same relation, $\sqsubseteq$, is used as in the case of bird's class hierarchy. The relation is a specialization on situations. In this case, specialization is applied to possibilities of the future. At t0 there were more possibilities on future events. One of them actually happened at t1. Therefore, t1 has more information than t0 and more specific in situation-wise.

Infons representing states, like $\langle\!\langle$alive$\rangle\!\rangle$, are semi-persistent. Semi-persistent means that it is persistent unless contradictory information is added. In this example, $\langle\!\langle$alive; 0$\rangle\!\rangle$ is contradictory to $\langle\!\langle$alive$\rangle\!\rangle$. Thus, from the above representation, the system concludes

$$s \models (t4 \models \langle\!\langle\text{alive; 0}\rangle\!\rangle)$$

successfully.

Infons representing actions, like $\langle\!\langle$shoot$\rangle\!\rangle$, should not be persistent, on the other hand. An action which takes place in one frame should not be inherited by the next frame.[7] PROSIT copes with this persistence and semi-persistence. It is possible to construct a temporal logic on top of PROSIT, but the details will be outside the scope of this paper and will be described in a future paper.

5.2   Further Problems and our Solution

There are several proposals to solve YSP (Hanks and McDermott 1987 gives a good summary of approaches). Their basic strategy is to choose the most preferred model, given a theory and a preference criterion. The preference criterion gives preference over different models. Thus either a meta-level sentence over models or some preprocessing (like circumscription in McCarthy 1980) should be provided to take the preference into account.

With IAS, on the other hand, the preference is given as ordering among situations, which is an object level sentence of situation theory. The reasoning system is then capable of choosing, as opposed to being given from outside, any proper ordering. It can, for example, reverse the temporal order by constructing a hypothetical situation:

$$hyp_1 \models t4 \sqsubseteq t3$$
$$hyp_1 \models t3 \sqsubseteq t2$$
$$hyp_1 \models t2 \sqsubseteq t1$$
$$hyp_1 \models t1 \sqsubseteq t0$$

The reasoning system can also change the strategy of its own reasoning. One example of such strategy is to first hypothesize the current status and see if it is consistent with the given sequence of actions and states. For example, one can just assume $t4 \models \langle\!\langle$alive$\rangle\!\rangle$ because it was true in t0 and check if it is consistent. A slight change of the structure suffices to make this happen. In this case, although we have the same amount of

---

[7]Here we assume that an action completes instantly.

information, our framework of inference is different. Instead of following the time sequence, we travel back and forth:

1. We assume ⟨⟨alive⟩⟩ at t4.
2. We conjecture ⟨⟨loaded⟩⟩ at t3.
3. We check if ⟨⟨alive⟩⟩ still holds at t4.
4. Since 2 contradicts with the assumption 1, we conclude ⟨⟨loaded; 0⟩⟩.

A simple PROSIT program will do the work. But showing the details of the program is outside the scope of this paper (see Nakashima 1990 for details). The bottom line is that if we do not use IAS, we cannot construct such a program.

6 Summary

We conjecture that intelligence requires the ability to use situations, not only as an external resource but also as objects of inference. We have shown that by moving some part of information into the situation side and by manipulating the relation of those situations, we can mimic human inference in various cases.

PROSIT is a test-bench to test the conjecture. The most important point is that situation governs inference and inference affects situation.

References

Barwise, J. 1981. Conditionals and Conditional Information. *The Journal of Philosophy*. Reprinted in Barwise 1989, 97–135.

Barwise, J. 1989. *The Situation in Logic*. CSLI Lecture Notes Number 17. Stanford: CSLI Publications.

Barwise, J., and J. Etchemendy. 1987. *The Liar: An Essay on Truth and Circularity*. New York: Oxford University Press.

Barwise, J., and J. Etchemendy. 1990. Visual Information and Valid Reasoning. In *Visualization in Mathematics*, ed. W. Zimmerman. Washington, DC: Mathematical Association of America.

Barwise, J., and J. Perry. 1983. *Situations and Attitudes*. Cambridge, MA: MIT Press.

Hanks, S., and D. McDermott. 1986. Default Reasoning, Nonmonotonic Logics, and the Frame Problem. In *Proceedings of AAAI-86*, 328–333.

Hanks, S., and D. McDermott. 1987. Nonmonotonic Logic and Temporal Projection. *Artificial Intelligence* 33(3).

McCarthy, J. 1980. Circumscription: A Form of Non-monotonic Reasoning. *Artificial Intelligence* 13:27–39.

McCarthy, J., and P. J. Hayes. 1969. Some Philosophical Problems from the Standpoint of Artificial Intelligence. In *Machine Intelligence 4*, ed. B. Meltzer and D. Michie, 463–502. Edinburgh University Press.

Nakashima, H. 1990. Inference about Situations (in Japanese). *Journal of Japanese Society of AI* 5(5):588–594.

Nakashima, H., H. Suzuki, P.-K. Halvorsen, and S. Peters. 1988. Towards a Computational Interpretation of Situation Theory. In *Proceedings of the International Conference on Fifth Generation Computer Systems*, 489–498. Tokyo. Institute for New Generation Systems.

Shoham, Y., and D. McDermott. 1988. Problems in Formal Temporal Reasoning. *Artificial Intelligence* 36(1):49–90.

11

Situation-Theoretic Aspects of Databases

BILL ROUNDS

The relational model for database theory, introduced by Codd (1970) has enjoyed widespread success, and many implementations and commercial versions are now available. However, there are not too many successful interfaces to these systems from natural language input. One of the reasons seems to be the difficulty of translating natural language queries (and sequences of these) into the language of first-order logic, which is at bottom the usual language for expressing relational queries.

One possible answer to this problem is that computational linguists do not understand well enough how to translate into logic; but another, possibly more appealing one, is that first-order logic itself is to blame. FOL, after all, was an initial attempt to capture mathematical reasoning in natural language. One explanation for the success of relational database theory might be that its semantics is closer to that of natural language than the language of disks and sectors. Continuing this analogy, it seems reasonable to design new database models using a better semantics for natural language, and therefore to consider situation theory as a source of ideas. The practical benefit will then presumably be better natural language interfaces to data bases.

In the present paper, then, we use situation theory as a guide to developing some semantical notions for databases. We do not, however, try to

This research was supported in part by the US National Science Foundation, grant IRI-8915282, and by the Science and Engineering Research Council of Great Britain, under a Visiting Fellowship at Edinburgh, grant number GR/G22046.

I would like to thank Jon Barwise, Robin Cooper, Mark Johnson, Hans Kamp, and Jerry Seligman for discussions, comments, corrections, and all sorts of other helpful advice while this paper was being prepared. A special debt is owed to Alexis Manaster Ramer, who suggested the linguistic "and-or" noun coordination problem as something which might be amenable to the methods described here.

Situation Theory and Its Applications, vol. 2.
Jon Barwise, Jean Mark Gawron, Gordon Plotkin, and Syun Tutiya, eds.

incorporate situations directly in a programming language, as in PROSIT (Nakashima et al. 1988). One reason is that the theory itself is still rather fluid, and another is that the problem of general inference is likely to be computationally intractable. What we do instead is to propose some programming language constructs which take advantage of nonwellfounded set-theoretical techniques (Aczel 1988) to define a class of structures which then can be used to encode the constructs of situation theory. These latter constructs (infons, relations, and types, for example,) are then just examples of types in our programming language. This design strategy has the advantage of possibly being able to accommodate changes in situation theory itself, and of being a way to implement PROSIT-like languages with suitable declarations. We try to attain computational tractability by choosing sufficiently simple structures, and severely restricting the language used to describe them. This is more like the approach of Mukai's CIL (1987).

There is currently a large body of research in what might be called the theory of complex objects in data bases. This started with the realization that flat relations (where tuples are allowed only to have atomic objects, like $1000, as values of attributes, like *salary*), are not as flexible in describing the world as one might like. (For example, one cannot say that "the author of *Logic for Children* is either Claire or Max, but I don't know which.") There are several lines that database researchers are pursuing; one is the extension of relational theory to these "non first normal form" databases; see van Gucht and Fischer 1988, for example. Another is the development of complex objects themselves; the first work along these lines seems to be Bancilhon and Khoshafian 1986; and another is the extension of logic programming to handle complex objects; early research in this line is Maier 1986, and subsequently, at Stony Brook, Chen, Warren, Kifer, and Wu 1989, 1989. Finally, there is work at Pennsylvania on complex objects in functional database programming languages. This includes, for example, Buneman, Davidson, and Watters 1988, which accounts for partial information using powerdomains, and Ohori 1988 which works out a theory of types. All of these design efforts address problems which situation theory is intended to handle: the non-flatness of relations (perhaps better expressed as making all citizens first-class), the inclusion of types in models; the question of partial information; the non-well-foundedness of the world; and so on.

It thus seems that much of this work has a remarkable affinity to situation theory, and that possibly there are some ideas from that theory and from Aczel's non-well-founded set theory (1988) which can contribute to the design of object-oriented databases. We will try do do some of this in what follows; we will first give the results in outline.

The initial attempt to model complex objects, by Bancilhon and Khoshafian (1986), is closest to the approach we give here. Their approach involves a simultaneous inductive definition of sets together with attributed tuples. We improve this definition by giving a coinductive definition of objects in AFA; this allows us to have truly circular objects, and provides a nice instance of AFA techniques.

Maier and the Stony Brook researchers have been concerned to integrate complex objects into the framework of logic programming. They also have been considering the question of *object identity*: the fact that there may be two employees with the same name and employee number, but only one object (tuple, record) with this information in the database. They solve this by thinking of unique names for all the distinct (atomic) entities in the system, and then by making up terms which combine the names with assertions qualifying them. These terms thus function both as entities and assertions in a Horn-like logic programming language environment. (Prolog does the same, mixing first-order terms inside predicates.) Our approach to this problem separates names and entities from assertions. The use of AFA to model objects allows us to have ordinary terms which denote these objects. It also allows us to assert equations between terms; these equations form the basic *constraint system* for logic programming over these objects. Use of the constraint formalism allows a clean separation of concerns, and seems to resolve certain anomalies which occur when terms are combined with assertions. We use the method of Höhfeld and Smolka 1988 for adding constraints to a Horn clause logic programming framework.

One of the fundamental concerns of situation theory is to provide a precise idea of *information*. Barwise and Etchemendy, in the first volume of these proceedings (1990), have provided a model of information called *infon algebras*. The idea is as follows. In an infon algebra, one develops a notion of information-bearing element (the infon). Then, one has the "makes factual" relation $\models$ between situations and infons, and a relation $\Rightarrow$ between infons, which denotes the "more information than" relation. Our concern is to explicate this latter relation for data bases, as is done by Buneman et al. 1988. (We use the Scott notation $\sqsubseteq$, a "less information than" relation, instead of $\Rightarrow$.) We thus view complex objects (data bases) as infons in the sense of Barwise and Etchemendy.

To specify the $\sqsubseteq$ relation, we introduce two set-ordering notions based on the Smyth and Hoare powerdomains. The Smyth ordering is appropriate for a notion of concrete "type", in which a set of objects gives a disjunctive possibility for describing some particular situation[1]. The Hoare powerdomain is appropriate for asserting the existence of multiple objects, so that a set of objects in the Hoare sense represents an actual aggregation. These notions are then combined into a single mixed ordering which allows types

---

[1] I am aware of the overuse of the word "type" in this context; perhaps a better word might be "sort". In any case, by using this word, we refer to a simple notion of set of objects.

to be pre-ordered in the Smyth sense, and other objects to be ordered in the Hoare sense. As an example, we can express the distinction between the facts

1. "the author of *Logic for Children* is either Claire or Max"
2. "The authors of *Logic for Children* are Claire and Max".

The former is expressed using a disjunctive type in the Smyth powerdomain, while the second is expressed as the Hoare aggregation of Claire and Max.

We extend our notion of object by allowing *parameters* to be basic objects. The introduction of parameters is intended to solve the problem of coreferring subobjects of a complex object, as well as to specify "unknown values" in the data base. This is a modeling technique borrowed directly from situation theory.

As a sample of what might be proved about such objects, we study least upper and greatest lower bounds in the Smyth preorder. We show that any two objects with an upper bound have a least such up to equivalence in the Smyth preorder. We also show that a set of complex objects can be viewed as the set of models of a simple modal propositional formula, and that there is a homomorphic map from conjunctions and disjunctions of propositions to Smyth least upper and greatest lower bounds.

The most complicated result in the paper is presented in Section 3, where we show how to prove the existence of least upper bounds and greatest lower bounds in the Smyth preorder on complex objects. This involves the use of the Solution Lemma of AFA both as a way of giving an existence proof for the required objects, and as an algorithmic specification of the objects, using a non-well-founded recursion. We believe (along with Barwise) that the semantics of many recursive functions defined on so-called "infinite" (read non-well-founded or circular) objects can be given this way, avoiding the need to introduce complicated partial orders (cpo's). This technique has appeared in several works; we present additional evidence of its usefulness in a case where a proof using explicit data structures is extremely messy.

At least two major tasks are not undertaken in this paper. The most important one is to specify (a mathematical model of) situations (the parts of the world actually described by data bases) and a definition of the "makes factual" relation, so that a full infon-algebraic picture of complex objects would be available. The other is to develop the logic programming aspects into a working language. At best we now have only a suggestion for the definition of the constraint language.

1 Complex Objects

We begin by assuming two disjoint alphabets L and A, called the sets of *features* and *atoms* respectively. Features are arguments to many-adic functions called *feature structures*, which are one kind of structured complex object. The atoms are used to denote individuals and unanalyzed types; we reserve the letters a, b, c for atoms. We also adjoin a set of *atomic parameters* X, with elements x, y, z and so forth. These will be used to stand for "unknown" objects, and to facilitate describing objects via terms. On the set of atoms A we assume a partial ordering $\sqsubseteq_A$; this is in analogy with order-sorted algebra (Goguen and Meseguer 1986). This ordering provides for the usual notion of inheritance. (We use the $\sqsubseteq$ relation of denotational semantics to indicate increasing specificity, so that the most general types are at the bottom.) We will also assume that in this order, any two objects with an upper bound have a least such, and similarly for lower bounds.

We are now ready for the definition of complex objects.

Definition 1 The class of of *complex objects* to be the largest class C such that if $u \in C$, then u is of one of the forms

- a, for $a \in A$;
- x, for $x \in X$;
- f, where f is a partial function from L to C,
- $\langle s, \tau \rangle$, where s is a subset of C;
- $\langle s, \alpha \rangle$, where s is a subset of C;

We intend the objects f and s to be structured objects. The function f evaluated on a feature l is thought of as the value of the l-attribute of the object denoted by s. Thus f is a version of a *feature structure* as in computational linguistics. The sets s are partitioned into either τ-sets (for types) or α-sets (for aggregates).[2]

1.1 An Example

This standard example of a set-valued complex object is in fact one from ordinary relational database theory, given by (Maier 1983, pp. 16–17). Imagine an airline which maintains a list of which types of aircraft may be used on each flight, and a list of the aircraft types which each pilot is certified to fly. The first list is called *usable*, and the second is called *certified*. These are shown in the following tables.

usable	
FLIGHT	EQUIPMENT
83	727
83	747
84	727
84	747
109	707

---

[2] Another possibility is to call the aggregate sets "conjunctive", and the types "disjunctive". But this usage seems to imply that the two kinds of sets could be combined using the conjunction and disjunction operators, which is not the case in our model.

The *certified* table:

certified	
PILOT	EQUIPMENT
Simmons	707
Simmons	727
Barth	747
Hill	727
Hill	747

Notice that in this example, there is a disjunctive quality to the information in the tuples. That is, it is not possible for flight 83 to be using a 727 and a 747 simultaneously. This is a perfect case to use the τ-sets in our model. We model the relations *usable* and *certified* by two τ-sets:

$$u = \{[flight : 83, equip : 727], [flight : 83, equip : 747], \ldots\}$$

$$c = \{[pilot : simmons, equip : 707], [pilot : simmons, equip : 727], \ldots\}.$$

Now the individual tuples in the relations are represented by feature structures. Thus $[flight : 83, equip : 727]$ is that function f whose value for $flight$ is 83, and for $equip$ is 747. (Later we will give this notation exactly.)

To preview our notion of Smyth order, we want a new τ-set combining the information in the two sets u and c above. What we want in this case is a list showing all of our possible options for flights, equipment, and pilots. This is the operation known as the *natural join* of the two relations, and is given as the table below:

usable ⋈ certified		
FLIGHT	EQUIPMENT	PILOT
83	727	Simmons
83	727	Hill
83	747	Barth
83	747	Hill
84	727	Simmons
84	727	Hill
84	747	Barth
84	747	Hill
109	707	Simmons

The natural join can be explained very simply using the notion of feature structure unification (Shieber 1986). For example, the unification of the two feature structures

$$f = [flight : 83, equip : 727] \text{ and } g = [pilot : simmons, equip : 727]$$

is the structure

$$f \cup g = [flight : 83, equip : 727, pilot : simmons].$$

The unification of f and g is really just their union as partial functions, and succeeds when the functions do not disagree.

The join of the two sets u and c can be thought of as the set consisting of all the pairwise unifications of the feature structures in u with those in c. We will see in what follows how the join can be given as a least upper bound in the *Smyth preorder* on complex objects.

We will not reproduce it here, but Barwise (1989) has a nice example of the use of aggregate sets of feature structures, using the *Hoare preorder*, in his chapter on the model theory of common knowledge. This example in particular is non-well-founded.

1.2 Terms Denoting Complex Objects

Our task is now to develop ways of describing the complex objects in the previous section. We will begin with a simple term language, in which the denotation of a term will be a particular element of C. Equalities between these terms can be used as the basis for a constraint logic in a logic programming system (see below).

We define the set of object-valued *terms* as follows. We use the set set $X = \{x_0, \ldots\}$ of parameters both as part of the term syntax, and as part of the semantic domain (so that we can speak of parametric objects). Notice that terms are well-founded, though their denotations need not be.

Definition 2 The set of terms over A and L is given by the following inductive clauses.

1. Each member of A and X is a term;
2. Every f-term, α-term, and τ-term is a term;
3. If $t_1, \ldots, t_n$ are terms, and $l_1, \ldots, l_n$ are distinct labels, then

$$[l_1 : t_1, \ldots l_n : t_n]$$

   is an f-term;
4. If $t_1, \ldots, t_n$ are terms, then $\{t_1, \ldots, t_n\}_\tau$ is a τ-term;
5. If $t_1, \ldots, t_n$ are terms, then $\{t_1, \ldots, t_n\}_\alpha$ is an $alpha$-term;
6. If u is a term, and $t_1, \ldots, t_n$ are non-variable terms, $x_1, \ldots, x_n$ are distinct variables, then

$$u[x_1 \mapsto t_1, \ldots, x_n \mapsto t_n]$$

   is a term.

We proceed to give meaning to these terms using AFA. For the last clause, recall that an *anchor* is a function mapping parameters to elements of the set-theoretic universe, and that the Solution Lemma says that every system of equations $\{x = b_x\}$, where b_x is a parametric set, has a unique solution—a function J assigning to each parameter x in the system a set $J(x)$ "solving" the system. (In fact, this can be used as the statement of the anti-foundation axiom.)

Definition 3 The *denotation* $[\![t]\!]$ of a term t is given by the following clauses.

1. $[\![a]\!] = a$; $[\![x]\!] = x$;
2. $[\![l_1 : t_1, \ldots, l_n : t_n]\!]$ is the function $f : L \to C$ such that $f(l_i) = [\![t_i]\!]$;
3. $[\![\{t_1, \ldots, t_n\}]\!] = \{[\![t_1]\!], \ldots, [\![t_n]\!]\}$ (this clause applies to α and τ-sets);
4. $[\![u[x_1 \mapsto t_1, \ldots, x_n \mapsto t_n]]\!]$ is determined as follows. Let J be the anchor which assigns to x_i the set obtained by the Solution Lemma from the system $x_i \doteq [\![t_i]\!]$. Then $[\![u[x_1 \mapsto t_1, \ldots, x_n \mapsto t_n]]\!]$ is $[\![u]\!]$ anchored by J.

For a precise statement of the notion of "u anchored by J" we refer the reader to Aczel's work on replacement systems (1990, pp. 15–16). The function J is a substitution on the parameters of u, and can be uniquely extended to u, because the class of complex objects is a special anti-founded replacement system over the set X. In particular, the result of such a substitution $u[J]$ is again a complex object.

2 Morphisms

We now define *Hoare* and *Smyth simulations*. We do this at first for set-valued objects in which there is no distinction between τ and α sets, for simplicity.

Definition 4 A *Hoare simulation* is a relation R on C such that if $u \, R \, v$, then

1. both u and v are atoms with $u \sqsubseteq v$; or u and v are both the same parameter x;
2. $u = f, v = g$, and f $f(l)\!\downarrow$, then $g(l)\!\downarrow$, and $f(l) \, R \, g(l)$;
3. u is a set s, v is a set t, and $(\forall s' \in s)(\exists t' \in t)(s' \, R \, t')$.

Example. Suppose we have the information that one of the authors of a certain well-known textbook is named Barwise. Then the object

[title:*Situations and Attitudes*, author:{Barwise}]

bears a Hoare simulation relation to

[title:*Situations and Attitudes*, author:{Barwise, Perry}].

Adding more elements to a set increases the information in that set under the Hoare preorder.

Definition 5 A *Smyth simulation* is just like a Hoare simulation, except that clause (3) reads

If $t' \in t$, then there is $s' \in s$ such that $s' \, R \, t'$.

Example. Suppose we have the information that the (unique) author of a certain well-known play is either Shakespeare or Elizabeth I of England. Then the object

[title:*Love's Labors Lost*, author:{S, QE1}]

bears a Smyth simulation relation to

[title:*Love's Labors Lost*, author:{S}].

Deleting elements from a set increases the information in that set under the Smyth preorder: namely, elements of a set represent disjunctive possibilities.

The distinction between Hoare and Smyth simulations may be remembered by considering the union of two sets A and B. Under the Hoare preorder, the union is the least upper bound of the two sets. Under the Smyth order, it is the greatest lower bound, because it represents the disjunction of all the possibilities in either of the two sets. This explains the understandable confusion of students when they first learn the definition of $A \cup B$ as the set of all x such that $x \in A$ or $x \in B$. They (quite naturally) understand the union as the aggregate notion of all x's in A and in B.

Working again without reference to aggregate or disjunctive sets, we say u *Hoare-subsumes* v, and write $u \sqsubseteq_H v$, if there is a Hoare simulation between u and v. Similarly for Smyth simulations.[3] Finally, we say that u and v are *Hoare-equivalent*, and write $u \equiv_H v$, if $u \sqsubseteq_H v$ and $v \sqsubseteq_H u$, and similarly for Smyth-equivalence.

Now let us return to the case when we distinguish aggregates α from types τ. We can combine these two notions into one, getting a *mixed* notion of simulation for all complex objects. (This definition is reminiscent of Buneman et al. 1988.)

Definition 6 An *M-simulation* is a relation R on C such that if $u\,R\,v$, then

1. both u and v are atoms and $u \sqsubseteq v$; or the same parameter x; or
2. $u = f, v = g$, and if $f(l)\!\downarrow$, then $g(l)\!\downarrow$, and $f(l)\,R\,g(l)$; or
3. u and v are α-sets s and t, and $(\forall s' \in s)(\exists t' \in t)(s'\,R\,t')$; or
4. u and v are τ-sets s and t, and $(\forall t' \in t)(\exists s' \in s)(s'\,R\,t')$.

Remark. We might want to use the notion of aggregate set to model functions from L to C, thereby simplifying the definition both of complex objects and simulation. But it turns out that using this definition, the Hoare preorder unifies two functions by taking their union as relations. Since we want the result to be a function, and to fail if two functions disagree, this approach will not work.

Let $\sqsubseteq_M$ be the preorder induced by the mixed notion of of simulation. We can see the use of this preorder as follows. Suppose that we receive two items of partial information about some one book. We remember in one case that there is more than one author, that one of them is Barwise, and that the title is either *Situations and Attitudes* or *Admissible Sets*. In

---

[3]Note that neither of these relations is a partial order.

the other case, we remember that the title is *Situations and Attitudes*, and that one of the authors is Perry. Now consider the two objects

$$[\text{ title:} \{SA, \ AS\}_\tau, \ \text{author:} \{\text{Barwise}\}_\alpha]$$

and

$$[\text{ title:} \{SA\}_\tau, \ \text{author:} \{\text{Perry}\}_\alpha].$$

We want these two objects to unify into the object which tells us that the title is *SA* and that the authors are Barwise and Perry. But plainly considering each as an unmixed object will not do; neither simulation notion alone will give the right answer.

Another remark is in order here: notice that according to our definitions so far, a parameter x will only "subsume" itself. This is at variation with the usual notion of term subsumption, where a parameter can subsume any term not involving it, because an appropriate substitution for that parameter always exists. There are two notions of "subsumption" which address this problem. One is to count parameters as being the same up to renaming; the other is to adopt a variant of the usual definition of "matching" for ordinary terms. These ideas are formalized in the following definitions. First we call an anchor which is an injective function from X to X a *parameter renaming*. (cf. Westerståhl 1990 for the same notion, which he calls a one-to-one parameter map.)

Definition 7 We say that $u \sqsubseteq v$ (u subsumes v) iff there is a renaming I for the parameters of u such that $u[I] \sqsubseteq_M v$. We say u *matches* v ($u \ \mu \ v$) if there is any anchor J such that $u[J] \sqsubseteq_M v$. (We also say in this case that v instantiates u.)

Example. The α-set $\{x, a\}$ subsumes $\{y, a, b\}$ via the renaming which sends x to y. The anchors which map x to y, a, and b, respectively, witness the instantiation relation. However, there is no M-simulation relation between these two sets.

The reason for considering these distinct notions of subsumption for objects lies in our desire to use parameters as names for unique objects. If we relaxed our notion of M-simulation to allow a parameter to simulate anything, then the τ-set $\{x\}$ would subsume $\{a, b\}$, violating the intuition that a singleton set is more informative than a disjunction. Another possibility would be to force simulations to be functions on parameters, but then the M-subsumption relation turns out not to be transitive. The notion of subsumption seems to be the strongest reasonable notion of "involvement", in the situation-theoretic sense of Barwise and Etchemendy, which accounts for the identity of objects. We will give an application later showing how this notion can be used for specifying "token identity" in linguistic feature structures without using so-called "path equalities." as in, say, Shieber 1986 or Kasper and Rounds 1990.

3 Properties of Preorders

In this subsection we establish some typical properties of our S, H, and M preorders. For simplicity, consider complex objects which have only τ-sets as their set-valued components. Call these τ-objects. Thus the M preorder is really the S preorder for this class.

Theorem 1 *If two τ-objects u and v have an upper bound in the Smyth preorder, then they have a least such, up to Smyth equivalence.*

We state, but do not show, the same result for the Smyth lower bound and both kinds of bounds in the Hoare and M-preorders.

By a it type we mean a τ-object which is in fact a set of (τ)-objects, identified up to S-equivalence.

Theorem 2 *The class of types forms a distributive lattice under the Smyth least upper bound and greatest lower bound operations.*

This result allows us to define the disjunction of types to be their Smyth greatest lower bound, and the conjunction to be their Smyth least upper bound. We also can define an "of-type" relation ":" by saying that $g :$ u, where g and u are τ-objects iff $u \sqsubseteq_S \{g\}$. We will say a bit more about types as propositions in the next section, but notice now that Smyth conjunction of sets of tuples, where the tuples are ordinary flat record structures, is exactly the notion of relational join. This follows from the equation

$$s \sqcup_S t = \{\sigma' \sqcup_S \tau' \mid \sigma' \in s, \tau' \in t\}$$

which expresses a characteristic property of the Smyth powerdomain. The idea turns up also in PROSIT, where it is called the unification of two situations; unification in this case proceeds by pairwise unifying infons in the two parts, in the manner of feature structure unification.

3.1 Proof of Theorem 1

The proof makes essential use of the Solution Lemma of AFA. Interestingly, the use of this lemma is tantamount to writing an algorithm to compute the required least upper bound, and can be seen as a way to formalize the process of recursive procedures on infinite data structures, common in functional programming languages.

Consider two complex objects of the form $u = f$ and $v = g$. A straightforward way to compute the unification of these objects is to try to unify the f and g as feature structures, which means that we recursively unify $f(l)$ with $g(l)$ for each common value of l, if that succeeds, and then join in the l values which are not in the common domain. On the other hand, suppose u and v are set values s and t. Referring to the example of the natural join, we should seemingly then try to pairwise unify all the elements of s and t. Both of these strategies lead to a nonwellfounded recursion, since the structures may be circular. But if we express the recursion using the Solution Lemma, we get our required existence result.

Before beginning the detailed proof, we define the *transitive feature closure* of an object u to be the smallest set $TF(u)$ such that $u \in TF(u)$, and if a function $f \in TF(u)$, then whenever $f(l)$ is defined, then $f(l) \in TF(u)$; and if a set $s \in TF(u)$, then every element of s is in $TF(u)$.

Now for the details: Let p and q be elements of $TF(u)$ and $TF(v)$ respectively. Introduce new parameters x_{pq} (not in X) for each pair p, q. Call the new parameter set Y. Consider the following system of equations, where the solution for x_{pq} stands for the result of unifying p and q:

$$x_{pq} \doteq \begin{cases} a & \text{if } p, q \in A \text{ and } p \sqcup q = a \text{ for some atom } a \in A \text{ (1)};\\ x & \text{if } p = q = x \text{ for some parameter } x \in X \text{ (2)};\\ h & \text{if } p, q \text{ are functional (3)};\\ w & \text{if } p, q \text{ are sets (4)}. \end{cases}$$

In this definition, the $\sqcup$ relation on line (1) is the least upper bound, if it exists, in the ordering $\sqsubseteq$ on A. On line (3), h is the function

$$h(l) = \begin{cases} p(l) & \text{if } p(l){\downarrow} \text{ and } q(l){\uparrow} \text{ ;}\\ q(l) & \text{if } q(l){\downarrow} \text{ and } p(l){\uparrow} \text{ ;}\\ x_{p(l)q(l)} & \text{if both converge;}\\ \text{undefined} & \text{otherwise.} \end{cases}$$

On line (4) w is the set

$$\{x_{p'q'} \mid p' \in p, q' \in q\}.$$

The system of equations defines an element of $C[X \cup Y]$, the complex objects over the parameter set $X \cup Y$, because there are no equations for parameters x_{pq}, where p is not "compatible" with q; that is, if p and q are atoms with no least upper bound, or if p and q are mismatched in the definition of simulation, for example, if p is a functional object and q is a set. But the Solution Lemma applied to the system still gives us a well-defined complex object.[4] We have to modify this object to get an element of $C[X]$. But first, notice that the definition of the object h and w are the obvious recursions mentioned at the beginning of the proof. And the required least upper bound of u and v will be the object assigned by the Solution Lemma to the parameter x_{uv}, subject to modification (which may cause the upper bound to become undefined).

Let $I(p, q)$ be the object assigned to x_{pq} by the Solution Lemma. We consider the modifications needed to the anchor I. First we need to exclude from the solution any objects containing "direct paths" to "incompatible" parameters in Y. This can be done informally by defining a *path* π to be a (possibly empty) finite sequence $l_1 l_2 \ldots l_n$ of labels. Let i be some complex object, and let $i(\pi)$ be the result (assumed to be defined) of evaluating i by

---

[4]In this system, we solve equations over Y, and treat the elements of X as atoms.

evaluating the arguments $l_1, \ldots, l_n$ in the successive functional components of objects inside i. More formally, $i(\epsilon) = i$, and $i(\pi l) = i(\pi)(l)$ assuming $i(\pi)$ is a functional object with the label l in its domain. If $I(p, q)(\pi) \in Y$, for some path π, then this value must in fact be an incompatible parameter, i.e., of the form x_{rs}, where r and s are not compatible as in the previous paragraph. We say that i is a *bad object* if there is a path π such that $i(\pi) \in Y$. Now change the original system of equations as follows. Remove all equations for x_{pq}, where $I(p, q)$ is a bad object. Notice that this will not remove any of the "basis equations"—those for atoms and parameters. In the remaining equations, let w be a right-hand side which is a set. Delete all occurrences of $x_{p'q'}$ from w, where $I(p', q')$ is a bad object. Notice that in the remaining equations, we cannot have a right hand side which is a functional object containing a parameter for a bad object, because the equation introducing that functional object would have had a parameter for a bad object on the left side. Now if $I(p, q)$ is not itself a bad object, then there will be an equation for x_{pq} in the modified system, and the Solution Lemma will again give a value to this parameter. But now this value will not contain any parameters in Y. And the equation for such a parameter x_{pq} will be the same as the original one, except that the parameters denoting bad objects will have been removed from the sets w. Let J be the anchor denoting the solution to the modified system.

Let u and v be arbitrary τ-objects and consider the system of equations constructed and modified as above, using the components of u and v. If there remains a solution for our given pair u and v, it is because there is no path in u which is simultaneously a path in v to an incompatible pair of objects. In this case, we have a value $u \sqcup v = J(u, v)$ for the unified structure, and otherwise the unification is not defined. Lastly, notice that if both p and q are related by Smyth simulations R_1 and R_2 respectively to some d in $C[X]$, then in fact $I(p, q)$ cannot be bad. In particular, if u and v are dominated by z in the Smyth preorder, there will be a solution $J(u, v)$ for x_{uv} in the modified system.

Now we have to show that (i) if in fact u and v are dominated by some object z in the Smyth preorder, $u \sqcup v$ (which we now know exists) is dominated by z. Also, we have to show (ii) that both u and v are dominated by $u \sqcup v$.

Proof of (i). Assume that $u \ R_1 \ z$ and $v \ R_2 \ z$. Then as above, $u \sqcup v$ exists. Let j and d be arbitrary objects. Define a relation R_3 as follows:

$$j \ R_3 \ d \iff j \ R_1 \ d \text{ or } j \ R_2 \ d$$

or

$$(\exists p, q)(j = J(p, q) \text{ and } p \ R_1 \ d \text{ and } q \ R_2 \ d)$$

where $J(p, q)$ is a solution to the (modified) system of equations above. By the last clause in the definition of R_3, we have $J(u, v) = u \sqcup v \ R_3 \ z$.

It remains to show that R_3 is a Smyth simulation. Let $j \ R_3 \ d$. The cases where j is an atom or parameter are straightforward, so we can assume that j is complex. Also, if j R_1 d or j R_2 d, the result is immediate. So we can assume that $j = J(p, q)$, where p R_1 d, and q R_2 d. Now there are a number of possibilities, depending on the form of p and q. Neither of these can be an atom or parameter, because then J would be an atom or parameter, by the form of the original equations in our system. We can thus assume that both p and q are complex. Now there are two cases depending on the form of the right hand side of the equation for x_{pq}.

Subcase (i). $J(p, q) = h$, where, as above, h is the function

$$h(l) = \begin{cases} p(l) & \text{if } p(l){\downarrow} \text{ and } q(l){\uparrow} \text{ ;} \\ q(l) & \text{if } q(l){\downarrow} \text{ and } p(l){\uparrow} \text{ ;} \\ J(p(l), q(l)) & \text{if both converge;} \\ \text{undefined} & \text{otherwise,} \end{cases}$$

We show that clause (2) in the definition of Smyth simulation is satisfied. Suppose that $j(l){\downarrow}$. If $p(l){\uparrow}$, then it must be that $q(l){\downarrow}$, so then $j(l) = q(l)$. But $q(l)$ R_2 $d(l)$, because q R_2 d. so $j(l)$ R_3 $d(l)$. A similar result obtains when $q(l){\uparrow}$. Suppose therefore that both $p(l)$ and $q(l)$ converge. In this case $j(l) = J(p(l), q(l))$. But $p(l)$ R_1 $d(l)$ and $q(l)$ R_2 $d(l)$, so again $j(l)$ R_3 $d(l)$.

Subcase (ii). $J(p, q) = w$, where w is the set

$$\{J(p', q') \mid p' \in p, q' \in q, \text{ and } \langle p', q' \rangle \in G\}$$

where G is the set of pairs denoting good objects in $I(p, q)$. In this case p and q must be sets, as is d. We satisfy clause (3) in the definition of Smyth simulation. Let $d' \in d$. Since p R_1 d and q R_2 d, we have an $p' \in p$, and a $q' \in q$ with both p' R_1 d' and q' R_2 d'. Therefore the solution $J(p', q')$ exists, is in the relation R_3 to d', and is in the set w, as was to be shown. This completes the proof of part (i).

Proof of part (ii). We show only that there is a Smyth simulation relating u with $u \sqcup v$, as the proof for v is symmetric. Define the relation R by

$$d \, R \, j \iff d = j \text{ or } (\exists q)(j = J(d, q)).$$

Again, we have $u \, R \, J(u, v) = u \sqcup v$, so we need only show that R is a Smyth simulation. Suppose that $d \, R \, j$, and that d is not an atom or parameter. If $d = j$, the result is clear. Assume that $j = J(d, q)$ for some q. Then q is not an atom or parameter either. So both d and q are complex, and we break into subcases as above.

Suppose that $j = J(d, q)$ is the function

$$h(l) = \begin{cases} d(l) & \text{if } d(l){\downarrow} \text{ and } q(l){\uparrow} \text{ ;} \\ q(l) & \text{if } q(l){\downarrow} \text{ and } d(l){\uparrow} \text{ ;} \\ J(d(l), q(l)) & \text{if both converge;} \\ \text{undefined} & \text{otherwise,} \end{cases}$$

Assume that $d(l){\downarrow}$. If $q(l){\uparrow}$, then $j(l) = h(l) = \delta(l)$, so suppose that $q(l){\downarrow}$.

Then $j(l) = J(d(l), q(l))$. But $d(l) \; R \; J(d(l), q(l))$, so clause (3) in the definition of Smyth simulation is satisfied.

Now, suppose $j = J(d, q)$ is the set

$$\{J(d', q') \mid d' \in d, q' \in q, \text{ and } \langle d', q' \rangle \in G\}$$

where G is as above. Again we satisfy clause(4) of Smyth simulations. Consider an element $j' \in j$ Then j' is of the form $J(d', q')$, where $d' \in d$, and $q' \in q$. Therefore, there is a $d' \in d$ such that $d' \; R \; j'$, as required. This completes the proof of Theorem 1.

This detailed proof gives a complete idea of the method, which we can use to prove other theorems of this type. One final remark on computability is in order. Suppose that u and v are *hereditarily finite* complex objects; that is, $TF(u)$ and $TF(v)$ are finite. Then u and v can be represented by finite data structures. The system of equations representing the unification is also finitely representable, and it is easy to see that the solution to such a finite system is always effectively computable. In fact, given a system, its solution can be obtained in time polynomial in the size of the system. Exact analysis, however, is outside the scope of this paper.

Next, let us consider other upper and lower bound proofs. For the Smyth preorder, the greatest lower bound of two set values is the union of those values. The greatest lower bound of two functional objects f and g is obtained by finding the lower bound of $f(l)$ and $g(l)$ for all l in the common domain. So we can modify the above proof to show the existence of a Smyth greatest lower bound (generalization) for any two objects with a common lower bound.

Moving to the Hoare preorder, we have a dual situation. This time the least upper bound is found by unifying functional values, and taking the union of set values. The greatest lower bound is found by generalizing function values, and taking pairwise generalizations of set values.

Next, consider upper bounds in the mixed preorder. We need only combine the two upper bound constructions to get the same result. Writing out the system of equations which is needed, we have

$$x_{pq} \doteq \begin{cases} a & \text{if } p, q \in A \text{ and } p \sqcup q = a \text{ for some atom } a \in A \text{ (1);} \\ x & \text{if } p = q = x \text{ for some parameter } x \in X \text{ (2);} \\ h & \text{if } p, q \text{ are functional (3);} \\ w_\alpha & \text{if } p, q \text{ are } \alpha\text{-sets (4);} \\ w_\tau & \text{if } p, q \text{ are } \tau\text{-sets (5).} \end{cases}$$

where the $\sqcup$ relation on line (1) is the least upper bound, if it exists, in the ordering $\sqsubseteq$ on A. On line (3), h is the function (as before)

$$h(l) = \begin{cases} p(l) & \text{if } p(l){\downarrow} \text{ and } q(l){\uparrow} \text{ ;} \\ q(l) & \text{if } q(l){\downarrow} \text{ and } p(l){\uparrow} \text{ ;} \\ x_{p(l)q(l)} & \text{if both converge;} \\ \text{undefined} & \text{otherwise.} \end{cases}$$

On line (4) the set w_α is just $p \cup q$, and on line (5) w_τ is, as before, the set

$$\{x_{p'q'} \mid p' \in p, q' \in q\}.$$

Of course the solution to these equations must undergo modification as in our proof above. Then we have to carry out a correctness analysis, but this will only be longer, not more difficult, than as above.

Finally, consider the same problem for upper bounds in the subsumption preorder. If u, v, and z are such that $u, v \sqsubseteq_0 z$, then there are renamings I and J such that $u[I] \sqsubseteq_M z$ and $v[J] \sqsubseteq_M z$. Define a new renaming $I + J$ as follows. ($I + J$ will only be defined on the union of the parameter sets of u and v) . If I and J do not agree on some set D of these parameters, then let $I + J$ have some arbitrary parameter not occurring in z, u or v assigned injectively to elements of D. (This requires an assumption about availability of parameters, which we will not bother with.) Otherwise let $I + J$ have the common value. Then $u[I + J] \sqcup_M v[I + J] \sqsubseteq_M z$, and is the least such up to M-equivalence. (The arbitrarily renamed parameters will never be involved in an M-simulation.)

We will not consider the instantiation preorder μ in this paper.

3.2 Proof of Theorem 2

First we establish some easy results.

Lemma 3 *The relational composition of two Smyth simulations is again a Smyth simulation.*

The proof is straightforward. As a corollary, the Smyth subsumption relation is transitive, and thus it is itself the largest Smyth simulation.

We will be concerned with τ-objects which are set objects; call these set values, and let s, t range over them.

Lemma 4 $s \sqsubseteq_S t \iff (\forall \tau \in t)(\exists \sigma \in s)(\sigma \sqsubseteq_S \tau)$.

Proof. The direction from right to left is an immediate consequence of the existence of a Smyth simulation from s to t. For the other direction, define the relation R as follows:

$$x \, R \, y \iff x \sqsubseteq_S y \text{ or } (\forall \tau \in y)(\exists \sigma \in x)(\sigma \sqsubseteq_S \tau).$$

It is immediate to check that R is a Smyth simulation, so $R \subseteq \sqsubseteq_S$, which gives the result.

Next we recall the definition of the "of-type" relation.

Definition 8 We say that $g : u$, where g and u are τ-objects, iff $u \sqsubseteq_S \{g\}$.

Lemma 5 $s \sqsubseteq_S t \iff (\forall \sigma)(\sigma : t \Rightarrow \sigma : s)$.

Proof. Again straightforward.

Lemma 6 $s \equiv_S t \iff (\forall \sigma)(\sigma : t \iff \sigma : s)$.

Proof. Immediate from the previous lemma.

Note that for set values, the Smyth least upper bound is always defined. Write $s \sqcup t$ (dropping the S subscript) for the least upper bound and $s \sqcap t$ for the greatest lower bound.

Lemma 7 $\sigma : (s \sqcup t) \iff \sigma : s$ *and* $\sigma : t$.

Proof. First notice that from the proof of Theorem 1,

$$s \sqcup t = \{s' \sqcup t' \mid s' \in s, t' \in t\}.$$

So $\sigma : s$ if and only if some $s' \sqcup t' \sqsubseteq \sigma$. This is the case iff some $s' \sqsubseteq \sigma$ and some $t' \sqsubseteq \sigma$, implying the result.

Lemma 8 $\sigma : (s \sqcap t) \iff \sigma : s$ *or* $\sigma : t$.

Proof. This is clear since $s \sqcap t = s \cup t$.

Now all these lemmas together imply Theorem 2.

Notice that our proofs above really show that the class of τ-sets is a distributive lattice under M-subsumption. We will see later, as an application of the logic to be discussed in the next section, that this use of τ-sets for types is entirely appropriate.

4   KR Logic and Types

Next we wish to make a simple logic based on the original KR logic Kasper and Rounds 1990 which defines classes of complex objects. Our use of this logic here (as in our previous work on this topic) will be technical, to characterize M-equivalence on the class of complex objects. Another use of logical constraints involving complex objects will be presented in the final section. The KR formulas which we are about to define look like the terms of Section 1.2. But those terms are singular terms, denoting individual complex objects. The logical formulas, on the other hand, have a set (actually a class) of complex objects associated with them—those objects satisfying the term. Were it not for the set/class distinction, our formulas would give us another term notation. In fact, the KR formulas we define here are an extension of the feature terms in Smolka 1989, which are another formulation of the original logic of Kasper and Rounds.

We define a modal logic $\mathcal{L}$. The formulas of $\mathcal{L}$ are defined to be the least set containing the Boolean constants tt and ff, all elements of the set A of atoms, and closed under the following formation rules:

1. If ϕ and ψ are formulas, then $\phi \wedge \psi$ and $\phi \vee \psi$ are formulas;
2. If ϕ is a formula, and $l \in L$, then $l : \phi$ is a formula;
3. If ϕ is a formula, then $\Diamond \phi$ and $\Box \phi$ are formulas.

The modalities $\Diamond \phi$ and $\Box \phi$ refer to the membership relation. An object u will satisfy $\Diamond \phi$ iff it is an α-object and there is some some v in u satisfies ϕ. The $\Box$ operator applies to a τ-set, and says that all members of the set have property ϕ. Finally, the $l :$ operator says that the object which is the l-value of the current functional object has property ϕ.

Next we give the formal definition of the *satisfaction predicate* $\models$. This is done with the usual inductive definition on formulas. We work with parameter-free objects u. The predicate $\models$ is the least relation between and $\mathcal{L}$ satisfying:

1. $u \models a$ iff $u \in A$ and $a \sqsubseteq u$, for $a \in A$;
2. $u \models$ tt always and ff never;
3. $u \models \phi \vee \psi$ iff $u \models \phi$ or $u \models \psi$, and analogously for $\wedge$;
4. $u \models l : \phi$ iff u is functional, $u(l){\downarrow}$ and $ul \models \phi$;
5. $u \models \Diamond\phi$ iff u is an α-set and for some $x \in u$, $x \models \phi$;
6. $u \models \Box\phi$ iff u is a τ-set and for all $x \in u$, $x \models \phi$.

For the next results, recall that the *transitive feature closure* of an object u is the smallest set $TF(u)$ such that $u \in TF(u)$, and if a function $f \in TF(u)$, then whenever $f(l)$ is defined, then $f(l) \in TF(u)$; and if a set $s \in TF(u)$, then every element of s is in $TF(u)$.

Say that a complex object u is *locally finite* if for any set-valued object $w \in TF(u)$, w is finite. We then have the next theorem, which is an analogue of the characterization in (Winskel 1985).

Theorem 9 *Let u and v be locally finite parameter-free complex objects. Then u M-subsumes v $\Leftrightarrow$ $\forall \phi \in \mathcal{L}$, $u \models \phi \Rightarrow v \models \phi$.*

Remark. This theorem says, in particular, that the logic $\mathcal{L}$ is *persistent*; that is, if $u \models \phi$ and $u \sqsubseteq v$ then $v \models \phi$.

Proof. We prove that for all ϕ, u and v, if u M-subsumes v, and $u \models \phi$, then $v \models \phi$. We do this by induction on the formula ϕ. The cases $\phi = $ tt and $\phi = $ ff are trivial. If $\phi = a$, and u R v and $u \models a$, for some Hoare simulation R, then $u = a$ and so $v = a$. The $\vee$ and $\wedge$ combinations are straightforward. For the $l :$ operator, if $u \models l : \phi$, Then $u(l){\downarrow}$, and $u(l) \models \phi$. By the M-simulation property, $v(l){\downarrow}$. By inductive hypothesis $v(l) \models \phi$, which means $v \models l : \phi$. We check the $\Diamond$ operator. If u R v and $u \models \Diamond\psi$, then u is an α-set and there is an $x \in u$ such that $x \models \psi$. Since R acts like a Hoare simulation on α-sets, there is a $y \in v$ such that x R y. By inductive hypothesis, $y \models \psi$, and so $s \models \Diamond\psi$, completing the induction. An analogous proof covers the $\Box$ case.

We have now proved the implication from left to right. Consider the opposite implication. Define for a complex object u:

$$Th(u) = \{\phi \mid u \models \phi\}.$$

Define the relation R on the class of complex objects as follows:

$$u \ R \ v \ \Leftrightarrow \ Th(u) \subseteq Th(v).$$

It will suffice to show that R is an M-simulation. So, if u is an atom a, then $Th(u) = \{w \mid a \sqsubseteq w\}$. This is a subset of $\{w \mid v \sqsubseteq w\}$. In particular, $v \sqsubseteq a$. So v is an atom, and $a \sqsubseteq v$, so $u \sqsubseteq v$. Next, suppose u R v and $u(l){\downarrow}$. u is a complex object f. Now $v(l)$ is also defined, because otherwise $u \models l : \mathrm{tt}$, but not v. We want $v(l)\ R\ u(l)$. If $\phi \in Th(u(l))$, then $l : \phi \in Th(u)$ and so also in $Th(v)$; hence $\phi \in Th(v(l))$, as desired. Next we consider the case where u is an α-set s. Clearly v must be an α-set too. Let $x \in s$. We want there to be some $r \in v$ such that and $x\ R\ r$. Suppose not. Let $t = \{r_1, \ldots, r_n\}$. Then for each of these r_i, there is a formula ϕ_i such that $q \models \phi_i$ but r_i does not. Then

$$u \models \Diamond(\phi_1 \wedge \ldots \wedge \phi_n)$$

but v does not satisfy this, a contradiction. The case of $\Box$ is proved similarly, using the formula

$$\Box(\phi_1 \vee \ldots \vee \phi_n).$$

This completes the proof of the theorem.

Finally, we state a theorem which relates $\mathcal{L}$ to types. To avoid set-class problems, we need to restrict ourselves to sets of complex objects. So we will assume that our universe is a set of objects which is closed under the transitive feature closure operation mentioned earlier, and also closed under application of the Solution Lemma; by this we mean that if $\{x = b_x\}$ is a system of equations with each b_x in our universe, then each solution set $J(x)$ is also in the universe. Plainly, given any set s_0 of complex objects, there is a smallest such universe s containing s_0.

Theorem 10 *Let s be a universe as above, and let ϕ and ψ be formulas of $\mathcal{L}$. Then*

$$Mod(\phi \vee \psi) \equiv Mod(\phi) \sqcap_S Mod(\psi)$$
$$Mod(\phi \wedge \psi) \equiv Mod(\phi) \sqcup_S Mod(\psi)$$

where $Mod(\phi) = \{u \in s \mid u \models \phi\}$ is considered as a τ-set, and equivalence means M-equivalence.

Proof. For the upper bound, by the characterization of the set upper bound of τ-sets (cf. Theorem 1) it suffices to show

$$Mod(\phi \wedge \psi) \equiv \{(g_1 \sqcup g_2) \mid g_1 \in Mod(\phi) \text{ and } g_2 \in Mod(\psi)\}.$$

Let V be the τ-set value on the right side. To show $Mod(\phi \wedge \psi) \sqsubseteq_M V$, apply Lemma 3.2 of Section 3. Choose $g_1 \in Mod(\phi)$, and $g_2 \in Mod(\psi)$, with $g_1 \sqcup g_2 \in V$. Then $g_1 \sqcup g_2 \in Mod(\phi \wedge \psi)$, because L is monotonic. Conversely, let $g \in Mod(\phi \wedge \psi)$. Then $g \in Mod(\phi)$ and $g \in Mod(\psi)$ by definition. But $g \sqsubseteq_M (g \sqcup g)$ trivially. Lemma 3.2 applies to give the desired equivalence. A similar proof, using the union of τ-sets instead of pairwise unifications of elements, works for the lower bound. This completes the proof of the theorem.

5 An Application: Redefining Feature Structures

In this section we use types to extend work of Barwise (1989, Chapter 12) for modeling linguistic feature structures using set theory. Barwise's article also treats the solution of constraint systems in set theory; more on constraints below.

Let us begin with an example. Consider the feature structure, from Pollard and Sag 1987, informing us about a certain department.

$$
\begin{bmatrix}
manager : \begin{bmatrix} name : abrams \\ ssno : 309532204 \\ secretary : [1]name : jones \end{bmatrix} \\
asstman : \begin{bmatrix} name : devito \\ ssno : 309532205 \\ secretary : [1] \end{bmatrix}
\end{bmatrix}
$$

This feature structure is a complex object, except for the bracketed [1], which means that Abrams and Devito share a secretary. In the data structure encoding this feature structure, Devito's secretary is a literal pointer to Abrams' secretary, so that there is sharing in the data structure as well. This means that any updates to the information about the manager's secretary will be automatically applied to the assistant's.

Now it turns out that the functional objects which we have been using to give an extensional model of feature structures, as coded in set theory, are not well suited to model this kind of sharing. This is because two functions may have the same value for two differing arguments, but not have any mechanism to indicate that if one of the values is changed, then the other must be changed as well. That is, the functions *always* have the same values.

Here is a case in which we can use parameters within objects. We could replace the [1] in the above object with the parameter x_1. We would model the $sec : [1]name : jones$ line using a *condition* on the parameter x_1, namely that any anchors for that parameter must be functional objects with the value *jones* for the *secretary* attribute. This could be accomplished by modeling conditioned parameters as pairs $\langle x, u \rangle$ where x is a parameter and u is an object representing the condition. We might decide to let u range over types (sets of feature structures, in the usual application). The change to the definition of simulation is then easy, just extending the M-simulations to such pairs. (The parameters x must be identical, and the objects u must continue to bear the relation.) We model our structure above as the following new object, where *NIL* is the null partial function:

$$
\begin{bmatrix}
manager : \begin{bmatrix} name : abrams \\ ssno : 309532204 \\ secretary : \langle x_1, \{name : jones\}_\tau \rangle \end{bmatrix} \\
asstman : \begin{bmatrix} name : devito \\ ssno : 309532205 \\ secretary : \langle x_1, \{NIL\}_\tau \rangle \end{bmatrix}
\end{bmatrix}
$$

We have used singleton type sets to indicate the conditions on these parameters. Look at the instantiation relation μ. We restrict anchors I so that $I(x, u)$ is an object of type u. Then the only legitimate instantiations of the above object will be structures where Devito's secretary is named Jones.

This attempt to use parameters to account for coreference is not complete by any means. More work will be required to see if this or other variations of parametric objects completely account for coreference problems, and for the notion of a conditioned parameter. But we do have at least one suggestion for an explicit model of restricted parameters here, a topic which is of special concern in situation theory.

6 Constraints for Logic Programs

In this section we briefly explore some proposals for incorporating complex objects into a logic programming language. This is the aim of the Stony Brook research as well, but we follow a different approach, using the general method of Höhfeld and Smolka for adding constraints to a language containing definite relations. We also notice that Ohori 1988 has in fact built an experimental *functional* language, called Machiavelli, which uses a type system and a semantics for complex objects like our notion. However, the objects are not constructed extensionally in set theory, but rather as "descriptions", which are formed from trees augmented with set constructor symbols. This approach is like our earlier work (Rounds 1988) where we used graphs as descriptions of the semantic objects. The advantage of set theory is that no equivalence relations on the syntactic objects need be used. We should also mention that Mukai (1991), in his contribution to this volume, presents a constraint logic for non-well-founded sets using a coinductive version of logic programming, and based on the scheme of Jaffar and Lassez 1987. There are many interesting questions suggested by the differing choices of CLP schemes, but these must be left for further work.

The basic material on constraint logic programming, from Höhfeld and Smolka 1988, appears in the appendix. We briefly recap the definition here.

First, let $\mathcal{L}$ be a *constraint language*. This is a language of assertions about *variables* expressed in a specialized language. (See below for examples) A *definite clause (Horn clause)* is a formula of the form

$$A_1 \wedge \ldots \wedge A_n \wedge \phi \to B$$

where $n \geq 0$, $A_1, \ldots, A_n$ are predicates of some arity, containing no terms, and $\phi \in \mathcal{L}$. (We could write this clause as $B ::= A_1 \wedge \ldots \wedge A_n \wedge \phi$, in a style reminiscent of Prolog.) A *definite clause specification* is a set of definite clauses. One then can give a fixed-point semantics for the meaning of such a definite-clause system, and a proof that an SLD-style resolution procedure works. The applicability of such a system depends on being able in general to solve (or at least test for satisfiability) systems of conjunctions of formulas in $\mathcal{L}$.

With the basic facts on constraints in place, it is a trivial matter to propose constraints involving complex objects. It is not so trivial, however, to ensure that the satisfiability problem for constraint formulas is decidable. We mention only a few results along this line.

Feature Constraints. We first require that all interpretations be in some set of complex objects. Our Horn clauses will have predicates ranging over elements of this set. Our *feature constraints* ϕ, ψ may be in general of one of the forms (as in Smolka 1989):

- $u(\pi) \doteq v(\rho)$, where u and v are terms (Section 2), π and ρ are strings of features (labels), possibly empty.
- $\phi \vee \psi$
- $\phi \wedge \psi$
- $\neg \phi$
- $\phi \rightarrow \psi$
- $\exists x \phi$
- $\forall x \phi$.

The semantics of these constraints can be given as a set of assignments. Let s be a set of complex objects. Then

$$[\![u\pi \doteq v\rho]\!]^s = \{ I : X \rightarrow s \mid [\![u]\!][I](\pi) = [\![v]\!][I](\rho) \}$$

where $[\![u]\!]$ is the term denotation in Section 2, and $[\![u]\!][I](\pi)$ is this denotation anchored by I, and then evaluated by the path I. Notice that this definition uses the semantic notion of anchoring, but is really equivalent to the usual syntactic definition. The rest of the constraints are given the standard meaning. For example, $[\![\phi \wedge \psi]\!]^s = [\![\phi]\!]^s \cap [\![\psi]\!]^s$.

Order constraints. In addition to the above constraints, we may allow constraints of the form $u(\pi) \sqsubseteq_M v(\rho)$ where u, v, π, and ρ are as before. ¿From these, we can define other constraints of interest. For example, $g : u$ could be defined as $u \sqsubseteq_M \{g\}$ (where we distinguish types syntactically), expressing our "of-type" relation. We could also consider constraints like $u \in v$. The semantics of these constraints is as before, with equality replaced by subsumption or membership.

Unfortunately, we do not have general proofs of decidability of satisfiability for all constraints above. It is known from Smolka's work that equality is decidable for "existential prenex" constraints, which include quantifier-free ones, but where terms are restricted to be atoms or variables. If simulations are not relations but functions, then conjunctions of subsumption constraints are an undecidable class over C, by the undecidability of the semiunification problem (Dörre and Rounds 1990). 1991 shows that if simulations are relations, as we have here, then satisfiability of conjunctions of inequalities is decidable in feature algebras. We conjecture that this result still holds in C, for any of the simulation notions.

7 Appendix: Constraint Logic Programming

We now review the basic notions of constraint logic programming. We use the formalism of Höhfeld and Smolka 1988.

7.1 Constraint Languages

We first introduce the notion of *constraint language*. The formulas of such a language specify the way in which individual variables are related one to another. The definition is general, in that it needs no particular notion of the syntax of a constraint formula. But for purposes of illustration, think of a constraint language formula as a conjunction of equations between first-order terms: $plus(b, x) = plus(b, times(y, z)) \land x = y$, for example.

A *constraint language* is a tuple (VAR, WFF, ν, INT) such that

1. VAR is a decidable, infinite set of *variables*;
2. WFF is a decidable set of *constraint formulas*;
3. ν assigns to each constraint formula ϕ a subset of VAR, called the set of variables constrained by ϕ;
4. INT is a nonempty set of *interpretations*, where every interpretation $\mathcal{A} \in$ INT consists of a nonempty set $D^{\mathcal{A}}$ called the *domain* of $\mathcal{A}$, and a *solution mapping* $[\![\cdot]\!]^{\mathcal{A}}$. Intuitively the solution mapping $[\![\cdot]\!]^{\mathcal{A}}$, applied to a constraint formula ϕ, tells which assignments to the variables of ϕ make ϕ true. Thus $[\![\cdot]\!]^{\mathcal{A}}$ maps VAR to subsets of ASGN$^{\mathcal{A}}$, where ASGN$^{\mathcal{A}}$ is the set of all functions from VAR to $D^{\mathcal{A}}$. The value $[\![\phi]\!]^{\mathcal{A}}$ is called the *solution set* of ϕ in $\mathcal{A}$. It is required that if an assignment α is in $[\![\phi]\!]^{\mathcal{A}}$, then any other β agreeing with α on $\nu(\phi)$ must also be in $[\![\phi]\!]^{\mathcal{A}}$.

Example. If our constraint language consists of conjunctions of equations involving "plus", "times", and so on, we can select an interpretation several ways. The Herbrand interpretation $\mathcal{H}$ has $D^{\mathcal{H}}$ as the set of all formal terms in these function symbols. Then an assignment α is just a substitution of terms for free variables. The solution set $[\![\phi]\!]^{\mathcal{H}}$ is the set of substitutions which would make each equation in ϕ an identity. So if ϕ is $plus(b, x) = plus(b, times(y, z))$, the substitution of $times(y, z)$ for x, and y and x for themselves, is in the solution set of ϕ. If however we add the equation $x = y$, then in the Herbrand interpretation, there are no solutions. But we can get another interpretation $\mathcal{N}$ by letting $D^{\mathcal{N}}$ be the set of natural numbers, and interpreting "plus" and "times" as ordinary integer functions. This time there are solutions to $plus(b, x) = plus(b, times(y, z)) \land x = y$ (where say $b = 1$); one solution is $x = 5$, $y = 5$, and $z = 1$. Yet another interpretation is the "string interpretation", where we let the alphabet $\Sigma = \{a, b, c, +, *, x, y, z\}$, and interpret variables over $D = \Sigma^*$; then we interpret $plus(\gamma, \delta)$ as the concatenation $\gamma + \delta$ using the literal symbol "+" in the middle of the strings α and δ.

A constraint formula ϕ is *satisfiable* if there is some interpretation $\mathcal{A}$ and some assignment α such that $\alpha \in [\![\phi]\!]^{\mathcal{A}}$. Another way of writing this last condition is $\mathcal{A}, \alpha \models \phi$. We then say that ϕ is *valid* in $\mathcal{A}$ if for all α, $\mathcal{A}, \alpha \models \phi$. We write this condition as $\mathcal{A} \models \phi$. Now let Φ be a set of constraint formulas. $\mathcal{A}$ is said to be a *model* of Φ if for all $\phi \in \Phi$, $\mathcal{A} \models \phi$.

Example. If ϕ is $times(x, y) = times(y, x)$, then ϕ is valid in the interpretation $\mathcal{N}$, but not in $\mathcal{H}$. The interpretation $\mathcal{N}$ is a model for the set Φ of all equations expressing familiar laws of arithmetic.

7.2 Relational Extensions

Next we repeat the method given by Höhfeld and Smolka (1988) for constructing a *relational extension* of a constraint language $\mathcal{L}$. We assume given a set $\mathcal{R}$ of *relation symbols*, each equipped with a number telling its *arity*, or number of arguments. This gives rise to a new language $\mathcal{R}(\mathcal{L})$. If the language $\mathcal{L}$ is the set of equations between first order terms, then $\mathcal{R}(\mathcal{L})$ gives the language of first-order predicate logic. It is technically elegant to regard $\mathcal{R}(\mathcal{L})$ as a constraint language in its own right. So we let the variables of $\mathcal{R}(\mathcal{L})$ be the variables of $\mathcal{L}$. We get the constraint formulas of $\mathcal{R}(\mathcal{L})$ inductively as follows.

1. Every formula of $\mathcal{L}$ is a formula of $\mathcal{R}(\mathcal{L})$;
2. Every relational atom $r(x_1, \ldots, x_n)$, where the x_i are distinct and n is the arity of r, is a formula of $\mathcal{R}(\mathcal{L})$;
3. The atom *FALSE* is in $\mathcal{R}(\mathcal{L})$; if F and G are in $\mathcal{R}(\mathcal{L})$, then so are $F \wedge G$ and $F \rightarrow G$;
4. If x is a variable, and $F \in \mathcal{R}(\mathcal{L})$, then $\exists x.F \in \mathcal{R}(\mathcal{L})$.

The variables constrained by an $\mathcal{R}(\mathcal{L})$-formula are the usual free variables. If the formula is an $\mathcal{L}$-formula, then the variables constrained are just those given by the original ν.

Let $\mathcal{A}$ be an interpretation of $\mathcal{L}$. We extend $\mathcal{A}$ to an interpretation $\mathcal{B}$ of $\mathcal{R}(\mathcal{L})$ as follows. Choose for each relation symbol r of arity n, an n-ary relation $r^{\mathcal{B}}$ on $D^{\mathcal{A}}$. Define $D^{\mathcal{B}} = D^{\mathcal{A}}$. Then let

1. $[\![\phi]\!]^{\mathcal{B}} = [\![\phi]\!]^{\mathcal{A}}$ if $\phi \in \mathcal{L}$;
2. $[\![r(x_1, \ldots, x_n)]\!]^{\mathcal{B}} = \{\alpha \in \mathrm{ASGN}^{\mathcal{A}} \mid (\alpha(x_1), \ldots, \alpha(x_n)) \in r^{\mathcal{A}}\}$;
3. $[\![FALSE]\!]^{\mathcal{B}} = \emptyset$; $[\![F \wedge G]\!]^{\mathcal{B}} = [\![F]\!]^{\mathcal{B}} \cap [\![G]\!]^{\mathcal{B}}$; $[\![F \rightarrow G]\!]^{\mathcal{B}} = [\![G]\!]^{\mathcal{B}} \cup (\mathrm{ASGN}^{\mathcal{A}} - [\![F]\!]^{\mathcal{B}})$;
4. $[\![\exists x.F]\!]^{\mathcal{B}} = \{\alpha \mid (\exists \beta \in [\![F]\!]^{\mathcal{B}})(\forall y \in \nu(F))(y = x \vee (\alpha(y) = \beta(y)))\}$.

7.3 Definite Clauses

A *definite clause* is an $\mathcal{R}(\mathcal{L})$-formula of the form

$$A_1 \wedge \ldots \wedge A_n \wedge \phi \to B$$

where $n \geq 0$, $A_1, \ldots, A_n$ are relational atoms, and $\phi \in \mathcal{L}$. We will write this clause as $B ::= A_1 \wedge \ldots \wedge A_n \wedge \phi$, in a style reminiscent of Prolog. A *definite clause specification* is a set of definite clauses.

Example. Consider the (partial) grammar for expressions

$$\text{EXPR} ::= \text{EXPR} + \text{TERM} \mid \text{TERM}$$

$$\text{TERM} ::= \text{TERM} * \text{FACTOR} \mid \text{FACTOR}$$

with its logical restatement

$$Expr(x) ::= Expr(y) \wedge Term(z) \wedge x = plus(y, z);$$

$$Expr(x) ::= Term(x).$$

This is a definite clause specification where the atoms $Expr$ and $Term$ form a relational extension of the language of equations over first-order function symbols *plus*, etc. A typical property of such specifications is that the variables x, y, etc., appear free. One way to think of these free occurrences is as if they were all universally quantified; but perhaps a better way is to think of them as actually being free, and the specification as constraining their possible values.

Now the above specifications are going to be used for defining sets recursively. To do this, we start with a definite clause specification Φ, and an interpretation $\mathcal{A}$ of the constraint language $\mathcal{L}$. Then we extend $\mathcal{A}$ to an interpretation $\mathcal{B}$ of $\mathcal{R}(\mathcal{L})$ which is a model of Φ. This extension corresponds to the usual process of grammatical derivations. Then we take (to get the generated language) the set of solutions for the "start predicate" of the grammar.

Suppose that $\mathcal{B}$ is an $\mathcal{R}(\mathcal{L})$-interpretation extending an $\mathcal{L}$-interpretation $\mathcal{A}$. We say that $\mathcal{A}$ is the *base* of $\mathcal{B}$. Two $\mathcal{R}(\mathcal{L})$-interpretations are *base equivalent* if they have the same base. We define a partial ordering $\sqsubseteq$ on the set of all $\mathcal{R}(\mathcal{L})$-interpretations by saying

$$\mathcal{B} \sqsubseteq \mathcal{C} \iff \mathcal{B} \text{ and } \mathcal{C} \text{ are base equivalent and } \forall r \in \mathcal{R}, r^{\mathcal{B}} \subseteq r^{\mathcal{C}}.$$

One can show that the set of all $\mathcal{R}(\mathcal{L})$-interpretations extending a given $\mathcal{A}$ is a complete lattice under this ordering. In particular, the *supremum* $\sqcup_i \mathcal{B}_i$ is formed by taking the union of all the relations $r^{\mathcal{B}_i}$ and extending to $\mathcal{R}(\mathcal{L})$ as above. We then have the following basic result from Höhfeld and Smolka (1988):

Theorem 11 (Definiteness) *Let Φ be a definite clause specification in $\mathcal{R}(\mathcal{L})$, and let $\mathcal{A}$ be an interpretation of $\mathcal{L}$. Then the equations*

$$r^{\mathcal{B}_0} = \emptyset;$$

$$r^{\mathcal{B}_{i+1}} = \{(\alpha(x_1), \ldots, \alpha(x_n)) \mid (r(x_1, \ldots, x_n) ::= G) \in \Phi \wedge \alpha \in [\![G]\!]^{\mathcal{B}_i}\}$$

define a chain $\mathcal{B}_0 \sqsubseteq \mathcal{B}_1 \sqsubseteq \ldots$ of $\mathcal{R}(\mathcal{L})$-interpretations with base $\mathcal{A}$. Moreover, the supremum $\mathcal{B} = \sqcup_i \mathcal{B}_i$ is the minimum model of Φ extending $\mathcal{A}$.

Many interesting consequences of these definitions can be shown; among them is that the standard completeness results for the SLD-resolution proof procedure continue to hold in a general setting.

References

Aczel, P. 1988. *Non-Well-Founded Sets.* CSLI Lecture Notes Number 14. Stanford: CSLI Publications.

Aczel, P. 1990. Replacement Systems and the Axiomatization of Situation Theory. In Cooper et al. 1990.

Bancilhon, F., and S. N. Khoshafian. 1986. A Calculus of Complex Objects. In *Proceedings of ACM SIGACT-SIGMOD-SIGART Symposium on Principles of Database Systems*, 53–59. March.

Barwise, J. 1989. *The Situation in Logic.* CSLI Lecture Notes Number 17. Stanford: CSLI Publications.

Barwise, J., and J. Etchemendy. 1990. Information, Infons, and Inference. In Cooper et al. 1990.

Buneman, P., S. Davidson, and A. Watters. 1988. A Semantics for Complex Objects and Approximate Queries. Proceedings of ACM Symposium on Principles of Database Systems, March 1988. To appear in *Journal of Computer and System Sciences.*

Chen, W., and D. S. Warren. 1989. C-Logic of Complex Objects. In *Proceedings of ACM Symposium on Principles of Database Systems.*

Codd, E. F. 1970. A Relational Model for Large Shared Data Banks. *Communications of the ACM* 13(6):377–387.

Cooper, R., K. Mukai, and J. Perry (ed.). 1990. *Situation Theory and Its Applications,* vol. 1. CSLI Lecture Notes Number 22. Stanford: CSLI Publications.

Dörre, J., and W. Rounds. 1990. On Subsumption and Semiunification in Feature Algebra. In *Proceedings of IEEE Symposium on Logic in Computer Science.* Washington. IEEE Computer Society Press. Also in IWBS Report, IBM Deutschland, Stuttgard, Dec. 1989.

Dörre, J. 1991. Feature Logic with Weak Subsumption Constraints. In *Proceedings of the 29th Annual Meeting of the ACL*, 256–263. Berkeley, CA.

Goguen, J. A., and J. Meseguer. 1986. Eqlog: Equality, Types, and Generic Modules for Logic Programming. In *Logic Programming, Functions, Relations, and Equations*, ed. D. deGroot and G. Lindstrom. New Jersey: Prentice-Hall.

Höhfeld, M., and G. Smolka. 1988. Definite Relations Over Constraint Languages. LILOG report 53, IBM Deustchland, Stuttgart, W. Germany, October.

Jaffar, J., and J.-L. Lassez. 1987. Constraint Logic Programming. In *Proceedings of the 14th ACM Symposium on Principles of Programming Languages.*

Kasper, R., and W. Rounds. 1990. The Logic of Unification in Grammar. *Linguistics and Philosophy.*

Kifer, M., and J. Wu. 1989. A Logic for Object-Oriented Logic Programming: Maier's O-Logic Revisited. In *Proceedings of ACM SIGACT-SIGMOD-SIGART Symposium on Principles of Database Systems*, 379–393. March.

Maier, D. 1983. *The Theory of Relational Data Bases.* Rockville, MD: Computer Science Press.

Maier, D. 1986. A Logic for Objects. In *Preprints of Workshop on Foundations of Deductive Database and Logic Programming*, ed. J. Minker. Washington, DC.

Mukai, K. 1987. Anadic Tuples in Prolog. Technical Report TR-239, ICOT, Tokyo.

Mukai, K. 1991. CLP(AFA): Coinductive Semantics of Horn Clauses with Compact Constraint. This volume.

Nakashima, H., H. Suzuki, P.-K. Halvorsen, and S. Peters. 1988. Towards a Computational Interpretation of Situation Theory. In *Proceedings of the International Conference on Fifth Generation Computer Systems*, 489–498. Tokyo. Institute for New Generation Systems.

Ohori, A. 1988. Semantics of Types for Database Objects. In *Proceedings of Second International Conference on Database Theory.* Bruges, Belgium. To appear in *Theoretical Computer Science.*

Pollard, C., and I. Sag. 1987. *Information-Based Syntax and Semantics, Volume 1: Fundamentals.* CSLI Lecture Notes Number 13. Stanford: CSLI Publications.

Rounds, W. 1988. Set Values for Unification-Based Grammar Formalisms and Logic Programming. Technical Report Number CSLI-88-129, CSLI, Stanford.

Shieber, S. 1986. *An Introduction to Unification-Based Approaches to Grammar.* CSLI Lecture Notes Number 4. Stanford: CSLI Publications.

Smolka, G. 1989. Feature Constraint Logics for Unification Grammars. IWBS Report 93, IBM Deutschland, Stuttgart, November.

van Gucht, D., and P. C. Fischer. 1988. Multilevel Nested Relational Structures. *Journal of Computer and System Sciences* 36:77–105.

Westerståhl, D. 1990. Parametric Types and Propositions in First-Order Situation Theory. In Cooper et al. 1990.

Winskel, G. 1985. A Note on Powerdomains and Modality. *Theoretical Computer Science* 36:127–137.

12

Physical Situations and Information Flow

JERRY SELIGMAN

Introduction

The question of how semantic concepts like 'information' fit into the physical world is an old one, central to many issues in the Cognitive Sciences. There are broadly speaking two kinds of approach to answering this question. Either some notion of *explicit representation* is invoked, whereby a distinct category of representations is introduced together with an assumed "interpretation", or appeal is made to certain *modal alternatives*: ways the world might have been. According to the first approach, informational relationships are studied in a way which is independent from the physical structure of the world and which is justified largely by linguistic intuitions about the cogency of forms of argument (i.e., logic). The second approach (which need not be incompatible with the first) views information in terms of the reduction of possibilities. Given that, in the absence of some information σ, the world might be in any one of a collection X of states, but only the states Y are compatible with σ, the information σ can be identified with the reduction in uncertainty that it involves: some function of the transition from X to Y. Probability theory, classical information theory and the standard model theory of intensional logic invoke this idea.

In Situation Theory, items of information (*infons*) are associated with *situations* in two different ways. A situation *supports* some infons and *carries* others. The infons supported by a situation are central to its identity as a situation. In some versions of the theory situations supporting the

Owing to space limitations all proofs have been omitted from this paper. They are all contained in my Ph.D. thesis (Seligman 1990b). Many thanks to Robin Cooper, under whose supervision that document was completed. Thanks also to Nick Chater and Richard Cooper for the lengthy discussions we have had on related matters. I am also grateful to the Human Communication Research Centre and the DYANA project (ESPRIT Basic Research Action 1195) for supporting this research.

Situation Theory and Its Applications, vol. 2.
Jon Barwise, Jean Mark Gawron, Gordon Plotkin, and Syun Tutiya, eds.
Copyright © 1991, Stanford University.

same set of infons are *identical* and consequently situations are often modeled as sets of infons. In contrast, infons are carried by a situation only in virtue of environmental *constraints*. The flexibility engendered by this two faceted approach enables the Situation Theorist to speak both of the locality of information (where it is situated) and the flow of information from one situation to another.

We propose to model situations[1] as parts of the physical world rather than as informational structures. By doing so we hope to show how physical entities can carry information without reference to modal alternatives or explicit representation. We feel that such a project is very much in the spirit of the original book on Situation Theory by Barwise and Perry (1983).

Our plan is to start from a fairly naive physicalist ontology and construct from it the notion of a situation. To capture informational relationships between situations we first adopt a traditional analysis in terms of "possible worlds" and then eliminate the dependence on modal alternatives using the idea of an *information channel*. Finally, we give an example of how to build a *perspective* on the physical world from within it. We regard this as an essential step towards the goal of explaining the place of information in the physical world. Following Seligman 1990a, perspectives can be used to define the information carried by a situation as well as the information it supports.

The physicalist ontology which we start with is that of Rosenschein (1987, 1989). Rosenschein is interested in designing robots by specifying constraints rather than by explicit internal representations. He therefore wants a model which is both very concrete (i.e., near to physics) and yet abstract enough to be able to specify complex conditions at a high level (i.e., near to semantics).

Rosenschein's (1989) model is made up of a set of (physical) locations which can be in various (physical) states at different times. The actual world is therefore a function assigning a state to every location at every time. This is the part that is close to physics. A specification of various environmental conditions is given in a (possibly modal) language which is interpreted in an algebra of *world conditions* (or propositions). This is the part that is close to semantics. The connection between the two parts is that the world conditions are taken to be sets of "possible world, time" pairs, where a *world* is a total function from locations and times to states. A world is "possible" if the distribution of states across the locations and times is physically possible.

The algebra on world conditions is just given by the normal set operations on the sets of possible world-time pairs. Implication is given by inclusion. The *information content* of a location's being in a certain state is given by the set of world-time pairs that are compatible with this.

---

[1] We do not claim that *all* situations are physical entities, merely that some are.

In Section 1 we generalize Rosenschein's model to account for locations which are aggregates of other locations, "locations" which are moving with respect to the frame of reference (*dynamic* locations) and the behavior of locations over time. At each stage we arrive at a new definition of information content. We use throughout the notion of a *state distribution function* which models the pattern of physical states over a regions of space and time. These functions are compared by means of spatial and temporal "invariants" which enable us to define complex behavioral 'states.'

In Section 2 the distribution functions are used to model situations. Rosenschein's world conditions are generalized to *situation conditions*. Intuitively, a situation condition holds between two situations if one situation satisfies some condition from the point of view of the other situation.

In Section 3 information flow between situations is characterized in terms of *information channels*. In this section and Section 4 the model of information flow along channels is developed and compared with alternatives based on Rosenschein's definition of information content and our generalizations of it.

In Section 5 we show how a perspective can be defined from a collection of information channels and a "point of view." Visual perspective is naturally thought of in this way.

1   World Systems

The world, for Rosenschein, is made up of *locations*, L, *times*, T, and *states* D. At any time each location is in a specific state determined by the *world function* $w : L \times T \to D$. The intuition for this metaphysics is presumably based on something like the following model of physical reality: locations can be thought of as points (or perhaps small quantized regions) of three dimensional physical space over which there is a distribution of energy (or matter) over time. The state of a location can be thought of as something like its energy level. No doubt a more sophisticated physicalist metaphysics could be given and Rosenschein's ideas could be extended to that setting. Here we will stay with the simple model, using 'physical state' and 'energy level' more or less interchangeably.

Rosenschein also makes use of a *computational interpretation* of L, T and D. The locations, L, are thought of as *registers* in a machine which hold *values* from D. T is thought of as *computational time*, as measured out by the machine's clock. Registers may hold different values at different times just as locations can be in different states. In fact, Rosenschein identifies the two interpretations, thinking of his robots as embedded in the physical world: their internal registers occupy physical locations and the values they store are determined by the physical state of those locations.

Attending the model of actual physical reality are two counterfactual notions, one local and one global. Firstly, for each location $a \in L$ there is

260 / Jerry Seligman

assumed to be a set $D_a \subset D$ of "possible states" that the location *could* be in as well as the actual state $w(a,t)$ it *is* in. The set of all states, D, is taken to be the union of all the D_a. Seen this way we can say that any function from $L \times T$ into D describes a "way the world might be", with w being the way the world actually is. But only some of these functions describe distributions of energy which are physically possible. The distinction is modeled by a subset W of the functions from $L \times T$ to D, which provides the second counterfactual aspect to the model. [2] Elements of W are called 'possible worlds' and, in particular, $w \in W$.

Definition 1 A *world system*, $\mathbf{W} = \langle L, T, D, W, w_0 \rangle$, consists of a set of locations, L, a set of times, T, a state function, D, a set of possible worlds, W, and a distinguished world, $w_0 \in W$. The state function, D, takes each location, $a \in L$, to the set, Da, of possible states it can be in. We abuse our notion by using D to refer to the set of all possible states, $\bigcup_{a \in L} Da$. Each possible world, $w \in W$, is a function which determines the state, $w(a,t) \in Da$, of each location, $a \in L$, at each time $t \in T$.

Example 1 For a "biological" example[3] of a world system consider Conway's *game of life*. Suppose L is a set of cells in an infinite grid which can be either 'alive' or 'dead'. Each generation a cell can come alive, die or stay the same as it was in the previous generation. The life and death of a cell are determined by various simple rules: a living cell dies if it is surrounded by too many or too few other live cells, and a dead cell comes alive if it is surrounded by enough live cells. At the start of a game some cells are chosen to be alive and successive generations are calculated according to the rules.

A game can be modeled as a function $w : L \times N \rightarrow D$ where D is the set {'alive', 'dead'} of states a cell can be in and N is just the natural numbers. So, for example, if in game w in the 9th generation cell c was dead then $w(c,9) =$'dead'. Suppose that we play the game w_0. With different initial conditions, we would have had different games: w_0 is only one of all the possible games we could have had. Let W be the set of all possible games of life. The structure $\langle L, N, D, W, w_0 \rangle$ is a world system.

Information about the world is modeled by sets of world-time pairs, i.e., subsets of $W \times T$. Rosenschein calls these *world conditions*, $\Phi = $ pow $(W \times T)$. A world condition is something that the world might satisfy at a given time. The idea is that $\langle w', t' \rangle$ is in world condition $\phi \in \Phi$ iff ϕ holds in world w' at time t'. For example, in the game of life world system, at some stage in a game all the cells may be dead. This condition is modeled as the set of pairs $\langle w, n \rangle$ where w is a game and n is a number and in the game g all the cells are dead at generation n.

---

[2] Presumably the two notions are connected by the fact that for all $w' \in W$, $a \in L$ and $t' \in T$, $w'(a, t') \in D_a$.

[3] Thanks to David Israel for suggesting this example.

World conditions are not simply predicates of the "total states" of worlds at different times. Whether or not a world w satisfies a condition ϕ at time t may depend on more than just the states of all the locations at time t. An example is the condition that all cells have been dead for the last ten generations. It would not be satisfied if the last living cell died out nine generations ago, but would then become satisfied at the next generation even though there would be no change in the instantaneous states of the cells.

The world conditions, Φ, form a boolean algebra under the usual operations of intersection, union and complementation. This ensures a classical interpretation of various logical operations on world conditions: conjunction, disjunction and negation. One world condition ϕ_1 *implies* another ϕ_2 just in case $\phi_1 \subseteq \phi_2$.

Definition 2 Associated with each state v that a location a can be in, there is a condition $M_a(v) \in \Phi$ which can be thought of as the "total information content" of a's being in state v. It is the set of all world-time pairs $\langle w', t' \rangle$ compatible with a's being in state v, i.e., $M_a(v) = \{\langle w', t' \rangle \mid w'(a, t') = v\}$. For any world condition, ϕ, we say that a's being in state v *carries the information that* ϕ iff $M_a(v) \subseteq \phi$.

Example 2 Suppose ϕ is the condition that the moon is eclipsed. The interpretation of ϕ consists of all the world-time pairs, $\langle w', t' \rangle$, such that at time t' in world w', the earth is directly in between the moon and the sun. For a location a in state v to have the information that the moon is eclipsed it must be the case that $M_a(v)$ is a subset of the interpretation of ϕ. So if, in world w', a is in state v at time t' (i.e., $w'(a, t') = v$) then the earth lies directly between the moon and the sun at time t'. In other words, a's being in state v is a reliable indicator of lunar eclipses. An example might be a location on the "sunny" side of the moon, which is in state '1' when illuminated by sunlight and in state '0' otherwise. The location's being in state '0' is an indicator of lunar eclipses.

Example 3 In the game of life there is very little information carried by a single cell's being alive or dead. Strong conditions like 'all the cells are dead' are of course refuted by a single cell's being alive, but no information is carried about other cells. If a and b are cells and $M_a(\text{'alive'}) \subseteq M_b(\text{'alive'})$ then $a = b$. The situation is quite different when we consider collections of cells. If all the cells surrounding cell a are dead then a will die out in the next generation, so the surrounding cells' being dead carries the information that cell a is about to die. But to capture this kind of informational dependency, we must look at aggregate rather than single locations.

1.1 Aggregate Locations

Rosenschein suggests a way of extending the notion of a state to aggregates of locations. On the computational interpretation, if a single location is a register, then an aggregate location is a collection of registers. The state of the aggregate is determined in terms of the states of its component locations. Rosenschein defines the value of a pair $\langle a_1, a_2 \rangle$ of registers to be the pair of their values, i.e., if a_1 is in value v_1 and a_2 is in value v_2 then $\langle a_1, a_2 \rangle$ is in value $\langle v_1, v_2 \rangle$. The definition is easily extended to sequences of registers.

On the physical interpretation, the state of a sequence of spatial locations is the sequence of energy levels of the component locations. This may not be specific enough for modeling physical phenomena. It is natural to think of the state of a spatial region as the distribution of the states over the region. For example, if the state of a point in a volume of fluid is given by the concentration of a certain chemical X at that point, then we would expect the state of the whole volume to be determined by the distribution of X in the fluid. If we adopted Rosenschein's definition then the state of the volume could only be specified relative to a certain ordering of its points. Not only could two different orderings give different states, but two different volumes of fluid could judged to be in the same state, given suitably chosen orderings, even if the distribution of chemical X in the two volumes was entirely different.

For our purposes Rosenschein's definition is both too specific and not specific enough. It is too specific since the same set of locations can be said to be in different states depending on the way the locations are ordered. It is not specific enough since two aggregates can be in the same state, relative to appropriately chosen orderings, even though, on our physical interpretation, they have very distinct properties. The reason for the inappropriateness of Rosenschein's definition in the physical case is that the notion of a spatial distribution of states takes into account more than just the states of the component locations. The geometrical relationships between component locations is also important.

Our approach is to model the distribution of states over an aggregate directly, and define an equivalence relation between distributions by looking at spatial transformations of various kinds. Two aggregates can then be said to be "in the same state" just in case they have equivalent distributions.

Definition 3 An *aggregate* location is a set $b \subseteq L$ of locations. Its state *distribution*, $\delta_{(b,w,t)}$ in world w at time t, is the function from b to D taking $a \in b$ to $w(a,t)$.

The choice of spatial transformations very much depends on the structure of space itself. Like Rosenschein, we have abstracted away from any specific model of space: L is just a set of locations, not a vector space nor a topology nor even a partial order. If we were to give L one of these structures then our choice of transformations of L would consist of those maps $g : L \to L$ which "preserved the structure" of L, in an appropriate sense (see the examples below). In the absence of any specific structure for L we provide a list of properties that we would expect any suitable set of structure preserving transformations to have. We call a set of transformations of L which has these properties a set of "spatial invariants."

Definition 4 A set G of bijections $g : L \to L$ is said to be a set of *spatial invariants* iff

1. G contains the identity transformation, is closed under composition and has inverses (i.e., G is a transformation group)
2. *Homogeneity.* For any two locations $a_1, a_2 \in L$ there is a $g \in G$ such that $g(a_1) = a_2$.
3. If $w \in W$ then for all $g \in G$ the world, $w' : L \times T \to D$, obtained by transforming L under g (i.e., for $a \in L$, $t \in T$, $w'(ga, t) = w(a, t)$) is also possible (i.e., $w' \in W$).

Condition 1 is satisfied by anything which can reasonably be said to be a set of transformations. Condition 2, the "homogeneity" condition, says that space is uniform. From any location you can find a transformation which gets you to any other location, so no location is unfairly privileged. Condition 3 is included to ensure that "physical laws" which determine the set W of possible worlds are blind to these transformations: if we transform the whole world then what we get is still a physically possible world.

Example 4 Suppose that we model physical space as a three dimensional vector space, L. A useful class of invariants of L is the translations, that is the maps $g_a : L \to L$ such that $a \in L$ and $\forall a' \in L$ $g_a(a') = a + a'$ (Here the $+$ is vector addition). The translations also capture the homogeneity of L, since for any two locations $a_1, a_2 \in L$ there is a translation $g_{(a_2 - a_1)}$ which maps a_1 to a_2. Another example is the class of rigid transformations of L (translations plus rotations).

We can now say what it is for two aggregate locations, b_1 and b_2 to be in the "same state": there must be some spatial invariant which maps elements of b_1 to elements of b_2 and preserves their elementary states. We describe this more precisely as an equivalence relation between state "distribution" functions.

Definition 5 State distributions $\delta_1 : b_1 \to D$ and $\delta_2 : b_2 \to D$ are *equivalent* iff there is a $g \in G$ such that $b_2 = \{g(a) \mid a \in b_1\}$ and for each $a \in b_1$, $\delta_1(a) = \delta_2(g(a))$. Two aggregate locations are in the *same state* iff their distribution functions are equivalent. We model the states of aggregate locations as equivalence classes of distribution functions. An aggregate b is in state d in world w at time t iff $\delta_{(b,w,t)} \in d$.

Example 5 In the case where L is a vector space and G is the set of translations, g_a, of L, we can find a canonical representative of each distribution equivalence class. For the finite aggregate $b \subseteq L$, define center(b) = $1/|b|\sum b$ where $|b|$ is the number of locations in L. Although the definition relies on b being finite, it can be extended to the infinite case. Informally, center(b) is the geometric center, or "balance point" of the aggregate. Each aggregate can be "normalized" by translating it so that its center is at the origin of L. We define norm(b) = $\{a - \text{center}(b) \mid a \in b\}$ Note that if there is a translation, $g_a \in G$, taking b_1 to b_2 (i.e., $g_a(b_1) = b_2$) then norm(b_1) = norm(b_2). Now the equivalence classes of distributions can be canonically represented by those distribution functions with a 0 center, i.e., $\{\delta : L \rightharpoonup D \mid \text{center}(\text{dom } \delta) = 0\}$. Aggregate location $b \subseteq L$ has canonical state δ iff δ is the distribution function of norm(b).

Such canonical representatives of states are not available in the general case. For example, if we include rotations in the set G then it is difficult to choose a "preferred" orientation for the representative of a class of rotation equivalent distributions.

Note how the homogeneity condition is important if aggregate states are to be conservative with respect to the elementary states of single locations. If $a_1, a_2 \in L$ are locations in the same state, d, then the distribution functions of the singleton aggregates $\{a_1\}$ and $\{a_2\}$ are just the functions assigning d to a_1 and a_2 respectively. These functions are equivalent iff there is a $g \in G$ such that $g(a_1) = a_2$. The existence of such a g for each pair $a_1, a_2 \in L$ is precisely what is guaranteed by homogeneity.

The definition of information content for an aggregate location b in state d is then given by $M_b(d) = \{\langle w, t \rangle \mid \delta_{\langle b,w,t \rangle} \in d\}$.

1.2 Dynamic Locations

The set of locations, L, provides a means of dividing up the world in a uniform way which allows information to flow. Rosenschein's definition of information content compares the current state of a location with its state at other times (and in other worlds) in order to constrain the possible states of its environment. It is not the location's current state which alone determines this constraint, but all of its possible histories.

On the computational interpretation, a location is a register, and its information content is the strongest world condition that must be satisfied given only that it is in its current state. Rosenschein uses this interpretation to ascribe knowledge (that the current environment satisfies this world condition) to a robot containing the register. The identification between location and register works fine as long as the robot is not moving relative to the environment (or whatever is at rest with respect to the location set L). If the robot moves then the register will occupy different locations at different times.

We could avoid this problem by modeling the world from a robot's eye view, in which case all locations would be at rest with respect to the robot.

But this does not seem satisfactory since we may want to model several different robots, or even a single robot with "moving parts."

Our proposal is to consider *dynamic* locations in addition to the locations in L, which we now call *static*. A dynamic location is a partial function $a : T \rightharpoonup L$. We write the collection of dynamic locations as $L^{(T)}$.[4] Every static location can be recaptured as a total, constant valued dynamic location. The definition of information content for dynamic locations must be modified to: $M_a(d) = \{\langle w, t \rangle \mid t \in \text{dom } a \text{ and } w(a(t), t) = d\}$.

Example 6 Suppose that LISA, the least intelligent situated automaton, is wandering aimlessly around the world. LISA has one register which is programmed to respond in a very simple way to the light conditions in LISA's immediate environment. In well lit environments LISA's register is in state '1'. In not so well lit environments LISA's register is in state '0'. As LISA wanders her register flips from '1' to '0' and back again approximately once a day. We model LISA's register by the dynamic location $r : T \rightharpoonup L$ which, for each moment t of LISA's life, determines the (static) spatial location $r(t)$ of the register. Let ϕ be the world condition: 'in world w at time t LISA is in a well lit environment'. For LISA to do what she is supposed to do, it must be the case that $M_r(1) \subseteq \phi$ and $M_r(0) \subseteq \neg\phi$.

1.3 Behavior Over Time

Another extension to Rosenschein's model of information concerns the information content of a location's behavior over time. In many cases of practical interest it is not the state of a location that conveys information, but a pattern of states adopted by a location over a period of time. For example, the instantaneous state of a telegraph wire transmitting Morse code tells us nothing: it is the sequence of states (off, on, off, on, off, on, off, on, on, off, on, on, off, on, on, off, on, off, on, off, on, off) that conveys a call for help. Similarly, it is the change in height of the column of fluid in a thermometer which carries the information that the temperature is rising.

What is meant by a "period of time" may well depend on the structure of time itself. For example, if we model time as a linear order we may only consider intervals to be genuine time periods. But, as in the space case, we will abstract over particular models of time and allow any subset τ of T to be a *time period*. Over time period τ a (static) location a may be in various instantaneous states. The question to be answered in this section is how we extend the notion of 'state' to a's behavior over τ. The solution we adopt is similar to that for aggregate locations, using distributions over time rather than space and temporal, rather than spatial, invariants.

Definition 6 The distribution $\delta_{(a,\tau,w)} : \tau \rightarrow D$ of a location a over a time period τ in world w is the function taking each $t \in \tau$ to $w(a, t)$.

---

[4]We use the notation $A^{(B)}$ for the set of partial functions from B to A.

Definition 7 A set H of bijections $h : T \to T$ is a set of *temporal invariants* for T iff

1. H contains the identity map, is closed under composition and has inverses.

2. *Homogeneity.* For any $t_1, t_2 \in T$ there is an $h \in H$ such that $h(t_1) = t_2$.

3. If $w \in W$ then for all $h \in H$ the world, $w' : L \times T \to D$, obtained by transforming T under h (i.e., for $a \in L$, $t \in T$, $w'(a, ht) = w(a, t)$) is also possible (i.e., $w' \in W$).

Example 7 For example, if we model time as a one dimensional vector space, then we can take H to be the set of translations in T; i.e., for each $t \in T$, there is an $h_t \in H$ such that for all $t' \in T$, $h_t(t') = t + t'$. Homogeneity is satisfied since for any $t, t' \in T$, $h_{(t'-t)}(t) = t'$.

Slightly more abstractly, if we model time as an order $\langle T, \leq \rangle$ then we could take the set of order preserving bijections on T as our set of temporal invariants. The homogeneity condition constrains the kind of order $\leq$ can be.

The definitions of distribution equivalence, state (in this case, "behavior") and information content follow the established pattern:

Definition 8 Distributions, $\delta_1 : \tau_1 \to D$ and $\delta_2 : \tau_2 \to D$ are *equivalent* iff there is an $h \in H$ such that $\tau_2 = \{h(t) \mid t \in \tau_1\}$ and for each $t \in \tau_1$, $\delta_1(t) = \delta_2(h(t))$. The *behavior* of a location a over time period τ in world w is the equivalence class [5] of $\delta_{(a,\tau,w)}$. The information content of location a's exhibiting behavior d is given by $M_a(d) = \{\langle w, \tau \rangle \mid \delta_{(a,\tau,w)} \in d\}$.

Note that $M_a(d)$ is not strictly a world condition in the technical sense we have been using so far. The elements of $M_a(d)$ are pairs consisting of a world and a time *period*. The new set Φ^+ of world conditions are therefore to be thought of as conditions which a world satisfies over a time period. Any "instantaneous" world condition $\phi \in \Phi$ can be recaptured as the world condition $\{\langle w, \{t\} \rangle \mid \langle w, t \rangle \in \phi\}$. It may be that the only conditions of any interest are those which can be reduced to instantaneous conditions in a uniform way, e.g., those $\phi \in \Phi^+$ for which $\langle w, \tau \rangle \in \phi$ iff for each $t \in \tau$, $\langle w, \{t\} \rangle \in \phi$. But, for the sake of generality, we will not adopt such a reduction here.

Example 8 Suppose that the temperature of a boiler is monitored by a thermometer which lights an LED when the temperature rises above a certain point. The LED goes out when the temperature fall below another (lower) point. If the temperature gets dangerously high, the LED starts to flash on and off to attract the attention of an operator. If we model

---

[5] If time is modeled as a vector space, then we can define canonical representatives of each equivalence class of temporal distributions in the same way as we did for spatial distributions.

the location of the LED by a, then "flashing" behavior can be captured by the equivalence class $[\delta]$ of the distribution $\delta : \{t_1, t_2, t_3\} \to D$ given by $\delta(t_1) =$'on', $\delta(t_2) =$'off', $\delta(t_3) =$'on' (for a suitably proximate sequence of times t_1, t_2, t_3). Then the flashing LED has information content $M_a([\delta])$ and if $\langle w, \tau \rangle \in M_a([\delta])$ then the boiler is dangerously hot in world w over time period τ. In this case the reduction to the instantaneous world conditions mentioned above would be sensible since being dangerously hot over a (short) period of time involves being dangerously hot at each instant of that period.

1.4 Complex Behavior

We have seen how information can be located across aggregates of locations, in moving ("dynamic") locations and in the behavior of a location over time. In this section we face the task of analyzing the informational content of complex behavior in terms of these simple cases.

There are several ways of extending the definition of dynamic locations to aggregates of locations. The first is to use *aggregates of dynamic locations*, i.e., sets $b \subseteq L^{(T)}$. We can define the state distribution of an aggregate b of dynamic locations in world w at time t to be the distribution of states across the aggregate of static locations which b occupies at time t, i.e., the function with domain $\{a(t) \mid a \in b$ and $t \in \operatorname{dom} a\}$ mapping each $a(t)$ to $w(a(t), t)$. Since we do not require that all the dynamic locations in b are defined over the same time period, this "instantaneous" aggregate may vary in size over time.

Example 9 In the game of life there are certain patterns of cells, called *gliders*, which "move" across the grid in straight lines: every four generations the pattern is replicated in a slightly different position. Figure 1 shows five generations of a glider's life. The labels illustrate one way of modeling the glider as an aggregate $\{a_1, a_2, a_3, a_4, a_5\}$ of dynamic locations. In each generation the cell marked by a_i is the instantaneous location of a_i in that generation. The distribution function in each generation will have the constant value 'live' but with a domain—the set of live cells of that generation—which changes over time. During the period depicted each dynamic location in the aggregate is defined at each generation and so the domain of the distribution function remains of constant size (5 cells).

The second approach uses *dynamic aggregate locations*, i.e., functions $b : T \to \operatorname{pow} D$, which determine an aggregate of "static" locations $b(t) \subseteq L$ at each time t. There is no need to use partial functions in this case, since b can be taken to be "undefined" when $b(t) = \emptyset$. The state distribution of a dynamic aggregate location b in world w at time t is the function mapping each $a \in b(t)$ to $w(a, t)$.

Example 10 The glider pictured in Figure 1 could also be modeled as a dynamic aggregate location, b, which maps each generation n to the set of

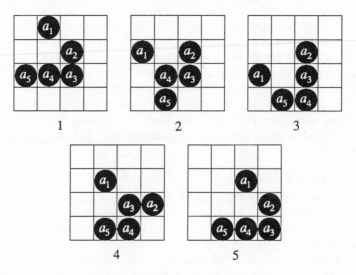

Figure 1 A "glider" modeled as the aggregate $\{a_1, a_2, a_3, a_4, a_5\}$ of dynamic locations.

live cells $b(n)$ of that generation. The distribution in each generation can be seen to be exactly the same as in the previous example.

In fact, as things stand, there is little to choose between these two approaches. For each aggregate of dynamic locations, b, there is a dynamic aggregate location, $b' : T \to \text{pow } L$, which determines the aggregate $b(t) = \{a(t) \in L \mid a \in b \text{ and } t \in \text{dom } a\}$ at each time, t. It is easy to see that b and b' have the same distribution function in every world and at every time. In the reverse direction, for a dynamic aggregate location, b', there may be more than one aggregate of dynamic locations which corresponds in this way, but since our definition of the state of an aggregate only depends on its distribution function there is no real difference.

A third approach is to change the definition of distribution functions for aggregates of dynamic locations. If we take a distribution to be a map from *dynamic* locations to states, then a subtle difference emerges between the two previous approaches. There is more information associated with an aggregate of dynamic locations, b, than with the corresponding dynamic aggregate location, b'. This fact is illustrated by Figure 2. For times $t_1, t_2 \in T$, there is no connection between locations in the aggregate $b'(t_1)$ and those in $b'(t_2)$, whereas b provides a connection between $a(t_1) \in b'(t_1)$ and $a(t_2) \in b'(t_2)$: they are instances of the same dynamic location. We loosely refer to the connections between location instances in an aggregate of dynamic locations as *dynamic bindings*. The intuition is that a dynamic location consists of "static" locations together with information about how

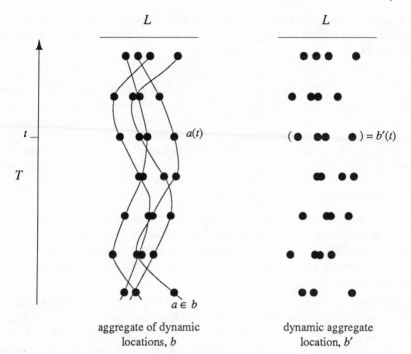

Figure 2 The difference between an aggregate of dynamic locations and its corresponding dynamic aggregate location.

they are connected, or "bound", in time. More precisely, we can think of an aggregate of dynamic locations as inducing a binary relation on space-time:

Definition 9 Let b be an aggregate of dynamic locations. For $l, l' \in L$ and $t, t' \in T$, we say that $\langle l, t \rangle$ is *bound* to $\langle l', t' \rangle$ in b iff $\exists a \in b$, such that $t, t' \in \text{dom } a$, $a(t) = l$ and $a(t') = l'$.

Because of the binding information contained in aggregates of dynamic locations we will use them to model a moving aggregate. To make use of the extra information, we define the distribution of states across a moving aggregate to be an assignment of states to *dynamic* locations.

Definition 10 The distribution $\delta_{(b,t,w)} : b \to D$ of an aggregate b of dynamic locations in world w at time t maps each $a \in b$ to $w(a(t), t)$. Distributions δ_1 and δ_2 are *equivalent* just in case there is a function $f : T \to G$ such that

1. $\text{dom } \delta_2 = \{a_f \mid a \in \text{dom } \delta_1\}$ where a_f is the dynamic location with domain $\text{dom } a_f = \text{dom } a$ and $a_f(t) = f(t)(a(t))$ for each $t \in \text{dom } a$, and

2. for each $a \in \text{dom } \delta_1$, $\delta_1(a) = \delta_2(a_f)$.

The *state* of an aggregate b of dynamic locations in world w at time t is the equivalence class of $\delta_{(b,w,t)}$. If b is in state d then it has information content $M_b(d) = \{\langle w, t \rangle \mid \delta_{(b,w,t)} \in d\}$.

Example 11 In the glider example, each of the five "parts" of the glider are instantiated by different live cells in different generations. The bindings between these cells are represented in Figure 1 by the labels a_1, a_2, a_3, a_4, a_5. If we were to rub out those labels then there would be no means of connecting the live cells of one generation to those of the next. The state distribution of the glider at each generation is just the constant 'live'-valued function with domain $\{a_1, a_2, a_3, a_4, a_5\}$. Since, according to our final definition, the glider never changes state, it's being in that state carries very little information about its environment.

Using similar techniques we can capture the information content of the temporal behavior of aggregates and single moving locations, and (finally) the temporal behavior of moving aggregates. We will spare the reader the details by merely stating and illustrating the notion of equivalence in the most complex case.

Definition 11 The distribution $\delta_{(b,w,\tau)} : L(T) \times T \rightharpoonup D$ of an aggregate b of dynamic locations in world w over time period τ has domain $\text{dom } \delta_{(b,w,\tau)} = \{\langle a_\tau, t \rangle \mid a \in b \text{ and } t \in \tau \cap \text{dom } a\}$ and, for each $a \in b$ and $t \in \text{dom } a \cap \tau$, $\delta_{(b,w,\tau)}(a_\tau, t) = w(a, t)$ where a_τ is the restriction of a to τ, i.e., the dynamic location with $\text{dom } a_\tau = \text{dom } a \cap \tau$ mapping each $t \in \text{dom } a_\tau$ to $a(t)$.

Distributions δ_1 and δ_2 are *equivalent* iff there is a function $f : T \to G$ and an $h \in H$ such that

1. $\text{dom } \delta_2 = \{\langle a_f, ht \rangle \mid \langle a, t \rangle \in \text{dom } \delta_1\}$ where a_f is the dynamic location with domain
   $\text{dom } a_f = \{ht \mid t \in \text{dom } a\}$ and $a_f(ht) = f(t)(a(t))$ for each $t \in \text{dom } a$, and
2. for each $\langle a, t \rangle \in \text{dom } \delta_1$, $\delta_2(a_f, ht) = \delta_1(a, t)$.

The *behavior* of an aggregate b of dynamic locations in world w over time period τ is the equivalence class of $\delta_{(b,w,\tau)}$. If b has behavior d then it has information content $M_b(d) = \{\langle w, \tau \rangle \mid \delta_{(b,w,\tau)} \in d\}$.

Example 12 Suppose that you and I collect two cars of the same model fresh from the Austin Rover assembly line. We fill them with the same amount of fuel and drive away in different directions. The engines in each of our cars are mechanically identical. Each is composed of a number of moving parts manufactured by the same machine. Each moving part traces out a trajectory in space and time, which we will model as a dynamic location. The engines of our two cars will therefore be modeled as aggregates of dynamic locations. Each part of each engine will be moving both with respect to other parts of the same engine and with respect to the corresponding part in the other engine. Nevertheless, when we are traveling at the same speed, there is a sense in which the behavior of your car's engine is the same as the behavior of mine. From hypothetical positions inside the two engines they would be physically indistinguishable. It is precisely this sense of equivalence which is captured by Definition 11.

2 Situations and Situation Conditions

In this section we consider how situations can be modeled in Rosenschein's framework. An event in the physical world consists of something happening at certain locations and certain times. On the physicalist metaphysics adopted in the previous section, anything that happens must involve a change in the state of a location (or dynamic location) over some time period. Rather than capturing the ontology of events, we follow situation theory by using the more neutral term *situation* to cover both events and states. We model situations by functions which take (dynamic) locations and times to elementary states.

Definition 12 A *situation* is a partial function, $s : L^{(T)} \times T \rightharpoonup D$, such that for all $a, a' \in L^{(T)}$ and $t, t' \in T$

1. if $\langle a, t \rangle \in \text{dom } s$ and $t' \in \text{dom } a$ then $\langle a, t' \rangle \in \text{dom } s$ and $t \in \text{dom } a$, and

2. if $\langle a, t \rangle, \langle a', t \rangle \in \text{dom } s$ and $a(t) = a'(t)$ then $s(a, t) = s(a', t)$.

Associated with each situation, s, is its *location*, loc$s$, and its *time period*, tim$s$. The location of a situation is the aggregate of dynamic locations over which it is defined: loc$s = \{a \mid \exists t, \langle a, t \rangle \in \text{dom } s\}$. The time period of a situation is the set of points of time at which at least one of its dynamic locations is defined: tim$s = \{t \mid \exists a, \langle a, t \rangle \in \text{dom } s\}$. Let Sit be the collection of all situations in the world system.

Condition 1 ensures that a situation determines the state of every location in loc$s$ at every time on which that location is defined, i.e., dom $s = \{\langle a, t \rangle \mid a \in \text{loc} s \text{ and } t \in \text{dom } a\}$. This imposes an identity condition on situations: two situations are the same if they have the same "underlying" distribution of states together with the same internal dynamic bindings (see Proposition 2).

Condition 2 ensures that there are no "clashes." If two dynamic locations in loc$s$ "cross," i.e., they occupy the same place at the same time, then s must be consistent about the state it assigns to them. Another, way of avoiding such clashes would be to insist that the dynamic bindings in the location of a situation never cross, but that seems unnecessarily restrictive.

In comparing situations we must bear in mind that they are defined with respect to *dynamic* locations. In other words, each situation carries with it a spatio-temporal "frame of reference" defined by the bindings between instantaneous events that are induced by its dynamic locations. It is quite possible that two situations with disjoint domains could "overlap": i.e., they could assign the same states to certain "static" locations at the same points of time. They would differ not because of the physical state of any region of space and time, but because they have different frames of reference.

In saying that one situation is "part of" another, we will mean that it is fully contained within it, i.e., the smaller situation is made up of instantaneous events, all of which are included in the larger situation. Whatever bindings there are between the instantaneous events are irrelevant to its being a part of the larger situation. On this conception, it is possible for a situation to have a part whose domain is entirely disjoint from its own. Such a part would be dependent on the same underlying distribution of elementary states, but would "cut up the world" differently with its own regimen of bindings between instantaneous events.

It is important to admit this possibility for the sake of a modular understanding of parts. A situation is structured by the bindings it imposes on its elementary parts. We should not expect it to say anything about the structure of those parts. For example, a car engine can be modeled as an aggregate of piston rods, valves, cylinders and other components. In such a model a single piston rod would be represented by the dynamic location which maps out its spatial trajectory. But the same piston rod can itself be modeled as an aggregate of *its* parts: vibrating molecules or whatever. The situation modeling the internal behavior of the piston rod is still a part of the situation modeling the engine, despite its distinct component structure.

For this reason, the "part of" ordering between situations is not determined by set inclusion of their graphs. Instead we use the idea of a "canonical" situation. A canonical situation is one in which the bindings are just those that are implicit in L itself, i.e., $\langle l, t \rangle$ is bound to $\langle l', t' \rangle$ iff $l = l'$. We proceed by defining an idempotent operator $*$ on Sit which takes each situation s to a canonical situation s^*. The $*$ operator can be thought of as an operator which "forgets" about the dynamic bindings in a situation. The 'part of' relation is then determined by graph inclusion of canonical situations.

Definition 13 The $*$ operator is defined indirectly using two auxiliary functions, $\vee$ and $\wedge$.

For $s : L^{(T)} \times T \rightharpoonup D$ let $s^{\vee} : L \times T \rightharpoonup D$ be such that (a) dom $s^{\vee} = \{\langle a(t), t \rangle \mid \langle a, t \rangle \in \text{dom } s\}$, and (b) for each $\langle a, t \rangle \in \text{dom } s$, $s^{\vee}(a(t), t) = s(a, t)$. Note that $s^{\vee}$ is well-defined by the "no clashes" condition (2) of Definition 12. We call $s^{\vee}$ the *underlying state distribution* of s.

For $f : L \times T \rightharpoonup D$ let $f^{\wedge} : L^{(T)} \times T \rightharpoonup D$ be such that (a) dom $f^{\wedge} = \{\langle a^{\wedge}, t \rangle \mid \langle a, t \rangle \in \text{dom } f\}$ where for $a \in L$, $a^{\wedge} : T \rightharpoonup L$ such that dom $a^{\wedge} = \{t' \mid \langle a, t' \rangle \in \text{dom } f\}$ and $a^{\wedge}(t') = a$ for all $t' \in \text{dom } a^{\wedge}$, and (b) for each

$\langle a,t \rangle \in$ dom f, $f^\wedge(a^\wedge,t) = f(a,t)$. $f^\wedge$ satisfies conditions (1) and (2) of Definition 12 and so is a situation. Note that $f^{\wedge\vee} = f$.

Now, for a situation, s, let $s^* = s^{\vee\wedge}$ and say s is *static* iff $s^* = s$, and *dynamic* otherwise. Finally, we say that situation s_1 is *part of* situation s_2, written $s_1 \trianglelefteq s_2$ iff dom $s_1^* \subseteq$ dom s_2^* and for all $\langle a,t \rangle \in$ dom s_1^*, $s_1^*(a,t) = s_2^*(a,t)$.

Proposition 1 *For all* $s, s_1, s_2 \in Sit$,

1. $s^{**} = s^*$, *i.e.,* s^* *is static*
2. $s_1 \trianglelefteq s_2$ *iff* $s_1^* \trianglelefteq s_2^*$
3. $\trianglelefteq$ *is a preorder*
4. *if* $s_1 \trianglelefteq s_2$ *and* $s_2 \trianglelefteq s_1$ *then* $s_1^* = s_2^*$
5. $\trianglelefteq$ *is a partial order on static situations*

Proposition 2 *Two situations are the same if they have the same "underlying" distribution of states together with the same internal dynamic bindings, i.e.,* $s_1 = s_2$ *iff* $s_1^\vee = s_2^\vee$ *and for all* $\langle l,t \rangle, \langle l',t' \rangle \in$ dom $s_1^\vee$ (= dom $s_2^\vee$), $\langle l,t \rangle$ *is bound to* $\langle l',t' \rangle$ *in* locs$_1$ *iff they are bound in* locs$_2$.

Situations can be regarded as partial specifications of Rosenschein's possible worlds. Not all situations will correspond directly to parts of worlds since they may divide up space using a different "grid" of dynamic locations than L. For situation, s, the partial function $s^\vee$ may be extendable to a possible world, but it may not: there are situations which distribute states in physically unrealizable ways. Conversely, we can lift Rosenschein's worlds to the level of situations using the map $\wedge$: for each world w, $w^\wedge \in Sit$. This allows us to apply the terms 'actual', 'possible' and 'world' to situations in a conservative manner.

Definition 14 If s is a situation then

s is *possible* iff there is some $w \in W$ for which $s \trianglelefteq w^\wedge$

s is *actual* iff $s \trianglelefteq w_0^\wedge$

s is a *world* iff for all $s' \in Sit$, if $s \trianglelefteq s'$ then $s' \trianglelefteq s$.

Let s^W to be the set of possible worlds that it *occurs* in, i.e., $s^W = \{w^\wedge \mid w \in W$ and $s \trianglelefteq w^\wedge\}$.

Proposition 3

1. *For* $w : L \times T \to D$, $w \in W$ *iff* $w^\wedge$ *is a possible world*.
2. *For situations* s_1 *and* s_2, $s_2^* \in s_1^W$ *iff* $s_1 \trianglelefteq s_2$ *and* s_2 *is a possible world*.

The first part of Proposition 3 shows that the definition of 'possible' and 'world' in Definition 14 is justified. It also permits us in identifying w with $w^\wedge$ which we will do for the sake of cleanliness. From this point on, except in detailed proofs, we will talk about w meaning $w^\wedge$ and vice versa.

Situations have already been studied in Section 1.3 under a different name. They are just the state distribution functions of aggregates of dynamic locations over a time period. So, in addition to the $\trianglelefteq$ ordering, we already have a classification of situations into "behavioral" types. The types are just the equivalence classes of distribution functions under the equivalence of Definition 11. However, in order to generalize this classification of situations we need to be more precise about the relationship between equivalent situations. To this end we will define a set of structure preserving maps for Sit called the set of *situation invariants*. A situation invariant will map situations to situations which are equivalent as distributions.

Definition 15 A function $e : Sit \rightarrow Sit$ is a *situation invariant* iff there is a function $f : T \rightarrow G$ and an $h \in H$ (where G and H are the sets of spatial and temporal invariants, respectively) such that, for each $s \in Sit$,

1. dom $es = \{\langle a_f, ht \rangle \mid \langle a, t \rangle \in \text{dom } s\}$ where a_f is the dynamic location with domain
   dom $a_f = \{ht \mid t \in \text{dom } a\}$ and $a_f(ht) = f(t)(a(t))$ for each $t \in$ dom a, and

2. for each $\langle a, t \rangle \in$ dom s, $es(a_f, ht) = s(a, t)$.

We say that two situations $s_1, s_2 \in Sit$ are *equivalent* and write $s_1 \approx s_2$ iff there is a situation invariant taking s_1 to s_2. A glance at Definition 11 will satisfy the reader that we are using our terminology consistently.

The equivalence relation between situations is intended to capture internal physical indistinguishability. Two situations are equivalent just in case it is physically impossible to distinguish between them by "looking" at their internal structure alone: it is only their external relational properties which tell them apart. Internal relational properties, however, may be sufficient to distinguish situations even when they "occupy" the same physical space. For example, if $s_1 \trianglelefteq s_2$ and $s_2 \trianglelefteq s_1$ it may be possible to distinguish between s_1 and s_2 on the basis of the dynamic bindings in their locations: one will be seen as moving with respect to the other and vice versa. In other words, $s_1 \trianglelefteq s_2$ and $s_2 \trianglelefteq s_1$ does not entail $s_1 \approx s_2$.

The role of a situation invariant is to specify *how* two situations are internally physically indistinguishable. A situation invariant provides a map between the location of one situation and the location of another situation from which it is indistinguishable. This map associates, point by point, locations and times in one situation with locations and times in another situation so that associated locations and times are assigned the same state in both situations. Moreover, it does this in a way that respects the underlying structure of space and time as represented by the spatial and temporal invariants, G and H. The following proposition establishes that the set of situation invariants has all the properties we would expect of a set of invariants on Sit.

Proposition 4

1. *The set of situation invariants contains the identity function, is closed under composition and has inverses.*

2. *If e is a situation invariant then $s_1 \trianglelefteq s_2$ iff $es_1 \trianglelefteq es_2$.*
3. *If w is a world and $s \approx w$ then s is also a world.*
4. *If s is possible and $s' \approx s$ then s' is also possible.*

Although space and time are taken to be homogeneous, the set of situations is not. Situations have a rich internal structure whereas points of space and time are taken to be atomic. So for situation invariants there is only a trivial version of the homogeneity property enjoyed by G and H. Given two equivalent situations there is, by definition, a situation invariant which maps one to the other. The question arises as to whether this invariant is *unique*. If for each pair of equivalent situations there is only one situation invariant connecting them, then we say that the collection of situation invariants has the *Uniqueness Property*. Whether or not we have the uniqueness property depends on underlying assumptions about G and H.

Definition 16 The set of situation invariants satisfies has the *Uniqueness Property* iff for any situation s and invariants e_1 and e_2, if $e_1 s = e_2 s$ then $e_1 = e_2$.

Example 13 If L and T are the Euclidean vector spaces R^3 and R, and G and H are the sets of translations on L and T respectively, then the induced collection of situation invariants has the Uniqueness Property. However, if we allow G to contain rotations on L, then the Uniqueness Property no longer obtains.

Just as for distribution functions, we define the *state* of a situation, s, to be the set $[s]$ of situations indistinguishable from it.

Definition 17 The collection *State* of *situation states* is given by

$$State = \{[s] \mid s \in Sit\}$$

where $[s]$ is the $\approx$-equivalence class of s. For $d \in State$, we say that a situation s is *in state d* iff $s \in d$.

We will now extend the notion of 'situation state' to give a broader classification of situations into *situation types*. A situation type is the union of some set of states. To say that a situation is of a certain type d is to say that it is in one of the states $d' \subseteq d$. In general, a situation type is a coarser classifier of situations than a state, although, of course, states are themselves situation types.

Definition 18 The collection *Type* of (unary) *situation types* is given by

$$Type = \{\bigcup X \mid X \subseteq State\}.$$

For each $d \in Type$ we say that a situation, s, is *of type d* iff $s \in d$.

This classification justifies our use of the term 'indistinguishable' for situations which are $\approx$-equivalent, since it is a trivial consequence of the above that for situations s_1 and s_2, $s_1 \approx s_2$ iff there no $d \in$ *Type* such that s_1 is of type d but s_2 is not.

In the classification of situations into types, we have the beginnings of an account of information content. To know that a situation is of type $d \in$ *Type* is to know *something*. If d is a state then knowing that a situation is of type d is knowing all we can know about its internal structure, but other aspects of the situation can be revealed through knowledge of its external properties. A generalization of the notion of a situation type is obtained by considering relational properties of situations which are dependent only on the relative locations of the participating situations (in addition to their internal structure).

Definition 19 The collection *Type*^{n} of *n-ary relational situation types* consists of those $d \subseteq Sit^n$ such that for all situation invariants, e, if $\langle s_1, \ldots, s_n \rangle \in d$ then $\langle es_1, \ldots, es_n \rangle \in d$. It is necessary but simple to check that *Type*^{1} = *Type*.

Relational situation types capture the simplest external properties of situations, but are still very restrictive. There are many sets of situations of interest which are *not* situation types; for example, the set, $\{s \in Sit \mid \text{tim}s = \tau\}$, of situations with time period τ.

The failure of situation types to characterize sets of situations like this is due to their lack of a "point of view". That a pair of situations is related by a type is a disembodied fact: any situation invariant will map the situations to another pair of related situations on the other side of world. It is instructive to note that we can capture the notion of time period as a higher level uniformity across situations since the relation, $\{\langle s_1, s_2 \rangle \mid \text{tim}s_1 = \text{tim}s_2\}$, of having the *same* time period is a binary situation type. This relation differs importantly from the property of having a particular time period τ since it is independent of any "point of view." If we are to attain the generality of Rosenschein's "world conditions" we must go beyond situation types, by re-introducing points of view.

Definition 20 A *situation condition* is a binary relation between situations. Let Σ be the set of situation conditions. We say that a situation s_1 *satisfies* situation condition $\sigma \in \Sigma$ *from the point of view of* s_0 iff $\langle s_1, s_0 \rangle \in \sigma$.

Pursuing the metaphor of a "point of view" we arrive at a translation of Rosenschein's "world conditions", Φ, into situation conditions. A world w satisfies world condition $\phi \in \Phi$ from the point of view of time period τ iff $\langle w, \tau \rangle \in \phi$. To make this correspondence more precise, we define a translation, $\dot{\phi} \in \Sigma$, of each $\phi \in \Phi$, viz.,

$$\dot{\phi} = \{\langle w^\wedge, s \rangle \mid \langle w, \text{tim}s \rangle \in \phi\}$$

The situation condition which we associate with an aggregate of dynamic locations α being in a temporal state d is given by $S_\alpha^{\text{tim}}(d) =$

$\{\langle s_1, s_2 \rangle \mid \delta_{(\alpha, \text{tim}s_2, s_1)} \in d\}$. This is the condition which is satisfied from the point of view of s_2 by those situations s_1 in which α is in state d *now*, i.e., over the time period of s_2. The contribution of the "point of view" situation is merely that of fixing the time period. This is directly analogous to $M_\alpha(d)$; in fact it is easily seen that $M_\alpha(d) \subseteq S_\alpha^{\text{tim}}(d)$ or, more precisely, that $M_\alpha(d) = \{\langle w^\wedge, s \rangle \mid \langle w^\wedge, s \rangle \in S_\alpha^{\text{tim}}(d)$ and $w \in W\}$.

The notion of a situation condition is more general than that of a world condition since, as well as the time, other aspects of the "point of view" situation may be relevant to the condition. For example we can express the condition, $S_\alpha^{\text{loc}}(d)$, which is satisfied from the point of view of s_2 by those situations s_1 in which α is in state d *here*, i.e., in the aggregate location occupied by s_2. Other examples of aspects of the "point-of-view" situation which may be called on include line of sight, relative speed, space occupied, and so forth.

Implication, or *involvement*, between two world conditions is given simply by set inclusion, but implication between situation conditions is slightly more involved. If one situation condition is contained in another then it will imply the later condition: i.e., from any given point of view, if a situation satisfies the first condition then it will also satisfy the second. But this notion of implication alone is too weak. It does not take into account the global notion of possibility implicit in the world system or anything that corresponds to it. Whereas world conditions are confined to applying to possible worlds ($\Phi = \text{pow } W \times T$) situation conditions apply indiscriminately to all situations, be they possible or impossible.

One way of rectifying this problem would be to restrict situation conditions to possible situations. But here we wish to consider an alternative to the global notion of possibility on which Rosenschein's account, and others like it, rely. We turn instead to the idea of an "information channel."

3   Information Channels

We introduce the notion of a *channel* to capture informational dependencies between situations. A channel is something which connects situations in a way which expresses their relative conditions of occurrence. Channels can be *active*, or not, possibly depending on the environment of the situations they connect. If an active channel links situation s to situation s' then if s occurs, i.e., if the location of s actually has the state distribution given by s, then s' also occurs.

For example, consider the simple communication system of Figure 3. The system consists of two devices: a "source" and a "receiver." Each device can be in one of six mutually exclusive states: $\{a, b, c, d, e, f\}$ and $\{1, 2, 3, 4, 5, 6\}$ respectively. Signals are transmitted from the source to the receiver, whose state is dependent on the information it receives. In particular, when the source is in state a it sends a signal to the receiver which

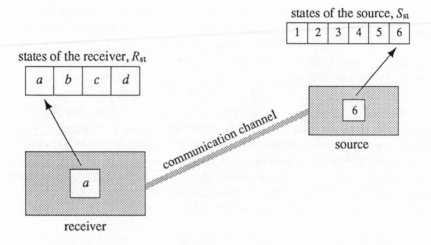

Figure 3 A two-device communication system.

reacts immediately by going into state 1. This dependence is captured using channels in the following way. We say that there is a channel which links the situation of the receiver's being in state 1 at a particular time, t, with the situation of the source's being in state a at the same time. If the receiver actually is in state 1 at time t then, as long as the channel is active, the source will be in state a at time t. The activity of the channel depends on many factors, such as the proper transmission of signals and the robustness of the receiving device.

One might think that the co-occurrence of *any* two situations can be "explained" by the existence of an active channel between them, but this is not so. We require that channels are only sensitive to genuine physical differences. If a channel links the situation s to the situation s' and s_1 is physically indistinguishable from s then s_1 must also be linked by the channel to a situation s'_1 which is indistinguishable from s'. Consequently, if s_1 is *not* linked to s'_1 then s cannot be linked to s' either.

In our example, this means that if in a new situation (at time t', say) the receiver is in a state physically indistinguishable from the state it was in at time t then this situation must be linked by the channel to a situation in which the source is in a state physically indistinguishable from the state *it* was in at time t. Moreover, the relation between this situation and the situation of the source at time t must be "parallel" to the relation between the situation of the receiver at times t' and t: in other words, the channel must link the situation of the receiver at time t' to the situation of the source *at time t'*.

Before we go any further a potential misconception should be dismissed. It is tempting to identify information channels with the physical objects which enable them to work: the wires and radar links of modern electronic communication systems. We avoid this identification because, amongst other reasons, it is in general very difficult to locate a physical object (a wire, say) which is solely responsible for the flow of information from one situation to another, and because, even when we can identify such an object, there are usually complex aspects of the environment which play a supporting role in ensuring that the "wire" performs as it should.

We model information channels as partial functions from situations to situations. The sense in which they respect the "parallel" indistinguishability criterion is made precise by our notion of a situation invariant. In our example, the situation invariant which connects the source's two situations, in virtue of which they are indistinguishable, must be the same as the invariant connecting the receiver's two situations. In this case, the situation invariant is induced by a simple translation from t to t' along the time line.

Definition 21 $c : Sit \rightharpoonup Sit$ is an *information channel* iff for all situations $s \in \text{dom } c$ and situation invariants $e : Sit \rightharpoonup Sit$, $es \in \text{dom } c$ and $ecs = ces$. In other words, channels commute with situation invariants. Let *Channels* be the collection of all channels in the world system.

We can use channels to describe the information which "flows" between situations on the basis of their classification into types. To do this we mimic Situation Theory's *constraints*. For a channel c and situation types t_1 and t_2 with $t_1 \subseteq \text{dom } c$ and $\text{ran } c \subseteq t_2$ we say that t_1 *involves* t_2 just in case c is active. From this we can derive the usual condition for constraint satisfaction used in Situation Theory: if s is a situation of type t_1 and t_1 involves t_2 then there is some other situation of type t_2. Moreover, with the dependency expressed as a channel we can be more precise, since the posited situation of type t_2 is determined by the channel to be the situation cs.

Note that for *any* two situations there is a channel which links them. In fact, if we have the Uniqueness Property for situation invariants, then there is a "minimal" channel linking any two situations, s_1 and s_2, namely the channel $c : [s_1] \rightarrow [s_2]$ defined for $s \in [s_1]$ by $cs = e_s s_2$ where e_s is the unique situation invariant mapping s_1 to s. This channel is minimal in the sense that its graph is contained in any other channel linking s_1 to s_2. The channel we appealed to in our discussion of the source/receiver system was an example of such a channel.

This abundance of channels may at first seem somewhat worrying, but all that should be concluded is that, potentially, there are dependencies between any two situations. Only when a channel is active will there be consequences of any substance. Clearly then, much of the work needed to make sense of an analysis of information flow in terms of channels will go in to saying what it is for a channel to be active.

As we have hinted, whether or not a channel works for a particular situation in its domain can, in general, depend on the environment in which that situation occurs. For example, the receiver's being in state 1 may be linked by a channel to the source's being in state a in virtue of a cable connecting the source to the receiver. Information only flows down the cable if certain conditions are met; the temperature must be within a reasonable range, the cable must not be fractured, there must be no strong external electromagnetic forces, etc. These are conditions which must be satisfied by the environment in which the situation of the receiver's being in state 1 occurs.

A first attempt at an analysis of channel activity may proceed by looking at the behavior of a channel in the *actual* world. We may require of active channels that they work ubiquitously in the actual world. For this to be the case the channel must map each actual situation in its domain to an actual situation. In other words, if $s \in \text{dom } c$ and $s \trianglelefteq w_0$ then $cs \trianglelefteq w_0$. For a general account channel activity, this is both too restrictive and too lax. It is too restrictive because it does not account for channels that work in some actual circumstances but not in others, and it is almost certain that any channel of interest will fail sometimes. It is too lax in that it counts a channel as active even if it links situations which only co-occur *by accident*: if every actual situation of a certain type is linked to an actual situation in a regular way (a "parallel" way) then the channel will be deemed to be active even if this correlation occurs "by chance."

Admittedly, for the kinds of channels we have been considering, this possibility is somewhat remote. If the cable between source and receiver was broken, but the state of the receiver continued to be correlated with the state of the source, then the cable is unlikely to have been responsible for the flow of information in the first place. This is further support for our wariness of identifying channels with physical objects.

There is another, potentially more worrying, reason why the account of channel activity is too lax. If d is a type of situation which does not occur in the actual world (i.e., there are no actual situations of type d) then *any* channel with domain d will be deemed active.

The traditional approach to these kind of problems (which arise in attempting to analyze law-like dependencies of any kind) is to appeal to a global notion of possibility. In this case, a putative solution would be to count as active those channels which only link situations s_1 and s_2 which co-occur in all possible worlds, i.e., for which $s_1^W \subseteq s_2^W$.

Definition 22 For world system $\mathbf{W}$, let Ch_W be the set of channels c such that for every $s \in \text{dom } c$, $s^W \subseteq cs^W$.

Taking Ch_W to be the active channels solves part of the problem of laxity. "Accidental" correlations cease to be active, as do channels from non-occurring types, but the latter problem re-emerges since all channels from *impossible* types will still be active. Also the account is still overly restrictive. Only channels which are genuinely ubiquitous are active.

Our approach to the problem is to reverse the direction of explanation. Instead of trying to explain the law-likeness of information flow along channels in terms of a global notion of possibility, we will reconstruct possibilities from the notion of an active channel. Instead of supposing that certain worlds are, as a matter of fact, possible whilst others are not, will will suppose that, in certain situations, certain channels are active whilst in other situations they are not.

To demonstrate the coherence of this proposal we will show how, given just the set *Sit* of situations, the set of situation invariants and taking the set of channels Ch_W to be ubiquitously active, we can recover all of the theory presented in the previous section. Moreover, the use of channels will enable us to state the relation of implication between situation conditions in a way that is conservative with respect to implication between world conditions.

The implications between situation conditions are dependent on which channels are active in the following way. Situation condition σ_1 implies situation condition σ_2 if, from every point of view, if s_1 satisfies σ_1 then there is an active channel linking s_1 to a situation s_2 satisfying σ_2 from the same point of view. To capture this dependence, we relativize implication between situation conditions to a set of channels. By doing this we mean to determine those implications that would exist between situation conditions on the assumption that the relativizing set of channels are all active.

Definition 23 Let $C \subseteq$ *Channels*. For $\sigma_1, \sigma_2 \in \Sigma$, we say that σ_1 C-implies σ_2 iff for all $s_0 \in Sit$, if $\langle s, s_0 \rangle \in \sigma_1$ then there is some $c \in C$ for which $\langle cs, s_0 \rangle \in \sigma_2$.

Now, supposing that the situations $S \subseteq Sit$ all occur and the set C of channels are ubiquitously active, we know at least that the situations cs, for each $s \in S \cap \operatorname{dom} c$ also occur. But do they occur in S? We say that S is C-closed if they all do. More precisely,

Definition 24 Given a collection S of situations and a channel c, we say that S is *closed* under c iff for all $s \in S \cap \operatorname{dom} c$, $cs \in S$. If $C \subseteq$ *Channels*, we say that S is C-*closed* just in case S is closed under each $c \in C$.

Proposition 5 *If s is C-closed and $s \approx s'$ then s' is C-closed.*

We extend the notion of C-closure to single situations. A situation is C-closed just in case the set of all its parts, $s_\lhd = \{s' \mid s' \unlhd s\}$, is C-closed. If a situation is C-closed then it is informationally isolated with respect to the channels C. We now show that the notion of 'possible world' can be recaptured as closure under Ch_W.

Proposition 6

1. *Every Ch_W-closed situation is possible.*

2. *Every possible world is Ch_W-closed.*

3. *A world is possible iff it is Ch_W-closed.*

Next we show that Ch_W-implication between situation channels is conservative with respect to implication between world conditions. We make use of the translation of world condition ϕ into situation condition $\dot{\phi}$ that was defined at the end of Section 2.

Proposition 7 *For world conditions ϕ_1 and ϕ_2, ϕ_1 implies ϕ_2 iff $\dot{\phi}_1$ Ch_W-implies $\dot{\phi}_2$.*

The above two propositions show that Rosenschein's model of information, which appeals to the notion of 'possible world' can be replaced by one which uses situations and information channels. Admittedly, the definition of Ch_W appeals to the set W of possible worlds, but Ch_W is just a set of channels. The question arises as to whether a set of possible worlds can be induced by an arbitrary set of channels. Motivated by Proposition 6, we define, for $C \subseteq Channels$,

$$Worlds(C) = \{w \mid w \text{ is a world and } w \text{ is } C\text{-closed}\}$$

Now for the set of channels, Ch_W, it is the case that $Ch_{Worlds(Ch_W)} = Ch_W$; i.e., the set of channels deemed active with respect to $Worlds(Ch_W)$ is just the set Ch_W. In other words, if, as a matter of fact, the channels, Ch_W, were the active ones then, taking $Worlds(C)$ to be our set of possible worlds, the possible world account of channel activity would be correct. In general, then, we can say that a possible worlds account of channel activity is forthcoming iff the set of all active channels, C, has the property $Ch_{Worlds(C)} = C$

For each $C \subseteq Channels$, let $C^o = Ch_{Worlds(C)}$. This defines a closure operator, i.e., $C \subseteq C^o$, $C^{oo} \subseteq C^o$ and $C_1 \subseteq C_2$ then $C_1^o \subseteq C_2^o$. Whether or not we can provide a possible worlds account of channel activity depends on whether or not the set of active channels, C, is closed with respect to this operator, i.e., $C^o = C$. We should examine some of the consequences of a set of channels being closed. The proofs of the following properties of closed sets of channels are omitted owing to their monotony and messiness. The importance is rather in the picture of closed sets of channels that emerges.

Proposition 8 *Let C be a closed set of channels, i.e., $C^o = C$.*

1. *For each $d \in Type$, the identity function on d is in C^o.*

2. *For situations $s, s' \in Sit$ such that $s' \trianglelefteq s$ the channel with domain $[s]$ taking es to es' for each situation invariant, e, is in C^o. (Assumes Uniqueness Property).*

3. *If $c, c' \in C$ and $\text{dom } c' \subseteq \text{ran } c$ then $c' \circ c \in C^o$.*

4. *If $c, c' \in C$ then the channel with domain $\text{dom } c \cap \text{dom } c'$ taking s to $cs \cup c's$ (which is defined) is in C^o.*

5. *If* $X \subseteq C$ *then the channel with domain* $\bigcap X$ *taking* s *to* $\bigcup_{c \in X} cs$ *(which is defined) is in* C^o.

For an arbitrary closed set C of channels, we can reconstruct the notion of a possibility as "C-coherence", which we now define.

Definition 25 Given a collection S of situations and a set of channels $C \subseteq Channels$, we say that S is C-coherent just in case there is a C-closed situation, $s \in Sit$ such that $S \subseteq s_{\lhd}$. A situation $s \in Sit$ is C-coherent iff $s_{\lhd}$ is.

Proposition 9 *If* $C = C^o$ *then a situation is* C-*coherent iff it is possible with respect to* $Worlds(C)$.

Finally, the notion of C-coherence enables us to define a negative implication, or "preclusion," between situation conditions.

Definition 26 Let $C \subseteq Channels$. For $\sigma_1, \sigma_2 \in \Sigma$, we say that σ_1 C-precludes σ_2 iff for all $s_0 \in Sit$, if $\langle s, s_0 \rangle \in \sigma_1$ and $\langle s, s_0 \rangle \in \sigma_2$ then s is not C-coherent.

In this section we have proposed that informational dependencies between situations should be modeled directly, by channels, rather than indirectly in terms of a set of possible worlds. Relative to a set C of channels, which we suppose to be ubiquitously active, we defined notions of C-closure, C-coherence, C-implication and C-preclusion. C-implication between situation conditions proved to be an appropriate generalization of implication between world conditions, whilst C-preclusion was new to this setting. We suggested that situations which are C-coherent can be regarded as "possible" and situations which are C-coherent can be regarded as "possible worlds." This correspondence with the terminology of Section 2 was shown to be exact when $C = Ch_W$ and, more generally, for any C such that $C^o = C$.

We can conclude, on the assumption of ubiquity, that if the set C of active channels is such that $C^o = C$ then it is amenable to analysis by the set $Worlds(C)$ of possible worlds. However, if $C^o \neq C$ then no such analysis is possible. In the next section we set out to question the assumption of ubiquity: can we analyze channel activity by supposing that there is a fixed set of active channels, or is it that channels are active on some occasions and not on others?

4 Channel Conditions and Conditional Channels

Suppose that we are concerned with a particular communication system, a telephone network, say, and that there is a set C of channels which are active in the network. These channels link situations in which sounds are produced by the receiver of a telephone, A, with situations in which sounds are made in the vicinity of the mouthpiece of another telephone; the telephone B to which A is connected by the network at that time.

What are the consequences of the channels C being active? For each channel $c \in C$ we can be sure that for all $w \in Worlds(C)$ and $s \in \mathrm{dom}\, c$, if $s \trianglelefteq w$ then $cs \trianglelefteq w$. In particular, if $w_0 \in Worlds(C)$ and s is actual then cs is actual. But, as we have been suggesting, this is too restrictive. For example, under normal circumstances, if I am speaking to you on the telephone and I hear nothing through my receiver then you are not saying anything; i.e., the silent situation in the vicinity of your telephone is actual. But if there is some technical problem with the telephone wires connecting us, then this may no longer be the case. There are certain conditions which must be satisfied for the channel to transmit information.

The set of worlds, $Worlds(C)$, contains those worlds in which the telephone network always works perfectly. For each of these worlds it must at least be the case that the telephone network *exists*. Worlds in which all telephones were fakes, or executive toys with no function, would be excluded from $Worlds(C)$. But these worlds are clearly not *impossible* in any physical sense, so that $Worlds(C) \neq W$.

More seriously, in all worlds in $Worlds(C)$ the telephone network must remain in working order for all time. This strongly suggests that the actual world is not in $Worlds(C)$. Consequently, if situations s_0 and s_1 are linked by an active channel c and s_0 is actual, we cannot decide whether or not s_1 is actual, since, in all probability, the actual world w_0 will not be closed under c.

The problem is that worlds are too big to capture the conditions under which information flows, so let us consider the set of C-closed *situations*, rather than just the set of C-closed worlds. We define,

$$Sits(C) = \{ s \mid s \in Sit \text{ and } s \text{ is } C\text{-closed } \}.$$

Now if $s \in Sits(C)$ occurs and $s' \trianglelefteq s$ then for appropriate $c \in C$, $cs' \trianglelefteq s$ and so cs' also occurs. In other words, inside a C-closed situation information is guaranteed to flow from cs to s. The advantage of considering $Sits(C)$ over $Worlds(C)$ is that there may be actual C-closed situations even though the actual world is not itself C-closed.

From an epistemological point of view we are no better off. If we know that s occurs then we can only be sure that cs occurs if we know that some $s' \in Sit(\{c\})$ occurs for which $s \trianglelefteq s'$. But if we knew that s' occurs then we would know that cs occurs anyway, since $cs \trianglelefteq s'$. Nevertheless, we need not be dismayed by this conclusion. As Dretske (1981) and others have argued at length, it is not necessary that we have such meta-knowledge about our environment. It need only be the case that a channel is working when we rely on it to gain knowledge. When we use a telephone, we are almost always ignorant of the state of the telephone network we rely on[6],

---

[6]In practice, we are not usually kept in ignorance for long if a telephone line breaks down. Apart from our knowledge of human behavior—you are unlikely to remain silent for *too* long—the telephone would probably make an unpleasant sound indicating to

but we still succeed in gaining information about what is said or unsaid at the other end of the line. The success of our acquisition of information depends not on the guarantee of certainty, but on our behavior. If we consistently confused real telephones with toy telephones, we would not gain information very effectively. But we don't, so we do.

Nevertheless, an account of the role of channels in supporting information flow would be incomplete without an analysis of the conditions under which channels work. The need for such an analysis is most acute in the explanation of implication between situation conditions. We have relativized implication to a set of channels C such that σ C-implies σ' just in case situations satisfying σ from some point of view are linked by channels in C to situation satisfying σ' from the same point of view. As above, the passage from σ satisfaction by an actual situation to σ' satisfaction is dependent on certain conditions. We capture this dependence in the following definition.

Definition 27 Let $C \subseteq$ *Channels* and $d \in$ *Type*. For situation conditions σ_1 and σ_2, we say that σ_1 C-implies σ_2 *given* d iff for all $s_0, s \in$ *Sit*, if $\langle s, s_0 \rangle \in \sigma_1$ and there is a $s' \in d$ such that $s \trianglelefteq s'$ then there is a $c \in C$ such that $\langle cs', s_0 \rangle \in \sigma_2$. d is called a *background* type.

The inclusion of a background type in statements of implication between situation conditions expresses at least some of the conditionality implicit in the channels on which the implication relies. Of course, we will only fully capture the background conditions in implications of the form σ_1 C-implies σ_2 given *Sits*(C). These implications are covered by our definition since

Proposition 10 *Sits*(C) *is a situation type.*

We now turn to a potentially more serious problems with the notion of an active channel. We have seen how the C-closure of a containing situation ensures the proper functioning of C channels, and this enables us to capture conditions under which a channel is active. But do these conditions adequately capture the conditionality of real informational dependencies? We will look at an example.

A channel makes an informational link between situations in a way that is dependent on their relative locations in time and space. If my telephone is connected to yours by the telephone network then, given that the network is working properly, situations in which the sound of a cough is emitted by my receiver are linked by an active channel to situations in which you cough (at more or less the same time). Moreover, if my receiver emits a second coughing sound later in our conversation, this new situation will be linked to another situation in which you cough (at the later time). In this case the relative locations of the cough sounds to the coughs remain constant: cough sounds are produced by my telephone and coughs are coughed at

---

me that something is wrong. But this is a fact which helps us recover from epistemic mistakes, not a precondition for the possibility of knowledge.

your telephone at the same time. The definition of a channel requires that this relationship be maintained.

However, it may be that the the informational connection between situations depends on more than their relative locations in time and space. For example, suppose we are speaking on the telephone. I am in my office and you are traveling down the M6. Your car telephone is therefore in motion relative to my office phone. Suppose I hear a cough in my receiver at 1.00pm whilst you are traveling past Carlisle. The situation of my receiver emitting the coughing sound is presumably linked by a channel to the situation of your coughing in your car at more or less the same time. Moreover, we would suspect that this channel is active: there is a genuine connection between the two situations.

Yet there is a problem with the way we have defined channels so far. If the situation in my office, s_0, is to be linked by c to the situation s_1 in your car, then it must be the case that every situation which is physically indistinguishable from s_0 is linked by c to a situation "parallel" to and indistinguishable from s_1. But consider the situation invariant e which maps situations three hours forward in time. If you cough whilst passing Manchester at 4 P.M., three hours after coughing in Carlisle, then I will hear a coughing sound in my receiver at more or less the same time. So the situation es_0 occurs. But c is required to link the situation es_0 at my receiver to the situation es_1. This is quite wrong since es_1 is the situation of your coughing in *Carlisle* and neither you nor your car phone are within a hundred miles of Carlisle at 4 P.M.

The problem resides in the fact that the relative locations of situations linked by a channel may not be the factor which determines *where* information flows. In the above example, it should be the relative locations of our *telephones* which determine which situations are linked. The situation that s_0 is linked to should be dependent on where your telephone *is*.

Our solution is to specify the location of an informational source (the situation at your telephone) relative to the background situation in which the information flow occurs (the situation of the telephone network). Indirect informational connections of this kind are captured by "conditional channels":

Definition 28 A *conditional channel* is a partial function c : $Sit \times Sit \to Sit$ such that for each situation invariant e and $\langle s_1, s_2 \rangle \in \text{dom } c$, $c(es_1, es_2) = ec(s_1, s_2)$. Let *CChannels* be the set of conditional channels.

The informational connection between my office phone and your car phone is expressed by a conditional channel, c, which maps pairs $\langle s_1, s_2 \rangle$, where s_1 is the situation at my telephone and s_2 is the network situation (which specifies the location of your telephone), to the situation $c(s_1, s_2)$ at your telephone.

Note that in a particular "environment" s, a conditional channel c determines an unconditional channel c' with domain $\{s' \mid \langle s', s \rangle \in \text{dom } c\}$ and such that for each $s' \in \text{dom } c'$, $c'(s') = c(s, s')$. Also, the set of unconditional channels are naturally embedded in the set of conditional channels by allowing the second (environment) argument to range freely over Sit. It is now easy to extend the definition of C-implication and C-closure to conditional channels by quantifying over the second argument:

Definition 29 Let $C \subseteq CChannels$. For $\sigma_1, \sigma_2 \in \Sigma$, we say that σ_1 C-*implies* σ_2 iff for all $s_0, s_1 \in Sit$, if $\langle s_1, s_0 \rangle \in \sigma_1$ then there is some $c \in C$ for which $\langle c(s_1, s), s_0 \rangle \in \sigma_2$ for all $s \in Sit$.

Definition 30 Given a collection S of situations and a conditional channel c, we say that S is closed under c iff for all $s \in S$ and $s' \in Sit$, if $\langle s, s' \rangle \in \text{dom } c$ then $c(s, s') \in S$. We extend the definition to C-*closure*, C-*coherence* and C-*preclusion* for a set C of conditional channels in exactly the same way as we did in the unconditional case.

Note that the conditionality of conditional channels is very different from the conditionality of conditional *constraints*. All channels are dependent on implicit "channel conditions" for their activity. So all channels induce conditional, rather than unconditional constraints. Conditional channels, even when active, depend on a "background" situation to determine which situations they link.

5 Perspectives on the World

As an application of the theory developed in the last two sections, we will show how to model perspectives in a world of situations and channels. A perspective[7] is a part of reality seen from some point of view. Within the current model, a part of reality is a (physical) situation, s. Given a point of view, s_0 (another situation), and a situation condition, σ, we can say which parts of s satisfy σ from the point of view of s_0; i.e., those situations $s_1 \trianglelefteq s$ such that $\langle s_1, s_0 \rangle \in \sigma$. This provides the basis for a classification of the parts of s by the conditions they satisfy from the point of view of s_0.

For example, take my office to be the situation, s; the part of reality being classified. The white-board on the wall defines a situation, s', consisting of the locations it occupies (over time) and their physical state. The white-board situation, s', is a part of my office situation, s. Now s' has certain geometrical properties. It has a well defined shape which is constant over time. We might say that its *internal* shape is square, meaning that in its primary plane (which in this case can be thought of as the wall) the locations it occupies at any time fill a square region of that plane.

We wish to model the (visual) perspective of my office from my (visual) point of view. My visual point of view, we will suppose, is given by the

---

[7]See Seligman 1990a. The technical definition of a perspective will be repeated at the end of this section.

situation of my eye[8], s_0, which is also a part of s. My eye, s_0, has various internal properties, one of which is the inclination of the plane of my retina[9]. That is, s_0, is related by a certain relation, d, to a situation s_0^p; its retinal plane. The relation, d, need not be restricted to eyes: an appropriately shape region of empty space can determine a plane in a similar fashion. However, d *is* a binary situation type since physically indistinguishable eyes will have physically indistinguishable retinal planes.

One condition that the white-board satisfies from my point of view is that its edges look parallel. We can make this more precise. We say that situations s' and s'' satisfy the condition σ_p iff s' has a well defined polygonal internal shape and opposite edges of the geometric projection of s' onto the retinal plane of s'' (the unique s''' such that $\langle s'', s''' \rangle \in d$) are parallel. In the current example, the white-board, s', does indeed satisfy σ_p from my point-of-view situation s_0. Strictly, we should refine the definition of σ_p further to account for changes in the position of either my eye or the white-board, but for the moment we will ignore the temporal dimension supposing s' to be a temporal slice of the white-board.

Following this approach, we could arrive at a classification of parts of my office according as to whether or not they satisfy σ_p from my point of view. Some parts of the room will fail to satisfy this condition because they fail to have a well defined polygonal internal shape. Others will fail because they have opposite edges which are not parallel, or because their primary plane is not parallel to the retinal plane of my eye. As I move around the room, the relative inclination of my retinal plane to the primary planes of various parts of the room will change and so the σ_p classification of them will also change. This is the phenomenon of visual perspective.

However, there is something missing from the story so far. If we extended s to include the whole building, rather than just my office, there will be white-boards in other offices which satisfy σ_p from my point of view even though I cannot see them. Extending s even further, across the globe, there will be white-boards in California which still possess the right geometric properties to satisfy, σ_p. We are failing to capture the important constraint which, in visual terms, amounts to the existence of a field of view. My visual perspective on the world around me is not only relative to my position in the world, but it is also constrained by what I can see.

A visual perspective exists because of light. That the geometric projection of the white-board onto my retina has a certain shape is a physical fact. It is the reflected light from surfaces in my office which carry information about their geometric properties. In the terms of the theory we have been developing, there are active information channels linking the situation in

---

[8] We will ignore the problems of binocular vision.

[9] Although my retina is in fact curved, we can take its plane to be defined in a suitable way, so that the line from the center of my pupil to the mid-point of my retina is orthogonal to it.

my eye to other parts of the room. But there are no such channels linking my eye to parts of other rooms in the building, or to offices in California. My field of view is defined by the range of a certain set of (visual) information channels.

To model this dependence on information channels, we suppose that there is some set C of (conditional) channels active in s. These are the channel concerned with the informational dependencies enabled by reflected light in the room. It is not that there are no other active channels between situations in the room, but the set of channels C are those which give rise to visual perspectives. Other channels would define other kinds of perspective.

Although we will not demand that $C^o = C$, we will need to ensure that C is at least closed under "iterated composition," i.e., for $c, c' \in C$, the channel $c; c'$ with domain

$$\{\langle s', s \rangle \mid \langle s', s \rangle \in \text{dom } c \text{ and } \langle c(s', s), s' \rangle \in \text{dom } c'\}$$

and mapping each $\langle s', s \rangle \in \text{dom } c; c'$ to $c'(c(s', s), s)$ is also in C.

Now, for a situation, $s_1 \trianglelefteq s$, to be classified at all, s_1 must be "visible" from the point of view of s_0, so there must be a (conditional) channel in C which links s_0 to s_1 in s.

Definition 31 For $s_1 \trianglelefteq s$, we say that the channel $c_1 \in C$ *locates* s_1 from s_0 in s iff $\langle s_0, s \rangle \in \text{dom } c_1$ and $c_1(s_0, s) = s_1$.

In the visual case we have been discussing, there would seem to be no need for a channel to locate the situation of the white-board since it is in a fixed location in the room. But in the general case, when either surfaces in the room are moving, or I am moving, we need a channel to locate the part of the world about which my eye is obtaining information. This can be seen in the example of my telephoning you whilst you are traveling down the M6. The channel must fix your location if the information I gain is to apply to you (or rather to your telephone).

To classify s_1 by some situation condition, σ, we also require that the channel c_1 which locates s_1 from s_0 in s is a channel along which information about σ satisfaction flows. That is, if the room outside s_0 was different from the way it is, say s', then, supposing c_1 to be active, the situation located by c_1 from s_0 in s' would still satisfy σ from the point of view of s_0.

Definition 32 For situation condition σ, we say that the (conditional) channel $c \in C$ *carries* σ to s_0 iff for all $s' \in Sit$, if $\langle s_0, s' \rangle \in \text{dom } c$ then $\langle c(s_0, s'), s_0 \rangle \in \sigma$.

Put more simply, this definition says that c carries σ to s_0 just in case whatever is at the "end" of c satisfies σ from the point of view of s_0.

Now we can use situation conditions carried by channels in C to classify situations located by channels in C. A perspective structure is added by considering the informational dependencies between the situation conditions, given by C-implication and C-preclusion.

Definition 33 Given a set C of (conditional) channels which is closed under iterated composition, a set Σ of situation conditions and C-coherent situations s and s_0, we define the structure $Persp(C, \Sigma, s, s_0) = \langle s_{\trianglelefteq}, \Sigma, :, \Rightarrow, \perp \rangle$ (where $s_{\trianglelefteq}$ is the set parts of s) by

1. $s_1 : \sigma$ iff there is a $c_1 \in C$ which locates s_1 from s_0 in s and which carries σ to s_0.
2. $\sigma \Rightarrow \sigma'$ iff σ C-implies σ'
3. $\sigma \perp \sigma'$ iff σ C-precludes σ'

Proposition 11 $Persp(C, \Sigma, s, s_0)$ *is a perspective in the sense of Seligman 1990a, i.e., it has the following properties:*

1. Facticity. *For all $s_1 \trianglelefteq s$ and $\sigma, \sigma' \in \Sigma$, if $s_1 : \sigma$ and $\sigma \Rightarrow \sigma'$ then there is some $s_2 \trianglelefteq s$ such that $s_2 : \sigma'$.*
2. Xerox. $\Rightarrow$ *is transitive.*
3. Local Preclusion. *For all $s_1 \trianglelefteq s$ and $\sigma, \sigma' \in \Sigma$, if $s_1 : \sigma$ and $\sigma \perp \sigma'$ then $s_1 \not\vdash \sigma'$.*
4. Mutual Preclusion. $\perp$ *is symmetric*

Conclusion

In this paper we have drawn certain connections between Situation Theory and the model of information used by Rosenschein in specifying and designing robots. We proposed answers to the two questions: how is information located in the physical world and how can information in one place be linked to information in another place?

On Rosenschein's account the information that ϕ is modeled as the condition the world must satisfy (at a time) in order for ϕ to be true. Technically this is captured by a *world condition*. The first question is answered by defining the information content $M_a(d)$ of a location a's being in state d in a natural way. The information ϕ is located at a just in case a is in state d and $M_a(d) \subseteq \phi$. Implication between ϕ_1 and ϕ_2 is given straightforwardly by the subset relation. This enables one to give a simple answer to the second question.

On the present account, certain modifications and generalizations have been made. Firstly, the sense in which information can be located was extended to *aggregates* of locations, *dynamic* locations, and *temporal* behavior. Rosenschein's suggestion of modeling distributed information by indexed sets (or tuples) of locations was abandoned in favor of *distribution functions* under various notions of equivalence based on spatial and temporal *invariants*.

The answer to our first question was given by combining these into the definition of a *situation*. On our account, a situation just is the sort of thing in which information can be said to be located. Situations were ordered by the *part-of* relation $\trianglelefteq$ and classified into *types* in a way commensurate with the underlying notion of physical indistinguishability. Given this ordering, the usual definitions of *possible* and *actual* situation and of a *world* were forthcoming.

Next, world conditions were generalized to *situation conditions* to suit the new setting. Rosenschein's definition of implication between world conditions was seen not to generalize in a straightforward way to implication between situation conditions. To fill the gap, the idea of an *information channel* (from Communication Theory) was introduced. The set W of possible worlds was used to define a collection Ch_W of *active* channels relative to which a sensible definition of Ch_W-*implication* between situation conditions could be given. Ch_W-implication between situation conditions was seen to be conservative with respect to implication between world conditions.

We then moved on to question whether channel activity could really be determined by the set of possible worlds. Arguing that it could not, we relativized implication and the notions of "possible situation" and "world" to *C-implication*, *C-coherence* and *C-closure* for an arbitrary set C of channels. The necessary theoretical apparatus can thus be obtained by supposing channel activity to be a unanalyzed theoretical primitive and dispensing with the notion of a possible world. Moreover, an analysis of channel activity by possible worlds was seen to be unavailable in the general case.

Nevertheless, some attempt was made to analyze the conditions under which a channel becomes active. An approach reminiscent of Situation Theory's *background types*, was deemed unsatisfactory and we fell back on the trick of including the activity conditions of a channel in the channel itself. This lead us to the definition of a *conditional channel*.

Finally, we gave a model of information flow within a situation, "seen" from a point-of-view situation and classified by situation conditions with respect to a collection of (conditional) channels. This model was shown to be a *perspective* in the technical sense of Seligman 1990a. This construction shows how perspectives can be introduced into a perspectiveless world. Starting from a Rosenschein world system with active channels Ch_W and world conditions $\Phi = \text{pow } W \times T$, we can build perspectives $Persp(Ch_W, \Phi, s, s')$ for each pair of actual situations s, s'. This collection of perspectives on actual situations can be seen as a metaphysical alternative to the collection of possible worlds W in Rosenschein's model.

Nevertheless we have not fully established the feasibility of this alternative. A collection of perspectives generated from a world system is in some sense consistent in virtue of being so generated, but this cannot be said of arbitrary collections of perspectives. Seligman 1990a showed how a collection of perspectives on an ordered set of situations (a *perspectival domain*) can give rise to notions of object and property as uniformities within perspectives and across perspective "shifts." Although providing a definition of predication in some simple cases, the account lacked a notion of consistency between perspectives to make sense of predication in general. Now we have a characterization of a class of perspectival domains which can be said to be internally consistent: those generated from Rosenschein's world systems and, more generally, those generated from (almost) arbitrary collections C and Σ, of (conditional) channels and situation conditions respectively. Much remains to be done in clarifying this connection. In particular, a place has to be found for objects and properties in the bodiless world of states and space-time.

References

Barwise, J. 1989. *The Situation in Logic*. CSLI Lecture Notes Number 17. Stanford: CSLI Publications.

Barwise, J., and J. Perry. 1983. *Situations and Attitudes*. Cambridge, MA: MIT Press.

Cooper, R., K. Mukai, and J. Perry (ed.). 1990. *Situation Theory and Its Applications,* vol. 1. CSLI Lecture Notes Number 22. Stanford: CSLI Publications.

Dretske, F. I. 1981. *Knowledge and the Flow of Information*. Cambridge, MA: MIT Press.

Rosenschein, S. 1987. Formal Theories of Knowledge in AI Robotics. Technical Report Number CSLI-87-84, CSLI, Stanford.

Rosenschein, S. 1989. Synthesizing Information-Tracking Automata From Environment Descriptions. Typescript, Teleos Research, Palo Alto.

Seligman, J. 1990a. *Perspectives: A Relativistic Approach to the Theory of Information*. PhD thesis, Centre for Cognitive Studies, Edinburgh.

Seligman, J. 1990b. Perspectives in Situation Theory. In Cooper et al. 1990.

Part III

Linguistic Applications

13

Persistence and Structural Determination

RICHARD P. COOPER

1 Introduction

The issue of infon persistence is one that has been widely discussed informally within the situation theoretic community. These discussions have, in general, raised many more issues than they have resolved, and consequently infon persistence remains a contentious issue—so contentious, in fact, that little has been committed to LaTeX. One of the few exceptions to this is Barwise's notes on branch points in situation theory (Barwise 1989b). His paper, which impartially states the space of possibilities for situation theories, illustrates the importance of the infon persistence question—six of Barwise's 19 branch points relate to infon persistence as discussed in this paper.

This paper attempts to bring infon persistence back into focus as a real and important issue by providing possible resolutions to some of the questions raised. The central issue of this paper—under what circumstances should an infon be persistent—is answered by making use of the full machinery offered by situation theoretic propositions. A version of situation theory is argued for in which all infons are taken to be persistent, and in which non-persistent phenomena are accounted for in terms of propositions. It is claimed that the key to the issue is what we call *structural determination*, which arises from dependencies between infons or propositions. The theory, which may be viewed as a branch on the tree of situation

This paper owes much to the comments and criticisms of Nick Braisby, Robin Cooper, Jerry Seligman, all other members of the STaGr Workshop in Edinburgh, Jon Barwise, Keith Devlin, Mark Gawron, David Israel, Stanley Peters, and all other participants of the 1990 Conference on Situation Theory and Its Applications, as well as two anonymous referees. This is not to say that any of the above agree with the position presented here. The research was carried out at the Centre for Cognitive Science, Edinburgh, and was supported by the Commonwealth Scholarship and Fellowship Plan, Award #AU0027.

Situation Theory and Its Applications, vol. 2.
Jon Barwise, Jean Mark Gawron, Gordon Plotkin, and Syun Tutiya, eds.
Copyright © 1991, Stanford University.

theories discussed by Barwise (1989b), yields a precise division between the persistent and the non-persistent, and allows the part-of ordering (which corresponds to a type rather than a relation) that holds between situations to be defined in purely extensional terms.

In arguing for this theory we take the situation semantic treatment of natural language quantification as providing an extended example. The reason for this is that there is at least a pre-theoretic sense in which it may be argued that natural language statements involving quantification should correspond to non-persistent infons: if every kitten is meowing in one situation then there is no guarantee that every kitten must be meowing in every larger situation. Natural language quantification also involves structural determination: if every kitten is meowing in some situation then each kitten must be meowing individually in that situation. Given the claim that structural determination is the key to the issue, the situation semantic treatment of natural language quantification is therefore a prime candidate for motivating the choices made in our arguments regarding persistence.

The paper begins with a presentation of some necessary background, essentially providing precise definitions for the terminology which we employ. In section 3, numerous approaches to natural language quantification are presented, and their persistence properties discussed. These approaches are reformulated in section 4 in terms of propositions, where the central thesis of the paper, that structurally determined "relations" should in fact be recast as types, is presented. Section 5 extends the discussion of structural determination by giving examples relating to areas other than natural language quantification. Finally, in section 6 the argument and its repercussions are summarized.

2   Background

2.1   Terminology

Of central importance to this paper is the distinction between the situation dependent, or the relative, and the situation independent, or the absolute. It is thus necessary to be absolutely clear about the precise variety of situation theory assumed, and the terminology employed, by this paper. Essentially this originates from Barwise's unpublished notes on a model of situation theory (Barwise 1987).

An *infon* is an object which is appropriate to stand in the supports relation with a situation. That is, an infon is something which may, or may not, hold in a situation. In this sense, an infon is situation dependent: whether or not it holds cannot be determined in isolation—it is dependent on a situation. A basic infon consists of an issue together with a polarity (either '+' or '−'). An issue in turn consists of a relation and an assignment of appropriate arguments to the argument roles of that relation. The dual of a basic infon is that infon consisting of the same issue resolved with the opposite polarity. Other, complex, infons will be considered below. The situation independent analogue of an infon is a *proposition*. A proposition consists of a type (the situation independent analogue of a relation) together with an assignment of appropriate arguments to the argument roles of the type.

One very important and familiar type is the binary type *supports*, written '$\models$'. Appropriate arguments for this type are a situation S and an infon σ. If the situation supports the infon then the proposition $(S \models \sigma)$ is true, otherwise it is false: propositions, unlike infons, are true or false—they are absolute. This has lead to the use of words such as "logical" to describe the domain of propositions and types. In contrast, the domain of infons and relations is often referred to as "informational", where information is taken to be inherently situation dependent.

In the interests of uniformity, propositions may be formally notated as:

$$(a : T)$$

where a is an appropriate assignment to the type T. Such propositions may be read as "the assignment a is of type T". For the most part, we adhere to the more common representation for propositions based on the supports type. That is, we write $(S \models \sigma)$ rather than $(a : \models)$ where a assigns σ to the infon argument role of $\models$ and S to the situation argument role of $\models$. Furthermore, when it is obvious which objects are being assigned to which roles, we shall often write the results of the assignment in place of the assignment itself.

There are many parallels between the logical and informational domains. In particular, parametric assignments to relations and types result in parametric infons and parametric propositions respectively. The parameters in these parametric objects may in each case be abstracted over, forming complex relations and complex types respectively.

2.2 Two Ways to Characterize a Situation

In allowing complex types we allow two ways of characterizing a situation. For every infon σ, there are corresponding parametric propositions, proposition of the form $\dot{s} \models \sigma$, where $\dot{s}$ is a parameter. Abstraction over this parameter yields the "situation type" $[\dot{s} | \dot{s} \models \sigma]$. A situation is appropriate for the sole argument role of this type, and a situation S is of this type just in case S supports the infon σ. Consequently, for every infon there is a corresponding type: the type of situation which supports that infon. There is nothing to suggest that the reverse should be true: there may be situation types which are not "infon based" in the above sense. Indeed, our theory requires such types.

Given any characterization of a situation in terms of the infons which it supports, there is therefore an equivalent characterization in terms of the types it is an instance of. If we then assume that a situation can be completely characterized by the infons which it supports (i.e., we assume that two situations are identical if and only if they support exactly the same infons), then any situation can be characterized in two equivalent, but entirely different, ways. Informally, the characterization in terms of infons might be seen as an *internal* characterization, being based on the internal make up, or internal properties, of the situation. The characterization in terms of types might be seen as an *external* characterization, being based on external properties of the situation. In a pre-theoretic sense, for every internal property ϕ, there is a corresponding external property, the property of having ϕ as an internal property. There may, of course, be other external properties not directly corresponding to any internal properties.

2.3 Persistence

We assume that the domain of situations comes with a partial ordering, $\trianglelefteq$, corresponding to the part-of type which may hold between situations. $S_1 \trianglelefteq S_2$ if and only if S_1 is a part of S_2. Persistence is a property of infons that derives from this ordering. An infon σ is persistent if and only if for every situation S, if $S \models \sigma$ then all situations S' of which S is a part also support σ. Persistence is meant to capture the notion that if a piece of information is supported by some situation, then it is supported by all larger situations—no amount of further information can deny the original information.

For this paper it is useful to extend the formal definition of persistence from infons to unary types whose sole argument role may be appropriately filled by a situation (i.e., "situation types"). We say that such a type T is persistent if and only if whenever a situation S is of type T, all situations S' of which S is a part are also of type T. Infon persistence as generally known is just a special case of this property when the type is an infon based situation type as described in the preceding section. The utility of this extension will become apparent when non-infon based situation types are introduced.

Infon persistence is generally regarded as being a desirable property. However, many varieties of situation theory must sacrifice infon persistence to maintain coherence. In particular, some varieties entertain non-basic infons—infons not composed of an issue and a polarity—such as quantified infons. Barwise (1989a), for example, allows quantified infons of the form $\forall \dot{x}^{\tau(\dot{x})} \sigma(\dot{x})$ and $\exists \dot{x}^{\tau(\dot{x})} \sigma(\dot{x})$, where $\tau(\dot{x})$ and $\sigma(\dot{x})$ are other infons dependent on the parameter $\dot{x}$, which is bound by the quantifier. Given such infons, it would seem that universally quantified infons need not be persistent (and similarly for the duals of existentially quantified infons, if duals of such infons are also entertained). This has lead Barwise to suggest, as a branch point of situation theory, that persistence should only apply to basic infons (Barwise 1989a).

Persistence is clearly intimately related to the $\trianglelefteq$ type that holds be-

tween situations. This type is normally taken to be a primitive type between situations. It is tempting to give an extensional definition in terms
of infon support: $S_1 \trianglelefteq S_2$ if and only if $\{\sigma | S_1 \models \sigma\} \subseteq \{\sigma | S_2 \models \sigma\}$. Such a
definition clearly leads to the consequence that all infons are persistent, and
so on most accounts is unsuitable. Note though that if we adopt Barwise's
branch point—that all basic infons are persistent—then this definition may
be salvaged by restricting attention to just those infons which are basic.

2.4 Structural Determination

One last area of central concern to this paper involves the notion of "structural determination". Precisely what we mean by this depends on whether
we are applying the term to an infon or a proposition, and our usage differs
from that of Barwise in his earlier writings.

We say that an infon is structurally determined if whether it holds in
a situation depends on other infons holding in that situation. That is, an
infon is structurally determined if and only if its support by a situation
is determined by the internal structure of (i.e., the other infons supported
by) that situation. Varieties of situation theory which admit compound
infons, infons consisting of a connective such as $\vee$ or $\wedge$ together with a
set of further infons, illustrate one variety of structurally determined infon:
a situation S supports the compound infon $\bigvee \Sigma$ if and only if it supports
some $\sigma \in \Sigma$. With respect to propositions the meaning is similar—the
term applies when the truth of one proposition is dependent on the truth
or falsity of other propositions.

3 Persistence and Approaches to Quantification

Under what conditions can an English sentence such as 'most kittens are
meowing' be said to accurately describe a situation? Furthermore, if a situation satisfies these conditions, will all situations of which that situation is a
part also satisfy the conditions? The answer to the second question, which
might be rephrased as "are those conditions persistent", depends crucially
on just what the conditions are, and on the part-of ordering between situations. In this section we consider several possible options for structurally
determined conditions on quantification along with their consequences for
infon persistence.

3.1 Two Caveats

A sentence such as 'most kittens meow' might be taken to describe a situation involving many kittens in which most of those kittens are meowing, or
it may be taken as a statement of a constraint holding more generally: it is
generally the case that most kittens are such that they meow. It is the first
of these readings which we are interested in here, and not the constraint
reading which states a generic property of kittens. In an attempt to avoid
any confusion between the readings we use the present progressive tense

in all examples, rather than the simple present: the constraint reading is less apparent in this tense (cf. 'most kittens meow' and 'most kittens are meowing').

The preferential interest in the first reading stems from the fact that this reading is clearly structurally determined. If 'most kittens are meowing' describes a situation, then it is because in that situation, when the kittens are considered individually, the ratio between those meowing and the total set is sufficient to justify the use of the determiner 'most'. The constraint reading, on the other hand, is not structurally determined—while we may wish to say that 'all unicorns have a single horn', it is not because there are no unicorns which do not have a single horn, rather having such a horn is a constraint on unicornhood.

Given that we are dealing with the reading where a quantified statement describes a situation, we must address the question of what the relationship is between the individuals in the situation and the properties ascribed to them by the quantified statement. Should the relationship be a conditional of the form "if some condition relating to individual kittens holds of a situation then the situation can be described by 'most kittens are meowing'", or a conditional of the form "if a situation can be described by 'most kittens are meowing' then some condition relating to individual kittens holds of the situation" or a bi-conditional: "a situation can be described by 'most kittens are meowing' if and only if some condition relating to individual kittens holds of the situation"? We assume a bi-conditional relation, though some comments on this issue are made below.

3.2   Determiners as Relations Between Properties

Following Cooper (1987), the treatment of determiners as generalized quantifiers (Barwise and Cooper (1981) within set-theoretic semantic formalisms may be translated into situation semantics by treating determiners as binary relations between properties. Under such an analysis, a sentence such as 'most kittens are meowing' describes a situation S_d such that:

$$S_d \models \langle\langle \text{most}, [\dot{x} \mid \langle\langle \text{kitten}, \dot{x}; + \rangle\rangle], [\dot{x} \mid \langle\langle \text{meowing}, \dot{x}; + \rangle\rangle]; + \rangle\rangle$$

where

$$S \models \langle\langle det, P, Q; + \rangle\rangle$$

iff

$$det'(\{a \mid S \models \langle\langle P, a; + \rangle\rangle\}, \{a \mid S \models \langle\langle Q, a; + \rangle\rangle\})$$

Here (and throughout this paper) det' denotes the extensional set theoretic generalized quantifier relation that corresponds to the situation theoretic relation det.

In Cooper (1987), a bi-conditional relationship between infons relating to quantificational statements and extensional set theoretic relations is not required. While Cooper requires that if a situation supports an infon of the form $\langle\langle det, P, Q; + \rangle\rangle$ then it also supports facts about individuals with the properties P and Q which justify the quantification, he does not require the reverse. Requiring the reverse effectively puts closure conditions on situations: the set of infons supported by a situation must be closed under all quantifier relations. Some justification for these closure conditions may be taken from similar closure conditions relating to compound infons suggested by Barwise (Barwise 1989a, 1989b). We return to this issue of closure conditions in section 4, where we treat structural determination in terms of situation types, rather than infons.

Cooper's treatment of quantification in terms of a relation between properties leads to a non-persistent infon. In one situation, it may be the case that most of the objects having the property of kittenhood also have the property of meowing, but there is no guarantee that in a larger situation there may be further kittens not meowing. Alternately a larger situation may resolve some of the issues regarding meowing kittens which were unresolved in the original situation, and thereby prevent the quantificational infon from holding.

3.3 Determiners as Relations Between Types

A further problem with treating quantifiers as relations between properties is that it does not correctly account for the exploitation of resource situations. In particular, with referential uses of noun phrases (we shall not be concerned with attributive uses), the restriction property is understood to be relative to a resource situation, while the scope property is relative to the described situation. We might thus propose that determiners should be treated as relations between object types, so that 'most kittens are meowing' describes a situation S_d such that:

$$S_d \models \langle\!\langle \text{most}, T_k, T_m; + \rangle\!\rangle \quad \text{for } T_k = [\dot{x} \mid S_r \models \langle\!\langle \text{kitten}, \dot{x}; + \rangle\!\rangle]$$
$$T_m = [\dot{x} \mid S_d \models \langle\!\langle \text{meowing}, \dot{x}; + \rangle\!\rangle]$$

where S_r is the resource situation exploited by the noun phrase and

$$S \models \langle\!\langle det, T_1, T_2; + \rangle\!\rangle$$

iff

$$det'(\{a \mid a : T_1\}, \{a \mid a : T_2\})$$

This approach is slightly worrying because, by building in the resource situation and described situation, the resulting infon losses the "situation relative" nature of infons. Under this definition, if any situation supports $\langle\!\langle det, T_1, T_2; + \rangle\!\rangle$, then every situation supports it. Note that of course this is a consequence of the bi-conditional in the structurally determined definition. It should also be noted that, because of the situation independence of the resulting infon, it is trivially persistent: if it is supported by one situation, it is supported by all situations, including those larger situations.

One way around the situation independence problem is to incorporate the requirement that we are only quantifying over objects of the situation in question. Thus we might have:

$$S \models \langle\!\langle det, \ T_1, \ T_2; \ +\rangle\!\rangle$$

iff

$$det'(\{a \mid a : T_1 \ \wedge \ a \in Obj(S)\}, \ \{a \mid a : T_2 \ \wedge \ a \in Obj(S)\})$$

This alteration leads to a non-persistent infon. A larger situation may involve further objects which may prevent the quantificational infon holding in that larger situation.

3.4 Determiners as Relations Between a Type and a Property

An alternate solution to the problem of situation independence above is to treat determiners as relations between an object type and a property. With this treatment, 'most kittens are meowing' describes a situation S_d such that:

$$S_d \models \langle\!\langle \text{most}, [\dot{x} \mid S_r \models \langle\!\langle \text{kitten}, \dot{x}; \ +\rangle\!\rangle], [\dot{x} \mid \langle\!\langle \text{meowing}, \dot{x}; \ +\rangle\!\rangle]; \ +\rangle\!\rangle$$

where again S_r is the resource situation exploited by the noun phrase. This is essentially the approach adopted by Gawron and Peters (1990a).

One possible definition of when a situation supports such an infon is:

$$S \models \langle\!\langle det, \ T, \ Q; \ +\rangle\!\rangle$$

iff

$$det'(\{a \mid a : T\}, \ \{a \mid S \models \langle\!\langle Q, \ a; \ +\rangle\!\rangle\})$$

Such an infon need not be persistent. Although the set of objects under consideration is fixed by the restriction type, in the case of monotone decreasing determiners, such as *no*, a larger situation may reveal further information about those objects preventing the quantificational infon from being persistent. That is, while 'no kittens are meowing' may describe some situation S, it need not describe some larger situation S'.

Persistence may be guaranteed by requiring complete information about those objects which the quantification concerns. That is, we might define the conditions under which quantificational infons hold as:

$$S \models \langle\!\langle det, \ T, \ Q; \ +\rangle\!\rangle$$

iff for all a such that $(a : T)$, either $S \models \langle\!\langle Q, \ a; \ +\rangle\!\rangle$ or $S \models \langle\!\langle Q, \ a; \ -\rangle\!\rangle$, and furthermore

$$det'(\{a \mid a : T\}, \ \{a \mid S \models \langle\!\langle Q, \ a; \ +\rangle\!\rangle\})$$

This does lead to a persistent infon (provided that Q is a persistent property). The objects under consideration are determined by the type contributed by the restriction. This set is thus fixed, and the requirement that everything relevant be known about those objects means that taking a larger situation cannot reveal anything more about those objects. Note though that this treatment does require complete information, whether it be positive or negative, about all objects under consideration, although in general there will not be many such objects: only those objects having the property of kittenhood in the resource situation.

3.5 Quantification via Quantified Infons

As mentioned in section 2.3, some versions of situation theory (e.g., Barwise (1989a), (1989b), Gawron and Peters (1990b), Devlin (forthcoming)) admit *quantified infons*, infons of the form:

$$\exists \dot{x}^{\tau(\dot{x})} \sigma(\dot{x})$$

and

$$\forall \dot{x}^{\tau(\dot{x})} \sigma(\dot{x})$$

In these infons the superscripted infon $\tau(\dot{x})$ acts as a restriction on the parameter $\dot{x}$ which is bound by the determiner (either $\exists$ or $\forall$). A situation S supports the existentially quantified infon iff there is some object a in S such that $S \models \tau(a)$ and $S \models \sigma(a)$. (Where $\tau(a)$ is the infon resulting from anchoring $\dot{x}$ to a in $\tau(\dot{x})$, and similarly for $\sigma(a)$.) Similarly a situation S supports the universally quantified infon iff for all objects a of S such that $S \models \tau(a)$, it is also the case that $S \models \sigma(a)$. Although these quantified infons are not normally intended to capture natural language quantification, Pollard and Sag (1987) extend the use of quantified infons for the HPSG treatment of natural language semantics. This is achieved by admitting determiners corresponding to the full range of natural language determiners. For example, their theory admits quantified infons of the form (modulo some syntactic conventions):

$$(most \ \dot{x}^{\tau(\dot{x})}) \ \sigma(\dot{x})$$

Pollard and Sag do not state structurally determined definitions giving the conditions under which a situation will support a quantified infon, though presumably such definitions follow the general pattern above:

$$S \models (det \ \dot{x}^{\tau(\dot{x})}) \ \sigma(\dot{x})$$

iff

$$det'(\{a \mid S \models \tau(a)\}, \ \{a \mid S \models \sigma(a)\})$$

Note that, as with our initial possible approach, such a definition takes the restriction to be with respect to the situation supporting the infon, not with respect to a resource situation. This proposal might be modified to correctly account for the exploitation of resource situations by treating restrictions in terms of propositions rather than infons. Persistence properties will of course be dependent on the precise details, but will in general follow those of the previous approaches.

3.6 Determiners as Properties of Properties

Gawron and Peters (1990b) point out a potential problem for all of the above analyses concerning the binding of pronouns. Under the above approaches, and assuming the absorption principle of Gawron and Peters (1990a) (which requires that, in the instance below, because of the dependence of $\dot{x}$ on $\dot{y}$, $\dot{y}$ be abstracted when $\dot{x}$ is), the sentence 'every psychiatrist who dates a patient of hers will be sued by him' (from their 65) would be required to have content:

$$\langle\!\langle\text{every}, [\dot{x}, \dot{y} \mid S_r \models \langle\!\langle\text{psych}, \dot{x}_{S_r \models \tau(\dot{x}, \dot{y})}; +\rangle\!\rangle], [\dot{x} \mid \langle\!\langle\text{will-sue}, \dot{y}, \dot{x}; +\rangle\!\rangle]; +\rangle\!\rangle$$

where

$$\tau(\dot{x}, \dot{y}) = \bigwedge\{\langle\!\langle\text{patient}, \dot{y}, \dot{x}; +\rangle\!\rangle, \langle\!\langle\text{dates}, \dot{x}, \dot{y}; +\rangle\!\rangle\}$$

Note that, because of the absorption principle we are lead to a two place type rather than a one place type. The second argument role may be interpreted as unsaturated, effectively existentially quantifying over that argument. This technical detail is not relevant to the point in question. What is relevant is that with the above translation, 'him' cannot be anaphoric to 'a patient of hers', because $\dot{y}$ is absorbed when $\dot{x}$ is abstracted over to form the restriction type, and so $\dot{y}$ is not, and cannot be, a parameter of the restriction.

To overcome this problem, Gawron and Peters (1990b) suggest an alternate treatment of determiners where the determiner expresses a property of a property and appropriateness conditions are employed to give a structurally determined definition. According to this proposal, the sentence 'most kittens are meowing' describes a situation S_d such that:

$$S_d \models \langle\!\langle\text{most}, [\dot{x}_{S_r \models \langle\!\langle\text{kitten}, \dot{x}; +\rangle\!\rangle} \mid \langle\!\langle\text{meowing}, \dot{x}; +\rangle\!\rangle]; +\rangle\!\rangle$$

The accompanying structurally determined definition is:

$$S \models \langle\!\langle det, P; +\rangle\!\rangle$$

iff

$$det'(\{a \mid a \text{ is appropriate for } P \text{ (in } S)\}, \{a \mid S \models \langle\!\langle P, a; +\rangle\!\rangle\})$$

The restriction on the abstracted parameter in the property is treated as an appropriateness condition on the argument role of the resultant property. Thus in the case of 'most kittens are meowing', this definition requires that the "most" relation hold between the set of things appropriate for "meowing kittens" and the set of things that actually have the "meowing" property in the described situation.

While this approach makes elegant use of the notion of appropriateness condition provided by situation theory, there are a number of difficulties which it presents. These have to do with the precise details of appropriateness conditions. For example, if a restricted parameter is abstracted, then the restriction on the parameter becomes an appropriateness condition on the resultant argument role. In the first instance this is what is required—the restriction on the relevant parameter, when translated as an appropriateness condition, restricts the domain of quantification. However, parameters may be restricted by other factors. 'Every kitten is chasing its tail', for example, might be taken to correspond to "everything that is appropriate for P has P", where P is the property (or type) of thing that is a kitten chasing its tail. Although the theory of appropriateness conditions is not sufficiently well defined to be definite, it seems reasonable to assume that manx kittens, kittens without tails, are not appropriate for P, and as such 'every kitten is chasing its tail' can still be supported by a situation even though that situation may contain manx kittens which are not chasing their tails. This seems counter to what is required.

These problems aside, this approach may lead to a non-persistent infon. While the appropriateness conditions, and hence the restriction, are expressed in terms of propositions concerning a particular resource situation (and hence provide an absolute set of individuals under consideration), the structurally determined definition above only requires positive information about the individuals in question, so that again monotone decreasing determiners such as *no* will lead to non-persistent infons. Persistence may be achieved by requiring complete (all positive and negative) information about the individuals under consideration.

4 Quantification in Terms of Propositions

4.1 Structural Determination and Completeness of Information

The various treatments of quantification and the consideration of persistence raise two principle issues: structural determination and completeness of information. If an infon is structurally determined, then clearly only if that structural determination has special properties will the infon necessarily be persistent. The structural determination of an infon has the immediate consequence of calling into question the persistence of that infon, simply because for a situation to support the infon the situation must satisfy certain structural conditions, conditions which, by their very nature, need not hold of all situations of which the original situation is a part. On the other hand, persistence of a structurally determined infon σ can be guaranteed by making the conditions relating to the structural determination sufficiently restrictive that they are effectively independent of any situation S in propositions of the form $(S \models \sigma)$. This route leads trivially to persistence. A second way to guarantee persistence in the cases above involves requiring complete information about the individuals involved in the quantification. Such completeness of information is at odds, however, with the underlying notion of a situation, in which partiality of information is crucial.

The above suggests that structurally determined phenomena might be treated not in terms of infons but in terms of situation types. By adopting this approach, only basic infons need be postulated, and persistence of all infons can be guaranteed. Such an approach places structurally determined phenomena at the level of logic, rather than at the level of information—at the level of external properties, rather that at the level of internal properties. This is consistent with the fact that the logic reflects our ability to stand back and look at situations from the "outside". Our ability to entertain structurally determined facts depends crucially on our ability to adopt this perspective.

4.2 Determiners as Types

In the light of this discussion of types, each of the above accounts of quantification may be revised to treat determiners as corresponding to types rather than relations. The first account, where the determiner corresponds to a relation between two properties, for example, might be revised so that the determiner corresponds to a three place type that holds between a situation and two properties if and only if the corresponding generalized quantifier relation holds between the set of things having the first property in the situation and the set of things having the second property in the situation. That is:

$$(S, P, Q) : det$$

iff

$$det'(\{a \mid S \models \langle\!\langle P,\ a;\ +\rangle\!\rangle\}, \ \{a \mid S \models \langle\!\langle Q,\ a;\ +\rangle\!\rangle\})$$

Similarly, the other accounts may be revised. For example, revising Gawron and Peters' property of property account, determiners could correspond to two place types that hold between a situation and a property iff the corresponding generalized quantifier relation holds between the set of individuals appropriate for the property (in the situation) and the set of individuals that actually have the property in the situation. That is:

$$(S, P) : det$$

iff

$$det'(\{a \mid a \text{ is appropriate for } P \text{ (in } S)\}, \ \{a \mid S \models \langle\!\langle P,\ a;\ +\rangle\!\rangle\})$$

Proceeding along these lines, the revision of the treatment of determiners as binary relations between types leads to perhaps the most natural formulation: that determiners correspond to two place types which hold of two object types iff the corresponding set-theoretic relation holds of the sets of objects of those types. The use of a type rather than a relation exactly captures the situation independence of this formulation, and maintains the intuition that determiners are like two place relations, the difference being that determiners are the situation *independent* analogues of two-place relations, where relations are situation *dependent*.

The use of types also avoids the issue of closure conditions on situations. Objects of the form $\langle\langle det,\ P,\ Q;\ +\rangle\rangle$ are not well-formed infons (as det is a type, and not a relation), and so there is no question of a situation supporting any such infons. Closure is instead accommodated at the logical level, the level of types. Consequently a situation may support just a small (finite) number of infons, yet be an instance of infinitely many situation types.

4.3 Quantification and Natural Language Semantics

The treatment of quantification in terms of types and propositions may easily be incorporated into the treatment of semantics by a unification-based grammar formalism such as HPSG if we interpret the semantic content of an HPSG sign not as modeling an infon but as modeling a situation type. In general this situation type will be the type of situation with supports the corresponding infon, but in the case of quantified sentences the situation type will not be infon based.

Given that determiners correspond to binary types that hold of two object types, abstraction allows a sentence such as 'most kittens are meowing' to be taken to correspond to the situation type:

$$[\dot{S} \mid (([\dot{x} \mid S_r \models \langle\langle\text{kitten}, \dot{x};\ +\rangle\rangle)], [\dot{x} \mid \dot{S} \models \langle\langle\text{meows}, \dot{x};\ +\rangle\rangle]) : \text{most})]$$

The described situation S_d is of this type if and only if:

$$(S_d : [\dot{S} \mid (([\dot{x} \mid S_r \models \langle\langle\text{kitten}, \dot{x};\ +\rangle\rangle)], [\dot{x} \mid \dot{S} \models \langle\langle\text{meows}, \dot{x};\ +\rangle\rangle]) : \text{most})])$$

This reduces to:

$$(([\dot{x} \mid S_r \models \langle\langle\text{kitten}, \dot{x};\ +\rangle\rangle)], [\dot{x} \mid S_d \models \langle\langle\text{meows}, \dot{x};\ +\rangle\rangle]) : \text{most})$$

The determiner 'most' may thus be associated with the type:

$$[\dot{S} \mid (([\dot{x} \mid S_r \models \langle\langle P, \dot{x};\ +\rangle\rangle)], [\dot{x} \mid \dot{S} \models \langle\langle Q, \dot{x};\ +\rangle\rangle]) : \text{most})]$$

where P is to be unified with the property contributed by the following noun and Q is a property contributed by the rest of the sentence.

5 Other Structurally Determined Types

Quantification provides one source of structurally determined proposition. In many versions of situation theory (see, for example, Cooper (1988)) an algebra is constructed on the domain of infons with the logical operators of conjunction, disjunction, and negation. Structurally determined definitions are then given for when a situation supports conjunctive, disjunctive or negative infons:

Conjunctive Infons:	$S \models \bigwedge\Sigma$	iff	$\forall\sigma \in \Sigma,\ S \models \sigma$
Disjunctive Infons:	$S \models \bigvee\Sigma$	iff	$\exists\sigma \in \Sigma,\ S \models \sigma$
External Negation:	$S \models \neg\sigma$	iff	$S \not\models \sigma$

Note that $\neg\sigma$ is not persistent, where as $\bigwedge\Sigma$ and $\bigvee\Sigma$ are.

In the version of situation theory developed here, we take the structural determination of these infons, which is a consequence of their logical character, as evidence that they should be treated as propositions, rather than infons. Rather than admitting compound infons, we take all infons to be basic, and treat all logic (i.e., situation independent, or absolute, things) at the level of types and propositions.

To effect this we may include amongst the types of our theory the types *and* and *or* which are structurally determined two place types that hold between a situation and a set of infons:

$$(S, \Sigma) : and \quad \text{iff} \quad \forall \sigma \in \Sigma \;\; S \models \sigma$$

and

$$(S, \Sigma) : or \quad \text{iff} \quad \exists \sigma \in \Sigma \;\; S \models \sigma$$

Persistence of the types *and* and *or* arises from a kind of upward monotonicity in their first argument role: if $S \unlhd S'$, then:

$$(S, \Sigma) : and \;\; \Rightarrow \;\; (S', \Sigma) : and$$

and likewise

$$(S, \Sigma) : or \;\; \Rightarrow \;\; (S', \Sigma) : or$$

We also have:

$$(S, \Sigma) : and \;\; \Rightarrow \;\; (S, \Sigma) : or$$

From a form of upward monotonicity in the second argument role of *or*, we have:

$$(S, \Sigma) : or \;\; \Rightarrow \;\; (S, \Sigma') : or$$

for any superset Σ' of Σ. And from a form of downward monotonicity in the second argument role of *and*, we have:

$$(S, \Sigma) : and \;\; \Rightarrow \;\; (S, \Sigma') : and$$

for any subset Σ' of Σ. Alternately, logical conjunction and disjunction may be treated in terms of unary types which are true of a set of propositions just in case all, or at least one, of those propositions are true, respectively.

We may also include a type corresponding to external negation, such as the two place type *not* which is true of a situation and an infon just in case the situation does not support the infon:

$$(S, \sigma) : not \quad \text{iff} \quad (S, \sigma) \not\models$$
$$\text{iff} \quad S \not\models \sigma$$

As in the case of logical conjunction and disjunction, negation might also be treated via a unary type, with a proposition being of that type just in case the proposition is false.

The development of situation theory advocated here also allows the part-of ordering between situations to be treated as a structurally determined type, with a purely extensional definition:

$$(S_1, S_2) : \unlhd \quad \text{iff} \quad \{\sigma \mid S_1 \models \sigma\} \subseteq \{\sigma \mid S_2 \models \sigma\}$$

6 Summary and Conclusion

We have argued for a version of situation theory in which all infons are both basic (and hence have duals) and persistent. In this theory, phenomena that have been treated in other theories via non-basic infons, such as quantified infons, conjunctive infons and disjunctive infons, all of which are structurally determined, may instead be treated in terms of propositions. Similarly, phenomena which in other theories might have been treated in terms of non-persistent infons may also be treated in terms of propositions, the claim being that non-persistent phenomena are necessarily structurally determined, and should thus be treated at the logical level, and not the informational level.

References

Barwise, J. 1987. Notes on a Model of a Theory of Situations. Unpublished manuscript.

Barwise, J. 1989a. Notes on Branch Points in Situation Theory. In *The Situation in Logic*, 255–276. CSLI Lecture Notes Number 17. Stanford: CSLI Publications.

Barwise, J. 1989b. Situations, Facts, and True Propositions. In *The Situation in Logic*, 221–54. CSLI Lecture Notes Number 17. Stanford: CSLI Publications.

Barwise, J., and R. Cooper. 1981. Generalized Quantifiers and Natural Language. *Linguistics and Philosophy* 4:159–219.

Cooper, R. 1987. Preliminaries to the Treatment of Generalized Quantifiers in Situation Semantics. In *Generalized Quantifiers: Linguistic and Logical Approaches*, ed. P. Gärdenfors. Studies in Linguistics and Philosophy Number 31. Dordrecht: Reidel.

Cooper, R. 1988. Facts in Situation Theory: Representation, Psychology or Reality. In *Mental Representations: The Interface Between Language and Reality*, ed. R. Kempson. Cambridge: Cambridge University Press.

Cooper, R., K. Mukai, and J. Perry (ed.). 1990. *Situation Theory and Its Applications*, vol. 1. CSLI Lecture Notes Number 22. Stanford: CSLI Publications.

Devlin, K. J. 1991. *Logic and Information*. Cambridge: Cambridge University Press.

Gawron, J. M., and S. Peters. 1990a. *Anaphora and Quantification in Situation Semantics*. CSLI Lecture Notes Number 19. Stanford: CSLI Publications.

Gawron, J. M., and S. Peters. 1990b. Some Puzzles About Pronouns. In Cooper et al. 1990.

Pollard, C., and I. Sag. 1987. *Information-Based Syntax and Semantics, Volume 1: Fundamentals*. CSLI Lecture Notes Number 13. Stanford: CSLI Publications.

14

Negation in Situation Semantics and Discourse Representation Theory

Robin Cooper and Hans Kamp

1 Introduction

The project of putting Situation Semantics and Discourse Representation Theory (DRT) together has a history going back to the early eighties when Barwise and Kamp investigated the topic. However, nothing concrete resulted from the research. After a decade we think it might be appropriate to try again in the hope that the two theories might illuminate each other.

The relationship Situation Semantics and DRT that Barwise and Kamp proposed was remarkably straightforward: With each DRS (DRS, discourse representation structure) K of the DRT fragment considered and each embedding function f for the universe of K one could associate a situation type $S(K)$, such that the situations supporting K would be precisely those of type $S(K)$. In particular, a maximal situation w (i.e., a situation comprehending the entire world in which it is situated) would be one in which f correctly embeds K iff w is of the type $S(K)$. The fragment investigated was that of Kamp 1981, in which the only complex DRS conditions are implications $K_1 \rightarrow K_2$; more complex DRS languages were meant to be considered, but the enterprise never got beyond this first stage. Since that early effort many things have changed, both within Situation Semantics and within DRT, and so the little that was then accomplished neither fits the terminology nor the prevalent conceptions of today. Nevertheless, the first part of the present investigation follows its predecessor quite closely. The main differences are (i) we no longer make use of the situation-theoretic notions of situation type and event type as they were conceived then; and

This research was supported by DYANA, ESPRIT Basic Research Action project 3175. We are grateful to Bill Rounds for discussion of parameters which was facilitated by SERC grant GR/G22046. We are also grateful for the comments made by anonymous referee for this volume.

Situation Theory and Its Applications, vol. 2.
Jon Barwise, Jean Mark Gawron, Gordon Plotkin, and Syun Tutiya, eds.

(ii) the basic DRS language with which we start is one in which complex conditions are not implications, but are formed with a one-place negation operator on DRS's. This second change is not occasioned by a change in DR-theoretical perspective, but motivated by a formal as well as by an expositional consideration. The formal motive is this: While arguably simpler than the DRS language of Kamp 1981, the DRS language which has negation as its only operator exceeds the earlier language in expressive power; in fact, unlike the earlier language it is equivalent to full classical first order predicate calculus.[1] The expositional consideration relates to our desire to investigate some of the alternatives that present themselves for the interpretation of the logical operators within a situation semantic framework. Here negation appears to be of particular interest, not least because the treatment of negation has been a topic of discussion within Situation Semantics quite independently from its potential connections with DRT. And it seemed to us that a first look at this matter would benefit from a stark environment, in which no other operators complicate the picture.

There are three approaches to putting together the two theories that we think might be fruitful to pursue:[2]

1. give a situation semantics for a language of DRSs as defined, for example, by Kamp and Reyle (forthcoming). This could be done by defining the conditions under which a DRS describes a situation. We could define a *describe* relation which holds between a DRS and a situation iff the situation is correctly described by the situation.

2. give a model of DRSs as objects in situation theory. This might be just another way of giving a situation semantics for a DRS language, but with the constraint that each DRS is related to a particular situation theoretic object (e.g., a parametric situation type). Now, since DRSs are identified with situation theoretic objects, the *describe* relation will be a relation between situation theoretic objects, so that the corresponding part of DRT becomes effectively a branch of situation theory.

3. start from some version of situation semantics, e.g., Cooper 1991 (in preparation) or Gawron and Peters 1990 and incorporate the dynamic aspects of DRT.

We pursue the first, which is the most conservative of these approaches, providing a simple DRS language with a very conservative situation semantics. We will discuss problems that arise with the interpretation of negation

---

[1] As it stands the fragment defined in Kamp 1981 is not able to express, for instance, classical negation. Of course, it would have been easy enough to add, say, the sentential constant F. To be precise, this would be a DRS condition which is never verified.

[2] A rather different approach which involves the situation schemata of Fenstad et al. 1987 is taken by Sem 1987.

and suggest that in order to give a reasonable account of negation we must give up one of the following:

1. the 'indefinite as variable' or 'singular noun-phrase' interpretation of indefinite noun phrases
2. persistence of the content of negative sentences
3. the situations described by sentences with indefinite NPs in the scope of negation do not need to support negative facts about all members of some universal set of individuals

The way that we choose to resolve these issues may have important consequences for situation theory since the discussion turns on characterizing the kind of situation which supports information corresponding to "John doesn't own a car". Is there a single negative infon corresponding to this information and, if so, what kind of infon is it? Or does this information correspond to a set of infons which must be supported and, if so, what is the structure of this set? Must all the infons in the set be supported by a single situation? It seems that detailed analysis of natural language might provide important input to the discussion of such situation theoretical questions. We should like to emphasize, however, that the paper's central focus is a semantic one. The problem of interpreting negative sentences is a central problem of semantics. That the exploration of this question should have led us to consider the kind of entities that the ontology supporting a satisfactory situation semantic treatment of natural language negation should include is hardly surprising. Modern semantic research has taught us that issues of ontology cannot be kept distinct from questions of (natural language) semantics any more than they can be kept separate from questions of logic and we therefore feel that the paper should have potential readers beyond those who have a declared interest in the functioning of natural language for its own sake.

2   DRS Language L_0

We shall start by defining a simple DRS language L_0 in the style of Kamp and Reyle (forthcoming).

1. Vocabulary
   a. a set V of discourse referents
   b. a set N of proper names
   c. a set R_1 of 1–place predicates
   d. a set R_2 of 2–place predicates
2. DRSs and DRS-conditions
   a. if U is a (finite) subset of V and Con a (finite) set of DRS-conditions, then $\langle U, Con \rangle$ is a DRS.
   b. if $x, y \in V$ then $x = y$ is a DRS-*condition*.
   c. if $x \in V$ and $\alpha \in N$, then $\alpha(x)$ is a DRS-*condition*.

    d. if $x \in V$ and $\alpha \in R_1$, then $\alpha(x)$ is a DRS-*condition*.

    e. if $x, y \in V$ and $\alpha \in R_2$, then $x\alpha y$ is a DRS-*condition*.

    f. if K is a DRS, then $\neg K$ is a DRS-*condition*.

Well-formedness

Suppose K is a DRS and γ a DRS- condition. The *set of undeclared discourse referents* of $K(\gamma)$, $\overline{U}(K)(\overline{U}(\gamma))$, is defined as follows:

    a. if $K = \langle U, Con \rangle$, then $\overline{U}(K) = (\bigcup_{\gamma \in Con} \overline{U}(\gamma)) - U$

    b. if $\gamma = x = y$, then $\overline{U}(\gamma) = \{x, y\}$

    c. if $\gamma = \alpha(x)$, then $\overline{U}(\gamma) = \{x\}$

    d. if $\gamma = x\alpha y$, then $\overline{U}(\gamma)) = \{x, y\}$

    e. if $\gamma = \neg K$, then $\overline{U}(\gamma) = \overline{U}(K)$

A DRS K is *well-formed* iff $\overline{U}(K) = \emptyset$.

3   Situation Semantics for L_0.

In this section we define a conservative situation semantics for L_0 using elements from the style of situation semantics used in Cooper 1989 and Cooper 1991 (in preparation).

We will characterize a relation *describe* which may hold between a use, $\underline{K}$, of a DRS, K or a condition γ in $\underline{K}$, a situation (a situation which could be described by $\underline{K}$ or γ), an environment for $\underline{K}$ and a lexicon for L_0.

For the purposes of this paper we will assume that the notion of a use of a DRS is clear. A full explication of this notion in situation theoretic terms would take us beyond the scope of this paper since it would involve modeling DRSs as situation theoretic objects, i.e., the second of the approaches we listed in section 1.

As usual, a situation is an object in situation theory which is defined by the collection of infons that it supports, where an infon is a situation-theoretic object which has a relation, an appropriate number of arguments (depending on the arity of the relation) and positive or negative polarity. Also as usual we use '$\models$' to represent the support relation. Thus we might characterize a situation as follows:

$$s \models \langle\langle \text{see}, a, b; 1 \rangle\rangle$$
$$s \models \langle\langle \text{see}, b, a; 0 \rangle\rangle$$

Here s is the situation which contains the information that a sees b and that b does not see a.

An environment for a DRS use $\underline{K}$ determines a partial anchoring for the discourse referents in U_K to individuals and a lexicon for the DRS language L_0 assigns the names in L_0 to individuals and the predicates in L_0 to relations. We shall construe both environments and lexica as special kinds of situations.

If $W \subseteq V$ and $U_K \subseteq W$ and e is a situation, then g is an *e-anchor for a use* $\underline{K}$ if g is a function with domain W and range included in the set of individuals such that for any $x \in W$ if $e \models \langle\!\langle \text{Anc}, \underline{K}, x, a; 1 \rangle\!\rangle$ then $g(x) = a$. (Intuitively the situation e is used here as an environment for $\underline{K}$. We may characterize a *proper environment* for $\underline{K}$, i.e., one that assigns something to at least one of the discourse referents in U_K, as a situation which supports an infon of the form

$$\langle\!\langle \text{Anc}, \underline{K}, x, a; 1 \rangle\!\rangle$$

for at least one discourse referent in U_K.)

For $W \subseteq V$ we define

$$g_1 \approx_W g_2 \ \text{ iff } \ \begin{array}{ll} \text{(i)} & W \subseteq \text{Dom}(g_1) \cap \text{Dom}(g_2), \text{ and} \\ \text{(ii)} & \text{for all } x \in W, g_1(x) = g_2(x) \end{array}$$

A *lexicon for* L_0 is a situation *lex* such that

(i) for each $\alpha \in N$ there is an individual a, such that

$$lex \models \langle\!\langle \text{Anc}, \alpha, a; 1 \rangle\!\rangle$$

(ii) for each $\alpha \in R_1$ there is a 1–place relation P such that

$$lex \models \langle\!\langle \text{Anc}, \alpha, P; 1 \rangle\!\rangle$$

(iii) for each $\alpha \in R_2$ there is a 2–place relation R such that

$$lex \models \langle\!\langle \text{Anc}, \alpha, R; 1 \rangle\!\rangle$$

If *lex* is a lexicon for L_0 and α is a name or predicate of L_0, we write $lex(x)$ for the entity e such that

$$lex \models \langle\!\langle \text{Anc}, \alpha, e; 1 \rangle\!\rangle$$

Suppose that K is the simple DRS:

x
John(x)
smile(x)

We shall say that a use $\underline{K}$ of K describes a situation which supports the infon $\langle\!\langle r, a; 1 \rangle\!\rangle$, with respect to an environment which anchors the discourse referent x to the individual a and a lexicon which anchors 'smile' to r and 'John' to a. We now make this notion of description more precise.

If $\underline{K}$ is a use of a DRS K, s and *env* are situations and *lex* a lexicon for L_0, $\underline{K}$ *describes* s with respect to *env* and *lex* iff there is some *env*-anchor g for $\underline{K}$ such that s satisfies K with respect to g and *lex* according to the following definition.

Where K is a DRS, γ a DRS condition, s a situation, g an *env*-anchor for some situation *env*, such that $\overline{U}(K) \subseteq \text{Dom}(g)$ and $\overline{U}(\gamma) \subseteq \text{Dom}(g)$, and *lex* a lexicon for L_0, we define the relation s *satisfies* K *(or* γ*) with respect to* g *and* lex, $_s[\![\{{K \atop \gamma}\}]\!]_{g,lex}$ by recursion:

(i) $_s[\![K]\!]_{g,lex}$ iff $_s[\![\gamma]\!]_{g,lex}$ for each $\gamma \in Con_K$.

(ii) if $\gamma = $ '$x = y$', then $_s[\![\gamma]\!]_{g,lex}$ iff $g(x) = g(y)$

(iii) if $\gamma = \alpha(x)$ where $\alpha \in N$, then $_s[\![\gamma]\!]_{g,lex}$ iff $g(x) = lex(\alpha)$

(iv) if $\gamma = \alpha(x)$ where $\alpha \in R_1$, then $_s[\![\gamma]\!]_{g,lex}$ iff $s \models \langle\!\langle lex(\alpha), g(x); 1\rangle\!\rangle$

(v) if $\gamma = x\alpha y$ where $\alpha \in R_2$, then $_s[\![\gamma]\!]_{g,lex}$ iff $s \models \langle\!\langle lex(\alpha), g(x), g(y); 1\rangle\!\rangle$

(vi) if $\gamma = \neg K$, then $_s[\![\gamma]\!]_{g,lex}$ iff $_{s'}[\![K]\!]_{g',lex}$ for *no* actual situation s' and *no* anchoring g' such that $g' \approx_{\mathrm{Dom}(g)-U_K} g$.

In clause (vi) we quantify over situations, and a brief elucidation is required of what that amounts to. We assume that intuitively each situation is situated in a given world, that, from its own perspective, it is *actual*, and that with it all other situations are actual that are also situated in that world. We prefer, however, to state this intuition without having to refer to the world as a distinct individual. So we assume instead that with each situation s is associated a class of situations $\mathrm{Sit}(s)$, whose members are precisely those situations that are actual from the perspective of s (are 'coactual with s', one might say). With $\mathrm{Sit}(s)$ (in fact with any class of situations, but we will need the notions here only for classes of this particular sort) we can associate a class of individuals or objects, $\mathrm{Ind}(\mathrm{Sit}(s))$, and a class of relations, $\mathrm{Rel}(\mathrm{Sit}(s))$. We do this by first defining the classes of individuals and relations associated with an infon.

(i) If σ is a basic infon of the form

$$\langle\!\langle R, a_1, \ldots, a_n; i\rangle\!\rangle$$

then $\mathrm{inds}(\sigma) = \{a_1, \ldots, a_n\}$, and
$\mathrm{rels}(\sigma) = \{R\}$

(ii) If σ is an infon of the form[3]

$$\tau_1 \wedge \tau_2 \text{ or } \tau_1 \vee \tau_2$$

then $\mathrm{inds}(\sigma) = \mathrm{inds}(\tau_1) \cup \mathrm{inds}(\tau_2)$, and
$\mathrm{rels}(\sigma) = \mathrm{rels}(\tau_1) \cup \mathrm{rels}(\tau_2)$

We can now define the sets of individuals, $\mathrm{inds}(s)$, and relations, $\mathrm{rels}(s)$ associated with a situation s as

$$\bigcup\nolimits_{s \models \sigma} \mathrm{inds}(\sigma)$$
$$\bigcup\nolimits_{s \models \sigma} \mathrm{rels}(\sigma)$$

respectively. Finally, the individuals and relations associated with a class of situations $\mathrm{Sit}(s)$, $\mathrm{Ind}(\mathrm{Sit}(s))$ and $\mathrm{Rel}(\mathrm{Sit}(s))$ can be defined as

$$\bigcup\nolimits_{s' \in \mathrm{Sit}(s)} \mathrm{inds}(s')$$
$$\bigcup\nolimits_{s' \in \mathrm{Sit}(s)} \mathrm{rels}(s')$$

$\mathrm{Sit}(s)$ is assumed to satisfy the following conditions:

---

[3] Other complex infons could be included here depending on the version of situation theory adopted.

(i) $s \in \text{Sit}(s)$

(ii) For each n place relation R in $\text{Rel}(\text{Sit}(s))$ and any sequence $a_1, \ldots, a_n$ of individuals in $\text{Ind}(\text{Sit}(s))$ that is appropriate[4] for R, there is an $s' \in \text{Sit}(s)$ such that

$$s' \models \langle\!\langle R, a_1, \ldots, a_n; 1 \rangle\!\rangle \text{ or } s' \models \langle\!\langle R, a_1, \ldots, a_n; 0 \rangle\!\rangle.$$

(iii) For any situations s_1 and s_2 in $\text{Sit}(s)$, there is a situation s_3 such that for every infon σ, if $s_1 \models \sigma$ or $s_2 \models \sigma$ then $s_3 \models \sigma$

(iv) for no $R \in \text{Rel}(\text{Sit}(s))$, $b_1, \ldots, b_n \in \text{Ind}(\text{Sit})(s))$ and $s' \in \text{Sit}(s)$ do we have $s' \models \langle\!\langle R, b_1, \ldots, b_n; 1 \rangle\!\rangle$ and $s' \models \langle\!\langle R, b_1, \ldots, b_n; 0 \rangle\!\rangle$[5]

The quantification over s' in the negation clause (vi) is to be understood as quantification over $\text{Sit}(s)$. All quantifications over situations in this paper will be understood in this way. Neither here nor later do we take the trouble of making the restriction to $\text{Sit}(s)$ explicit.

4   The Treatment of Negation

In this section we will discuss the treatment of negation in clause (vi) and some alternatives to it.

One comment concerns the role of the described situation s in the negation clause (vi). s does not occur on the right hand side of this clause. So $\neg K$ describes an actual situation s (according to the given env and lex) if and only if it describes (according to env and lex) any other actual situation. The "locality" of the described situation, which might be thought to be of the essence of situation semantics, has thus been obliterated. According to (vi) utterances of negated sentences relate to the described situation only in a trivial sense; what they really describe is the world at large. This may seem so much at variance with the spirit of situation semantics that the reader might be inclined to think that we simply chose the wrong clause. Perhaps we did; but we did have a reason. The reason is that sentences which give rise to DRS conditions of the form $\neg K$, with U_K non-empty, often appear to have the force of quantifying over all there is. Consider for instance the sentence 'John doesn't own a car'. Often such a sentence is

---

[4] The restriction to $a_1, \ldots, a_n$ that are appropriate to R is to avoid category violations, such as would occur, say, if the property of being green were to be combined with the number 19. The matter is of no importance to what is to come and we will henceforth ignore it.

[5] The values of the function Sit, as characterized here, are closely related to the *infon algebras* defined in Barwise & Etchemendy 1990, p. 39. Indeed, $\text{Sit}(s)$ is much like an infon algebra stripped of its lattice structure, provided by '$\Rightarrow$'. Part of this structure can be reintroduced by defining: $s \leq s'$ iff for each infon σ: if $s \models \sigma$ then $s' \models \sigma$, where the set of infons is defined as the set of all combinations $\langle\!\langle R, b_1, \ldots, b_n; i \rangle\!\rangle$ where $b_1, \ldots, b_n$ is a sequence, of the right length and appropriate to R, of individuals from $\text{Ind}(\text{Sit}(s))$, and i is a polarity. Our conditions do not guarantee that $\langle \text{Sit}(s), \leq \rangle$ is a lattice, however, let alone a distributive lattice. We have opted here for the comparatively weak conditions (i)–(iv) we have given, since they are all we need in this paper.

used to assert that there is no car owned by John anywhere in the world. There being no car owned by him in the local situation s is not enough to make the sentence true; if there happened to be a car he owned but which was not part of this situation, the sentence would still be false. It was with the intention to capture this intuition that we formulated (vi) the way we did. We wish to emphasize, however, that we do not offer this as a conclusive argument for defining negation as in (vi), but only as prima facie motivation. There are other ways to achieve this intuitive effect in situation semantics and we will come back to this point below.

The effect of (vi), we just observed, is to make negated sentences global in their semantic import: they describe the world, not the local situation. The logic going with this, one would expect, is classical logic, not the weaker logic associated with the partiality that is inherent in the description relation between utterances and situations. In fact, the logic generated by (i)–(vi) turns out to be a curious mixture of classical logic (for those DRSs in which all relevant components are in the scope of $\neg$) and a weaker partial logic (the by now quite well-known "Strong Kleene Logic") for the DRS for which this is not so.

An alternative that immediately comes to mind in a situation semantics is one that makes use of the part-of relation, $\trianglelefteq$, between situations. We assume a simple part-of relation such that

$$s \trianglelefteq s' \quad \text{iff} \quad \forall \sigma \, s \models \sigma \rightarrow s' \models \sigma$$

Using this notion we can formulate (vi.1).

(vi.1) If $\gamma = \neg K$, then ${}_s[\![\gamma]\!]_{g,lex}$ iff for no actual situation s' such that $s \trianglelefteq s'$, and no anchoring g', such that $g' \approx_{\mathrm{Dom}(env) - U_K} g$, ${}_{s'}[\![K]\!]_{g',lex}$

Interestingly, replacing (vi) by (vi.1) in the above definition does not alter the extension of the *describe* relation.

Let us define: $s \vdash^1_{g,lex} K$ iff ${}_s[\![K]\!]_{g,lex}$ according to clauses (i)–(v), (vi) and $s \vdash^2_{g,lex} K$ iff ${}_s[\![K]\!]_{g,lex}$ according to clauses (i)–(v), (vi.1). We first observe

(1) Each DRS K that does not contain any occurrences of $\neg$ is persistent, i.e., whenever $s \trianglelefteq s'$ and ${}_s[\![K]\!]_{g,lex}$, then ${}_{s'}[\![K]\!]_{g,lex}$. Evidently, this fact is independent of the choice between (vi) and (vi.1), since these clauses do not come into play for such K.

The relevant claim is proved by induction on the complexity of K; more precisely, we show by induction on K

(2) (a) for all $K, s, g, lex,$
  (∗) $s \vdash^1_{g,lex} K$ iff $s \vdash^2_{g,lex} K$.
  (b) K is persistent. (Both as regards $\vdash^1$ and as regards $\vdash^2$; the two are by (a) indistinguishable!)

Base Case: for K $\neg$-free (∗) is obvious.

Inductive Case:

(1) Suppose K has the form
$$\langle\{\vec{x}\}C_1(\vec{x}_1),\dots,C_n(\vec{x}_n),\neg K_1,\dots,\neg K_m\rangle$$
where $C_1(\vec{x}_1),\dots,C_n(\vec{x}_n)$ are atomic conditions and $\neg K_1,\dots,\neg K_m$ are all the complex conditions in Con_K. Suppose that $s\vdash^1_g K$ (we keep *lex* fixed throughout the argument and won't mention it explicitly). Then

    (i) s supports $\langle\langle lex(C_i),g(\vec{x}_{i1}),\dots,g(\vec{x}_{ik});1\rangle\rangle$
        (with $i=1,\dots,n$ and k the length of the sequence x_i)

    (ii) for no s' and no $g'\approx_{V-\vec{x}} g$, $s'\vdash^1_{g'} K_j$ $(j=1,\dots,m)$. Then by the induction hypothesis for no s' and no $g'\approx_{V-\vec{x}} g$, $s'\vdash^2_{g'} K_j$. So obviously for $s'\trianglerighteq s$ and $g'\approx_{V-\vec{u}} g$, $s'\vdash^1_{g'} K_j$. So by clause (vi') $s\vdash^2_g K$.

(2) Suppose that $s\vdash^2_g K$. Then again

    (i) above holds, together with

    (ii) for no $s'\trianglerighteq s$ and no $g'\approx_{V-\vec{x}} g$, $s'\vdash^2_{g'} K_j$ $(j=1,\dots,m)$. So by the induction hypothesis for no $s'\trianglerighteq s$ and no $g'\approx_{V-\vec{x}} g$, $s'\vdash^1_{g'} K_j$. By persistence of K_j there is no actual situation s'' such that $s''\vdash^1_{g'} K_j$. For suppose s'' were such a situation. Then for any actual situation s''' such that $s''\trianglelefteq s'''$ and $s\trianglelefteq s'''$ $s'''\vdash^1_{g'} K_j$.
Since s and s'' are both actual situations, s''' exists and we have a contradiction. So we have shown for $j=1,\dots,m$ that there is no s' and no $g'\approx_{V-\vec{x}} g$ such that $s'\vdash^1_{g'} K_j$. It follows by (vi) that $s\vdash^1_g K$. □

The equivalence of $\vdash^1$ and $\vdash^2$ supports the claim made in Kratzer 1989 that her generic negation is persistent and independent of the situation described. Kratzer defines her generic negation semantically by a clause which formally resembles (vi.1) rather than (vi). So a proof of these claims seems called for. Exactly how to carry out such a proof on the basis of the semantics she develops is not straightforward, as the details of (something corresponding to) the relation of support—and thus of the verification or truth of atomic sentences by, or in, situations—is not made fully explicit. However, even if we assume that verification of atomic sentences is to be made precise along the lines assumed here (which, we believe, are consonant with the received views on this matter within situation semantics), some indispensable ingredient to the proof of Kratzer's claim is still missing.

In order to push the induction through we must consider not only negation but also each of the other operators which the object language may contain. In the proof just given we were spared this additional effort, as '¬' is the only operator for forming complex conditions that can be found in the DRS language we are studying. But in general things won't be that simple, and in particular for Kratzer, whose central concern is with counterfactual conditionals, a formalization of the language she studies would be bound to have additional operators. As our proof shows, these additional operators will not interfere with the argument as long as they preserve persistence. Indeed this is a property that Kratzer seems to want (and that seems to be warranted by the truth clauses for conditionals she proposes). So it may be presumed that an argument like the one we have just given would apply for her languages, too. Still it ought, we thought, to be pointed out that an argument is required.

Thus, somewhat surprisingly perhaps, the restriction in (vi.1) to extensions of the described situation s does not have any locality effect at all. So, if a local notion of negation is what we want we will have to try something else. The next characterization we consider is (vi.2) in which we still quantify over anchors, but in which the quantification over situations has been done away with.

(vi.2) If $\gamma = \neg K$, then $_s[\![\gamma]\!]_{g,lex}$ iff for no $g' \approx_{\mathrm{Dom}(g) - U_K} g$, $_d[\![K]\!]_{s,g',lex}$

This is like the previous definition except that there is no quantification over described situations. This, however, is not persistent in that situations of which s is a part could support infons required by K, i.e., K could describe situations parts of which could be described by $\neg K$. The previous version maintained persistence but at the expense of quantifying over all actual situations to make sure that there would be no larger situation which would support the offending infons. It is still the case that no negative information is required locally in the described situation, i.e., there is no requirement that any negative infons be supported.

This leads us to a third alternative which follows the lead of partial semantics as originally used by Kleene (1952). (For a more linguistic application see Kamp 1975). It uses a negative satisfaction relation, $[\![\,]\!]^-$, in addition to the satisfaction relation we have already used.

(vi.3) If $\gamma = \neg K$, then $_s[\![\gamma]\!]_{g,lex}$ iff for all g' such that $\mathrm{Dom}(g') = \mathrm{Dom}(g) \cup U_K$ and $g' \approx_{\mathrm{Dom}(g) - U_K} g$, $_s[\![K]\!]^-_{g',lex}$

Now, of course, we need to characterize $[\![\,]\!]^-$.

Definition of $[\![\,]\!]^-$.

  (i) $_s[\![K]\!]^-_{g,lex}$ iff $_s[\![\gamma]\!]^-_{g,lex}$ for some $\gamma \in Con_K$

  (ii) if $\gamma = 'x = y'$, then $_s[\![\gamma]\!]^-_{g,lex}$ iff $g(x) \neq g(y)$

 (iii) if $\gamma = \alpha(x)$ ($\alpha \in N$), then $_s[\![\gamma]\!]^-_{g,lex}$ iff $g(x) \neq lex(\alpha)$

 (iv) if $\gamma = \alpha(x)$ where $\alpha \in R_1$, then $_s[\![\gamma]\!]^-_{g,lex}$ iff $s \models \langle\!\langle lex(\alpha), g(x); 0 \rangle\!\rangle$

  (v) if $\gamma = x\alpha y$ where $\alpha \in R_2$, then $_s[\![\gamma]\!]^-_{g,lex}$ iff $s \models \langle\!\langle lex(\alpha), g(x), g(y); 0 \rangle\!\rangle$

 (vi) if $\gamma = \neg K$, then $_s[\![\gamma]\!]^-_{g,lex}$ iff $_s[\![K]\!]^-_{g',lex}$ for some g' such that $\mathrm{Dom}(g') = \mathrm{Dom}(g) \cup U_K$ and $g' \approx_{\mathrm{Dom}(g) - U_K} g$.

Now finally we have the presence of negative information in the described situation. It is required that the described situation support a negative infon in the case of clauses (iv) and (v). Thus we have persistence. We also have a doubly negated DRS describing exactly the same situations as the DRS without negation.

However, we have gained this at some expense. We have introduced two satisfaction relations and we seem to have partial semantics twice in the system: once with the satisfaction relations where we can talk of a DRS being positively or negatively satisfied by a situation or neither and once again in the situation theory where we can talk of a situation as settling an issue by supporting a positive or negative infon or not settling the issue. It seems that there is overkill in the system.

There is another potential problem. Consider the DRS corresponding to *John doesn't own a car*:

$$
\boxed{
\begin{array}{|l|}
\hline
x \\
\hline
\text{John}(x) \\
\quad
\neg\;\boxed{
\begin{array}{|l|}
\hline
y \\
\hline
\text{car}(y) \\
\text{own}(x, y) \\
\hline
\end{array}
} \\
\hline
\end{array}
}
$$

According to the present proposal, this DRS will only describe situations which support negative facts for all objects in the universe since we universally quantify over anchors. Thus again we have maintained persistence at some considerable expense. While we only have one situation, that situation is required to support a great deal of negative information and it seems unintuitive to require that somebody perceiving a situation supporting the information that John does not own a car should be aware of this large number of negative facts. For an example that seems to us to be particularly compelling, consider the sentence 'John does not have a child', and the situation *s* which supports the information that John is a one month old baby, peacefully asleep in his cot. Such a situation can surely support the information corresponding to the content of an utterance of this sentence without supporting information about every single human being in the world.[6]

One way that we could try to solve this problem is to use a negative parametric infon with a restricted parameter. Thus we could say that the

---

[6]The referee for this paper points out that this could be ameliorated by placing restrictions on the domain of quantification by limiting the domain of anchors provided for the DRS. While this would certainly be better than quantifying over all objects in the universe it still means that for every object provided by the context there would have to be a negative fact supported by the described situation. This still seems undesirable in a case where there might be a thousand relevant cars or where there is no obvious relevant context set as in the example 'John does not have a child'.

DRS corresponding to 'John doesn't own a car' describes a situation which supports the infon

$$\langle\!\langle \text{own}, j, X | \langle\!\langle \text{car}, X; 1 \rangle\!\rangle; 0 \rangle\!\rangle$$

We could place the following constraints on support for parametric infons.

1. If $\sigma(\vec{X})$ is a positive basic parametric infon with parameters $\vec{X}$ then

$$s \models \sigma(\vec{X}) \;\rightarrow\; \exists g \exists s' \in \text{Sit}(s)\, s' \models \sigma(\vec{X})[g]$$

2. If $\sigma(\vec{X})$ is a negative parametric basic infon with parameters $\vec{X}$ then

$$s \models \sigma(\vec{X}) \;\rightarrow\; \sim\exists g \exists s' \in \text{Sit}(s)\, s' \models \overline{\sigma(\vec{X})[g]}$$

We could introduce similar clauses for complex infons.

There are three problems with trying to pursue a solution along these lines. Firstly, there may be problems inherent in the notion of restricted parameters. (See Westerståhl 1990 for a discussion from the point of view of formalizing situation theory, and Cooper 1991 for a discussion from a more linguistic perspective.) Secondly, it is not currently standard to talk of parametric infons being supported, although unsaturated infons may be supported. However, nobody has to our knowledge suggested that unsaturated infons can have their argument roles restricted in the manner that it has been suggested that parameters can be restricted. Thirdly, and perhaps most importantly for the present discussion the DRT syntax does not provide us with an adequate base for deriving this infon since it does not distinguish the status of the two conditions that would lead to the restriction and the infon in which the restricted parameter occurs.

It may be thought that we can get around these problems by using quantified infons rather than parametric infons and relating the DRS under discussion to the infon

$$\overline{\exists x \langle\!\langle \text{car}, x; 1 \rangle\!\rangle \wedge \langle\!\langle \text{own}, j, x; 1 \rangle\!\rangle}$$

This would, of course, involve using a situation theory which allows such infons which are suspicious because they do not appear to be persistent. Given normal assumptions about duals this infon is identical with

$$\forall x \langle\!\langle \text{car}, x; 0 \rangle\!\rangle \vee \langle\!\langle \text{own}, j, x; 0 \rangle\!\rangle$$

If we wish to avoid problems with lack of persistence we might make use of our collections of coactual situations and say that a situation s supports this infon just in case

$$\forall x \in \text{Obj}(\text{Sit}(s))\; s \models \langle\!\langle \text{car}, x; 0 \rangle\!\rangle \vee \langle\!\langle \text{own}, j, x; 0 \rangle\!\rangle$$

i.e.,

$$\forall x \in \text{Obj}(\text{Sit}(s))\; s \models \langle\!\langle \text{car}, x; 0 \rangle\!\rangle \text{ or } s \models \langle\!\langle \text{own}, j, x; 0 \rangle\!\rangle$$

This means that our potentially local negation represented by the dual of an existentially quantified infon turns out to be local at the expense of introducing a large number of negative facts into the described situation. Thus in this respect a treatment along these lines would not improve on the Kleene negation represented by clause (vi.3) above.

Another way of trying to avoid this predicament is to use the other kind of quantified infons which is provided by situation theory, namely those whose relations are generalized quantifier relations with two argument roles for properties, as discussed, for example, in Gawron and Peters 1990, Richard Cooper 1991a, 1991b, and Cooper 1991. For the treatment of indefinites this would involve a return to the traditional view that indefinites are existential quantifiers (combined with some kind of E-type account in the spirit of Cooper 1976 and Evans 1980 to explain the recalcitrant facts about donkey pronouns that File Change Semantics and DRT explain via the "indefinites = free variables" assumption). On such a treatment a situation s will be described by a sentence such as

John owns a car.

if s supports an infon of the form $\langle\langle \text{Exist}, P, Q; 1 \rangle\rangle$, where, roughly, P and Q are the properties of being a car and being something owned by John, respectively, and **Exist** is the generalized quantifier which holds between P and Q if their extensions have something in common. Similarly, s is described by

John doesn't own a car.

if it supports the corresponding negative infon $\langle\langle \text{Exist}, P, Q; 0 \rangle\rangle$. If we treat generalized quantifiers along the lines suggested in Cooper 1991 then there need be no implication that a situation s that supports this negative infon also needs to support all the basic negative infons which we wish to avoid, although these infons would need to be supported somewhere in a coherent collection of situations including s. (For the purposes of this paper we can take coherent collections of situations as discussed in Cooper 1991 to correspond to the notion Sit(s) discussed here.)

To explore the implications of the proposal somewhat more closely, let us begin by looking in greater detail at its implications for a quantificational sentence which does not raise the problem of indefinites, say, (1).

(1)   Every executive is happy.

will describe a situation s in virtue, and only in virtue, of s supporting the fact that the property of being an executive is included in the property of being happy. Similarly,

Some executive is happy.

correctly describes s in virtue of s supporting the fact that the property of being an executive and the property of being happy overlap. In other words, the first sentence describes s in virtue of $s \models \langle\langle \text{Every}, P_1, Q_1; 1 \rangle\rangle$

where P_1 and Q_1 are the relevant properties and the second describes s in virtue of $s \models \langle\!\langle \text{Exist}, P_1, Q_1; 0 \rangle\!\rangle$.

We can apply this proposal also to the *describe* relation for DRSs. For instance, for the DRS for *John doesn't own a car*,

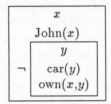

it entails that a situation s is described by it if there is an anchor a such that $a(x) = \text{John}$, $s \models \langle\!\langle \text{named},\text{'John'},a(x);1 \rangle\!\rangle$ and $s \models \langle\!\langle \text{Exist}, P_2, Q_2; 0 \rangle\!\rangle$, where P_2 is the property of being a car and Q_2 the property of being owned by John.

It seems possible to hold that a situation might support this last infon without having to support, for each and every car c in the entire world, the negative infon $\langle\!\langle \text{own},j,c;0 \rangle\!\rangle$. This is not to deny that information directly supported by s might enable us to infer, for any car c that c is not owned by John. As standardly assumed in situation theory, we want to distinguish between information that is directly supported by a situation and further information that is implied by that information (in virtue of constraints), i.e., information that is *carried* by the situation but not supported by it.

Before we can say any more about the constraints that are relevant in this connection, there are a number of issues that we must address first. To begin with, note that the present proposal seems particularly well suited to DRSs in which quantification is represented by a duplex condition, as in the following DRS for the sentence "Every executive owns a car".[7]

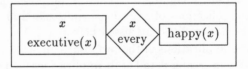

---

[7]This kind of representation, involving a so-called 'duplex condition'

to represent the quantificational information of the sentence has been current in DRT for some time. (See Kamp and Reyle (forthcoming), Chapter 4). However, the point at issue now obtains equally well for the original representation

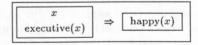

According to our proposal the duplex condition of this DRS describes s just in case s supports $\langle\!\langle$Every,$P_2, Q_2; 1\rangle\!\rangle$, where P_2 and Q_2 are the properties of being an executive and of being a car, respectively; and the same goes for the DRS itself. We can generalize this to duplex conditions of the general form given in footnote 7. A situation s is described by a duplex condition

(2)

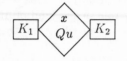

relative to an anchor g and lexicon lex iff s supports an infon with the relation Qu, arguments P and Q (the properties determined by the DRSs K_1 and K_2) and polarity 1:

(3)　$_s[\![(2)]\!]_{g,lex}$ iff $s \models \langle\!\langle Qu, P, Q; 1\rangle\!\rangle$

In order that (3) may be considered as part of a compositional account of the *describe* relation, we must clarify how in general the properties P and Q are determined by K_1 and K_2. Trying to do this leads us to a number of issues in the comparison between DRT and situation semantics which we will point out here but not at this point attempt to resolve.

The first issue involves the use of complex infons. If we wish to represent a property corresponding to a DRS with conditions $C_1, \ldots, C_n$ obtained say by abstracting over a parameter X corresponding to a discourse referent x then the obvious candidates are properties such as

(4)　a.　$[X \mid s \models C_1 \wedge \ldots \wedge C_n]$
　　b.　$[X \mid \models_{\mathrm{Sit}(s)} C_1 \wedge \ldots \wedge C_n]$
　　c.　$[X, S \mid S \models C_1 \wedge \ldots \wedge C_n]$

defined in terms of the complex parametric infon $C_1 \wedge \ldots \wedge C_n$.[8] However, the careful reader will have noted that we have not used complex infons so far. This reflects the DR-theoretic intuition that "the building blocks of reality are simple," i.e., that the constituents of those structures—be they possible worlds, models or situations—in relation to which DRSs can be true, or verified or supported, correspond to atomic DRS conditions, but that the structures do not in general have constituents which correspond in a similar way to complex formulae or DRS conditions. Hence it might be regarded as undesirable to rely on a complex algebra of infons and properties in order to be able to account for the simple conditions in DRT.

A second issue involves the notion of resource situation. There is nothing in a DRS to determine which resource situation s should be used in the property (4a). We might elect to use the more general properties (4b)

---

[8]See Cooper 1991 for a simple characterization of the kinds of properties we are using here.

or (4c). But that would seem to preclude an essential feature of context dependence for quantified sentences. (See Cooper 1991, for more discussion.) One approach to this issue would be to say that the DRS itself, as an expression of a language, should not explicitly refer to a resource situation (after all, natural languages do not refer explicitly to resource situations). Rather the resource situation should be introduced by interpreting the DRS relative to a context which provides a resource situation. This might suggest that resource situations do not play any role in the kind of discourse phenomena which are treated in the construction of DRSs and this seems to us an open question.

A third issue involves the compositional use of the kind of *describe*-relation we have been defining. It is not obvious how to construct the properties (4) given our definitions. Rather what is suggested by this is the assignment of complex (conjunctive) infons as the situation theoretic interpretation of simple DRSs, from which then it would be straightforward to construct the properties. This raises the reservations about the relationship between complex infonic structure and simple DRS conditions which we noted above. In order to construct something appropriate in terms of description conditions it seems that we might be forced to use sets rather than properties, interpreting the abstraction over the discourse referent x in DRS K as something like

$$\{a \mid \exists g(\mathrm{Dom}(g) = \mathrm{U}_K \cup \{x\} \land g(x) = a \land {}_s[\![K]\!]_{g, lex})\}$$

However, the remarks about resource situations apply equally to this proposal.

It is now time to remember that the reason we had for bringing up this discussion had to do not with duplex conditions (or the sentences thereby represented) but with negative existentials such as 'John doesn't own a car'. Unfortunately, standard DRT does not represent such sentences or their unnegated counterparts with the help of duplex conditions. For instance, (5)

(5)   John owns a car.

is represented, in line with the DRT thesis that "indefinites act as free variables" as

(6)
x y
John(x)
car(y)
owns(x,y)

Applying the kind of proposals we have been discussing to a DRS of this form is problematic because the DRS does not tell us which of its parts contribute to the characterization of the property P and which to that of the property Q. For example, the proposal is meant to yield that s is described by the sentence (5) iff s supports the infon

$$\langle\!\langle \text{Exist}, [Y \mid s_r \models \langle\!\langle \text{car}, Y; 1\rangle\!\rangle], [y \mid \models_{\text{Sit}(s)} \langle\!\langle \text{own}, j, y; 1\rangle\!\rangle]; 1\rangle\!\rangle$$

(where j is the referent of the given use of 'John'). But how is this infon to be reconstructed from (6)? What tells us that the property of being a car is to become the first property and that of being owned by j part of the second? With DRSs for quantifying NP's involving other determiners, such as for instance *every*, this problem does not arise. For instance, the DRS of *Every executive is happy* has the form

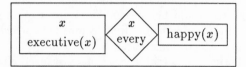

Here the conditions that identify restrictor and nuclear scope are formally separated, and so a systematic identification of the properties P and Q is straightforward. To guarantee an unambiguous interpretation of the DRSs representing existential information we need a similar representation, involving something like duplex conditions for sentences containing indefinites. For instance, for (5) we ought to have some such DRS as

(7)

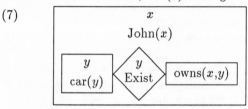

To represent indefinites along these lines means giving up on DRT's original explanation of donkey anaphora. For now it has become quite opaque why the discourse referents introduced by indefinites should be available to pronouns in cases where those introduced by quantifying NPs such as those beginning with *every* are not. We should note in this connection, however, that that original account has been much under attack recently.[9] In the light of these recent criticisms representations of indefinites along the lines of (7) now appear a good deal more defensible than they seemed four or five years ago; rather different principles are then to be held responsible for the distinct anaphoric properties of a-phrases and **every**-phrases.

Even if we retained the original principle according to which indefinites introduce discourse referents at their "own" levels, it would of course be possible to refine DRS-structure in such a way that a DRS for a sentence containing an indefinite NP directly encodes the information needed to separate its material into restrictor and nuclear scope. For instance, we

---

[9]See, e.g., Kadmon 1987, 1990, Heim 1990, Chierchia 1991, Neale 1990.

could simply mark the two sets of conditions as belonging to the restrictor and the nuclear scope of the relevant discourse referents, as in

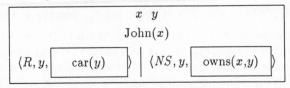

This looks very much like a paradigm case of eating one's cake and having it, without bothering to give a justification for either.

A proposal along these lines may well come to look a good deal less ad hoc, however, if it could be embedded within a more general account of how utterance material is to be divided into that which contributes to the topic and that which contributes to the comment. Admittedly the topic-comment distinction is still in need of substantial clarification at the conceptual and methodological level, and consequently a detailed theory of how utterances are divided into topic and comment may still be a long way off. But it is nevertheless evident that the distinction—whatever it may come to precisely—is crucial to the explanation of a considerable variety of linguistic phenomena, especially those relating to discourse and text. For the further development of a theory such as DRT, with its commitment to confront precisely those aspects of semantics, a viable topic-comment theory is therefore an eventual must. If and when a thus revised DRT will be in place, the question of how to represent indefinites will have to be assessed again.

In what follows we will ignore the present problem and simply assume that the parts of a given DRS that identify restrictor and nuclear scope of the infons of the form $\langle\!\langle \text{Exist}, P, Q; i \rangle\!\rangle$ can somehow be recognized as such.

The second problem relates, as we said, also to DRT's treatment of indefinites as variables. It is a problem that does not arise for the sentences we have so far considered, but it does arise for a sentence such as

(8)   If an executive owns a car he has a credit card.

The DRS for (8) is

(9)

$$
\boxed{\;\boxed{\begin{array}{c} x \ \ y \\ \text{executive}(x) \\ \text{car}(y) \\ \text{owns}(x,y) \end{array}} \;\Rightarrow\; \boxed{\begin{array}{c} z \\ \text{credit card}(z) \\ \text{has}(x,z) \end{array}}\;}
$$

Here we have a universal quantification over two variables, not one. What would it be for this condition (or, if you prefer, the DRS (9) which consists of this condition only) to describe the situation s? Again, if we stand by our present proposal, s should support a corresponding infon. But which infon? The structure of (9) suggests that its constituents ought to be (i) the *relation* that holds between x and y when x is an executive, y is a car and x owns y, (ii) the *relation* which holds between x and y if x owns a credit card, and (iii) the *polyadic* quantifier **Every** which holds between two binary relations R and S if the extension of the former is included in that of the latter.

It would be unproblematic to admit such polyadic quantifiers. However, doing so would involve a certain amount of work and would distract from the issues that interest us here. An alternative where indefinites are treated as generalized quantifiers might be obtained by extending the kind of quantification over situations introduced in Cooper 1991 to the analysis of conditionals. Here we merely note the problem as one for further investigation.

At last, we return to the sentence which prompted this long excursus into the treatment of quantification, namely,

(10) John doesn't own a car.

with its DRS

(11)

$$
\boxed{
\begin{array}{c}
x \\
\mathrm{John}(x) \\
\neg \;
\boxed{
\begin{array}{c}
y \\
\mathrm{car}(y) \\
\mathrm{own}(x,y)
\end{array}
} \\
K_1
\end{array}
}
$$

According to the proposal now before us, (11) describes s, in an environment of which we may assume that it anchors x to the actual referent j of 'John' iff

$s \models \langle\!\langle \text{named}, \text{'John'}, x; 1 \rangle\!\rangle$ and

$s \models K$ iff $s \models \langle\!\langle \text{named}, \text{'John'}, x; 1 \rangle\!\rangle$ and

$s \models \langle\!\langle \text{Exist}, [\text{Y} \mid s_r \models \langle\!\langle \text{car}, \text{Y}; 1 \rangle\!\rangle], [\text{Y} \mid \text{Sit}(s) \models \langle\!\langle \text{owns}, \text{j}, \text{Y}; 1 \rangle\!\rangle]; 0 \rangle\!\rangle$

We have not yet discussed veridicality of the support relation for such negative infons, but the implications of what has been said above are clear: s supports the infon $\langle\!\langle \text{Exist}, P, Q; 0 \rangle\!\rangle$ if there is *no* overlap in extension between P and Q; more explicitly if there is no object $b \in \text{Ind}(\text{Sit}(s))$ such that $s_r \models \langle\!\langle \text{car}, b; 1 \rangle\!\rangle$ and $\models_{\text{Sit}(s)} \langle\!\langle \text{owns}, \text{j}, b; 1 \rangle\!\rangle$. Alternatively, we may take the dual condition: for every object $b \in \text{Ind}(\text{Sit}(s))$ such that $s_r \models \langle\!\langle \text{car}, b; 1 \rangle\!\rangle$ and $\models_{\text{Sit}(s)} \langle\!\langle \text{owns}, \text{j}, b; 0 \rangle\!\rangle$.

It should be kept in mind in this connection that the analysis we have proposed here does *not* entail that an utterance of (10) can only be true if there is no car anywhere in the world that is owned by John. The resource situation s_r could restrict the cars that (10) excludes from being owned by John in any one of a number of ways.

For instance, there might be uses of (10) in which the resource situation restricts the range of the existential quantifier to cars in the United Kingdom; when used this way (10) asserts that there is no car in Britain which John owns. If it happens nevertheless that he owns a car in the US—say, one which he left with friends upon his permanent return to Europe a couple of years earlier—this would not count against the statement being true. (Admittedly, with the verb *own*, such restricted uses appear marginal.)

The role of resource situations in the semantics of quantified utterances holds a particular significance in the context of the juxtaposition of situation semantics and DRT that is our general concern in this paper. For this is one of the points on which the two theories suggest distinct mechanisms for dealing with the same phenomenon. The treatment of contextual restriction of quantificational domains within DRT is something that is treated in connection with the analysis of plurals by Kamp and Reyle (forthcoming), Chapter 4.

5   Conclusion

Except for the issue concerning the treatment of indefinites, the analyses of negation that we have presented could be seen as independent of DRT since they might arise if one tried to provide a situation semantics for predicate logic or some fragment of English with negation in the conservative style that we explored. Thus the main conclusion that we draw concerning the relationship between DRT and situation semantics is that if we are to maintain the 'indefinite as variable' idea of DRT (or classical situation semantics) and use a partial semantics in the style of situation semantics, then it seems that we have either to give up the notion of persistence and with it the notion that all negative sentences in natural language correspond to the presence of negative information as opposed to the lack of positive information or we may have to countenance the possibility that certain negative DRSs do not express "local" information in that they only describe situations which support negative facts about a whole universe of individuals. However, if we return to Montague's proposal that indefinites correspond to generalized quantifiers then we may have a partial semantics that allows "local" negation which is persistent.

It is difficult to make this into a general result about partial semantics for quantification and negation. However, it seems to us that it holds true for some of the standard tools available in DRT and situation semantics. It remains an open question whether there is not some variant of the 'indefinite as variable' analysis or of partial semantics that would allow us to have the best of both worlds.

An interesting suggestion for such a variant was made by the referee of this paper. The idea would be to use a quantifier relation **exist** which has just one argument role for a property or relation of any number of arguments. Intuitively the relation **exist** would hold just in case the relation has a non-empty extension. A DRS would then correspond to such an existential infon where the relation abstracts over parameters corresponding to the domain of the DRS. A conjunction of infons corresponding to the conditions of the DRS would provide the body of the relation. There are two ways in which we could begin to implement this suggestion. We could say that a DRS of the form

$$\boxed{\begin{array}{c} X_1, \ldots, X_n \\ C_1 \\ \vdots \\ C_m \end{array}}$$

describes a situation s iff

$$s \models \langle\!\langle \text{exist}, [X_1, \ldots, X_n \mid s \models C_1 \wedge \ldots \wedge C_m]; 1 \rangle\!\rangle$$

Alternatively we could say that this DRS describes a situation s iff

$$s \models \langle\!\langle \text{exist}, [X_1, \ldots, X_n \mid \models_{\text{Sit}(s)} C_1 \wedge \ldots \wedge C_m]; 1 \rangle\!\rangle$$

A problem with this approach seems to be that we need the second of the two alternatives for negative cases and the first alternative for positive cases. Thus we might want to require that the DRS (11) describes a situation s just in case

$$s \models \langle\!\langle \text{exist}, [X \mid \models_{\text{Sit}(s)} \langle\!\langle \text{car}, X; 1 \rangle\!\rangle \wedge \langle\!\langle \text{own}, j, X; 1 \rangle\!\rangle]; 0 \rangle\!\rangle^{10}$$

However, we would want the positive DRS (6) to describe a situation s according to the first alternative, i.e., iff

$$s \models \langle\!\langle \text{exist}, [X \mid s \models \langle\!\langle \text{car}, X; 1 \rangle\!\rangle \wedge \langle\!\langle \text{own}, j, X; 1 \rangle\!\rangle]; 1 \rangle\!\rangle$$

unless we were to give up the locality of any infons corresponding to the individual conditions of a DRS. Nevertheless, it seems like this suggestion might be an important direction in which to go, not least because it moves us closer to providing a situation theoretic object corresponding to a DRS (namely the quantified infon with relation **exist**). The idea would thus get us closer to the second approach mentioned in the introduction to this paper, that of modeling DRSs as situation theoretic objects. However, as with the discussion of properties above, it has the disadvantage of relying on complex infonic structure to deal with simple DRS conditions.

We hope at least that the discussion in this paper shows that it would be dangerous to assume that an appropriate partial semantics for indefinites as

---

[10]Or perhaps something which makes the embedded structure explicit like

$$s \models \langle\!\langle \text{exist}, T_y; 1 \rangle\!\rangle \quad \text{where}$$
$$T_y = [Y \mid \models_{\text{Sit}(s)} \langle\!\langle =, Y, j; 1 \rangle\!\rangle \wedge \langle\!\langle \text{exist}, T_x; 0 \rangle\!\rangle]$$
$$T_x = [X \mid \models_{\text{Sit}(s)} \langle\!\langle \text{car}, X; 1 \rangle\!\rangle \wedge \langle\!\langle \text{own}, j, X; 1 \rangle\!\rangle]$$

free variables can be obtained in a straightforward manner—an assumption that was perhaps made in classical situation semantics as put forward by Barwise and Perry 1983.

References

Barwise, J., and J. Etchemendy. 1990. Information, Infons, and Inference. In Cooper et al. 1990.

Barwise, J., and J. Perry. 1983. *Situations and Attitudes*. Cambridge, MA: MIT Press.

Chierchia, G. 1991. Anaphora and Dynamic Logic. In *Quantification and Anaphora I*. DYANA Deliverable R2.2.A, ed. M. Stokhof, J. Groenendijk, and D. Beaver. Edinburgh University: Centre for Cognitive Science.

Cooper, R. P. 1991a. *Classification-Based Phrase Structure Grammar: an Extended Revised Version of HPSG*. PhD thesis, University of Edinburgh.

Cooper, R. P. 1991b. Persistence and Structural Determination. This volume.

Cooper, R. n.d. Introduction to Situation Semantics. In preparation.

Cooper, R. 1989. Information and Grammar. Research Paper 438, Department of AI, University of Edinburgh.

Cooper, R. 1991. Three Lectures on Situation Theoretic Grammar. In *Natural Language Processing: EAIA 90 Proceedings*. Lecture Notes in Artificial Intelligence, no. 476, ed. M. Filgueiras, L. Damas, N. Moreira, and A. P. Tomás, 101–140. EAIA, Springer-Verlag.

Cooper, R., K. Mukai, and J. Perry (ed.). 1990. *Situation Theory and Its Applications*, vol. 1. CSLI Lecture Notes Number 22. Stanford: CSLI Publications.

Evans, G. 1980. Pronouns. *Linguistic Inquiry* 11(2):337–362.

Fenstad, J. E., P.-K. Halvorsen, T. Langholm, and J. van Benthem. 1987. *Situations, Language and Logic*. Dordrecht: Reidel.

Filgueiras, M., L. Damas, N. Moreira, and A. P. Tomás (ed.). 1991. *Natural Language Processing: EAIA 90 Proceedings*. Lecture Notes in Artificial Intelligence no. 476. Springer Verlag.

Gawron, J. M., and S. Peters. 1990. *Anaphora and Quantification in Situation Semantics*. CSLI Lecture Notes Number 19. Stanford: CSLI Publications.

Groenendijk, G., T. Janssen, and M. Stokhof (ed.). 1981. *Formal Methods in the Study of Language*. Amsterdam: Mathematisch Centrum.

Groenendijk, G., and M. Stokhof. 1989. Dynamic Montague Grammar: A First Sketch. Prepublication Series X-89-04, ITLI.

Heim, I. 1990. E-Type Pronouns and Donkey Anaphora. *Linguistics and Philosophy* 13(2):137–177.

Kadmon, N. 1987. *On Unique and Non-Unique Reference and Asymmetric Quantification*. PhD thesis, University of Massachusetts, Amherst.

Kadmon, N. 1990. Uniqueness. *Linguistics and Philosophy* 13(3):273–324.

Kamp, H. 1975. Two Theories About Adjectives. In *Formal Semantics of Natural Languages*, ed. E. Keenan. Cambridge: Cambridge University Press.

Kamp, H. 1981. A Theory of Truth and Semantic Representation. In *Formal Methods in the Study of Language*, ed. G. Groenendijk, T. Janssen, and M. Stokhof. Amsterdam: Mathematisch Centrum.

Kamp, H., and U. Reyle. n.d. From Discourse to Logic. Forthcoming from Reidel.

Kleene, S. 1952. *Introduction to Metamathematics*. Princeton, NJ: D. van Nostrand.

Muskens, R. 1989. *Meaning and Partiality*. Academisch Proefschrift, University of Amsterdam.

Neale, S. 1990. Descriptive Pronouns and Donkey Anaphora. *Journal of Philosophy* 87(3):113–150.

Sem, H. 1987. Discourse Representation Theory, Situation Schemata and Situation Semantics: A Comparison. Cosmos Report 2, Department of Mathematics, University of Oslo.

Stokhof, M., J. Groenendijk, and D. Beaver (ed.). 1991. *Quantification and Anaphora I*. DYANA Deliverable R2.2.A. Edinburgh University: Centre for Cognitive Science.

Westerståhl, D. 1990. Parametric Types and Propositions in First-Order Situation Theory. In Cooper et al. 1990.

15

The Absorption Principle and E-Type Anaphora

JEAN MARK GAWRON, JOHN NERBONNE, AND STANLEY PETERS

1 Introduction

In Gawron and Peters (1990a), henceforth G&P, we discussed a generalization we called the Absorption Principle (AP), which constrains scope-relations between NP's.

The Absorption Principle is a principle of situation theory which rules out certain kinds of parametric contents. If a parameter x occurs in a restriction on a parameter y, we say y depends on x. The Absorption Principle says that in such cases, any type formed by abstracting on x must also abstract on y. That is parametric types of the following form do not exist:

(1) $[x \mid \langle\langle \ldots y_{\langle\langle \ldots x \ldots \rangle\rangle} \ldots \rangle\rangle]$

However there are types of both the following forms:

(2) $[x, y \mid \langle\langle \ldots y_{\langle\langle \ldots x \ldots \rangle\rangle} \ldots \rangle\rangle]$
$[x \mid \exists y \langle\langle \ldots y_{\langle\langle \ldots x \ldots \rangle\rangle} \ldots \rangle\rangle]$

Thus, y can be absorbed anywhere within the scope of the type, but it cannot be a parameter of the type as a whole. The situation-theoretic motivations for the Absorption Principle need not concern us here. Suffice it to say that the restrictions on the existence of the forbidden types appear necessary for any theory countenancing restricted parameters.

Among its many effects, the AP prevents a pronoun utterance from be-

---

This paper owes a great deal to conversations with Makoto Kanazawa in its early formative stages. The authors would also like to thank Christa Hauenschild, Jean-Yves Lerner, Manfred Pinkal, and Barbara Zimmermann for discussions of this paper. As usual, the authors are responsible for its content.

Situation Theory and Its Applications, vol. 2.
Jon Barwise, Jean Mark Gawron, Gordon Plotkin, and Syun Tutiya, eds.
Copyright © 1991, Stanford University.

ing anaphorically related to the NP *his car* in any utterance of the following sentence in which *his* is anaphorically linked to *Every boy*:

(3) *Every boy* washed *his* car. #I inspected it.

Roughly, this is because the pronoun parameter x, which occurs in a restriction on the parameter y belonging to the NP *his car*, is abstracted on by either the content of the VP *washed his car* or the quantifier's scope:

(4) $[x \mid \exists y \langle\!\langle \text{WASH}, x, y_{\langle\!\langle \text{CAR},y \rangle\!\rangle \wedge \langle\!\langle \text{POSS},x,y \rangle\!\rangle} \rangle\!\rangle]$

In such cases, the Absorption Principle requires that the resulting type not be parametric in y. Since the VP content can have no parameter for y, no anaphoric relation to the NP *his car* was possible in the system of G&P.

In some contexts where the Absorption Principle would appear to apply, however, anaphoric uses of the pronoun do appear possible. In Sem, Sæbø, Verne, and Vestre (1990), Norwegian sentences of the following sort are raised as evidence against use of the Absorption Principle in explaining the deviance of examples like (3):

(5) John kysset sin kone og det gjorde Bill også.
     John kissed his wife and Bill did too.

Here the only reading possible for the sentence with the elliptical VP is the sloppy reading, on which Bill kisses his own wife. But this means the content of the first clause must be roughly:

(6) $\langle\!\langle [x \mid \exists y \langle\!\langle \text{KISS}, x, y_{\langle\!\langle \text{WIFE},y \rangle\!\rangle \wedge \langle\!\langle \text{POSS},x,y \rangle\!\rangle} \rangle\!\rangle], z_{\langle\!\langle \text{NAMED},z,\text{"John"} \rangle\!\rangle} \rangle\!\rangle$

That is, John has the property of being an own-wife kisser:

(7) $[x \mid \exists y \langle\!\langle \text{KISS}, x, y_{\langle\!\langle \text{WIFE},y \rangle\!\rangle \wedge \langle\!\langle \text{POSS},x,y \rangle\!\rangle} \rangle\!\rangle]$

Crucially, the property John has cannot be a property parametric in y: that would be just the sort of property which the Absorption Principle says does not exist. Since the parameter y has x in its restriction, when x is absorbed, y cannot be a parameter of the resulting type. But if y is not a parameter of the content of any utterance of (5), then one would expect that no pronoun could enter into an anaphoric relation with the NP *sin kone*.

Yet Sem, Sæbø, Verne, and Vestre discuss numerous examples in which an anaphoric relation is possible with an NP containing *sin*:[1]

(8) John vasket bilen sin. Den ble skinnende ren nå.
     John washed his car. It is spanking clean now.

Before commenting on (8),[2] we turn to some other examples which pose

---

[1] The Norwegian constructions appear to be a kind of event (or event-type) anaphora, more closely analogous to the English "do it" construction than to VP ellipsis. But whether or not the ellipsis analysis should be applied here, the issues raised are significant.

[2] Analogous problems may arise in conjunction with constructions using the pronoun modifier *own* in English:

related problems for the Absorption Principle. Consider the ambiguous discourse:

(9)   Only John washed his car. It got spanking clean.

Here the first sentence can be interpreted to mean either that John was the only one to wash his *own* car, or that he was the only one to wash John's car. On the first of these readings, the VP content will be analogous to (7); again the point is that this VP content cannot have y, the parameter associated with *his car*, as a parameter. Yet an anaphoric relation with *it* still seems possible, even on this reading. This is in marked contrast to (3), where no such anaphoric relation is possible. Intuitively, the difference between these examples is clear. In (9), on the relevant reading, there is a salient car for the pronoun to exploit. In (3), there is no such car. The issue before us now is whether capturing this difference will entail weakening or abandoning the Absorption Principle.

We summarize the problem as follows: in G&P, we followed a basic strategy of trying to account for all anaphora by means of parameter-sharing, either directly by a pronoun and its antecedent, or by a pronoun and a role to which the antecedent was linked. This meant that if a pronoun's parameter fell outside the scope in which its antecedent's parameter was absorbed, there was no way for the two to be anaphorically related. Our problems concerning the action of the Absorption Principle and the anaphoric relations exhibited above can be viewed as a special consequence of this property of the system in G&P. In all cases, a pronoun falls outside the scope of its antecedent.

A somewhat different case of the same general problem involves a phenomenon first discussed in Grinder and Postal (1971), known as Missing Antecedents. The Missing Antecedents Phenomenon can be illustrated with contrasting discourses like the following:

(10)   John has never ridden a camel. # And it stank.

(11)   John has never ridden a camel. But Bill has. And it stank.

In the first discourse, the pronoun cannot be understood as anaphoric to the NP *a camel*; in the second, it can.

The data suggest that the antecedent of the pronoun in (11) is not the overt NP in the first VP, but the "missing NP" that would have occurred if the VP of the second clause weren't elliptical. One might try to account

---

(i) John washed his own car. It got spanking clean.

In (i), it seems perfectly acceptable to understand the pronoun as anaphoric to the NP *his own car*. Many speakers find that *own* forces sloppy readings, so that a sentence like *The baby washed his own face before his mother could* is odd on the most pragmatically natural interpretation: the baby washed his face before the mother could wash it. Other speakers, however, accept these examples. Sentences with *own* only present a problem for the Absorption Principle if in fact they force a sloppy reading. The analogous data in Norwegian appear to be clear.

for such examples by resorting to a parametric content for the minimal VP *ridden a camel*. If this VP content has a parameter for the camel, then even though that parameter is absorbed in the first clause as a whole, the parameter is reused when the VP content is reused in ellipsis, this time without being absorbed, and is thus able to license further anaphora. This sort of account crucially relies on always being able to produce a VP content which is parametric in Missing Antecedent cases. However, the Absorption Principle can sometimes make it impossible to produce such a parametric VP content. Consider:

(12)   John has never read a Russian novel he disliked. But Bill has. It was *War and Peace*.

We are concerned here with the sloppy reading of the VP-ellipsis, the reading on which what is at issue is John's reading novels John dislikes and Bill's reading novels Bill dislikes. On this reading, the content of the VP *read a Russian novel he disliked* must be

(13) $[\, x \mid \exists y \langle\!\langle \text{READ}, x, y \langle\!\langle \text{RUSSIAN-NOVEL}, y \rangle\!\rangle \wedge \langle\!\langle \text{DISLIKE}, x, y \rangle\!\rangle \rangle\!\rangle \,]$

Note, that, in order to get the desired sloppy reading, the parameter y must depend on x. But in that case, the Absorption Principle requires that the scope of y can be no greater than x. There is thus no way to obtain a VP content which has abstracted over x but is still parametric in y.

Worse yet, Nerbonne, Iida and Ladusaw (1990) (henceforth NI&L) demonstrate that missing antecedent cases interact directly with standard cases of donkey anaphora, demonstrating that "missing antecedent" mechanisms must in principle be available in donkey anaphora as well.

(14)   No [farmers who own several donkeys$_j$]$_i$ beat them$_j$. Few $\emptyset_i$ even scold them$_{j'}$.

This is an example of an $\bar{\text{N}}$ anaphor (*few* $\emptyset_i$) which contains an example of a "missing antecedent", i.e., a case in which the pronoun *them* could NOT have been licensed by the explicit NP *several donkeys*, but could only be licensed by material "missing" in the anaphor *few* $\emptyset_i$. The pronoun *them*$_{j'}$ could not be licensed by the explicit NP *several donkeys* because it necessarily falls outside its scope, closed by the "trapping" quantifier *No*. So *several donkeys* is an unavailable antecedent for parameter-reusing anaphora. One might try to avoid the conclusion that this is a missing antecedent, for example by noting that the plural anaphor *they* does not obey scope restrictions as strictly as its singular counterparts, *she*, *he* and *it*. For example, the following is certainly felicitous:

(15)   No farmers who own several donkeys beat them$_i$. They$_i$ are too valuable.

But this use of the pronoun can only refer to a group of donkeys *simpliciter*, NOT to a group of donkeys owned, but not beaten by farmers. Given the simpler sort of binding, we would expect the second sentence in (14) to mean that few of the farmers scold the group of donkeys in question—which it apparently can mean. Nonetheless, the more prominent reading is the one, roughly, that few farmers who own several donkeys scold THE DONKEYS THEY OWN. This is the reading we're interested in. And on this reading, there is simply no appropriate antecedent in the sentence for *them$_{j'}$*—it's missing.

The combination of donkey anaphora and missing antecedent licensing arises in VP ellipsis as well:

(16) Farmer Brown has never owned a donkey she hated, but every farmer who has has beaten it.

Thus, there appears to be a significant class of cases which raise questions about the Absorption Principle. We believe, however, that these are not counterexamples to the Absorption Principle.

In G&P, a pronoun and an antecedent were linked in content by parameter-sharing. Because the basic idea behind this account of pronouns was first argued for by Quine, we shall call this a Q-Type account.

We assume that the above data falsify the following conjunction, implicitly assumed in G&P: (a) all anaphora can be accounted for by a Q-Type account; and (b), the Absorption Principle is correct.

In order for the above data to be accounted for at least one of these assumptions must be weakened or dropped. It is our purpose in this paper to argue that an illuminating account is open to us if we modify only assumption (a).

To begin with, assumption (a) can be falsified on grounds quite independent of the Absorption Principle. As Evans (1977) points out, pronouns *can* have antecedents whose scope they lie outside of.

(17) Mark owns exactly one car. It's green.

We cannot assume that the pronoun in the second sentence falls under the scope of the quantifier, *exactly one*, because that would yield the wrong interpretation, that there is exactly one car which is owned by Mark and is green. Clearly, thus, there are pronoun utterances whose interpretations fall outside the scope of their antecedents. To distinguish these pronoun occurrences from those open to a Q-Type account, we will follow the lead of a number of authors in the wake of Evans (1977), and call them E-Type.

Such uses of pronouns are quite widespread. Other examples have a (possibly non-monotone) quantifier with scope inside another operator outside of whose scope the pronoun lies.

(18) If you take at most one cookie, it won't be missed.

(19) The fact that John denies he has an offshore bank account means we're going to have a hard time locating it.

E-Type uses of pronouns are so ubiquitous it is somewhat surprising in retrospect that they were apparently not noticed prior to the 1970s.[3]

To summarize: we think that examples like (8), (9), (11) and (12) show that the conjunction of the Absorption Principle with the claim that there is only Q-Type anaphora is false. But (17) alone shows that there must also be E-Type anaphora. We think that (8), (9), (11) and (12) are all cases of E-Type anaphora: the NP parameters in these examples are absorbed, just as the Absorption Principle predicts. But a pronoun outside the scope of that absorption is still able to relate anaphorically to the NP by taking it as an E-Type antecedent.

In this paper we try to explore some of the consequences of this view. The paper divides up as follows: sections 2 and 3 lay out the requirements for an analysis of E-Type pronouns, specifically pointing out a number of areas where the exact truth-conditions are problematic. Section 4 shows how a minimal account of E-Type anaphora deals with the putative counterexamples to the Absorption Principle. Section 5 discusses the status of the Absorption Principle in a system which allows E-Type anaphora, and argues that there are a number of important predictions which it still makes, particularly as regards possible quantifier scopes. Section 6 presents an analysis that tries to account for some of the basic facts about E-Type pronouns.

2 Some Puzzles about E-Type Pronouns

Puzzle 1. What is the propositional content of a statement involving an E-Type use of a pronoun, such as might be made using (20) or (21):

(20) Mark owns exactly one car. He should take good care of it.

(21) Few senators support the immigration bill. They will have to convert a lot of their colleagues.

Puzzle 2. If the discourse

(22) Noam wrote a book. It was not well received.

entails that Noam wrote just one book (as Evans has claimed), why isn't (23) parallel? How can the second sentence be true?[4]

(23) I bought a sage plant yesterday. I bought eight others with it.

Puzzle 3. What's odd about the following?

---

[3] While Kadmon's recent (1990) paper might be read as implying that example (17) doesn't prove the existence of E-Type uses as Evans claimed, we believe his argument is sound. For any generalized quantifier Q, the conservativity property guarantees equivalence of the proposition $\ldots Q(A, B) \ldots$ with the proposition $\exists X (X = A \cap B \wedge \ldots Q(A, X) \ldots)$. The price of analyzing quantified propositions in the latter way, as Kadmon does, is to empty the accessibility condition on reference markers in DRT of predictive power.

[4] The example and the puzzle are due to Heim.

(24)   Nobody is at the door. I'm not going to let him in.

(25)   John didn't plant any daisies. They need water.

Puzzle 4. Why doesn't (26) entail that a doctor examined Bill?[5]

(26)   Either no doctor has examined Bill today or she didn't write anything on this chart.

(27)   Either John has no children or they haven't been in touch with him
in years.

Puzzle 5. If (26) requires that *any* doctor who has examined Bill have
refrained from chart-writing, why doesn't (28) require that you hand over
any quarter that you have to that beggar?[6]

(28)   If you have a quarter, you should give it to that beggar.

3   The Analysis: Basic Cases

We begin by discussing a central problem confronting any analysis of E-
Type pronouns, the apparent quantificational variability of singular E-Type
pronouns. We then discuss plural E-Type pronouns and some extra quantificational wrinkles they give rise to.

Consider the case of an anaphoric utterance of the pronoun *it* in a
discourse like (29).

(29)   Mark owns exactly one car. It's green.

Assume that the antecedent in the given discourse is the NP *exactly one
car*. The content for a statement using the first sentence is something like:

(30) $(\text{EXACTLY-ONE}, T)$
          where
          $T = [\, x : (r \models \langle\!\langle \text{CAR}, x \rangle\!\rangle) \mid (s \models \langle\!\langle \text{OWNS}, \text{mark}, x \rangle\!\rangle) \,]$

Then the question is: what is the content of a statement using the second
sentence? As a first approximation, we might try the the following content.

(31) $(s' \models \langle\!\langle \text{GREEN}, z_{(z\,:\,T)} \rangle\!\rangle)$

An important point here is that the pronoun parameter z occurs outside
the scope of its antecedent's quantification. We take this to be diagnostic of
E-Type anaphora. That is, two conditions must hold: first, the pronoun's
antecedent must be quantified away (it cannot be referential); and second,
the content of the pronoun must fall outside its antecedent's quantification.

In (31), the pronoun parameter is restricted to be of Type T, the same
type that is the argument of the quantifier EXACTLY-ONE in the previous
sentence.[7] In general, let us call the type the pronoun depends on (here, the

---

[5]This example is modeled on one pointed out by Barbara Partee.

[6]This example is modeled on one pointed out in Schubert and Pelletier (1989).

[7]For arguments that motivate this treatment of determiners as types of types, see
Section 5 of this paper and G&P (1990b).

type of x such that x is a car owned by Mark in s) the Evans-type.[8] Clearly the Evans type depends both on the content of the previous utterance, and on determining the pronoun's antecedent in that utterance. In fact, it is just the conservative scope of the antecedent's quantification.[9]

If (31) were the content of an utterance of the second sentence in (29), the circumstances would be responsible for somehow anchoring the parameter z. In that sense, we could speak of the pronoun-use as "referential." However, we might just as well have prefixed the content with some operator, call it ∇, which quantified the pronoun parameter away. For the moment, let us consider ∇ simply a placeholder, to be filled by a specific quantifier, perhaps an existential, perhaps a definite, or perhaps a universal. A central issue in the analysis of E-Type pronouns is whether E-Type pronouns are (at least sometimes) referential, or whether there is always some operator ∇ which quantifies them away, and if so, what it is.

3.1 Quantificational Variability of E-Type Pronouns

We now try to show why there is an issue about the quantificational force of E-Type pronouns. We proceed by examining a sampling of relevant examples which suggest referentiality or various quantificational forces that might be assigned to E-Type pronouns.

Our intuitions about the truth conditions of (29) are of little help here. If the first sentence is true, there will only be one such car. So, for this particular example, it is all the same if we analyze the pronoun as referential or quantify it away using existential, definite, or universal force. If it never mattered at all, we would doubtless settle on the weakest of the possibilities, the existential account. Then $\nabla = \exists$ and (31) can simply become (32):

(32) $\exists z (z : T)(s' \models \langle\!\langle \text{GREEN}, z \rangle\!\rangle)$

It is worth pointing out that in all the examples of E-Type pronouns discussed below, the pronoun has at least existential force (though not always an existential with widest possible scope). Thus (32), if not the correct analysis, at least captures a minimal requirement on the correct analysis. That is, all viable alternatives will have to entail (32). And in fact, all the alternatives we discuss do entail it.

There are examples that indicate that the quantificational force of E-Type pronouns is something stronger than the existential in (32). It is sometimes argued (in Kadmon (1987), for example), that the correct analysis must build in an implicature of the uniqueness of the description which the pronoun exploits. Thus, take (33).

---

[8] Throughout this discussion we follow the convention of representing a parameter such as $y_{\langle\!\langle \text{NAMED}, y, \text{"MARK"} \rangle\!\rangle}$ simply as $mark$.

[9] The conservative scope of a quantification incorporates both the restriction type (the type of being a car in the example) and the scope type (the type of being an x owned by Mark in the example).

(33)   Noam wrote a book last year. It was not well received.

This discourse appears to implicate that Noam wrote just one book last year. In support of this claim, consider the oddness of

(34)   Bill had a quarter. He gave it to a beggar, and later gave it to another beggar.

What this discourse seems to describe is a situation in which Bill generously gave a quarter to a beggar, somehow got it back, and then gave *the same quarter* to another beggar.[10] If we take both occurrences of *it* to be anaphoric to *a quarter*, then the existential analysis would allow for the possibility of two quarters. But the discourse simply cannot be understood that way.[11]

To capture the uniqueness entailment of (33), we might represent the content of an utterance of the second sentence as:

(35)   *the* $z\,(z:T)(s' \models \langle\!\langle \text{WELL-RECEIVED}, z; 0\rangle\!\rangle)$
where
$$T = [\, x : (x : T') \mid (s \models \langle\!\langle \text{WRITE-LAST-YEAR}, \text{noam}, x\rangle\!\rangle)\,]$$
$$T' = [\, x \mid (r \models \langle\!\langle \text{BOOK}, x\rangle\!\rangle)\,]$$

We define *the* $z\,\psi\phi$ to be true if and only if there is only one appropriate anchoring for z, i.e., satisfying ψ, and moreover that anchoring satisfies ϕ. The difficulties of this sort of analysis are discussed extensively in Kadmon (1987); the general outline of the problem can be illustrated with the help of a simple example due to Heim:

(36)   I bought a sage plant yesterday. I bought eight others with it.

If we follow the view that $\nabla = the$, then the semantics of the second sentence of the above discourse becomes something like *I bought eight other sage plants (yesterday) with the unique sage plant I bought yesterday.* The assigned interpretation would be self-contradictory, but the discourse does not appear to be. Thus, if there is a uniqueness implicature associated with E-Type pronoun use, that implicature must somehow be made defeasible.

Indeed, the same sort of defeasibility of a uniqueness implicature can be observed with respect to (33):

(37)   Noam wrote a book last year. It was not well received. So he wrote a second book that very same year.

There is nothing desperately wrong with this discourse. Nevertheless, there is a clear sense that the facts in question might better have been expressed:

---

[10] For this example, we are indebted to Makoto Kanazawa.
[11] One might claim that the second *it* is anaphoric to the first, in which case, the existential analysis would associate it with the description *a quarter which Bill had which he gave to a beggar.* This would force the same quarter to occur in both transactions. However, that still doesn't explain why the second *it* cannot be anaphoric to *a quarter*; on an analysis in ∇ was simply existential quantification, this would allow for the possibility of two quarters.

(38) Noam wrote a book that was not well received last year. So he wrote a second book that very same year.

We can roughly capture the facts by assigning a third quantificational force to ∇:

(39) $\exists \wedge \forall\, z(z:T)(s' \models \langle\!\langle \text{BUY-8-OTHERS-WITH}, \text{I}, z \rangle\!\rangle)$
where
$T = [\, x : (s \models \langle\!\langle \text{SAGE-PLANT}, x \rangle\!\rangle) \mid (s \models \langle\!\langle \text{BUY}, \text{I}, x \rangle\!\rangle) \,]$

Here, $\exists \wedge \forall$ amounts to non-vacuous universal quantification: $\exists \wedge \forall\, z\, \psi\phi$ is true if and only if ϕ is true for all appropriate anchorings of z, i.e., all that satisfy ψ, and moreover there is some appropriate anchoring that makes ϕ true. Since z in (39) is a restricted parameter, the quantification is over sage plants bought by the speaker in s. What the second sentence in (36) says, then, is that any such sage plant has to be such that eight others were bought with it, and that moreover there is such a sage plant.

Another sort of case that may illustrate a non-vacuous universal force for an E-Type pronoun is (26), repeated here:

(40) Either no doctor has examined Bill today or she didn't write anything on this chart.

Suppose Bill in fact has been examined by two doctors, one who did in fact write something on the chart, one who didn't. Many speakers judge the sentence false in such circumstances; others are undecided. No speakers feel comfortable awarding it an unqualified "true." Assigning an existential value to ∇ makes (40) come out true. Assigning a definite value to ∇ makes (40) entail that at most one doctor examined Bill today, which intuitively the sentence does not seem to do.

In (40), we thus have a fairly clear case in which fixing ∇ to be universal appears to give the best account of the available candidates. We also have our first clear example of a non-referential use of an E-Type pronoun. In the previous examples, we could have given the pronouns widest possible scope, or even treated them as referential. In (40), it is clear that making the pronoun referential or giving it the widest possible scope, gives the wrong results. The reading we would get would entail that *there is a doctor x such that x examined Bill, and for all such x, either no doctor examined Bill or x didn't write anything on this chart.*

What we want is to allow for the possibility that (40) is true even though there is no such doctor:

(41) $(\text{NO}, T) \vee \nabla z(z:T)(s' \models \langle\!\langle \text{WRITE-ON-CHART}, z \rangle\!\rangle)$
where
$T = [\, x : (x:T') \mid (s \models \langle\!\langle \text{EXAMINE}, x, \text{bill} \rangle\!\rangle) \,]$
$T' = [\, x \mid (r \models \langle\!\langle \text{DOCTOR}, x \rangle\!\rangle) \,]$

Thus, (41) gives us a clear case in which treating an E-Type pronoun as referential gives unsatisfactory results; some version of ∇ appears unavoidable. (42) is another such case:

(42)   Every farmer who owns exactly one donkey beats it.

Here the same argument we used to motivate an E-Type analysis to begin with applies. Any attempt to extend the scope of the antecedent quantifier to include the pronoun will give us the wrong truth conditions.

An analysis of this example along the lines we have been sketching is straightforward:

(43) $(\text{EVERY}, [\, x : S \mid \nabla z(z : T)(s' \models \langle\!\langle \text{BEATS}, x, z \rangle\!\rangle) \,])$
       where
       $S = (s \models \langle\!\langle \text{FARMER}, x \rangle\!\rangle) \wedge (\text{EXACTLY-ONE} : T)$
       $T = [\, y : (y : T') \mid (s \models \langle\!\langle \text{OWNS}, x, y \rangle\!\rangle) \,]$
       $T' = [\, y \mid (r \models \langle\!\langle \text{DONKEY}, y \rangle\!\rangle) \,]$

We have thus far seen examples that point in two different directions for the value of ∇: a definite quantifier in (35), and a non-vacuous universal quantifier in (39). The sage plant shows that uniqueness implicatures are defeasible, but (37) shows that the conditions of that defeasibility are not easy to state. What we have not seen yet is an example that requires ∇ to be existential, as in (32). Puzzle 5 was meant to provide just such an example:

(44)   If you have a quarter, please give it to me.

This example, from Schubert and Pelletier (1989) does not require that the addressee have only one quarter, nor if (s)he has more than one quarter, does (s)he have to give all of them up. One will do. Thus both the universal and the definite analysis seem to fail.[12]

3.2   Donkey Anaphora and E-Types

More examples in which ∇ is existential can be found if we assume donkey pronouns are E-Type. In some cases, both universal and definite values for ∇ get the truth-conditions flat-out wrong, as pointed out in Rooth 1987. Speakers consistently judge sentences like

(45)   No farmer who owns a donkey beats it

false if there is *any* farmer-donkey pair where the farmer owns the donkey and beats it. The universal treatment makes the sentence come out true if there is a farmer who owns two donkeys and (s)he beats only one of them. Note that the definiteness analysis of (45) would fare just as badly: the sentence comes out true, because none of the donkey-owning farmers are such that they have exactly one donkey and beat it.

It is worth pointing out here that the classical DRT analysis of Kamp 1981 and the parallel analysis of Heim (1982) gets the above facts just

---

[12]Note that a standard DRT-style analysis of the sort given in Kamp (1981) fails as well, since it is equivalent to the universal analysis in this case.

right, in both cases by not taking the pronoun to be E-Type. However the classical DRT analysis has other problems, in particular, the proportion problem, as it is referred to in Kadmon 1987:

(46) Most farmers who have a donkey beat it.

Here one does not get the right truth conditions by quantifying over farmer-donkey pairs, for there may be many such, but still only a few farmers. Thus if there are five farmers, one of whom owns and beats a thousand donkeys, while the other four own a donkey apiece without beating them, then we still want the sentence coming out false. In such a case, however, quantifying over farmer-donkey pairs makes the sentence comes out true. This problem is easy enough to fix, by restating the truth-conditions for quantifiers, but then one immediately gets into the business of deciding between what we have here called the existential and universal analyses. Example (45) shows that sometimes the existential analysis is wanted. But for many speakers, the corresponding quantification with *every* requires the universal analysis: for every farmer x and every donkey x owns, x beats it. It is not at all clear that there is any single generally satisfactory answer for quantificational donkeys. Heim (1990) offers this gloomy summary:

> A number of authors, including Bauerle and Egli (1985), Root (1986), Rooth (1987), and Reinhart (1987), have advocated variants of the following strategy. Suppose we view donkey sentences with relatives as involving not one but two quantifying operators. One is the QDet, and that binds only the variable corresponding to the head noun; the other is an implicit quantifier of sometimes universal, sometimes existential force, and this binds the indefinite and pronouns anaphoric to it.

Summarizing now: only the existential analysis gets the truth conditions right for (45) and (44). Only the universal analysis gets the truth conditions right in (40). Only the definite analysis satisfies our intuitions about uniqueness in simple discourses like (22) or (34). Yet those same intuitions seem to evaporate in other cases, such as (36). Something makes the quantificational force of the pronoun appear to vary. What seems clear is that in some cases at least, the particular quantificational force that is used seems to be a matter for the pragmatics to decide:

(47) If you catch a Medfly, please bring it to me.

Consider a case in which the speaker is a biologist looking for samples on a field trip to Northern California. Then a single Medfly will do. This context gives a reading exactly parallel to that in (44); the existential analysis is called for. But now consider a case in which the speaker is a health department official engaged in eradicating the Medfly from Northern California. Then every instance of a Medfly may be crucial, and what the speaker has in mind is that *any* Medfly found should be brought. For this reading the universal analysis will be required.

Note that the same indeterminacy applies to an analogous quantificational donkey-sentence:

(48) Anyone who catches a Medfly should bring it to me.

In Section 6, we present a uniform analysis that we believe accounts for the apparent quantificational variability of E-Type pronouns.

3.3 Plurals, Scope of ∇ and Extra Parameters

We turn now to some other issues, first, plural E-Type pronouns, which are often simpler than singular E-Type pronouns, and then some difficult cases involving more unusual quantificational antecedents. Consider (49):

(49) Few senators support the immigration bill. They will have to win support from a lot of their colleagues.

Here in a discourse in which the pronoun *they* is anaphoric to *few senators*, it appears to pick out those senators who support the immigration bill. The content of an utterance of the second sentence with that anaphoric relation would be:

(50) $\nabla_2 z(z = \text{EXT}(T))(s' \models \langle\langle\text{WIN-SUPPORT}, z\rangle\rangle)$
      where
      $$T = [\, x : (r \models \langle\langle\text{SENATOR}, x\rangle\rangle) \mid (s \models \langle\langle\text{SUPPORT-BILL}, x\rangle\rangle)\,]$$

Here $\nabla_2 z$ means "z has a cardinality of at least 2," for whatever quantificational force is chosen. Thus, the analysis of this plural case is exactly like the singular case, with two differences (a) z is constrained to be equal to the extension of the Evans-type, not in it; and (b) there must be at least two members of z. Note that, with plurals, the distinction between the three solutions for ∇ vanishes. Necessarily there is exactly one z such that z is equal to the extension of the Evans-type.

We turn now to Puzzle 3.

(51) Nobody is at the door. I'm not going to let him in.

(52) John didn't plant any daisies. They need water.

All we need in order to account for these examples is existential import for the E-Type pronoun, which all versions of ∇ and ∇_2 have. On any account which grants the pronoun at least existential import, it is clear that these examples are self-contradictory. If the antecedent of *him* in (51) is *nobody* then the only available interpretation is roughly: *nobody is at the door and there is a person at the door and I'm going to let the person at the door in*. Analogously, (52) must have the interpretation *John didn't plant any daisies and there are daisies John planted and all the daisies John planted need water*. We give a provisional semantics for (51) here; we will deal with (52) in detail below.

(53) $(\text{NO}, T) \wedge \nabla z (z : T)(s' \models \langle\langle \text{LET-IN}, \text{I}, z; 0 \rangle\rangle)$

where

$$T = [\, x : (r \models \langle\langle \text{PERSON}, x \rangle\rangle) \mid (s \models \langle\langle \text{IS-AT-THE-DOOR}, x \rangle\rangle) \,]$$

Here the crucial point is that ∇ gets wider scope than the negation in the second clause, so that the second clause still has existential import: there is someone x who is at the door and I'm not going to let x in.

The right generalization about ∇ seem to be the following: it takes the widest scope it can without including its antecedent. Examples like the following provide independent justification for giving ∇ such wide scope:

(54)   The US has a president. He used to be a Democrat.

(54) has no reading which makes it true at the time of the writing of this article. That is, it has no reading paraphrasable as *there was a time t at which the president of the US at t was a Democrat*. Hence we might characterize the *only* possible scope for the E-Type pronoun as the widest scope that does not include its antecedent.[13]

We turn now to a question which arises very naturally given the E-Type analysis sketched thus far: E-Type anaphora is by definition anaphora where the pronoun lies outside the scope of its antecedent. To accommodate such pronouns, we have assumed some simple machinery for determining the type which restricts the pronoun parameter with conditions that combine the restrictions on the antecedent with what was predicated of it. But what happens when the antecedent falls under the scope of other parameter absorptions, that is, when the restrictions placed on it, and the predications made of it, are themselves parametric? One might guess that E-Type anaphora becomes impossible, but as it turns out, this is not at all the case.

Let us consider a simple case:

(55)   John didn't plant any pansies, but Bill did.

If the content of the sloppy reading of (55) were:

(56) $\neg\exists x \langle\langle \text{PLANT}, \text{john}, x_{r \models \langle\langle \text{PANSY}, x \rangle\rangle} \rangle\rangle \wedge \exists x \langle\langle \text{PLANT}, \text{bill}, x_{r \models \langle\langle \text{PANSY}, x \rangle\rangle} \rangle\rangle$

then it would be easy to obtain the content of (57) along the lines we have sketched.

(57)   They all came up.

It would be:

---

[13] One difficulty with this characterization arises in opaque contexts, as in Geach's famous hob-nob examples, if these are indeed E-Type anaphora: *Hob believes a witch blighted his mare and Nob believes she burned down his barn*. A similar case, *John thinks that he will catch a fish and he hopes I will grill it tonight*, is discussed in Heim (1990). In both cases "the widest scope not including the antecedent" will assign the pronoun a *de re* reading with respect to the attitude verb. That the issues involved in such cases may be orthogonal to issues about E-Type anaphora is suggested by the treatment in Saarinen (1978).

(58) $\nabla_2 z(z = \text{EXT}([x \mid \langle\!\langle \text{PLANT}, \text{bill}, x_r \models \langle\!\langle \text{PANSY}, x \rangle\!\rangle \rangle\!\rangle]))\langle\!\langle \text{CAME-UP}, z \rangle\!\rangle$

However, an appropriate content for an utterance of (55) would be:

(59) $\langle\!\langle [y \mid \exists x \langle\!\langle \text{PLANT}, y, x_r \models \langle\!\langle \text{PANSY}, x \rangle\!\rangle \rangle\!\rangle], \text{john}; 0 \rangle\!\rangle \wedge$
        $\langle\!\langle [y \mid \exists x \langle\!\langle \text{PLANT}, y, x_r \models \langle\!\langle \text{PANSY}, x \rangle\!\rangle \rangle\!\rangle], \text{bill}; 1 \rangle\!\rangle$

When interpreting (57), we cannot just get the Evans-type by picking up the type of x that is the scope of that quantification, namely,

(60) $[x \mid \langle\!\langle \text{PLANT}, y, x_r \models \langle\!\langle \text{PANSY}, x \rangle\!\rangle \rangle\!\rangle]$.

Not only is (60) not the type we want, it is inappropriate because of containing a 'free floating' parameter y, which would not get anchored or abstracted away by the operation of any rule of the language. The secret of success here is to recognize that the role to be filled by the E-Type use of the pronoun is outside the scope not only of the quantification,

(61) $\exists x \langle\!\langle \text{PLANT}, y, x_r \models \langle\!\langle \text{PANSY}, x \rangle\!\rangle \rangle\!\rangle$,

but also of the abstraction,

(62) $[y \mid \exists x \langle\!\langle \text{PLANT}, y, x_r \models \langle\!\langle \text{PANSY}, x \rangle\!\rangle \rangle\!\rangle]$.

Since the abstract (62) enters into the content of the utterance by having its argument role filled with b, the natural thing to do is replace y by b in (60) to get the actual restriction (63) on the parameter corresponding to the E-Type pronoun:

(63) $[x \mid \langle\!\langle \text{PLANT}, \text{bill}, x_r \models \langle\!\langle \text{PANSY}, x \rangle\!\rangle \rangle\!\rangle]$

This, then, is the simplest case of E-Type anaphora in which the pronoun falls outside the scope not only of its antecedent, but of other absorptions. Typically, such cases will involve a type like the type in (62), a type formed by abstracting on a parameter occurring in the restriction on the pronoun's antecedent. In the case we looked at, that type is a VP content given an argument. Another possibility is that the abstract (62) enters into the content of the utterance not by having its argument role filled, but instead by itself filling an argument role, e.g., of a quantifier. In this case, we will see two different subcases: (i) some other parameter could substitute for the one abstracted over by the quantifier, (ii) no other parameter could. Cases of the second sort were discussed by Webber (1977):

(64) Every farmer bought a cow. My job is to keep watch over them as they graze.

Cases of the first sort also occur, e.g.,

(65) Every student wrote a paper. John submitted it to L&P.

Note that this discourse as a whole appears to presuppose that John is a student. A precise treatment of both types of cases is beyond the scope of the present paper; the important point here is simply this: it often happens that the type formed when the antecedent of an E-Type pronoun is absorbed is itself parametric. In such cases the formation of the Evans type involves some extra complication. Nevertheless, E-Type anaphora is still possible.

4 The Absorption Principle and Putative Counterexamples

We return now to the putative counterexamples to the Absorption Principle discussed in the Introduction. These were cases where a pronoun appeared to be anaphoric to an NP whose parameter must be absorbed, according to the Absorption Principle. We will discuss (8), repeated here:

(66)   John vasket bilen sin. Den ble skinnende ren nå.
        John washed his car. It is spanking clean now.

The right account of these cases, we believe, is that the the antecedent NP's parameter is absorbed in the first sentence; therefore, since the pronoun occurs outside the scope of its antecedent, the anaphoric relation is E-Type.

Assuming that sloppy readings are obligatory with the Norwegian reflexive *sin*, the content for an utterance of the first sentence in (66) is:

(67) $\langle\!\langle [\, x, y \mid \langle\!\langle \text{WASH}, x, y_{(r \models \langle\!\langle \text{CAR}, y \rangle\!\rangle \wedge \langle\!\langle , \text{OWNS}, x, y \rangle\!\rangle)} \rangle\!\rangle \,], \text{john} \rangle\!\rangle$

Now suppose in an utterance of the second sentence of (66), the pronoun *den* is taken to be anaphoric to *bilen sin*, setting up circumstances in which E-Type anaphora is required. Now when we try to form the Evans type from the scope of the absorption of the pronoun, we find that it is parametric:

(68) $[\, y \mid \langle\!\langle \text{WASH}, x, y_{(r \models \langle\!\langle \text{CAR}, y \rangle\!\rangle \wedge \langle\!\langle , \text{OWNS}, x, y \rangle\!\rangle)} \rangle\!\rangle \,]$

As discussed in the last section, such a parametric Evans type cannot be directly used unless the pronoun falls inside the scope of whatever binds the parameter x. In this case, the parameter x is bound in the VP *washed his own car* and the pronoun is in the next clause. Thus, a non-parametric type must be constructed. In this case, the parameter x is abstracted on to make the subject role of the VP, and that role is labeled with the subject parameter. Thus, we replace x above with that parameter to yield:

(69) $[\, y \mid \langle\!\langle \text{WASH}, \text{john}, y_{(r \models \langle\!\langle \text{CAR}, y \rangle\!\rangle \wedge \langle\!\langle \text{OWNS}, \text{john}, y \rangle\!\rangle)} \rangle\!\rangle \,]$

This is now non-parametric and can be used to restrict the pronoun parameter. Using T to stand for the above Evans-type, the content of an utterance of the second sentence in (66) would be:

(70) $\nabla z(z : T)(s \models \langle\!\langle \text{SPANKING-CLEAN}, z \rangle\!\rangle)$

The same approach will work for the missing antecedent cases discussed in Section 1.

(71)   John has not read a Russian novel he hated. But Bill has. It was
        War and Peace.

We are concerned here with the sloppy reading of the VP-ellipsis, the reading on which what is at issue is John's reading novels John dislikes and Bill's reading novels Bill dislikes. On this reading, the content of the VP *read a Russian novel he disliked* must be

(72) $[\,x \mid \exists y \langle\!\langle \text{READ}, x, y_{(r \models \langle\!\langle \text{RUSSIAN-NOVEL},y\rangle\!\rangle \wedge \langle\!\langle \text{HATE},x,y\rangle\!\rangle)}\rangle\!\rangle\,]$

We will now attempt to determine the content of an utterance of the third sentence of discourse (71). Intuitively, the antecedent for the pronoun is the NP *a Russian novel he disliked*, with parameter y, but when we try to find the Evans-type that corresponds to that antecedent, we find, first of all, that the antecedent is absorbed in type (72) (whose body is parametric in x), and second, that that type is used in two places in the content of the discourse. We first consider the case where the occurrence of the type we use is the second occurrence, that is the occurrence predicated of Bill; this will lead us to the intended interpretation of the discourse. Then we consider the alternative analysis, which will lead to a contradictory interpretation of the discourse.

The situation here is entirely analogous to the situation discussed for example (55). The argument-role formed by abstracting on the parameter x is fed the argument *Bill*. To find the Evans-type, we substitute that parameter into the relevant part of (72). The result is:

(73) $T = [\,y \mid \langle\!\langle \text{READ}, \text{bill}, y_{(r \models \langle\!\langle \text{RUSSIAN-NOVEL},y\rangle\!\rangle \wedge \langle\!\langle \text{HATE},\text{bill},y\rangle\!\rangle)}\rangle\!\rangle\,]$

The only parameters in this type are parameters accounted for by the circumstances (the parameter *bill*, which will be anchored to some individual named "Bill"). This then is an appropriate type to use as our Evans-type. Calling (73) T, the content of the third sentence of (71) is:

(74) $\nabla z (z : T) \langle\!\langle \text{EQUAL}, z, \text{W\&P} \rangle\!\rangle$

Suppose that we had instead used the first occurrence of type (72) in the content of the discourse to form our Evans type. There the argument fed to the type is the parameter for John rather than the parameter for Bill. The result of our substitution would have been:

(75) $T' = [\,y \mid \langle\!\langle \text{READ}, \text{john}, y_{(r \models \langle\!\langle \text{RUSSIAN-NOVEL},y\rangle\!\rangle \wedge \langle\!\langle \text{HATE},\text{john},y\rangle\!\rangle)}\rangle\!\rangle\,]$

But then our content for the discourse as a whole would have contained the conjunction:

(76) $\langle\!\langle [\,x \mid \exists y \langle\!\langle \text{READ}, x, y_{(r \models \langle\!\langle \text{RUSSIAN-NOVEL},y\rangle\!\rangle \wedge \langle\!\langle \text{HATE},x,y\rangle\!\rangle)}\rangle\!\rangle\,], \text{john}; 0 \rangle\!\rangle$
$\wedge \nabla z (z : T')(s \models \langle\!\langle \text{EQUAL}, z, \text{W\&P} \rangle\!\rangle)$

But, since ∇ always has at least existential force, this claims there is no Russian novel that John has read and hated and that there is a Russian novel that John has read and hated, and it's *War and Peace*. This is contradictory.

We can also provide an account of the $\bar{\text{N}}$ anaphora facts exhibited in (14) if we assume that $\bar{\text{N}}$ contents are nonparametric types.[14] We first consider a simple case in order to show the basic lines of the treatment. Let $*P$ refer to the plural predicate holding of an entity e iff P holds of all the atoms in e (cf. Link, 1983). Furthermore, let

$$T = [\, d \mid r \models \langle\!\langle *\text{DONKEY}, d\rangle\!\rangle \,].$$

Then we represent the first sentence in (77) as (78):

(77) Pedro owned several donkeys. Raul bought two $\emptyset$.

(78) $\langle\!\langle \text{OWNED}, p, x_{\langle\!\langle T,x\rangle\!\rangle \wedge \langle\!\langle >,|x|,1\rangle\!\rangle} \rangle\!\rangle$

NI&L distinguish two readings of $\bar{\text{N}}$ anaphors. The less common, but logically simpler reading is the "unrestrained" reading. On this reading the content of the second utterance is merely that that Raul bought two donkeys:

(79) $\langle\!\langle \text{BOUGHT}, r, y_{\langle\!\langle T,y\rangle\!\rangle \wedge \langle\!\langle \geq,|y|,2\rangle\!\rangle} \rangle\!\rangle$

The more common, and logically more complex, reading is the "restrained" one, with the content that Raul bought two of the donkeys THAT PEDRO OWNED.

In order to represent the restrained reading, we need an Evans-type as well as (80), which leads to a representation of content (81). This can only hold if Raul bought two of the several donkeys that Pedro owned—exactly the restrained reading.

(80) $T_E = [\, d:(d:T) \mid (s \models \langle\!\langle \text{OWN}, p, d\rangle\!\rangle) \,]$

(81) $\langle\!\langle \text{BOUGHT}, r, y_{\langle\!\langle T_E,y\rangle\!\rangle \wedge \langle\!\langle \geq,|y|,2\rangle\!\rangle} \rangle\!\rangle$

We omit illustrating the treatment of simple quantified antecedents, and turn directly to $\bar{\text{N}}$ anaphors with missing (donkey) antecedents.[15] We represent the first sentence in (83) as (84), given the definition of T:

(82) $T = [\, f:(f:T'') \mid (r \models \exists d(d:T')\langle\!\langle \text{OWN}, f, d\rangle\!\rangle) \,]$

where

$T' = [\, d \mid (r \models \langle\!\langle *\text{DONKEY}, d\rangle\!\rangle) \,]$

$T'' = [\, f \mid (r' \models \langle\!\langle *\text{FARMER}, f\rangle\!\rangle) \,]$

(83) P knows several [farmers who own donkeys$_j$]$_i$. Most $\emptyset_i$ beat them$_{j'}$.

---

[14] This deviates from the proposal in NI&L, in which $\bar{\text{N}}$ contents were plural entities. The more familiar type denotations ease presentation here, particularly that of donkey anaphora.

[15] We should note, however, that the NI&L treatment provides an explanation for the apparent absence of restrained readings with genuinely quantificational antecedents, i.e., the apparent failure of sequences such as the following to admit a restrained interpretation:

Few men smoked. Some drank.

But we note that an explanation should follow from whatever mechanism explains the normal failure of these genuinely quantificational examples to support pronominal anaphora—provided that this explanation makes the E-Types unavailable.

(84) $\langle\!\langle \text{KNOW}, p, x_{\langle\!\langle T,x\rangle\!\rangle \wedge \langle\!\langle >, |x|, 1\rangle\!\rangle} \rangle\!\rangle$

And the unrestrained reading of the anaphoric utterance is just:

(85) $\langle\!\langle \text{MOST}, [\, x_{\langle\!\langle T,x\rangle\!\rangle \wedge \langle\!\langle \text{ATOM},x\rangle\!\rangle} \mid \langle\!\langle \text{BEAT}, x, \text{PRO}\rangle\!\rangle \,]\rangle\!\rangle$

We note a potential antecedent for **PRO** in the restriction on the variable bound by MOST, viz., the variable d in T (defined above). The associated E-Type is just:

$$T_E' = [\, d : (d : T') \mid (r \models \langle\!\langle \text{OWN}, x, d\rangle\!\rangle) \,]$$

N.B. that the variable f in T (cf. 82) has been renamed x above, reflecting the fact that T has been required to hold of x. Given this E-Type, we can specify the content of the anaphoric utterance more exactly:

$$\langle\!\langle \text{MOST}, [\, x_{\langle\!\langle T,x\rangle\!\rangle \wedge \langle\!\langle \text{ATOM},x\rangle\!\rangle} \mid \nabla z_{\langle\!\langle T_E',z\rangle\!\rangle} \langle\!\langle \text{BEAT}, x, z\rangle\!\rangle \,]\rangle\!\rangle$$

So the second utterance describes a situation in which most farmers who own donkeys beat (at least) some of the donkeys they own. The restrained reading of the $\bar{\text{N}}$ anaphor is straightforwardly obtained by adding a condition to T above (which amounts to using the E-Type construal of *farmers*).

This treatment here preserves the benefits of the NI&L analysis even while maintaining the Absorption principle. What has been emphatically abandoned is the hypothesis that anaphora always involves the re-use of the content of some previous linguistic form; but the mere existence of E-Type anaphora demonstrates that anaphora cannot (always) merely reuse contents.

5   The Status of the Absorption Principle

In G&P, we claimed that the Absorption Principle explains why sentence (86) has no "sloppy identity" reading when *she* is anaphoric to *her mother* if *her* is simultaneously anaphoric to *my wife*,

(86)   My wife forgot her mother's birthday this year, and so did she

While it is true that no Q-Type analysis will license this anaphoric relation, there is an E-Type analysis that will. The question arises then, what force does the AP have in our revised system? In this section we argue that the AP still makes important predictions; first, about anaphora; second, about Quantifiers, particularly, for the revised account of Quantification given in G&P 1990b.

Even with the availability of an E-Type analysis, the Absorption Principle, taken together with some rather natural restrictions on E-Type anaphora, makes a number of predictions. Consider:

(87)   Every student revised *a paper he wrote*. # *It* was accepted by L&P.

Here the indicated anaphoric relation is impossible. The Absorption Principle rules out the possibility of a Q-Type analysis.[16]

We turn now to predictions made by the Absorption Principle for cases of Q-Type anaphora. These basically concern what readings are available. Here is an example discussed in detail in G&P.

(88)   Alice praised the book she hated and Betty did too.

The claim about this case is that there is no *reading* of this sentence in which the elliptical VP is given a sloppy interpretation and Alice and Betty are *understood* as praising the same book. Contrast:

(89)   Alice praised the book because she hated it and Betty did too.

Here there is a *reading* available on which the elliptical VP is assigned the sloppy interpretation, and yet Alice and Betty praise the same book. It is important to stress here that we are not claiming that the truth conditions of (88) require that Alice and Betty praise different books. Rather we are saying there is no *reading* which requires that they praise the same book. This contrasts with the facts for (89), where there is such a reading, namely the one on which the definite is given wide scope over both VP's. The Absorption Principle entails that there is no such wide-scope option for (88).

Finally there are predictions made by the Absorption Principle that concern scope directly, and do not involve anaphora. Consider another example discussed in G&P:

(90)   Carol hasn't yet met the author of a book about anaphora.

The general tendency is for indefinites inside the VP to take narrow scope inside negation, and for definites to take wide scope. Yet there is no way in (90) for both the definite and the indefinite to take their "natural" scopes. This is because the analysis of the NP *the author of a book about anaphora* is:

(91) y_ρ
     where
     $\rho = (s_\mu \models \langle\!\langle \text{AUTHOR-OF}, y, x_\tau \rangle\!\rangle)$
     $\tau = (s'' \models \langle\!\langle \text{BOOK-ABOUT-ANAPH}, x \rangle\!\rangle)$

Here the restriction μ is what makes the definite NP definite:

(92) $\mu = \text{UNIQUE}(s, [\, y \mid \langle\!\langle \text{AUTHOR-OF}, y, x_\tau \rangle\!\rangle \,])$

---

[16] In order to explain why no anaphora at all is possible here, we must also explain why no E-Type analysis is possible. Since E-Type anaphora allows a pronoun to be anaphorically related to a quantifier whose scope the pronoun lies outside of, the question arises of why this isn't possible in every case. Possibly some constraint of the following sort is required:

> *The Distinguishability Requirement*: The antecedent clause must not implicate that there is more than one witness to the Evans-type.

Here UNIQUE is a relation holding between a situation s and a property P, if and only if there is exactly one individual that has P in s. The important point here is that y depends on x in (91). Thus if x is absorbed, y must be. Thus, if the indefinite takes scope inside the negation in (90), the definite must too.

There is another another more theory-internal function served by the Absorption Principle. In a system which recognizes the distinction between Generalized Quantifiers and Referential NP's, it gives us a unified explanation of certain scoping facts common to both Generalized Quantifiers and Referential NP's. Consider:

(93)   *Every student* revised at least two papers *he* wrote.

When the indicated anaphoric relation holds, the Quantificational NP *at least two papers he wrote* must take scope inside that of *every student*. This is simply because that NP is associated with a parameter dependent on the subject NP's parameter. Hence, when subject quantifier is quantified in, the object quantifier must already be quantified in. This is entirely parallel to the judgment for (87). The explanation for both facts is the same, and that explanation crucially involves an appeal to the Absorption Principle.

Although the facts in (93) and (87) are quite analogous, there was no single explanation for them in the system of G&P. G&P relied on the Absorption Principle to rule out the unwanted reading of (87), but appealed to their analysis of GQ to rule out the unwanted reading of (93).

For this and related reasons, G&P (1990b) abandoned the Generalized Quantifier analysis. Instead of being relations on properties, Quantificational Determiners became types of types.

To illustrate first with a simple example, consider (94):

(94)   Most elephants don't fly.

On the Generalized Quantifier analysis this is:

(95) $\langle\!\langle \text{MOST}, [x \mid (r \models \langle\!\langle \text{ELEPHANT}, x \rangle\!\rangle)], [x \mid (s \models \langle\!\langle \text{FLY}, x; 0 \rangle\!\rangle)]\rangle\!\rangle$

We propose instead that it is:

(96) $(\text{MOST}, [x_{(r \models \langle\!\langle \text{ELEPHANT}, x \rangle\!\rangle)} \mid (s \models \langle\!\langle \text{FLY}, x; 0 \rangle\!\rangle)])$

Note that the quantified noun phrase *most elephants* fills the subject argument role of the VP *don't fly* with a parameter restricted to elephants, just as the noun phrase *an elephant* would. Thus Quantified NP's on this account are more like Referential NP's than they were on the old account.

We are now in a position to give a unified explanation of the "scope" facts in (93) and (87). In both cases the NP containing a pronoun is treated as restricted parameter, y. In both cases, y depends on the pronoun parameter x. Thus, in both cases, the maximal scope of the pronoun parameter is also the maximal scope of y.

As a bonus, the G&P analysis of Quantification makes a unified treatment of NP semantics possible, one which will still maintain the distinction necessary for an adequate analysis of Q-Type anaphora. The Described Objects of both kinds of NPs are restricted parameters.

With this view, we can now give the semantics for Referential NPs and Quantificational NPs with a single semantic composition rule. That rule will simply place the restriction given by the NP's $\bar{\text{N}}$ on the NP's described object. Quantifying in is a separate phenomenon, mediated by facts in the circumstance, as sketched in G&P. But even there, Referential NPs and Quantificational NPs can be alike. Both kinds of NP can quantify in.

The revised analysis of Quantification proposed in Gawron and Peters (1990b), taken together with the Absorption Principle, thus allows a very natural account of some basic facts of NP semantics.

6 The Proper Treatment of E-Type Anaphora

In closing, let us summarize our final analysis of E-Type uses of pronouns, which both captures their existential import for the quantification that is their antecedent and explains the apparent fluctuation in their force.

Singular and plural pronouns behave slightly differently in E-Type use; so we have two cases to consider:

(i) E-Type uses of the singular pronouns *he*, *she*, *it* and their accusative and genitive congeners,

(ii) E-Type uses of the plural pronoun *they* and its accusative and genitive congeners.[17]

Singular and plural are alike, however, in that E-Type uses of *he*, *she*, *it* and *they* impose restrictions (as do deictic and Q-Type uses) on the value the pronoun can take on (roughly that they be male, female, inanimate and at least two in number, respectively). Recall also that, in contrast with Q-Type anaphoric uses of non-reflexive, third person pronouns, E-Type uses are possible only when the scope of the antecedent does not include the pronoun.

To bring out a distinguishing feature of singular E-Type pronouns, we consider the discourse

(97) Noam wrote a book last year. It was not well received.

Together with the rules of English, the circumstances of utterance of the discourse (97) determine that the content of the first statement in it is (98).

(98) $\exists y \langle\!\langle [\, x \mid \langle\!\langle \text{WROTE LAST YEAR}, x, y_{\langle\!\langle \text{BOOK},y\rangle\!\rangle}, \rangle\!\rangle \,], \text{noam} \rangle\!\rangle$

The circumstances of utterance determine that the antecedent of *it* in the second statement is the constituent

$\exists y \langle\!\langle [\, x \mid \langle\!\langle \text{WROTE LAST YEAR}, x, y_{\langle\!\langle \text{BOOK},y\rangle\!\rangle}, \rangle\!\rangle \,], \text{noam} \rangle\!\rangle$

---

[17]Reflexive pronouns (*himself*, *herself*, *itself*, and *themselves*) and non-third person pronouns (*I*, *you*, *we*, and their accusative and genitive congeners) do not have E-Type uses.

of (98). So the semantic rules determine that the Evans type T_E for this use of *it* is

$$[\, y \mid \langle\!\langle [\, x \mid \langle\!\langle \text{WROTE LAST YEAR}, x, y_{\langle\!\langle \text{BOOK}, y \rangle\!\rangle}, \rangle\!\rangle \,], \text{noam}\rangle\!\rangle\,].$$

Intuitively, we want this E-Type use of *it* to have as its content the object that is of this type, provided that the object is nonhuman. That is, we want the pronoun's content to be $z_{(z\,:\,T_E)\wedge\langle\!\langle \text{HUMAN},z;0\rangle\!\rangle}$.[18]

The obvious question is: What if nothing is of the Evans type, or more than one thing is of that type? The question gets different answers in the two cases. If nothing is of the Evans type, the clause containing the E-Type pronoun should be false, giving E-Type pronouns existential import for their antecedent. We accomplish this by insisting that the restricted parameter as which an E-Type pronoun is interpreted be existentially quantified away. We mentioned in Section 3 that the scope of this quantification is as large as possible without including the quantification that is the pronoun's antecedent.

If the Evans type has more than one object in its extension, we must account for the fact that the E-Type pronoun picks out a single object. We capture this by using a choice function *Index*choice function χ in interpreting E-Type uses of singular pronouns.[19] We interpret an E-Type use of *it* for which the Evans type is T_E as $\chi(ext(T_E))$ provided this object is nonhuman. All E-Type uses of pronouns with the same antecedent will thus get the same interpretation. Accordingly the restricted parameter (the E-Type pronoun *it*'s content) above should instead be

$$z_{(z=\chi(ext(T_E))\wedge\langle\!\langle \text{HUMAN},z;0\rangle\!\rangle)}.$$

Therefore, an E-Type use of *it* gets a well-defined value if and only if neither of two conditions obtains:

(i) $ext(T_E)$ is the empty set,

(ii) $\chi(ext(T_E))$ exists and is human.

In the event no value is defined for an E-Type use of *it* or another pronoun, any basic proposition is false which is supposed to have the pronoun's interpretation as an immediate constituent, there being no object of the type to which the existentially quantified parameter is restricted.

We explain the apparent fluctuation in force of singular E-Type pronouns, described in Section 3, with the aid of the following hypothesis:

(99) The choice function χ used in interpreting E-Type uses of singular pronouns is fixed for a discourse and is not under the control of any speaker participating in that discourse.

---

[18] When an object of an Evans type is human, an E-Type utterance of *it* cannot have that person as its content. This fact is what prevents an E-Type use of *it* with antecedent *an astrologer* in

(i) Noam quoted an astrologer last year. # It was flattered.

[19] A choice function is a function χ such that $\chi(S) \in S$ for any nonempty set S.

The key fact is that no speaker controls χ; neither the speaker whose utterance provides the antecedent for an E-Type use of a singular pronoun, nor the possibly different speaker who makes E-Type use of the pronoun fixes χ with their utterance. Because of this, the only way someone who utters a singular E-Type pronoun can be sure of speaking truthfully (or otherwise accurately) is to take care that the truth (accuracy) of his utterance is not affected by whatever choice χ may make out of the extension of the Evans type that the pronoun picks up from its antecedent. We appeal to this fact in explaining all of the apparently different forces (purely existential, definite singular, non-vacuous universal) encountered in Section 3.

The fact that the pronoun may denote any object of the Evans type allows one to be sure of speaking the truth in stating:

(100) I bought a sage plant yesterday. I bought eight others with it.

just in case one did buy (at least) nine sage plants the previous day.

Let us first discuss why

(101) Either no doctor has examined Bill today or she didn't write anything on this chart

appears to claim that *every* doctor who examined Bill today refrained from writing anything on the chart. The explanation is, in fact, straightforward. The E-Type pronoun *she* is interpreted as the restricted parameter

$$z_{(z=\chi(\,ext(T_E))\wedge\langle\!\langle\mathrm{FEMALE},z\rangle\!\rangle)}.$$

where the Evans type T_E is

$$[\,y \mid \langle\!\langle[\,x \mid \langle\!\langle\mathrm{EXAMINED\ TODAY},x,\mathrm{bill}\rangle\!\rangle\,],\, y_{\langle\!\langle\mathrm{DOCTOR},y\rangle\!\rangle}\rangle\!\rangle\,].$$

This restricted parameter is existentially quantified with scope over just the second disjunct of (101). So the proposition that is asserted to be true unless the first disjunct is

$$\exists z\,\langle\!\langle[\,x \mid \exists v\,\langle\!\langle\mathrm{WROTE\ ON\ CHART},x,v\rangle\!\rangle\,],\, z_{(z=\chi(\,ext(T_E))\wedge\langle\!\langle\mathrm{FEMALE},z\rangle\!\rangle)};0\rangle\!\rangle.$$

If the first disjunct of (101) is false, the Evans type T_E has a nonempty extension, S; in that case, the truth of the second disjunct, and therefore of the whole statement, depends just on whether the member of S that χ chooses didn't write anything on the chart (and is female). So if more than one doctor examined Bill today, the statement's truth depends entirely on which one of them the function χ chooses. Since the speaker has no control over which one is chosen, the speaker's responsibility to assure that his statement is true can be met only if all of those doctors wrote nothing on the chart (and are female).

Note that this pragmatic explanation of the appearance of universally quantified force does not claim that the content of the speaker's assertion is a universally quantified proposition. The actual content, according to our analysis, is more like a singular proposition. If two doctors examined Bill today and one wrote something on the chart but the other didn't, an utterer of (101) might be lucky enough to speak the truth because χ happened to choose the doctor who didn't write on the chart. However, it would not be responsible to make the statement in such a situation since the speaker might just as easily be unwittingly making the false statement that the other doctor didn't write on the chart. Thus one should assert (101) only if no examining doctor wrote on the chart.

We similarly derive an explanation of the fact that it is incorrect to state:

(102)   No farmer who owns a donkey beats it

if every donkey-owning farmer refrains from beating at least one donkey she owns but some farmer owns more than one donkey and beats at least one of them. The speaker has no control over which donkey the pronoun *it* will denote for each of the farmers. Thus the appearance of something akin to universal quantification comes from the fact that if more than one witness is of the Evans type of the antecedent, then the pronoun must be able to denote any of them without detracting from the accuracy of what is said. The only added twist in this case is that the Evans type T_E is

$$[\, y \mid \langle\!\langle \text{OWNS}, x, y_{\langle\!\langle \text{DONKEY}, y \rangle\!\rangle} \rangle\!\rangle \,]$$

which has a parameter x for a farmer. It is precisely this, of course, which allows the value of E-Type *it* to vary with the farmer who owns the donkey.

E-Type use of a pronoun can appear to carry the quantificational force of definiteness arise because all E-Type pronouns with the same antecedent denote the same value. Thus

(103)   Bill had a quarter. He gave it to a beggar, and later gave it to another beggar.

describes two events involving the same quarter.

The appearance of mere existential force in

(104)   If you have a quarter, you should give it to that beggar.

comes from the fact that the pronoun does actually denote just one single object of the Evans type (if it denotes at all). The content of the conditional assertion is that the addressee should give the beggar the one quarter in his or her pocket which *it* denotes. Thus no assertion is made that the addressee should give more than one quarter to the beggar. Of course, the injunction asserted in (104) nevertheless applies indifferently to any quarter the addressee has in his or her pocket, not singling out one above the others as the one that should be given away, for the same reason we discussed in connection with apparently universal E-Type cases.

Our account gives no uniqueness entailment from an E-Type pronoun. If there is an implicature following from

(105)   Noam wrote a book. It was not well received.

that Noam wrote exactly one book, then that is a separate matter. Note that uniqueness can at most be an implicature, since examples like (100) show uniqueness is cancellable. Moreover, in the face of examples like (101) and (102), it is hard to even argue for a generalized conversational implicature.

E-Type uses of the plural pronouns *they*, *them*, and *their* are interpreted as a parameter

$$z_{(z = ext(T_E)) \wedge (\mathrm{Card}(z) \geq 2)}.^{20}$$

In these plural cases, no choice is needed of one member from the multi-membered extension of the Evans type.

Recall that the antecedent of an E-Type pronoun is not a syntactic NP but rather a constituent of content, in particular the counterpart of the closure of an utterance of a syntactic NP. For example, the antecedent of the E-Type use of *they* in (106) is not the NP *any pansies*.

(106) John didn't plant any pansies. But Bill did. They all came up.

Instead the antecedent is the constituent of the content of *But Bill did* that is the counterpart of the closure of *any pansies*. (The circumstances of utterance of *they* determine this fact.) More precisely, in the content

$$(107) \quad \langle\!\langle [\, x \mid \exists_2 y \langle\!\langle \mathrm{PLANT}, x, y_{\langle\!\langle \mathrm{PANSY}, y \rangle\!\rangle} \rangle\!\rangle \,], \mathrm{john}; 0 \rangle\!\rangle \wedge$$
$$\langle\!\langle [\, x \mid \exists_2 y \langle\!\langle \mathrm{PLANT}, x, y_{\langle\!\langle \mathrm{PANSY}, y \rangle\!\rangle} \rangle\!\rangle \,], \mathrm{bill}; 1 \rangle\!\rangle$$

of the first two subutterances in (106), the antecedent of the E-Type use of *they* is the second occurrence of the closure

$$\exists_2 y \langle\!\langle \mathrm{PLANT}, x, y_{\langle\!\langle \mathrm{PANSY}, y \rangle\!\rangle} \rangle\!\rangle.$$

Now this closure, and thus the type

$$[\, y \mid \langle\!\langle \mathrm{PLANT}, x, y_{\langle\!\langle \mathrm{PANSY}, y \rangle\!\rangle} \rangle\!\rangle \,],$$

have a parameter x for the planter of the pansies in question, while the Evans type for this pronoun should have the anchored parameter 'bill' in place of x. To obtain the Evans type, we observe that when a parameter of the closure that serves as antecedent is abstracted on with a scope that does not include the E-Type pronoun (as x is in (107) in forming a property), and the argument role produced by this abstraction is filled (with 'bill' for the relevant occurrence of the property), then the Evans type is the result of replacing the first parameter by what fills the argument role.[21] Therefore, in this case T_E is

$$[\, y \mid \langle\!\langle \mathrm{PLANT}, \text{'bill'}, y_{\langle\!\langle \mathrm{PANSY}, y \rangle\!\rangle} \rangle\!\rangle \,].$$

---

[20] In a fragment more closely concerned with plural logic, one might follow Link's lead and take the pronoun to denote the 'individual sum' of the set.

[21] If the argument role produced by abstracting over parameters like x is not filled, other cases arise, as in Webber's

(i) Every farmer bought a donkey. It's my job to feed them.

So the content of the final subutterance of (106) is

$$\exists z \langle\!\langle [\, x \mid \forall y \langle\!\langle \text{CAME UP}, y_{y \in x} \rangle\!\rangle \,], z_{(z = ext(T_E)) \wedge (\text{Card}(z) \geq 2)} \rangle\!\rangle.$$

This analysis fully captures the behavior of E-Type *they* except for two facts, which we stipulate:

(i) the NP whose closure is the counterpart of the pronoun's antecedent must have the same grammatical number as the pronoun, and

(ii) no E-Type pronoun can c-command (what would have been) its antecedent (if that weren't missing).[22]

References

Barwise, J. 1989a. Notes on Branch Points in Situation Theory. In *The Situation in Logic*, 255–276. CSLI Lecture Notes Number 17. Stanford: CSLI Publications.

Barwise, J. 1989b. *The Situation in Logic*. CSLI Lecture Notes Number 17. Stanford: CSLI Publications.

Barwise, J., and R. Cooper. 1981. Generalized Quantifiers and Natural Language. *Linguistics and Philosophy* 4:159–219.

Cooper, R. 1975. *Montague's Semantic Theory and Transformational Syntax*. PhD thesis, University of Massachusetts, Amherst.

Cooper, R. 1987. Preliminaries to the Treatment of Generalized Quantifiers in Situation Semantics. In *Generalized Quantifiers: Linguistic and Logical Approaches*, ed. P. Gärdenfors. Studies in Linguistics and Philosophy Number 31. Dordrecht: Reidel.

Cooper, R., K. Mukai, and J. Perry (ed.). 1990. *Situation Theory and Its Applications*, vol. 1. CSLI Lecture Notes Number 22. Stanford: CSLI Publications.

Devlin, K. J. 1991. *Logic and Information*. Cambridge: Cambridge University Press.

Evans, G. 1977. Pronouns, Quantifiers and Relative Clauses. *Canadian Journal of Philosophy* 7:467–536.

Evans, G. 1980. Pronouns. *Linguistic Inquiry* 11(2):337–362.

Gärdenfors, P. (ed.). 1987. *Generalized Quantifiers: Linguistic and Logical Approaches*. Studies in Linguistics and Philosophy Number 31. Dordrecht: Reidel.

Gawron, J. M., and S. Peters. 1990a. *Anaphora and Quantification in Situation Semantics*. CSLI Lecture Notes Number 19. Stanford: CSLI Publications.

Gawron, J. M., and S. Peters. 1990b. Some Puzzles About Pronouns. In Cooper et al. 1990.

Geach, P. 1962. *Reference and Generality*. Ithaca: Cornell University Press.

Grinder, J., and P. Postal. 1971. Missing Antecedents. *Linguistic Inquiry* 2(3).

Heim, I. 1982. *The Semantics of Definite and Indefinite Noun Phrases*. PhD thesis, University of Massachussetts, Amherst.

---

[22]This can be stated by means of a relatively minor revision of the binding theory formulated in G&P.

Heim, I. 1990. E-Type Pronouns and Donkey Anaphora. *Linguistics and Philosophy* 13(2):137–177.

Kadmon, N. 1987. *On Unique and Non-Unique Reference and Asymmetric Quantification.* PhD thesis, University of Massachusetts, Amherst.

Kadmon, N. 1990. Uniqueness. *Linguistics and Philosophy* 13(3):273–324.

Link, G. 1983. The Logical Analysis of Plurals and Mass Terms: A Lattice-Theoretic Approach. In *Meaning, Use, and the Interpretation of Language*, ed. R. Bäuerle, C. Schwarze, and A. von Stechow. Berlin: de Gruyter.

Nerbonne, J., M. Iida, and W. Ladusaw. 1989. Semantics of Common-Noun Phrase Anaphora. In *WCCFL-9*. Stanford Linguistics Association.

Pollard, C., and I. Sag. 1987. *Information-Based Syntax and Semantics, Volume 1: Fundamentals.* CSLI Lecture Notes Number 13. Stanford: CSLI Publications.

Rooth, M. 1987. NP Interpretation in Montague Grammar, File Change Semantics, and Situation Semantics. In *Generalized Quantifiers: Linguistic and Logical Approaches*, ed. P. Gärdenfors, 237–268. Dordrecht: Reidel.

Saarinen, E. 1978a. *Game-Theoretical Semantics.* Dordrecht: Reidel.

Saarinen, E. 1978b. Intentional Identity Interpreted: A Case Study of the Relations Among Quantifiers, Pronouns, and Propositional Attitudes. In *Game-Theoretical Semantics*, 245–327. Dordrecht: Reidel.

Schubert, L. K., and F. J. Pelletier. 1989. Generically Speaking, or Using Discourse Representation Theory to Interpret Generics. In *Properties, Types, and Meaning. Vol. 2: Semantic Issues.* Netherlands: Kluwer.

Sem, H. F., K. J. Sæbø, G. B. Verne, and E. J. Vestre. 1991. Parameters: Dependence and Absorption. This volume.

Webber, B. 1977. *A Formal Approach to Discourse Anaphora.* New York: Garland Outstanding Dissertations.

16

Questions without Answers, Wh-Phrases without Scope: A Semantics for Direct Wh-Questions and their Responses

JONATHAN GINZBURG

1 Introduction

What does a wh-question mean? A naive response might go as follows: "...
we have an unknown 'quantity' exactly as in an algebraic equation; we may
therefore use ... the term x-question for a question aiming at finding out
what x stands for." (Jespersen 1965.) This proposal actually accomplishes
much of what is required of a semantics for direct wh-questions: it predicts
that the felicitous responses elicited by a given question will be those that
provide information, through linguistic or other means, that enables the
interrogated role to be filled. Second, it explains why wh-sentences[1] cannot
be used in assertoric acts: contents which contain uninstantiated variables
cannot be associated with a (world/situation) in a way that enables truth
or falsity to be determined.

This view has been hard to formalize in and reconcile with a Model
Theoretic Semantics which insists that every expression be interpreted as a
"non-parametric" object. I will propose a semantics for wh-sentences, cast
within the framework of Situation Semantics (Barwise and Perry 1983,
Gawron and Peters 1990). The essence of the proposal will be to inter-

---

Thanks to Stanley Peters for continuous discussion and much encouragement. Thanks
also to Aaron Halpern, Smita Joshi, Craige Roberts, Ivan Sag, Peter Sells. Especial
thanks to Mark Gawron and an anonymous reviewer for comments on earlier drafts.

[1]In what follows, the term 'wh-sentence' is used for the uninterpreted interrogative
sentence. 'Wh-question' denotes a semantic object which is the content of a wh-
sentence.

Situation Theory and Its Applications, vol. 2.
Jon Barwise, Jean Mark Gawron, Gordon Plotkin, and Syun Tutiya, eds.
Copyright © 1991, Stanford University.

pret an interrogative pronoun such as 'which book' as a parameter for a book that is neither anchored, nor subject to existential closure. By compositionality, a wh-question has as its content a parametric infon (also known as a "state of affairs"), that is, an infon containing a (unanchored) parameter.[2]

Since on this view wh-phrases are not scope-bearing elements, in particular wh-phrases do not necessarily scope over each other. Thus, multiple-wh-sentences can be assigned contents without recourse to quantification-into-wh rules. I will propose that even in such cases where quantifiers or wh-phrases have been taken to take scope over wh-phrases no quantification-into-wh rules are required or desirable. Instead, I offer a unified account for these (henceforth "dependent") readings by refining the parametric interpretation of interrogative sentences. The essential idea is that this reading utilizes a mechanism similar to and converse with that proposed by Gawron and Peters 1990 for the "capture" of definites by quantifiers, a parallel already pointed out in Engdahl 1988.

The approach to questions taken here will be compared with a view of questions that has been predominant since the dawn of Montague Grammar. This view was originally put forward in Hamblin's ground breaking 1973 paper, revised and extended by Karttunen, Engdahl, Groenendijk and Stokhof, Higginbotham and May and others. The leading idea of this (henceforth "Hamblinian") approach is that a wh-question can be characterized by (the set of) its possible answers. This is usually taken to be the singular propositions obtained by instantiating the open sentence underlying the question. (Or alternatively, some object constructed from the open sentence and all possible instantiating entities.) This set will be referred to as a question's *Hamblin Set*.[3]

---

[2]It is worth pointing out, for those who are queasy about semantic parameters, that the proposal is, apparently, reformulatable without using parameters. What is needed is a framework in which argument roles of a state-of-affairs can be left unfilled. As part of a wider scoping constituent, these roles can be either abstracted, as part of a complex relation, or remain unfilled, in which case that constituent contains unfilled roles. Systems with parameters happen to be particularly convenient and elegant implementations of such a framework. Crimmins 1991 has proposed a parameter-less such system. For a model theory of Situation Theory with parameters see Westerstahl 1990.

[3]In *Situations and Attitudes*, Barwise and Perry gave a sketch of a theory of questions. They rejected the letter, though not the spirit of a Hamblinian approach. Their stated bone of contention with respect to Hamblin sets (= sets of possible answers) was essentially formal: given the set theoretic modelling they proposed, in which propositions were modelled as proper classes, sets of propositions were not constructible. Their proposal was to model the *meaning, though not the interpretation* of a wh- question as a type containing an indeterminate. This, however, was really just a different way of getting at a Hamblin set: "The insight that the meaning of a question has something to do with the possible answers is still present, for there are all the ways to anchor the indeterminate and *when asked on a particular occasion there all the ways to anchor it which give you a factual situation.*" (emphasis added –J.G.) (p. 286) In contemporary Situation Theory there is nothing foundational that prevents the formation of

I will argue that the possible answers denotation is not well motivated either in terms of its integrability in a theory of interrogative speech acts or embedded questions, and appears to face significant problems in its construal as a cognitive object. Specifically, I will argue against the following assumptions that underlie the Hamblinian approach:

1. The semantic answers of a wh-question are all and only the propositions obtained by instantiating the open sentence underlying the question.

2. In embedded-question constructions, the semantic object corresponding to the question is, in all cases, a direct argument of the (relation denoted by the) verb.

3. Wh-phrases are quantifiers, (or, alternatively, there exists an operator, "Q," which binds the wh-variable.)

The structure of the paper is as follows: in Section 2, I introduce the framework, and illustrate how it works for various representative cases: argument-wh-phrases, adjunct-wh-phrases, multiple-wh-questions. In Section 3, I discuss the notion of a parametric content, in particular its relation to the unassertability of wh-sentences. Sections 4 and 5 contain a treatment of interrogative speech acts (INSA): I discuss the notion of a felicitous response and offer a characterization of the responses that the contents provided by the proposed semantics predict to be felicitous. Sections 6 and 7 compare the current approach to Hamblinian approaches with respect to INSA's and embedded questions respectively. Section 8 offers an appraisal of arguments adduced to show that wh-phrases are quantificational, and a reanalysis of some phenomena from a non-quantificational viewpoint. Finally, in Section 9 the semantics will be extended to cover "dependent uses" of wh-phrases: interactions of wh-phrases with quantifiers will be accounted for. A semantic account of subject/object asymmetries exhibited in such interactions will be offered. An account will also be provided for the differing uniqueness conventional implicatures associated with the wh-determiner 'which' in unary and multiple-wh-questions.[4]

Hamblin sets. A Hamblinian approach is, consequently, quite consistent with Situation Theory.

[4] I do not offer a semantics for y/n questions, or alternative questions in this paper. Some of the problems of the Hamblinian approach in the domain of wh-questions apply equally to these other types of questions, for instance the distinction between "embedded answers" and "embedded questions" (see Section 7) and the inadequacy of the Hamblin set of a y/n question to predict felicitous responses. A natural way of generalizing the approach taken here to wh-questions to these other types of questions consists in revising a proposal sketched in Barwise and Perry 1983. If we assume that what is parametric about yes/no question is a property of propositions, (a "degree of confirmation" of the proposition: "true," "possible," "probable," "false") marked syntactically in various languages by a "question particle," or morphologically on the verb (this is also one possible analysis of the inversion typical of Indo-European languages), the analysis goes through with some interesting consequences. See Ginzburg 1991a for details.

2 A Semantics for Wh-Phrases and Wh-Sentences

2.1 Situation Theoretic Notation and Terminology

This section contains a brief introduction to the Situation Theoretic notation and terminology that will be used throughout. More details on current Situation Theory notation and terminology can be found in Devlin 1991. The semantic framework used in this paper is that of Gawron and Peters 1990a, whence further details and motivation for what is telegraphically conveyed here is to be found.

Each relation R is endowed with a set of argument roles $r_1, r_2, \ldots, r_n$ together with certain appropriateness restrictions on these roles. When appropriate objects $a_1, a_2, \ldots, a_n$ are assigned to the argument roles of a relation R an issue arises: do these assigned objects stand in the relation R or do they not. The former possibility is denoted by the *infon*

$$\langle\!\langle R, r_1{:}a_1, r_2{:}a_2, \ldots, r_n{:}a_n; 1 \rangle\!\rangle$$

while the latter possibility is denoted by the infon

$$\langle\!\langle R, r_1{:}a_1, r_2{:}a_2, \ldots, r_n{:}a_n; 0 \rangle\!\rangle$$

In the text I follow the established convention of omitting the *polarity* '1', where no confusion can arise.

The factuality of an infon is determined by some situation, that is, if the possibility represented by some infon σ is realized, there must be some real situation s in the world which supports the factuality of σ: this is denoted

$$s \models \sigma$$

Issues need not be determinate, that is, one of the argument roles of a relation can be left unfilled by an individual. The argument role is then *parametrized*, filled by a parameter. The issue will become determinate once some object is assigned to the argument role. The mapping assigning an object to a parameter is termed an *anchor*. Referents, in other words objects filling argument roles will be denoted by bold faced characters in what follows. Restrictions can also be placed on parameters; these serve as restrictions on anchors: any anchor on a restricted parameter must assign the parameter to an object which satisfies the restriction. A restriction is, then, somewhat like a presupposition that is added onto the filler of the parametrized role. A restricted parameter is denoted as follows:

$$x_{\langle\!\langle R,\ldots,x,\ldots;i \rangle\!\rangle} \cdot$$

An anchor f will be a proper anchor for x if f maps x to some object a and $\langle\!\langle R, \ldots, a, \ldots; i \rangle\!\rangle$ is a fact.

The following, for instance, is a parametric infon representing the fact that an object, restricted to individuals named 'John', runs at a time t.

$$\langle\!\langle R, x_{\langle\!\langle \text{NAMED},x,\text{'John'} \rangle\!\rangle}, t \rangle\!\rangle$$

By abstracting over roles that are parametrized in an infon, one can form types and relations. Thus, given the infon $\langle\!\langle\text{EAT}, \text{eater:}x, \text{eatee:}hummus\rangle\!\rangle$, where the role of the eater is parametrized, one can form the property 'eater of hummus', denoted

$$[x_{eater} \mid \langle\!\langle\text{EAT}, \text{eater:}x, \text{eatee:}hummus\rangle\!\rangle].$$

Where no confusion can arise, the subscript denoting the role abstracted over will be omitted. This is used particularly in constructing VP's from V's: the basic idea is that a content for a V has both object and subject roles parametrized. Forming the VP involves filling the object role and abstracting over the subject role. Thus, in order to form the VP 'ate that hummus' from the infon $\langle\!\langle\text{EAT}, \text{eater:}x, \text{eatee:}y\rangle\!\rangle$ which is parametric in both *eater* and *eatee* roles, the latter role is assigned its semantics, in this case anchoring to *that hummus*, and then the *eater* role is abstracted over. The content of the VP is, then,

$$[x_{eater} \mid \langle\!\langle\text{EAT}, \text{eater:}x, \text{eatee:}that\ hummus\rangle\!\rangle]$$

The content of 'John ate that hummus' is then constructed by predicating the content of the VP, given by the above type, of the content of the subject NP, namely *John*:

$$\langle\!\langle[x_{e}ater \mid \langle\!\langle\text{EAT}, \text{eater:}x, \text{eatee:}that\ hummus\rangle\!\rangle], John\rangle\!\rangle$$

Quantified sentences are interpreted by means of infons whose main relation is the quantificational force, and whose arguments are the restrictive term and the nuclear scope. Thus, the content of 'Every man met Jane.' is denoted

$$\langle\!\langle\text{EVERY}, [x \mid \langle\!\langle\text{MAN}, x\rangle\!\rangle], [v \mid \langle\!\langle[y \mid \langle\!\langle\text{MET}, \text{meeter:}y, \text{meetee:}Jane\rangle\!\rangle], v\rangle\!\rangle]$$

Similarly, the content of 'Jane met every man.' where, say, 'every man' takes widest scope is generated as follows: the object role is filled by a parameter, which is abstracted over to form the nuclear scope. The restrictive term is at that point fed in as second argument to the relation denoted by the determiner:

$$\langle\!\langle\text{EVERY}, [x \mid \langle\!\langle\text{MAN}, x\rangle\!\rangle], [v \mid \langle\!\langle[y \mid \langle\!\langle\text{MET}, \text{meeter:}y, \text{meetee:}v\rangle\!\rangle], Jane\rangle\!\rangle]$$

2.2 The Semantics of Wh-Phrases

In this section, a semantics for wh-phrases will be introduced. This semantics is supposed to cover all "individual" uses of wh-phrases. In order to get the basic idea across, I will use simplified contents, that blur various distinctions that are, in general, crucial: thus, I will ignore the hierarchical nature of sentential content (e.g., SUBJ/PRED structure), interpreting sentences simply as an infon consisting of a main relation and its arguments. This simplification will be remedied in later sections, which follow the framework and notation of Gawron and Peters 1990a fairly closely.

In providing a formal account, I utilize the framework and general semantic assumptions of Situation Semantics (Barwise and Perry 1983, Gawron and Peters 1990a, 1990b). In particular, I presuppose something like the relational theory of meaning (RTM). The basic idea of the RTM is that meaning should be viewed as a relation between two independent dimensions, contextual and contentual. So that the meaning of a syntactic object is the relation between the contexts in which that syntactic object can be used, and an object (the "described object") specified by the content. How this will be of use will become clearer a little later on.

Consider first wh-NP's. Ever since Frege, with the noted exception of Montague, there has been a distinction between two types of NP's: name-like and quantificational. Operationally, this distinction is cashed out as follows: The name-like expressions "refer directly" by contributing objects that fill argument roles. The quantificational expressions denote higher order entities, so that first they contribute a place holder and then a restricting type and binding operator, and a quantificational relation (= force). At the point where the quantifier is to be scoped, the binding operator binds the place holder to form a property. This property together with the restricting type are the arguments of the quantificational relation. The way wh-phrases are going to be treated here is as half-breeds: They are name-like in the fact that all they contribute is an argument role filler. But the argument role filler they contribute is not any specific object (as with proper names), but just a parameter, a place holder. Thus, the contribution to (asserted) content of a wh-NP is threadbare: a place-holder, no more.[5]

As an example, consider the contents assigned respectively to a referential NP such as 'Jill', a wh-NP 'which man' (ignoring for the present the uniqueness conventional implicature), and a quantificational NP 'Every man':

(1) a. Content of 'Jill': *jill* (= the referent of the particular use of 'Jill'.)
     b. Content of 'Which Man': $x_{\langle\langle MAN, x \rangle\rangle}$ (= a parameter restricted to men.)
     c. Content of 'Every Man':
        Contributed-content: x (a parameter)
        Restricting type: $[x \mid \langle\langle MAN, x \rangle\rangle]$
        Quantificational force: Every.

We can see the contrasting contributions to content of these NP's in the following sentences:

---

[5]It should be pointed out that although I am assuming all wh-phrases have the same *type* of contribution to content, this does not preclude the emergence of meaning differences, for instance pertaining to distinctions in "definiteness" along the lines of D-linking, cf. Bolinger 1978, Pesetsky 1987 and Comorowski 1988. These distinctions are naturally captured in the circumstantial component of an expression's meaning.

(2) a. Content of 'Jill came': $\langle\!\langle$ CAME,comer:*jill* $\rangle\!\rangle$

  b. Content of 'Which man came': $\langle\!\langle$ CAME, comer:$x_{\langle\!\langle\text{MAN},x\rangle\!\rangle}$ $\rangle\!\rangle$

  c. Content of 'Every man came':

  $\langle\!\langle Every, [x \mid \langle\!\langle \text{MAN}, x\rangle\!\rangle], [x \mid \langle\!\langle \text{CAME}, \text{comer:}x\rangle\!\rangle]\rangle\!\rangle$

The contents in (2) illustrate the assertion above about wh-phrases being half way between referential phrases and quantificational phrases: (2b) is like (2a) in that the only contribution of the syntactic NP associated with the semantic role of *comer* is an argument role filler, to the exclusion of a binding operator, a restricting type and a quantificational force. (2b) is like (2c) in that the filler of the argument role of 'COME' is a parameter, not an individual.

Notice, then, that on this view, all a wh-NP contributes to content is a variable-like object with its associated restriction. Neither binding operator, nor quantificational force is contributed. It is important to stress that parameters are semantic, rather than syntactic objects. So that the content (2b) *is* a content, rather than a syntactic object that depends on a variable assignment for meaning.

What explanatory use can be made of a content like (2b)? Loosely speaking the idea is this: because the content is parametric, it is intrinsically not assertible. However, the role filled by a parameter is marked out in such a way that in subsequent discourse this role can be filled. Thus, in (2b) since the role of *comer* is parametrized, it is available for filling. More precisely, from a parametric proposition a relation-like object (the "queried type") can be formed by abstracting over its parameters. The queried type can then be used in the formation of an answer from the information provided in the response. Thus, if (2b) is used in an interrogative speech act, and a suitable response, say 'Jill', is supplied, then by predicating the queried type of the referent of 'Jill', the proposition 'Jill came' arises as an answer.

2.3 Wh-Movement and Questions

How are we to deal with the effects of wh-movement? As far as the syntax goes, the current approach makes few commitments: all we assume is that the dislocated phrase is "coindexed" in some fashion with the argument position it is supposed to fill: this can be viewed as an instruction to unify the (syntax and semantics of the) two positions (as in frameworks like LFG or H/G-PSG), or as a reflex of movement (as in GB). As far as the semantics goes, however, the basic assumption made is that the "trace position" makes no independent semantic contribution to the content, but gets unified entirely with the semantics of the wh-phrase. Thus, the content of a sentence that has a dislocated wh-phrase is constructed in identical fashion to that of a topicalized sentence:

(3) a. Mary, John adores:
      Syntax: $Mary_i$, John adores t_i
      Content: $\langle\!\langle$ADORES, adorer:*john*, adoree:*mary*$\rangle\!\rangle$
   b. Which woman does John like:
      Syntax: Which *woman*$_i$ does John adore t_i
      Content: $\langle\!\langle$ADORES, adorer:*john*, adoree:$x_{\langle\!\langle \text{WOMAN},x\rangle\!\rangle}\rangle\!\rangle$

The contents of (3a) and (3b) are identical, save for the following: the argument role of the adoree in (3a) is filled by an individual, Mary, in (3a), but by a restricted parameter in (3b). This means, in effect, that the "adoree role" takes widest scope in (3b): the semantic role that the question makes salient for filling in the discourse is the role of 'adored by John'. The corresponding queried type is

$$[x \mid \langle\!\langle \text{ADORES, adorer:}john, \text{ adoree:}x_{\langle\!\langle \text{WOMAN},x\rangle\!\rangle}\rangle\!\rangle]$$

I stress that these are simplified contents: They ignore the informational structure of these sentences, the fact that Mary is "new information," or the "focus," etc. The claim made for these simplified contents is that however we decide to embellish (3a) to account for these additional factors, the same can be applied to (3b).[6] Alternatively put, whatever long-distance mechanism is adduced to assign the topicalized NP in (3a) to its argument structure role, the same is to apply to the dislocated wh-phrase.

Consequently, wherever a wh-phrase occurs *in situ*, it is interpreted *in situ*. Whenever, a wh-phrase is dislocated, it is interpreted analogously to a topicalization. Since this position is not particularly novel, I will not provide arguments in its favor in the current work, though it has noticeable repercussions concerning such phenomena as "pied piping," in that it eliminates the need for "reconstruction."[7] Given that no commitment is made with regards to the *syntactic* status of the "trace position," it is still possible to maintain accounts of phenomena that make reference to the relative position of filler and gap. Explanations that are not open to us are those that make reference to a semantic operator/variable relation. The consequences of this are discussed further in Section 8.

2.4 Adjunct-Questions

It should be clear that everything that has been said about wh-NP's can be generalized directly to other types of wh-phrases, used typically as adjuncts, 'when', 'why', 'where', etc. Thus assuming the content of 'Bill met Jill,

---

[6]The importance of these effects is not to be underestimated, e.g., in explaining why in certain contexts wh-movement is not needed: A: I'm going. B: You're going where? But I will not discuss this phenomenon further here.

[7]Engdahl 1986 utilizes the framework PLG, in which this assumption is built in. It is also implicit in such works as Kaplan and Zaenen 1987, and Pollard and Sag (to appear). Although these are all non-GB works, this position is also compatible with a syntax that utilizes GB S-structures.

because he liked her' is (4a), the content of 'Why did Bill meet Jill' will be (4b):

(4) a. $\langle\!\langle$REASON-FOR, $\langle\!\langle$MEET, meeter:*bill*, meetee:*jill*$\rangle\!\rangle$,
        $\langle\!\langle$LIKE, liker:*bill*, likee:*jill*$\rangle\!\rangle$ $\rangle\!\rangle$

     b. $\langle\!\langle$REASON-FOR, $\langle\!\langle$MEET, meeter:*bill*, meetee:*jill*$\rangle\!\rangle$, $r\rangle\!\rangle$

So again, the sole difference in content between the (4a) and (4b) is that in the former the second argument of the REASON-FOR operator it is a particular proposition, the proposition with content $\langle\!\langle$LIKE, liker:*bill*, likee:*jill*$\rangle\!\rangle$, while in the latter example, it is an unfilled parameter for a proposition, r.[8]

2.5 Multiple-Questions

It should now be apparent how multiple wh-questions are to be interpreted: they differ from unary wh-questions only in that their content contains multiple parameters. A simple example would be

(5) a. Who likes whom?

     b. Content: $\langle\!\langle$LIKES, liker:$x_{\langle\!\langle \text{HUMAN},x\rangle\!\rangle}$, likee:$y_{\langle\!\langle \text{HUMAN},y\rangle\!\rangle}$ $\rangle\!\rangle$

In fact, it is here that the current approach is particularly attractive: multiple-wh-questions pose a problem for non-parametric accounts, since one has to "wh-quantify in" to a question. Special wh-quantification rules have to be posited to deal with these cases. On the account proposed here, however, nothing additional whatsoever need be said to accommodate multiple-wh-questions. Parameterizing the subject-role of a parametrized VP is no more nor less problematic than parametrizing the subject role of a non-parametric VP.

However, even on this approach there is something different about multiple-wh-questions, when one inspects the types of responses we expect them to elicit. For a start, since more than one role is parametrized, we expect responses that will provide more than one filler. However, notice that the parametrized roles are linked to each other in a way that leads one not to expect responses to provide solely a filler for each role. Compare the proposed content for 'Who adores whom' with the content of 'Who does Jill adore':

(6) a. Content: $\langle\!\langle$ADORES, adorer:$x_{\langle\!\langle \text{HUMAN},x\rangle\!\rangle}$, adoree:$y_{\langle\!\langle \text{HUMAN},y\rangle\!\rangle}$ $\rangle\!\rangle$.

     b. Content: $\langle\!\langle$ADORES, j, $x_{\langle\!\langle \text{HUMAN},x\rangle\!\rangle}$ $\rangle\!\rangle$

In (6b), the parametrized role is that of 'adoree of John'. So, (an interrogative use of) the question seeks out to fill or quantify over that role. However, in (6a), the analogous role is 'adoree of x'. Unless information about x exists, it is not clear how to fill this role. Similarly, for the subject argument, which is best described as 'adorer of y'. This suggests a natural account for the tendency multiple wh-questions exhibit for eliciting (exhaustive)

---

[8]Needless to say, I am not offering this as a serious analysis of motive adjuncts.

list-like rather than single filler responses: the roles such questions make salient are parametric, so that they evoke a relation between roles, rather than just fillers of specific roles. In terms of their queried type, apart from adicity, there is no formal distinction between individual uses of unary and multiple-wh-questions. So that the queried type of (6a) is

(7) $[x, y \mid \langle\!\langle \text{LIKES}, \text{liker:}x_{\langle\!\langle \text{HUMAN},x\rangle\!\rangle}, \text{likee:}y_{\langle\!\langle \text{HUMAN},y\rangle\!\rangle} \rangle\!\rangle]$

This is, I claim, as it should be, since the list-like tendency of multiple-wh is not categorical: non-exhaustive responses can be felicitous, depending on the contextual setup, as discussed in Ginzburg 1991a. In fact, my claim there is that multiple-wh questions are ambiguous, where the second type of reading, the exhaustive, arises from a "dependent" use of a wh-phrase, discussed in Section 6.

The important thing to notice for the present is that in a multiple-wh-question, where both phrases are used "individually" (viz. according to the semantics provided in this section), neither phrase has scope over the other, and there are good reasons for this, as argued in Ginzburg 1991a. This might appear to cause problems because scope has been invoked to account for various phenomena connected to multiple-wh-questions, most convincingly perhaps Baker 1970's examples: the ambiguity of a sentence like 'Who remembers where John bought which book.' However, the problem is only apparent: In Sections 8 and 9, I show how variable scopes for wh-phrases can be generated, without assuming that any binding operator emanating from the wh-phrase is responsible. This type of explanation figures in our account of the Baker examples, pair-list readings of questions, and "uniqueness filtering" in multiple-wh-questions.

Summing up for the moment, a wh-phrase denotes a restricted parameter. A wh-sentence denotes a propositional content one or more of whose roles is parametrized. Answers can arise by predicating of objects supplied in a response a property or relation that arises from the parametrized content.

3 Parametric Content

Declarative sentences can be used in assertoric speech acts. Following Russell, Kaplan, Situation Theory and others, it will be assumed that a propositional content is a structured (semantic) object consisting of a relation and certain objects that fill (some or all of the) arguments of the relation. Following Austin, one can view an assertion as associating a situation with a propositional content, a claim that a particular situation is of a type specified in the propositional content. Thus, in the case of the sentence 'John came', an assertion involves an agent picking out a certain situation and claiming it is of the type specified in (2a), namely $[s \mid s \models \langle\!\langle \text{CAME}, john\rangle\!\rangle]$ (read "The type of situation that supports the infon $\langle\!\langle \text{CAME}, john\rangle\!\rangle$." More informally 'A situation in which John came.').

In contrast to declaratives, wh-questions cannot be asserted, nor do they bear truth values:

(8) a. # I claim the following: What did Bill eat last night(?/.)
     b. # Who left is false/true.

The question is, then, why the only (direct) speech act a wh-sentence can be used in is interrogative? Alternatively: why can't a wh-question get a truth value?[9] In either case, it is incumbent upon us to explain why the assertion/wh-sentence association is impossible.

The semantics proposed above for wh-sentences provides a natural explanation for this. The described situation type which a wh-sentence denotes is *parametric*.[10] Hence it lacks the right ingredients to be used in an assertoric act, where a situation-type, consisting of a relation coupled with specific objects is measured against an (actual) situation. If the situation is of the given situation type, the assertion is true, otherwise it is false.[11] A situation cannot be definitively adjudged to be of a parametric type, hence the assertoric act cannot go through.

Thus, 'Who came' denotes the situation type

$$[s \mid s \models \langle\!\langle \text{CAME}, x_{\langle\!\langle \text{HUMAN}, x \rangle\!\rangle} \rangle\!\rangle]$$

and since the role of the *comer* is parametrized, this type is not assertible.[12] It is important to emphasize yet again that it is the *content* of an utterance of a wh-sentence that is parametric, rather than just the meaning of the wh-sentence. Many declarative sentences are analyzable as possessing parametric *meanings*, so that each utterance has to *fix* the value of the parameter.[13] Nonetheless, the *content* of each utterance of such a sentence is definitely *not* parametric. In contrast, the claim advanced here is that each utterance of a wh-sentence involves a content that contains an uninstantiated parameter.

---

[9] I am assuming, for the present, that exclamatives such as 'What a kid Georgie is!' use a content that is different from a wh-question. One motivation for this being that the existential implicature of wh-questions, which is cancellable, 'Which friends, if any, does Bill have?' seems to be uncancellable: '# What friends, if any, he has!'. Further research on exclamatives will hopefully clear this issue up.

[10] This is a slight oversimplification which I will continue to adopt throughout this paper. The actual denotation should be an equivalence class of parametric objects, relative to the equivalence induced by being alphabetic variants of each other.

[11] In a quantified propositional content, the relation is specified by the determiner, and the objects are sets or types: 'Every man came' denotes a structured object consisting of the relation 'Every' and the types 'is a man' and 'had the property of coming'.

[12] See Westerståhl 1990 for a model theory for parametric objects, in particular, parametric propositions.

[13] Null complement anaphora seem good candidates for such an analysis: an utterance of 'Bill won' must fix the value of the competition which Bill is asserted to have won. This cannot be done by existentially quantifying away the competition role as indicated by negation: 'Bill didn't win' entails that Bill didn't win a particular competition, rather than the lack of a competition in which he won.

4   Wh-Sentences and Interrogative Speech Acts

In the previous section, we saw one argument for the adequacy of the semantics for wh-sentences proposed here: it offers a natural account of the non-assertibility of wh-sentences. In this section, the adequacy of the proposed semantics will be tested with respect to its integrability into a theory of interrogative speech acts.[14]

Wh-sentences can be used interrogatively, to perform an interrogative speech act. One of the characteristics of such speech acts is that they evoke responses whose felicity is directly influenced by the content of the question. Some, but by no means all, felicitous responses have a further property: they cause a proposition which has a close semantic relation to the question to be asserted, in other words, they convey an "answer," or as I shall phrase it, the response *ostends* (from ostension) to an answer.

There are two main issues on which a semantics for questions can be judged, with respect to its integrability into a theory of interrogative speech acts:

(a) For a question Q what is the class $R(Q)$ of possible felicitous responses to Q?

(b) Given a question Q and a felicitous response r, which answer, if any, does r ostend to?

Before showing how this framework deals with these tasks, I discuss some issues concerning the felicity of responses, and the different types of answers that can be provided to a wh-question.

4.1   Response Felicity

In actual use, whether a response is felicitous and which answers, if any, it ostends to depend on various pragmatic factors such as the goals and knowledge state of the questioner.[15] However, in utilizing response patterns as a probe that will help us characterize the meaning of a question, we would like to abstract away from such factors. In other words, the notion of "response felicity" we are after is one that derives from an intuition competent language users possess that is independent of their non-linguistic knowledge and goals. This is the ability to judge whether a response "coheres" with a question, regardless of its informative potential for the addressee or its *truth*. Similarly, what interests us from a semantic point of view about answers is which answer, if any, does a response ostend to utilizing purely semantic means. Consider the following examples:

---

[14] This topic is updated and discussed in detail in Ginzburg 1991a: it contains explicit discussion of the components of the illocutionary force of different types of interrogative speech acts, in particular what the different types of preconditions on these speech acts are and what the contribution of different types of interrogative operators is to the content of the interrogative speech act.

[15] See Ginzburg 1989 for an articulation of the factors underlying Informativeness of responses.

(9)   a. Who committed the crime?
    b. John Dean.
    c. Someone did.
    d. Dan Quayle was out of town.
    e. I haven't got the foggiest idea.

Both (9b) and (9e) are clearly felicitous responses: (9b) ostends to the answer 'John Dean committed the crime'; (9e) does not ostend to an answer. What of (9c) and (9d)? (9c) is, I would claim, a semantically felicitous response which is, in most contexts, not pragmatically felicitous. By uttering (9c) as a response, a speaker does demonstrate basic semantic competence—no one would be entitled to think 'Gosh, where did this person learn English, he just didn't understand the question.' In fact, an utterance of (9c) ostends, using entirely conventional means, to the answer 'Someone committed the crime', not a particularly useful proposition for many purposes, but an answer nonetheless.

(9d), in contrast, is a response that is not semantically felicitous, but, in certain contexts, could become felicitous, on pragmatic grounds. A reasonable reaction to (9d) might be 'I didn't ask *who was out of town*, I asked *who committed the crime*.' However, in a certain context (9d) might be felicitous: if it is known that only George Bush and Dan Quayle could possible have committed the crime, (9d) would be felicitous and could be taken to implicate that Dan Quayle did not commit the crime, or perhaps even that George Bush was the culprit. In this case, the answer 'George Bush committed the crime' has been ostended to, but not by conventional means.

4.2   Excursus on Quantified Answers, Exhaustiveness and Presupposition

In this section, I'd like to discuss further the status of responses that ostend to quantified answers, and claim that they are on par, semantically, with referential answers. This will have some importance for us when we compare the current approach to Hamblinian "set of all possible answers" approaches to questions. Consider the following examples, which show that quantified and referential responses can be equally and simultaneously (viz. uttered in the same context) felicitous:

(10)   a. Who voted for the proposal?
    b. At most thirty Democrats.
    c. Most Southern Senators.
    d. Moe Flatbush and Joe Cannelli.

(11)   a. What did the patient eat last night?
    b. Nothing.
    c. Some carrots.
    d. No carbohydrates.
    e. The remainder of the boiled vegetables.

The claim made here is not only that responses that are quantified are felicitous, but moreover that even if they ostend necessarily to quantified answers, they are felicitous. In other words, a quantified response can be felicitous, *even* if it cannot be construed as indirectly pointing to a referential answer. One might, for instance, claim that when one responds to the question 'Who came' with 'Every syntactician.', this is construed to be indirectly ostending to the answer 'The group consisting of all syntacticians came'. The claim here, then, is that even when such an analysis is impossible, as is typically the case with monotone-decreasing quantificational forces, the response can be felicitous, semantically, as the examples above indicate. In so doing, we explicitly reject two common assumptions concerning wh-questions.

The first concerns exhaustiveness for interrogative uses. It is claimed that part of the semantic force of a wh-question is a specification that a response provides exhaustive (modulo domain selection) specification of the extension of the queried type. It is assumed that this force can be canceled "metalinguistically," during the INSA.[16] A full discussion of this issue would take me farther afield than I have space here, a few brief remarks will have to suffice. No one denies that responses that ostend to non-exhaustive answers can be felicitous. Consequently, the issue becomes one of division of labor between Semantics and Pragmatics. Given that a more complicated semantics is needed to ensure that exhaustiveness is asserted by the response,[17] and moreover that exhaustiveness is quite clearly a feature that *is* derivable from Gricean principles of cooperative communication, special motivation is required in order not to assume that it is a specifically pragmatic feature. This additional motivation is supposed to be provided by the exhaustiveness putatively exhibited by embedded questions. Given the fact that the semantics of embedded questions are, as is argued in Section 7, not directly the semantics of direct questions, this is no longer a compelling argument. In any case, various data, originating with Belnap and Hintikka, and extensively discussed in Berman 1990 show that even in such contexts, exhaustiveness is cancellable or modifiable. Whatever the outcome of that debate, as far as direct questions go, a semantics that leaves exhaustiveness to be dealt with by pragmatics is to be preferred.

A second common misconception is that wh-questions, in general, presuppose the existence of an instantiating answer (see, e.g., Comorowski 1988 for a recent statement of this claim). It is clear that when a question such as

---

[16]See Karttunen 1977, p. 10, and Groenendijk and Stokhof 1984, chapter 5.

[17]Presumably this has to be implemented by associating exhaustiveness in some manner with the queried type the INSA makes salient, so that 'Who came' provides as queried type one identical to that provided by 'Who are all humans that came.'

(12)   What did John eat last night?

is uttered, the normal expectation is that there exists something that John ate last night. But equally clearly, this expectation is cancellable, both during questioning:

(13)   What, if anything, did John eat last night?

and during responding

(14)   (He ate) nothing.

This response is, after all, as felicitous as any instantiating response. It is undeniable that in many contexts, a negative response of this type will be surprising to the questioner. However, it is not difficult to construct contexts in which no pragmatic accommodation need be made. Thus, a doctor making his rounds in the post-surgery recovery ward will be quite ready to receive precisely such a negative answer to his question (12). The infelicity of 'I know no one came, but who came?' is *not*, as Comorowski claims, an illustration that the putative presupposition is not cancellable. Rather, it is an illustration of a violation of the pre-conditions on the felicity of an interrogative speech act (roughly, that an answer not be salient): 'I know John came, but who came?' is equally infelicitous.

4.3   Responses, Subsequents, and Answers

Our tasks in this and the coming section are two: first, to provide a characterization of the class of felicitous responses an interrogative speech act use of a given wh-sentence elicits. Second, to explain how given the contents of both a question and a response to the question, a particular answer is ostended to.

First, for some terminological distinctions. An object provided in a response that fills or quantifies over a role r parametrized in a wh-question q will be called r's *subsequent*, or when no confusion can ensue, q's subsequent.[18].

We have, then, three distinct notions, all of which an interrogative use of a wh-question is intended to elicit. Once an interrogative speech act has been made, a verbal or non-verbal response must be provided, for the discourse to maintain its felicity. Broadly speaking, felicitous responses can be classified into two types: ones that provide subsequents, and ones that do not. The term *answer* is reserved here for a proposition that certain responses directly or indirectly assert. Thus, in (15)

(15)   a. Who committed the crime?
        b. John Dean.
        c. (Responder silently points to John Dean.)
        d. Someone committed the crime.
        e. I haven't got the foggiest idea.

---

[18] To be suggestive of being a converse to the anaphoric notion of *antecedent*.

(15b), (15c), and (15d) are all responses that provide subsequents; in the first two cases they are *John Dean* (the referent), and in the latter case the quantifier 'Someone'. Only in the case of (15d) is the content of the response identical with the content of the answer which has been ostended to, namely the proposition 'Someone committed the crime'. In both other cases, the content of the response is simply (the individual) John Dean. The *answer* that gets ostended to in both cases is the proposition (expressed by the sentence) 'John Dean committed the crime.'[19] (15e) is a felicitous response that does not contain a subsequent. We might choose to say that it ostends to the proposition 'I haven't the foggiest idea who committed the crime.'

Felicitous responses that do not provide subsequents are not uniquely elicited by wh-questions. They are acceptable as responses to any interrogative speech act. Consequently, I will not dwell on a precise generation of this class and concentrate instead on the class of subsequent-containing responses.

This latter class is, then, the class we are interested to characterize, using the contents we have provided for wh-sentences, starting initially with unary wh-sentences. Given a wh-sentence q with parametrized role r, this class is

(16) {Informational Acts R | R contains a subsequent for r}

The phrase requiring formalization is "R contains a subsequent for r." This will be interpreted as the following conjunction:

(17) (A constituent of the content of R is s) and (s is in $S(r, q)$, the set of subsequents for r.)

Observing this conjunction we see that what remains to do is to define the set of subsequents for each wh-question, in terms of its content. Subsequents are either objects that can fill r, or quantifiers that can quantify over r:

(18) $S(r, q) =_{def} \{o \mid o$ is appropriate for the role $r\} \cup \{q \mid q$ is appropriate for quantifying over the role r of $q\}$

Generalizing this to multiple-wh-questions is straightforward:

(19) $S(r_1, r_2, \ldots, r_n, q) =_{def} \{\langle o_1, \ldots, o_n \rangle \mid o_i$ is appropriate for the role $r_i\} \cup \{\langle q_1, \ldots, q_n \rangle \mid q_i$ is appropriate for quantifying over the role r_i of $q\}$

4.4 The Generation of Answers

In the previous section, we showed how using the content we assigned wh-sentences, we could provide a characterization of the class of felicitous

---

[19] Actually, it is plausible to argue that (15b) is an elliptical construction along the lines of "sluicing" (see Ross 1969). So that there is more linguistic structure and content there than meets the eye. This does not detract from the general point, namely that the content of the response can differ from the content of the answer ostended to.

responses elicited by an interrogative use of such a sentence. What remains to be shown is how an answer gets generated, on the basis of the semantics of the response and the question. The basic idea is this: an interrogative speech act makes the parametrized role(s) and the queried type salient. A subsequent-containing response contains a (or more than one) prominent constituent, namely the subsequent(s). Together, the queried type and the subsequent(s) form an answer by predication or quantification.

The current proposal interacts nicely and gains motivation from work on *focus* in Jackendoff 1972 and Rooth 1985.[20] Jackendoff proposed to derive a level of representation for old information by (i) substituting variables for focused phrases, and (ii) lambda abstracting the focus variables to produce a relation, the "presuppositional set" of the sentence. This relation is what must be salient for a felicitous use of a focused phrase. Our own proposal mirrors this: wh-sentences have contents in which the interrogated roles are filled by phrases that denote parameters (read "variables" for current discussion). These phrases serve as templates into which the new information, the subsequent, can be inputted. This makes for a simple characterization of the interrogative speech act: it makes the *queried type*, analogously to Jackendoff's presuppositional set, salient.[21]

A subsequent provided by a response is that speech act's "new information." Jackendoff and Rooth assume that such focused constituents are syntactically marked with a feature F. This is required by the "model T" organization of the grammar that both of them assume. Although one could follow this line in our case, I will assume that such marking is provided by a different source: Since subsequents can also be provided non-verbally, it will be assumed that the circumstances of utterance are those that provide information as to which constituent is intended to be the subsequent for any given role. This is represented by means of a relation 'Subsequent-for' that holds between a role and an utterance.

4.4.1 Generating the Same Answer from Different Responses

It should now be clear how the same answer is generated from a wide range of responses:

(20) a. Who arrived last night?
  b. Jill.
  c. (Responder points at Jill.)
  d. I believe it was Jill.

---

[20]I am indebted to Mark Gawron for pointing out the relevance of Rooth's work to me. Discussion of Jackendoff 1972 is based entirely on Rooth's exegesis.

[21]I depart from Rooth's characterization of the set of alternative answers, his p-sets, since I assume quantificational answers are also possible alternatives. Clearly, nothing in his account precludes this revision.

(21) a. Content of question: $\langle\!\langle \text{ARRIVED-LAST-NIGHT}, x_{\langle\!\langle\text{HUMAN}\rangle\!\rangle} \rangle\!\rangle$
Effect of INSA:

$\langle\!\langle \text{Salient}, [x \mid \langle\!\langle \text{ARRIVED-LAST-NIGHT}, x_{\langle\!\langle\text{HUMAN}\rangle\!\rangle} \rangle\!\rangle] \rangle$

b. Content of response: *jill*
Circumstance of Utterance: $\langle\!\langle \text{Subsequent-for, arriver}, \textit{jill} \rangle\!\rangle$
Ostended Answer:

$\langle\!\langle [x \mid \langle\!\langle \text{ARRIVED-LAST-NIGHT}, x_{\langle\!\langle\text{HUMAN}\rangle\!\rangle} \rangle\!\rangle], \textit{jill} \rangle\!\rangle$

c. Content of response: *jill*
Circumstance of Utterance: $\langle\!\langle \text{Subsequent-for, arriver}, \textit{jill} \rangle\!\rangle$
Ostended Answer:

$\langle\!\langle [x \mid \langle\!\langle \text{ARRIVED-LAST-NIGHT}, x_{\langle\!\langle\text{HUMAN}\rangle\!\rangle} \rangle\!\rangle], \textit{jill} \rangle\!\rangle$

d. Content of response:

$\langle\!\langle \text{Believe, speaker}, \langle\!\langle \text{Filler-of-arriver-role}, \textit{jill} \rangle\!\rangle \rangle\!\rangle$
Circumstance of Utterance: $\langle\!\langle \text{Subsequent-for, arriver, Jill} \rangle\!\rangle$
Ostended Answer:

$\langle\!\langle [x \mid \langle\!\langle \text{ARRIVED-LAST-NIGHT}, x_{\langle\!\langle\text{HUMAN}\rangle\!\rangle} \rangle\!\rangle], \textit{jill} \rangle\!\rangle$

4.4.2 Quantified Answers

Nothing more needs to be said to accommodate quantified answers:

(22) a. Who arrived last night?
b. Many men.
c. To the best of my knowledge, no one did.

(23) a. Content of question: $\langle\!\langle \text{ARRIVED-LAST-NIGHT}, x_{\langle\!\langle\text{HUMAN}\rangle\!\rangle} \rangle\!\rangle$
Effect of INSA:

$\langle\!\langle \text{Salient}, [x \mid \langle\!\langle \text{ARRIVED-LAST-NIGHT}, x_{\langle\!\langle\text{HUMAN}\rangle\!\rangle} \rangle\!\rangle] \rangle$

b. Content of response: Quantificational Force: Many.
Ascribed Type: $[x \mid \langle\!\langle \text{MAN}, x \rangle\!\rangle]$
Circumstance of utterance:

$\langle\!\langle \text{Subsequent-for, arriver, Utterance-of ('Many men')} \rangle\!\rangle$
Ostended Answer:

$\langle\!\langle \text{MANY}, [x \mid \langle\!\langle \text{MAN}, x \rangle\!\rangle],$
$[x \mid \langle\!\langle \text{ARRIVED-LAST-NIGHT}, x_{\langle\!\langle\text{HUMAN}\rangle\!\rangle} \rangle\!\rangle] \rangle\!\rangle$

c. Content of utterance:

$\langle\!\langle \text{KNOW, speaker}, \langle\!\langle \text{NO}, [x \mid \langle\!\langle \text{MAN}, x \rangle\!\rangle],$
$[x \mid \langle\!\langle \text{ARRIVED-LAST-NIGHT}, x_{\langle\!\langle\text{HUMAN}\rangle\!\rangle} \rangle\!\rangle] \rangle\!\rangle \rangle\!\rangle$
Circumstance of utterance:

$\langle\!\langle \text{Subsequent-for, arriver, Utterance-of ('No one')} \rangle\!\rangle$
Ostended Answer:

$\langle\!\langle \text{NO}, [x \mid \langle\!\langle \text{MAN}, x \rangle\!\rangle],$
$[x \mid \langle\!\langle \text{ARRIVED-LAST-NIGHT}, x_{\langle\!\langle\text{HUMAN}\rangle\!\rangle} \rangle\!\rangle] \rangle\!\rangle$

5 Justification for a Parametric Content

In this section, I would like to summarize the motivation for providing wh-sentences with a parametric content, as a prelude to comparison with other approaches. In so doing, I will provide some arguments for the particular division of labor given here between the *content* of a wh-sentence, and the effect on context produced by an INSA which utilizes that content.

The content of a syntactic object is a semantic object that must remain constant across use in various syntactic contexts. The two contexts which a wh-sentence appears in are matrix sentence, used in INSA's, and as embedded questions.

Let us first concentrate on the matrix sentence context. The first use we made of parametricity of the proposed content was to explain why matrix wh-sentences cannot be used in an assertoric speech act. The idea was that contents which contain uninstantiated parameters cannot be associated with a (world/situation) in a way that enables truth or falsity to be determined.

A parametric content is used to explicate what goes on in an INSA: the role that is parametrized is made salient for filling by the new information provided by the response.[22] So, the content is directly used in characterizing the felicitous responses: all responses that provide an instantiator for or quantifier over the parametrized role. An INSA makes a certain property salient, namely the property formed by abstracting the parametrized role from the content of the question. It is this property, the queried type, that is combined with the new information about the parametrized role provided in the response to yield an answer. This view of what happens in an INSA and in a responsive act allows us to account for the wide variety of possible responsive acts: why responses can be linguistic and non-linguistic, why they can be sentential or phrasal (a phrase providing the filler of the parametrized role) and so on. An answer will be generated as long as information supplying an appropriate filler for the parametrized role is provided, regardless of the form that information takes.

Nonetheless, it is important to understand that the queried type is *not* the content of the question, rather its salience arises as an effect of the speech act. Given that as far as predicting responses and generating answers, we can make do with the queried type rather than the parametric content, one might be tempted to ask why, in fact, we don't posit *the queried type* as the content of the question?

Briefly, the answer is that such a move would produce some unwanted side effects, as well as lacking motivation in the domain of embedded questions:

(a) A familiar problem this move would bring about is that wh-sentences containing different numbers or types of wh-phrases would differ in semantic type, e.g., unary wh-sentences and binary wh-sentences, whose distribution is identical, end up as bearing different semantic types.

---

[22] All this applies to the case where more than one role is parametrized *mutatis mutandis*.

(b) Conversely, there is no independent distributional motivation for the assumption that the denotation of a wh-sentence is property or relation-like: it is syntactically saturated.

(c) Wh-sentences can be used rhetorically, which suggests that the content is also semantically saturated, in other words propositional.

As we shall see in Section 7, parametric contents allow us to make the proper distinctions among the different classes of embedded questions. Some verbs actually take the content of the wh-sentence as their argument: these are "question-embedding" verbs such as 'ask' and 'wonder'. Other verbs, such as 'know' and 'tell', embed the answers to questions, in which case the argument of the verb is a proposition that constitutes an answer to the question. In this case, the content of the question is a constituent of the semantic object that is the argument to the verb.

6   Comparisons with Hamblin-Inspired Approaches

In this section, I compare the approach proposed here to approaches based on the idea that a wh-sentence denotes the set of its possible instantiations. I will argue that the possible answers denotation is not well motivated either in terms of its integrability in a theory of INSA's or embedded questions, and appears to face significant problems in its construal as a cognitive object.

The two main motivations for positing the denotation of a question to be the set of its possible instantiations have been the following:

(a) *The set of all instantiations is the set of possible (semantic) answers.* Hamblin was under the impression that "Semantically, an answer to a question on a given reading is any statement whose denotation set is contained in that of the question" (Hamblin 1973, p. 52). In other words, membership in the denotation of the question could be set up as a criterion for answerhood.

(b) *The set of all instantiations serves as the denotation of an embedded question.* (Karttunen) Assuming the semantic rule for question-embedding VP's to be simply

$$(**)\quad [\![VP]\!] = [\![V]\!]([\![Q]\!])$$

one can then "solve" for the denotation of Q, which appears to be precisely the Hamblin set, the set of all instantiations of the open sentence underlying the question.

I will argue that both assumptions are false, and consequently the original motivations for the Hamblinian approach are correspondingly significantly weakened.

6.1 The Set of All Instantiations is (not) the Set of Possible (Semantic) Answers

The passage cited above from Hamblin 1973 suggests that Hamblin was under the impression that membership in the set of instantiations of the open sentence underlying a wh-question could serve as a criterion for answerhood:

(24) p is an answer to q iff $p \in \{r \mid r \text{ is an instantiation of } q\}$

This assumption is false: as was discussed in Section 4, responses that ostend to quantified answers are as semantically felicitous as ones that ostend to instantiated answers. Consequently, we may ask what explanatory role does a denotation such as this serve in explaining what goes in an interrogative use of a wh-sentence?

As we have seen above, there are two basic components of an INSA that a semantics for questions must provide for: characterize the set of felicitous responsive acts and show how a subsequent-containing response ostends to an answer. Although it was intended to perform the first task, the Hamblin set falls short in this respect. There are a number of moves one could make to remedy this problem. The most obvious would be to expand the Hamblin set to include also quantified answers. It is fairly clear that the resulting set is not appropriate for the denotation of an embedded question. Hence, the expansion of the denotation for purposes of INSA's, viz. addition of the quantified component, requires some motivation. Whatever it is, it is clear that a theory such as the present one, where both types of answers are accommodated symmetrically is to be preferred, just as a theory of bound variable anaphora which accommodates with equal ease quantified and referential antecedents is to be preferred over one that requires additional apparatus for one type of antecedent.

The second task required of a content of a question is that it explain how subsequent-containing responses ostend to answers. In other words, what we have called the "queried type" needs to be recoverable from the content of the question. It seems plausible that at least in certain implementations of the Hamblinian idea, e.g., in frameworks that utilize structured meanings, this can be done. Nonetheless, even if it is possible, it represents an unnecessary complication, over and above what is proposed here, namely abstraction over the parametrized role.

Consider now the fact that wh-sentences are not assertible. Can positing a Hamblin set denotation help to explain this fact? Hamblin thought that this could be captured by saying that assertions could be performed only with Hamblin sets whose cardinality is one, namely unit sets. This seems reasonable, but is only interesting as an explanation if some independent motivation is provided for the postulation of set-like propositional contents (viz. contents that are sets of one or more propositions.)

Summing up for the present, in the domain of INSA, the idea of Hamblin set-like denotations for wh-sentences is not well motivated: not in terms of characterizing the class of felicitous responses, nor in the generation of answers, nor in accounting for the unassertability of wh-sentences. And yet, if all these problems can, for better or worse be patched up, insofar as explicating INSA's, the idea seems to possess an intrinsic cognitive flaw. As I point out briefly in the next section, it is not at all clear that the Hamblin set (independent of its implementation in a particular semantic framework) can be assumed to be "cognitively available" to arbitrary participants in an INSA.

6.2 Cognitive Concerns

In this section, I will raise a psychological objection to this set as a representation of the denotation of a wh-question. Whatever steps are taken to correct this problem point, I will claim, to an object very much like a parametric object proposed in this paper. In so doing, I do not claim any particular "psychological reality" for the framework I propose, rather I claim a certain psychological unreality for the Hamblinian approach, as it stands. Note that this accusation, assuming it is valid, is applicable to any particular implementation of the Hamblinian approach, whether in possible worlds semantics, situation semantics, DRT, etc.

One uncontroversial characteristic of wh-questions is that they can be used without acquaintance with any possible (instantiated) answers they can evoke. This is, in fact, one of their distinct advantages, although it does make them somewhat more complex cognitively. Consider, for example, the following sentence

(25) What is the word for 'relaxation' in Chukotian?

uttered by someone such as myself who does not know what language family Chukotian belongs to, let alone possible word forms in the language. Clearly, one can ask this question without reference to or acquaintance with *any* singular proposition which instantiates an answer. Similarly, with respect to comprehension, though not, of course, ability to provide a true answer—ostending response.

Now an apparently similar situation exists with quantification, and has lead to a move from a substitutional construal of quantified statements ('Every dog barks' means 'x barks' is true for any dog instance) to an objectual construal that views quantification as describing relations that hold between types (or sets) of entities. ('Every dog barks' means that doghood is a subattribute of 'being a barking producing entity'.)[23]

So, the question arises—is there an objectual construal of "the set of all possible answers" that would resolve the cognitive quandary a substitutional construal of it poses? In the current work, I will not argue the point

---

[23] See Quine 1974 for extensive discussion of this problem.

beyond providing a plausibility sketch that if an objectual construal of this set exists, then what it amounts to is an object that is parametric in all but name.

Assume as given a wh-question $q(x)$ that has some role r interrogated. We are supposed to provide a "schematic" construal of the Hamblin-set $H(q)$ of this question, one that does not make reference to particular instantiations of $q(x)$. Presumably, this will consist in filling the role r with some prototypical filler, or equivalently, viewing r as filled by an unspecified type of some kind. But, whatever the precise details, this representation does not have as constituents any actual singular propositions, instantiations. Rather, it is utilizes a parametric content.

Thus, plausibly, even if some use could be found for a Hamblin-like denotation for wh-questions, cognitive constraints force one to construe it as a parametric object in all but name.

7 Embedded Questions and the Content of Questions

Consider the sentence

(26) Jill knows who came yesterday.

A reasonable intuition about (26) (following Karttunen 1977) is that it makes essentially the following claim (∗) 'Jill has represented in her mental knowledge box *all true* instantiations of the open sentence 'x came home yesterday''.

If the rule for interpreting a VP consisting of a V and an embedded question were:

(∗∗) $[\![VP]\!] = [\![V]\!]([\![Q]\!])$

then we would well on our way to discovering the denotation of a wh-sentence such as 'Who came yesterday.' By a simple application of compositionality to (26), it turns out that the denotation of 'Who came yesterday' is none other than "all true instantiations of the open sentence 'x came home yesterday'."[24]

The basic claim made here concerning embedded questions is that the rule (∗∗) above is false. The basic semantic argument for this is the following: it will be shown that different verbs embed questions in systematically (as contrasted with verb-specific) different ways. This is somewhat analogous to the existence of indicative and subjunctive sentential complements. The wh-question is clearly a semantic constituent common to all embedded question constructions. Thus, if it ends up contributing a different object for different classes of verbs, there must exist some mediating "filters" or "operators" that given a question as input, yield one of these different objects as output that can then serve as the argument of the embedding verb. I propose that the correct rule for embedded-question VP's is schematically

---

[24] Or perhaps some more complex intensional object.

$(**')$ $\llbracket \text{VP} \rrbracket = \llbracket \text{V} \rrbracket \text{OP}_i(\llbracket \text{Q} \rrbracket)$

In other words, the embedded question is a mediated argument of the relation denoted by the verb, mediated by an operator OP_V. The nature of this operator depends on the nature of the embedding verb, so that if the verb embeds propositions (e.g., 'know'), then OP_V constructs a propositional object out of Q which denotes, roughly speaking, an answer to Q. While if V is actually a verb whose argument is question-like (e.g., 'ask'), then OP_V is essentially "quotative." In other words it performs much of the same duties assigned to 'that' in embedded proposition contexts, which is to signal that the content following it is a description of a mental state or paraphrase of illocutionary act. The question embedding operator has the added task of binding (or more precisely limiting the scope of) uninstantiated parameters, if the embedded question is a wh-question.

If $(**')$ is indeed the correct rule for embedded question VP's, then the motivation for a Hamblinian content for wh-sentences is lost: one can no longer directly "solve" for the denotation of Q, as assumed by, e.g., Karttunen 1977 and Groenendijk and Stokhof 1984. Rather, the contribution to content of the operator must also be taken into account. A content resembling to some degree a Hamblinian content will be the content of *a certain type* of question that has undergone embedding, namely those embedded by proposition embedding verbs. But it is *not* the content of the question. The proper analogy to bear in mind is with embedded y/n questions: one cannot deduce the content of 'John came' by "solving" for its denotation in the content 'Bill knows whether John came', while ignoring the contribution of 'whether' to the embedded question.

In this section, I will limit myself to providing arguments for the rule $(**')$.[25]

I will point to distinctions between *two* types of embedding. I propose that verbs such as 'know', 'remember', 'find out' and 'tell', embed questions differently from verbs such as 'ask', 'ponder' and 'investigate'.

Object of attitude. The most basic difference is this: the verbs of the 'know' class all denote relations whose semantic argument is a proposition (or more precisely whose content is propositional). Whatever a question is, it cannot be known, found out, told or remembered. This is reflected in the following:

(27) Jill knew/told/found out/remembered the question.

---

[25] But see Ginzburg 1991b for a semantics for embedded questions. It is shown that dividing up embedded questions in this way, an idea clearly anticipated by Vendler's (1972) perceptive discussion of embedded questions, allows for various simplifications in the syntax and semantics of embedded questions, in particular in eliminating completely the need for semantic selection for embedded questions. Other recent treatments that advocate postulating different types of embedded question include Munsat 1986 and Berman 1990, though neither take it as grounds for abandoning a Hamblinian semantics for wh-questions.

These sentences can only be interpreted as "concealed questions," wherein 'John knew the question' means "John know what the question was.," which does not express the fact that part of John's mental knowledge state had a question represented in it, but rather that it had represented in it the correct identity of a certain question.

In contrast, the relations denoted by verbs of the 'ask' type class all concern themselves with attitudes or action whose content *is* a question: asking, pondering, investigating, puzzling-over all involve objects whose content is question-like. Thus, the following can be interpreted as assertions that the relation of asking/pondering/puzzling over/investigating held between John and a certain question:

(28)   Jill asked/pondered/puzzled over/investigated the question.

Paraphrase. With verbs of the 'know' class, 'J V'ed who came' means roughly "J V'ed that p," where p is a proposition that provides a resolution of the issue raised by the question 'who came'.

In contrast, with the verbs of the 'ask' class, 'J V'ed who came' means roughly "J is in the relation V to a certain question: who came." Notice that the paraphrase provided for 'know'-type verbs is impossible here because 'ask' class verbs do not embed propositions, a fact that is surely of more than syntactic origin. This does have syntactic reflexes though. One example: Plann 1982 shows that in Spanish only embeddings of this latter type can co-occur with the complementizer "que."[26]

(29)   a. Ya supieron /entendieron/ recordaron (*que) por que lo habias hecho.
        b. They already found out/understood/remembered why you had done it.

(30)   a. El psiquiatra nos pregunta/ se pregunta que por que lo habriamos hecho.
        b. The psychiatrist asked us/ wondered why we could have done it.

There is also motivation for the distinction in paraphrase, provided by differing inference patterns exhibited by these verbs. For the 'know' class, there is a clear connection between the embedded question use and embedded (instantiated) sentence use: if someone came and J V'ed who came, it is entailed that J V'ed that x came, for some specific *instantiation* of the open sentence 'x came'. Thus, if someone came, to the party and Jill knows who came to the party, then there is someone such that Jill knows that he/she came to the party.

However, for the 'ask' class, there is no clear connection between the embedded wh-question use and any instantiation, embedded sentence (which these verbs do not embed after all), or even an embedded y/n question. Thus, an inference of the following type is simply not valid: if someone

---

[26]I am indebted to the anonymous reviewer who pointed out this reference to me.

came, and J V'ed who came, then J V'ed whether x came, for some specific instantiation of the open sentence 'x came'. Thus, if Jill wondered who she would meet at the party, and it turns out that she would meet some people there, it need not be the case that there be someone that she wondered whether she would meet him/her.[27]

Exhaustiveness. Berman 1990 has pointed out a distinction between 'know' class verbs and 'ask' class verbs with respect to modification by adverbs of quantification, which he calls the "Quantificational Variability Effect" (QVE). The former, but not the latter, can display differing forces of exhaustiveness, induced by the adverb:

(31) a. Sue mostly remembers what gifts she got for her birthday last year. (The wh-phrase can be understood as having the quantificational force of the adverb. Thus, it can be understood as asserting that she remembers most instantiations of the open sentence 'x is a gift Sue got for her birthday last year.)
  b. Sue mostly wonders what gifts she got for her birthday last year. (The wh-phrase cannot be understood as having the quantificational force of the adverb. The adverb must be interpreted as quantifying over the different cases of wonderment of Sue, asserting that most of them concern the nature of her gifts.)

NPI felicity. Munsat 1986 has pointed out that 'ask' class verbs, but not 'know' class verbs, can license NPI's questions. Assuming, after Ladusaw 1979, that NPI's operator with a characteristic semantic property, this is quite suggestive of the existence of different embedding operators (operations), given that the same question is input to both types of embedding verb:

(32) a. I wonder how he ever did it.
  b. #I know how he ever did it.

(33) a. I wonder why anyone bothers to listen to him.
  b. #I know why anyone bothers to listen to him.

Summing up, we have seen that there are good grounds to assume that (at least) two wh-question embedding processes exist: the argument of 'know' class verbs seems to be an instantiated object, most plausibly a proposition given the fact that all such verbs embed propositions, which

---

[27]It is true that this inference can be blocked by assuming, following Groenendijk and Stokhof 1984, that these verbs utilize the intension of the question, while the verbs of the 'know' class utilize the extension of the question. Such an analysis, however, suffers from a number of problems. By assuming that all differences among question embedding verbs arise via meaning postulates, it can account for differing inference patterns, but not for differences in felicity of wh-complement (see NPI facts below), differences in modification by adverbs (see exhaustiveness facts below), nor for differences in the ontological status of the embedded object, which is reflected in the lack of declarative sentence embedding in 'ask' type verbs. Groenendijk and Stokhof's 1989 version of this account is more immune to some of these problems, see Ginzburg 1991b for discussion.

is an answer to the question. The argument of 'ask' class verbs seems to be an object very similar, perhaps even identical in content, to the content of direct wh-questions. If this is in fact the case, it can be accommodated quite easily by our account: for the first type of embedded content, one utilizes simply the content of the question. For the second case, where answers are embedded, the content of the question is a constituent of the description for the answer providing proposition.

On the other hand, a demonstration of the Hamblinian nature of the content of wh-sentences on the basis of their apparent Hamblinian contribution to meaning in embedded questions is flawed, since there exists a class of embedded questions where a different, apparently more basic, meaning is contributed.

8 On the Quantificational Status of Wh-Phrases

It is commonly assumed that wh-phrases are "quantificational." That is, their contribution to content consists inter alia in a binding operator that fixes the scope of the wh-phrase along with some type of quantificational force. The binding and quantification are essential components in the construction of a non-parametric semantic object that is to serve as the content of a wh-sentence.[28]

Given that the current proposal argues for a parametric interpretation for wh-sentences, the binding of and quantification over the "variable" introduced by a wh-phrase are explicitly abolished. A precondition for this is that phenomena previously accounted for in terms of variable scoping and binding can find alternative explanations.

In this section, I discuss briefly a number of phenomena previously explained using the assumption that wh-phrases are quantificational. In the next section, I will discuss quite extensively the phenomena of pair-list readings of questions, a phenomenon that appears at first sight to cause serious problems for a parametric account of wh-questions.

8.1 Inter-Scope-Island Anaphora

It has been widely believed that inter-scope-island anaphora is impossible with wh-phrases. If this were indeed the case, it would find a ready explanation in the following syllogism: wh-phrases are quantifiers, quan-

---

[28]However, one can maintain that wh-phrases are variable-like, and yet construct a Hamblin-like denotation by postulating the existence of a binding operator that binds the variable. Proposals along this line have been suggested recently by a number of researchers including Comorowski 1989, Berman 1990 and Nishigauchi 1990. In many respects, positing the existence of such a binding operator is only syntactically different from a quantificational approach, that is, the same semantic object ultimately gets constructed, though from different syntactic constituents: it permits many of the same explanations to go through, e.g., narrow scoping of wh-phrases, with respect to quantified NP's can be accounted for by saying that "Q," rather than a wh-quantifier gets scoped inside the quantifier.

tifiers cannot license (so called "bound variable," or Q-type) anaphora across scope islands,[29] hence wh-phrases cannot license anaphora across scope islands. Empirically, however, it appears that wh-phrases *can* license anaphora across scope islands:

(34) a. *Which Stanford student* was late? Was *she* also rude?
      b. Tell me *which book* was written by *which author* and whether *he* sent *it* in with the required changes?
      c. *Who* killed the Red Queen? Was *he* a dark and swashbuckling Englishman?
      d. *When* is the next neurolinguistics professor going to be appointed? I sure hope *it* will be before the turn of the century.
      e. Where were you born? Does your family still live *there*?

One might invoke some form of pragmatic accommodation to account for these facts: so that the anaphora feeds on the existential conversational implicature associated with an INSA use of a wh-phrase. However, cancellation of the implicature, explicitly or in a fashion reminiscent of Partee's 'bathroom in a funny place' sentence, does not prevent the possibility of anaphora:[30]

(35) a. *Which Stanford student, if any* was late?? Was *she* also rude?
      b. *Who, if anyone* killed the Red Queen?? Was *he* a dark and swashbuckling Englishman?
      c. *Which journalist* insulted Mrs. Simpson? Or was *he* only trying to be funny?
      d. *Which car* can get 60 mpg on Kuwaiti crude? Or did the advertising people fake *its* performance statistics?

8.2   Baker Multiple-Wh-Questions

The putative quantificational status of wh-phrases has been invoked to explain the ambiguity of sentences first pointed out by Baker in his 1970 dissertation. In this section I show how the current approach can offer an account that has something of the flavor of the original proposal. In Section 7 above I sketched the approach offered here to embedded questions. The basic idea is this: there are two semantic types of VP's of the form 'V Q'. Verbs that embed propositions, such as 'know', 'remember' and 'tell' utilize a "coercion operator" that converts the embedded question into a proposition that is an answer to the question: 'John knows Q' means roughly 'John knows a proposition that is a true answer to Q.' This coercion operator can bind parameters that are in its scope, in fact

---

[29] Of course, arguably, certain quantifiers do license anaphora across scope-islands, as in dynamic or E-type accounts.

[30] It must be emphasized that I have not demonstrated that a different anaphoric process might not be at work here, such as E-type anaphora. I leave this issue open for the present.

it must bind at least one, otherwise vacuous binding occurs, which results in semantic malformedness. This means that in principle three contents are predicted to be possible for 'Who remembers where John bought which book. Schematically:

(36)　a. $\langle\!\langle\text{Remembers}, x, \text{COERCE-OP}_l \langle\!\langle \text{Bought}, j, z_{book}, \text{at location } l \rangle\!\rangle^{31}$
　　　b. $\langle\!\langle\text{Remembers}, x, \text{COERCE-OP}_{z,l} \langle\!\langle \text{Bought}, j, z_{book}, \text{at location } l \rangle\!\rangle$
　　　c. $\langle\!\langle\text{Remembers}, x, \text{COERCE-OP}_z \langle\!\langle \text{Bought}, j, z_{book}, \text{at location } l \rangle\!\rangle$

(36a) corresponds to a question that elicits a list response ('Bill remembers where John bought the Physics book, Mike remembers where John bought the yoga book, ...'), (36b) corresponds to a question eliciting a response of the type ('Bill knows where John bought which book'), while (36c) corresponds to a question eliciting the response (Bill remembers which book John bought in London, Mike remembers which book John bought in Milan, ...') As is well known, the latter type of response is uneducible in English, but does exist in wh *in situ* languages such as Turkish and Japanese. Hence, it can be attributed to be a syntactic correlate of wh-movement, captured, e.g., by stipulating that "Wh phrases in COMP must be absorbed by COERCE-OP."

Thus, for "answer-embedding" predicates (essentially all question embedders that also embed declaratives) we have a straightforward semantic account for the Baker effect. What of "question embedding" predicates such as 'ask', 'wonder' and 'investigate'? Here the claim of the current approach is that the nature of the embedding is similar to embedding of declarative sentences, in other words it is "quasi-quotative." 'John asked Q' means essentially 'John asked a question whose content is Q'. Thus, in the formation of the meaning of the VP, an operator exists that can restrict the scope of the parameters to be embedded-question internal. Thus, essentially the same considerations as above obtain, and we can account yet again for Baker effects. Interestingly, Ross 1972 has claimed that predicates of this latter type do not manifest the Baker effect, rather the embedded wh-phrases cannot "take matrix scope." Comorowski 1988 appears to endorse this judgment. The judgments are very subtle and seem to involve quite strong dialectal variation. If this contrast does exist, the current account offers an avenue for explanation of this effect, based on different binding properties of the respective operators.

8.3　Weak Crossover Phenomena

Wh-phrases appear to exhibit weak crossover effects. The traditional account for this is based on the assumption that such phrases are quantificational. Quantifiers are supposed to exhibit weak crossover because in such a configuration some violation of a condition on operator/variable pairs ensues.

---

[31] COERCE-OP$_i$ indicates that the parameter i has been bound by the coercion operator.

(37) a.* *Who* does *his* mother like?
      b.* *Every man, his* mother likes.
      c.* *Some man, his* mother likes.
      d. *John, his* mother likes.

Heim 1982 points out in a different context (she is trying to defend the claim that indefinites are not quantifiers) that the weak crossover facts can be accounted for as adequately by assuming that the relevant parameter is *lack-of-definiteness*, rather than quantifierhood. Within the analysis proposed here, it seems plausible to view interrogatives as lacking definiteness, and thus have Heim's proposal apply to them as well.[32]

9   Narrowly Scoping Interrogatives: Functional and Pair-List Understandings

The existence of question/answer pairs such as (38) is traditionally taken to show that quantifiers can take scope over interrogatives:

(38) a. Who does every English person admire most?
      b. Arthur admires Paul Gascoigne, Betty admires Barbara Bush, Charlie admires Mr. Thatcher, ...

Question/answer pairs such as (39), although assumed to have a different source from (38) also clearly involve a different reading for the question than the standard "individual use" which the semantics in Section 4 provides for directly:

(39) a. Who does *every English person* admire most?
      b. *Her* mother.

(38) and (39) cannot be accommodated by the semantics for wh-phrases provided in Section 3: in that semantics wh-phrases are unbound parameters, and hence always take widest scope. This means that, e.g., in (38) the admiree role does not vary with different admirers. Hence, a response such as (38b) cannot be accommodated. Similarly for (39), where the response is supposed to be construed as a function, mapping each English person to her mother.

In this section, I show how to extend the semantics for wh-phrases in a way that uniformly accommodates both types of responses. The basic ingredient in interrogative semantics, namely *parametricity*, remains as in Section 4, but some extra refinements will be needed. The essential idea will be that this reading utilizes a mechanism similar and at the same time converse to that proposed by Gawron and Peters 1990a for the "capture" of definites by quantifiers.[33] In advocating a unified account, I will be defending a conflation that has been explicitly argued against in the recent literature. My claim, contra Groenendijk and Stokhof 1984 and Engdahl

---

[32] I am indebted to Mark Gawron for pointing out this possibility to me.
[33] This parallel was already pointed out in Engdahl 1988.

1988,[34] is that "relational" readings and "pair-list" readings correspond to different ways of responding to one and the same question. Which form the response takes in a given context depends on a number of pragmatic factors. In order to avoid any confusion, I will call this use of an interrogative a "dependent" use, to emphasize the cause of this reading-dependence of the interrogative on another argument. No new semantic rules are invoked, in contrast to frameworks where wh-phrases are quantificational (or bound by Q) in which rules allowing quantifying into questions need to be invoked. A more detailed comparison with other proposals in this area will be found in Ginzburg 1991a.

9.1 Recognizing the Dependent Use

My approach to dependent uses will build on the notion of "dependence," a generalization of the notion of anaphora.[35] Anaphora can be viewed as the imposition of a dependency, in fact an identity dependency, between two argument roles. The dependent argument is the anaphor and the depended upon argument is the antecedent. Identity, nonetheless, is not the only condition of dependence that can be placed, others include "possession," inequality (both in switch-reference constructions, and utilizing the element 'other') and various relations denoted by relational nouns such as 'teacher' and 'mayor'. Although definites entail/conventionally implicate uniqueness, if the definite is dependent on another argument, it can lose the uniqueness:

(40) a. Every father thinks his kid is a star.
      b. (In the winter, all the girls broke their left leg.) Then, two months later, Sasskija and Melissa broke their other leg.
      c. Every town hates the mayor, unless he gives them a tax-break.

Gawron and Peters 1990a, 1990b account for such cases by invoking a basic principle of a Situation Theory that has restricted parameters—the Absorption Principle.[36] This states that whenever a parameter x is absorbed, all parameters that are dependent on x must also be absorbed (i.e., must undergo existential closure). The content for the VP in (40a) when 'Every father' and 'his' are anaphorically construed will consequently be:

(41) $[x \mid \exists y \langle\!\langle \text{THINK}, x, \langle\!\langle \text{STAR}, y_{\langle\!\langle \text{POSS}, x, y \rangle\!\rangle \wedge \langle\!\langle \text{KID}, y \rangle\!\rangle} \rangle\!\rangle \rangle\!\rangle]$

---

[34] Groenendijk and Stokhof 1984 and Engdahl 1988 were both arguing against reducing the "relational" reading to the "pair-list" reading. If anything, my reduction proceeds in the opposite direction, from "pair-list" to "relational." This does not face the same objections.

[35] See also Keenan and Clark 1986 for discussion of an apparently similar notion of "dependence."

[36] This was first proposed by them in their 1990a. They provide extensive linguistic and situation theoretic motivation for the principle (pp. 90–113), and in the appendix (pp. 176–8).

The parameter y, corresponding to the definite 'his kid', gets existentially quantified away because of its dependence on a parameter that gets absorbed, the x parameter. Because y has gotten existentially quantified away, the uniqueness of the definite is lost, it becomes scoped within the subject argument, and hence dependent on it.

Something very similar, I claim, takes place in cases like (38). If the interrogative parameter p is dependent on another parameter that gets absorbed, then p gets existentially quantified away. The question is—how is it that a wh-phrase become existentially quantified away and yet the wh-question does not lose its interrogative, i.e., parametric character? The simplest explanation would be to assume that a dependency of a wh-phrase on another role must itself be *parametric*. What characterizes the dependent reading is, then, that once an interrogative parameter gets existentially quantified away the dependency remains as the sole parameter of the question.[37] One way of viewing the "individual" use is as having a unary dependency of the interrogative parameter, one that depends on no other NP, and thus does not cause absorption of the interrogative parameter.

How does this idea work informally? Consider a question like

(42)   *Who*$_{dependent}$ does [Each *man*]$_{depended\text{-}upon}$ like?

where 'who' is being used dependently on 'each man'. A schematic content for this will look as follows:

(43) $\langle\!\langle \text{LIKES}, \text{liker}{:}Each\ Man\ x, \text{likee}{:}f(x) \rangle\!\rangle$

or somewhat more fleshed out:

(44) $\langle\!\langle \text{EACH}, [x \mid \langle\!\langle \text{MAN}, x \rangle\!\rangle], [x \mid \exists y \langle\!\langle \text{LIKES}, x, y_{\langle\!\langle y=f(x) \rangle\!\rangle} \rangle\!\rangle] \rangle\!\rangle$

Notice that the parameter corresponding to the likee role, y, is not a parameter of the sentential content, neither of course is the parameter corresponding to the liker role, which gets universally quantified. This content contains solely one uninstantiated parameter, none other than f, the parameter for the dependency between liker and likee.

We can repeat the question asked before when we provided contents for individual uses of wh-phrases: what explanatory use can be made of a content such as (44)? The first thing we note is that the explanation for the unassertability of a wh-question is retained: The content in (44) is parametric and hence unassertable. What kind of effect will an interrogative use of (44) have on the context ? With individual uses, an INSA made a role, the parametrized role, and a type of objects, the queried type, salient. Analogously, an INSA using (44) makes a *dependency between roles*, in this case between liker and likee, and a type of functions, salient. The queried type is

---

[37]The debt this perspective owes to Engdahl 1986's approach should be clear. The dependencies in her case are viewed as quantificational, rather than parametric, and so have to be assured widest scope, when they are quantified away.

(45) $[f \mid \langle\!\langle \text{EACH}, [x \mid \langle\!\langle \text{MAN}, x\rangle\!\rangle], [x \mid \exists y \langle\!\langle \text{LIKES}, x, y_{\langle\!\langle y=f(x)\rangle\!\rangle}\rangle\!\rangle]\rangle\!\rangle]$

That is, the type of relations that relate a man to a human he likes. Thus, a response to a INSA using this content should provide a specification of such a function. How are functions specified? One way is by provision of a schematic rule. Thus, for instance

(46)   His best friend.

We can view, informally for the moment, this NP in this context as providing a rule that maps each man to his best friend. We shall soon see how this actually ties in with a proposal for conceiving (a certain use of) NP's as functional. This response then ostends to the proposition

(47)   His best friend is (the person) who each man likes.

Another possibility for specifying a relation is by provision of its extension:

(48)   man$_1$ likes person A, man$_2$ likes person B, ...

In this case, the response ostends to the proposition

(49)   (man$_1$ likes person A, man$_2$ likes person B, ...) is who each person likes.

Summing up for the moment: we have extended the semantics for wh-phrases as follows: there are two ways to use wh-phrases. One way, the individual use, causes a role to remain uninstantiated and be (potentially) focusable by a INSA. The other use, a dependent use, subordinates a role to be dependent on some other role and causes this dependency to be (potentially) focusable by a INSA. One interesting consequence of this proposal is that, just like with bound variable anaphora, since the dependency is on roles, rather than on specific entities (as is the case with deictic anaphora), it is expected that such readings should arise with any type of antecedent (viz. depended upon) NP, referential or quantificational. This, as we shall see, is indeed the case.

9.2   A More Detailed Look at the Dependent Use

Our analysis of examples like (38) and (39) has two components: (a) the role filled by a wh-phrase is subordinated to another role. As a result, when the latter role is absorbed, (b) the role filled by the wh-phrase *must* be existentially quantified away. Thus, in order to obtain this type of reading, the depended-upon role must get absorbed at some point. Absorption in the Gawron and Peters framework can occur at essentially two junctures: first, during role-linking, when a subcategorized role is passed up from one level of phrase structure to another, without being filled at the lower level, e.g., when the "subject" role is transmitted from the V level to the VP. Second, when the scope of a role is fixed, e.g., during the formation of the nuclear scope of a quantified proposition. (examples)

To make this more concrete, let us consider examples involving each of these types of absorption. First, one involving absorption of the subject

argument during VP formation. Since in this example the semantic identity
of the subject makes no difference to the existence of the reading we're
interested in, I will parametrize it for the time being:

(50) a. Who does $\langle Subject \rangle$ admire most?

    b. $\langle\!\langle [x \mid \exists y \langle\!\langle \text{ADMIRE-MOST}, \text{admirer:}x, \text{admiree:}y_{\langle\!\langle y=f(x)\rangle\!\rangle} \rangle\!\rangle],$
         $subject \rangle\!\rangle$

What has happened in this example, is that when the VP content is formed
by absorbing over the admirer role, the admiree role must be existentially
quantified away, because it depends on the admirer role. The VP property
$[x \mid \exists y \langle\!\langle \text{ADMIRE-MOST}, \text{admirer:}x, \text{admiree:}y_{\langle\!\langle y=f(x)\rangle\!\rangle} \rangle\!\rangle]$ is then parametric
in the dependency f, but not in the parameter filling the admiree role.
Since the semantic identity of the subject has not figured at all in this, the
prediction is that whatever NP fills the subject role, essentially the same
type of response should be elicited, namely responses that specify relations
belonging to the queried type

(51) $[f \mid \langle\!\langle [x \mid \exists y \langle\!\langle \text{ADMIRE-MOST}, \text{admirer:}x, \text{admiree:}y_{\langle\!\langle y=f(x)\rangle\!\rangle} \rangle\!\rangle],$
       $subject \rangle\!\rangle]$

Let us consider some concrete examples by instantiating the subject argument:

(52) a. Who does each boy admire most?

    b. Content: $\langle\!\langle \text{EACH}, [x \mid \langle\!\langle \text{BOY}, x \rangle\!\rangle],$
                $[v \mid \langle\!\langle [x \mid \exists y \langle\!\langle \text{ADMIRE-MOST},$
                       $\text{admirer:}x, \text{admiree:}y_{\langle\!\langle y=f(x)\rangle\!\rangle} \rangle\!\rangle], v \rangle\!\rangle] \rangle\!\rangle$

    c. Queried-Type: $[f \mid \langle\!\langle \text{EACH}, [x \mid \langle\!\langle \text{BOY}, x \rangle\!\rangle],$
                      $[v \mid \langle\!\langle [x \mid \exists y \langle\!\langle \text{ADMIRE-MOST},$
                           $\text{admirer:}x, \text{admiree:}y_{\langle\!\langle y=f(x)\rangle\!\rangle} \rangle\!\rangle], v \rangle\!\rangle] \rangle\!\rangle]$

Hence, felicitous subsequent containing responses will provide specifications
of relations that are of the queried-type. Namely, functions that (inter alia)
map boys to their most-admired (humans). Thus, either of the following
should do:

(53) a. His cousin.

    b. John admires Billy most, Mike admires Saddam most, . . .

This ties in with a proposal made in Gawron and Peters 1990b regarding
such sentences as 'Its title is the best thing about every Oscar Wilde play.'
A number of reasons lead Gawron and Peters to propose that NP's such as
'its title', as it occurs in this sentence be analyzed as NP's that denote functions, rather than bound variable anaphora. This fits in with the proposal
made here, since 'its title' used as a function could then be a subsequent
for a dependency in a dependent use of 'what' in 'What is the best thing
about every Oscar Wilde play?'.

    If instead of a quantificational term, we plug a group-denoting term, an
almost identical content is obtained:

(54) a. Who do Jill, Melissa and Harriet admire most?

b. Content: $\langle\!\langle [v \mid \langle\!\langle [x \mid \exists y \langle\!\langle$ ADMIRE-MOST,

$\qquad$ admirer:x, admiree:$y_{\langle\!\langle y = f(x)\rangle\!\rangle}$ $\rangle\!\rangle], v\rangle\!\rangle],$

$\qquad$ $gr(Jill,Melissa,Harriet)\rangle\!\rangle$

c. Queried-Type: $[f \mid \langle\!\langle [v \mid \langle\!\langle [x \mid \exists y \langle\!\langle$ ADMIRE-MOST,

$\qquad$ admirer:x, admiree:$y_{\langle\!\langle y = f(x)\rangle\!\rangle}$ $\rangle\!\rangle], v\rangle\!\rangle],$

$\qquad$ $gr(Jill,Melissa,Harriet)\rangle\!\rangle]$

The sole difference between this latter type and (52c) is the domain over which the relation is constrained to be defined over.

A third possibility for a filler of the subject role is, none other than an interrogative. In English this causes a syntactic change as well, though one that, due to our *in situ* commitment, does not reflect on the content:

(55) a. Who admires whom most?

b. Content: $\langle\!\langle [v \mid \langle\!\langle [x \mid \exists y \langle\!\langle$ ADMIRE-MOST,

$\qquad$ admirer:x, admiree:$y_{\langle\!\langle y = f(x)\rangle\!\rangle}$ $\rangle\!\rangle], v\rangle\!\rangle],$

$\qquad$ $v_{\langle\!\langle \text{HUMAN},x\rangle\!\rangle}\rangle\!\rangle$

This question is parametric in x and f, and the queried type is, hence a relation:

c. $[v, f \mid \langle\!\langle [x \mid \exists y \langle\!\langle$ ADMIRE-MOST, admirer:x, admiree:$y_{\langle\!\langle y = f(x)\rangle\!\rangle}$ $\rangle\!\rangle],$

$\qquad$ $v_{\langle\!\langle \text{HUMAN},x\rangle\!\rangle}\rangle\!\rangle]$

Since subsequent-containing responses provide both a relation and a domain for this relation, seeming responses to such a question are not much different from those elicited by run of the mill contents for multiple-wh-sentences. However, below I will show that contents such as (55) allow us to solve a puzzle concerning the loss of uniqueness-implicature associated with "which-phrases" that occurs in multiple-which-sentences.

The second trigger for absorption is the creation of a type that is the nuclear scope of a quantified infon. Consider a question such as (56) on a dependent use of 'who':

(56) a. Who proved each lemma?

In (56b), the nuclear scope for (56) is supplied. Here the trigger for existentially quantifying away the subject parameter is the absorption of the object role to create the nuclear scope:

b. $[y \mid \exists v \langle\!\langle [x \mid \langle\!\langle$ PROVE, prover:x, provee:$y\rangle\!\rangle], v_{\langle\!\langle \text{HUMAN},v\rangle\!\rangle \wedge \langle\!\langle v = f(y)\rangle\!\rangle}$ $\rangle\!\rangle]$

The content of the whole question is

c. $\langle\!\langle$ EACH, $[x \mid \langle\!\langle$ LEMMA, $x\rangle\!\rangle],$

$\qquad$ $[y \mid \exists v \langle\!\langle [x \mid \langle\!\langle$ PROVE, prover:x, provee:$y\rangle\!\rangle],$

$\qquad\qquad$ $v_{\langle\!\langle \text{HUMAN},v\rangle\!\rangle \wedge \langle\!\langle v = f(y)\rangle\!\rangle}$ $\rangle\!\rangle]\rangle\!\rangle$

d. Queried-Type:

$[f \mid \langle\!\langle$ EACH, $[x \mid \langle\!\langle$ LEMMA, $x\rangle\!\rangle],$

$\qquad$ $[y \mid \exists v \langle\!\langle [x \mid \langle\!\langle$ PROVE, prover:x, provee:$y\rangle\!\rangle],$

$\qquad\qquad$ $v_{\langle\!\langle \text{HUMAN},v\rangle\!\rangle \wedge \langle\!\langle v = f(y)\rangle\!\rangle}$ $\rangle\!\rangle]\rangle\!\rangle]$

Hence, subsequent-containing responses will specify a relation constrained to hold between lemmas and their provers. For instance,

(57) a. The person who conjectured it.
      b. Bill proved the snake lemma, Jill proved the pumping lemma, . . .

9.3 Asymmetries

The discussion above shows that an asymmetry in the availability of dependent readings is to be expected. Wh-phrases can be made dependent on roles that inherently trigger absorptions, such as subjects, quite independently of the scopal properties of the filler of this latter, depended-upon role. In contrast, wh-phrases can only be used dependently on a "dominated" role, typically an object, if the filler of that role can take scope over the role filled by the wh-phrase. Notice that, although one can construe this statement purely configurationally, one can also construe the statement more generally, e.g., to account for different scoping properties of object roles of psychological verbs. This caveat should be presupposed when reading the following summary of asymmetries predicted:

- wh-phrases filling an object role can be used dependently on any subject filler, quantificational, group-denoting, interrogative.
- wh-phrases filling a subject role can be used dependently only on object fillers that can scope over the subject.

Support for these contrasts is found in familiar minimal pairs such as the following, where the (a) examples lack, but the (b) examples possess a dependent reading:

(58) a. Which person likes every man?
      b. Which person does every man like?

(59) a. Which person likes them?
      b. Which person do they (each) like?

The subject/object asymmetry predicted here is reminiscent of a prediction made on the basis of the Empty Category Principle of GB (May 1985). The ECP prediction is tantamount to saying that *no* dependent readings whatsoever are permitted with subject interrogatives, regardless of the scopal abilities of the quantifier. Examples such as (56) above, repeated here as are an (acknowledged) problem for that account since it clearly does have a dependent reading.[38]

A more detailed examination of this type of data can be found in Engdahl 1988.

---

[38] May states in May 1988 that 'each' has a special "focusing" property that independently allows in the desired for configuration despite violating the ECP.

9.4 Uniqueness-Filtration in 'Which' Questions

A direct consequence of the existence of the dependent use is an account for the "uniqueness-filtration" effect noted in Higginbotham and May 1981. The effect they describe concerns questions featuring the interrogative determiner 'which'. It has been noticed that in unary wh-questions featuring 'which', a uniqueness of the subsequent is conventionally implicated:

(60) a. Which Canadian athlete was suspended in 1988?
      b. # Ben Johnson, Debbie Brill, ...

However, in multiple "which-questions," as noted by Higginbotham and May, the uniqueness effect disappears, as long as the specification providing the answer is 1–1: thus (61b) is a possible response to (61a).

(61) a. Which Canadian athlete won which competition in 1988?
      b. Ben Johnson won the 100 meters, Debbie Brill won the high jump,
          ...

This is something of a mystery for a univocal non-parametric theory of interrogatives, which should provide the multiple-which-sentence with a content like $\{p \mid \exists!x\exists!y(p = R(x,y))\}$.

The typical way this problem is eliminated is by assuming that in these contexts the wider scoping 'which' somehow gets universal quantificational force.[39] This is countenanced by such frameworks formulation of their quantification-into-wh rule. There is something somewhat unsavoury about this, though if multiple-wh-sentences only had this type of reading, this would be mitigated. In Ginzburg 1991a, however, I discuss cases which show that unique readings are available for multiple-wh-sentences.

Here I will show how to obtain a non-unique reading, without resorting to any special rule or device, solely as a consequence of a dependent use of the object interrogative.

Higginbotham and May, who acknowledge the existence of an ambiguity,[40] propose to account for the existence of this reading through polyadic quantification, utilizing a technique they call "absorption" (only coincidentally related to Situation Theoretic absorption), which creates polyadic quantifiers out of unary ones. Nonetheless, Engdahl 1986 points out a problem for their account: since absorption cannot apply when one wh-quantifier contains a variable bound by the other, the following is predicted to lack a non-unique reading:

(62) Which boy likes which one of his sisters?

However, this seems to be a false prediction, as indicated in (50a), and especially in (50b).

---

[39] See, e.g., Karttunen and Peters 1980, Groenendijk and Stokhof 1984, Comorowski 1989.

[40] May 1989 contains discussion of cases where he claims only the unique reading is available.

(63) a. John admires (his sister) Mary, Mike admires (his sister) Beth, ...

b. Bill likes his elder sister, Mike likes his younger sister, ...

Utilizing a dependent use of the object interrogative, we can account for the uniqueness filtration, without running into the problem pointed out by Engdahl. In (64) the content for (62) is provided:

(64) $\langle\!\langle [x \mid \exists y \mid \langle\!\langle \text{ADMIRES}, x, y_{\langle\!\langle y=f(x) \rangle\!\rangle \wedge \langle\!\langle \text{UNIQUE}, y \rangle\!\rangle}\rangle\!\rangle$
$\wedge \langle\!\langle Sister, x, y\rangle\!\rangle \rangle\!\rangle], v_{\langle\!\langle Unique, v \rangle\!\rangle}\rangle\!\rangle$

Since the object interrogative has to be absorbed, the property any subsequent for the subject interrogative will have is to love a unique, rather than a fixed sister, who also stands in a relation f to him. Different f's will give different subsequents for the subject. What we do know is that for any f, there will be a unique admirer. Putting all this together, we predict that this question can have a "list" answer, but the list will be 1-1. This is exactly as desired.

9.5 Dependent Uses and Their Responses: Arguments for the Semantic Unity of "Pair-List" and "Relational" Understandings

We have seen how to generate readings for questions in which the of the filler of the interrogative argument role depends on some other role. The dependency, nonetheless, remains a parameter, whose content is to be fixed by subsequent discourse. There are, I claim, two basic ways of responding to this use of a question. The first is in the form of a list which specifies the pairs ⟨value-of-independent-argument, value-of-dependent-argument⟩, as in (38b). The other option is to specify a general description of this dependency, as in (39b). And, there is, in principle, nothing that prohibits a combination of these two options:

(65) Who does every graduate student admire most and who do John and Mary? The syntacticians admire their adviser, the semanticists admire Jespersen, John admires Billy Hatcher and Mary admires Di Feinstein.

In this section I defend the conflation proposed here between pair-list and functional understandings of a wh-sentence. No one, including the defenders of the semantic nature of the distinction, will deny that, at least in certain contexts, which of the two response patterns gets used does depend on essentially pragmatic features. The relational response is briefer, more succinct, and is better suited for generic and nomic statements. The pair-list response can be more (pragmatically) specific, and will tend to be used when the domain of the characterizing function is salient and small. So what appears to be a pair-list reading could, claim the ambiguity theorists, actually be a relational one, presented in pair-list fashion. This would be a way out of example (65).

The defenders of this distinction have been intent on showing that the "relational" use cannot be reduced to the "pair list" use, in which putatively some element has scope over the interrogative quantifier. Given the perspective advanced in this paper, the question which arises is this: are there any arguments that force one into the reverse position, namely that the "pair-list" use is not a special case of the "relational use"?

Let us consider the two main arguments for a semantic distinction. The first argument is a distributional one: it is claimed that there are questions which can be responded to relationally, but not in pair-list fashion, the classic case being

(66)   What does no man like?

In fact, the claim is that the universal quantifiers are the only quantifiers that permit a "pair-list" use. I believe this is a false generalization, based on what are, admittedly strong, *pragmatically conditioned* preferences. Detailed discussion of this point can be found in Ginzburg 1991a. For present purposes, it will suffice to discuss why (66) is thoroughly resistant to a pair-list response on a dependent reading.

The queried-type in this case is

(67) $[f \mid \langle\!\langle \text{NO}, [x \mid \langle\!\langle \text{MAN}, x \rangle\!\rangle], [x \mid \exists y \langle\!\langle \text{LIKES}, x, y_{\langle\!\langle y = f(x) \rangle\!\rangle} \rangle\!\rangle] \rangle\!\rangle]$

The function sought is one, call it f_0, constrained to make the type $[x \mid \langle\!\langle \text{MAN}, x \rangle\!\rangle]$ disjoint from $[x \mid \exists y \langle\!\langle \text{LIKES}, x, y_{\langle\!\langle y = f_0(x) \rangle\!\rangle} \rangle\!\rangle]$. A pair-list response in this case provides pairs of likers and likees, where the likers cannot be in the type $[x \mid \langle\!\langle \text{MAN}, x \rangle\!\rangle]$. In other words, it provides no direct information whatever about men and their liking tendencies. If, for instance, this question were asked by someone wishing to avoid giving the wrong present to a man, a pair-list response would not help in the least, since the fact that a non-man has a certain like is quite irrelevant.

A response that provides a canonical function can be, however, very informative in such cases: thus responding 'his teacher' in this case provides positive information concerning men and their likings, namely that teachers are universally not liked by men.

The second argument concerns cases such as

(68)   Which politician does Bill know every sane Canadian admires?

Unless the pair-list/relational distinction is available how is one to distinguish between a case where Bill is acquainted personally with each sane Canadian and his politics, and a case in which Bill is, say, a political scientist who has ideas about the average sane Canadian's political tendencies?

I will limit my response in this case to showing how in the framework proposed here we can generate readings that distinguish these cases:

Case 1: 'every sane Canadian' has embedded sentence scope, 'which politician' used dependent on the subject.

(69) Queried type:

$$[f \mid \langle\!\langle \text{KNOWS}, \textit{Bill}, \langle\!\langle \text{EVERY}, [x \mid \langle\!\langle \text{SANE-CANADIAN}, x \rangle\!\rangle],$$
$$[x \mid \exists y \langle\!\langle \text{ADMIRES}, x, y_{\langle\!\langle \text{POLITICIAN},y \rangle\!\rangle \wedge \langle\!\langle y=f(x) \rangle\!\rangle} \rangle\!\rangle]\rangle\!\rangle\rangle\!\rangle]$$

This corresponds to the 'Bill as political scientist' case.

Case 2: 'every sane Canadian' has matrix sentence scope, 'which politician' used dependent on the subject.

(70) Queried type:

$$[f \mid \langle\!\langle \text{EVERY}, [x \mid \langle\!\langle \text{SANE-CANADIAN}, x \rangle\!\rangle],$$
$$[x \mid \exists y \langle\!\langle \text{KNOWS}, \textit{Bill}, \langle\!\langle \text{ADMIRES}, x, y_{\langle\!\langle \text{POLITICIAN},y \rangle\!\rangle \wedge \langle\!\langle y=f(x) \rangle\!\rangle} \rangle\!\rangle]\rangle\!\rangle\rangle\!\rangle]$$

Here the required function will be one that makes the type

$$[x \mid \langle\!\langle \text{SANE-CANADIAN}, x \rangle\!\rangle]$$

a subtype of

$$[x \mid \exists y \langle\!\langle \text{KNOWS}, \textit{Bill}, \langle\!\langle \text{ADMIRES}, x, y_{\langle\!\langle \text{POLITICIAN},y \rangle\!\rangle \wedge \langle\!\langle y=f(x) \rangle\!\rangle} \rangle\!\rangle]\rangle\!\rangle]$$

which corresponds exactly to the "individual acquaintance" scenario.

References

Baker, C. L. 1970. *Indirect Questions in English.* PhD thesis, University of Illinois, Urbana-Champaigne.

Barwise, J., and J. Perry. 1983. *Situations and Attitudes.* Cambridge, MA: MIT Press.

Belnap, N. 1982. Questions and Answers in Montague Grammar. In *Processes, Beliefs and Questions,* ed. Peters and Saarinen. Dordrecht: Reidel.

Berman, S. 1990. Towards the Semantics of Open Sentences: Wh-phrases and Indefinites. To appear in Proceedings of 7th Amsterdam Colloquium.

Bolinger, D. 1978. On Asking More than One Thing at a Time. In *Questions,* ed. H. Hiz. Dordrecht: Reidel.

Comorowski, I. 1989. *Discourse and the Syntax of Multiple Constituent Questions.* PhD thesis, Cornell University, Ithaca.

Cooper, R., K. Mukai, and J. Perry (ed.). 1990. *Situation Theory and Its Applications,* vol. 1. CSLI Lecture Notes Number 22. Stanford: CSLI Publications.

Crimmins, M. 1991. States of Affairs Without Parameters. Cornell University.

Devlin, K. J. 1991. *Logic and Information.* Cambridge: Cambridge University Press.

Engdahl, E. 1986. *Constituent Questions.* Dordrecht: Reidel.

Engdahl, E. 1988. Relational Interpretation. In *Mental Representations: The Interface between Language and Reality,* ed. Kempson. Cambridge: Cambridge University Press.

Evans, G. 1977. Pronouns, Quantifiers and Relative Clauses. *Canadian Journal of Philosophy* 7:467–536.

Frege, G. 1918. Thoughts. In *Gottlob Frege: Logical Investigations.* trans. P. Geach and R. H. Stoothoff. New Haven: Yale University Press (1977).

Gawron, J. M., and S. Peters. 1990a. *Anaphora and Quantification in Situation Semantics.* CSLI Lecture Notes Number 19. Stanford: CSLI Publications.

Gawron, J. M., and S. Peters. 1990b. Some Puzzles About Pronouns. In Cooper et al. 1990.

Ginzburg, J. 1989. Informativeness Evaluated. Paper delivered at LSA meeting, Washington, DC.

Ginzburg, J. 1991a. A Semantics and Pragmatics for Questions and Responses. Stanford University Dissertation (in progress).

Ginzburg, J. 1991b. Semantic Selection and Embedded Questions. Presented at the 7th meeting of the ITLA, Hebrew University, Jerusalem.

Groenendijk, J., and M. Stokhof. 1984. *Studies on the Semantics of Questions and the Pragmatics of Answers.* PhD thesis, University of Amsterdam.

Groenendijk, J., and M. Stokhof. 1989. Type Shifting and the Semantics of Interrogatives. In *Properties, Types, and Meaning,* vol. 2, ed. G. C. (et al.). Dordrecht: Reidel.

Hamblin, C. L. 1973. Questions in Montague English. *Foundations of Language* 10:41–53.

Hausser, R. 1983. On Questions. In *Questions and Answers,* ed. F. Kiefer. Dordrecht: Reidel.

Heim, I. 1982. *The Semantics of Definite and Indefinite Noun Phrases.* PhD thesis, University of Massachussetts, Amherst.

Higginbotham, J., and R. May. 1981. Questions, Quantifiers and Crossing. *The Linguistic Review* 1:41–80.

Hintikka, J. 1983. New Foundations for a Theory of Questions and Answers. In *Questions and Answers,* ed. F. Kiefer. Dordrecht: Reidel.

Hiz, H. (ed.). 1978. *Questions.* Dordrecht: Reidel.

Huang, C. T. J. 1982. Move WH in a Language without WH Movement. *The Linguistic Review* 1:369–416.

Jackendoff, R. 1972. *Semantic Interpretation in Generative Grammar.* Cambridge, MA: MIT Press.

Jespersen, O. 1965. *The Philosophy of Grammar.* New York: Norton.

Kaplan, R., and A. Zaenen. 1989. Long Distance Dependencies, Constituent Structure and Functional Structure. In *Alternative Conceptions of Phrase Structure,* ed. M. Baltin and A. Kroch. Chicago: University of Chicago Press.

Karttunen, L. 1977. The Syntax and Semantics of Questions. *Linguistics and Philosophy* 1:1–44.

Karttunen, L., and S. Peters. 1980. Interrogative Quantifiers. In *Times, Tense, and Quantifiers,* ed. C. Rohrer. Tubingen: Niemeyer.

Keenan, E. L., and R. Clark. 1986. On the Syntax and Semantics of Binary Quantification. In *WCCFL-5,* 13–27. Stanford Linguistics Association.

Kiefer, F. (ed.). 1983. *Questions and Answers.* Dordrecht: Reidel.

Ladusaw, W. 1979. *Polarity Sensitivity as Inherent Scope Relations.* PhD thesis, University of Texas, Austin.

May, R. 1985. *Logical Form in Natural Language.* Cambridge, MA: MIT Press.

May, R. 1988. Ambiguities of Quantification and Wh. *Linguistic Inquiry* 19:118–134.

Munsat, S. 1986. Wh-Complementizers. *Linguistics and Philosophy* 9:191–217.

Pollard, C., and I. Sag. 1987. *Information-Based Syntax and Semantics, Volume 1: Fundamentals.* CSLI Lecture Notes Number 13. Stanford: CSLI Publications.

Quine, W. V. O. 1974. *The Roots of Reference.* La Salle, IL: Open Court.

Rooth, M. 1985. *Association with Focus.* PhD thesis, University of Massachusetts, Amherst.

Ross, J. R. 1972. Q-binding and Conjunctive Questions. *Foundations of Language* 10:331–332.

Vendler, Z. 1972. *Res Cogitans.* Ithaca, NY: Cornell University Press.

Westerståhl, D. 1990. Parametric Types and Propositions in First-Order Situation Theory. In Cooper et al. 1990.

17

Reducing Complexity of Constraint-Based Grammars

Kôiti Hasida

1 Introduction

It is practically impossible to delimit the scope of information potentially relevant to the survival or benefit of a cognitive agent. On the other hand, the information-processing capacity of a cognitive agent is severely limited. Only a very small part of the relevant information can therefore actually be reflected in the actions (including inferences) by the cognitive agent at each context. This gives rise to a very complex flow of information in cognitive processes, because the information really exploited should vary drastically from one context to another, in order to encompass as much of the relevant information as possible across various contexts.

Due to this complexity, descriptive formalisms which stipulate and hence restrict information flow fail to capture subtleties of cognition. In this connection, the major advantage of constraint-based approaches, among other intertwined benefits, is that they are basically free from stipulation of (restriction on) information flow, providing a basis on which to construct scientific theories with tractable complexity.

The transformation operations employed in some linguistic theories (Chomsky 1981, 1986) are officially claimed to be free from processing order. This claim may well be justified, but still those theories impose too much limitation on information flow, because successive transformations give birth to sequences of intermediate structures, and information flow is restricted to be along this sequence. Transformations are procedural by nature, and the claim that transformations impose no processing directions is as vacuous as a claim that FORTRAN and LISP programs do not restrict information flow because they are regarded as constraints on the structure of the chronological sequence of working memory contents. Just like those

Situation Theory and Its Applications, vol. 2.
Jon Barwise, Jean Mark Gawron, Gordon Plotkin, and Syun Tutiya, eds.
Copyright © 1991, Stanford University.

procedural programming languages, transformational grammars postulate intermediate stages of computation, inviting excessive complexity in the resulting theories.

The linguistic theories often termed 'unification-based,' 'non-transformational,' 'information-based' and so on (Bresnan 1982, Gazdar et al. 1985, Pollard and Sag 1987, Gunji 1987) provide a basis for designing grammars genuinely exempt from such a restriction on information flow and the resulting complications of theories. For instance, the slash feature in some of those theories may be regarded as a genuine constraint-based mechanism, in the sense that it captures long distance dependencies in terms of relationships within a single grammatical structure rather than in terms of procedure (relationships among many intermediate structures).

However, those constraint-based theories are not yet entirely free from the procedural line of reasoning. Still they have several aspects which involve what appear to be intermediate structures. The major purpose of this paper is to point out some of those aspects and propose genuinely constraint-based alternatives. There are primarily two of such aspects which we discuss below. One is the phrase-structure based description of the relationships among words, and the other is quantifier storage (Cooper 1983) to deal with scopings. So-called mother categories, together with a the subcat feature, may be regarded as encoding intermediate stages of the computation to work out intrasentential relationships. Quantifier storages would be more readily recognized as intermediate structures.

In place of phrase structure and subcat feature, we will propose an alternative treatment based on what could be called *potential energy*. The system of constraints we employ below consists of a symbolic (digital) and an analog aspect. The symbolic aspect is a sort of first order logic program, and the analog aspect is potential energy, which represents the degree of dissatisfaction of constraints. A common usage of such an analog component is to provide preferences among *possible* combinations of propositions, but we consider that simply every combination is possible, and that potential energy defines an analog measure of consistency. In this view, potential energy does not serve as a secondary means used when the symbolic aspect fails to determine the answer, but plays a primary role to be tightly coupled with the symbolic aspect. This results in a reduction of the symbolic (combinatorial) complexity of the overall design of the constraints, parts of constraints formerly encoded symbolically being substituted with energy minimization.

The alternative approach we propose below to handle quantifier scopes will be obtained also by eliminating intermediate stages of computation encoded in linguistic structures. Potential energy will be employed here as well, though playing a somewhat minor role in determining preferred readings.

2 Constraints and Potential Energy

We assume that what the world might be like is captured in terms of constraints of various sorts, which are represented uniformly as first order logic programs of a clausal form plus some analog component. For example, a piece of aa constraint might look like the following clause, when we restrict our attention to the symbolic aspect.

(1) $p(X) \leftarrow q(X,Y) \wedge r(Y)$.

Names beginning with capital letters are variables. The other names and special symbols are constants, including predicates and functors. As usual, each clause is a disjunction of atomic formulas which is universally quantified with respect to every variable it contains. So clause (1) is an abbreviation of the following first order formula.

(2) $\forall X \{p(X) \Leftarrow \exists Y \{q(X,Y) \wedge r(Y)\}\}$

For any binary predicate ρ_i $(1 \leq i \leq n)$, an object α satisfying (3) may be written as a record-like term shown in (4).

(3) $\rho_1(\alpha, \beta_1) \wedge \rho_2(\alpha, \beta_2) \wedge \cdots \wedge \rho_n(\alpha, \beta_n)$

(4) $\{\rho_1/\beta_1, \rho_2/\beta_2, \cdots, \rho_n/\beta_n\}$

Some binary predicates, called *features*, stand for partial functions. For instance, if ρ is a feature, then $\rho(\alpha, \beta) \wedge \rho(\alpha, \gamma)$ implies $\beta = \gamma$. An atomic formula with a feature is called a *feature specification*. Although the record notation used in (4) is restricted to cases where every ρ_i is a feature in usual practices (Johnson 1988), we use this notation more loosely for expository conveniences.

Clauses are regarded as identical in as far as they are transformed to each other by syntactic transformations preserving the logical equivalence. For instance, one and the same clause may be represented in many different ways including the following three.

(5) $p(f(X)) \leftarrow q(\{a/X,b/Y\},Y) \wedge r(Y)$.

(6) $\neg q(B,Y) \vee A{\neq}f(X) \leftarrow \neg p(A) \wedge r(Y) \wedge B{=}\{a/X,b/Y\}$.

(7) $p(A) \vee \neg q(B,Y) \vee \neg r(Y) \vee A{\neq}f(X) \vee \neg a(B,X) \vee \neg b(B,Y)$.

Information processing concerns hypotheses. A hypothesis is the negation of a clause: that is, a conjunction of atomic formulas existentially quantified in terms of all the variables appearing in it. Computation begins given an initial hypothesis, which is successively rewritten to new hypotheses by abduction (backward chaining) and factoring (unification), while checking consistency by deduction (forward chaining).[1] Abduction may be regarded as resolution in the standard sense, and factoring is also

---

[1] A more serious account of information processing could be based on transformation of the entire constraint instead of simply rewriting the top-level hypothesis. For further details, see Hasida and Ishizaki 1987, Tuda, Hasida and Sirai 1989, and Hasida and Tuda 1991, among others.

understood in the standard fashion. Deduction is mainly for consistency checking. Some factorings are obligatory, as a part of consistency checking. A typical example is the unification of two feature specifications sharing both the feature and the first argument. That is, if ρ is a feature, then $\rho(\alpha, \beta)$ and $\rho(\alpha, \gamma)$ must unify, so that β and γ unify.

The atomic formulas and literals are classified into two categories, *defined* and *free*. Defined atomic formulas and defined literals are those with *defined* predicates. A predicate is defined if it has *definition clauses*; otherwise it is free. A definition clause has the form '$H :- B.$'. H is an atomic formula called the *head* of this definition clause, and B is a conjunction of literals. A definition clause of a defined predicate is one whose head has that predicate. The approximate logical meaning[2] of a defined predicate is given in terms of a necessary and sufficient condition obtained from its definition clauses. For instance, if predicate p has the two definition clauses in (8), its meaning is roughly defined by (9).

(8) p(X) :- q(X,a). p(f(X)) :- r(X).

(9) $\forall A\{p(A) \Leftrightarrow \{\exists Y (q(A, Y) \wedge Y = a) \vee \exists X (A = f(X) \wedge r(X))\}\}$

Predicates like =f as in atomic formula (binding) X=f(Y) are free, and thus variable bindings are typical free atomic formulas. Most features are also free predicates, and thus most feature specifications are free atomic formulas. Computation may stop when the current hypothesis contains only free literals and there is no need for consistency checking.

Out of various aspects of potential energy, in this paper we consider only what we will call the *cost* of literals and hypotheses. Like *assumability cost* of Hobbs et al. 1990, our cost is the cost of maintaining hypotheses. That is, a cost increases potential energy and thus degrades the plausibility of the relevant hypothesis. Smaller cost corresponds to better interpretation of a sentence, for example. Thus a hypothesis with a large cost should be transformed through inferences so as to reduce the cost, or the hypothesis will be abandoned. For simplicity, we assume that costs are primarily assigned to literals in the top-level hypothesis, and that the cost of the entire hypothesis is the sum of the costs of the literals it contains. In this section we do not care about small differences of the cost, but just distinguish very costly literals by emboldening their predicates, like **p**(X).

Throughout the rest of the paper, we employ a very tentative and simplified version of cost dynamics. That is, when two literals with costs α and β unify (factor), the resulting literal has cost $\min(\alpha, \beta)$. This means that literals with larger costs should unify with others with smaller costs, so that the overall cost of the hypothesis should be reduced.

Note that costs cannot be eliminated freely, because the computational scheme described above does not allow free introduction of assumptions

---

[2]Potential energy underlies the full meaning of the constraints, which is much more delicate than the logical meaning.

whether or not those assumptions are known to be consistent with the current hypothesis. Introduction of any literal must be based explicitly on some clause. Thus, attempts at cost elimination trigger nontrivial inferences. At any rate, it is in order to capture the behavior of costs that we should be as explicit about representation and computation as we are above.

3 Encoding Linguistic Constraints

Before entering the main part of the paper, some introductory comments are in order about how to represent constraints pertaining to natural language.

The domain of interpretation of our first order language includes the domain of syntactic objects and the domain of semantic objects of natural language. Let us refer to the former as SYN and the latter as SEM.

We organize SYN incorporating methods of the constraint-based grammars concerning the use of record-like structures. SYN includes grammatical categories and other syntactic constructs. Grammatical categories are represented in terms of records (alias feature bundles or attribute-value pairs). For instance, the following grammatical category says that the part of speech of the linguistic (Japanese, in this case) expression in question is postposition of form 'ga,' and it is directly associated with a semantic object X.

(10) $\{\mathsf{pos}/\mathsf{p},\mathsf{form}/\mathsf{ga},\mathsf{sem}/\mathsf{X}\}$

pos, form, and sem are features. p and ga are syntactic objects that are not categories. X is a semantic object.

SEM is organized on the basis of Situation Theory and Situation Semantics (Barwise and Perry 1983, Barwise and Etchemendy 1987, Barwise 1989), with some amalgamation with Discourse Representation Theory (DRT hereafter; Kamp 1981, 1988). SEM includes *situations, states of affairs* (soas henceforth), *types, individuals,* and so on. *Collections* include types, quantified objects and situations, and regarded as sets, masses, and other sorts of complex objects. Some semantic objects are members or parts of collections. Atomic formula $\alpha \in \beta$ means that semantic object α is a member of another semantic object β, and $\alpha \sqsubseteq \beta$ means that α is a subset or a part of β. Binary relation $\rightsquigarrow$ is the union of $\in$ and $\sqsubseteq$. That is, $\alpha \rightsquigarrow \beta$ holds iff either $\alpha \in \beta$ or $\alpha \sqsubseteq \beta$ holds. Note that α and β here are first order individuals, and that the infix operators $\in$, $\sqsubseteq$, and $\rightsquigarrow$ are first order predicates.

Soas are record-like semantic objects of the form $\{\rightsquigarrow/\alpha\}$, where α is some type. For instance, the soas $\langle\!\langle$kiss, kisser:john, kissed:mary$\rangle\!\rangle$ and $\langle\!\langle$drink, drinker:X, drunk:Y$\rangle\!\rangle$ are regarded as (11) and (12), respectively.

(11) $\{\in/\mathsf{kiss},\mathsf{kisser}/\mathsf{john},\mathsf{kissed}/\mathsf{mary}\}$
(12) $\{\sqsubseteq/\mathsf{drink},\mathsf{drinker}/\mathsf{X},\mathsf{drunk}/\mathsf{Y}\}$

A kissing event, which is atomic, is a member of type kiss, whereas a drinking event is a part of drink. Binary predicates such as kisser, kissed, drinker, and drunk are called *roles*. We remain undecided about whether roles are features.[3] We do not assume that soas carry polarity of Situation Theory.[4] Unlike in the other versions of Situation Theory, a dog is represented as a soa $\langle\!\langle dog \rangle\!\rangle$: that is, an individual α such that $\alpha \in$ dog. Some quantity of water is also a soa $\langle\!\langle water \rangle\!\rangle$, but it is $\{\sqsubset/\text{water}\}$ rather than $\{\in/\text{water}\}$.

Incorporating an aspect of DRT, we postulate that there is a quasi-order relation[5] $\preceq$ in SEM which may be regarded as the reflexive and transitive closure of the scoping relation in the traditional sense. So $\alpha \preceq \beta$ means that α belongs to a scope larger than or equal to the one β belongs to. The definition of $\preceq$ and related constraints are listed below.

(13) $X \preceq Y$:– $X \simeq Y$.

(14) $X \preceq Y$:– $X \prec Y$.

(15) $X \prec W$:– $X \simeq Y \wedge \text{col}(Y,Z) \wedge Z \preceq W$.

(16) $X \leadsto Y \leftarrow \text{col}(X,Y)$.

(17) $X \prec_1 W$:– $X \simeq Y \wedge \text{col}(Y,Z) \wedge Z \simeq W$.

(18) $\neg X \simeq Y \vee \neg X \prec Y$.

(19) $X \simeq Y \leftarrow U \simeq V \wedge \text{col}(U,X) \wedge \text{col}(V,Y)$.

(20) $\{\rho/\text{ARG}\} \preceq \text{ARG}$. (for each role ρ)

(13), (14), and (15) together mean that $\preceq$ is the transitive closure of $\simeq \cup \text{col}$. $\simeq$ is an equivalence relation in SEM. $\alpha \simeq \beta$ means that α and β belong to the same minimal scope of quantification (or abstraction). That is, each quantifier scope is encoded as an equivalence class of $\simeq$. In (16), $\text{col}(\alpha,\beta)$ means that α is the representative element or part of collection β. col is a special feature whose inverse is also a partial function. That is, if $\text{col}(\alpha,\beta) \wedge \text{col}(\gamma,\delta)$ then either $\alpha{=}\gamma \wedge \beta{=}\delta$ or $\alpha \neq \gamma \wedge \beta \neq \delta$. So if a collection has a scope, it has just one representative element or part in the scope. Also, each semantic object is the representative of at most one collection. Due to (17), $\alpha \prec_1 \beta$ means that α and β belong to two adjacent equivalence classes of $\simeq$. (18) implies that col must always encompass two distinct equivalence classes of $\simeq$, and that $\prec$ does not constitute any cycle,[6] as should be expected from the viewpoint that $\preceq$ is the scoping relation. (19) means that $\preceq$ does not fork upwards. So the equivalence classes of $\simeq$ constitute a tree branching only downwards. (20) is the accessibility constraint.

---

[3] If they are, there is exactly one lover for each loving event, for instance.

[4] Although we do not spell out further details, we can represent negation more along traditional lines, assigning a scope to each negation. This still leaves at least three different affirmation statuses for a soa: true, don't care, and false. The variety turns out to be larger when we take cost assignments into account.

[5] A binary relation R is a quasi-order iff it is both reflexive (xRx for every x) and transitive (if xRy and yRz then xRz).

[6] The circularity as in the Liar sentence (Barwise and Etchemendy 1987) can obtain within an equivalence class of $\simeq$.

4 Local Dependency

Here we take a look at a role our cost may play in putting smaller expressions together to form bigger ones. Consider the following Japanese sentence.[7]

(21) Gakusei -ga   sake -wo   nonda.
       student NOM sake ACC drank
       'A student drank sake.'

In constituency-based approaches, including GPSG, HPSG, JPSG, LFG, and transformational grammars, this sentence will be assigned a syntactic structure in (22).

(22)

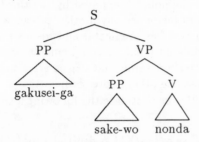

Given this, a suspicion might arise: perhaps the grammatical categories such as VP and S here encode intermediate steps in the computation to work out the entire sentential structure. That is, the relationship between a category and its mother in a local tree might be similar to the relationship between the input and the output structural descriptions in transformation. If this suspicion turns out true, and if this case is parallel to the case with transformations, then it should be possible to recast the relationship between a category and its mother to a relationship between two different states of computation probably just before and after an operation to set up local dependency, so that the head/mother distinction be abandoned. Such an approach has been called dependency grammars (Sgall and Panevová 1989). In this viewpoint, sentence (21) has the structure in (23).[8]

(23)   V(nonda)

          P(gakusei-ga)   P(sake-wo)

An edge in this dependency tree means that the category at its lower end depends on the category at the upper end. The comparison of the two structures in terms of the number of the categories suggests that the

---

[7] The English translation of *gakusei* may also be 'the student,' 'students' or 'the students'; the Japanese language does not usually mark definiteness and number.

[8] Throughout the paper, we treat each postpositional phrase as a word for simplicity.

dependency-based approach will reduce the combinatorial complexity of the theory.

The mother-head relationship in the constituency-based account is captured in the dependency-based account by using cost. To show this, let us first postulate the following dependency-based rule for head-final constructions.

(24) expr(Head,Left,Right) :−
        expr(Cat,Left,Middle) ∧ expr(Head,Middle,Right) ∧ dep(Cat,Head).

Predicate expr means that the first argument is the grammatical category of the linguistic expression beginning at the point designated by the second argument and ending at the point designated by the third argument. Note that the this rule does not introduce any mother category as separate from the head category. dep is a free predicate, and means that the first argument syntactically depends on (that is, complements or adjoins) the second argument. We tentatively assume that dep is a feature. So every expression depends on at most one other expression.

To account for sentence (21), we postulate the following lexical entries.[9]

(25) expr(Cat, "gakusei-ga") :−
        Cat={pos/p,form/ga,sem/{↝/X}} ∧ dep(Cat,{pos/v}).
(26) expr(Cat, "sake-wo") :−
        Cat={pos/p,form/wo,sem/{↝/X}} ∧ dep(Cat,{pos/v}).
(27) expr(Cat, "nonda") :−
        Cat={pos/v,sem/DRANK} ∧
        col*(⟪drank, drinker:X, drunk:Y⟫,DRANK) ∧
        dep({pos/p,form/ga,sem/X},Cat) ∧
        dep({pos/p,form/wo,sem/Y},Cat).

The apparently second argument of expr(···) is the part of the utterance between the two points designated by the actual second argument and the third argument. col* is the reflexive and transitive closure of col. As discussed later, the literal of the form col*(···) in (27) makes room for optional quantifications of arbitrary depth. The intuitive meaning of the cost assignment here is: *gakusei-ga* and *sake-wo* should depend on some verbal category, and *nonda* should be modified by a *ga*-phrase and a *wo*-phrase.

The interpretation of sentence (21) begins with the following unit hypothesis, which means that *gakusei-ga sake-wo nonda* should be a well-formed linguistic expression.

(28) expr(Cat, "gakusei-ga sake-wo nonda")

---

[9]Note the form of the semantic object associated with *gakusei-ga* (essentially *gakusei*). This reflects the fact that the Japanese language lacks morphological marking of singularity, as mentioned in Note 7.

We consider that to interpret (21) is to derive from (28) a new hypothesis (approximately) all of whose implications are consistent with the given constraints. Let us call such a new hypothesis an *interpretation* of (21). To get an interpretation, (28) is transformed into the following through resolution with (25), (26) and (27).[10]

(29) Cat0={pos/p,form/ga,sem/{$\rightsquigarrow$/student}} $\wedge$ dep(Cat0,Cat) $\wedge$
      Cat1={pos/p,form/wo,sem/{$\rightsquigarrow$/sake}} $\wedge$ dep(Cat1,Cat) $\wedge$
      Cat={pos/v,sem/DRANK} $\wedge$
      col*($\langle\!\langle$drank, drinker:X, drunk:Y$\rangle\!\rangle$,DRANK) $\wedge$
      dep({pos/p,form/ga,sem/X},Cat) $\wedge$
      dep({pos/p,form/wo,sem/Y},Cat).

The compulsory unifications among literals of the form dep($\cdots$) have been finished here, leaving two literals dep(Cat0, Cat) and dep(Cat1, Cat). A better interpretation is one with smaller cost. The minimum cost is obtained by further factoring the literals of the form dep($\cdots$) in the expected combination, and accordingly unifying other literals:[11]

(30) dep({pos/p,form/ga,sem/X},Cat) $\wedge$ X$\rightsquigarrow$student $\wedge$
      dep({pos/p,form/wo,sem/Y},Cat) $\wedge$ Y$\rightsquigarrow$sake $\wedge$
      Cat={pos/v,sem/DRANK} $\wedge$
      col*($\langle\!\langle$drank, drinker:X, drunk:Y$\rangle\!\rangle$,DRANK).

This interpretation subsumes various quantificational possibilities, to which we return in the next section.

As is illustrated by this example, the above grammar fragment captures the following principle.

(31) A specified argument place of a verb requires a complement to be associated with it.[12]

This principle is embodied in terms of the literals of the form $\mathbf{dep}(\alpha,\mathsf{Cat})$ in (27) and (29). These literals are assigned costs, so that they must unify with other literals. It is easy to see that the expected combination of unifications is the only possible one in the case of (29). Even in more complicated cases where there are other literals of the form dep(α,β) with β distinct from Cat, the expected unifications are as strongly preferred, provided another principle as follows.

(32) Two grammatical categories do not unify when they are associated with different parts of utterance.

---

[10] We have omitted the resolved literals, though they might be necessary for consistency checking.

[11] We have done resolution entirely before cost-driven factoring here, but this processing order is just for explanatory ease. Of course it is possible to interpret the sentence on a more incremental basis, for instance.

[12] The optionality of complements in Japanese may be formulated in terms of a lexical rule which deletes argument slots from a verb, for instance.

This is regarded as a very general principle. In fact, it also predicts the badness of the following.

(33) Gakusei -ga   gakusei -ga   kita.
     student NOM student NOM came
     'A student a student came.'

A straightforward way to implement principle (32) is to assign distinct indices to categories to be distinguished in terms of feature specifications for feature, say, ind. Indices can simply be associated with positions in the utterance.

Note also that the above grammar fragment captures the freedom of the order among the elements (complements and adjuncts) locally depending on a verb. For instance, it allows *sake-wo gakusei-ga nonda* as well as *gakusei-ga sake-wo nonda*. In this connection, constraints on word order, if any, may be stated separately.

Owing to the cost-based component, our account of complementation is much simpler than constituency-based accounts, with respect to combinatorial complexity. For instance, GPSG and HPSG implement (31) and (32) in terms of subcat feature and the Subcat Feature Principle (SFP), both of which are of combinatorial nature. The value of subcat feature is a list, a combinatorial syntactic object, and the application of SFP accompanies combinatorial operations where a new list is made by deleting (or inserting, if you look at it on a top-down basis) an element in a subcat list, in order to embody (32). (31) is captured by requiring that subcat lists at the maximally projected categories should be empty except for the controlled elements. JPSG assumes that the subcat value is a set instead of a list. Although a set might appear less combinatorially complex than a list, the application of SFP is no less complicated with a set than with a list; you must look at possibly all the elements of a set when you tailor another set from it by adding or subtracting some elements. In contrast, the account presented here involves unifications among categories but no unifications among lists or sets.

Further, our approach naturally extends to adjunction as well. So we have adopted the general name for predicate dep, in a sense neutral between complementation and adjunction. In the case of adjunction, the lexical entry of the verb does not contribute a literal of the form dep($\cdots$), so that the thematic role of the adjunct is determined by the adjunct itself and the semantic property of the verb. Thus complementation and adjunction are given very analogous accounts. Namely, both phenomena are accounted for equally in terms of unifications among literals of the form dep($\cdots$), and the only difference between them is that the verb contributes some syntactic information to determine the thematic role of a complement but not that of an adjunct. So our approach contrasts again with the accounts based on subcat feature, which sharply distinguish between complements and adjuncts, in the sense that complementation is accounted for in terms of subcat feature and adjunction in terms of some other feature.

Incidentally, such a treatment of local dependency fits the intuition that complementation is less costly (in a pretheoretic sense) and hence more preferable than adjunction, because the former reduces cost but the latter does not.[13] Some delicate linguistic phenomena are accounted for on the basis of the different processing loads with complementation and adjunction (Hasida 1988, among others). Our current framework might provide a formal basis for these accounts.

The so-called θ-criterion is formulated in terms of cost assignment, as a purely semantic rather than syntactic constraint. For example, the semantic structure of *wo*-phrase of Japanese (postpositional phrase having the accusative case by default) might include a literal of the form $\mathbf{patient}(\alpha,\beta)$. β is the sem value of this *wo*-phrase. patient is a general role subsuming loved, drunk, and so on. That is, we have constraints like the following.

(34) patient(X,Y) ← loved(X,Y).

All of this means that a *wo*-phrase requires a soa to which it supplies a patient-type role parameter.[14] In a typical case of computation triggered by the above cost, a soa with a patient-type role such as loved is found, a rule such as (34) is applied to yield a literal of the form $\mathbf{patient}(\cdots)$ without cost, and this literal is unified with $\mathbf{patient}(\cdots)$ to eliminate the cost. In this connection, our approach will also contribute to the investigation of children's language use and more drastic attempts to minimize syntax (Suzuki and Tutiya 1989) where syntactic constraints do not play major roles.

5 Quantifier Scoping

The discussion in the previous section has been motivated by the suspicion that constituent structures encode intermediate states of computation which should be unnecessary in a genuine constraint-based framework. A similar and probably stronger suspicion arises regarding a prevailing treatment of quantifier scoping. That is, quantifier storage (Cooper 1983, Keller 1988) appears to explicitly encode intermediate states of computation (Hobbs and Shieber 1987), and is very probably dispensible. Here we propose a simple treatment of quantifier scoping without any explicit storage mechanism. In doing so, we pay attention to the quasi-order relation $\preceq$, which corresponds to the scoping relation, as mentioned already.

The Japanese sentence (35)[15] has two plausible (minimal) readings, (36) and (37), of which the former is the default interpretation.

---

[13] The author is grateful to the anonymous referee for drawing attention to this respect.
[14] Of course the story would not be that simple if we take into consideration *wo*-phrases which do not play a patient role, as in *sora-wo tobu* 'fly in the sky.'
[15] *-nin* and *-hon* are classifiers of Japanese, for counting people and long objects, respectively. The latter becomes *-ppon* after some numerals.

(35) Gakusei -ga   san -nin   sake -wo   ro -ppon nonda.
      student NOM three person sake ACC six bottle drank
      '3 students drank 6 bottles of sake.'

(36) 3 students and 6 bottles of sake were involved in a drinking event.
      (cumulative reading)

(37) Each of 3 students drank 6 bottles of sake. (wide scope reading of
      san-nin)

To account for this, we further postulate the following lexical entries for the
floating quantifiers *san-nin* and *ro-ppon*, plus some additional constraints.

(38) expr(QCat,"san-nin") :—
      QCat={pos/n,sem/QSem} $\wedge$ dep(QCat,VCat) $\wedge$
      PCat={pos/p,form/F,sem/PSem} $\wedge$ ga_wo(F) $\wedge$
      dep(PCat,VCat) $\wedge$ VCat={pos/v,sem/VSem} $\wedge$
      quant(PSem,3nin) $\wedge$ PSem $\prec_1$ QSem $\wedge$ col*(QSem,VSem).

(39) expr(QCat,"ro-ppon") :—
      QCat={pos/n,sem/QSem} $\wedge$ dep(QCat,VCat) $\wedge$
      PCat={pos/p,form/F,sem/PSem} $\wedge$ ga_wo(F) $\wedge$
      dep(PCat,VCat) $\wedge$ VCat={pos/v,sem/VSem} $\wedge$
      quant(PSem,6pon) $\wedge$ PSem $\prec_1$ QSem $\wedge$ col*(QSem,VSem).

(40) ga_wo(F) :— F=ga.

(41) ga_wo(F) :— F=wo.

(42) col*(X,Y) :— X=Y.

(43) col*(X,Z) :— col(X,Y) $\wedge$ col*(Y,Z).

Here a floating quantifier is regarded as an adjunct of a verb. Due to the
general dependency rule (24), VCat is to unify with the category of the
verb. Just as with complementation, literal dep(PCat,VCat) is to unify
with another literal with dep to eliminate the cost. As a result, PCat is to
unify with the category of a *ga*-phrase or *wo*-phrase which depends on the
verb.

   The semantic structure encoded in the body of (38) and (39) may be
depicted as in (44), if we pay attention to scoping relationships only.

(44)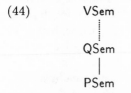

Relation $\preceq$ is represented by dotted lines, and $\prec_1$ by solid perpendicular
lines. The lower end of each such line is smaller than ($\prec$) or equivalent to
($\simeq$) the higher end. The dotted line in (44) reflects QSem $\preceq$ VSem, which
is implied by col*(QSem,VSem). In the box notation of DRT, (44) would
look like the following:

(45)

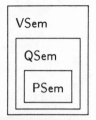

Each box corresponds to an equivalence class of $\simeq$. The outermost box and the second may be identical, VSem and QSem belonging to the same minimal box; otherwise there may be zero or more boxes between the two outer boxes.

quant(α,β) means that α may be instantiated so much as to reach quantity β. In the case of (38), for instance, the copy of Student may produce up to three different instances of Student. β may also be every, most, and so on, but further details are irrelevant to the current purpose. QSem stands for the minimal quantified event involving three people in the case of (38) and six bottles (or long objects in general) in the case of (39). PSem is the bound parameter of this quantification, as indicated by PSem $\prec_1$ QSem, and an instantiation of PSem due to quant(α,β) accompanies a copy of the whole equivalence class of $\simeq$ containing PSem. col*(QSem,VSem) implies that a floating quantifier cannot outscope the minimal sentence containing it. Such a constraint may be associated with other syntactic constructs as well.

A literal of the form col*($\cdots$) in the lexical entry of a verb (such as (27)) accounts for why a sentence such as *tori-wa tobu* 'a bird flies' may be interpreted as if it involved a universal quantifier. Although (43) allows infinitely many different interpretations, it is not the case that just anything goes. col($\cdots$) in (43) indicates that there should be an abstraction (quantified soas and some types) introduced elsewhere in order to use (43). As seen below, this explains why (35) has the interpretation preference mentioned above.

From (46) we can infer (47) as an abductive explanation, after reducing the cost of the literals of the form dep($\cdots$) by factoring.

(46) expr(Cat, "gakusei-ga san-nin sake-wo ro-ppon nonda").

(47) col*(StudentsDrank,DRANK) $\wedge$
      col*(DrankSake,DRANK) $\wedge$
      Student $\prec_1$ StudentsDrank $\wedge$
      Sake $\prec_1$ DrankSake $\wedge$
      Drank $\preceq$ Student $\wedge$
      Drank $\preceq$ Sake $\wedge$
      col*(Drank,DRANK) $\wedge$
      Drank=$\langle\langle$drank, drinker:Student, drunk:Sake$\rangle\rangle$ $\wedge$

dep({pos/n,sem/StudentsDrank},Vcat) ∧
dep({pos/n,sem/DrankSake},Vcat) ∧
dep({pos/p,form/ga,sem/Student},VCat) ∧
dep({pos/p,form/wo,sem/Sake},VCat) ∧
VCat={pos/v,sem/DRANK}.

This inference involves deductions by (20), which gave rise to the two literals Drank ⪯ Student and Drank ⪯ Sake. The constraints on quantifier scoping contained in (47) is depicted as follows.

(48)

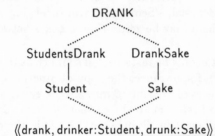

《drank, drinker:Student, drunk:Sake》

DRANK is the quantified soa associated with the entire sentence, and stands for a complex drinking event involving three students and six or more bottles of sake. StudentsDrank is the quantified soa standing for the minimal drinking event involving three students, and Student is the parameter bound by this quantification. Similarly, DrankSake is the minimal drinking event involving six bottles of sake, and parameter Sake is bound in it. Note that (48) does not have any concise box representation like (45).

As mentioned earlier, (19) rules out upward forking of ⪯. So all the six nodes in (48) must be linearized in terms of ⪯. This linearization is obtained by further resolutions on the literals with predicates ⪯ and col* together with some factorings and deductions. Let us consider only those interpretations minimal in terms of the number of times clauses are exploited. Such interpretations come out quickly, gaining preferences. In addition, stronger preferences result from fewer exploitations of clauses introducing costs. So we are interested in minimizing the use of (43) in particular here. That is, we will substitute as many occurrences of col* with equality as possible.

There are three minimal interpretations worked out accordingly, as shown below with illustrations of the associated scoping relations.

(49) 3 students and 6 bottles of sake were involved in a drinking event. (cumulative reading)

DRANK = StudentsDrank = DrankSake
|
《drank, drinker:Student, drunk:Sake》 ≃ Student ≃ Sake

(50) Each of 3 students drank 6 bottles of sake. (wide scope reading of *san-nin*)

$$\text{DRANK} = \text{StudentsDrank}$$
$$|$$
$$\text{DrankSake} \simeq \text{Student}$$
$$|$$
$$\langle\!\langle \text{drank, drinker:Student, drunk:Sake} \rangle\!\rangle \simeq \text{Sake}$$

(51) Each of 6 bottles of sake was drunk by 3 students. (wide scope reading of *ro-ppon*)

$$\text{DRANK} = \text{DrankSake}$$
$$|$$
$$\text{StudentsDrank} \simeq \text{Sake}$$
$$|$$
$$\langle\!\langle \text{drank, drinker:Student, drunk:Sake} \rangle\!\rangle \simeq \text{Student}$$

Out of these, only (51) is barred. This seems to be a sort of subject-object asymmetry, but we do not go into details here because it is irrelevant to the purpose of the present paper.

As for the remaining two interpretations, it is natural to consider that (49) (=(36)) tends to have stronger preference than (50) (=(37)), because the former is a smaller explanation in terms of the number of exploitations of (43). This accounts for why it is the default interpretation. The cost-based dynamic account thus straightforwardly captures some aspects, such as the complexity of inferences, which have been abstracted away from the underlying symbolic logic.

In the above example, the two quantified noun phrases are not related directly and thus all the permutations involving unification are possible, except that one interpretation is ruled out by the subject-object asymmetry. So let us consider some different patterns.

To begin with, we can account for the two possible (minimal) scopings of the following sentence.

(52) Every man loves a woman.

As mentioned before, the word-order constraints of English may be stated in addition to the local dependency constraints. A universal quantification is assigned a semantic structure totally parallel to the one in (38) and (39). A singular indefinite does not create any quantification but just introduces a parameter, following the DRT approach. Further details are omitted. The scoping relationships involved in a half-cooked interpretation of (52) look like (53).

(53)

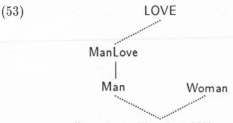

$$\langle\!\langle \text{love}, \text{lover}:\text{Man}, \text{loved}:\text{Woman}\rangle\!\rangle$$

Similarly to the previous case, LOVE is the semantic object associated with the whole sentence. ManLove is the soa quantified by *every*, and Man is the parameter bound by this quantifier. The scope to this quantification is the equivalence class of $\simeq$ containing Man. Woman is the semantic object associated to *a woman*. The linearization of the diagram in (53) forces us to choose between the wide-scope reading and narrow-scope reading of *every*. The former is characterized by Woman $\prec$ Man, and the latter ManLove $\prec$ Woman. All the possible cases fall in either of these two.

Next example (taken from Hobbs and Shieber 1987) is a little more complicated:

(54) Every representative of a company saw most samples.

This sentence cannot be interpreted so that *every representative* outscopes *most samples* and *most samples* outscopes *a company*. So there are just five rather than six (=3!) different minimal scopings here. This is accounted for as follows in the present approach. The constraints on scopings look like (55).

(55)

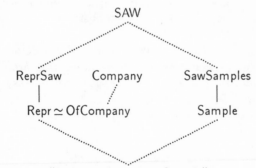

$$\langle\!\langle \text{saw}, \text{seer}:\text{Repr}, \text{seen}:\text{Sample}\rangle\!\rangle$$

As above, SAW is the soa associated with the entire sentence, ReprSaw is the soa quantified by *every*, and SawSamples is the soa quantified by *most*. Although we do not go into details here, OfCompany and Repr $\simeq$ OfCompany are introduced by copying from the content of the type associated with *representative of a company*; the same mechanism underlying so called E-type anaphora. OfCompany is a copy of the soa associated with *of a company*, and Company may be the corresponding copy of the parameter associated with *a company*. OfCompany will look like

$$\langle\!\langle \text{represent, representative:Repr, represented:Company} \rangle\!\rangle.$$

Repr $\simeq$ OfCompany holds because *of a company* is a restrictive modification to *representative*. This characterization of restriction is essentially the same as the *Absorption Principle* of Gawron and Peters (1990).

Again (55) must be linearized. But note that SawSamples cannot cut in between ReprSaw and Company if Company $\prec$ ReprSaw in the resulting linear ordering, because either Company $\simeq$ Repr or ReprSaw $\preceq$ Company holds.

After all, our account of quantification does not involve quantifier storage. The quasi-order relation encoding constraints on quantifier scoping is directly handled instead. In this connection, note that our approach exploits minimal syntactic structures. As we have discussed, we postulate a dependency hierarchy but no constituency hierarchy of syntax. This is all right because we have enough structure in semantics, such as the quasi-order hierarchy of semantic objects.

6 Concluding Remarks

A grammar fragment has been worked out to demonstrate that combinatorial complexity of constraint-based linguistic theories can be reduced by eliminating explicit encoding of intermediate states of computation. This is along the same line on which transformational rules have been abandoned in those theories. We have discussed how to eliminate the subcat feature, constituent structure, and quantifier storage. Subjects of further investigation will include binding features such as slash and que. The chances are that they will be reduced to a large extent, if not entirely eliminated.

We have employed a notion of cost, mainly in dealing with local dependencies and, in a somewhat complementary manner, in handling quantifier scopings. Cost is a part of potential energy, which constitutes the analog aspect of constraint. Although here we have used this analog aspect just to obtain truth values (alias preferences of interpretation), potential energy is quite naturally used for providing preferences of computation, based on energy minimization principle.

Such a unified treatment of truth conditions and computation control is not simply due to the convenience in theory construction, but necessitated by more essential reasons. That is, since the standard methods of defining truth conditions (or consistency) are computationally intractable, truth values can be obtained at best as preferences of interpretation depending on local computational contexts. Under this intractability, purely logical approaches to truth conditions, typically represented by non-monotonic logics (McCarthy 1980, McDermott and Doyle 1980), are useless as long as they disregard partial processing.

From a viewpoint of linguistics, this direction is to eliminate the distinction of linguistic competence (concerning determination of truth values) and linguistic performance (concerning control of computation). From a wider perspective, we face a need for restructured descriptive formalisms, such as those found in Situation Theory, so that the notion of truth and consistency should be defined in tight conjunction with processing control. It is a small first step into this direction that we have marked in this paper.

References

Barwise, J. 1989. *The Situation in Logic.* CSLI Lecture Notes Number 17. Stanford: CSLI Publications.

Barwise, J., and J. Etchemendy. 1987. *The Liar: An Essay on Truth and Circularity.* New York: Oxford University Press.

Barwise, J., and J. Perry. 1983. *Situations and Attitudes.* Cambridge, MA: MIT Press.

Bresnan, J. (ed.). 1982. *The Mental Representation of Grammatical Relations.* Cambridge: MIT Press.

Chomsky, N. 1981. *Lectures on Government and Binding.* Dordrecht: Foris.

Chomsky, N. 1986. Barriers. *Linguistic Inquiry Monograph* 13.

Cooper, R. 1983. *Quantification and Syntactic Theory.* Vol. 21 of Synthèse Language Library. Dordrecht: Reidel.

Gawron, J. M., and S. Peters. 1990. *Anaphora and Quantification in Situation Semantics.* CSLI Lecture Notes Number 19. Stanford: CSLI Publications.

Gazdar, G., E. Klein, G. K. Pullum, and I. A. Sag. 1985. *Generalized Phrase Structure Grammar.* Cambridge: Harvard University Press.

Gunji, T. 1987. *Japanese Phrase Structure Grammar.* Dordrecht: Reidel.

Hasida, K. 1988. A Cognitive Account of Unbounded Dependency. In *Proceedings of the 12th International Conference on Computational Linguistics*, 231–236. Budapest.

Hasida, K., and S. Ishizaki. 1987. Dependency Propagation: A Unified Theory of Sentence Comprehension and Generation. In *Proceedings of the 10th International Joint Conference on Artificial Intelligence*, 664–670.

Hasida, K., and H. Tuda. 1991. Parsing without Parser. In *Proceedings of the 2nd International Workshop on Parsing Technologies*, 1–10. Cancun.

Hobbs, J., and S. Shieber. 1987. An Algorithm for Generating Quantifier Scopings. *Computational Linguistics* 13(1–2):47–53.

Hobbs, J., M. Stickel, D. Appelt, and P. Martin. 1990. Interpretation as Abduction. Technical Note 499, SRI International, Menlo Park.

Johnson, M. 1988. *Attribute-Value Logic and the Theory of Grammar.* CSLI Lecture Notes Number 16. Stanford: CSLI Publications.

Kamp, H. 1981. A Theory of Truth and Semantic Representation. In *Formal Methods in the Study of Language*, ed. G. Groenendijk, T. Janssen, and M. Stokhof. Amsterdam: Mathematisch Centrum.

Kamp, H. 1988. Discourse Representation Theory: What It Is and Where It Ought to Go. In *Natural Language at the Computer*, ed. A. Blaser. Proceedings of Scientific Symposium of Syntax and Semantics for Text Processing and Man-Machine Communication. Lecture Notes in Computer Science 320. Springer-Verlag.

Keller, W. R. 1988. Nested Copper Storage: The Proper Treatment of Quantification in Ordinary Noun Phrases. In *Natural Language and Linguistic Theories*, ed. U. Reyle and C. Rohrer, 432–447. Dordrecht: Reidel.

McCarthy, J. 1980. Circumscription: A Form of Non-monotonic Reasoning. *Artificial Intelligence* 13:27–39.

McDermott, D., and J. Doyle. 1980. Non-Monotonic Logic I. *Artificial Intelligence* 13:41–72.

Pollard, C., and I. Sag. 1987. *Information-Based Syntax and Semantics, Volume 1: Fundamentals*. CSLI Lecture Notes Number 13. Stanford: CSLI Publications.

Sgall, P., and J. Panevovă. 1989. Dependency Syntax—A Challenge. *Theoretical Linguistics* 15:73–89.

Suzuki, H., and S. Tutiya. 1991. A Strictly Incremental Approach of Japanese Grammar. This volume.

Tuda, H., K. Hasida, and H. Sirai. 1989. JPSG Parser on Constraint Logic Programming. In *Proceedings of the European Chapter of ACL*.

18

Perspectivity and the Japanese Reflexive '*zibun*'

Yasuhiro Katagiri

1 Introduction

Intelligent agents acting in an environment are not outside observers of what is happening in the world. They are embedded in and are interacting with their surrounding environments. They perceive, recognize and even describe facts of the environment not from a detached, god's eye view, but from where they stand in it. Perspectivity has its origin in this kind of situatedness of agents within environments.

On the other hand, we could and do sometimes imagine a situation from another person's perspective. How things would look like if I were her? This mode of recognition and reasoning is a fairly common practice in our daily activities, especially when we are thinking of, trying to explain, or making sense of another person's behaviors, be they real or imaginary.

Since perspectivity is deeply rooted in human nature as situated agents, it is quite natural that systems of our languages be prepared with mechanisms to reflect and express perspectivity. The use of the Japanese reflexive '*zibun*' is considered to reflect and to be somehow correlated with perspectivity. Several Japanese linguists have been claiming that usage of '*zibun*' is, at least partly, determined by discourse-related factors pertaining to perspectivity. The various accounts which have been proposed for the behavior of '*zibun* differ considerably from one another; proposals include such factors as the person whose awareness the speaker is reporting (Kuno 1973), whom the speaker identifies herself with (Kuno and Kaburaki 1977; Kuno 1978, 1987; Kameyama 1984), and whose point of view, in the sense of physical location, the speaker is taking on (Iida and Sells 1988, Sells 1987). In all of these accounts, however, it is commonly assumed that a certain noun phrase referent in a sentence is linguistically marked as occupying a specific role with respect to perspectivity. The referent is the person from

Situation Theory and Its Applications, vol. 2.
Jon Barwise, Jean Mark Gawron, Gordon Plotkin, and Syun Tutiya, eds.
Copyright © 1991, Stanford University.

whose perspective the speaker is uttering the sentence, or the person who is nearer to the speaker's perspective than any other noun phrase referent. It is then assumed that the reflexive '*zibun*' has to co-refer with that particular referent.

Close examination of data, however, reveals that this type of account is not all-embracing. Some occurrences of '*zibun*' certainly follow that coreference pattern, but we can also find other occurrences that do not. There seem to be conflicting intuitions for the relationship between the usage of '*zibun*' and the notion of "perspectivity."

In this paper, we first reexamine relevant data for the use of '*zibun*' to show that, in contrast to English reflexives, the use of '*zibun*' cannot be captured only by syntactic conditions, and that although the notion of perspectivity has to do with the use of '*zibun*', accounts of '*zibun*' in terms of coreference with a perspectivity role are too simple, and a richer model for the notion of perspectivity is necessary. We then propose, as a model of perspectivity, perspectival mental states that have two components, which we call *indexical perspectivity* and *inferential perspectivity*. By assuming that these perspectival mental states constitute part of the discourse situations in perspectival utterances, we will then proceed to give an account of the use of the Japanese reflexive '*zibun*'. In doing so, we will claim that, contrary to the currently wide-spread explications, the use of '*zibun*' is not *directly* related to point of view location; rather, the relationship is indirect. We will show that the apparent correlation of '*zibun*' and perspectivity is mediated by an independently motivated default principle, which captures our intuition that, in normal situations, agents are aware of facts pertaining to their actions and experiences.

2 Japanese Long-Distance Reflexive '*zibun*'

2.1 Possibility of Syntactic Binding of '*zibun*'

The Japanese reflexive '*zibun*' is known to behave differently from English reflexives in that while the latter are almost always bound clause internally, the former can be non-clause-bounded; '*zibun*' can have its antecedent outside the clause where the reflexive appears. To use Government Binding theory terms, '*zibun*' need not be bound in its Governing Category.

So, whereas English sentences in (1) exhibit the fact that, in contrast to ordinary pronouns, English reflexives have to be bound within a certain minimal syntactic domain, the corresponding Japanese sentences in (2) show that Japanese reflexives do not obey similar syntactic constraints.[1]

---

[1] It has been pointed out that English, too, has non-clause-bounded usages of reflexive pronouns, and that those usages somehow seem to be related to the speaker's point of view (Jackendoff 1972, Kuno 1987, Pollard and Sag 1990).

(1) a.   Taro$_i$ loves himself$_i$.

    *b.   Taro$_i$ loves him$_i$.

    *c.   Hanako$_i$ thinks that Taro loves herself$_i$.

    d.   Hanako$_i$ thinks that Taro loves her$_i$.

(2) a.   Taro$_i$-wa   zibun$_i$-wo   aishiteiru.
              TOP   SELF-OBJ   love
              (Taro$_i$ loves self$_i$.)

  ?b.   Taro$_i$-wa   kare$_i$-wo   aishiteiru.
              TOP   he-OBJ   love
              (Taro$_i$ loves him$_i$.)

    c.   Hanako$_i$-wa   Taro-ga   zibun$_i$-wo   aishiteiru-to
              TOP   SUBJ   SELF-OBJ   love-COMP
       omotteiru.
       think
       (Hanako$_i$ thinks that Taro loves self$_i$.)

    d.   Hanako$_i$-wa   Taro-ga   kanojo$_i$-wo   aishiteiru-to
              TOP   SUBJ   she-OBJ   love-COMP
       omotteiru.
       think
       (Hanako$_i$ thinks that Taro loves her$_i$.)

As an alternative to the English-like binding condition, a proposal has been made to the effect that '*zibun*' has to be bound by one of the subjects of the sentence, possibly a subject of a higher clause. This proposal is not only valid for many '*zibun*' occurrences, including those in (2), but is also capable of providing a viable explanation of the ambiguity of '*zibun*' binding in causative constructions like (3).[2]

(3) Taro$_i$-wa   Hanako$_j$-ni   zibun$_{i/j}$-no   hon-wo   yoma-seta.
      TOP   IOBJ   SELF-GEN   book-OBJ   read-CAUSE
    (Taro$_i$ made Hanako$_j$ read self$_{i/j}$'s book.)

Considering that, in a causative construction, the '*ni*'-marked NP, 'Hanako' in (3), syntactically controls the subject of the embedded verb phrase, 'zibun-no hon-wo yomu' (read self's book), the subject binding rule for '*zibun*' correctly predicts that '*zibun*' in (3) can be bound either by the matrix clause subject 'Taro' or by the embedded subject, which is realized as the '*ni*'-marked NP 'Hanako' (Gunji 1987).

But there are also exceptions to this subject binding rule. The following sentence (4) is acceptable, where '*zibun*' is bound by the matrix object, and there is no possibility of control in this construction (McCawley 1976).

---

[2] Subjects include NPs marked by the topic marker '*wa*'.

(4) Hanako–ga   zibun$_i$–wo   hihansita   koto–ga   Taro$_i$–wo
       SBJ   **SELF–OBJ**   criticize   **COMP–SBJ**   **OBJ**
     nayama–seta.
     annoy–**CAUSE**
     (The fact that Hanako criticized self$_i$ annoyed Taro$_i$)

Furthermore, the referent of '*zibun*' can be pragmatically provided. In addition to the intrasentential binding described above, '*zibun*' in (2a), (2c), (3) and (4) can be interpreted as referring to the speaker. This point may be made clearer if we look at sentence (5) below, which contains no possible antecedents for '*zibun*'.

(5) Zibun–wa   Tokyo–de   umaremasita.
       SELF–TOP   in   born
     (I was born in Tokyo.)

Looking at these examples, it seems fair to say that no purely syntactic account can fully explain all of the usages of the Japanese long-distance reflexive '*zibun*'.

2.2   Interaction Between '*zibun*' and Perspectivity

In contrast to the syntactic accounts discussed in the previous subsection, it has also been observed that the Japanese long-distance reflexive '*zibun*' shows a certain pattern of interactions with perspectivity sensitive expressions (Kuno and Kaburaki 1977; Kuno 1978, 1987; Kameyama 1984). Individual languages have their own repertoires of perspectivity sensitive expressions. Directional movement verbs and ownership transfer verbs are probably most common across languages. In addition to these, there is a group of auxiliary verbs in Japanese whose sole function it is to present the locus of the speaker's point of view.

In (6), the lexical item '*iku*' (go)[3] signals that the speaker's point of view is placed nearer than any other **NP** referent to the person at the source of the movement, which is realized as the subject of the sentence, e.g., 'Taro' in (6a). In the limiting case it could mean that the speaker's point of view is placed exactly on Taro. Naturally, the speaker herself has to be given the highest priority in the set of people on which to place the speaker's point of view, and no other person can be nearer to the speaker's point of view than the speaker herself. Sentence (6b), which signals that the speaker's point of view is nearer to Taro than to the speaker herself, violates this requirement, and is judged bad by most Japanese native speakers.[4]

---

[3]'*itta*' is the agglutination of the root of the verb '*iku*' (go) and the past tense marker '*ta*'.

[4]Strictly speaking, the requirement for the speaker priority of the point of view has only to be satisfied at the time of the utterance. This is exemplified by the fact that the only interpretation acceptable for (6b) is the one in which the speaker is not in her place at the time of the utterance.

(6) a. Taro–ga   Hanako–no   tokoro–ni   itta.
          SBJ   GEN   place–GOAL   go
          (Taro went to Hanako's place.)

    *b. Taro–ga   watasi–no   tokoro–ni   itta.
          SBJ   I–GEN   place–GOAL   go
          (Taro went to my place.)

Similarly, the auxiliary verb 'kureru'[5] indicates that the speaker is describing a certain fact, not from a neutral standpoint, but from a standpoint that is closer to the person at a non-subject position, e.g., indirect object (IOBJ) in (7), than to the person at the subject position. In the limiting case it could mean that the speaker's point of view is placed exactly on the person in a non-subject position and the speaker herself is identifying with that person. Due to this information supplied by 'kureru', together with the speaker priority for the point of view, while (7a) is acceptable with the speaker's point of view being placed nearer to the indirect object 'Hanako', than to the subject 'Taro', (7b) is judged bad because the information supplied by 'kureru', that the speaker's point of view is nearer to the indirect object 'Hanako' than to the subject 'watasi' (I), is in conflict with the speaker priority requirement.

(7) a. Taro–ga   Hanako–ni   hon–wo   yonde–kureta.
          SBJ   IOBJ   book–OBJ   read–EMP–IOBJ
          (Taro read a book for Hanako.)

    *b. Watasi–ga Hanako–ni   hon–wo   yonde–kureta.
          I–SBJ   IOBJ   book–OBJ   read–EMP–IOBJ
          (I read a book for Hanako.)

The distribution of 'zibun' is apparently correlated with the use of these perspectivity sensitive expressions. Comparable to the contrast between (6a)/(7a) and (6b)/(7b), the sentences (8a)/(9a) are acceptable, whereas (8b)/(9b) are not.

(8) a. Hanako$_i$–wa   zibun$_i$–ga   Taro–no   tokoro–ni
                 TOP   SELF–SBJ   GEN   place–GOAL
          itta   koto–wo   oboeteiru.
          went   COMP–OBJ remember
          (Hanako$_i$ remembered that self$_i$ went to Taro's place.)

    *b. Hanako$_i$–wa   Taro–ga   zibun$_i$–no   tokoro–ni
                 TOP   SBJ   SELF–GEN   place–GOAL
          itta   koto–wo   oboeteiru.
          went   COMP–OBJ remember
          (Hanako$_i$ remembered that Taro went to self$_i$'s place.)

---

[5] 'kureta' is the agglutination of the root of the auxiliary verb 'kureru' and the past tense marker 'ta'.

(9) a. Hanako$_i$–wa   Taro–ga   zibun$_i$–ni   hon–wo
       TOP   SBJ   SELF–IOBJ   book–OBJ
       yonde–kureta   koto–wo   oboeteiru.
       read–EMP–IOBJ   COMP–OBJ   remember
       (Hanako$_i$ remembered that Taro read a book for self$_i$.)

   *b. Hanako$_i$–wa   zibun$_i$–ga   Taro–ni   hon–wo
       TOP   SELF–SBJ   IOBJ   book–OBJ
       yonde–kureta   koto–wo   oboeteiru.
       read–EMP–IOBJ   COMP–OBJ   remember
       (Hanako$_i$ remembered that self$_i$ read a book for Taro.)

In (8), the directional movement verb '*iku*' requires the speaker's point of view to be placed nearer than any other NP referent to the person at the source of the movement, that is, '*zibun*' in (8a) and Taro in (8b). Similarly, in (9), the use of the auxiliary verb '*kureru*' requires the speaker's point of view to be placed nearer to the indirect object, that is, '*zibun*' in (9a) and Taro in (9b), than to the subject, that is, Taro in (9a) and '*zibun*' in (9b). So, if we assume that there is a discourse role that concerns the person whose perspective the speaker is taking on, and '*zibun*' is to be bound by that discourse role, or at least by an NP whose referent is closest to this discourse role, the acceptability judgments of (8) and (9) could well be explained. These observations apparently suggest that the function of '*zibun*' is to refer to the person who is closest to the speaker's point of view.

If this were actually the case, then '*zibun*' would always have to refer to the speaker whenever '*watasi*' (I) appears in a perspectival sentence, since the speaker herself has the highest priority for the point of view assumed by the speaker. But the sentences below are known to be perfectly acceptable Japanese sentences (Iida and Sells 1988).

(10) Taro$_i$–wa   zibun$_i$–ga   kaita   hon–wo   watasi–ni
      TOP   SELF–SBJ   write   book–OBJ   I–IOBJ
      yonde–kureta.
       read–EMP–IOBJ
      (Taro$_i$ read the book self$_i$ wrote to me.)

(11) Taro$_i$–wa   watasi–ga   zibun$_i$–wo   butta   koto–wo
       TOP   I–SBJ   SELF–OBJ   hit   COMP–OBJ
      oboeteiru.
      remember
      (Taro$_i$ remembers that I hit self$_i$.)

Both in (10) and (11), '*zibun*' is acceptable without referring to the speaker. Notice, in (10), the use of '*zibun*' violates the speaker priority requirement, even though '*kureru*' explicitly marks that the sentence is perspectival. The use of '*kureru*' indicates that the speaker is uttering the sentence from her own perspective ('*watasi*' (I)), whereas '*zibun*' refers successfully to Taro.

These sentences seem to suggest, contrary to the contrast exhibited in sentences (8) and (9), that the use of '*zibun*' may not have any straightforward relationship to the notion of perspectivity. Any account of the use of '*zibun*' has to give a reasonable explanation to these conflicting intuitions for the relationship between perspectivity and '*zibun*'.

The contrast between sentences (8)and (9) on the one hand, and (10) and (11) on the other, tells us that as long as we acknowledge the speaker priority requirement, it cannot be the case that all occurrences of '*zibun*' are bound by a unitary perspectivity role. Kameyama (1984) proposed that '*zibun*' has to be bound either by a subject NP or an NP marked, in her feature system, as [+log], which is specified by predicates of communication, consciousness, and other perspectivity sensitive expressions like '*kureru*'. Although her theory provides us with a set of possible binders of '*zibun*', it does not give any account of why, among possible binders, certain cases are acceptable whereas others are not. Compare (9b) above with (12) below.

(12) Hanako$_i$–wa   zibun$_i$–ga   watasi–ni   hon–wo
   TOP   SELF-SBJ I-IOBJ book-OBJ
  yonde–kureta koto–wo oboeteiru.
  read–EMP-IOBJ COMP-OBJ remember
(Hanako$_i$ remembered that self$_i$ read a book for me.)

The only difference between (9b) and (12) is that whereas 'Taro' is the NP marked [+log] in (9b), '*watasi*' (I) is used instead in (12). But (12) is considerably better than (9b). Her theory does not give any explanation to this difference in acceptability.

Sells 1987 and Iida & Sells 1988 propose three different discourse roles that are relevant to perspectivity related phenomena: SOURCE, one who does a report; SELF, one whose mind is being reported; and PIVOT, one from whose point of view, in the physical sense, the report is being made. They then claim that '*zibun*' is bound by the PIVOT role. Although their distinction correctly dissects the intermingled intuitions we have of the notion of perspectivity, their PIVOT binding condition for '*zibun*' is incorrect. The point of view in the physical sense, their PIVOT, can be different from '*zibun*' referent. In the following sentence, '*migi*' (right) can be interpreted with respect to Hanako's point of view even though '*zibun*' refers to Taro.

(13) Hanako–ga   zibun$_i$–no   nimotu–wo   tukue–no
   SBJ   SELF-GEN baggage-OBJ desk-GEN
  migi–ni   oita koto–wo Taro$_i$–wa
  right–to put COMP-OBJ TOP
  sira–nakatta.
  know–NEG
(Taro$_i$ did not know that Hanako$_j$ put self$_i$'s baggage onto the right$_j$ of the desk.)

Kuno (1978, 1987) introduces the notion of a domain to explain interaction of *'zibun'* and *'watasi'*. He stipulates that a perspectivity requirement has to be observed only within a certain syntactically specified domain. Although this explanation is applicable to the sentences like (10), he has to stipulate a different rule for sentences like (11) which have psychological predicates.

To summarize the discussion, although the usage of *'zibun'* and the speaker's perspective interact with each other, *'zibun'* cannot be explained solely in terms of the notion of binding by a discourse role for perspectivity. Examination of *'zibun'* sentences and previous accounts given of them seems to suggest that we need a richer structure for the notion of perspectivity.

3 Requirements for a Theory of Perspectivity

Perspectivity comes from our situatedness within environments. Our situatedness itself is independent of our ability to use language. Our perspectival recognition of environments must primarily be reflected in the structure and organization of our representations. Hence, before we start talking about language, we have to think about the situatedness of our representation. Our perspectival representation of the environment provides us with the basis to use expressions of a language that are sensitive to perspectivity. And perspectivity in our representation must then be reflected not only in our day-to-day use of the language but also in the system of our language itself.

Missing arguments and transferability are the two important characteristics of the perspectivity of our representation.

Missing Arguments: An agent's perspectival recognition of facts amounts to the omission of certain arguments for relations in them. To put it differently, in a perspectival representation an agent is adopting argument-reduced relations. Think of the relation LEFT-OF. My coffee cup being left of my computer terminal is actually a fact consisting of the three-place relation LEFT-OF$_3$, my coffee cup, my computer terminal, and myself; my coffee cup is left of my computer terminal seen from me. But I do not and need not be aware of the third argument, myself, when I move my left hand to reach for the cup. This argument is missing in my representation. I am, in that case, conceiving of this fact as if it consisted of the two-place relation LEFT-OF$_2$, my coffee cup, and the terminal.

Transferability: Not only can we recognize our environment from our own points of view, we can take on others' perspectives and conceive of what the environment might look like if we were them. This ability of assuming other agent's perspective is one of the central functions that differentiates perspectivity from self-identity.[6]

When we have a theory of perspectival representation, we will then be able to proceed to consider the relationship between our perspectival representation and expressions used in utterances. In addition to the fact that in perspectival utterances the person whose perspective the speaker is assuming is often omitted and made implicit in expressions uttered, each language has a set of perspectivity sensitive expressions. The theory of perspectivity could then give an account of the usage of these expressions in terms of interaction between perspectival representation of the speaker and the expression used in utterances. The usage of 'zibun' must be discussed in this context.

4 Structure of Perspectivity

The apparent conflict in usages of 'zibun' and perspectivity we saw in Section 2 suggests that the notion of perspectivity needs clarification. We will propose below a model for perspectivity which consists of two different notions, which we call *indexical perspectivity* and *inferential perspectivity*.

4.1 Indexical Perspectivity

The first constituent of perspectivity is related to the situatedness of agents in their surrounding environments. An agent is located at a certain point in space-time, and she conceives of her environment from her location. She is not an objective observer from outside, but an embedded agent striving for her own interest. So it is natural that her conception of the world reflects her situatedness in the world, that is, her conception of the world should primarily be relative to herself. It should consist of facts like whether an object is near to or far from her, to the left or to the right of another seen by her, or whether an event is in the past or in the future relative to her current *now*, rather than of facts of absolute nature like whether two objects are near to or far from each other, whether one object is located to the east or to the west of another, or whether one event occurs earlier or later than another. Moreover, we can also think of an agent being located at a certain point in a space of personal relationship. In this space, the agent's conception must again primarily be relative to herself. So a person is intimate with, familiar with, or a stranger to the agent herself. And somebody is high or low, in terms of the social status, relative to the agent. The agent plays the particular role of the indexical center, the center of the coordinates in her conception of the world, both physical and personal. All

---

[6]The goal of perspective transfer is not necessarily restricted to animate agents. For objects that have canonical and salient orientations such as a car or a house, missing arguments of 'left of the car', 'in front of the house' can be filled with those objects.

perceptual information converges on the agent, and all actions originate from the agent.

Granted that the primary conception of her environment is agent-relative or indexical in nature, this does not necessarily mean that the agent always assumes herself as the center of the coordinates. We all know that we sometimes can take on another person's perspective and imagine what the world would look like. This is manifested in many of our utterances like 'Put your luggage to the left of the chair', or 'John saw the building across the street'. An intelligent agent can move the locus of indexical center from its actual value, the agent herself, to a hypothetical position in the space.

Let us define the indexical perspective of an agent as the particular point relative to which the agent conceives of her surrounding environment. It has several components: spatial location, time, and personal relationship. Naturally, an agent is, in most cases, assuming herself, e.g., her spatial location, her current time, and her current person, as her own indexical perspective.[7] But she could from time to time assume, for some or all of its components, other points as her indexical perspective.

An agent representing a certain state in the outside world is in a mental state that is in some sense structurally isomorphic to the objects and states represented. Under a situation semantical framework (Barwise and Perry 1983), an agent A's believing, for example, that a block U is on another block V is a situation classified by the following state of affairs (SOA).

$$\langle\!\langle \mathtt{Bel}, \mathtt{A}, [\dot{s}|\dot{s} \models \langle\!\langle \mathtt{on}, \dot{x}, \dot{y}\rangle\!\rangle] \rangle\!\rangle \wedge \langle\!\langle \mathtt{of}, \dot{x}, \mathtt{U}\rangle\!\rangle \wedge \langle\!\langle \mathtt{of}, \dot{y}, \mathtt{V}\rangle\!\rangle$$

A's mental state itself is classified by a parametric type of situation, $[\dot{s}|\dot{s} \models \langle\!\langle \mathtt{on}, \dot{x}, \dot{y}\rangle\!\rangle]$. Parameters $\dot{x}$ and $\dot{y}$ correspond respectively to A's concepts of blocks U and V. The second and the third conjuncts in the above formula show that these two concepts are anchored to the real objects U and V, and guarantees that A's mental state is really a representation of the state of the world. Agent A's reasoning is the process of manipulating her concepts. She need not and cannot get hold of facts about what objects her concepts are anchored to in her reasoning processes.

The identity of a concept is established by what functional role it plays internally in the agent's reasoning processes, which is mostly determined by what facts the agent associates with it. Two concepts playing different functional roles have to be distinguished, even if they share a referent in the external world. This is manifested in examples of paradoxical beliefs, e.g., beliefs of an ignorant student about Cicero and Tully, where an agent has apparently incoherent beliefs about one and the same object (Barwise and Perry 1983).

---

[7]This does not necessary imply that she knows what her spatial location, etc., is in absolute terms.

The individuation of concepts does not always have to be finer than the individuation of their corresponding external objects. Think of the concept of self, i. Each agent has her own self concept. Since each of them is anchored to its holder by its nature, the referent of the self concept is different from agent to agent. But its function as the self concept, namely the recipient of perceptual information and the originator of actions, stays the same irrespective of its holders. We will use the same parameter i for the self concept to indicate this common functional role. But the referent of this concept depends on who holds this concept.

We observed that, in an indexically perspectival representation of an environmental state, the entity relative to which the state is represented, typically the agent herself, is omitted and functions as a missing argument. We proposed elsewhere (Katagiri 1989) to represent this kind of indexicality in representation by incorporating a complex relation that has a reduced number of arguments to classify the agent's perspectival mental states. Consider that the block U, this time, is located to the left of another block V seen from the agent A. A's perspectival recognition of this situation can be classified by the SOA below, which incorporates a two-place complex relation $\text{LEFT-OF}_{p\dot{o}v}$ constructed out of the three-place relation LEFT-OF.

$$\langle\!\langle \text{Bel}, \text{A}, [\dot{s}|\dot{s} \models \langle\!\langle \text{LEFT-OF}_{p\dot{o}v}, \dot{x}, \dot{y} \rangle\!\rangle \wedge \langle\!\langle =, p\dot{o}v, i \rangle\!\rangle] \rangle\!\rangle$$
$$\wedge \langle\!\langle \text{of}, \dot{x}, \text{U} \rangle\!\rangle \wedge \langle\!\langle \text{of}, \dot{y}, \text{V} \rangle\!\rangle$$

where the relation $\text{LEFT-OF}_{p\dot{o}v}$ is a complex relation,

$$[\dot{x}, \dot{y} | \langle\!\langle \text{LEFT-OF}, \dot{x}, \dot{y}, p\dot{o}v \rangle\!\rangle].$$

The SOA $\langle\!\langle =, p\dot{o}v, i \rangle\!\rangle$ in A's belief shows that she is taking on her own indexical perspective. Since LEFT-OF is a spatial relation, the component of indexical perspective in question is its spatial location. Hereafter, we will use $p\dot{o}v$ for the spatial location component, and $e\dot{m}p$ for the personal relationship component.[8] Since we introduced a set of parameters, $\{p\dot{o}v, e\dot{m}p\}$, for indexical perspectivity, we can represent cases where the agent is taking on other agent's perspective by having the SOA of the form $\langle\!\langle =, p\dot{o}v, \dot{a} \rangle\!\rangle$ for $\dot{a} \neq i$. The point of this representation is that the use of two-place complex relation $\text{LEFT-OF}_{p\dot{o}v}$ is not merely for notational convenience; the relation itself has significance in actual reasoning processes within A's perspectival mental states.

4.2 Inferential Perspectivity

Mental states can represent not only our own physical and interpersonal environments but also other agents and the way other agents conceive of their surrounding environments. Sometimes, an agent comes to realize that there are discrepancies between what she takes to hold of a state/event in

---

[8] The name $e\dot{m}p$ is from the term empathy (Kuno and Kaburaki 1977; Kuno 1978, 1987). We will not discuss problems related to the time component in this paper.

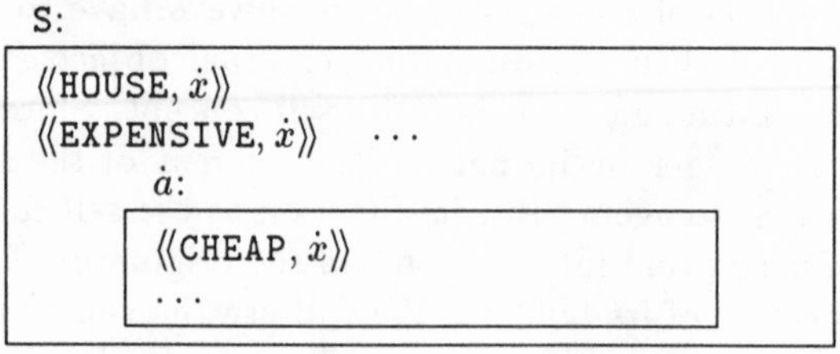

S:

$\langle\!\langle\text{HOUSE}, \dot{x}\rangle\!\rangle$
$\langle\!\langle\text{EXPENSIVE}, \dot{x}\rangle\!\rangle$ $\cdots$

$\dot{a}$:

$\langle\!\langle\text{CHEAP}, \dot{x}\rangle\!\rangle$
$\cdots$

Figure 1 Inferential perspective of speaker S and agent A

the world and what other agents take to hold of the same state/event. You may find that your friend estimates a certain house in Tokyo as cheap, while you yourself think it is quite expensive. Or you may be surprised to find that your colleague does not know the time of the next group meeting. It is often useful for an agent to have information on how other agents conceive of their environments, since she could then use the information to obtain explanations of their past behaviors and predictions of their subsequent behaviors. In reasoning about other agents' behaviors and reasoning processes, an agent can utilize both information she herself owns and information that she takes to belong to other agents. Moreover, as is shown in many of the sentences discussed in Section 2, utterances often describe actions and mental states of agents other than the speaker. In these utterances, we can think that each of the clauses and descriptions is based either on the information held by the speaker herself, or on what she takes to be the information held by the agent. In narrative style compositions, for example, the author often assumes that the information is held by the protagonist of the narrative.

Let us define the inferential perspective of a piece of information as the person whose information the agent takes that to be. The inferring agent or the speaker can take either her own inferential perspective or the other agent's inferential perspective for each piece of information. The notion of inferential perspective is primarily concerned with an agent's ability to simulate other agents' reasoning processes and to utilize that simulation in constructing her utterances.

Under the situation semantical formulation described above, the essential constituent determining an agent's mental state is the type of situation classifying the mental state, e.g., the second argument of the Bel SOA. And the type of situation in turn is determined by the set of parametric SOAs that are constituents of that type. So, we take the set of parametric SOAs as representatives of the agent's mental state.

The difference in inferential perspective of a certain piece of information can then be represented as whether the corresponding SOA resides in the speaker S's space or in the agent A's space embedded inside S's space. An example of this difference is depicted in Figure 1. qThe speaker S has two sets of SOAs, one for her own conception of the environment, and another for (her conception of) the other agent A's conception of the environment. SOAs at the top level comprise S's inferential perspective, whereas the SOAs in the embedded box constitute the agent A's inferential perspective (within S). We used *à* rather than A for the internal box to indicate that it includes, not the information that the agent A actually has, but the information which S ascribes to the agent A.

4.3 Utterance Production and a Relational Theory of Meaning

We can think that there is a certain set of beliefs of a speaker behind an utterance. Every utterance has to be caused by an intention to make it, together with a set of beliefs corresponding to the content. In a more serious model of language production, we have to take into account the fact that the speaker actually chooses an expression in uttering a sentence based on her conception of what is mutually believed by both the speaker and the hearer (Appelt 1985, Cohen and Perrault 1979). But in this paper we will simply ignore the mutual belief aspect involved in language production, and simply assume that the speaker S's utterance production is based on her beliefs about what to say and her intention to say it.

When the sentence uttered is one describing another agent's actions and states, the notion of inferential perspective in the speaker's belief structure becomes particularly important. The speaker has the choice of inferential perspective for each of the descriptions and for each of the clauses comprising the sentence. For example, the belief configuration depicted in Figure 1 can be a consistent set of beliefs of a speaker when she utters the following sentence.

(14) Taro–wa   ano   kookana   ie–wo   yasui   to   itta.
     TOP   that expensive house–**OBJ** cheap **COMP** say
     (Taro said that that expensive house is cheap.)

The relational theory of meaning pictures the meaning of a sentence as a constraint between a discourse situation, which is a situation of a certain person issuing the sentence in a certain space-time location, and the described proposition, e.g., the content of the utterance (Barwise and Perry 1983). The beliefs of the speaker behind an utterance should have a place in a discourse situation. We need not think of them as part of the content of the utterance. The task of an individual upon hearing an utterance is not necessarily limited to finding what its content is. She may obtain additional information via meaning constraints about the discourse situation. A piece of information about the configuration of the speakers' beliefs is one such example. This *inverse* information is what makes utterances of sentences like (14) meaningful to both the speaker and the hearer.

4.4   Structural Constraints on Perspectivity

There are several constraints that perspectivity structure has to satisfy. We can distinguish two types of constraints among them. The first type of constraint is that which must be strictly observed for a perspectival mental state to be a valid mental state. The second type only specifies a default preference among valid alternative structures.

There are three constraints that have to be observed by all perspectival mental states. They are (a) asymmetry in accessibility of concepts in embedded mental states, (b) uniqueness of the indexical perspective, and (c) priority of self as the indexical perspective. We assume here only one constraint, the agent awareness default, which specifies the default preference among alternatives. This constraint concerns the choice of inferential perspective for an utterance.

Accessibility of Concepts in Embedded Mental States

In a nested structure of an agent's mental state, one structure that is embedded inside another corresponds to the agent's beliefs about another agent's beliefs. Since the embedded structure itself is also a part of the beliefs of the outer agent, even though she herself does not believe the very same thing as the other agent, she has to have at least some belief about what the other agent's belief is based on. But we cannot conversely assume that for each piece of an agent's belief, she believes that the other agent also has some corresponding beliefs.

More precisely stated: every concept in an embedded inferential perspective has a counterpart in its embedding inferential perspective and hence is available for the reasoning process in the outer inferential perspective. But concepts in an inferential perspective may not have their counterparts in an inferential perspective embedded in it, hence they are not necessarily available for the reasoning process in the inner inferential perspective.

An important consequence of this constraint is that in a case where a speaker S utter a sentence describing another agent A's actions and states, while S has always concepts of both the speaker herself and the agent, the agent A may not have a concept for the speaker S.

Uniqueness of the Indexical Perspective

The indexical perspective of an agent has to be unique at a time in each inferential perspective. This constraint captures the fact that the point relative to which environmental states are represented in an agent stays the same among a set of beliefs for a certain period of time. Since the indexical perspective has spatial and personal components, it can have different values for each of the components.

Priority of Self as the Indexical Perspective

One of the important relations in the indexically perspectival representation is the relation between two objects, $\text{CLOSER}_{\dot{p}\dot{o}v}$, that holds when one object is located closer to the indexical perspective $\dot{p}\dot{o}v$ than another object. There is also a similar relation for the parameter $e\dot{m}p$. We will see that many perspectivity sensitive expressions carry information about the structure of the speaker's beliefs that is classified in terms of these relations.

By definition, the indexical perspective has to be the closest to itself.

> In all of the inferential perspectives, for any $\dot{x}$, $\langle\!\langle \text{CLOSER}_{\dot{p}\dot{o}v}, \dot{x}, \dot{p}\dot{o}v \rangle\!\rangle$ does not hold; and the same for $e\dot{m}p$.

Since the speaker or the inferring agent herself has the highest priority for the indexical perspective, we additionally assume the following.

> In all of the inferential perspectives, for any $\dot{x}$, $\langle\!\langle \text{CLOSER}_{\dot{p}\dot{o}v}, \dot{x}, i \rangle\!\rangle$ does not hold; and the same for $e\dot{m}p$.

This implies that when i appears in an inferential perspective of beliefs for an utterance, both $\dot{p}\dot{o}v$ and $e\dot{m}p$ have to be equal to i in that inferential perspective.

Agent Awareness Default

When uttering a sentence that describes the actions and states of an agent, the speaker adopts the inferential perspective of that agent by default.

Agents usually perform actions consciously. They are conscious of the fact that they will perform, are performing, and have performed the actions. And they are aware of facts that held before, have been held throughout, and were established by the actions. Hence it is natural to have as a default constraint that, in an utterance reporting an agent's behavior, the inferential perspective for descriptions and clauses is usually taken to be that of the agent.

5 Perspectivity and '*zibun*'

5.1 Coreference Rule for '*zibun*'

Having developed the underlying theory of perspectivity, we can now state the hypothesis concerning the usage of '*zibun*' in the form of a coreference rule. Note that the coreference rule below is not itself directly related to the notion of perspectivity.

Coreference Rule for '*zibun*'

The use of '*zibun*' is based on the identity of the referent of '*zibun*' to the semantic agent of an action or to the semantic experiencer of a mental state described in the sentence.[9]

---

[9]By "semantic" I mean here that we take these case roles as relations at the level of semantic representation, which are relatively independent of their surface syntactic realizations. Semantic roles lexically assigned by verbs and nouns are the most typical

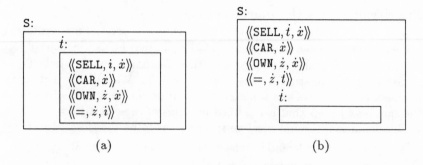

Figure 2 Two possible readings for (16)

The point of the coreference rule above is that the identity of the referent of '*zibun*' may be established either in the speaker's inferential perspective or in the agent's inferential perspective. Although by the agent awareness default, the identity should be primarily established in the agent's inferential perspective by default, in a special circumstances where the default could be defeated, the identity judgment can be strictly from the speaker's inferential perspective. The following sentence with '*zibun*' referring to Taro can be used without any problem to describe Taro's amnesia story. Since Taro, being amnesiac, does not have the knowledge of his having been a baseball player, the agent awareness default has to be defeated and the hearer should interpret the utterance by assuming that the identity of '*zibun*' with Taro is from the speaker's inferential perspective.

(15) Taro–wa zibun–ga yakyuusensyu datta koto–wo
   TOP SELF–SBJ baseball-player was COMP–OBJ
   sira nai.
   know NEG
   (Taro$_i$ does not know that self$_i$ was a baseball player.)

5.2 Agent Awareness Default and Priority of the 'de se' Reading

Kuno 1973 notes that in addition to the usual coreference function as a pronoun, the use of '*zibun*' often implies that the agent referred to by the antecedent NP is actually aware that the referent of '*zibun*' is herself. An utterance of the sentence below strongly suggests that Taro knowingly sold his own car, i.e., he knew that the car he sold was his own car, rather than that Taro happened to have sold his car without the knowledge of its identity.

---

cases. But examination of several borderline sentences seems to suggest that there might be some other cases where these semantic roles are inferentially derived. We will discuss some related phenomena in a later section, but determining exactly how and what roles are inferentially derived needs further study.

(16) Taro$_i$-wa   zibun$_i$-no   kuruma-wo   utta.
      TOP   SELF-GEN   car-OBJ   sell
(Taro sold his car.)

This dominance of what is known as a *de se* reading (Castañeda 1968, Lewis 1979) can also be explained by our agent awareness default. Figure 2 shows two possible readings for (16). The agent awareness default dictates that the (a) reading should be the default interpretation, where the speaker believes that Taro knows the identity of '*zibun*' z with his self i.

5.3   Defeating the Default

Given the constraint on indexical and inferential perspectives, and the coreference rule for '*zibun*', we can give an explanation of the possibility of apparent conflict between the usage of '*zibun*' and perspectivity phenomena noted in Section 2. The crux of the matter is the default nature of the agent awareness constraint. When the agent awareness constraint is in force, identity of '*zibun*' with semantic agent/experiencer is established in the agent/experiencer's inferential perspective. Since the semantic agent/experiencer is the same as the inferential perspective, '*zibun*' ends up referring to the inferential perspective, which is also usually equal to indexical perspective. But once this default is defeated, identity of '*zibun*' and agent/experiencer would be established in the speaker's inferential perspective, and '*zibun*' reference could be independent from perspectives.

Before going into the details of defeating of the agent awareness default, we will first give characterizations of some of the perspectivity sensitive expressions. Directional movement verbs are used when the speaker's indexical perspective in spatial location is either located closer to the source or to the goal of the movement. For example, the use of Japanese verb '*iku*' (go) implies that the speaker perceives the event from a point of view in spatial location which is closer to the source than to the goal of the movement:

$$\langle\!\langle \text{CLOSER}_{\dot{p}\dot{o}v}, \dot{s}, \dot{g} \rangle\!\rangle$$

where $\dot{s}$ and $\dot{g}$ respectively stand for the source and the goal of the movement.

The perspectival spatial relation expressions '*migi*' (right), '*hidari*' (left), and others simply do not express reference points, and they have to be interpreted relative to the spatial location component of the indexical perspective.

On the other hand, the Japanese auxiliary '*kureru*' indicates that the indexical perspective in personal space is closer to one of the non-subject NP referents than to the subject NP referent within the clause to which the auxiliary is attached:

$$\langle\!\langle \text{CLOSER}_{e\dot{m}p}, \dot{o}, \dot{s} \rangle\!\rangle$$

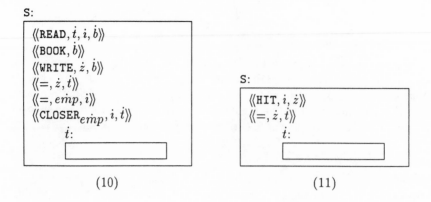

Figure 3 Mental states behind utterances of (10) and (11).

where $\dot{o}$ stands for one of the non-subject NP referent, and $\dot{s}$ stands for the subject NP referent.

Although elucidation of exactly what and how the agent awareness default is to be defeated requires further investigation, we will discuss here several defeating factors and their effects on the use of '*zibun*'. The following three can be counted as possible defeaters of the default.

- Appearance of the speaker; or the use of the first of pronoun '*watasi*'.
- Negation of the existence of mental states.
- Use of the perspectivity sensitive auxiliary '*kureru*'.

The constraint on concept accessibility tells us that the concept for the speaker is not always available in the agent's inferential perspective. Hence, utterances of a sentence that refers to the speaker may well be from the inferential perspective of the speaker herself, thus defeating the agent awareness default. The nonexistence of a mental state, either explicitly stated or contextually established, may also defeat the default, since it implicates that the content of the mental state is not from the agent's but from the speaker's inferential perspective. The use of '*kureru*' also functions as a defeater when the semantic agent occupies the subject NP, which is usually the case, since the perspectivity requirement imposed by '*kureru*', that is, a non-subject NP is closer to the personal indexical perspective than the subject NP, cannot be satisfied in the agent's inferential perspective.

We can now give explanations of the apparently conflicting interactions between perspectivity and '*zibun*' we saw in Section 2. In both sentences (10) and (11), the use of '*watasi*' signals the defeat of the agent awareness default, and the hearer is to interpret them in the speaker's inferential perspective, especially the identity of '*zibun*' with Taro, who is the agent of reading the book in (10), and the experiencer of remembering in (11),

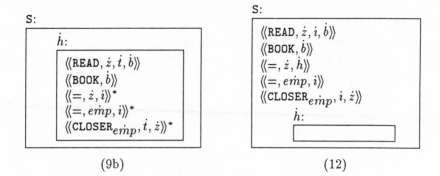

Figure 4 Perspectival mental states behind utterances
of *(9b) and (12).

has to be ascribed to the speaker's own beliefs. Under this interpretation both sentences are acceptable without any problem. Note that in (10), the use of '*kureru*' also contributes to the defeat of the agent awareness default. The speaker's belief structures behind the utterances of these sentences are depicted in Figure 3.

The indexical perspective can have different values for each component. This combined with the default defeat force of '*kureru*' explains why the following sentence (17) is acceptable from Taro's perspective in the sense of spatial location, and Hanako's perspective in the sense of personal relations: $pov = t$, $emp = i$, and Hanako is closer to emp than Taro.

(17)   Taro–wa   hasira–no   migi–no   nimotu–wo
       TOP   pillar–GEN   right–GEN   baggage–OBJ
       Hanako–ni   totte–kureta.
       IOBJ   hand–EMP-IOBJ
       (Taro$_i$ handed the baggage which was to the right$_i$ of the pillar
       to Hanako.)

The notion of the agent awareness default and its defeat can also give us an account for why the small change in the choice of words between (9b) and (12) makes a difference in acceptability. The speaker's belief states behind utterances of these sentences are shown in Figure 4. The use of '*oboeteiru*' (remember) in (9b) enforces the agent awareness default, and the complement clause, what is remembered, is taken by default to be within the agent Hanako's inferential perspective.[10] But once Hanako's

---

[10] Since '*kureru*' is embedded in the complement clause of '*oboeteiru*' (remember), it does not have the force of making the speaker as the inferential perspective for the clause. It only defeats the default at that level, preventing the agent of reading from becoming the inferential perspective. But this defeat is vacuous since the agent of reading and the experiencer of remembering are both Hanako in this sentence.

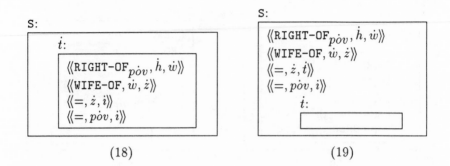

(18)   (19)

Figure 5 Negation as a defeater of the agent awareness default.

inferential perspective is chosen, identity of '*zibun*' $\dot{z}$ with Hanako herself i conflicts with the configuration of the personal relationship space specified by the use of '*kureru*', since they violate the condition that emp has to be CLOSER$_{emp}$ than any other concepts. Conflicting SOAs are indicated by * in the figure. On the other hand, in (12), the use of '*watasi*' works as a defeat for the agent awareness default, and the inferential perspective for the complement clause can be the speaker's. Within the speaker's perspective, identity of '*zibun*' $\dot{z}$ with Hanako h does not cause any conflict with the requirement on indexical perspective imposed by '*kureru*', and the sentence becomes acceptable.

The subtlety of the interaction of agent awareness default and perspectivity may be seen by the following pair of sentences.

(18) Taro$_i$–wa   Hanako–ga   zibun$_i$–no   tuma–no   migi–ni
      TOP   SBJ   SELF–GEN   wife–GEN   right–to
      iru   noni   kigatuita.
      be   COMP   notice
      (Taro$_i$ noticed that Hanako was to the right of self$_i$'s wife.)

(19) Taro–wa   Hanako–ga   zibun–no   tuma–no   migi–ni
      TOP   SBJ   SELF–GEN   wife–GEN   right–to
      iru   noni   kigatuitei–nai.
      be   COMP   notice–NEG
      (Taro$_i$ has not noticed that Hanako was to the right of self$_i$'s wife.)

The corresponding mental states of the speaker are shown in Figure 5. In (18), the relation RIGHT-OF$_{p\dot{o}v}$ is usually interpreted from Taro's point of view. At least, it does not have the interpretation from the point of view of the speaker. This is because the use of '*kigatuita*' (noticed) in (18) enforces the agent awareness default, and the complement clause, what was noticed, is taken to be in Taro's inferential perspective. Since the concept for the speaker is not necessarily available in Taro's inferential perspective, the indexical perspective *pòv* may not be equal to the speaker. In contrast to this, the negation of noticing in (19) can defeat the agent awareness default, and consequently the RIGHT-OF$_{pòv}$ of (19) can additionally have an interpretation from the point of view of the speaker.[11]

5.4 Inferential Perspective as an Experiencer

As noted in Section 2, although sentence (4), which has been a representative example against syntactic subject binding account for '*zibun*', becomes in our model an example of '*zibun*' coreference with an experiencer role lexically specified by the psychological predicate '*nayamu*' (annoy), there are several similar '*zibun*' sentences in which it looks somewhat difficult to find corresponding lexically specified experiencer roles. Look at the following sentences.[12]

(20) Hanako–ga   zibun$_i$–wo   hihansita   koto–ga   Taro$_i$–wo
       SBJ   SELF–OBJ   criticize   COMP–SBJ   OBJ
       zetuboo–e   oiyatta.
       despair–GOAL drive
       (That Hanako criticized self$_i$ drove Taro$_i$ into despair.)

(21) Uwayaku–no   taido–ga   Taro$_i$–ni   zibun$_i$–no
       Boss–GEN   behavior–SBJ   IOBJ   SELF–GEN
       kangae–ga   matigatte ita   koto–wo osieta.
       idea–SBJ wrong   be   COMP–OBJ teach
       (His boss$_i$'s behavior taught Taro$_i$ that self$_i$'s idea was wrong.)

(22) Zibun$_i$–no   hon–wo syuppansita   syuppansya–kara
       SELF–GEN   book–OBJ publish   publisher–from
       kyou   Taro$_i$–ni   kozutumi–ga   todoita.
       today   IOBJ   parcel–SBJ   reach
       (A parcel reached Taro$_i$ today from the publisher which published self$_i$'s book.)

With the coreference relation for '*zibun*' indicated, it becomes progressively difficult to find corresponding experiencer roles in these sentences. Predicates of these sentences '*oiyaru*' (drive), '*osieru*' (teach), and '*todoku*' (reach) themselves do not lexically subcategorize arguments for experiencers, although it might be possible to argue for (20) that the experiencer role of '*zetuboo*' (despair) is somehow transferred to the entire predicate,

---

[11]When we replace '*zibun*-no tuma' with '*zibun*', the resulting sentences, both affirmative and negative, seem to show stronger preference toward the interpretation of RIGHT-OF$_{pòv}$ from Taro's point of view. This could partly be because, as we noted in footnote 6, when we talk of an object which has its own salient orientation, we often take on the point of view of the object itself.

[12]Sentences (20) and (21) are from McCawley 1976. This type of sentence was originally noted by Kuroda and Kuno, respectively. (22) is from Momoi 1985.

and similarly for (21) that Taro is implicitly playing an experiencer role, since teaching implies learning.

A promising way out of this might be to think that an inferential perspective can work as a kind of experiencer role for belief SOAs in that inferential perspective even though it is not lexically specified as such, and that descriptions containing 'zibun' in the sentences above are all within the agent Taro's inferential perspective. Since by definition SOAs in an inferential perspective are beliefs of the corresponding agent, it would be natural to assume that inferential perspective also functions as an experiencer for these SOAs. For the second point, we can note that sentences (20)–(22) all strongly suggest that Taro himself is recognizing the states of affairs described in the phrases containing 'zibun', and it is virtually impossible to think of a context in which this does not hold.

Further evidence for an inferential perspective functioning as an experiencer role could be found in the first pronoun usages of 'azibun' exemplified in the sentence (5) in Section 2. In (5), 'zibun' refers to the speaker, which is the inferential perspective for the entire sentence, even though the predicate does not specify the speaker as an experiencer.

6 Conclusions

We proposed our theory of perspectivity as a basis for the theory of situated agents. Situatedness has two aspects; agents are situated in their physical-personal environments, but they can also infer how other agents are situated in their respective environments. These two aspects have repercussions in the organization of the representation they use in inference. An agent can exploit the environment as an extension of its representational medium and put as much information as possible into the environment rather than into her own representation. An agent can also use her own representation in reasoning about reasoning performed by other agents. Our notions of indexical perspective and inferential perspective, together with constraints on the interaction between the two, capture these two aspects of situatedness.

Based on the theory of perspectivity, together with coreference rule for 'zibun', we argued that the use of the Japanese long-distance reflexive 'zibun' is not directly related to perspectivity, and gave an alternative explanation for the interaction of 'zibun' and perspectivity. We showed that the interaction of 'zibun' and perspectivity can be explained in terms of an independently motivated preference constraint, the agent awareness default, which applies to utterances in general. One notable point of the account we gave of the use of 'zibun' is that, although simple, the account is in the form of a process theory, which explains the usage of 'zibun' in terms of the structure of underlying representation and the mechanism of language production. We think that this type of theory has far wider potential, compared with purely syntactic approach conventional in linguistics, for explaining *uses* of linguistic expressions.

References

Appelt, D. E. 1985. *Planning English Sentences.* Cambridge University Press.

Barwise, J., and J. Perry. 1983. *Situations and Attitudes.* Cambridge, MA: MIT Press.

Castañeda, H.-N. 1968. On the Logic of Attributions of Self-knowledge to Others. *The Journal of Philosophy* 65:439–456.

Cohen, P. R., and C. R. Perrault. 1979. Elements of a Plan-based Theory of Speech Acts. *Cognitive Science* 3:177–212.

Gunji, T. 1987. *Japanese Phrase Structure Grammar.* Dordrecht: Reidel.

Iida, M., and P. Sells. 1988. Discourse Factors in the Binding of Zibun. In *Papers from the Second International Workshop on Japanese Syntax*, ed. W. J. Poser, 23–46. Stanford: CSLI Publications.

Jackendoff, R. 1972. *Semantic Interpretation in Generative Grammar.* Cambridge, MA: MIT Press.

Kameyama, M. 1984. Subjunctive/logophoric Bound Anaphora *zibun. Chicago Linguistic Society* 20:228–238.

Katagiri, Y. 1989. Semantics of Perspectival Utterances. In *Proceedings of the Eleventh International Joint Conference on Artificial Intelligence*, 1474–1479. Morgan Kaufman.

Kuno, S. 1973. *The Structure of the Japanese Language.* MIT Press.

Kuno, S. 1978. *Danwa-no Bonpou (Grammar of Discourse).* Taishu-kan.

Kuno, S. 1987. *Functional Syntax: Anaphora, Discourse and Empathy.* The University of Chicago Press.

Kuno, S., and E. Kaburaki. 1977. Empathy and Syntax. *Linguistic Inquiry* 8:627–672.

Lewis, D. K. 1979. Attitudes *de dicto* and *de se. The Philosophical Review* 88:513–543.

McCawley, N. A. 1976. Reflexivization: a Transformational Approach. In *Syntax and Semantics 5*, ed. M. Shibatani, 51–116. New York: Academic Press.

Momoi, K. 1985. Semantic Roles, Variation, and the Japanese Reflexive. In *University of Chicago Working Papers in Linguistics*, 73–92. University of Chicago.

Pollard, C., and I. A. Sag. 1990. Anaphora in English and the Scope of Binding Theory. To appear.

Sells, P. 1987. Aspects of Logophoricity. *Linguistics Inquiry* 18:445–479.

19

A Formalization of Metaphor Understanding in Situation Semantics

TATSUNORI MORI AND HIROSHI NAKAGAWA

1 Introduction

Metaphor—a rhetorical device—is used not only in literary writings, but also in many conversations in our everyday life (see Lakoff and Johnson 1980, Lakoff 1987b). Therefore, metaphor understanding is one of the most important themes which we must deal with to have a sophisticated natural language understanding system. The metaphor understanding process has been discussed from various points of view by a number of researchers (see Tanaka et al. 1989, Indurkhya 1987, Gentner et al. 1987, Ortony and Fainsilber 1987, Plantinga 1987, Lakoff 1987a, Nunberg 1987, Holyoak 1989).

It is the essence of metaphors that one thing or idea (we will call it α) is expressed by means of something else (β). For example, in a metaphorical phrase "A man like a wolf", "a man" corresponds to α and "a wolf" corresponds to β. In the rest of this paper, we will use the term *target* (or *target domain*) to refer to a thing α and *source(source domain)* to refer to β. According to the interaction theory of metaphors proposed by Black, an "implicative complex", which is a set of inferences that can be drawn about a domain, is associated with the domain. A metaphorical expression works by projecting an implicative complex of a source domain upon a target domain (Indurkhya 1987). There are a number of studies of the metaphor understanding based on this theory, in which such projections, or correspondences, are found by an analogical mapping (Gentner et al. 1987, Holyoak 1989, Indurkhya 1987). Most of these studies, however, deal only with understanding an isolated metaphorical sentence, and regard the metaphor understanding process simply as establish-

Situation Theory and Its Applications, vol. 2.
Jon Barwise, Jean Mark Gawron, Gordon Plotkin, and Syun Tutiya, eds.
Copyright © 1991, Stanford University.

ing correspondences by some analogical mapping. Indeed the establishment of correspondences is the main part of the metaphor understanding process, but in order to deal with the information obtained from a metaphorical expression in a discourse, it is necessary that the part of semantics which deals with metaphor understanding should harmonize with the rest of semantics which deals with ordinary discourse understanding. There is no research based on such a viewpoint, that is, which refers to the analysis of metaphorical expressions in discourse.

In this paper, in view of this point, we present a new theory which can account for understanding metaphorical expressions in a discourse. It is a typical case of the metaphor understanding in a discourse that the information which the hearer obtains from a metaphorical expression depends on the context in which the expression is uttered. For example, let us consider the following sentence:

(1)   With a new strategy, I wiped him out.

This sentence can convey some different kind of information according to contexts in which it is embedded:

Case 1. A description about a war: The head of a winning state utters the sentence about the victory, referring to the head of the defeated state.

Case 2. A description about an argument: Someone utters the sentence about the argument in which he/she refuted his opponent.

(2)   *A:* "I argued with *B* about his theory last night."
             C: "How did it come out?"

Case 3. A description about a game: The manager of a soccer team utters the sentence about the result of the game, referring to the manager of the opponent team.

As this example shows, the sentence (1) connotes different situations according to the contexts in which it is uttered. These connotations of the sentence (1), however, seem to share some common structure, rather than to be quite different from each other.

Generally speaking, the information in an expression may vary with hearer's circumstance, or *resource situations*, such as contexts, background knowledge, and so on. The context sensitivity like this can be explained by drawing a distinction between the interpretation of an utterance and the information in the utterance, which is one of the ideas in situation semantics. Accordingly we adopt the formalization based on situation semantics, in which by dealing with the interpretation of a metaphorical expression and the information in the expression separately the metaphor understanding is done according to the hearer's resource. That is, an actual meaning connoted by either a word or a phrase in a metaphorical expression may vary from its ordinary meaning. As a result, metaphorical expressions can convey some other new information. We would like to formulate this variation as a process of introducing new resources, namely, establishing correspondences between a source domain and a target domain, with which a hearer can project information about a source domain onto a target domain.

2 The Outline of Metaphor Understanding in Situation Semantics

In our theory, metaphor understanding consists of the following steps and semantic representations with which this metaphor understanding process are represented in terms of situation semantics:

Step 1. Hear a fragment uf^i of an utterance and construct states of affairs corresponding to it by the convention of the language use. Then a described situation s^i_{uf} corresponding to uf^i is obtained.

Step 2. By supposing that uf^i describes the same situation which is described by the current context s^{i-1}_d, we obtain a situation s^{new}_d such that:

$$(3) \qquad s^{new}_d = s^i_{uf} = s^{i-1}_d$$

Then examine whether the situation s^{new}_d satisfies the following requirements:

1. Every relation in the situation s^{new}_d satisfies the appropriateness of its argument assignment.
2. The situation s^{new}_d is coherent.
3. All of constraints holding in the situation s^{new}_d are satisfied.

Step 3. If the requirements in Step 2 are satisfied, let the new context s^i_d be s^{new}_d and increase i by 1, then go to Step 1.

Step 4. Since the requirements in Step 2 are not satisfied at this point, introduce a new resource to cancel the inappropriateness and to obtain a meaningful interpretation. In metaphor understanding, as described later, the new resource is a set of constraints which represents the correspondence between the source domain and the target domain. Thus, the new situation s^i_r in which these constraints hold is regarded as a new resource situation. Now pay attention to states of affairs carried relative to the resource situation s^i_r by the described situation s^i_{uf}, which is a situation related to the source domain in this case. Since the situation $s^{i,t}_{uf}$ supporting these states of affairs corresponds to a situation related to the target domain, return to Step 2 after replacing the described situation s^i_{uf} with $s^{i,t}_{uf}$.

Not only in ordinary sentence understanding, but also in metaphor understanding, it does not seem to be plausible that the hearer begins to interpret a sentence just after he/she finished hearing all of the sentence. As described in Step 1, whenever the hearer hears/reads a fragment of an utterance such as a noun phrase, a verb (phrase), and so on, he/she starts to interpret the fragment under the current context made by the discourse.

It is Step 2 that is the process which integrates fragments of interpretation newly obtained with the current context. The way of the integration depends on the convention of the language used. For example, the grammar of the language is one of the constraints which are effective within one sentence.

In Step 4, the described situation s^i_{uf} constitutes a part of the context about the source domain, which is going on in parallel with the main context. We call this context about the source domain the *parallel context* and denote it s^i_p. If there already exists a parallel context s^{i-1}_p, Step 2 is also applied to the parallel context and s^i_{uf}. When the requirements in Step 2 are satisfied, a new parallel context s^i_p such that

$$(4) \qquad s^i_p = s^{i-1}_p = s^i_{uf}$$

is made. In this case, the situation which includes both s^i_r and the resource situation which has already introduced for the parallel context s^{i-1}_p serves as a new resource situation. When one of the requirements in Step 2 is not satisfied, a new metaphor has been introduced and another parallel context is made. By allowing for multiple parallel contexts which describe multiple source domains of metaphors, the case that several different metaphors are introduced one after another into a discourse can be accounted for.

3 The Details of Each Step

This section will give details of these steps roughly described in the previous section through the process of understanding the example sentence (1)

"With a new strategy, I wiped him out."

in the Case 2, in which a topic about an argument is described.

3.1 Construction of a Fragment of a Described Situation

As described in the previous section, we assume that whenever the hearer hears/reads a fragment of an utterance, he/she interprets the fragment to some extent. While the size of the unit of fragments to be interpreted depends on the language used and his/her ability in language use, it seems that the most primitive unit is the phrase, such as a noun phrase or a verb phrase, which is determined by the grammar of the language. Assuming that the phrase is the unit of an utterance fragment, the example sentence is regarded as the following sequence of three fragments:

[With a new strategy]$_{\text{PP}}$, [I]$_{\text{NP}}$ [wiped him out]$_{\text{VP}}$

As the result of the constraint satisfaction such as the grammar of the language, the described situation s^i_{uf} corresponding to each fragment described above is obtained as follows:

(5) $s_{uf}^1 \models \langle\!\langle with, agent:A, object:ST \rangle\!\rangle \wedge \langle\!\langle strategy, object:ST \rangle\!\rangle$

(6) $s_{uf}^2 \models \langle\!\langle speaker, agent:A \rangle\!\rangle$

(7) $s_{uf}^3 \models \langle\!\langle wipe\_out, agent:A, patient:B \rangle\!\rangle$

We also assume the following situation s_d^0 as the initial context corresponding to the context (2):

(8) $s_d^0 \models \langle\!\langle argue, agent:A, participant:B, object:TH \rangle\!\rangle \wedge$

$\langle\!\langle theory, TH \rangle\!\rangle \wedge \langle\!\langle own, agent:B, object:TH \rangle\!\rangle$

In the following subsections, first we will show how the described situation s_{uf}^1 is interpreted by Step 2, Step 3 and Step 4 in the process described above. Then we will describe the interpretation of s_{uf}^2 and s_{uf}^3 briefly.

3.2   Examining the Appropriateness of a Described Situation

According to Step 2, let us consider the situation s_d^{new} such that:

(9) $s_d^{new} = s_{uf}^1 = s_d^0$

This situation is a candidate for the context of s_{uf}^2. If only the condition (9) is imposed on s_d^{new}, the situation satisfies the requirements in Step 2. The hearer, however, usually uses some background knowledge to fill the lack of information, whenever he/she interprets an utterance fragment. For example, the typical situation supporting a state of affairs *argue*, and the knowledge that what state of affair is involved by the state of affair *strategy*, are derived from these background knowledge. In the following part of this subsection, first we show how to represent background knowledge, then we consider how s_d^{new} is interpreted with the background knowledge which we usually have in our mind.

3.2.1   Representing Background Knowledge

An utterance itself usually gives little information to a hearer. The hearer can receive useful information from an utterance with some background knowledge, rather than from the utterance only. In this paper, by the term *resources* we mean some information which does not appear in utterances and can be used to interpret utterances by a hearer. We will pay attention particularly to the following resource, from which the hearer will be able to obtain useful information for metaphor understanding:

The domain knowledge of a concept such as the typical context
in which the concept is used.

Since the speaker assumes that the hearer has sufficient knowledge about a source domain to retrieve some information intended by the speaker from an expression related to the source domain, the speaker may inform the hearer about something related to the current context, that is, the target domain intentionally by comparing the two domain. Therefore, in order to formulate metaphor understanding, it should be assumed that a hearer has some knowledge both of source and target domains to a certain extent. Such a knowledge includes common sense and typical scenes, which the hearer is usually supported to have or be able to associate in his/her mind.

We treat this background knowledge as a situation type, that is,

$$(10) \qquad [s \mid s \models \sigma]$$

which somehow the hearer has. Then an instance of a typical scene actually used as a resource becomes the situation which is of this situation type, where parameters are anchored to fit individual situations. These resource situations may also include knowledge such as causal relations between states of affairs in typical scenes.

We also define the type hierarchy in terms of the relation *subtype* in order to express the conceptual hierarchy as follows:

- R_1 *subtype* R_2 is true, if all assignments of the type R_1 are of the type R_2.
- Types in the same type hierarchy can have the same assignment, only if they have a common lower bound.

3.2.2 Interpretation with Background Knowledge

We suppose that the noun "strategy" recalls the situation type T_{war} to the hearer's mind as the background knowledge of the "war".[1] Suppose also that T_{war} is the type of the situation which supports the following constraints about a strategy:

$$(11) \qquad \langle\!\langle \Rightarrow, \langle\!\langle strategy, object{:}x \rangle\!\rangle, \langle\!\langle method, object{:}x, event\text{-}type{:}ET_{use\ m.p.} \rangle\!\rangle \rangle\!\rangle$$

where

$$(12) \qquad ET_{use\ m.p.} =$$
$$[s \mid s \models \langle\!\langle use, agent{:}y, object{:}mp \rangle\!\rangle \wedge \langle\!\langle mil\text{-}power, object{:}mp \rangle\!\rangle]$$

Now, a positive constraint $\Rightarrow$ is defined as follows. If $s_0 \models \langle\!\langle \Rightarrow, \sigma(\vec{x}), \tau(\vec{x}) \rangle\!\rangle$ then for every situation $s \trianglelefteq s_0$ and every anchor $f : \vec{x} \to Obj(s)$ such that $s \models \sigma(f)$, there is a situation s' such that $s' \models \tau(f)$. A negative constraint $\perp$ is also defined as follows. If $s_0 \models \langle\!\langle \perp, \sigma(\vec{x}), \tau(\vec{x}) \rangle\!\rangle$ and there is a situation $s \trianglelefteq s_0$ and an anchor f such that $s \models \sigma(f)$, then there is no situation s' such that $s' \models \tau(f)$.

For the initial context s_d^0, we also suppose that to the hearer's mind, the verb "argue" recalls the type T_{argue} of the situation, in which the following states of affairs hold, as the background knowledge of the "argue":

$$(13) \qquad \langle\!\langle argue, agent{:}a, participant{:}p, object{:}x \rangle\!\rangle \wedge$$
$$\langle\!\langle use, agent{:}a, object{:}y \rangle\!\rangle \wedge \langle\!\langle reasoning, object{:}y \rangle\!\rangle$$

---

[1] To do this, such a mechanism as the association is necessary in implementation.

Moreover, we suppose that T_{misc} is the situation type which represents the miscellaneous background knowledge and a situation of T_{misc} supports the following constraints:

(14) $\quad\quad \langle\!\langle \Rightarrow, \langle\!\langle with, agent{:}a, object{:}x \rangle\!\rangle \;\wedge$
$\quad\quad\quad\quad\quad \langle\!\langle method, object{:}x, event\text{-}type{:}[s \mid s \models \sigma] \rangle\!\rangle,$
$\quad\quad\quad\quad \sigma(agent{:}a) \rangle\!\rangle$

(15) $\quad\quad \langle\!\langle \perp, \langle\!\langle mil\text{-}power, object{:}y \rangle\!\rangle, \langle\!\langle reasoning, object{:}y \rangle\!\rangle \rangle\!\rangle$

The state of affairs (14) represents the constraint about the case that the preposition "with" occurs with a "method". The state of affairs (15) represents the constraint about the conceptual structure.

Now, let us apply the background knowledge described above to s_d^{new} such that (9), that is, assume the following conditions:

(16) $\quad\quad\quad\quad\quad s_d^{new} : T_{argue}$

(17) $\quad\quad\quad\quad\quad s_d^{new} : T_{war}$

(18) $\quad\quad\quad\quad\quad s_d^{new} : T_{misc}$

The proposition (16) leads to:

(19) $\quad s_d^{new} \models \langle\!\langle argue, agent{:}A, participant{:}B, object{:}TH \rangle\!\rangle \;\wedge$
$\quad\quad\quad\quad \langle\!\langle use, agent{:}A, object{:}y \rangle\!\rangle \;\wedge\; \langle\!\langle reasoning, object{:}y \rangle\!\rangle$

where we assume that the state of affair $argue$ supported by s_d^{new} was merged with one in T_{argue}.

On the other hand, (17) and (18) imply that the constraints (11) and (14) hold in s_d^{new}, there exists the following situation s_d':

(20) $\quad s_d' \models \langle\!\langle method, object{:}ST, event\text{-}type{:}ET_{use\ m.p.} \rangle\!\rangle \;\wedge$
$\quad\quad\quad\quad \langle\!\langle use, agent{:}A, object{:}mp \rangle\!\rangle \;\wedge\; \langle\!\langle mil\text{-}power, object{:}mp \rangle\!\rangle$

Assuming that states of affairs carried relative to the constraints, that is, the right hand side of (21) is used as parts of the main context, the condition $s_d' = s_d^{new}$ should be satisfied. Under the condition, it seems to be natural that we presume the state of affair use in (20) is merged with one in (21). For this presumption leads to:

(21) $\quad\quad\quad\quad s_d^{new} \models \langle\!\langle reasoning, y \rangle\!\rangle \;\wedge\; \langle\!\langle mil\text{-}power, y \rangle\!\rangle$

it is clear that the situation s_d^{new} violates constraint (15). Since the requirement 3 of Step 2 is not satisfied, to assume the condition (9), that is, $s_{uf}^1 = s_d^0$ has turned out to be false. Therefore s_{uf}^1 constitutes the parallel context s_p^1.

(22) $\quad\quad\quad\quad\quad s_p^1 = s_{uf}^1$

Generally speaking, there exists some inappropriateness about the content in metaphorical expressions. What a pair of domains is compared with in a metaphor understanding is shown by the background knowledge recalled using associations. In the example, the initial context s_d^0 and the new described situation s^1_{uf} recall the background knowledge T_{argue} of an argument and the background knowledge T_{war} of a war respectively. This means that the target domain is the "argument", and the source domain is the "war." Finally we obtain the following conditions as the result of Step 2:

$$(23) \qquad\qquad\qquad s^0_d \neq s^1_{uf}$$

$$(24) \qquad\qquad s^0_d : T_{argue} \wedge s^0_d : T_{misc}$$

$$(25) \qquad\qquad s^1_{uf} : T_{war} \wedge s^1_{uf} : T_{misc}$$

That is, the new described situation s^1_{uf} constitutes a parallel context which is not equal to the main context s^0_d. The main context s^0_d and the described situation s^1_{uf} are the situations related to an argument and a war, respectively.

3.3 Introducing New Resources to get Meaningful Information

In the previous subsection, we examined the inappropriateness which might occur when a described situation is combined with the hearer's circumstances. In metaphor understanding, however, the clue is what kinds of information are carried by an utterance and are combined with the context to make a new context. But, as described in the previous subsection, the hearer's background knowledge of both a war and an argument is insufficient for information which contributes to the main context to be able to obtained from s^1_{uf}. Therefore, it can be presumed that the hearer should introduce some new resource to get meaningful information.

In addition to the interaction theory mentioned in Section 1, the following two studies serve to figure out the new resource. First, Lakoff (1980) points out that about the example, we can consider that *a part of conceptual network in the concept "war" partially characterizes the concept "argument"*. Secondly, the pragmatic function proposed by G.Nunberg, whose importance is pointed out by G. Fauconnier (1985), is worthy of notice. The pragmatic function connects objects whose characters are different from each other according to psychological, cultural, domestic pragmatic grounds. Nunberg shows that a reference to an object can be done by another object which is appropriately connected with the former object. Both studies suggest that the correspondence is important. As the consequence we come up with having the following supposition:

> First, the hearer introduces some correspondence between a source domain and a target domain as a new resource. Then, according to this resource, he/she converts information, that is,

he/she converts some states of affairs in the source domain into the corresponding states of affairs in the target domain[2].

Domain "war" $\quad\boxed{\rightleftharpoons}\quad$ Domain "argument"

CONVERTER

Figure 1 Construction of an Information Converter

Descriptions of "war" $\Rightarrow$ $\boxed{\rightarrow}$ $\Rightarrow$ Descriptions of "argument"

Figure 2 Conversion of Information

In the case of simile understanding or metaphor understanding, what connects the source domain with the target domain is a set of correspondences such as those which are given by a general metaphor[3] and are made by some analogical mapping. On the other hand, in metonymy understanding and so on, pragmatic functions may give some correspondences.

3.3.1 A Description of Correspondences between a Target Domain and a Source Domain

In this section, we will show what correspondences we should deal with and how to express them. Since a source domain and a target domain are generally distinct from each other, in a strict sense we should treat correspondences between the schemes of individuation for each situation in order to express correspondences between the situations. However, since it is important for metaphor understanding what kinds of information about the target domain are obtained from descriptions about the source domain, the following constraints are sufficient to express correspondences between the source domain and the target domain:

(26) $\qquad \langle\!\langle \Rightarrow, \langle\!\langle r_{source}, \vec{x}; p_s \rangle\!\rangle, \langle\!\langle r_{target}, \vec{y}; p_t \rangle\!\rangle \rangle\!\rangle$

where s_{target} and s_{source} are the situations related to the target domain and the source domain respectively, and $r_{target} \in Rel_{s_{target}}$, $r_{source} \in Rel_{s_{source}}$. The hearer's attunement to these constraints means that he/she is aware of the correspondence between the two domains by comparing them. Intuitively, these constraints are descriptions of the hearer's inference or association between a source domain and a target domain.

---

[2] From now on, let the terms "source domain" and "target domain" mean also situations related to a source domain and a target domain, respectively.

[3] See also Section 3.3.2 for further information about general metaphors.

3.3.2 How to Obtain Correspondences

How can we obtain the constraints which represent the correspondence between the source domain and the target domain? General metaphors (Lakoff and Johnson 1980) are an important concept relevant to this question. Lakoff points out that a metaphorical expression in a certain text is an instance of a general metaphor. For instance, the example sentence can be regarded as an instance of the general metaphor "ARGUMENT IS WAR." At first sight, it seems to be sufficient for metaphor understanding to prepare all of the correspondences obtained from all of the general metaphors. However, since metaphorical expressions can be and indeed are likely to be flexibly extended by a speaker according to the context, it seems unlikely that we prepare a universal set of correspondences. If so, how can we get correspondences which should be set up according to the context? In the next section, we show that some heuristics can give us some useful correspondences.

3.3.3 Heuristics for Analogical Mapping in Metaphor Understanding

Basically, there may be many possible correspondences between two domains. However, it seems that we use some heuristics to establish correspondences which can be used to retrieve some useful information from metaphorical utterances during our interpretation process. Let us enumerate some heuristics useful for metaphor understanding:

H1 Coherence of information.

There are no incoherent situations when constraints, representing correspondences, are applied.

H2 Similarity between corresponding states of affairs.

This heuristic is based upon our assumption that it is difficult even for human beings in metaphor understanding to find correspondences between two domains containing no pairs of states of affairs closely related to each other. On this assumption, we expect that some corresponding pairs of states of affairs may be found easily.

H2.1 Make correspondences between the same states of affairs in two domains as far as possible.

H2.1.1 Especially when a state of affairs $\sigma = \langle\!\langle r, \vec{x}; p \rangle\!\rangle$ holding in the source domain does not appear in the target domain, check whether the state of affairs can be used in the target domain, that is, check whether the assignments to the argument roles of the state of affairs are appropriate in the target domain. If the condition is satisfied, the following constraint becomes one of the assumptions:

$$\langle\!\langle \Rightarrow, \sigma, \sigma \rangle\!\rangle$$

H2.2 When the heuristic H2.1 is not applicable, make correspondences between *similar* states of affairs in two domains to whatever extent possible. Similarity among relations is defined in
terms of the relation *subtype*, by which the type hierarchy is
defined.

H2.2.1 If in the target domain the assignment is not appropriate
for the state of affairs σ obtained by applying the heuristic
H2.1.1, generalize the relation r by obtaining a super type
r_{sup} such that:

$$\sigma' = \langle\!\langle r_{sup}, \vec{x}; p \rangle\!\rangle$$
$$r \ subtype \ r_{sup}$$

from the type hierarchy and check whether the assignment
is appropriate for this super type. If the condition is satisfied, the following constraint becomes one of the assumption:

$$\langle\!\langle \Rightarrow, \langle\!\langle r, \vec{x}; p \rangle\!\rangle, \langle\!\langle r_{sup}, \vec{x}; p \rangle\!\rangle \rangle\!\rangle$$

This generalization, however, gives us a weaker assumption.

H2.2.2 If the heuristic H2.2.1 is applicable, examine subtypes r_{sub}
of the relation r_{sup} obtained by applying H2.2.1 such that:

$$\sigma'' = \langle\!\langle r_{sub}, \vec{x}; p \rangle\!\rangle$$
$$r_{sub} \ subtype \ r_{sup}$$

If the assignment is appropriate for one of the subtypes,
r_{sub}, the following constraint becomes one of the assumption:

$$\langle\!\langle \Rightarrow, \langle\!\langle r, \vec{x}; p \rangle\!\rangle, \langle\!\langle r_{sub}, \vec{x}; p \rangle\!\rangle \rangle\!\rangle$$

This assumption is stronger than the result of H2.2.1.

H3 Coherence of objects in two domains.

Each object in one domain corresponds to an object in another domain according to correspondences between relations. There must be
no incoherence in these correspondences between objects. For exam-
ple, suppose that the relations r^1_{target} and r^2_{target} in the target domain
correspond to the relations r^1_{source} and r^2_{source} in the source domain
respectively. Suppose also that the following states of affairs hold in
the target domain and the source domain respectively.

$$\langle\!\langle r^1_{target}, w, x \rangle\!\rangle \ \wedge \ \langle\!\langle r^2_{target}, y, z \rangle\!\rangle$$
$$\langle\!\langle r^1_{source}, l, m \rangle\!\rangle \ \wedge \ \langle\!\langle r^2_{source}, n, o \rangle\!\rangle$$

While it is an appropriate case that the equations

$$x = y \quad \& \quad w \neq z$$
$$m = n \quad \& \quad l \neq o$$

are obtained from some other relations, it is an inappropriate case
that the equations

$$x = y \quad \& \quad w \neq z$$
$$m \neq n \quad \& \quad l = o$$

are obtained, because objects in one domain do not correspond to
objects in another domain coherently.

H4 Isomorphism of constraints.

Make correspondences which preserve the isomorphism of constraints
in two domains. For example, Suppose the following causal relations
hold in the target domain and a source domain respectively.

$$\langle\!\langle \Rightarrow, A_{target}, B_{target} \rangle\!\rangle$$
$$\langle\!\langle \Rightarrow, A_{source}, B_{source} \rangle\!\rangle$$

It seems to be natural to assume that the consequence B_{target} corresponds with the consequence B_{source}, if it is known that the premise
A_{target} corresponds to A_{source}, and vice versa.

H4.1 Strengthening the definition of constraints

Since the definition of the positive constraint, which is described
in the Section 3.2.2, is weaker than the implication of the predicate logic, we cannot combine several constraints into a new
constraint. Therefore, the heuristic H4, which depends on the
isomorphism of constraints, will not always work well. In order
to cope with this, we introduce the heuristic which strengthens
the definition of the positive constraint only while the heuristic
H4 is applied to make some correspondences. The strengthening
is achieved by the following two restrictions.

o The situation s' which supports the state of affairs τ, which
is carried relative to a constraint, should be a part of the
situation s_0, which supports the constraint. That is, add the
condition $s' \trianglelefteq s_0$ to the definition of the positive constraint.

o This definition should be bidirectional. Replace "if" in the
definition of the positive constraint with "if-and-only-if".

These may correspond to the plausible restriction on the domain
of consideration, with which we usually do not have to examine
unrelated matters.

These restrictions contribute to the derivation of the following
relations, which can be used in H4, rather than to finding new
constraints[4].

o Transitivity

$$s \models \langle\!\langle \Rightarrow, \sigma, \sigma' \rangle\!\rangle \wedge \langle\!\langle \Rightarrow, \sigma', \sigma'' \rangle\!\rangle \quad \rightsquigarrow \quad s \models \langle\!\langle \Rightarrow, \sigma, \sigma'' \rangle\!\rangle$$

---

[4]The size of search spaces for finding new constraints based on these restrictions is
often very large.

○ Monotonicity

$$s \models \langle\!\langle \Rightarrow, \sigma, \sigma' \rangle\!\rangle \quad \leadsto \quad s \models \langle\!\langle \Rightarrow, \sigma \wedge \sigma'', \sigma' \rangle\!\rangle$$

○ Conjoining of consequence

$$s \models \langle\!\langle \Rightarrow, \sigma, \sigma' \rangle\!\rangle \wedge \langle\!\langle \Rightarrow, \sigma, \sigma'' \rangle\!\rangle \quad \leadsto \quad s \models \langle\!\langle \Rightarrow, \sigma, \sigma' \wedge \sigma'' \rangle\!\rangle$$

○ Disjoining of consequence

$$s \models \langle\!\langle \Rightarrow, \sigma, \sigma' \wedge \sigma'' \rangle\!\rangle \quad \leadsto \quad s \models \langle\!\langle \Rightarrow, \sigma, \sigma' \rangle\!\rangle \wedge \langle\!\langle \Rightarrow, \sigma, \sigma'' \rangle\!\rangle$$

○ Weakening

$$s \models \langle\!\langle \Rightarrow, \sigma, \sigma' \rangle\!\rangle \quad \leadsto \quad s \models \langle\!\langle \Rightarrow, \sigma \wedge \sigma'', \sigma' \wedge \sigma'' \rangle\!\rangle$$

where $\leadsto$ means that assuming the restriction described above, the right hand side is derived from the left hand side logically.

The following points may be paid attention to when these heuristics are used.

- We consider that a *partial* correspondence between two domains will be enough for metaphor understanding. Here, by *"partial"* we mean:
  ○ One domain is allowed to have some relations which correspond to no relations in another domain.
  ○ All argument roles about a relation do not have to be considered. That is, it may be sufficient that projections of relations in one domain correspond to projections of relations in another domain. An object which corresponds to another object in the source domain does not have to exist in the target domain as long as it is not referred to in metaphorical expressions.
- Some measure, that is, some evaluating functions for application of heuristics may be required for the efficient search of a plausible correspondence.

3.3.4 An Example of Establishing Correspondences

Let us examine correspondences for the example sentence. As described in the Section 2, the described situation s_{uf}^1 forms a certain part of the parallel context s_p^1 in parallel with the main context s_d. Therefore correspondences we should obtain are those that connect states of affairs which hold in s_{uf}^1 to states of affairs which meet the requirements of Step 2 in the context s_d^0 relative to the conditions (23), (24) and (25).

First let us spell out the states of affairs which hold in s_{uf}^1 under the condition (25). The states of affairs which hold in s_{uf}^1 are given in (5). By applying the constraints in T_{misc} to s_{uf}^1, it is derived that there exists a situation s_d' such that (21). Now, supposing that s_d' is also used as a part of the parallel context, the condition $s_d' = s_{uf}^1$ should be satisfied. Under the condition, states of affairs holding in s_{uf}^1 are as follows:

$$(27) \qquad s_{uf}^1 \models \langle\!\langle with, agent{:}A, object{:}ST \rangle\!\rangle \wedge$$

(28) $\langle\!\langle strategy, object{:}ST\rangle\!\rangle\ \wedge$

(29) $\langle\!\langle method, object{:}ST, event\text{-}type{:}ET_{use\ m.p.}\rangle\!\rangle\ \wedge$

(30) $\langle\!\langle use, agent{:}A, object{:}mp\rangle\!\rangle\ \wedge$

(31) $\langle\!\langle mil\text{-}power, object{:}mp\rangle\!\rangle$

Let us construct the constraints which connect the states of affairs (27), ..., (31) to the states of affairs which may hold in the target domain. For the states of affairs (27) and (30), the following constraints are obtained by the heuristic H2.1, which generates correspondences related to the states of affairs which can be used also in the target domain:

(32) $C^1_{w \to a}\ =\ \{\langle\!\langle \Rightarrow, \langle\!\langle with, agent{:}A, object{:}ST\rangle\!\rangle,$
$\langle\!\langle with, agent{:}A, object{:}ST\rangle\!\rangle\rangle\!\rangle,$

(33) $\langle\!\langle \Rightarrow, \langle\!\langle use, agent{:}A, object{:}mp\rangle\!\rangle,$
$\langle\!\langle use, agent{:}A, object{:}y\rangle\!\rangle\rangle\!\rangle\}$

To the states of affairs (31), (29) and (28), however, the heuristic H2.1 cannot be applied, since they cannot be used in the target domain for the following reasons:

- (31) violates the constraint (15).
- (29) leads to (31) with both (27) and (14).
- (28) leads to (29) with (11).

For the state of affairs (31), the correspondence constraint is obtained by comparing s^1_{uf} with the main context s^0_d under the correspondences (33) and (34). Under the condition (24) the main context s^0_d is as follows:

(34) $s^0_d\ \models\ \langle\!\langle argue, agent{:}A, participant{:}B, object{:}TH\rangle\!\rangle\ \wedge$
$\langle\!\langle theory, TH\rangle\!\rangle\ \wedge\ \langle\!\langle own, agent{:}B, object{:}TH\rangle\!\rangle\ \wedge$
$\langle\!\langle use, agent{:}A, object{:}y\rangle\!\rangle\ \wedge\ \langle\!\langle reasoning, object{:}y\rangle\!\rangle$

Since the parameter mp in the source domain is connected to the parameter y in the target domain by (34), by applying the heuristic H3, the following constraint is obtained:

(35) $C^2_{w \to a}\ =\ \{\langle\!\langle \Rightarrow, \langle\!\langle mil\text{-}power, object{:}mp\rangle\!\rangle, \langle\!\langle reasoning, object{:}y\rangle\!\rangle\rangle\!\rangle\}$

Since the relation *method* itself can be used also in the target domain, for the state of affair (29) the correspondence constraint is obtained by translating the situation type, which is in the argument of the state of affair and is related to the source domain, into the situation type related to the target domain. Since the correspondence constraints (34) and (35) are applied to any situation s, such that $s : ET_{use\ m.p.}$, related to the target domain, it is derived that there exists a situation s' such that $s' : ET_{use\ reas}$ for every situation s, where

(36) $ET_{use\ reas} =$

$$[s \mid s \models \langle\!\langle use, agent{:}y, object{:}reas \rangle\!\rangle \wedge \langle\!\langle reasoning, object{:}reas \rangle\!\rangle]$$

We suppose the following constraint, for s' can be regarded as a situation related to the target domain:

(37) $\quad C^3_{w \to a} \;=\; \{ \langle\!\langle \Rightarrow, \langle\!\langle method, object{:}ST, event\text{-}type{:}ET_{use\ m.p.} \rangle\!\rangle,$

$$\langle\!\langle method, object{:}ST, event\text{-}type{:}ET_{use\ reas} \rangle\!\rangle \rangle\!\rangle \}$$

Lastly we examine the case of the state of affairs (28). It seems to be natural that we assume the following constraint about the "logic" holds in a situation s which is of the situation type T_{argue} about the "argument."

(38) $\quad \langle\!\langle \Rightarrow, \langle\!\langle logic, object{:}x \rangle\!\rangle, \langle\!\langle method, object{:}x, event\text{-}type{:}ET_{use\ reas} \rangle\!\rangle \rangle\!\rangle$

Now, applying the heuristic H4 to the constraints (11) and (38), the following correspondence constraint are obtained:

(39) $\quad C^4_{w \to a} \;=\; \{ \langle\!\langle \Rightarrow, \langle\!\langle strategy, object{:}ST \rangle\!\rangle, \langle\!\langle logic, object{:}ST \rangle\!\rangle \rangle\!\rangle \}$

We have obtained all constraints which connect each state of affairs holding in s^1_{uf} to a state of affairs related to the target domain "argument."

3.4 Metaphor Understanding with Resources Related to Correspondences

The resource situation s^1_r in Step 4 becomes the situation which supports the constraints $C^1_{w \to a}, \ldots, C^4_{w \to a}$ in the previous subsection. In order to apply these constraints to s^1_{uf}, suppose the condition $s^1_r = s^1_{uf}$. Then it is derived that there exists the following situation $s^{1,t}_{uf}$:

(40) $\qquad s^{1,t}_{uf} \;\models\; \langle\!\langle with, agent{:}A, object{:}ST \rangle\!\rangle \;\wedge$

(41) $\qquad\qquad\quad \langle\!\langle logic, object{:}ST \rangle\!\rangle \;\wedge$

(42) $\qquad\qquad\quad \langle\!\langle method, object{:}ST, event\text{-}type{:}ET_{use\ reas} \rangle\!\rangle \;\wedge$

(43) $\qquad\qquad\quad \langle\!\langle use, agent{:}A, object{:}y \rangle\!\rangle \;\wedge$

(44) $\qquad\qquad\quad \langle\!\langle reasoning, object{:}y \rangle\!\rangle$

This situation corresponds to a described situation related to the target domain. Return to Step 2 after replacing the described situation s^1_{uf} with $s^{1,t}_{uf}$. Then all requirements in Step 2 are satisfied under the condition $s^{1,t}_{uf} = s^0_d$. Therefore $s^{1,t}_{uf}$ forms part of the new main context s^1_d such that:

(45) $$s^1_d = s^0_d = s^{1,t}_{uf}$$

Generally speaking, the semantic representation of metaphor understanding can be formulated as the following constituents:

- A described situation s^i_{uf} related to the source domain, that is , a part of the parallel context

- An application of the background knowledge of the source domain $s^i_{uf} : T_{source}$
- A resource situation s^i_r which supports constraints representing the correspondence between two domains
- A described situation $s^{i,t}_{uf}$ related to the target domain, which satisfies the following conditions:

$$s^i_r = s^i_{uf}$$

$$s_{uf} \;\Vdash_{s^i_r}\; \sigma$$

$$s^{i,t}_{uf} \models \sigma$$

- The following condition, which represents the construction of a new context:

$$s^i_d = s^{i-1}_d = s^{i,t}_{uf}$$

- An application of the background knowledge of the target domain $s^i_d : T_{target}$

3.5 Understanding the Remaining Described Situations

In this section, we will briefly examine the interpretation for the remaining described situations s^2_{uf} and s^3_{uf}. First, let us consider s^2_{uf} as in (6). The described situation s^2_{uf} satisfies each requirement in Step 2 under the condition $s^2_{uf} = s^1_d$, which is imposed in Step 2. Thus we obtain a new main context s^2_d as follows:

$$(46) \qquad\qquad s^2_d = s^1_d = s^2_{uf}$$

Secondly, let us examine s^3_{uf} such that (7). By taking s^3_{uf} into account, we should describe the situation types T_{war} and T_{argue}, which have been already used as the background knowledge, in more detail. For the situation type T_{war}, we suppose that a situation of T_{war} holds not only (28), but also the following states of affairs:

$$(47) \qquad \langle\!\langle \Rightarrow, \langle\!\langle wipe\_out, agent{:}a, patient{:}b, object{:}z \rangle\!\rangle,$$
$$\langle\!\langle own, agent{:}b, object{:}z \rangle\!\rangle \;\wedge$$
$$\langle\!\langle make, agent{:}a, event{:}E_{not\_func} \rangle\!\rangle \;\wedge$$
$$\langle\!\langle can, agent{:}b, event\text{-}type{:}ET_{repair}; - \rangle\!\rangle \rangle\!\rangle \;\wedge$$

$$(48) \qquad \langle\!\langle purpose, agent{:}a, event{:}E_{make\_not\_func} \rangle\!\rangle$$

where

$$(49) \qquad E_{not\_func} \;:\; ET_{not\_func}$$

$$(50) \qquad ET_{not\_func} = [s \mid s \models \langle\!\langle function, object{:}z; - \rangle\!\rangle]$$

$$(51) \qquad ET_{repair} = [s \mid s \models \langle\!\langle repair, agent{:}b, object{:}z \rangle\!\rangle]$$

$$(52) \qquad E_{make\_not\_func} \;:\; ET_{make\_not\_func}$$

(53) $ET_{make\_not\_func} = [s \mid s \models \langle\langle make, agent:a, event:E_{not\_func}\rangle\rangle]$

Similarly, for the situation type T_{argue}, we suppose that a situation of T_{argue} holds not only (14), but also the following states of affairs:

(54) $\langle\langle\Rightarrow, \langle\langle refute, agent:a, patient:b, object:w\rangle\rangle,$

$\langle\langle own, agent:a, object:w\rangle\rangle \wedge$

$\langle\langle prove, agent:a, event:E_{not\_func}\rangle\rangle\rangle\rangle \wedge$

(55) $\langle\langle purpose, agent:a, event:E_{prove\_not\_func}\rangle\rangle \wedge$

(56) $\langle\langle make, agent:a, event:E_{not\_func}; -\rangle\rangle$

where

(57) $ET_{prove\_not\_func} = [s \mid s \models \langle\langle prove, agent:a, event:E_{not\_func}\rangle\rangle]$

and (56) means "in an argument, an agent does not damage anything. " Since the constraint about the state of affairs $wipe\_out$ holds in a situation of the type T_{war}, which represents the source domain, we can suppose that s^3_{uf} is a described situation related to the target domain, namely, a part of the parallel context as the following conditions:

(58) $s^3_{uf} : T_{war}$

(59) $s^3_p = s^3_{uf} = s^1_p$

Since the constraint (48) is applied to s^3_{uf} by these conditions, it is derived that there exists a situation $s^{3'}_{uf}$ such as:

(60) $s^{3'}_{uf} \models \langle\langle own, agent:B, object:z\rangle\rangle \wedge$

(61) $\langle\langle make, agent:A, event:E_{not\_func}(f)\rangle\rangle \wedge$

(62) $\langle\langle can, agent:B, event\text{-}type:ET_{repair}(f); -\rangle\rangle$

where f is an anchor such that $f(a) = A$ and $f(b) = B$. We also assume that $s^{3'}_{uf}$ constitutes a part of the parallel context, that is,

(63) $s^3_p = s^3_{uf} = s^1_p = s^{3'}_{uf}$

Now, the constraints which connect the states of affairs (7), (48), (60), (61) and (62) which hold in s^3_{uf} to the states of affairs of the target domain are obtained as follows:

(64) $C^5_{w \rightarrow a} = \{\langle\langle\Rightarrow, \langle\langle own, agent:B, object:z\rangle\rangle,$

$\langle\langle own, agent:B, object:TH\rangle\rangle\rangle\rangle,$

(65) $\langle\langle\Rightarrow, \langle\langle make, agent:A, event:E_{not\_func}(f)\rangle\rangle,$

$\langle\langle prove, agent:A, event:E_{not\_func}(f)\rangle\rangle\rangle\rangle,$

(66) $\langle\langle\Rightarrow, \langle\langle can, agent:B, event\text{-}type:ET_{repair}(f); -\rangle\rangle,$

$\langle\langle can, agent:B, event\text{-}type:ET_{repair}(f); -\rangle\rangle\rangle\rangle,$

(67) $\qquad \langle\!\langle \Rightarrow, \langle\!\langle purpose, agent:A, event:E_{make\_not\_func}(f)\rangle\!\rangle,$

$\qquad\qquad\qquad \langle\!\langle purpose, agent:A, event:E_{prove\_not\_func}(f)\rangle\!\rangle\rangle\!\rangle,$

(68) $\qquad \langle\!\langle \Rightarrow, \langle\!\langle wipe\_out, agent:A, patient:B, object:z\rangle\!\rangle,$

$\qquad\qquad\qquad \langle\!\langle refute, agent:A, patient:B, object:TH\rangle\!\rangle\rangle\!\rangle\}$

The constraints (65),(67) and (68) are obtained by applying the heuristic H2.1. The constraint (66) is obtained as the result of the heuristic H3 by taking account of the correspondence (68). The constraint (69) is obtained by using the heuristic H4 under the correspondence (48), (55),(65), and (66). Thus, the situation supporting the constraints $C_{w \rightarrow a}^5$ becomes the resource situation s_r^3. In order to apply the constraints to s_{uf}^3, suppose the condition $s_r^3 = s_{uf}^3$. Then there exists a situation $s_{uf}^{3,t}$ such that:

(69) $\qquad s_{uf}^{3,t} \models \langle\!\langle own, agent:A, object:TH\rangle\!\rangle \wedge$

$\qquad\qquad\qquad \langle\!\langle prove, agent:A, event:E_{not\_func}(f)\rangle\!\rangle \wedge$

$\qquad\qquad\qquad \langle\!\langle can, agent:B, event\text{-}type:ET_{repair}(f); -\rangle\!\rangle \wedge$

$\qquad\qquad\qquad \langle\!\langle refute, agent:A, object:TH\rangle\!\rangle$

This situation corresponds to the described situation related to the target domain.

As the result of understanding the example sentence, the situation which satisfies the following condition is obtained as the main context:

(70) $\qquad\qquad\qquad s_d^0 = s_{uf}^{1,t} = s_{uf}^2 = s_{uf}^{3,t}$

and the situation which satisfies the following condition is obtained as the parallel context:

(71) $\qquad\qquad\qquad s_{uf}^1 = s_{uf}^3$

where

$$s_d^0 \neq s_{uf}^1$$
$$s_d^0 : T_{argue} \wedge s_d^0 : T_{misc}$$
$$s_{uf}^1 : T_{war} \wedge s_{uf}^1 : T_{misc}$$

4 Conclusion

In this paper, we give a formal description of metaphor understanding in terms of situation semantics. In this formulation, we propose a model in which the hearer introduces correspondences between a target domain and a source domain. These correspondences serve as a resource for obtaining useful information about the target domain in terms of the source domain. We expect that this formal description of metaphor understanding may be used as a guide to natural language understanding systems which can accommodate discourse involving metaphor. Since we have concentrated on a formal description in this paper, we have not mentioned how to search a plausible correspondence. The concrete method of how to search a plausible correspondence will be developed in future work. (For related works of plausible search in metaphor understanding, several methods have been proposed (see Tanaka et al. 1989, Indurkhya 1987).)

References

Barwise, J. 1989. *The Situation in Logic*. CSLI Lecture Notes Number 17. Stanford: CSLI Publications.

Barwise, J., and J. Perry. 1983. *Situations and Attitudes*. Cambridge, MA: MIT Press.

Fauconnier, G. 1985. *Mental Spaces: Aspects of Meaning Construction in Natural Language*. Cambridge, MA: MIT Press.

Gentner, D., B. Falkenhainer, and J. Skorstad. 1987. Metaphor: The Good, the Bad and the Ugly. *Theoretical Issues in Natural Language Processing* 3:176–180.

Holyoak, K. J. 1989. Analogical Mapping by Constraint Satisfaction. *Cognitive Science* 13:295–355.

Indurkhya, B. 1987. Approximate Semantic Transference: A Computational Theory of Metaphors and Analogies. *Cognitive Science* 11:445–480.

Lakoff, G. 1987a. Position Paper on Metaphor. *Theoretical Issues in Natural Language Processing* 3:194–197.

Lakoff, G. 1987b. *Women, Fire, and Dangerous Things*. Chicago: University of Chicago Press.

Lakoff, G., and M. Johnson. 1980. *Metaphors We Live By*. Chicago: University of Chicago Press.

Nunberg, G. 1987. Poetic and Prosaic Metaphors. *Theoretical Issues in Natural Language Processing* 3:198–201.

Ortony, A., and L. Fainsilber. 1987. The Role of Metaphors in Description of Emotions. *Theoretical Issues in Natural Language Processing* 3:181–184.

Plantinga, E. 1987. Mental Models and Metaphor. *Theoretical Issues in Natural Language Processing* 3:185–193.

Tanaka, H., M. Iwayama, and T. Tokunaga. 1989. A Computational Model of Understanding Metaphors. In *Proceedings of Nagoya International Symposium on Knowledge, Information and Intelligent Communication*, 17–26. November.

20

Relational Semantics and Scope Ambiguity

MASSIMO POESIO

Relational Semantics can be used to give a denotation to the unscoped logical forms used by Natural Language Processing systems—representations in which the quantifiers are 'left in place' rather than extracted. In this way, the system is no longer required to compute all the disambiguated interpretations of a sentence before storing its representation in the knowledge base. Rules of inference can also be defined so that the disambiguation process can be modeled by formal derivations, and 'weaker' versions of the standard rules of inference can be specified so that conclusions can be drawn without requiring a complete disambiguation.

1   Introduction

In using (1), a speaker could mean that there is some one undergraduate that is dating all male students, or merely that all male students date some undergraduate or other.

(1)   Every male student dates an undergrad.

The conventional view is that each sentence with multiple interpretations is to be seen as ambiguous, that is, each interpretation has to be represented by a distinct formula. The two interpretations of (1) are represented by (2a) and (2b).

This work was supported in part by the ONR/DARPA research contract number N00014-82-K-0193 and the NSF research grant number CDA-8822724.

I am grateful to my advisor Len Schubert and to Sandro Zucchi, James Allen, Jeff Pelletier and Graeme Hirst for their comments. I have profited considerably from discussions with Mats Rooth, Mark Gawron, John Nerbonne, David Israel, Dag Westerståhl, Fernando Pereira, Barbara Di Eugenio, Heinz Marburger, Michael Fliegner, and Rolf Eberle. I also thank an anonymous referee for editorial comments, suggestions to sharpen the focus of the paper, and for pointing out unclarities.

(2)   a. $((\forall x)\ (MS(x) \supset ((\exists y)\ U(y) \wedge D(x,y))))$
        b. $((\exists y)\ (U(y) \wedge ((\forall x)\ (MS(x) \supset D(x,y)))))$

'Traditional'[1] Natural Language Processing (NLP) systems, such as TEAM (Grosz et al. 1987) or the Core Language Engine (Alshawi et al. 1988), are built according to this view, and analyze (1) more or less as follows. First, the parser computes a *logical form* (Webber 1978, Schubert and Pelletier 1982, Allen 1987, Alshawi and van Eijck 1989) similar to the S-structure representation of (1) before Quantifier Raising:

(3)   [⟨every x male-student⟩ dates ⟨a y undergrad⟩]

All the unambiguous interpretations of (1) are then extracted from (3) by algorithms like that proposed by Hobbs and Shieber (1987). Finally, the system has to choose an interpretation, which is normally done using preference heuristics (Hurum 1988).

The disadvantages of this way of doing things have not gone unnoticed (see Kempson and Cormack 1981, Hobbs 1982, and Allen 1991). In this paper I will especially focus on two problems. The first problem is that a system built in this way cannot use the information which comes later in the discourse. Yet, this information could save the system a lot of work. Suppose, for instance, that sentence (1) is followed by sentence (4); one could immediately conclude that *an undergrad* in (1) has to take wide scope.

(4)   I met her yesterday.

The second problem is that because of the great number of possible interpretations, computing all of them can be very expensive. Two factors combine to multiply the number of interpretations. First, the number of (scopally) distinct interpretations grows as the factorial of the number of NPs. Sentence (5) has $5! = 120$ interpretations, all distinct (in the sense that no two interpretations are such that one entails the other).

(5)   In most democratic countries most politicians can fool most of the people on almost every issue most of the time (Hobbs 1983).

Yet, it seems obvious that people do not entertain 120 possibilities when hearing (5b). In addition, scope is just one of the reasons why a sentence may have more than one interpretation. By just considering the fact that in a sentence with numerical quantifiers like (6a) the examiners may be involved to a different degree in the grading, Kempson and Cormack (1981) are able to find at least four interpretations for it:

(6)   a. Two examiners marked six scripts.
        b. Three Frenchmen visited five Russians.

(6a) can be used to mean (a) that the same six scripts were each marked by two examiners, (b) that two examiners marked six (not necessarily the

---

[1]The use of 'traditional' here should not be thought of as derogatory. Actually, it is almost synonymous with 'working'.

same) scripts each, (c) that two examiners marked a group of six scripts between them, and (d) that two examiners each marked the same set of six scripts. As for (6b), Partee (1975, quoted by Bunt 1985) argues that it has eight readings; Bunt, counting also collective and distributive interpretations, is able to find 30 different readings for it! Even 30 interpretations seems to be too large a number to be actually considered. And yet, people do understand (5b) and (6b).

The aim of this article is to show that a fairly simple solution to the two problems just presented is possible within the 'relational' semantic framework developed in Barwise and Perry 1983, Barwise 1987, and Rooth 1987. The basic idea of relational semantics is that certain expressions 'change' the conditions of interpretation, represented by the variable assignments. For example, after the sentence *A man came in* has been added to a discourse, every variable assignment f which satisfies the new discourse has to assign a value to the variable used to represent the NP *a man*. This process can be modeled most effectively by using partial variable assignments and by requiring each variable assignment which satisfies the whole discourse to be an extension of a variable assignment which satisfies the portion of discourse prior to the last sentence. The value of a sentence will not be a truth value, but a *relation*, that is, a set of pairs of assignments, where the first element of each pair will be a variable assignment which satisfies the discourse prior to the addition of the expression, and the second element will be a variable assignment which satisfies the discourse after the sentence has been added (Barwise 1987, Rooth 1987).

My solution will be to give to the 'unscoped' expressions proposed in the NLP literature a denotation which is the union of the denotations of the disambiguated interpretations, and to use semantically justified inference rules to derive from the unscoped representation a new representation which is consistent with a smaller number of interpretations, possibly just one.[2] A system which uses a representation like the one I will present does not have to compute all the interpretations of (1) right away. Once such a system has translated (1) into an unscoped logical form, this logical form can be immediately stored in the discourse representation. As a matter of fact, it is not necessary for the system to disambiguate at all, unless it is required to do so: I will also show rules to derive certain types of conclusions from an unscoped representation. If a sentence like (4) is also asserted, however, and if the system is able to conclude that *her* in the

---

[2]To dissipate possible misunderstandings, it may be useful to add that even though the logic I will present is strictly monotonic, I'm not claiming that discourse disambiguation is a monotonic process. Some of the aspects of discourse inference can be explained as the result of the interaction of a number of different constraints, and at the moment I am mostly interested in exploring these interactions. Nothing however prevents extending the treatment I'll propose with nonmonotonic or probabilistic rules. I will return on this topic at the end of the paper.

second sentence is anaphoric to *an undergrad* in the first one, it will also be able to conclude that *an undergrad* takes scope over *every male student*. It should be clear that in this way both problems with the previous kind of architecture are solved.

I will use a DRT style of representation of the kind proposed in Kamp 1981. I needed a discourse representation which would make it easier to talk about anaphoric relations, and I chose DRT with the hope that this kind of representation would be better known than, say, Dynamic Montague Grammar (Groenendijk and Stokhof 1990) or the logic of Schubert and Pelletier 1988. However, I will redefine Kamp's semantics for DRT, and in such a way that the difference between the different kinds of representations will reduce considerably.

The organization of the paper is as follows. I will first discuss three solutions for the two problems of using later information and having to compute all the interpretations: the idea of using disjunction, the 'radical vagueness proposal' of Kempson and Cormack, and Hobbs' solution based on 'dependency functions'. I will explain why these solutions are all incomplete in one way or the other. After having introduced my DRT notation, and having shown how one can write a relational semantics for it preserving the properties of the representation proposed in Kamp 1981, I will show in Section 4 that one can use this semantics to add to the logic a construct to represent scopally ambiguous sentences, the *scope forest*, as well as to give a semantic justification to the disambiguating inference rules. Before introducing the logic more formally, I will give examples of 'disambiguation by deduction' in Section 5. I will close with a discussion of some issues raised by the solution I propose.

2 Previous Work

I am aware of three kinds of solutions to the two problems with the conventional view. In this section I will review them in turn.

2.1 Disjunction

The easiest way for representing a sentence with multiple interpretations without losing any information is to represent that sentence with a disjunction of all the interpretations. Sentence (1), for example, would be represented by the disjunction (7).

(7) $((\forall x) \, (\mathrm{MS}(x) \supset ((\exists y) \, \mathrm{U}(y) \wedge \mathrm{D}(x, y))))$
          $\vee \; ((\exists y) \, (\mathrm{U}(y) \wedge ((\forall x) \, (\mathrm{MS}(x) \supset \mathrm{D}(x, y)))))$

In this way, it is possible to take advantage of disambiguating information that may come later. This solution has several problems, however. First of all, as Kempson and Cormack point out, there is the *Mapping Problem*—there are a number of reasons for preferring as the semantic representation of a sentence a logical structure as close as possible to its syntactic structure, which isn't the case for (7). A second, and I think decisive, argument against this method is that it requires all the interpretations to be computed, and therefore is not a solution to the combinatorial explosion problem.[3]

2.2 Vagueness

Kempson and Cormack (1981) contend that the conventional view is misled. Even if (1) or (6a) have different interpretations (as Kempson and Cormack put it, they are *logically* ambiguous), they claim that those sentences are not *linguistically* ambiguous, that is, they have a single semantic representation. In their view, the representation of a sentence with multiple interpretations is the weakest representation entailed by all interpretations. This proposal works fairly well for sentences like (1), because in fact the two interpretations of that sentence are not really distinct: the reading in which a single undergraduate is dating all male students entails the other. The representation initially proposed by Kempson and Cormack for sentence (1) is (8).

(8) $\exists M \ \forall m_{m \in M} \ \exists U_1 \ \exists u_{u \in U} \ D(m, u)$

In order to extend this method to represent sentences like (6a), however, something more drastic is called for, since none of the interpretations of (6a) is entailed by all other three; the 120 interpretations of (5b) are also all distinct. In order to give a unique semantic representation to sentences like these, Kempson and Cormack introduce a second version of the theory in which a much weaker representation is used. The representation of (6a) is (9a), and the new representation of (1) is shown in (9b).

(9)   a. $\exists X_2 \ \exists S_6 \ \exists x_{x \in X_2} \ \exists s_{s \in S_6} \ M(x, s)$
       b. $\exists M \ \exists U_1 \ \exists m_{m \in M} \ \exists u_{u \in U} \ D(m, u)$

All that (9b) says is that there are a set of male students and a set of undergrads, and that one male student dated one undergrad. These truth conditions are of course much too weak a representation of (1): a NLP system using (9b) as the representation for (1) would have to pay a high price to eliminate the problems discussed above.

This is not, however, what Kempson and Cormack have in mind. Their idea is that (9b) is not the final representation of (1), but only the 'basis' from which the real interpretations can be generated by means of two operations: *uniformizing*—when an existential quantifier follows a universal, reverse their order; and *generalizing*—turn an existential quantifier into a universal. But if this is what they have in mind, we are left with something not much different from a 'traditional' system; the extraction operations do the job that in a traditional system would be done by an algorithm like Hobbs and Shieber's (assuming of course than one can justify these oper-

---

[3] Finding the logical representation for (5) is left as an exercise to the reader.

ations semantically, which Kempson and Cormack don't) and the 'filters' that Kempson and Cormack use to choose one interpretation are not much different from the preference heuristics mentioned above.

2.3 Dependency Between Sets

The proposal advanced by Hobbs (1983) falls in a third class of solutions, based on finding dependencies between sets. First of all, Hobbs wants to use a first-order representation, with variables ranging over sets. Second, he represents determiners as relations between sets. The sets he has in mind are not, however, the set of sets denoted by the NP and the set denoted by the VP. For example, he paraphrases a sentence like *Most men work* as 'there exists a set s which represents a majority of the set of all men, and for each individual y in s, y works'. This paraphrase becomes in his representation the formula (10).

(10) $(\exists s)\ (\text{MOST}(s, \{x|\text{MAN}(x)\}) \land (\forall y)(y \in s \supset \text{WORK}(y)))$

Hobbs' third assumption is that sets have *typical elements*. The typical element of a set s is an individual $\tau(s)$ defined by the following axiom:

(11) $(\forall s)P_s(\tau(s)) \equiv (\forall y)(y \in s \supset P(y))$

Where P_s is a predicate which is like P except that it is also true of $\tau(s)$ iff P is true of all the elements of s. Hobbs' representation for (1) is (something like) (12), which can be read as follows: there is a set m which includes all the male students, a set u which contains one undergrad, and the typical element of m dates the typical element of u.

(12) $(\exists m, m_1, u, u_1)\ (\text{EVERY}(m, m_1) \land \text{A}(u, u_1) \land$
       $\text{MALE-STUDENT}_{m_1}(\tau(m_1)) \land$
       $\text{UNDERGRAD}_{u_1}(\tau(u_1)) \land \text{DATES}(\tau(m), \tau(u)))$

Finally, scope relations are represented using *dependency functions*. A dependency function f returns, for each male student x, the set of undergrads that x dates:

$$f(x) = \{y|\ \text{UNDERGRAD}(y) \land \text{DATES}(x, y)\}.$$

If the inferencing component discovers there is a different set u for each element of the set m, u can be viewed as referring to the typical element of this set of sets, and the fact $u = \tau(\{f(x)|x \in m\})$ can be added to the knowledge base. There are two problems with this solution. First of all, as Hobbs points out, the representation in (10) can only be used with monotone increasing determiners, like *most* and *every*. For, if we were to represent *No man works hard* in Hobbs's representation, we would be able to conclude that no man works, which doesn't follow—*no* is not monotone increasing. The second problem, common to other dependency function-based solutions, is that only sentences with two quantifiers can be given a scope-neutral information, and not, say, sentences with a quantifier and negation, as *John doesn't have a car*.

3   A Relational Semantics for DRT

This section has two purposes: to introduce the DRT-based representation I will use in the rest of the paper, together with some terminology[4], and to show how one can specify a 'relational' semantics for such a representation. I will call the resulting logic DRT_0. The reader to whom both DRT and relational semantics are familiar may want to skip this section.

3.1   The Syntax of DRT_0

The set of symbols of DRT_0 includes a set of *property symbols* (unary predicates), a set of *relational symbols*, and a set of *markers*: $x_0, \ldots, x_n, \ldots$. (I will sometimes use for simplicity letters without indices like x, y, etc., for the markers.) The set of expressions of DRT_0 consists of:

1. *marker introducers* like α^{x_i}, where x_i is a *new* marker, that is, a marker not used for any other marker introducer. (That is, i must be strictly greater than any previously used marker index.)

2. *conditions*:
   a. *unary conditions* like $P(x_i)$, where x_i is a marker and P is a property symbol.
   b. *binary conditions* like $R(x_i, x_j)$, where x_i and x_j are markers and R is a relation symbol.
   c. *coindexing conditions* like $x_i = x_j$, where x_i and x_j are markers.
   d. *negated DRSs* of the form $\neg K$, where K is a DRS.
   e. *conditional DRSs* of the form $K_1 \to K_2$, where K_1 and K_2 are DRSs.

3. *Discourse Representation Structures*: a DRS is an expression containing one or more conditions and zero or more marker introducers, usually written as in (13), where α^{x_0} and α^{x_1} are marker introducers, FARMER(x_0) and DONKEY(x_1) are unary conditions, and OWNS(x_0, x_1) is a binary condition.

(13)

α^{x_0} α^{x_1}
FARMER(x_0)
DONKEY(x_1)
OWNS (x_0, x_1)

In keeping with the standard conventions, I will reserve the symbol K, possibly with subscripts, to indicate DRS's. Subscripted x's like x_0 will always indicate markers. Let a marker x be *free in* K if no marker introducer α^x is in K. A DRT_0 *formula* is a DRS with no free markers. The donkey sentence *Every farmer who owns a donkey beats it* is represented in DRT_0 by (14).

---

[4]The amount of space at my disposal prevents a complete introduction to DRT.

(14)

$$
\boxed{
\begin{array}{l}
\alpha^{x_0} \; \alpha^{x_1} \\
\hline
\text{FARMER}(x_0) \\
\text{DONKEY}(x_1) \\
\text{OWNS} \; (x_0, x_1)
\end{array}
}
\;\rightarrow\;
\boxed{
\begin{array}{l}
\alpha^{x_2} \\
\hline
x_2 = x_1 \\
\text{BEATS}(x_0, x_2)
\end{array}
}
$$

The only significant difference between DRT_0 and 'standard' DRT is the distinction between 'use' and 'introduction' of markers. This distinction makes it easier to enforce the constraint that each marker has to be new, as well as simplifying the definition of the semantics of a DRS, but otherwise has no semantic consequences.

3.2 The Semantics

A model M for DRT_0 is a pair $\langle U, F \rangle$: U is a nonempty set, and F an interpretation function. Assignments are called *embedding functions* in DRT; embedding functions are partial functions from markers to objects of the domain. An embedding function over M is a function which associates to the markers values from U. The denotation with respect to M of an expression of DRT_0 is a set of pairs of embeddings over M defined as follows:

1. $\|\alpha^{x_i}\|^M = \{\langle f, g \rangle |\ f \subseteq g,\ x_i \notin \text{DOM}(f)\ \text{and}\ g = f\ \cup \langle x_i, a \rangle,$
   for some $a \in U\}$

2. $\|\text{FARMER}(x_i)\|^M = \{\langle f, f \rangle |\ f(x_i) \in F(\text{FARMER})\}$

3. $\|\text{OWNS}(x_i, x_j)\|^M = \{\langle f, f \rangle |\ \langle f(x_i), f(x_j) \rangle \in F(\text{OWNS})\}$

4. $\|x_i = x_j\|^M = \{\langle f, f \rangle |\ f(x_i) = f(x_j)\}$

5. $\left\|\ \boxed{\begin{array}{l} \alpha^{x_1}, \ldots, \alpha^{x_n} \\ \hline C_1 \\ \vdots \\ C_m \end{array}}\ \right\|^M = \{\langle f, f \rangle |\ \text{there exist}\ f_1 \ldots f_n\ \text{such that}$
   $\langle f, f_1 \rangle \in \|\alpha^{x_1}\|^M, \ldots, \langle f_{n-1}, f_n \rangle \in \|\alpha^{x_n}\|^M$
   $\text{and}\ \langle f_n, f_n \rangle \in \|C_1\|^M, \ldots, \|C_m\|^M\}$

6. $\|\neg K\|^M = \{\langle f, f \rangle | \langle f, f \rangle \notin \|K\|^M\}$

7. $\|K_1 \rightarrow K_2\|^M = \{\langle f, f \rangle |\ \text{for all}\ f\ \text{such that for all extensions}\ g\ \text{such}$
   that $\langle f, g \rangle \in \|K_1\|^M$, there exists h such that $\langle g, h \rangle \in \|K_2\|^M\}$

It is easy to check that the verification conditions in DRT_0 are analogous to those of standard DRT, and to verify that by requiring that a marker x be coindexed with a marker y only if the assignment x is defined on both, one also obtains the same accessibility conditions of DRT. Truth can be defined as follows. A formula K is *true* in a model M iff $\|K\|^M \neq \emptyset$. A simple notion of entailment for DRT_0 can be defined as follows: if K_1 and K_2 are formulas, $K_1 \models K_2$ iff for all models M in which K_1 is true, $\|K_1\|^M \subset \|K_2\|^M$.

3.3 The Inference Rules

I am not aware of any definition of inference rules for DRT in the literature, so I will introduce one that will do for the purposes of this article. A *rule of inference* in DRT_0 is a way of deriving a *conclusion* from a set of *premises*, precisely as in first order logic. That it, the rules of inference of DRT are of the form

$$\frac{K_1, \ldots, K_n}{K}$$

where both the premises $K_1, \ldots, K_n$ and the conclusion K are conditions. The only difference is that these inference rules will be DRS-specific, in the sense that the argument is applicable only when the premises $K_1, \ldots, K_n$ are all conditions of a single *formula* K'; the conclusion will also be added to the same DRS, obtaining a new DRS K''. An inference rule is *acceptable* iff K'' is still a formula. A rule of inference will be *sound* iff it is acceptable, and $K' \models K''$. An example of sound rule of inference for DRT$_0$ is the following version of *Modus Ponens*:

$$\frac{\boxed{P} \longrightarrow \boxed{Q}, \; P}{Q}$$

4 The Proposal

DRT$_0$ is not a solution to our problems: the two interpretations of sentence (1), in fact, still have to be represented by distinct DRT$_0$ formulas:

(15) *a.*

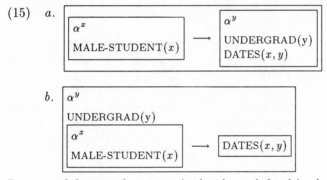

    b.

Because of the way the semantics has been defined in the previous section, however, it will be relatively easy to extend DRT$_0$ with a new construct which will be used to give a unique representation to (1). In this section I will introduce a model of disambiguation in which sentences are represented as *scope forests* whose denotation is the union of the denotations of the scopally disambiguated interpretations, and the number of possible interpretations can be restricted using inference rules which reflect either logical or referential facts.

4.1 Scope Forests

Consider first a slightly modified version of (1).

(16)   Every male student dates most undergrads.

The 'unscoped logical form' of (16) proposed in the literature (Schubert and Pelletier 1982, Allen 1987, Alshawi and van Eijck 1989) has a form that in DRT terms could be something like (17).

(17)
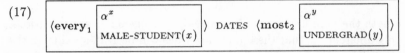

My goal is to give a denotation to a DRS of this type. The relational semantics sketched in Section 3 can be used to this end, as follows. There are two quantified NPs in the sentence, *every male student* and *most undergrads*, and two ways of 'ordering' them to get an interpretation. The interpretation of (16) in which the universal takes wide scope (assuming a representation for generalized quantifiers in DRT roughly analogous to the one suggested in Kamp 1988) is shown in (18).

(18)
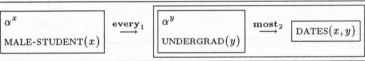

If we think of the restrictions of the quantifiers and of the DRS which represents the scope of *most undergrads* in (18) as nodes of a graph, we can see each way of ordering the quantifiers as a path which starts from the antecedent of the quantifier with wider scope and ends with the consequent of the quantifier with narrower scope. I will therefore call each such way of ordering the NPs a *path*. In the relational semantics of section 3, each path denotes a set of pairs. The denotation of the logical form in (17) can therefore be defined as the union of these sets. I will call DRS's like (17) *scope forests*. If the denotation of a scope forest SF is the union of the denotation of the paths in a set PS, I will say that the paths in PS are *associated* with SF. The translation rules in the grammar will be such that the interpretation of a sentence like (16) is a scope forest[5].

4.2 Ordering Constraints and Scope Forest Disambiguation

As new facts about the relative scope of the NPs in a sentence S are discovered, the number of paths (that is, interpretations) associated with the scope forest SF representing S is reduced. The inference rules for scope disambiguation (below) model this process. These rules derive from a scope forest SF a new scope forest SF′ which has more *ordering constraints* (using logical truths, facts about reference, etc.)Each ordering constraint of a scope forest SF is a label of the form $i < j$, where i and j are indices of operators in SF, and indicates that only paths in which the operator with

---

[5]The logical form is generated as proposed by Schubert and Pelletier (1982). The fragment cannot be included in the paper, because of space constraints.

index i precedes the operator with index j are associated to SF. For example, the scope forest equivalent to the subset of interpretations of (16) in which *most undergrads* takes scope over *every male student* is represented by the DRS in (19).

(19)
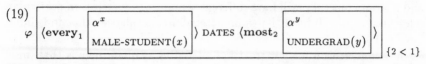

Since only one path is associated to the scope forest in (19), we can derive from it the equivalent disambiguated interpretation, as shown below.

4.3 Negation and Indefinites

Before introducing the rules of inference I need to fill in a few details. The first question is what to do with other operators with scope, like negation. The answer is that the tools introduced so far are in fact sufficient to represent scope ambiguities originated by negation, provided that we also index the negation operator. The representation of the sentence *John doesn't have a car*, for example, will be the scope forest (20).[6]

(20)

$$\varphi \left| \; j \quad \neg_1 \text{HAVE} \; \langle a_2 \; \boxed{\begin{array}{c} \alpha^x \\ \text{CAR}(x) \end{array}} \rangle \right| \; \emptyset$$

The second question is how to make the 'path' idea work with sentences like (1), since the representation for indefinites in DRT_0 does not consist of a restriction and a scope. My answer is that it is possible to represent indefinite NPs with structures similar to those used for quantifiers. For example, it is possible to represent the disambiguated reading of (1) in which *every student* scopes over *an undergrad* as in (21) without changing the properties that indefinites have in standard DRT.

(21)
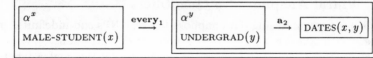

Two such properties seem especially important. The first property is that indefinites, unlike quantifiers, are not subject to the scope constraint, as clearly shown by the contrast in acceptability between (22a) and (22b):

(22) a. A dog$_i$ came in. It$_i$ sat under the table
      b. Every dog$_i$ came in. ??It$_i$ sat under the table

The work on relational semantics and Dynamic Montague Grammar has however shown that we can model this distinction semantically, and still represent indefinites as having a scope (Rooth 1987, Schubert and Pelletier

---

[6] This method can also be used for modal operators.

1988). It is enough to introduce two separate classes of DRS's: one of *referential* DRSs,[7] used to represent determiners like *a*, *the*, and the pronouns; another of *quantified* DRSs $index$ DRS *!quantified*, used to represent determiners like *most* and *every*. Both classes of DRS's will have a restriction and a scope, but they will have different semantic properties: in particular, referential NPs will have the same accessibility properties that indefinites have in DRT.

A second reason for not treating indefinites as quantifiers is that unselective operators like the universal and the conditional seem able to bind indefinites, but not generalized quantifiers. Again, this does not prevent a representation in which indefinites have a restriction and a scope. If desired[8], one can achieve the same semantic effects of DRT by giving to generalized quantifiers the capability of imposing constraints on the set of satisfying embeddings, as shown in more detail in section 6.

In a word, representing indefinite NPs as in (21) won't require a change in the way they participate to anaphoric relations, nor will require a change in the properties of generalized quantifiers, unless this change is otherwise motivated. If desired, we could even define 'simplification rules' for transforming the structures associated to referential NPs into the representation more traditionally associated to indefinites in DRT.

A note on the notation: in order to distinguish between referential NPs and quantifiers in the scope forest representation, I will use parentheses instead of angle brackets for referential NPs; brackets will be used when any determiner is possible. The scope forest into which (1) is translated will be as follows:

(23)

$$\langle \text{every}_1 \begin{array}{|c|} \hline \alpha^x \\ \hline \text{MALE-STUDENT}(x) \\ \hline \end{array} \rangle \quad \text{DATES} \quad (\text{a}_2 \begin{array}{|c|} \hline \alpha^y \\ \hline \text{UNDERGRAD}(y) \\ \hline \end{array})$$

4.4 Plural Anaphora To Quantifiers

While intersentential singular anaphora to every-NPs and indefinites in the scope of a quantifier is subject to a number of restrictions[9], intersential plural anaphora is generally possible, as shown by the contrast between (22b) and (24), as well as by the contrast between (25a) and (25b).

(24) Every dog$_i$ came in. They$_i$ sat under the table.

---

[7]Bad as this name sounds, the only alternative that came to my mind was 'article DRS's', which is also misleading, because pronouns will also be represented in this way.

[8]That is, leaving aside the well-known objections raised against the unselective quantification account: the *proportion problem*, presented in more detail in section 6, puts under discussion the claim for generalized quantifiers, while Schubert and Pelletier (1988) present counterexamples to the claim for conditionals.

[9]Roberts (1987) discusses some cases in which it is possible; see also Poesio and Zucchi 1991.

(25) a. Every person with a dog$_i$ came in.
      ??It$_i$ was put under the table.
  b. Every person with a dog$_i$ came in.
      They$_i$ were put under the table.

Without attempting a complete description of the phenomenon, I'll incorporate into the inference rules some facts about plural anaphora to quantifiers which will be useful to disambiguate on the basis of referential information.

I'll borrow the necessary notation from Link's *LP* logic (Link 1987). Link proposes a model in which the universe of discourse is not a set, but a complete semilattice $\langle E, \bigvee \rangle$ which contains all the 'sums' of the (atomic) individuals of a set $A \subset E$. With this model we can give an interpretation to the logical predicates ATOM(x), true iff the value associated to x in Link's model is an element of A, and GROUP(x), true iff that value is in $E - A$.[10] The following lemma holds:

Lemma 1 *For every marker x it is either the case that ATOM(x) or that GROUP(x), but not both.*

The semantics of quantified DRS's like $K_1 \xrightarrow{\text{every}_i} K_2$ will be defined in terms of a *distancing* operation to be performed on the set of pairs $\langle f, g \rangle$ of embeddings such that f verifies the truth conditions of $K_1 \xrightarrow{\text{every}_i} K_2$ and g is one of the extensions of f which associate values to the markers which verify both restriction and scope. If we think of embeddings as ways of encoding situations, this operation is like a 'change in perspective': in the situation resulting from distancing we do not perceive the individual events and the single objects any more, but only the situation in its totality and the sets of objects involved. This means that after distancing, only the *projections* of the NPs, that is, the sets of objects playing certain roles in the global situation, are available for discourse anaphora. According to this account, the contrast between (22a) and (22b), as well as the acceptability of (24), are due to the fact that the projection of *a dog* in (22a) is a unique individual, and therefore available for individual anaphora, while the projection of *every dog* in (22b) and in (24) is the set of all dogs.[11]

---

[10]Link's model has already been proposed by Kamp as a way to represent conjoined and plural NPs in DRT (Kamp 1988). Both ATOM and GROUP are mine.

[11]This account provides a justification for the operation of *summation* introduced in Kamp 1988, but of course doesn't solve the well-known problems raised by (a) and (b):

(a) Each student walked to the stage. He shook hands with the dean and left. (Partee)
(b) Each Italian loves his car. He rides it every Sunday.

Poesio and Zucchi (1991) propose that distancing is blocked if the discourse has a certain structure—typically, the sentence which contains the anaphoric reference is an elaboration of a generic description or the continuation of an episode along a known 'script'.

4.5 Inference Rules for Scope Disambiguation

At this point, I can begin to answer the questions: How can we infer the intended scope relations? Do we really need to infer them completely? What consequences can we infer from a non-disambiguated interpretation? The rules presented in this section are a way for using disambiguation information to infer the intended scope relations. The information about scope relations comes from a variety of sources. Three kinds of sources seem especially important:

1. Logical facts, like the fact that the sentence *A male student is dating an undergrad* has only one interpretation.
2. Anaphoric facts: If sentence (1) is followed by *They meet them at parties*, and we may conclude that either *them* or *they* is anaphoric to *an undergrad* in (1)—that is, we may conclude that the projection of *an undergrad* in (1) is not a single person, but a group of people—then we may also conclude that *every male graduate* scopes over *an undergrad*.
3. World knowledge. For example, one may use facts about the social rules of dating to infer that the most likely interpretation of (1) is the one in which *every student* takes scope over *an undergrad*. As this very example shows, however, most of this information cannot be taken as conclusive, and therefore rules of this type are only appropriate with a logic which allows for revisions. My ideas on this problem are still tentative, and will be discussed at the end of the paper.

I will present an example of scope forest reduction rule based on 'logical' facts and two examples of rules based on 'anaphoric' facts. There is no pretense of completeness: the only reason why I introduce these specific rules is that they will get the examples in section 5 through. I'll then present the *Scope Forest Elimination* rule. The rules will be in the format specified in Section 3.

ROR (Referential Over Referential): This rule reflects the logical fact that referential NPs do not create scope ambiguities: in *A man saw a dog*, for example, the relative scope of *A man* and *a dog* does not matter.

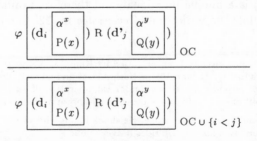

RAOQ (Referential Atom Over Quantifier): This rule allows the reduction of the scope forest associated with sentences like *Every male student dates an undergrad* once it has been concluded that *an undergrad*

refers to a single individual, that is, the projection of *an undergrad* is an atom in Link's sense. It is worth remembering that because of the way the denotation of the scope forest is defined, y gets different values 'inside' and 'outside' of a quantified DRS (therefore, of a scope forest): 'outside' it denotes the *projection* of the referential NP.

$$\varphi \left| \langle d_i \left[\begin{array}{c} \alpha^x \\ \hline P(x) \end{array} \right] \rangle \; R \; (d'_j \left[\begin{array}{c} \alpha^y \\ \hline Q(y) \end{array} \right]) \right| \text{OC}$$

$$\text{ATOM}(y)$$

$$\varphi \left| \langle d_i \left[\begin{array}{c} \alpha^x \\ \hline P(x) \end{array} \right] \rangle \; R \; (d'_j \left[\begin{array}{c} \alpha^y \\ \hline Q(y) \end{array} \right]) \right| \text{OC} \cup \{j < i\}$$

QORG (Quantifier Over Referential Group): This rule enables us to conclude, from the fact that the projection of an indefinite NP is a group and the indefinite NP is in a scope forest with a quantifier, that the quantifier takes wide scope. (Consider for example the case when (1) is followed by *They meet them at parties.*)

$$\varphi \left| \langle d_i \left[\begin{array}{c} \alpha^x \\ \hline P(x) \end{array} \right] \rangle \; R \; (d'_j \left[\begin{array}{c} \alpha^y \\ \hline Q(y) \end{array} \right]) \right| \text{OC}$$

$$\text{GROUP}(y)$$

$$\varphi \left| \langle d_i \left[\begin{array}{c} \alpha^x \\ \hline P(x) \end{array} \right] \rangle \; R \; (d'_j \left[\begin{array}{c} \alpha^y \\ \hline Q(y) \end{array} \right]) \right| \text{OC} \cup \{i < j\}$$

Last but not least, we need to be able to derive a disambiguated DRS from a scope forest associated to a single path. The simplest way for doing this is to introduce a rule of inference whose premise is a scope forest associated to a single path, as follows:

SFE (Scope Forest Elimination): a scope forest which associated to a single path can be replaced by the corresponding interpretation.

$$\varphi \left| \langle d_i \left[\begin{array}{c} \alpha^x \\ \hline P(x) \end{array} \right] \rangle \; R \; \langle d'_j \left[\begin{array}{c} \alpha^y \\ \hline Q(y) \end{array} \right] \rangle \right| \{i < j\}$$

$$\left[\begin{array}{c} \alpha^x \\ \hline P(x) \end{array} \right] \xrightarrow{d_i} \left[\begin{array}{c} \alpha^y \\ \hline Q(y) \end{array} \right] \xrightarrow{d'_j} \boxed{R(i,j)}$$

This way of writing the rules makes it simple to show how the derivations work in Section 5, but, of course, one then needs one such rule for each permutation of the indices—120 rules for a sentence with 5 quantifiers, for example. In addition, one would require one such rule for every number of arguments. In a word, it would seem that the combinatorial explosion that I was throwing out of the door is coming back through the window.

It is not so in practice, however. First of all, the particular notation for scope forests I have been using has been chosen to preserve the similarity with the logical forms proposed in the NLP literature as much as possible. With this notation, however, one can only write rules which apply to scope forests with a fixed number of arguments, and these rules are normally asymmetrical, in the sense that the argument position is significant. It should be clear however how rules for n-arguments scope forests could be written, as well as rules in which the argument position is reversed. There are notations in which more general rules can be written, but I preferred not to use them, since they are pretty opaque.

As for the potentially more dangerous problem of requiring $n!$ rules to disambiguate a scope forest with n arguments, a moment's thought will reveal that all that is really needed to trigger these rules is a way of checking that the ordering constraints define a total order, that is, there is a path of length $n-1$ from an index to another index. The inference procedure can do that without really going through $n!$ rules. A very simple minded algorithm exists to add a new constraint and discover if the constraints define a total order in $O(n^2)$. Once it has been determined that the constraints define a total order, the operators can be 'extracted' from the scope forest one after the other in linear time using a procedure similar to the one that will be used in Section 6 to define the set of paths associated to a scope forest.

4.6 Reasoning with Scope Forests

I mentioned before three reasons for assigning a semantics to unscoped logical forms: first, one doesn't need to compute all the possible interpretations; second, one can use information which comes later in the discourse to disambiguate; third, if one is able to draw the interesting conclusions on the basis of the ambiguous sentence alone, one may not need to disambiguate at all.

So far, however, I haven't said anything about how to go about performing inferences not related to disambiguation. We can do that by defining inference rules analogous to first order logic's Universal Instantiation (UI) and Existential Generalization. It's easy to see how such rules can be defined (and semantically justified) in the framework I have been proposing. I will give as an example the scope forest version of UI; 'weak' versions of Existential Generalization and Existential Instantiation can be defined in the same way.

[WUI (Weak Universal Instantiation:] from *Every male student dates an undergrad* and *John is a male student* conclude *John dates an undergrad*.

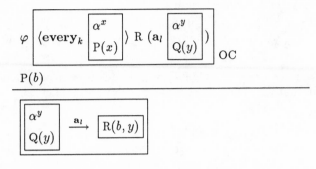

$$P(b)$$

Similar rules hold when a is replaced by *many, most*, etc.[12]

5 Reasoning with an Ambiguous Logic: Examples

In this section I will show how one can formally derive an unambiguous interpretation from a scope forest using the inference rules presented in the previous section, as well as facts about world knowledge and anaphoric relations. I will not give explicit examples of application of WUI, for reasons of space; hopefully, the derivations presented below will be explicit enough that the reader will be able to reconstruct the derivation of, e.g., *John dates and undergrad* from the scope forest representation of *Every male student dates an undergrad* and of *John is a male student*. of examples to show how scope disambiguation can interact with other discourse disambiguation processes, in particular, with reference disambiguation. I will first present a simple model of reference disambiguation, then show the derivations.

5.1 An Elementary Model of Reference Disambiguation

The set of possible anaphoric antecedents of a pronoun x (its *anchoring set*) initially includes all the markers accessible to x according to a definition of accessibility which is essentially that of DRT, modulo the accessibility of plural markers for quantifiers. The initial anchoring set does not include those markers ruled out by binding principles (Reinhart 1983), since the parser introduces a disjointness condition $x \neq y$ for each such marker y.

I will need a logical predicate for talking about accessibility in the object language. The relation between two markers $x_i \prec x_j$ holds whenever x_i is accessible from x_j, that is, whenever x_i is introduced 'before' x_j. Semantically, $x_i \prec x_j$ will be defined to hold whenever $i < j$ (remember that each new marker has a greater index than any of the markers introduced before, and that no two markers are allowed to have the same index). $x_i \prec x_j$ is

---

[12]This observation is due to Len Schubert.

reflexive and transitive but not symmetrical. I will also make the simplifying assumption that if the marker x is the representation of a pronoun, then x is coindexed with one of the accessible markers. This assumption is encoded by the following axiom[13]:

Axiom 1 Let $x_1 \ldots x_n$ be all the markers introduced before x_{n+1} (that is, all the markers for which $x_j \prec x_{n+1}$ is true), and let x_{n+1} be introduced by a pronoun. Then $x_{n+1} = x_1 \vee \ldots \vee x_{n+1} = x_n$ is also true.

The first reference disambiguation rule adds new disjointness conditions, thus eliminating elements from the anchoring set. Let the * operator be defined as follows:

$$(\text{*OP}) \quad P^*(x) \equiv_{\text{def}} (\text{ATOM}(x) \wedge P(x))$$

$$\vee \; (\text{GROUP}(x) \wedge \boxed{\begin{array}{l} \alpha^y \\ y \in x \end{array}} \overset{\text{every}_i}{\longrightarrow} \boxed{P(y)} \,)$$

The ASTR rule says that if two markers x and y are not of the same type, i.e., a predicate P is true of the marker x but not of y, then y and x are disjoint.

ASTR (Type Reduction):

$$\frac{P^*(x), \; \neg P^*(y)}{x \neq y}$$

When the anchoring set of x reduces to just one element z the *parameter anchoring* (PA) rule applies. Parameter anchoring lets us infer a coindexing relation $x = y$ between a marker x and a marker y whenever every other marker z accessible from x has been found to be distinct from x:

PA (Parameter Anchoring):

$$\frac{\begin{array}{c} y \prec x \\[4pt] \boxed{\begin{array}{l} \alpha^z \\ z \prec x \\ y \neq z \end{array}} \overset{\text{every}_i}{\longrightarrow} \boxed{x \neq z} \end{array}}{x = y}$$

5.2 Disambiguation By Deduction

In this section I demonstrate the ideas presented up to this point by showing how each disambiguated interpretation of sentence (1) can be derived

[13]This axiom is too strong in general. Consider the sentence *He came in*, and suppose that John and Bill are the only available referents. Using the disjunction method, we would obtain as a representation of the sentence that it is either the case that John came in or that Bill came in. Imagine, however, that neither John nor Bill came in. The axiom would lead us to conclude that *He came in* is false, which doesn't seem the right prediction: most people would conclude instead that the referent of *he* is neither John nor Bill. This is, I think, yet another argument against identifying ambiguity with disjunction.

```
1. [<every 1 [x male-student(x)]> dates (a 2 [y undergrad(y)])], 0
                 (translation of 'Every male student dates an
                 undergrad')

2. x <> y        (translation of 'Every male student dates an
                 undergrad', possibly incorporating some form
                 of indefiniteness effect)

3. [speaker met (her 3 [z woman(z)])], 0
                 (translation of 'I met her')

4. x < z         (acessibility condition)

5. y < z

6. woman*(z)     (part of the translation of 'I met her')

7. ~woman*(x)    (world knowledge)

8. z <> x        (4, 6, 7, ASTR)

9. z = y         (5, 2, 4, 8, PA)

10.atom(z)       (world knowledge)

11.atom(y)       (9, 10, Theorem 2)

12.[<every 1 [x male-student(x)]> dates (a 2 [y undergrad(y)])],
                 {2 < 1}
                 (1, 11, RAOQ)

13.[y undergrad(y)] -a-> [[x male-student(x)] -every-> [x dates y]]
                 (12, SFE)
```

Figure 1 Wide scope for *an undergrad*

from the scope forest representation, given the appropriate context. The following theorem (a simple corollary of a lemma presented in Section 4) will be used in the derivations:

Theorem 2 *Given any two markers x and z, if* ATOM(z) *is true and $x = z$ is true, then* ATOM(x) *is also true.*

Let us consider again sentence (1), repeated here for convenience.

(26)   Every male student dates an undergrad.

Let us now suppose that sentence (26) is followed by the sentence in (27).

(27)   I met her.

```
1. and 2.           as before.

3. [<they 3 [z group(z)]> meet-at-parties <they 4 [w group(w)]>], 0
                    (translation of 'They meet them at parties.')

4. and 5.:          as before

6. z <> w           (translation of 'They meet them at parties.')

7. w = x or w = y   (Axiom 1)

8. z = x or z = y   (Axiom 1)

9. y = w or y = z   (6, 7, 8)

10.group(z)         (part of the meaning of 'they')

11.group(w)         (part of the meaning of 'they'

12.group(y)         (9, 10, 11)

13.[<every 1 [x male-student(x)]> dates (a 2 [y undergrad(y)])],
                    {1 < 2}
                    (1, 12, QORG)

14.[x male-student(x)] -every-> [[y undergrad(y)] -a-> [x dates y]]
                    (13, SFE))
```

Figure 2 Narrow scope for *an undergrad*

In Figure 1 I show how one can deduce a wide scope reading for *an undergrad* in (26) using the fact that it is coindexed with *her* in (27).

For an example of disambiguation in which *every male student* takes wide scope, suppose that (26) is followed by the following sentence:

(28)   They meet them at parties.

The derivation of a wide scope reading for *every male student* is shown in Figure 2.

6   A More Formal Presentation of DRT$_1$

6.1   The Syntax

The main syntactic differences between DRT$_0$ and DRT$_1$ are the following:

1. Universally quantified sentences and conditionals are now represented as two different classes of expressions: the class of *quantifier* DRSs, and the class of *connective* DRSs.

2. A new class of complex conditions is introduced, the class of *referential* DRSs, to represent indefinites, definites and pronouns. These kinds of NPs are therefore syntactically separated from proper names.

3. Another new kind of complex condition is introduced, the *scope forest*.

4. Operators like quantifiers and negation are given *indices*.

The set of symbols of DRT$_1$ includes, in addition to the set of symbols of DRT$_0$, a set of *indices* $0 \ldots i \ldots$; a set QDet $=$ {**every, most**} of *quantifier operators*; and a set RDet $=$ {**a, the, he, it, she, they**} of *referential operators*. The set of expressions of DRT$_1$ consists of marker introducers (defined as in DRT$_0$), conditions, and DRSs. In addition to the unary, binary and coindexing conditions of DRT$_0$, DRT$_1$ includes the following types of conditions:

1. *disjointness conditions* of the form $x \neq y$, where x and y are markers.

2. *accessibility conditions* of the form $x \prec y$, where x and y are markers.

3. the *structural conditions* ATOM(x) and GROUP(x), where x is a marker.

4. *negated* DRSs, that are expressions of form $\neg_i K$, where K is a DRS and i an index;

5. *connective* DRSs, like $K_1 \overset{\text{if-then}_i}{\longrightarrow} K_2$ (used to represent the conditional), where K_1 and K_2 are DRSs;

6. *quantifier* DRSs, which are expressions of the form

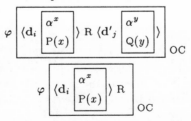

where $\mathbf{d} \in$ QDet, and K_1 and K_2 are DRSs; K_1 will be called *restriction*, K_2 *scope*, and x the *main marker*;

7. *referential* DRSs, again of the form $K_1 \overset{\mathbf{d}_i}{\longrightarrow} K_2$, where $\mathbf{d} \in$ RDet, and K_1 and K_2 are DRSs; again, K_1 will be called restriction and K_2 will be called scope;

8. *scope forests*, which are expressions of one of the following types:

$$\varphi \; \boxed{ \langle \mathbf{d}_i \; \boxed{\begin{array}{c} \alpha^x \\ \hline P(x) \end{array}} \rangle \; R \; \langle \mathbf{d}'_j \; \boxed{\begin{array}{c} \alpha^y \\ \hline Q(y) \end{array}} \rangle } \; \text{OC}$$

$$\varphi \; \boxed{ \langle \mathbf{d}_i \; \boxed{\begin{array}{c} \alpha^x \\ \hline P(x) \end{array}} \rangle \; R } \; \text{OC}$$

where $\mathbf{d}$ and $\mathbf{d}'$ are in QDet $\cup$ RDet; R is either a relation or a *negated relation* of the form $\neg_i R'$ where R$'$ is a relation; and OC is a set $\{ i \prec j, \ldots k \prec l \}$ of *ordering constraints* among the indices of the operators in the scope forest.

A *formula* of DRT_1 is a DRS with no free markers, and in which no two operators are given the same index. The donkey sentence *Every farmer who owns a donkey beats it* is represented as in (29) (which the reader should compare to the DRT_0 representation (14), Section 3).

(29)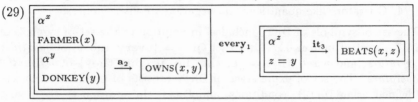

6.2 The Semantics

A model M for DRT_1 is a pair $\langle U, F \rangle$: F is an interpretation function, and U is a Link-type boolean algebra $\langle D, A, \leq, \sqcup \rangle$ in which $\leq$ models the inclusion relation, A is the set of *atoms* of D, i.e., those elements of D such that no other element is included in them, and $\sqcup$ models sum ($x \sqcup y$ is the minimal element of U which includes both x and y).

The denotation of a DRT_1 expression with respect to M is defined as follows. The denotation of basic conditions and marker introducers is the same as in DRT_0. The new atomic conditions have the following denotations:

1. $\|x \neq y\|^M = \{\langle f, f \rangle| \; f(x) \neq f(y)\}$
2. $\|\text{ATOM}(x)\|^M = \{\langle f, f \rangle| \; f(x) \in A\}$
3. $\|\text{GROUP}(x)\|^M = \{\langle f, f \rangle| \; f(x) \in U - A\}$
4. $\|x_i \prec x_j\|^M = \emptyset$ if $i > j$, $\{\langle f, f \rangle| \; x_i, x_j \in \text{DOM}(f)\}$ otherwise.

The denotation of the basic DRS changes, since accessibility is now controlled by discourse structure and the type of NP. Rather than pairs $\langle f, f \rangle$, a basic DRS will denote pairs $\langle f, g \rangle$ where g contains additional values for the markers introduced by the DRS:

$$\left\| \begin{array}{|l|} \hline \alpha^{x_1}, \ldots, \alpha^{x_n} \\ C_1 \\ \vdots \\ C_m \\ \hline \end{array} \right\|^M = \{\langle f, g \rangle| f \subset f_1 \subset \ldots \subset f_n \subset g_1 \subseteq \ldots \subseteq g_{m-1} \subseteq g,$$
$$\langle f, f_1 \rangle \in \|\alpha^{x_1}\|^M, \ldots, \langle f_{n-1}, f_n \rangle \in \|\alpha^{x_n}\|^M, \text{ and}$$
$$\langle f_n, g_1 \rangle \in \|C_1\|^M, \ldots, \langle g_{m-1}, g \rangle \in \|C_m\|^M\}$$

The semantics of quantifier and referential DRSs will be a straightforward extension of the semantics of the conditional DRS in DRT_0. Let us first introduce the following definitions. Let $K_1 \xrightarrow{d_i} K_2$ be a quantifier or referential DRS, with determiner $\mathbf{d}$, index i, and main marker x. Let f be an embedding such that $x \notin \text{DOM}(f)$. The set of DRS-*Satisfying Embeddings*, DSE, is defined as follows:

$$\text{DSE}(f, K) = \{h| \; \langle f, h \rangle \in \|K\|^M\}$$

and extended as follows to sets of embeddings:

$$\text{DSE}(\{f_1, \ldots, f_n\}, K) = \{h| \; \langle f_i, h \rangle \in \|K\|^M \text{ for some } i \in 1 \ldots n\}$$

I need now to make the notion of 'distancing' introduced in Section 4 more precise. As said there, distancing has the effect of 'changing the perspective' on a certain situation, that is, making available 'outside' the DRS only the sets of participants to a situation 'as a whole', so that whereas before the closure the markers are available for singular anaphora, after they are only available for plural anaphora.

Definition 1 Let E be a set of embedding pairs $\{\langle f, g \rangle\}$. DIST(E) is the set of embedding pairs $E' = \{\langle f, h \rangle\}$ defined as follows. Let $x_i \ldots x_j$ be the markers over which g extends f. Then $\langle f, h \rangle$ will be in DIST(E), where h is the embedding which is like g for the markers up to x_{i-1}, and then for $l = i \ldots j$, $h(l) = \sqcup\, h'(l)$, for any h' such that $\langle f, h' \rangle \in E$.

For example, an output embedding h in the denotation of a quantified DRS like

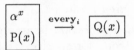

gives as a value to the marker x the group of all individuals which satisfy both the restriction and the scope of the quantified DRS.[14] We can now specify the denotations of quantified and referential DRSs:

1. $\| K_1 \overset{\text{every}_i}{\longrightarrow} K_2 \|^M = \text{DIST}(\{\langle f, g \rangle, \text{ where } f \text{ is an embedding such that}$ for every $h \in \text{DSE}(f, K_1)$ there is an h' such that $h' \in \text{DSE}(h, K_2)$, and $g \in \text{DSE}(\text{DSE}(f, K_1), K_2)\})$

2. $\| K_1 \overset{\text{most}_i}{\longrightarrow} K_2 \|^M = \text{DIST}(\{\langle f, g \rangle \,|\, \text{where } f \text{ is an embedding such that}$ for most $h \in \text{DSE}(f, K_1)$ there is an h' such that $h' \in \text{DSE}(h, K_2)$, and $g \in \text{DSE}(\text{DSE}(f, K_1), K_2)\})^{15}$

---

[14]This semantics is correct for the examples in the previous section, but also predicts that in texts like *Every man who has a donkey beats it. They hate him.*, *They* would refer to the set of all donkeys beaten by any man. To fix this problem it would be necessary to stipulate an ambiguity.

[15]This definition suffers from the so called *proportion problem* (Heim 1982, and Rooth 1987). Let us consider a model with 100 farmers, 99 of which own a donkey and don't thrive whereas one, Pedro, owns 1000 donkeys and thrives. The definition of the semantics of $K_1 \overset{\text{most}_i}{\longrightarrow} K_2$ above would predict that this model would make *Most farmers who own a donkey thrive* true, which is rather counterintuitive. The reason is that if the restriction is a DRS K like

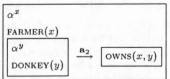

DSE(f,K) will include a different embedding for each *pair* of values for the markers x and y, and the fact that Pedro owns 1000 donkeys will make him a participant in 1000 pairs. The source of the problem, in short, is that the pairs are counted, rather than the

3. $\|K_1 \xrightarrow{\text{a}_i} K_2\|^M = \{\langle f, g \rangle | \text{ DSE}(\text{DSE}(f, K_1), K_2) \neq \emptyset \text{ and } g \in \text{DSE}(\text{DSE}(f, K_1), K_2)\}$

4. $\|K_1 \xrightarrow{\text{he}_i} K_2\|^M = \{\langle f, g \rangle | f(x) = f(y) \text{ for some marker } y \text{ and } \langle f, g \rangle \in \|K_2\|^M\}$

(Analogous rules could be developed for $K_1 \xrightarrow{\text{she}_i} K_2$ and $K_1 \xrightarrow{\text{they}_i} K_2$, of course.) Next, the denotations of the negated DRS and the conditional, almost identical to those in DRT_0:

1. $\|\neg_i K\|^M = \{\langle f, f \rangle | \text{ there is no } g \text{ such that } \langle f, g \rangle \in \|K\|^M\}$

2. $\| K_1 \xrightarrow{\text{if-then}_i} K_2\|^M = \{\langle f, f \rangle | \text{ for every } h \text{ such that } \langle f, h \rangle \in \|K_1\|^M$ there is an l such that $\langle h, l \rangle \in \|K_2\|^M$, and g is one such $l\}$

Finally, in order to define the semantics of scope forests, we have to specify more precisely the set of paths associated to them. This definition will be given in terms of an *extraction procedure*.

Definition 2 An *extraction procedure* is an algorithm which 'pulls out' all the operators from a scope forest $\varphi[i_1 \ldots i_n]\text{OC}$, one after the other, and returns a *disambiguated* DRS (a DRS not a scope forest), under the constraint that if the ordering constraint $i < j$ is in OC, then the operator with index i is extracted before the operator with index j.

What the 'extraction rules' do is fairly obvious, and is analogous to what Quantifier Raising does. I will just give two examples:

Negation:

$$\varphi \boxed{T_1 \ \neg_i R \ T_2} \quad \Rightarrow \quad \neg_i \ \varphi \boxed{T_1 \ R \ T_2}$$

Indefinites:

$$\varphi \boxed{T_1 \ R \ (\text{a}_i \boxed{\begin{array}{c} \alpha^x \\ \hline P(x) \end{array}})} \quad \Rightarrow \quad \boxed{\begin{array}{c} \alpha^x \\ \hline P(x) \end{array}} \xrightarrow{\text{a}_i} \boxed{T_1 \ R \ x}$$

number of possible distinct values that may be given to x. R. Root presented a solution to the problem which could easily be accommodated in my framework. Her idea was to partition a set of embeddings into equivalence classes according to the value that the embeddings associate to x:

$\text{EP}(E, x)$, where E is a set of embeddings, and x is a marker, $= \{E_a |$ each $h \in E_a$ is a member of E, and for all $h \in E_a \ h(x) = a$ for some $a \in U\}$

and then replacing the definition of $K_1 \xrightarrow{\text{most}_i} K_2$ above with the one below:

$\|K_1 \xrightarrow{\text{most}_i} K_2\|^M = \{\langle f, g \rangle | \text{ for most } E \in \text{EP}(\text{DSE}(f, K_1), x) \text{ there is an } h \in E \text{ such that } h' \in \text{DSE}(h, K_2) \text{ for some } h' \ldots\}$ (g is defined as before)

However, even if this definition does not suffer from the problem above, it does not explain why the semantics of *most* should be defined in terms of equivalence classes, while the semantics of *every* should be based on pairs. A more illuminating solution would be to assume an ambiguity, originated by the possibility of choosing different farmers-owning-donkeys 'cases' in the restriction of a quantifier; developing this solution in detail, however, would go outside the scope of this paper.

The first extraction rule pulls out a negation operator from a scope forest, and produces a negated DRS with the scope forest from which the operator has been extracted in the scope of the negation operator. T_1 and T_2 can be either unextracted terms or markers. The rule for indefinites extracts an indefinite term from a scope forest, and produces a referential DRS in whose scope there is a new scope forest in which the marker x has replaced the indefinite term. It is worth observing that nothing prevents having more than one extraction rule per determiner, or extraction rules which operate on the scope forest as a whole (this will take care of the additional readings of examples like *Two examiners marked six scripts*). An 'empty extraction rule' will replace a scope forest without operators left with a basic DRS.

Definition 3 Let K be the scope forest $\varphi[i_1 \ldots i_n]$OC with indices $i_1 \ldots i_n$ and ordering constraints OC. The *paths associated to* SF are all the disambiguated DRS's K' which can be derived from K by an extraction procedure.

We can now define the denotation of a scope forest as follows:

$$\| K : \varphi[i_1 \ldots i_n]\text{OC} \|^M = \bigcup \|P\|^M, \text{ for every path } P \text{ associated to } K$$

6.3 The Inference Rules

The set of inference rules of DRT$_1$ includes, in addition to the traditional rules (Modus Ponens, Universal Instantiation, etc.) all the rules defined in Section 4 and 5. Because of the change in the semantics of the basic DRS, we need to modify the definition of logical entailment given in Section 3.2 as follows: if K_1 and K_2 are formulas, $K_1 \models K_2$ iff for all models M in which K_1 is true, for every pair $\langle f, g \rangle \in \|K_1\|^M$, there is an embedding h, $g \subseteq h$, such that $\langle f, h \rangle \in \|K_2\|^M$. With this new definition, the following theorem holds:

Theorem 3 MP, UI, ROR, RAOQ, QORG, SFE, WUI, PA *and* ASTR *are sound* DRT$_1$ *inference rules.*

7 Discussion

I have shown that relational semantics can be used to give a denotation to certain expressions, called scope forests, used to represent scopally ambiguous sentences. As a consequence, certain types of scope disambiguation can be performed by a deductive procedure. I have also shown examples of such derivations. In this section I would like to discuss more in detail what the theory predicts and what it doesn't.

First of all, I do not claim that people do not disambiguate unless they can use world knowledge or referential information. This position is hard to defend: there seems to be psychological evidence that, at least for simple sentences like *Every boy climbed a tree*, people do have interpretation preferences (Kurtzman and McDonald 1991). Giving a semantics to un-scoped logical forms does not rule out scope forest reduction rules based on preferences, however, although these preferences should be incorporated as defeasible rules, with consequent problems in formalization.[16]

An interesting question is whether these preferences always apply, that is, whether people always attempt to come out with a unique unambiguous interpretation. The theory just presented is neutral with respect to this question (although it would be most useful for the cases when disambiguating is very expensive). My hypothesis is that the cost of disambiguating is a factor in determining whether or not people try to disambiguate. Kurtz-man and MacDonald only studied sentences with two quantified NPs, and the only determiners that appeared in those sentences were *every*, *the*, *a* and *a different*. These quantifiers are 'easy to compute'—they can all be computed by DFAs (van Benthem 1987). It would be interesting to repeat the experiment with determiners which are 'harder' than the determin-ers above, such as *most* and *few*: for example, to try sentences like *Most male students date few undergrads*. Another source of complexity is the number of possible interpretations: the prediction would be that as the number of interpretations gets larger, it should be less likely that people disambiguate. This hypothesis could be tested by running experiments on sentences containing numerical quantifiers, such as *Two examiners marked six transcripts.*.

Another question left open by Kurtzman and MacDonald's experiments is whether people, when they do disambiguate, compute only one interpre-tation (as predicted by the theory presented in this paper) or compute all interpretations in parallel, as predicted by the disjunction theory. The tim-ings of the experiments (approximately 3.5 seconds) were not strict enough to guarantee that only one interpretation could be computed [Kurtzman, p.c.]. Testing people on sentences with numerical quantifiers would be an interesting test for this hypothesis also. The sheer number of interpre-tations should make it possible to verify whether indeed people compute them all and then 'filter', or rather compute a few (possibly using preference heuristics).

One should not read the theory as claiming that syntactic constraints play no role in determining scope relations either. There is evidence to the contrary: as May (1985) argues, sentences like *Some student admires every professor* may be ambiguous in isolation, but in a VP-deletion context, like (30), the ambiguity evaporates.

(30)   Some student admires every professor, but John doesn't.

---

[16]Kurtzman and MacDonald's results do seem to be in contrast with the predictions of approaches based on using the weakest possible interpretation, like Kempson and Cormack's, since people do not seem to favor the weakest interpretation, and actually at times have a definite preference for the strong one.

All that my theory claims is that scope determination is not an entirely syntactic operation. In this, it is less radical than the theory proposed in Gawron and Peters 1990 (cf. pp. 53–56), in which the determination of the scope of NPs is also attributed to contextual factors (Gawron and Peters call them *circumstances*). The two theories are however trying to answer different questions. As I mentioned before, I am interested in questions like: How can we infer the intended scope relations? Do we really need to infer them completely? What consequences can we infer from a non-disambiguated interpretation? Instead, Gawron and Peters are concerned with questions like: How do SCOPES-OVER facts get into the circumstances? How do we capture the constraints on scoping and anaphora reflected, for example, by data about sloppy and strict anaphora?

8 Conclusions

8.1 Status of the Implementation

A GPSG grammar for a fragment of English more or less equivalent to that of 'standard' DRT has been developed, which produces DRT_1 expressions. A parser which carries on the translation 'bottom up' in a fashion similar to that proposed by Johnson and Klein (1986) has also been implemented in PROLOG, together with a module which carries on the inferences presented in this paper, using a logical form very similar to that use in the Core Language Engine (Alshawi and van Eijck 1989).

8.2 Future Work

A crucial question is whether we get any actual performance improvement by adopting this method, that is, whether inferencing with DRT_1 is so expensive as to offset the advantages gained from not having to produce all the interpretations. A general answer would require determining the complexity of reasoning with DRT_1. Even an experimental answer is hard to get, since that requires, in addition to implementing two or three different scope disambiguation methods (which we have actually already done in part), making sure that their coverage is actually the same, and elaborate appropriate tests.

A second, very important problem is to have some way of jumping to conclusions on the basis of uncertain knowledge, and of choosing between different possibilities. A logic of this form seems necessary to formalize the kind of preferences discussed by Kurtzman and MacDonald; in addition, we'll probably need it to represent the disambiguating information originated from lexical and world knowledge. For example, a lexical property of the predicate *comes with* is that the argument in subject position takes scope over the argument in object position, so that *Every chess set comes with a spare pawn* has no reading in which *a spare pawn* scopes over *Every chess set*. In order to express such 'defeasible disambiguation axioms' we have developed the *Disambiguation Schema*, whose general form is S --> {i<j}, where S is the scope of the quantifier with the strictest scope and i and j are indices of operators. For example, the disambiguation schema for the predicate *comes with* would be [i comes-with j] --> {i<j}. This schema is an abbreviation for a list of axiom schemata each of which adds the ordering constraint $i < j$ to a scope forest. Unfortunately, schemata of this kind do not always hold.

A question that needs to be addressed in more detail is the relation between scope ambiguities and, for example, collective/distributive ambiguities, in order to see better the relation between this approach and, for example, the approach proposed by Bunt (1985). The reference interpretation model also needs to be extended. I'm in particular interested in studying sentences like *Every chess set comes with a spare pawn. It's taped to the bottom.*, in which the interface between reference and scope disambiguation seems totally different from the one presented in the examples in Section 5.

References

Allen, J. 1987. *Natural Language Understanding*. Menlo Park: Benjamin Cummings.

Allen, J. 1991. Natural Language, Knowledge Representation, and Logical Form. Technical Report 367, University of Rochester, Rochester, NY.

Alshawi, H., D. M. Carter, J. van Eijck, R. C. Moore, D. B. Moran, F. C. Pereira, and A. G. Smith. 1988. Interim Report on the SRI Core Language Engine. Technical Report CCSRC-5, SRI International, Cambridge, England.

Alshawi, H., and J. van Eijck. 1989. Logical Forms in the Core Language Engine. In *Proceedings ACL-89*. Vancouver, CA.

Barwise, J. 1987. Noun Phrases, Generalized Quantifiers and Anaphora. In *Generalized Quantifiers*, ed. P. Gärdenfors, 1–30. Dordrecht: Reidel.

Barwise, J., and J. Perry. 1983. *Situations and Attitudes*. Cambridge, MA: MIT Press.

Bunt, H. 1985. *Mass Terms and Model Theoretic Semantics*. Dordrecht: Reidel.

Gärdenfors, P. (ed.). 1987. *Generalized Quantifiers: Linguistic and Logical Approaches*. Studies in Linguistics and Philosophy Number 31. Dordrecht: Reidel.

Gawron, J. M., and S. Peters. 1990. *Anaphora and Quantification in Situation Semantics*. CSLI Lecture Notes Number 19. Stanford: CSLI Publications.

Groenendijk, J. A. G., and M. J. B. Stokhof. 1990. Dynamic Montague Grammar. In *Papers from the 2nd Symposium on Logic and Language*, ed. L. Kalman and L. Polos. Budapest: Akademiai Kiado.

Grosz, B., D. Appelt, P. Martin, and F. Pereira. 1987. TEAM: An Experiment in the Design of Transportable Natural Language Interfaces. *Artificial Intelligence* 32(2):173–244.

Heim, I. 1982. *The Semantics of Definite and Indefinite Noun Phrases*. PhD thesis, University of Massachussetts, Amherst.

Hobbs, J. 1982. Representing Ambiguity. In *WCCFL-1*, 15–28. Stanford Linguistics Association.

Hobbs, J. 1983. An Improper Treatment of Quantification in Ordinary English. In *Proceedings ACL-83*, 57–63. Cambridge, MA.

Hobbs, J., and S. Shieber. 1987. An Algorithm for Generating Quantifier Scopings. *Computational Linguistics* 13(1–2):47–53.

Hurum, S. 1988. Handling Scope Ambiguities Using Domain-independent Heuristics. Technical Report TR 88-12, University of Alberta, Edmonton, Canada.

Johnson, M., and E. Klein. 1986. Discourse, Anaphora and Parsing. Report Number CSLI-86-63, CSLI, Stanford.

Kamp, H. 1981. A Theory of Truth and Semantic Representation. In *Formal Methods in the Study of Language*, ed. G. Groenendijk, T. Janssen, and M. Stokhof. Amsterdam: Mathematisch Centrum.

Kamp, H. 1988. Some Remarks about the Semantic Representation of Certain Plural Constructions of English, and Suggestions for a Procedural Treatment of Plural Pronoun Anaphora. Contribution to Acord Workshop.

Kempson, R., and A. Cormack. 1981. Ambiguity and Quantification. *Linguistics and Philosophy* 4(2):259–310.

Kurtzman, H. S., and M. C. McDonald. 1991. Interpretation Preferences for Quantifier Scope Ambiguities. In *Proceedings SALT-1*.

Link, G. 1987. Generalized Quantifiers and Plurals. In *Generalized Quantifiers*, ed. P. Gärdenfors, 151–180. Dordrecht: Reidel.

May, R. 1985. *Logical Form in Natural Language*. Cambridge, MA: MIT Press.

Partee, B. 1975. Comments on C.J. Fillmore and N. Chomsky's Papers. In *The Scope of American Linguistics*, ed. D. Austerlitz. The Netherlands: De Ridder Press.

Poesio, M., and S. Zucchi. 1991. On Some Alleged Violations of the Scope Constraint. In preparation.

Reinhart, R. 1983. *Anaphora and Semantic Interpretation*. London: Croom Helm.

Roberts, C. 1987. *Modal Subordination, Anaphora, and Distributivity*. PhD thesis, University of Massachusetts, Amherst.

Rooth, M. 1987. NP Interpretation in Montague Grammar, File Change Semantics, and Situation Semantics. In *Generalized Quantifiers: Linguistic and Logical Approaches*, ed. P. Gärdenfors, 237–268. Dordrecht: Reidel.

Schubert, L. K., and F. J. Pelletier. 1982. From English to Logic: Context-free Computation of 'Conventional' Logical Translations. *American Journal of Computational Linguistics* 10:165–176.

Schubert, L. K., and F. J. Pelletier. 1988. Generically Speaking. In *Properties, Types and Meaning, vol. II*, ed. G. Chierchia, B. H. Partee, and R. Turner, 193–268. Dordrecht: Kluwer.

van Benthem, J. 1987. Towards a Computational Semantics. In *Generalized Quantifiers*, ed. P. Gärdenfors, 31–72. Dordrecht: Reidel.

Webber, B. L. 1978. *A Formal Approach to Discourse Anaphora*. Report 3761. Cambridge, MA.

21

Parameters: Dependence and Absorption

Helle Frisak Sem, Kjell Johan Sæbø,
Guri B. Verne, and Espen J. Vestre

Introduction

During the spring of 1989, the authors studied and discussed a draft for "Anaphora and Quantification in Situation Semantics" by Jean Mark Gawron and Stanley Peters. The book, hereafter referred to as G&P, was published in the autumn of 1990 and "is an investigation into the semantics of anaphora with third person singular pronouns" in a framework of Situation Semantics (G&P, page 1). The following presents some results from our discussion, centering on the use of the *Absorption Principle* and its effect on anaphoric relations.

This paper does not attempt at giving a representative picture of G&P. In particular, we do not discuss the authors' account of interactions between quantifier scope and ellipsis or of quantifier scope ambiguities as differences in the circumstances of an utterance. In general, we do not assess the broader implications of their work for the theory of grammar.

Our paper focuses on some Norwegian data which we consider inconsistent with the use of absorption and its effect of blocking certain anaphoric relations. We also show that the same phenomena can be found in English if we go beyond the fragment of G&P.

The first section introduces some central concepts along with the Absorption Principle. Readers acquainted with Situation Theory and with G&P may skip this section. The next two sections discuss the difficulties facing the analysis of G&P, and we present some English counterexamples. In section 4, we discuss briefly some ways to go in order to remedy the shortcomings of G&P. In an appendix we discuss some Norwegian examples that are alleged counterexamples to our position.

Situation Theory and Its Applications, vol. 2.
Jon Barwise, Jean Mark Gawron, Gordon Plotkin, and Syun Tutiya, eds.
Copyright © 1991, Stanford University.

1 Some Central Concepts

G&P uses Situation Theory as its basic theory. Assuming that the reader is acquainted with Situation Theory, we offer a short introduction to the notation and the formalism that G&P uses, as well as to the vocabulary and basic techniques that it makes use of[1].

The central concept in Situation theory is the *situation*, a slice of the world consisting of facts, or *states of affairs*, abbreviated *soa*. A soa is built up from the basic features *relations*, *entities* or objects, *locations*, and *polarities* (truth values). A soa is on the form

(1) $\langle\langle at\ l, R, r_1{:}e_1, \ldots, r_n{:}e_n; p\rangle\rangle$

where l is a location, R a relation, $r_1, \ldots, r_n$ are argument roles of R (no order of roles is implied by the indexing), $e_1, \ldots, e_n$ are entities *filling* the given argument roles, and p is a polarity. For convenience, G&P adopts the convention that positive polarity may be omitted. In a soa like (1) n must be less than or equal to the number of argument roles defined by R. If n is equal to the number of argument roles of R, the soa is said to be *saturated*, otherwise, as in (2), the soa is said to be *unsaturated*.

(2) $\langle\langle at\ June\text{-}9th\text{-}1990\text{-}in\text{-}Oslo, \text{SOOTHES}, soother{:}Marit\rangle\rangle$

The missing arguments in an unsaturated positive soa are submitted to an existential quantification, restricted by the appropriateness condition defined by the omitted role; if Marit is soothing, there has to be something appropriate for soothing that she soothes.

It is important not to confuse the unsaturated soa with the *parametric soa*, *psoa* for short, which is a soa where some of the argument roles are *labeled* by *parameters*:[2]

(3) $\langle\langle \text{HUGS}, hugger{:}x, hugged{:}Signe\rangle\rangle$

A psoa allows for abstraction over the free parameters, or what is also called *absorption* of parameters. From the psoa (3) we can by absorption on x construct the following *type*:

(4) $[x \mid \langle\langle \text{HUGS}, hugger{:}x, hugged{:}Signe\rangle\rangle]$

This type can be taken to represent the VP *hugs Signe*, serving as a suitable building block in a linguistic theory. (4) is seen as a property (or relation, possibly with several argument roles, if more parameters are absorbed). The property in (4) has one argument role. Relations that come from abstraction of more arguments will have more than one argument role, one for each abstracted parameter. Using this as the relation of a new soa, we can construct the soa (5):[3]

(5) $\langle\langle [x_{subj} \mid \langle\langle \text{HUGS}, x, Signe\rangle\rangle], subj{:}e_{Eskil}\rangle\rangle$

---

[1] For ease of readability, we have simplified the formalism of G&P to some extent. The questions raised in this paper will of course have the same impact on the full formalism.

[2] The location argument is omitted here and in the following for simplification.

[3] Role names are omitted here and in the following provided no confusion arises.

representing an analysis of the sentence *Eskil hugs Signe*. The NP *Eskil* *covers* the role *subj* of the VP *hugs Signe*, *utilizing* the parameter *e*. The role *subj* is said to be a (non-trivial) *projection* of the hugger role. The relation of projection is transitive.

The index *subj* on the *x* has been put there by the grammar or by the lexicon. Indexed roles are roles like *subj*, *tns* (tense), and *obj*, and the grammar decides for each type (representing a V, a VP,...) which roles are indexed. This has consequences for the construction of objects representing more complex constructions, as "only indexed roles can be labeled by parameters that are anchored or quantified away. Thus the unindexed roles of a VP introduced by the Absorption Principle are inaccessible, they cannot be given arguments. In effect, they function as if they were Existentially Quantified away" (G&P, page 94).

In (5) we wrote e_{Eskil} instead of just *Eskil* as in the first examples. This is shorthand for $e_{\langle\langle \text{NAMED},e,Eskil\rangle\rangle}$, restricting the parameter *e* to be anchored to an individual named Eskil. The restrictions that occur when, intuitively speaking, some of the agents enter into more than one straightforward role is of particular interest. A simple example is the sentence

(6) Eivind likes his teddy bear.

where Eivind is both liking and the owner of the teddy bear. A (somewhat simplified) analysis of *his teddy bear* in the framework of "Anaphora and Quantification in Situation Semantics" is for example

(7) $y_{\langle\langle \text{TEDDY-BEAR-OF},owner:x,teddy-bear:y\rangle\rangle}$

Here a parameter other than *y* itself enters into the restrictions on *y*. The parameter *y* is said to *depend* on the parameter *x*, since a suitable anchoring of *y* will depend on what *x* is anchored to. If *x* is anchored to Eivind, *y* must be anchored to (one of) Eivind's teddy bear(s), if *x* is anchored to someone else, *y* must be anchored to a teddy bear belonging to this other person. The concept *depends* is defined as follows (G&P, page 93):

> We'll say that a parameter *y* depends on *x* if *x* is a parameter of a restriction on *y*.

In the analysis of (6) there are according to G&P two ways in which the teddy bear can become Eivind's. Either the subject role of *likes* is labeled by the same parameter as the owner role, as in (8), or the owner role is labeled by the same parameter as the subject role of the full VP *likes his teddy bear*, as in (9).

(8) $\langle\langle [x_{subj} \mid \langle\langle \text{LIKES}, x, y_{\langle\langle \text{TEDDY-BEAR-OF},x,y\rangle\rangle}\rangle\rangle], subj:e_{Eivind}\rangle\rangle$

(9) $\langle\langle [x_{subj} \mid \langle\langle \text{LIKES}, x, y_{\langle\langle \text{TEDDY-BEAR-OF},e,y\rangle\rangle}\rangle\rangle], subj:e_{Eivind}\rangle\rangle$

In the former case, the VP is analyzed as *liking one's own teddy bear* whereas in the latter case it is analyzed as *liking the teddy bear of someone*, and since the parameter used for this 'someone' happens to be the same as the parameter labeling the subject role of the full VP, it must be anchored to the same person, analyzing (6) as *Eivind likes Eivind's teddy bear*.

G&P distinguishes between the *content* and the *circumstances* of a linguistic utterance. The content of a linguistic utterance is a parametric soa. The circumstances given by the utterance situation, appropriateness conditions on the words etc., guide us as hearers in finding a correct anchoring. Correctly anchored, the content gives us the *interpretation* of the utterance. Contextually governed relations like anaphoric relations and scope are stated in the circumstances, a somewhat extended discourse-situation. Circumstantial information in general will not be of major interest in this paper. The only kinds of circumstantial information we will mention at all are the COVARIES-WITH facts. The relation COVARIES-WITH is a relation between "an anaphoric NP utterance and what it is anaphoric to." G&P claims that this cannot be an "unchanging relation role, but must be something that varies across utterances" (G&P, page 117). These "role-aspects" are represented by a pair of an utterance and some relation-index assigned by grammar. Analyzing the VP as *liking one's own teddy bear* the circumstances must contain the soa

(10) $\langle\!\langle$COVARIES-WITH, *'his'*, [*'likes'*, *subj*]$\rangle\!\rangle$

and following the analysis of (9) the circumstances must contain

(11) $\langle\!\langle$COVARIES-WITH, *'his'*, [*'likes his teddy bear'*, *subj*]$\rangle\!\rangle$

A problem with the analysis of the VP given in (8) is that the parameter x is bound by the type abstraction, whereas the parameter y remains free though it depends on x. VP ellipsis is in G&P treated by making an exact copy of the analysis of the VP, so that for instance the property of *liking one's own teddy bear*,

(12) $[x_{subj} \mid \langle\!\langle\text{LIKES}, x, y_{\langle\!\langle\text{TEDDY-BEAR-OF},x,y\rangle\!\rangle}\rangle\!\rangle]$

is ascribed to two different subjects. If the same free parameter, y, is used in both cases, we are forced to anchor y to the same teddy bear in both cases, thus understanding the sentence *Eivind likes his teddy bear and so does Aksel* as if Eivind and Aksel each likes their own teddy bear, this being one and the same teddy bear.

The solution to this problem offered in G&P (page 93) is the Absorption Principle (AP), a central principle in the framework:

> If x is a parameter of some object o, then every parameter that x depends on is a parameter of o.

The absorption principle is in the essence of understanding what dependent parameters are. If a dependent parameter can remain free while the parameter it depends on becomes abstracted, the parameter does not depend on the abstracted parameter any more.

The analysis in (8) is then changed to

(13) $\langle\!\langle[x_{subj}, y \mid \langle\!\langle\text{LIKES}, x, y_{\langle\!\langle\text{TEDDY-BEAR-OF},x,y\rangle\!\rangle}\rangle\!\rangle], subj{:}e_{Eivind}\rangle\!\rangle$

The parameter y in $[x_{subj}, y \mid \langle\!\langle \text{LIKES}, x, y_{\langle\!\langle\text{TEDDY-BEAR-OF},x,y\rangle\!\rangle} \rangle\!\rangle]$ is bound, and we have in (13) an unsaturated soa, and thus in effect an appropriate existential quantification over teddy bears owned and liked by the subject. Note that y is not indexed by the grammar, and the corresponding role can thus not be labeled by a parameter.

We will in the following study the effects of the absorption of dependent parameters that do not have their roles indexed by the grammar. We will show first for Norwegian, and then give some examples from English too, that the specific use that absorption is put to in G&P restricts the number of anaphoric relations too much, and that instead of explaining anaphoric behavior, it cuts off a number of important phenomena for the benefit of explaining some facts that are at best marginal.

2 Some Facts About the Norwegian Reflexive Possessive Pronoun

This section centers on the 'sloppy' reading of VP ellipsis conjunctions like (14) and on consequences of absorbing dependent parameters incompatible with relevant data in a language like Norwegian.

(14) John washed his car and Bill did too.

In the formalism of G&P, strict versus sloppy ambiguities are represented as ambiguities in the antecedent clause in VP ellipsis contexts. The two readings are distinguished in terms of the antecedent VP content, so that any simple sentence like

(15) John washed his car

is ambiguous too. The distinction is captured in a *co-parametric* versus a *role-linking* analysis of the pronoun, correlated with distinct facts in the circumstances:

   Co-parametric:
   Clause Content:

   $\langle\!\langle [x_{subj} \mid \langle\!\langle \text{WASH}, x, y_{\langle\!\langle\text{CAR-OF},j,y\rangle\!\rangle} \rangle\!\rangle], subj{:}j\text{JOHN} \rangle\!\rangle$

   Circumstances:

   $\langle\!\langle \text{COVARIES-WITH}, \text{'his'}, [\text{'washes his car'}, subj] \rangle\!\rangle$

   Role-linking:
   Clause Content:

   $\langle\!\langle [x_{subj}, y \mid \langle\!\langle \text{WASH}, x, y_{\langle\!\langle\text{CAR-OF},x,y\rangle\!\rangle} \rangle\!\rangle], subj{:}j\text{JOHN} \rangle\!\rangle$

   Circumstances:

   $\langle\!\langle \text{COVARIES-WITH}, \text{'his'}, [\text{'washes'}, subj] \rangle\!\rangle$

AP does not apply to the co-parametric case, because the object parameter does not depend on the subject parameter but on John: "Consequently, the same y parameter is shared by both VP-contents, and it is the same car that John and Bill wash" (G&P, page 95).[4].

Sloppily, the role-linking VP content is the relation of washing one's car, whereas the co-parametric VP content is the property of washing John's. The parameter y depends on x in the role-linking case, and is thus absorbed in the role-linking VP content. Thus, *John* and *Bill* wash two different cars (as far as (14) describes it). In each case there is an appropriate existential quantification over cars, and the *car* parameters are "therefore unavailable for anaphoric relations with anything outside the VP" (G&P, page 91). That is, on the role-linking reading (16) does not make sense.

(16) John washed his car. It's spanking clean now.

The theory predicts that it is impossible to append an anaphoric pronoun to a discourse like (15) in the role-linking sense. It would be very interesting to test this prediction, as one could if there were some linguistic device that would force the role-linking reading. A disambiguating device does not seem to exist in English, and insofar, the prediction cannot be falsified, as the theory explains phenomena in English without claiming universal validity. However, the analyzes are so principled that some transfer to languages other than English must be expected. And in fact, there are languages, i.e., Norwegian, where the sloppy reading of a sentence like (14) is forced. Indeed, this fact supports the assumption that there is a separate "role-linking" reading of the antecedent clause.

Norwegian possesses a reflexive possessive pronoun alternating with the ordinary 3rd person possessive pronouns. Not surprisingly, this dichotomy interacts with co-parameterization and role-linking. There are the following facts: If the example

(17) John kissed his wife and Bill did too

is rendered with the reflexive possessive pronoun 'sin'

(18) John kysset sin kone og det gjorde Bill også

the co-parametric (strict) reading is excluded. That is, Bill necessarily kissed his own wife. If, on the other hand, it is rendered with the ordinary possessive pronoun

(19) John kysset hans kone og det gjorde Bill også

both the role-linking reading and the (co-parametric) reading where the pronoun covaries with the role eventually covered by John are excluded.

---

[4] This remains valid for cases where the object NP is indefinite, like the following.

John resents a teacher who flunked him, and Bill does too.

John has invited a friend of his, and Bill has too.

That is, there is no reading on which Bill resents a teacher who flunked John but not necessarily the same, and none on which Bill has invited just some friend of John's—either there is the sloppy reading, or there is the strictest reading where the two parameters are anchored alike. Judgments may differ on this issue.

That is, both John and Bill must have kissed the wife of some third man.[5] The only way to express the (normal) co-parametric relationship with pronouns is to duplicate the VP, not using ellipsis, and substitute the nonreflexive for the reflexive possessive pronoun:

(20) John kysset sin kone og Bill kysset hans kone.

The only way to have a strict reading using ellipsis is to repeat the proper name in the VP:

(21) John kysset Johns kone og det gjorde Bill også.

Can these facts of Norwegian be accounted for in the framework of G&P? When translating into Norwegian, surface structure of (17) forces a choice between

- the role-linking analysis of the example and
- a co-parametric (or a 'deictic') analysis where the pronoun cannot covary with the subject ("John") role.

(Assuming VP ellipsis and the use of a pronoun.) Thus with respect to the following underspecified sentence content for (17)

$$\langle\!\langle [x_{subj}, \ldots) \mid \langle\!\langle \text{KISS}, x, y_{\langle\!\langle \text{WIFE-OF}, u, y\rangle\!\rangle} \rangle\!\rangle], subj\!:\!j\text{JOHN}\rangle\!\rangle$$

it appears that the following is not a possible circumstance fact in Norwegian:

$$\langle\!\langle \text{COVARIES-WITH}, pronoun\ utterance, [VP utterance, subj]\rangle\!\rangle$$

So the following sentence content is only possible as translating *John kysset Johns kone*:

$$\langle\!\langle [x_{subj} \mid \langle\!\langle \text{KISS}, x, y_{\langle\!\langle \text{WIFE-OF}, j, y\rangle\!\rangle} \rangle\!\rangle], subj\!:\!j\text{JOHN}\rangle\!\rangle$$

If the reflexive possessive pronoun is used, *sin* must covary with the subject of *kysset* (and consequently y must be absorbed); if the non-reflexive pronoun is used, *hans* must covary with some role-aspect distinct from the subject of *kysset* and any projections thereof. The former is the role-linking case; the latter is a case of "discourse" co-parameterization (or 'deixis').

Clearly, G&P must provide a minimum of Government and Binding to account for well-known facts about reflexive and non-reflexive personal pronouns in English:

---

[5] Note that this is not to indicate that *hans* is a necessarily 'deictic' pronoun—it may well be anaphoric, though like the corresponding personal pronoun *han* normally not to the nearest subject. The reflexive possessive pronoun *sin* is complementary to the nonreflexive possessive pronoun *hans*, etc., in a similar manner as the reflexive personal pronoun *seg* to the nonreflexive personal pronoun *han*, etc. Thus the following two sentences are perfect translations:

Mary promised John to wash his car.
Mary lovte John å vaske bilen hans.

John admires him

only has a reading where the pronoun is 'deictic' ("discourse" co-parametric), whereas

John admires himself

only has a reading where the pronoun is 'anaphoric' (role-linking or co-parametric with the subject NP). Sloppily, the reflexive pronoun corefers with the subject and the non-reflexive pronoun does not. These simple data are captured in Binding Principles:[6]

> If the circumstances contain the fact $\langle\!\langle \text{COVARIES-WITH}, NP_1, r \rangle\!\rangle$, then for any noun phrase NP_2 that covers a projection of r, if NP_2 is independent, it governs NP_1 iff NP_1 is reflexive.

This principle excludes the following two simplified sentence contents for *John admires him*:

$$\langle\!\langle [x_{subj} \mid \langle\!\langle \text{ADMIRE}, x, j \rangle\!\rangle], j_{\text{JOHN}} \rangle\!\rangle$$

$$\langle\!\langle [x_{subj} \mid \langle\!\langle \text{ADMIRE}, x, x \rangle\!\rangle], j_{\text{JOHN}} \rangle\!\rangle$$

The former (co-parametric) content results from covarying *him* with the role-aspect the governing NP *John* covers; the latter (role-linking) content results from covarying *him* with the subject role-aspect of *admires*, that is, of a role the governing NP role projects.

However, the principle fails to distinguish between these two analyzes of *John admires himself*. It seems to say that if an NP governs a reflexive pronoun, the pronoun covaries with a role of which the role the NP covers is a trivial or a nontrivial projection. This permits a co-parametric interpretation of the sentence. But is it possible to read

John admires himself and Bill does too.

as expressing that both John and Bill admire John? Peters (pc) refers to

(22) John cannot save himself, but his brother can

to defend the claim that in principle, it is possible to interpret an English reflexive pronoun in the co-parametric sense—covering a role merging with the role covered by the governing NP. Be that as it may; in Norwegian,

(23) John kissed *his*_{reflexive} wife and Bill did too

can only be read as expressing that John kissed John's wife and Bill kissed Bill's wife. That is, the first conjunct expresses that John has the property of being an "own wife kisser," and only that. In other words, the reflexive possessive pronoun can only covary with a role of which the role covered by the antecedent NP is a nontrivial projection, which is to say that the NP is a role-linking antecedent.

---

[6]G&P, page 140. The formulation here is simplified with respect to the formulation in G&P.

The reflexive possessive pronoun does not have to be role-linked to the minimal VP in which it is contained. G&P discusses the sentence *John revised his paper before the teacher did and so did Bill*. It is claimed to have three readings, either (i) everybody revises Johns paper, (ii) everybody revises their own paper or (iii) John revises John's paper before the teacher revises John's paper and Bill revises Bill's paper before the teacher revises Bill's paper. Reading (i) is obtained by co-parametrization, and the two latter by role-linking. Reading (ii) where everybody revises their own paper has role-linking in the minimal VP, viz., *revised his paper*, whereas reading (iii) has role-linking in the greater VP, viz., *revised his paper before the teacher did*. For the Norwegian translation *Jon så gjennom stilen sin før læreren (gjorde det), og det gjorde Bill også*, there are two readings, namely the two role-linking ones. Reading (iii) is clearly the preferred one, maybe for pragmatic reasons.

Thus, the pronoun *sin* is inherently role-linked.

3 The Necessity of Referring to Dependent Parameters

On the sloppy reading of (24), it is almost impossible to continue with (25).

(24) John washed his car and Bill did too.

(25) It is spanking clean now.

This is in harmony with the analysis of G&P. The absorption of the *car* parameters inside their respective VP-contents explains why none of the cars are available for anaphoric reference. We feel that this is not a good explanation for the oddity of continuing (24) with (25). The two cars are in principle different, and the case is parallel to *A man and a boy entered. He was wet.* Having established that "sin" in Norwegian must have a role-linking analysis, the Norwegian version of this example gives further evidence that it is not a good solution to absorb the *car* parameter in the VP object.

The Norwegian version of *John washed his car* is, if *his* is to be coreferent with *John*,

(26) John vasket bilen sin.

Sin must have a role-linking analysis, so the content must in this case be something like

$$\langle\!\langle [x_{subj}, y \mid \langle\!\langle \text{WASH}, x, y_{\langle\!\langle \text{CAR},y\rangle\!\rangle \wedge \langle\!\langle \text{OWN},y,x\rangle\!\rangle}\rangle\!\rangle], subj{:}j\text{JOHN}\rangle\!\rangle$$

It is perfectly acceptable to continue (26) with the Norwegian translation of (25):

(27) Den er skinnende ren nå.

There is on the account of G&P, however, no way for the pronoun *den* to be anaphoric to the car mentioned in (26). One way to try to overcome this is to adopt the following hypothesis for the interpretation of Norwegian *sin* (Peters' proposal (pc)):

- "*sin* is role-linking if a co-parametric interpretation is not explicitly demanded."

This would account for the fact that *sin* in *John vasket bilen sin, og det gjorde Bill også* has to have a role-linking interpretation, but at the same time allow for a co-parametric interpretation in the discourse *John vasket bilen sin. Den ble skinnende ren.* Unfortunately, as the following discourse shows, this cannot be the right solution:

(1) Jon vasket bilen sin. Den ble skinnende ren.
    Bill prøvde også. Resultatet var imidlertid skuffende.

    (John washed $his_{reflexive}$ car. It became spanking clean.
    Bill tried to too. The result was disappointing, however.)

The interpretation of this discourse is that John's car became spanking clean, and that Bill tried to wash his own car with a disappointing result. The elliptic sentence *Bill prøvde også* having only the sloppy reading requires a role-linking interpretation of *sin* in *John vasket bilen sin.* On Peters' proposal, the fact that the car of John's is anaphorically referred to in *Den ble skinnende ren* is an explicit demand for a co-parametric reading of the same occurrence of *sin*. (1) should thus not have the reading which we claim is the only one in Norwegian.

We can find similar phenomena in English as well. Consider the following discourse:

(2) This was a miserable Christmas for Mary.
    First, John returned the present she had sent him. It wasn't even opened.
    Then Bill did too!
    She was all in tears when I found her.

This discourse contains exactly the same problems with respect to a choice between a role-linking and a co-parametric reading as (1). On a role linking reading of the *him* parameter, *it* cannot refer to *the present*. On a co-parametric reading, Bill is returning the very same present as John.

There are also problems in connection with quantification. G&P offers the following solution to the canonical donkey-sentence (G&P, page 173):

(3) $\langle\langle EVERY, \{y\},$

$\qquad [x \mid s' \models \langle\langle FARMER, x\rangle\rangle \wedge \langle\langle OWNING, x, y\rangle\rangle \wedge \langle\langle DONKEY, y\rangle\rangle],$

$\qquad [x \mid \langle\langle BEATING, x, y\rangle\rangle]]\rangle\rangle$

The solution here is to let *it* covary with *a donkey* and have EVERY bind a specified set of parameters in the same way as INVOLVES: "Let the first parametric property argument of EVERY, *R*, be called the *restrictor-property*, and the second, *S*, the *scope-property*. The idea is that the above state-of-affairs is a fact if and only if for every anchor f for y, every bearer of $R[f]$ has the property $S[g]$ where g is some extension of f" (G&P, page 173).

G&P (page 80) discusses another donkey sentence together with the sentence

(4)   Every woman who leaves *her husband* eventually gives *him*
      a second chance.

After having proposed a co-parametric analysis for the donkey case parallel to (3) G&P says: "Again we would propose a co-parametric analysis in which the parameters shared by the two NP's is simply captured by the quantifier" (G&P, page 80). But in this case, the parameter for *her husband* depends on *woman*, and with some simplifications we can construct the following content:[7]

(5) $\langle\!\langle\text{EVERY},\{y\},$

$[v \mid \langle\!\langle[x,y \mid s' \models \langle\!\langle\text{WOMAN}, x\rangle\!\rangle \wedge \langle\!\langle\text{LEAVES}, x, y_{\langle\!\langle\text{HUSBAND-OF},x,y\rangle\!\rangle}\rangle\!\rangle],$

$scope{:}v\rangle\!\rangle],$

$[x \mid \langle\!\langle\text{EVENTUALLY-GIVES}, x, y, z_{\langle\!\langle\text{SECOND-CHANCE},z\rangle\!\rangle}\rangle\!\rangle]]\rangle\!\rangle$

Even though we have used the same parameter, y, for *her husband* and *him*, the two NPs do not covary. The dependent parameter for *her husband* is absorbed in the restrictor-property for EVERY, and thus unavailable for anaphoric relations from outside of this property. So as far as we can see, G&P is unable to supply (4) with the desired interpretation.

4   Discussion

The aim of G&P is to construct a compositional semantics for English in the framework of Situation Semantics. They claim that their use of absorption can explain anaphoric phenomena, or to be more exact, the lack of certain anaphoric relations. Using absorption has the effect of blocking reference to dependent parameters labeling roles without grammatical function higher up in the analysis. When absorption is used on every level of composition, the blocking may take place too soon. G&P's remedy to that is to use non-dependent parameters in the case where we have a referential use of the antecedent. We have shown that the Norwegian reflexive *sin* forces dependent readings, where the dependent parameter is not blocked from anaphoric reference. We have also shown that the analysis in G&P fails to capture the behavior of English fully.

Montague raised the interpretation of proper names like *John* from the individual referred to by the name to the set of properties of the individ-

---

[7]Absorbing the parameter for *woman* in *woman who leaves her husband* yields a two-argument relation due to AP and the dependence of the parameter for *her husband*. EVERY expects two properties as arguments. The solution is to project the role in question one more time. See G&P, page 121.

ual, so that the composition of NP interpretations and VP interpretations could be uniform for all NPs. In our opinion the analysis of G&P is in some ways analogous to this. Absorption is needed in order to liberate the parameter from a (locally) referential interpretation. This is called for when the parameter is bound (directly or through dependence to some bound parameter) by a generalized quantifier, or when the parameter lies within the scope of negation or a modal operator. In a plain referential VP there is no need for absorption; *John washes his car* has only one reading where *his* is anaphoric to *John*, the coparametric and the role-linking readings are equivalent in the sense that it is a necessary constraint that whenever John washes his own car, John also washes John's car, and vice versa.

In G&P there is an implicit interpretation of ellipsis: The elliptical VP content is exactly identical to the antecedent VP content. Thus, for ellipsis it is necessary to have more than one reading of the VP *washes his car* also in the cases where we intend to let the *his* corefer with the subject to be combined with the VP. Using absorption to create VP contents, G&P obtains the result that the VP content of the elliptic sentence is the very same object as the VP content of the antecedent sentence. This blocks for reference to any non-indexed dependent parameter in the VP content, thus preventing reference to the *car* of either subject of the VP in the sloppy case. How are we to avoid the undesired effects of absorption? We see four ways out:

1. Only use absorption for constructs of generalized quantifiers, negation and modal operators and find some other way than absorption to construct normal VP and other complex constituent contents.
2. Simplify as far as possible in the construction of the sentence content.
3. Allow for projection of other roles than the roles given by the grammar.
4. Use E-type analysis or some other way to pick up the same objects to refer to without going through the parameters[8].

Solutions 3. and 4. seem to us to give rise to at least as many problems as they solve. Allowing reference to blocked objects opens for too many cases of coreference. Along with such a solution comes the demand for classification of when such mechanisms may be used and when not. To get a uniform analysis the simple cases have been raised to a higher level of complexity than necessary for their own purpose. The need for repair of undesired effects of this complexification calls for a reidentification of the simple cases in order to allow for the possibility of something that would have been easy if the simple cases had been analyzed in a very simple way. We think that solutions that can give a more direct way to the desired effect are to be preferred. Solution 2. would in the framework of G&P

---

[8]See Gawron et al. 1991, Heim 1990

mean the counterpart of λ-application in all simple cases[9], so that the VP content

$$[x_{subj}, y \mid \langle\!\langle \text{WASHED}, x, y_{\langle\!\langle\text{CAR-OF},x,y\rangle\!\rangle} \rangle\!\rangle]$$

combined with the NP *John* yields the sentence content

(28) $\quad [\langle\!\langle \text{WASHED}, w_{\text{JOHN}}, y_{\langle\!\langle\text{CAR-OF},w,y\rangle\!\rangle} \rangle\!\rangle]$

rather than the content

$$\langle\!\langle [x_{subj}, y \mid \langle\!\langle \text{WASHED}, x, y_{\langle\!\langle\text{CAR-OF},x,y\rangle\!\rangle} \rangle\!\rangle], subj{:}w_{\text{JOHN}} \rangle\!\rangle$$

In the case of the non-role-linking VP content

$$[x_{subj} \mid \langle\!\langle \text{WASHED}, x, y_{\langle\!\langle\text{CAR-OF},x,w\rangle\!\rangle} \rangle\!\rangle]$$

combined with the same NP, the sentence content should be the same as in the first case, namely (28), rather than

$$\langle\!\langle [x_{subj} \mid \langle\!\langle \text{WASHED}, x, y_{\langle\!\langle\text{CAR-OF},x,w\rangle\!\rangle} \rangle\!\rangle], subj{:}w_{\text{JOHN}} \rangle\!\rangle$$

For VP ellipsis, the full VP content of the right kind must of course be combined with the NP *Bill* to yield the sloppy reading. In the meaning construction of the content for the elliptic VP, the VP content rather than the sentence content of the antecedent must be used (and then simplified in the sentence content for the elliptic sentence) to get the two different readings. This reflects that the VP is ambiguous whereas the antecedent sentence is not.

There is still a problem with respect to quantification. We cannot simplify to get rid of the absorption, since the quantified parameters and the parameters that depend on them must be quantified over. In (5), we see that the absorption has taken place on a too early level even when it takes place on the highest possible level according to G&P's format for quantified phrases. Another format for quantification, like $(D, x_1, \ldots, x_n, R, S)$, where D stands for determiner, R for restrictor and S for scope, where R and S are soas, and $x_1, \ldots, x_n$ are the parameters quantified over and the parameters that depend on them (ignoring the need for representing which are which), would be adequate.

---

[9]Upon completion of this manuscript, we were introduced to the manuscript "Ellipsis and Higher-Order Unification" by Mary Dalrymple, Fernando Pereira and Stuart Shieber (1990). The authors claim that their analysis requires no hidden ambiguity in the antecedent, or source, clause. However, it does rely on the "Primary Occurrence Constraint" requiring the abstraction of a primary occurrence of a term. A primary occurrence is defined as an occurrence of a subexpression in the semantic form directly associated with one of the parallel elements (page 7). And in order to cope with cases where only sloppy readings are available, they are forced to postulate that the reflexive possessive pronoun in Serbo-Croatian—the same would apply to Norwegian—engenders primary as opposed to secondary occurrences (page 39). Thus since primary occurrences are marked in semantic forms, the authors do provide a method for a "role-linking" representation of the antecedent clause. On the whole, their analysis appeals to us as elegant, although they defer discussion of identity of dependent parameters ("*car* parameters") to a companion paper in preparation.

Where did the need for types in the sentence contents go? Do we need types at all? In the intermediary stages solution 2. used types to distinguish between readings that were equivalent on the sentence level. A suggestion for solution 1. is to take care of this bookkeeping either on an intermediary representation level, or by viewing the $[x_1, \ldots, x_n \mid \ldots x_i \ldots], r_i{:}y$ as syntactic sugar placed there to keep track of the construction and of the possible disambiguation in case of ellipsis[10].

On a very strict understanding of compositionality, neither solution 1. nor solution 2. yields compositional analyzes. The sentence content does not carry all the information about the content of its parts, and the parts of the sentence cannot directly be found as parts of the content.

The Absorption Principle and the concept of dependent parameters are central concepts in Situation Theory. We agree with the intuitions these concepts are based upon, and think it right to demand dependent parameters to be absorbed whenever the parameters they rely upon are. It is the use of absorption on every level of construction even in the higher level constructs we question.

We think that reserving the power of absorption for the cases in which the parameters are cut off from a referential reading will explain almost all of the cases that Gawron and Peters use to motivate their stand, and some cases that G&P cannot explain, e.g., (2) and (4). The cases that Gawron and Peters use as a motivation for their analysis, but that the more restricted use of absorption does not capture in the same way, are a few cases where there is no quantification, negation, or modal operators. One example is

(29) Mary corrected her mother's errors before she did.

G&P claims that (29), as opposed to *Mary corrected her mother's errors before I did*, only has the co-parametric reading. This is in accordance with their use of absorption: since *she* is coparametric with *mother*, the parameter utilized by *mother* cannot depend on the parameter labeling the subject role of the VP *corrected her mother's errors*. We feel that this is a somewhat marginal case, and there are parallel examples where a role linking reading should be available. The following examples are reported to have originated with Karttunen:

---

[10] Discarding AP and having some bookkeeping mechanism instead, one could alter the concept of ellipsis slightly, from the very strict notion that every character is copied unconditionally to a copying mechanism that substitutes fresh parameters for the indexed parameters and the parameters that depend on them. Such a reinterpretation will come close to attempts at describing strict versus sloppy ambiguities in the framework of Discourse Representation Theory—Klein (1987) unites the advantage of antecedent ambiguity with the advantage of parameter variation, G&P itself renders a proposal communicated to Gawron and Peters personally by Hans Kamp, and similar ideas have been implemented by Lerner and Schatz (1989), who present an elaborate analysis of anaphoric ambiguities in sentences with scalar particles as well as in VP ellipsis, based on general principles of a DRT with events and roles, and a Prolog implementation.

When Reagan took office, he denounced his predecessor's policies, as he had done before him.

Mary resembles her mother even more than she did when she was her age.

The analysis of G&P predicts that on the sloppy reading of *Reagan denounced his predecessor's policies* and *Mary resembles her mother* the parameter utilized by *his predecessor* or *her mother* is absorbed—inaccessible to anaphoric reference from elsewhere in the discourse. The examples are VP ellipsis contexts strongly suggesting the sloppy reading, and yet the parameter utilized by the pronoun *he* or *she*, subject NP of the elliptical VP, clearly corefers with that parameter. Gawron and Peters must dispute these data by attributing the sloppy reading to accommodation.

According to G&P, the blocking of accessibility of absorbed parameters other than the subject parameter from outside of the VP has yet another semantic confirmation in the Bach-Peters sentences. Consider the following sentence:

(30) The pilot who first spotted it, downed the MIG that chased him.

G&P argues that on a Bach-Peters reading of (30) one cannot continue with *so did his squadron mate*. This is in accordance with the effects of The Absorption Principle. A sloppy reading of *him* calls for absorption of the MIG parameter in the VP, thus blocking an anaphoric relation between *it* and the MIG. A strict reading of *him* does not have the effect of absorption of the MIG parameter, and thus opens for the Bach-Peters reading of (30). To G&P, this is a confirmation that there is a reason to distinguish between Generalized Quantifiers and referential NPs. We feel that this analysis is not correct. For one thing, it seems possible to understand (30) in the Bach-Peters way, continuing with *and so did his squadron mate* meaning that the squadron mate downed the MIG he was chased by. Another objection is that the same Bach-Peters structure is found in the sentence (31).

(31) The Russian pilot who first entered it, started his MIG.

The Norwegian translation of (31) would have to use the reflexive pronoun *sin* in order to have coreference between the MIG-owner and the pilot:

(32) Den russiske piloten som entret den først, startet MIG-en sin.

Sin must have a role-linking interpretation, but the Bach-Peters reading of (32) is possible, though maybe slightly less likely than the Bach-Peters reading of (31).

5 Conclusions

Our aim in this paper has not been to provide a linguistic theory in Situation Semantics. We only wanted to point out some shortcomings of the analysis given in G&P. The brief sketches we have given for directions to move in order to remedy these shortcomings function more to give an idea of what the shortcomings really are than as solutions to replace the analysis of G&P. To do that a considerable amount of work is required, far beyond the scope of the present paper. We regret that the analysis of G&P, elegant in its simplicity despite the almost unreadable notation, does not solve the problems put forward here.

6 Appendix

Lars Hellan's Counterexamples to the Obligatory Role-Link of *sin*.

We have put forward a rather strong claim regarding the interpretation of the Norwegian possessive, namely that it is obligatorily bound by the subject-role of (one of) its VP(s). This is in tune with Isabelle Haïk's proposal (1985) for the syntactical analysis of sloppy identity, giving the prediction that "none of those anaphors which require c-command between binder and bindee, or some version of co-argumenthood, can have strict identity readings in constructions corresponding to (1) and (2a)" (Hellan 1988, page 231), where (1) is the sentence *John drank his coffee willingly, and Bill did it reluctantly* and (2a) is the sentence *John admires his dog, and Mary does too*. Hellan claims that this prediction is wrong for Norwegian, presenting several examples which he claims have strict readings (the typesetting is as in Hellan 1988), i.e.:

> **Jon** *gir* **sin** *kone* *et* *grått* *hår* *per* *dag*, *og* **det** **gjør**
> Jon gives his wife a grey hair per day and it does
>
> deres sønn også
> their son too

'Jon gives his wife one grey hair per day, and so does their son.'

Can we use this sentence with a strict reading of *sin*? If so, is this really a violation of the boundness of *sin*?

We find that the example is difficult to understand, and that this reflects the unlikeliness of a sloppy reading. There is no strict interpretation of *sin* in our opinion. As communication normally is a cooperative process, even if an utterance does not literally have the meaning intended by the speaker, the hearer is often willing to make a robust guess as to what the speaker means, based on world knowledge and pragmatics. It is of course extremely difficult to determine whether an alleged reading of a sentence is a real reading or only a cooperative guess. Let us therefore first state why a sloppy reading may be difficult to get at, before we try to explain what mechanisms may be at work in case a strict reading is possible after all. We are presented with a completely unknown family with a father, mother and son. The concept of a typical family will make you think of the son as a child. It is difficult to think of him as having a wife.

Let us now assume that the sentence has the strict reading as claimed by Hellan. Replacing *deres sønn* by the proper name *Per*, it is clear that the sentence only and unproblematically has the sloppy reading. What properties of *deres sønn* is it that could possibly open for the strict reading? In addition to the fact that replacing *deres sønn* with *Per* only has the normal bound reading, our reason to believe that the intended reading is not an unbound reading of *sin* is based on the following:

Jon gir sin kone et grått hår hver dag, og det gjør deres sønn også.

Hva gjør deres sønn? (What does their son do?)

If we accept the allegedly strict reading, the natural answer is:

Han gir sin mor et grått hår hver dag.
(He gives his*reflexive* mother a grey hair every day.)

It is not:

Han gir Jons kone et grått hår hver dag.
(He gives Jon's wife a grey hair every day.)

It seems to us that the boundness of *sin* is maintained by a weakening of the interpretation of *kone*, such that *sin kone* goes to *sin mor*. If so, we are still faced with a bound occurrence of *sin*. It seems that such a weakening is possible, though not always likely, when there is a relation with a lexicalized converse between the nouns in question. It seems possible to get the same kind of reading also if we replace *deres sønn* with *hennes elsker*, *hennes bror* (her lover, her brother). Note also that the intended reading is less likely if *deres sønn* is replaced by *hans sønn* (his son):

Jon gir sin kone et grått hår hver dag, og det gjør hans sønn også.

This is particularly clear if we replace *kone* by *nye kone* (new wife), in which case the intended reading may be possible with *deres sønn*, but not with *hans sønn*. In the latter case, the natural reaction is to say something like "oh, is his son remarried too?" Maybe *hennes*, or *deres*, together with a relational noun establishes a link between Jon's wife and the whatever being *hennes/deres*, making an opening for the possibility that Jon's wife is *sin* also to this other person, though perhaps not *sin kone*.

Two Final Remarks

We definitely feel the acceptability of

John vasket bilen sin. Den ble skinnende ren.
John washed his*reflexive* car. It became spanking clean.

is in no way exceptional. That is, the sequence does not even remotely resemble Hellan's alleged counterexamples, as it would if we had to read the antecedent in the strict sense, in accordance with AP. The interpretation does not require any robustness whatsoever.

And we would like to appeal to general principles of linguistic theory. The reflexive possessive certainly has a certain syntactic property: Like the reflexive personal pronoun, it requires C-command in the antecedent—the subject. In terms of a version of the Binding Principles of G&P, the reflexive personal pronoun covaries with a role-aspect of a role of which the role the subject NP covers is a (trivial or nontrivial) projection. And quite possibly, it has a semantic property too: Then it requires a role-linking antecedent— it covaries with a role-aspect of a role of which the role the antecedent NP covers is a nontrivial projection. Hellan will dispute this, as Peters disputes the notion that the English reflexive personal pronoun requires a role-linking antecedent, but they cannot dispute the strong preference there is for role-linking antecedents. And in fact, in terms of a strengthened Binding Principle, the latter property subsumes the former property:

> A reflexive pronoun covaries with a role-aspect of a role of which the role the subject NP covers is a nontrivial projection.

The stronger assumption provides a neat correlation between syntax and semantics: The distinction between reflexivity and personality in syntax carries over to the distinction between nontrivial and trivial projection in semantics. We feel that when there is an interesting generalization—e.g., every reflexive pronoun is role-linked—and counterexamples are dubious, they should be ignored.

References

Dalrymple, M., F. Pereira, and S. Shieber. 1990. Ellipsis and Higher-Order Unification. Unpublished.

Gawron, M., S. Peters, and J. Nerbonne. 1991. Anaphora, Quantification and Absorption. This volume.

Haïk, I. 1985. *The Syntax of Operators.* PhD thesis, MIT.

Heim, I. 1990. E-Type Pronouns and Donkey Anaphora. *Linguistics and Philosophy* 13(2):137–177.

Hellan, L. 1988. *Anaphora in Norwegian and the Theory of Grammar.* Dordrecht: Foris.

Klein, E. 1987. VP Ellipsis in DR Theory. In *Studies in Discourse Representation Theory and the Theory of Generalized Quantifiers*, ed. J. Groenendijk, D. de Jongh, and M. Stokhof, 161–187. No. 8 Groeningen-Amsterdam Studies in Semantics. Dordrecht: Foris.

Lerner, J., and U. Schatz. 1989. Does the sloppy/referential ambiguity reflect two uses of pronouns? *Zeitschrift für Sprachwissenschaft* 8:3–52.

22

A Strictly Incremental Approach to Japanese Grammar

HIROYUKI SUZUKI AND SYUN TUTIYA

1 Introduction

In this paper, we propose a computational linguistic approach to semantic interpretation of utterances in Japanese. We call this approach *incremental* in the sense that the parsing system built on the approach tries to provide a semantic interpretation by adding up the information given by utterances of words in sequence, rather than by depending for its interpretation on the syntactic structure of the whole sentence. Our approach is called *strictly* incremental as opposed to the conventional bottom-up parsing, because the sequence of utterances of words is always given a (partial) interpretation at any point of the sequence.

The parser we build on this approach does not depend on the syntactic structure of a sentence for its semantic interpretation. Natural language understanding systems which assume this type of parser are expected to be robust enough to cope with utterances of fragmentary sentences with abrupt endings as well as flexible enough to incorporate contextual factors appropriately.

The strictly incremental approach is inspired by an insight and an intuition. The insight is that the utterance of a sentence is done by uttering

The authors are grateful to the following people for suggestions, improvements and criticisms: Jon Barwise, Takao Gunji, Yasunari Harada, Masayo Iida, Roberta Ishihara, David Israel, Hideyuki Nakashima, John Nerbonne, John Perry, Stanley Peters, Carl Pollard, Peter Sells, Takenobu Tokunaga, ICOT NLU working group members and all the participants of the conference at Asilomar. Thanks are due to the anonymous referee who suggested that we compare our theory with more "conventional" theories. We also thank Matsushita Electric Industrial Company and the Ministry of Education, Culture and Science and CSLI for enabling us to spend time together in one place to discuss the contents of this paper.

Situation Theory and Its Applications, vol. 2.
Jon Barwise, Jean Mark Gawron, Gordon Plotkin, and Syun Tutiya, eds.

words in sequence, that is, by producing a sequence of actions of uttering a word. The intuition is that utterances in Japanese can best be processed in this incremental manner. Interpretation of Japanese utterances does not have to turn to the structure.[1] In this paper, we talk exclusively about the processing of Japanese utterances, but our hope is that this approach will shed some light on the machine processing of utterances in other languages, such as English, which appear to be more structured. Notice now that we do not speak of "the parser of sentences" but of "the parser of utterances".

The basic idea is this. An utterance of a sentence consists of a sequence of acts, each of which is an uttering of a token word belonging to a certain language. The constraints or rules of the language associate the type of utterance of those tokens in particular circumstances with a certain content and other items of information conveyed by the utterance. That is, an utterance of the first word conveys certain information, conditional on which the utterance of the second word of the sentence conveys a further piece of information. In this sense, the conveyance of information by uttering a sentence is an essentially incremental action. This action ends with the ending of the sentence. Needless to say, the utterance of the first word conveys incremental information on top of information that the discourse and other situations provide. The properties of the discourse are characterized by facts about the utterance and other relevant facts including those related to the preceding utterance(s), if any. The interpretation of the sentence as a whole, therefore, is also incremental in the sense that the interpretation is an addition to the information (content) given by the context. Our approach is designed to follow this picture as faithfully as possible.[2]

In this paper, we concentrate on the basic ideas of our approach. To do that, we describe the way our method works with an utterance of a simple yet typical Japanese sentence. Next we discuss apparent problems with the approach, namely how we could handle "embedding structures," like Passives, Causatives, Adverbial Clauses, and Adnominal Clauses[3], arguing that the semantic interpretation of utterances using sentences with such structures does not pose any essential difficulty, given the rich theoretical resources of situation theory and impartial observations on Japanese grammatical phenomena. We conclude the paper by comparing our ideas with

---

[1] Of course, we do not claim that Japanese sentences have no syntactic structures or constituent structures but just that if there were any syntactic structures, they might not play an important role in the (semantic) interpretation of the sentence.

[2] But in this paper we do not take contextual factors into account explicitly, though their inclusion is understandably straightforward.

[3] The sense in which Passives give rise to "embedded structures" will be shown in later sections.

Hozumi Tanaka's right-branching bottom-up parser and the traditional approach to Japanese grammar.

2 Simple Analytic Paradigm

Here we introduce our approach by first presenting the intuitive picture, then illustrating the procedure and finally arguing for a principle, which we call the Principle of Integrity, and its implementation.

2.1 The Idea

First we look at our approach by showing what happens when the system processes a simple, typical Japanese sentence. The sentence is this:

syunbun-no-hi	ni	zinbotyo	de	taroo	ga	hon
spring equinox	on	Jinbocho	in	Taro	*nom.*	book

o	kau	yo
acc.	buy	

Taro buys books in Jinbocho on the spring equinox.

Simple as it may look, this sentence embodies the basic features of Japanese sentences.

- The last element is a particle to end a sentence with.
- The penultimate element of the sentence is a predicative expression.
- The predicative expression is preceded by noun expressions, each of which is followed by a particle of a certain kind[4] (**ga**, **o**, **ni**, **de**, **e**, and so forth).
- The nouns are not prefixed with any article or determiner.

To explain how the system works, we borrow some basic notions from situation theory. A *state of affairs*, or *soa* for short, is a sequence consisting of a major constituent and minor constituents, which we write $\langle\!\langle R, a_1, \ldots, a_n; p \rangle\!\rangle$, where the major constituent R is a relation, and each minor constituent $a_1, \ldots, a_n$ is either an object or a parameter, and p is a polarity, either 0 or 1. A soa is a *parametric soa* if one or more of its constituents are parameters. A *situation* is part of the world that makes soas factual. We say a situation s *supports* a soa σ, and write $s \models \sigma$ if the former makes the latter factual. For any soa there is a *type* of a situation which supports the soa, which we call the *conditioning soa* of the type. Given a type T, there is a *proposition* P that says there is a situation of the type. The proposition P is *true* if there is a situation which supports the conditioning soa of the type T. We allow conjunction operation over types. A situation s is of the type of $T \wedge T'$, i.e., the conjunction of the types, T and T', if it is of both types. We call this conjunction a conjunctive type. We assume conjunction is associative.

---

[4] The particles of this kind have been categorized as particles marking "cases," though what is a "case" is still an unsettled problem.

The system takes in one word[5] after another and specifies, at each word, the conditioning soa induced by the utterance thus far made. Each particle, **ga, o, ni**, etc., picks out a relation between a situation and an object. Thus a noun followed by a particle induces a parametric soa. The major constituent of the soa is the relation the particle picks out, the first minor constituent is the object referred to by the noun. The second minor constituent is a parameter for a situation.[6] This parametric soa determines a type of situation. All the nouns and particles thus induce a set of parametric soas which, in turn, determines parametric types severally. All the types obtained up to a certain point of utterance constitute a conjunction thereof.

We assume the interpretation of an utterance is a proposition. The utterance gets interpreted as expressing a proposition that there is a situation of that type.[7] So the content conveyed by an utterance of an unambiguous sentence is to the effect that there is a situation which satisfies the conditions induced by the uses of the particles,the nouns and verbs. Now the problem is how to get this kind of proposition from the conjunctive type. To see this problem more closely, we have to break down the whole procedure into several steps and see exactly what is required to happen.[8]

2.2 The Step-by-Step Exposition

We assume **ni, de, ga**, and **o** pick out the relations, DATE, PLACE, AGENT, and OBJECT respectively.[9]

For the time being we assume the following simple lexicon containing our "content" word.

[[kau]]= *buy*;
[[hon]]= *book*;
[[syunbun-no-hi]]= *spring equinox*;

---

[5]The concept of word in Japanese has been a chronic problem for linguists, but we do not go into the details of the long history of the discussion here. Our tentative decision on this problem is that we follow a commonsensical agreement, namely that the strings which are listed as words in Japanese dictionaries are words. We hope the final correct definition, if any, of the word will be reached in a way that the essence of the approach advised in this paper is not substantially jeopardized. Our worry mainly concerns the wordhood of those morphemes attached to the verbs, which are called *auxiliary verbs* in Japanese.

[6]In what follows, we always assume all the occurrences of lexical items are anchored. Therefore the parameters thus introduced are all that are *un*anchored. Also in this paper, when we say *parameters*, we mean only the parameters thus introduced for situations.

[7]Here by *propositions* we mean the propositions of Russellian type discussed in Barwise and Etchemendy 1987.

[8]This is *pure* information in the sense used in Israel and Perry 1990.

[9]This means that we do not follow the conventional treatment of the particles as mere case markers. Of course the alternative we give here is an oversimplification, but we believe only by giving due credits to the jobs of those particles could we really appreciate their "meanings." We have a fairly interesting generalization about the meaning of de on this line.

$[\![\text{taroo}]\!] = tr$;

$[\![\text{zinbotyo}]\!] = jinbocho$;

$_C[\![\text{yo}]\!] = \phi$, where in C, the speaker is convinced of the content.

When the sentence is read to the end, the system gets the following conjunctive type:

$$[\dot{s} \mid \dot{s} \models \langle\!\langle \text{DATE}, spring\ equinox, e_1; 1\rangle\!\rangle] \wedge$$
$$[\dot{s} \mid \dot{s} \models \langle\!\langle \text{PLACE}, jinbocho, e_2; 1\rangle\!\rangle] \wedge$$
$$[\dot{s} \mid \dot{s} \models \langle\!\langle \text{AGENT}, tr, e_3; 1\rangle\!\rangle] \wedge$$
$$[\dot{s} \mid \dot{s} \models \langle\!\langle \text{OBJECT}, book, e_4; 1\rangle\!\rangle] \wedge$$
$$[\dot{s} \mid \dot{s} \models \langle\!\langle \text{BUY}, e_5; 1\rangle\!\rangle].$$

The construction of this structure is quite straightforward. The interpretation is "produced" one by one as the words are fed into the system. The first word **syunbun-no-hi** refers to a spring equinox, and **ni** introduces a parameter e_1 and the relation DATE between e_1 and the spring equinox. **Zinbotyo** picks up a place, Jinbocho, and the **de** introduces a new parameter e_2, specifying a parametric soa, $\langle\!\langle \text{PLACE}, jinbocho, e_2; 1\rangle\!\rangle$.

Based on this conjunction, we derive the following proposition. It is the proposition expressed by the utterance of this sentence, relying on the principle we explain shortly.

$$s : [\dot{s} \mid \dot{s} \models \langle\!\langle \text{BUY}, \text{AGENT} : tr, \text{OBJECT} : book,$$
$$\text{DATE} : spring\ equinox, \text{PLACE} : jinbocho; 1\rangle\!\rangle].$$

But the intuitive idea should be clear at this stage. We had five e's in the conjunction. From the conjunction, we get a proposition as the content of the utterance.

2.3 The Principle

What is required of the principle is to allow us to think of the type parameterized to an unmanageable number of situations as that which one situation is of. We observe the following principle working in two steps in our approach. We call the principle *the principle of integrity*.

(π) **Principle of Integrity:** People talk about one thing at one time.

This principle does two jobs. First, when people speak, they talk about one thing or one situation. It is clearly inconceivable that with the first word we talk about this, with the second about that, with the third about yet another thing and so on and so forth. We expect a normal, truthful speaker who utters a sentence to talk about one thing in the sense of what the topic of reference is. This licenses us to assume there exists a situation which is of the type of the conjunction we gave. Now of what type would the situation we talk about be? Is there a unique conditioning soa which determines the type of which our situation is? If there is a conditioning soa, then we call it a *solution* to the conjunctive type induced, and we say that the respective proposition—that the situation is of the type determined by the solution—is the content of the utterance. The principle does not guarantee the existence of a unique solution but does specify a way to get to a solution if there are any. Where there is no unique solution, application of the principle might end up only with ambiguity. Thanks to the fact that all the utterances are situated and supplied with contexts, normally we have some unique solution.[10]

When is this principle invoked? In Japanese, we propose that any input of any one of the conjugational endings of predicative expressions (verbs, adjectives, and certain auxiliary verbs) cues the system to apply this principle.

We specify the computational procedure which implements the principle π as follows:[11]

1. Use one symbol to replace all the parameters. Collapse the conjunctive type into a type whose conditioning soa is the conjunction of the conditioning soas of the conjunct type.[12]

2. If there is a situation which supports all the conjuncts, we get a proposition of the form $s : [\dot{s} \mid \dot{s} \models \Sigma]$, where Σ is the conjunction of the conditioning soas of the conjunctive type.

Notice that the principle is twice made essential use of in the implementation. At the first step, the principle works in the way that it guarantees the substitution of one and the same E for all the e_i's, and at the second step, the principle is again invoked to allow us to posit one and the same situation as a situation supporting the type induced at the first step. Let us describe the steps more formally by way of situation theoretic notations. In general, what we get from reading the words in the sentence is:

$$\bigwedge_{i \leq n} [\dot{s} \mid \dot{s} \models \langle\!\langle R_i, a_i, e_i; 1 \rangle\!\rangle].$$

At the first step, the principle gives us the following by replacing the $e_1, \ldots, e_n$ with E.

$$\bigwedge_{i \leq n} [\dot{s} \mid \dot{s} \models \langle\!\langle R_i, a_i, E; 1 \rangle\!\rangle].$$

---

[10]Note that two senses of integrity exactly correspond to the two uses of this principle. Honesty of the speakers provides the uniqueness of the situation which the utterance is about, and unity of the type leads to a unique conditioning soa. If the reader is at a loss about the striking paucity and commonplaceness of this principle he should be reminded of the principle and maxims Grice introduced.

[11]The computational implementation of the following algorithm is now at the stage where the basic part of our fragment covered in this section is processed with satisfactory results.

[12]This operation is similar to the operation in first-order logic whereby, from a conjunction of closed formulas, one derives a closed formula whose open formula is the conjunction of the open formulas of the original conjunction. Obviously this operation is not necessarily truth-preserving, and neither is our operation, hence the lack of uniqueness of the solution. That is similar to the operation which derives $\exists x (Px \land Qx)$ from $\exists x\, Px \land \exists x\, Qx$.

The principle justifies the transition from the above to the following because it says the meaning of the sentence is associated with a type of situation:

$$[\dot{s} \mid \dot{s} \models \bigwedge_{i \leq n} \langle\!\langle R_i, a_i, E; 1 \rangle\!\rangle].$$

By uttering a declarative sentence, we normally pick up a described situation in virtue of the demonstrative convention[13] induced by the rules of the language. This is the second meaning of what the principle says. Let the situation so picked up be s, and then we might be entertaining the following proposition:

$$s : [\dot{s} \mid \dot{s} \models \bigwedge_{i \leq n} \langle\!\langle R_i, a_i, E; 1 \rangle\!\rangle]$$

This is reduced to the following by simply referring to the meaning of R.

$$s : [\dot{s} \mid \dot{s} \models \langle\!\langle R, a_1, \ldots, a_n; 1 \rangle\!\rangle]$$

Let us go back to our example sentence. When the sentence:

syunbun-no-hi ni zinbotyo de taroo ga hon
spring equinox on Jinbocho in Taro *nom.* book

o kau yo
acc. buy

Taro buys books in Jinbocho on the spring equinox.

is read to the end, the system gets the following:

$[\dot{s} \mid \dot{s} \models \langle\!\langle \text{DATE}, spring\ equinox, e_1; 1 \rangle\!\rangle] \wedge$
$[\dot{s} \mid \dot{s} \models \langle\!\langle \text{PLACE}, jinbocho, e_2; 1 \rangle\!\rangle] \wedge$
$[\dot{s} \mid \dot{s} \models \langle\!\langle \text{AGENT}, tr, e_3; 1 \rangle\!\rangle] \wedge$
$[\dot{s} \mid \dot{s} \models \langle\!\langle \text{OBJECT}, book, e_4; 1 \rangle\!\rangle] \wedge$
$[\dot{s} \mid \dot{s} \models \langle\!\langle \text{BUY}, e_5; 1 \rangle\!\rangle].$

Then our system makes the following conjunctive type as a result of the first step.

$[\dot{s} \mid \dot{s} \models \langle\!\langle \text{DATE}, spring\ equinox, E; 1 \rangle\!\rangle] \wedge$
$[\dot{s} \mid \dot{s} \models \langle\!\langle \text{PLACE}, jinbocho, E; 1 \rangle\!\rangle] \wedge$
$[\dot{s} \mid \dot{s} \models \langle\!\langle \text{AGENT}, tr, E; 1 \rangle\!\rangle] \wedge$
$[\dot{s} \mid \dot{s} \models \langle\!\langle \text{OBJECT}, book, E; 1 \rangle\!\rangle] \wedge$
$[\dot{s} \mid \dot{s} \models \langle\!\langle \text{BUY}, E; 1 \rangle\!\rangle].$

The second step is to remake the above conjunctive type into the following situation-type.

$[\dot{s} \mid \dot{s} \models \langle\!\langle \text{DATE}, spring\ equinox, E; 1 \rangle\!\rangle \wedge \langle\!\langle \text{PLACE}, jinbocho, E; 1 \rangle\!\rangle$
$\wedge \langle\!\langle \text{AGENT}, tr, E; 1 \rangle\!\rangle \wedge \langle\!\langle \text{OBJECT}, book, E; 1 \rangle\!\rangle \wedge \langle\!\langle \text{BUY}, E; 1 \rangle\!\rangle].$

And the third and the fourth step give us the proposition

---

[13]See *The Liar*.

$$s : [\dot{s} \mid \dot{s} \models \langle\langle \text{BUY}, \text{AGENT} : tr, \text{OBJECT} : book,$$
$$\text{DATE} : spring\ equinox, \text{PLACE} : jinbocho; 1\rangle\rangle].$$

Note that the order makes no difference. Suppose the same assortment of words as our example is uttered in the following order.

syunbun-no-hi ni taroo ga hon o   kau yo
spring equinox on Taro *nom.* book *acc.* buy
zinbotyo de
Jinbocho in

The interpretation of this utterance remains the same in our system and this is exactly what is the case.[14]

Furthermore, we do not postulate any constraint of syntactic nature. To make the proposition expressed of the following sentence, we may have to violate the rule against crossover.[15]

eiga o   zinbotyo ni taroo ga   mi ni iku
movie *acc.* Jinbocho in Taro *nom.* see go
Taro goes to see the movie in Jinbocho.

3   Problems and Solutions

Facts that (Seem to) Challenge our Approach

Although our incremental approach covers the basic part of our fragment with sufficient plausibility, as has been shown in the previous section, there are still several problems which might endanger the whole idea of our approach. These involve some very obvious features of Japanese grammar which require its semantics to take into account syntactically structured information in an essential manner. These are the two problems we think are most important.

Passives and Causatives. In Japanese, these constructions are considered to constitute embedded structures, following the prevalent conception of Japanese "auxiliary verbs" as matrix verbs. The typical structure of a passive construction in Japanese could be envisioned as follows:

$$[_S\ [_S\ \text{inu ga john o kam}]\ [_{Pred}\ \text{areru}]],$$

which realizes in the surface form as

john ga inu ni kam-areru.

---

[14]It is also remarkable that if yo is omitted, this sentence does not seem to be accepted naturally by as many people as those who accept the sentence in its original order.

[15]One may claim that the mi ni iku is one word and make a tree structure accordingly. Our objection to this treatment is that we find no reason to treat the following two sentences in different ways. Both orders are used to express the same content.

eiga o zinbotyo ni mi   ni iku
eiga o mi   ni zinbotyo ni iku

This analysis is prima facie convincing in that it predicts the desired semantic interpretation of the sentence in which the agent of the action of biting is the dog and the patient John. Given the facts about Japanese passives, especially of adversative passives,[16] however, the uniformity of the phenomena escapes this kind of analysis. Problems the passive construction of Japanese presents are the following:

- Our analysis predicts that the word followed by **ga**, "john" in this case, denotes the agent of an action, but John is obviously the patient of the act of biting.
- Closely related is the problem of how to interpret the noun followed by **ni** as the agent of the action of biting.

The causative construction poses the same kind of problem.[17]

In both constructions, some particles, **ni** in particular, seem test to be given different interpretations than we assumed they do in the previous section. We need to accommodate this apparent "shift" in meaning in ways which are consistent with our incremental/solution approach, which, though seems, at the first glance, quite impossible, because the system proposed here can *not* talk about the structure of sentences at face value.

Determinacy. In most Japanese sentences, the interpretation of nouns (verbs) relative to the verbs (nouns, resp.) in the same sentence can be determined structurally, but our approach appears to be incapable of utilizing this kind of structural information, thus giving only ambiguous interpretations to sentences which have a definite, unambiguous sense.

3.1 Passives and Causatives

Look at the following sentences as uttered.

Taroo o Jiroo ga tataku	Jiro hits Taro.
Taroo ga Jiroo ni tatak-areru	Taro is hit by Jiro.

We admit any utterance of either sentence expresses the same type given a fixed anchor for **Taroo** and **Jiroo**, namely the following:

$$[\dot{s} \mid \dot{s} \models \langle\!\langle \text{HIT}, \text{AGENT}: jr, \text{OBJECT}: tr; 1 \rangle\!\rangle].$$

But apparently our principle π produces two different interpretations, if we give **areru** the type

$$[\dot{s} \mid \dot{s} \models \langle\!\langle \text{PASSIVE}, \text{EVENT-1}, \text{EVENT-2} \rangle\!\rangle$$

---

[16]As defined and discussed in the following section.

[17]Notice that in Japanese the causative construction is on a par with the passive construction in that both constructions are triggered, so to speak, by the suffixation of the verbs and involve certain systematic deviance from the expected roles played by the nouns "marked by case particles."

which roughly reads: EVENT-2 is a passive counterpart of EVENT-1. That is, we would get:

$$[\dot{s} \mid \dot{s} \models \langle\!\langle \text{OBJECT}, tr, e_1; 1 \rangle\!\rangle] \wedge [\dot{s} \mid \dot{s} \models \langle\!\langle \text{AGENT}, jr, e_2; 1 \rangle\!\rangle]$$
$$\wedge [\dot{s} \mid \dot{s} \models \langle\!\langle \text{HIT}, e_3; 1 \rangle\!\rangle]$$

$$[\dot{s} \mid \dot{s} \models \langle\!\langle \text{AGENT}, tr, e_4; 1 \rangle\!\rangle] \wedge [\dot{s} \mid \dot{s} \models \langle\!\langle \text{PATIENT}, jr, e_5; 1 \rangle\!\rangle]$$
$$\wedge [\dot{s} \mid \dot{s} \models \langle\!\langle \text{HIT}, e_6; 1 \rangle\!\rangle] \wedge [\dot{s} \mid \dot{s} \models \langle\!\langle \text{PASSIVE}, e_6, e_7; 1 \rangle\!\rangle]$$

How could we get the same content from these two apparently different readings without adding syntactic information about the passive construction? And what does the relation PASSIVE mean? To answer these questions, we observe the uses of **areru** a little more extensively and draw attention to the uses of what Japanese linguists have called the "adversative passive." The adversative passive phenomena are thought to be observed in cases where the immediately preceding verb is an intransitive verb. A case in point is

> **Taroo ga titi   ni sin areru**
> Taro   father   die

which means that Taroo's father dies.[18] **Sinu**, i.e., "die," is no doubt an intransitive verb, and this phenomenon has drawn linguistic curiosity for some time. This construction of a passive with an intransitive verb has been traditionally called *an adversative passive* because the construction suggests the experience of suffering on the part of the referent of the subject expression, namely Taroo in this case.

But closer observation provides evidence that such a use of **areru** is not restricted to those cases but also allows cases where transitive verbs are involved. In other words, we are required not only to explain the semantic nature of the use of **areru** with an intransitive verb but also, by positing a a uniform relation expressed by **areru**, to derive the adversative and non-adversative, ordinary, passive meaning. We propose to introduce the relation AFFECTED as associated with the use of the word **areru**, and show how the existence of this more general relation predicts reasonable interpretations of both kinds of passive sentences.

First consider the following two sentences.

> **Taroo ga Jiroo ni tatak-areru**
> Taro is hit by Jiro.

> **Taroo ga Jiroo ni Hanako o tatak-areru**
> Jiro's hitting Hanako affects Taro.

They have the same "tatak-areru" at the end of the sentence and, therefore, are "passive sentences." The first sentence has the reading expected from

---

[18] Japanese has another form expressing the same content, namely the death of Taroo's father: **Taroo no titi ga sin-u**, the meaning of which is thought commonly to be more "objective" than the "passive sentence" in question.

the grammatical concept of passivity, while the second sentence could not be the passive in the normal sense because there is a Noun marked with o, traditionally a mark for Object case. We call the interpretation of such sentences *adversative passive*.

Where does this reading come from? One might argue that the extra argument **Hanako o** requires the adversative reading, based on the above contrast. However, it is not a valid argument. Consider the following pair.

> **Taroo ga Hanako to kekkon suru**
> Taro marries Hanako.

> **Hanako ga Taroo ni kekkon sareru**
> *Hanako gets married to Taro.
> Taro's marrying somebody affects Hanako.

Although there is no extra argument in the second sentence, the adversative reading is preferred to the passive reading. In other words, the adversative reading is the basic analysis for Japanese "passive" sentences. We can now show that the so-called passive readings are derivable from the adversative readings.[19]

Now when the sentence

> **Taroo ga Jiroo ni Hanako o tatak-areru**
> Jiro's hitting Hanako affects Taro.

is read, the following sequential conjunction is generated.

$$[\dot{s} \mid \dot{s} \models \langle\!\langle \text{AGENT}, tr, e_4; 1 \rangle\!\rangle] \wedge [\dot{s} \mid \dot{s} \models \langle\!\langle \text{PATIENT}, jr, e_5; 1 \rangle\!\rangle] \wedge$$
$$[\dot{s} \mid \dot{s} \models \langle\!\langle \text{OBJECT}, hnk, e_6; 1 \rangle\!\rangle] \wedge [\dot{s} \mid \dot{s} \models \langle\!\langle \text{HIT}, e_7; 1 \rangle\!\rangle] \wedge$$
$$[\dot{s} \mid \dot{s} \models \langle\!\langle \text{AFFECTED}, e_8, e_7; 1 \rangle\!\rangle]$$

Note that we have switched the lexical entry of **areru** from PASSIVE to AFFECTED to avoid the confusion.

It is true that we cannot replace all e's with only one E. Since the relation AFFECTED is a relation between a situation and a person, we need two E's to interpret the so-called passive sentences. The solutions for this given by the equations

$$E_8 = e_4 = e_5 = e_8 \neq e_6 = e_7 = E_6$$

give us two propositions.

$$E_8 : [\dot{s} \mid \dot{s} \models \langle\!\langle \text{AFFECTED}, \text{AGENT}: tr, \text{PATIENT}: jr, \text{EVENT}: E_6; 1 \rangle\!\rangle]$$
$$E_6 : [\dot{s} \mid \dot{s} \models \langle\!\langle \text{HIT}, \text{AGENT}: jr, \text{OBJECT}: hnk; 1 \rangle\!\rangle]$$

The reason why the AGENT of the second soa become jr, the PATIENT of the first soa, is a constraint about the relation AFFECTED.

---

[19]This explains the reason why Japanese passive sentences in general tend to be perspectival expressions (Katagiri).

One may argue that there are equations other than the equations given above which also qualify as a solution, say,

$$E_8 = e_5 = e_8 \neq e_4 = e_6 = e_7 = E_6.$$

What these equations say is that the Taro is the agent of event HIT, not of the event AFFECTED. However, we claim here that the constraint about the relation AFFECTED is so strong that this interpretation is excluded at the stage of constructing a proposition.

The same applies to the sentence:

Taroo ga Jiroo ni tatak-areru   Taro is hit by Jiro.

The conjunction

$$[\dot{s} \mid \dot{s} \models \langle\!\langle \text{AGENT}, tr, e_9; 1 \rangle\!\rangle] \wedge [\dot{s} \mid \dot{s} \models \langle\!\langle \text{PATIENT}, jr, e_{10}; 1 \rangle\!\rangle]$$
$$\wedge \, [\dot{s} \mid \dot{s} \models \langle\!\langle \text{HIT}, e_{11}; 1 \rangle\!\rangle] \wedge [\dot{s} \mid \dot{s} \models \langle\!\langle \text{AFFECTED}, e_{12}, e_{11}; 1 \rangle\!\rangle]$$

is generated and the feasible minimal solution

$$E_{12} = e_9 = e_{10} = e_{12} \neq e_{11} = E_{11}$$

gives us two propositions.

$$E_{12} : [\dot{s} \mid \dot{s} \models \langle\!\langle \text{AFFECTED}, \text{AGENT} : tr, \text{PATIENT} : jr, \text{EVENT} : E_{11}; 1 \rangle\!\rangle]$$
$$E_{11} : [\dot{s} \mid \dot{s} \models \langle\!\langle \text{HIT}, \text{AGENT} : jr, \text{OBJECT} : Y; 1 \rangle\!\rangle]$$

The difference is that in this case the OBJECT position is not filled by the thing mentioned in the sentence. At this stage some contextual environment is considered and fills that gap.[20] One candidate is of course the thing filling the AGENT position of the AFFECTED soa. Thus in most cases we get,

$$E_{12} : [\dot{s} \mid \dot{s} \models \langle\!\langle \text{AFFECTED}, \text{AGENT} : tr, \text{PATIENT} : jr, \text{EVENT} : E_{11}; 1 \rangle\!\rangle]$$
$$E_{11} : [\dot{s} \mid \dot{s} \models \langle\!\langle \text{HIT}, \text{AGENT} : jr, \text{OBJECT} : tr; 1 \rangle\!\rangle]$$

The second content is the same as the content of the sentence

Jiroo ga Taroo o tataku   Jiro hits Taro.

Causatives have the same kind of problem. Consider the following sentences.

Jiroo ga hon   o   kau
Taroo ga Jiroo ni hon o kaw aseru
Jiro buys books.
Taro makes Jiro buy books.

The parsing by introducing the relation CAUSATIVE for the meaning of **aseru** will face the problem, but our solution to the Passive *mutatis mutandis* applies to this case too.

---

[20]Of course, the information necessary for this stage is already there, but it is only at this stage that use is made of the information.

The sequential conjunction derived from the second sentence above:

$$[\dot{s} \mid \dot{s} \models \langle\!\langle \text{AGENT}, tr, e_{13}; 1 \rangle\!\rangle] \wedge [\dot{s} \mid \dot{s} \models \langle\!\langle \text{PATIENT}, jr, e_{14}; 1 \rangle\!\rangle] \wedge$$
$$[\dot{s} \mid \dot{s} \models \langle\!\langle \text{OBJECT}, book, e_{15}; 1 \rangle\!\rangle] \wedge [\dot{s} \mid \dot{s} \models \langle\!\langle \text{BUY}, e_{16}; 1 \rangle\!\rangle] \wedge$$
$$[\dot{s} \mid \dot{s} \models \langle\!\langle \text{CAUSATIVE}, e_{17}, e_{16}; 1 \rangle\!\rangle]$$

and the feasible minimal solution

$$E_{17} = e_{13} = e_{14} = e_{17} \neq e_{15} = e_{16} = E_{16}$$

gives us two propositions.

$$E_{17} : [\dot{s} \mid \dot{s} \models \langle\!\langle \text{CAUSATIVE}, \text{AGENT} : tr, \text{PATIENT} : jr, \text{EVENT} : E_{16}; 1 \rangle\!\rangle]$$
$$E_{16} : [\dot{s} \mid \dot{s} \models \langle\!\langle \text{BUY}, \text{AGENT} : jr, \text{OBJECT} : book; 1 \rangle\!\rangle]$$

3.2 Determinacy

The sentence,

Jiroo ga hon o zinbotyo de kau Taroo o tataku
Jiro hits Taro, who buys books at Jinbocho

is commonly thought to have only one constituent structure, namely:

[[Jiroo ga] [[[hon o] [zinbotyo de] kau] Taroo o] [tataku]].

However, our approach does produce that interpretation that **zinbotyo de** modifies the verb **tataku** which is not admitted by the supposed above structure. We call this the *adverbial determinacy problem*.

Problems of the same kind occur in the adnominal case. Consider the uses of the noun phrases below.

ookii kyou hako kara ochiru tama
big   today box from drop   ball
Balls dropping from a box today

The structure of this noun phrase is normally assumed to be the following:

[[ookii] [[kyou] [hako kara] ochiru] tama]

Using this structure, the possibility of "big box" is excluded by the reason that **hako** is embedded in the adnominal verb phrase or clause. However our approach again produces this "big box" interpretation. We call this the *adnominal determinacy problem*.

They are pseudoproblems, though. Unbiased closer observation will lead us to conclude that these utterances are not utterances of structurally unambiguous sentences. Let's look at the above expressions again. First look again at the sentence we analyzed in the previous section.

eiga o zinbotyo ni taroo ga mi ni iku

Another typical sentence is

Taroo ga hon o Jiroo ni kaw aseru
Taro makes Jiro buy books.

We point out that even if we could adopt the notion of constituency as explanatory in the above cases, the notion could not explain *indeterminacy* in the following cases.[21] Our approach, however, grants us enough tools to treat the indeterminacy in question. That can be done by introducing a relation ADNOMINAL, which is to be induced by the adnominal form of verbs and adjectives.

Now we claim that **ookii** does not "modify" **hako** in the sentential fragment, contrary to what the alleged constituency of the phrase might suggest,

ookii	kyou	hako	kara	tataku	tama	e	iku
big	today	box	from	hit	ball		to go

while it is not unnatural to think that **ookii** "modifies" **hako** in the following sentence.

ookii	hako	kara	tataku	tama	e	iku
big	box	from	hit	ball		to go

And we would like to point out that in most cases the adnominal determinacy only results from the semantic idiosyncrasies of the word involved as follows:[22]

nagai	akage	no	syouzyo
long	red hair	of	girl

kireina	akage	no	syouzyo
beautiful	red hair	of	girl

se-no-takai	akage	no	syouzyo
tall	red hair	of	girl

4 Discussion

In this section, we compare our approach with two proposed theories for processing Japanese sentences. One comes from a purely computational consideration about parsing, and the other is a traditional view of so-called "te–ni–o–wa" particles. Both theories share our underlying intuition into the structural nature of Japanese sentences. We do not go into the details of the comparison, but rather leave the reader to verify the similarities by manually simulating the processes they are supposed to undergo.

Right Branching Analysis for Semantics

The traditional concept of parsing as building has been challenged, though unbeknownst even to the critics, by researchers in machine translation involving Japanese. It generates, they have complained, so many unnecessary

---

[21] Actually it is not difficult to make an equivalent system in our framework.
[22] This means that our "conjunctive approach" is required.

candidate trees for a humanly unambiguous sentence that the natural language processing system later has a hard time determining which is *the* right tree for the sentence. Our approach is free from this difficulty in the most trivial sense: it does not generate any tree.

Some researchers tried to figure out the most economic structural representation for the purpose of semantic interpretation (Tanaka et al. 1984). Although Tanaka describes the goal of his parsing mechanism as development of a right-branching grammar for Japanese which generates only one tree structure for any Japanese sentence, nonetheless the tree his grammar is supposed to most parsimoniously generate for each sentence does not reflect its syntactic structure in the normal sense. His right branching trees merely serve as well-formatted data structures that are input to the semantic processing phase, at which point sentences are given semantic interpretations. The tree carries little more information than we employ to give semantic interpretation in our system. For example, to the sentence:

Jiroo ga zinbotyo de hon o kau Taroo o tataku
Jiro hits Taro who buys books at Jinbocho.

Tanaka gives the following structure.

[[Jiroo ga] [[zinbotyo de] [[hon o] [[kau Taroo o] [tataku]]]]]

Then from this structure he derives two readings. As far as the simple sentences go, there is no difference between our representation and Tanaka's.

However, since his main concern is to reduce unnecessary trees for interpreting sentences, Tanaka does not propose to abandon the whole idea of trees or syntactic structures. In spite of that, his conclusions confirm our basic ideas. Of course we are more prepared to cope with fragmentary inputs than his system is, but this does not depreciate his contributions. We repeat here that the major advantage of our approach over his has been made possible by taking the particles to induce real relations rather than merely as marking the accompanying noun's syntactic roles.

Conventional Treatment in the Tradition of Japanese Grammar

The tradition of Japanese grammatical study of the particles dates from the 17th century. The history of the field was well surveyed by Motoki Tokieda (1940). We basically follow his view of the history. In the 18th century the study of the language which was used in *waka* (Japanese short poems with 31 syllables) emerged because without serious academic study of the poems handed down from the 8th century, people or *waka* authors could not have decided on what word to use with what other words. Motoori Norinaga surveyed the extensive literature and established laws of co-occurrences. In his theory, words of a certain kind, called "te–ni–o–wa," [23] were supposed to

---

[23] The category is not exhausted by these four words.

occur in a sentence or *waka* which contains a word form of a corresponding type, to unite and organize a sentence. In his metaphor, "te–ni–o–wa" is like "threads running through beads (*tama no o*)." Fujitani Nariaki, on the other hand, studied the morphological interaction between immediately neighboring words, though he shared interest in the locutions used in *waka* with Norinaga. Typical of his study is the functional distinction between the verb endings with the same morphological realization according to the different words permitted to follow. The modern classical studies of verb endings in Japanese linguistics are viewed as attempts at synthesis of these two traditions.

We regard our theory of the semantics of the word which have once been called "te–ni–o–wa" and then later "case markers" as yet another attempt to synthesize Norinaga's and Nariaki's views. Those particles are not just "markers" but words with their own meanings and functions. Their functions are both unifying a sentence, just as our Principle of Integrity and Norinaga's view of "threads through beads" dictate, and at the same time connecting two neighboring words, as our use of parameters and Nariaki's theory suggest.

5 Conclusion

In this paper, we have proposed a strictly incremental approach to the parsing of Japanese utterances and confirmed that the system based on the approach gives appropriate semantic interpretations to Japanese utterances without assuming that the sentences used in the utterances have definite syntactic structures. Apparent problems to our approach have been proved to be really apparent. We have compared our approach with the precursors to attest that their basic ideas are consistent with ours.

References

Barwise, J., and J. Etchemendy. 1987. *The Liar: An Essay on Truth and Circularity*. New York: Oxford University Press.

Israel, D., and J. Perry. 1990. What is Information? In *Information, Language, and Cognition*. Vancouver Studies in Cognitive Science, Volume 1, ed. P. P. Hanson, 1–19. Vancouver: University of British Columbia Press. Also available as Report No. CSLI-91-145, CSLI Publications, Stanford.

Katagiri, Y. n.d. Point of View in Situation Semantics. Manuscript.

Shirai, K., and S. Tutiya. n.d. Situation Theoretic Semantics of Japanese. Manuscript.

Tanaka, H., H. Koyama, and M. Okumura. 1984. The Extension of Bottom Up Parsing System BUP and its Application to a Japanese Grammar (in Japanese). In *Proceedings of the Logic Programming Conference 84*, 12–13.

Tokieda, M. 1940. *The History of Japanese Linguistics* (in Japanese). Iwanami Shoten.

23

Probing the Iroquoian Perspective: Towards a Situated Inquiry of Linguistic Relativity

Dietmar Zaefferer

1 Introduction

This paper may seem a little exotic among the contributions to the present volume, not because its concern is the application of Situation Theory to Situation Semantics—there are other contributions that share this concern—but because its concern is furthermore the application of Situation Semantics to so-called exotic languages like the Iroquoian languages, which may seem premature at this stage of the development of the theory.

So why apply Situation Semantics to Iroquoian instead of, say, English or Norwegian? And why use Situation Semantics for the analysis of Iroquoian, instead of, say, Montague Semantics or the Principles and Parameters theoretical frame? The answer to the first question is that I want Situation Semantics to be tailored right from the beginning in a way that it fits any natural language, not just English or Norwegian. So I have to look for languages that are as different as possible from the well-known Standard Average European languages (or SAE languages for short, as Whorf (1956) has dubbed them), and the Iroquoian languages seem to be located at one extreme point of a scale in that they are extremely verb-oriented, whereas SAE languages are both noun and verb oriented. I will come back to what that means shortly.

In preparing this paper I have profited from the interesting discussion and encouraging comments by the participants of the Kinloch Rannoch conference as well as from remarks by Hans-Jurgen Sasse and Godehard Link. Special thanks are due to an anonymous referee whose to-the-point comments greatly helped me to clarify and revise my main issue. Remaining shortcomings should be blamed, as usual, to the author, and not to anyone of the aforementioned.

Situation Theory and Its Applications, vol. 2.
Jon Barwise, Jean Mark Gawron, Gordon Plotkin, and Syun Tutiya, eds.
Copyright © 1991, Stanford University.

The answer to the second question can be easily derived from a quotation from Barwise: "I think of this [the view of inquiry as crucially a situated activity] as part of a larger reaction against the dominant theme in Western thought, the idea that agents ever step back and have a God's eye view of the world, as Thomas Nagel has called it, 'a view from nowhere'. As Hilary Putnam has observed, the rejection of the view from nowhere idea is something that ties together disciplines as diverse as quantum mechanics and the work on semantical paradoxes. To my mind, it is what drives situation theory and situation semantics." (Barwise 1989, p. 251)

I may add that it is also what drives modern linguistic typology and research into linguistic universals, as well as the investigation of how much of the Humboldt-Sapir-Whorf hypothesis about linguistic relativity, if anything, remains, if the presently available data are taken into account. A situated inquiry of linguistic relativity is aware of the fact that it starts out from a view of natural languages that takes Indo-European languages (Whorf's SAE languages) as a prototype. It then looks for languages that are as far as possible from this common conception of what a language should look like. A prominent feature of this common conception is the centrality of the NP-VP-dichotomy. So languages that make only marginal use of what might be justifiably called a noun phrase, like Cayuga and other Northern Iroquoian languages are of special interest for this enterprise. Therefore, the bulk of this paper is devoted to a sketch of a situation semantics for Cayuga. The final section will assess (a) the consequences of this challenge for situation theory and (b) how well the linguistic relativity hypothesis fares in the light of the proposed analysis.

2   Stepping Back from the SAE-Perspective

If we want to develop Situation Semantics towards universal applicability we have to step back from our SAE-perspective of what a natural language looks like, and have to ask ourselves what remains constant if we compare all kinds of natural languages. One thing that has to remain stable are our basic categories such as nouns, verbs and adjectives. Within X-bar theory, the framework most recent work in the so-called generative grammar paradigm is based on, there is a widespread tendency (going back to Chomsky 1970) to reduce the four central lexical categories noun, verb, adjective, and preposition to the even more fundamental categorial features $[\pm N]$ and $[\pm V]$ in the following way:

$$V := [+V, -N]$$
$$N := [-V, +N]$$
$$A := [+V, +N]$$
$$P := [-V, -N]$$

It may be hard to see why the neither-nor case should characterize the category P instead of all the rest, but what is obvious is the view that the N-V opposition is considered something very fundamental.

In linguistic typology it is a widely accepted fact that there are languages which get along without any adjectives (the example Givón (1984, p. 53) cites is Toposa, a Nilotic language), but not all linguists agree that there are languages that collapse the N-V distinction, a possibility brought into the discussion some 70 years ago by Edward Sapir with respect to Nootka, an American Indian language of the Wakashan family. The plausibility of the assumption that there are languages which get along basically without an N-V distinction has gained new support through data from the Northern Iroquoian languages which suggest that NP's play at most a very marginal role in these languages.[1]

The interesting thing is that even if a language without any N-V distinction cannot be attested, it can be argued that it is still a possible human language, i.e., that it is learnable and that it has the same general-purpose functionality and expressive power as any other full-fledged human language, and the question comes up of how this can be. Furthermore, for Situation Semantics the question of Barwise's branch point 9 (Barwise 1990, p. 267) concerning the relation between situations and objects comes up: Verbs and the sentences they head are about situations, nouns and the NP's they head are about objects (directly or indirectly). But if the N-V distinction can collapse in some languages, one should reconsider seriously Ken Olson's choice at branch point 9 such that the situation-object distinction may collapse as well, at least for some perspectives, and that where it exists it is a perspectival one. Here is the branch point as Barwise puts it:

Alternative 9.1: Every object is a situation.

Alternative 9.2: Some objects are situations, some are not.

Ken Olson's choice is 9.1, that every object is a situation. This seems to be at odds with Barwise's thesis 3 (1989, p. 232), which can be rendered schematically as follows (where '<' is to be read as 'is metaphysically prior to'):

$$\text{situations} < \text{facts/soas}^2/\text{objects/properties/relations} < \text{propositions}$$

and which entails that situations are metaphysically prior to objects. But the views can be reconciled, if one takes into account Piaget's observation that objects arise in the development of human cognition at the moment where recurring situations are attributed to something more stable which causes them to come about. So objects may be considered as the result of

---

[1] In fact, the data are less new than their interpretation in the indicated way. See Sasse 1988, 1991, n.d.

[2] The term 'soa' is short for 'state of affairs'. Instead of this term, I will use in what follows its successor, 'infon', which stands for 'unit of information'.

associating prima facie situations with certain stability conditions, which yields those time-stable 'situations' that are called objects.

But the quotation marks around 'situations' in the last sentence point at another reason for rejecting Olson's choice, a terminological one. It looks like some terminological clarifications are needed before we can assess it seriously.

3 Terminological Considerations

A third alternative not mentioned by Barwise comes into mind if one thinks about the pretheoretical use of the notions involved:

Alternative 9.3: Objects and situations are disjoint.

Pretheoretically, situations are always situations of some object(s), the situations these objects are in, and most of the time, these situations are not objects themselves. Consider for instance your current financial situation: You are an object, your financial situation is not. But how about local situations? Maybe you are sitting in a building. Then the building may be considered one of the local situations you are in. But at the same time it continues to be an object. So alternative 9.3 does not seem to be very plausible. On the other hand, if a necessary condition for situationhood is the possibility for an object to be in that situation, alternative 9.1 can be excluded as well if one assumes that there are (given some granularity) minimal objects (with respect to that granularity), namely those objects that cannot contain any other object, since these objects cannot be a situation for any other object.

But now the question comes up how closely the pretheoretical use of the notion of situation and its use in Situation Theory are tied together. In Situation Theory, situations are parts of some world that support infons relative to some scheme of individuation. Intuitively this characterization holds equally well of situations and of objects in the pretheoretical sense. But there may be other, theoretical reasons for excluding some kinds of objects from the domain of the supports relation. Without them, the only reason for rejecting Olson's choice is a terminological one.

Technical and everyday use of a term may diverge, but they should not diverge to such a degree that it hurts. Your reading this here now is a situation, part of the situation you are in right now, but you are not a situation. It may be funny to say that everybody is precisely the situation he is necessarily in all his life long, but it seems preferable not to overload the notion situation and to coin a new term that covers both situations and objects.

You are not a situation, but you are, among other things, a reader, or, equivalently, a case of a reader. The activity you are engaged in is reading, or, equivalently, a case of reading. So my proposal for a term covering both situations and objects is *case*. Now we can discuss Olson's choice in

PROBING THE IROQUOIAN PERSPECTIVE / 537

an unbiased way, since we can say that a proposition is something that relates a (possibly concrete) case and a (necessarily abstract) infon (alias state of affairs, type, or concept) via a relation that is written '$\models$', which can be read as 'is a model of' or 'supports' or 'is correctly classified by' or 'instantiates' or 'is characterizable by'. For the sake of readability I will however stick to the conventional notation ($s \models \sigma$), asking the reader to bear in mind that s stands for cases, where cases can be conceived of as subsuming either all objects or only part of them.

Situations or cases that are of central relevance for Situation Semantics are situations or cases of language use. According to a very attractive proposal made by Jon Barwise in his Branch Point paper (1989, p. 275), we need in addition to Austinian propositions what he calls Holmesian propositions, which differ from the former in that their situations support their infons not directly, but via a collection of constraints. Holmesian propositions are at the heart of my picture of language, since cases of language use carry the important part of their information not on their sleeves, but only indirectly via certain constraints, namely the conventions defining the language in question. But instead of saying 'situation s, in addition to supporting infon σ, carries the information τ with respect to some collection of constraints C', we can now also say 'case s, in addition to instantiating concept σ, C-indicates concept τ', where C is again a collection of constraints holding in some supercase of s, i.e., a case that s is a part of.

So my basic picture of language use looks like follows. A case of language use is a case that instantiates some concept of a perceivable action trace pattern like the utterance of [*mira*] and that C-indicates some concept of an abstract social interaction pattern such as putting the cooperative addressee under the obligation to look, if the collection of constraints C includes the rules of Spanish grammar (in German, the outcome would be different). Symbolically: If s is a case of language use, then there are σ, C and τ such that $s \models \sigma$ and $s \models_C \tau$, where σ is a concept of a perceivable action trace pattern, C is a collection of conventions of language use, and τ a concept of an abstract social interaction pattern.

In order to compensate the reader for following me through these rather abstract terminological preliminaries I would now like to invite him to an imaginary field trip to the area north of lake Erie, where several Iroquoian Indian tribes live.

4 Comparing the English and the Iroquoian Perspective

Based on what we have heard about the Northern Iroquoian languages and their tendency to neglect the nouns and noun phrases Europeans are so fond of, our imaginary journey has at least three purposes:

1. We want to find out whether Situation Semantics is flexible enough to deal equally well with Mohawk or Cayuga as it does with English or Norwegian.

2. We want to see whether the Iroquoian languages are more easily describable if the objects are subsumed under the situations, i.e., whether their structure can be turned into an argument for Olson's choice.[3]

3. We would like to find some evidence for or against the Humboldt-Sapir-Whorf hypothesis of linguistic relativity, which would entail that the dramatically different structure of the Iroquoian languages forces or induces their speakers to see the world from a very different perspective.

Let us assume that the first Iroquoian Indians we come across are Cayugas, and that we immediately meet a reliable Indian informant. But before we start to ask him questions let us recapitulate what we already know about the English-Cayuga differences.

The English perspective seems to distinguish at least two kinds of cases, cases of objects and cases of situations, be they activities, events or states. This is correlated with the fact that English noun phrases denote either single objects (as with proper names and (in)definite descriptions) or sets of sets thereof (at least according to the Generalized Quantifier analysis), whereas verbs denote properties which together with appropriate arguments can characterize situations. Cayuga speakers get along in general quite well without nouns or noun phrases and it seems rather plausible that the few exceptions could fade away without doing any harm. How do the Cayugas do that?

Let us look first at the Cayuga lexicon. What we find here is basically a two-fold distinction between (a) particles, i.e., uninflected words, and (b) paradigms, i.e., inflected words with all their word forms. Some of the word forms have acquired an idiomatic reading, which is the main reason why most Iroquoianists assume that Cayuga does have nouns. But Sasse (1988) correctly points out that these forms include the same morphological marking as the other word forms, and the categories which are encoded in this morphological marking are person, number and gender of both actor and undergoer. These are typical features of conjugation rather than declension, so the conclusion seems to be warranted that these word forms are verb forms and not noun forms. It turns out furthermore that each such verb form is autonomous, i.e., its use expresses by itself a complete proposition without the need for any syntactical complements.

This is strongly reminiscent of the so-called pro-drop languages like Italian or Spanish, where single word forms like 'habla' without any comple-

---

[3] In Zaefferer 1988 I have argued for the same option, sketching a case-based semantics which is spelled out in Zaefferer 1989.

ments can encode complete propositions ('he talks'). There are, however, two important differences with the pro-drop languages. The first is that Cayuga is double-pro-drop: Not only subjects are dropped, but also objects. This can happen in Hungarian as well and, without morphological reflexes, in languages like Japanese or Korean. So the second difference is more important and more surprising: Pro-drop languages do have complements with their verbs; these complements *can* be dropped, especially if they are pronominal, in which case dropping may be obligatory for nonemphatic proforms, but in principle, they can be there as overt constituents.

Cayuga, by contrast, does not have any complements as separate constituents; arguments are (a) always morphologically encoded by means of a prefix, and (b) only pronominal in nature. So it looks as if something like 'She has prepared it' is expressible in Cayuga, whereas 'Your mother has prepared the meal' is not. How can this seeming restriction be overcome? In order to find out, we ask our informant to translate an English sentence with a two-place verb and two non-pronominal arguments into Cayuga. The sentence we choose is (1).

(1)   My younger Brother has many potatoes.

Sentence (1) contains two noun phrases, 'my younger brother' and 'many potatoes', and the only verb around is 'has'. How can our informant possibly express this proposition in Cayuga without using any noun phrases? Before we look at his translation, let us first express (1) in a Situation Semantics style. I assume with Barwise (e.g., 1989, pp. 228f) that every proposition consists of the situation or case it concerns (called focus situation by Barwise, thematic situation or case by me, since in linguistic terminology, focus is something different), and the state of affairs or infon which is used to classify it, together with the supports relation that is claimed to hold between the two.

As mentioned above, the notation I use for propositions is the usual one: $(s \models \sigma)$. Following a suggestion of Barwise's,[4] restricted parameters are written to the left of the parametric proposition in which they occur, followed by a colon and the restricting proposition; the list of restrictions is closed by a vertical stroke. In order to enhance readability, parameter restrictions are pulled as far to the left as possible.[5] An atomic infon is written between double angles, its relation before its arguments (postspecifying constituent order), arguments are preceded by the corresponding argument role label, followed by a colon. If there is only one argument, hence no need to distinguish between arguments, no argument role is indicated; positive polarities are omitted, and tense is ignored. So a Situation Semantics representation of (1) looks like the following:

(1') $s : (s_{utt} \models \langle\!\langle \text{thematic}, s \rangle\!\rangle)$

---

[4] Personal communication, September 1990.
[5] I am grateful to an anonymous referee for this notational hint.

$$x : (s \models \langle\langle \text{younger-brother, possessum:}x, \text{possessor:speaker}(s_{utt}) \rangle\rangle)$$
$$y : (s \models \langle\langle \text{many-potatoes}, y \rangle\rangle) |$$
$$(s \models \langle\langle \text{have, possessor:}x, \text{possessum:}y \rangle\rangle)$$

(1') expresses a parametric proposition whose supporting situation is restricted by the requirement that it is thematic in the utterance situation, and whose infon is parametric in both arguments of 'have', the possessor being restricted to a younger brother of the speaker, the possessum to a large quantity of potatoes. The relations involved are: speaker in the utterance situation ('my'), 'younger brother of', i.e., 'male' and 'younger sibling of', large quantity ('many'), 'potato', and possession ('my', 'have'). The same relations will have to be expressed in the Cayuga translation of (1), but how are they expressed? Here is the translation our informant gives:[6]

(2)   he-'kẹ:'-ẹ́ ho-họn'at-á-k'ate'

Its analysis yields the following results. Syntactically, (2) consists of two words, hence two clauses, and forms a two-membered complex sentence. Its morphological building blocks are the following: -'kẹ:'-, "younger-sibling", -họn'at-, "potato", and -k'ate'-, "be-many", are roots. The latter is prespecified by the second one, yielding the complex stem -họn'at-á-k'ate'- with the semantically empty linker -á- and the meaning "be many with respect to potatoes", or in Sasse's (1991) wording, "be many potatowise". The first stem is also complex, the root -'kẹ:'-, "younger sibling", is modified by the diminutive suffix -ẹ, and the resulting stem 'kẹ:'-ẹ therefore means "little younger sibling."

Now comes the interesting part: the prefixes he- and ho- are both person prefixes and, as mentioned above, Cayuga person prefixes encode pairs of feature structures for the features thematic role, person, number, and gender. The value for the first feature is always actor for the first coordinate and undergoer for the second one. The values for the person feature can be first (exclusive and inclusive), second, and third; for the number feature singular, dual, and plural; for the gender feature masculine, feminine, and neuter. The he-prefix of the first clause in (2) encodes ⟨⟨actor, first, singular, any⟩,⟨undergoer, third, singular, masculine⟩⟩, or, shorter, 'I-him'. But in order to fully understand the first word-clause, our informant tells us, we need one additional piece of information, namely that for inalienable possessive relations 'actor' can also encode 'possessor' and 'undergoer' 'possessed'. (With alienable possession, the converse holds.) Now we are able to interpret the first part of (2) as expressing the proposition that the speaker has a male person as little younger sibling or as an equivalent of "I have a little younger brother." A Situation Semantics style representation is (2a'):

---

[6]The example is taken from Mithun and Henry 1982 (p. 381), its analysis mostly from Sasse 1988.

(2a′) $s : (s_{utt} \models \langle\!\langle \text{thematic}, s \rangle\!\rangle)$,
 $x : (s_{utt} \models \langle\!\langle \text{speaker}(s_{utt}), x \rangle\!\rangle) \cap (s \models \langle\!\langle \text{sg}, x \rangle\!\rangle)$,
 $y : (s_{utt} \models \langle\!\langle \text{third}, y \rangle\!\rangle) \cap (s \models \langle\!\langle \text{male}, y \rangle\!\rangle \wedge \langle\!\langle \text{sg}, y \rangle\!\rangle)|$
  $(s \models \langle\!\langle \text{little-younger-sibling}, \text{possessum}{:}y, \text{possessor}{:}x \rangle\!\rangle)$

(2a′) expresses a parametric proposition whose situation is restricted by the requirement that it is thematic in the utterance situation, and whose infon is parametric in both arguments of 'little-younger-sibling-of', the possessum being restricted to some non-speaking non-addressed male, the possessor to the speaker.

For an analogous interpretation of the second part of (2) we need the information encoded in the prefix ho-. It is $\langle\!\langle \text{actor, third, singular, neuter} \rangle$, $\langle \text{undergoer, third, singular, masculine} \rangle\!\rangle$. So the meaning of the whole word-clause is "it, namely being many potatowise, concerns him", or, with Sasse's transliteration "it manies him potatowise" (Sasse 1991). A Situation Semantics style representation of this is (2b′):

(2b′) $s' : (s_{utt} \models \langle\!\langle \text{thematic}, s' \rangle\!\rangle)$,
 $z : (s_{utt} \models \langle\!\langle \text{third}, z \rangle\!\rangle) \cap (s' \models \langle\!\langle \text{neuter}, z \rangle\!\rangle \wedge \langle\!\langle \text{sg}, z \rangle\!\rangle)$,
 $u : (s_{utt} \models \langle\!\langle \text{third}, u \rangle\!\rangle) \cap (s' \models \langle\!\langle \text{male}, u \rangle\!\rangle \wedge \langle\!\langle \text{sg}, u \rangle\!\rangle)|$
  $(s' \models \langle\!\langle \text{be-many-potatowise}, \text{concerning}{:}z, \text{concerned}{:}u \rangle\!\rangle)$

(2b′) expresses a parametric proposition whose situation is restricted by the requirement that it is thematic in the utterance situation, and whose infon is parametric in both arguments of 'be-many-potatowise', the concerning entity being restricted to some non-speaking non-addressed thing, the concerned entity to some non-speaking non-addressed male. Joining both clauses of (2) yields a maximally coherent sentence if we identify all compatible parameters, namely s with s' and y with u.

Now we can almost fully understand the literal meaning of the whole two-clause sentence (2). Our informant tells us the last missing piece of information: In Cayuga, he says, focused items come first. The literal translation "I have him as little younger sibling, he is someone who is concerned by a large potato quantity" fails to express this. A better translation would be "My younger brother has many potatoes" with focus accent on 'brother', or "Someone who does have many potatoes is my younger brother", but all these translations, in one way or the other, distort the way the information is organized in the Cayuga sentence. The Situation Semantic representation in (2′) does not. It puts the background information into the restrictions of the parameters and the focal information into the infon of the proposition expressed by the whole two-clause sentence:

(2′) $s : (s_{utt} \models \langle\!\langle \text{thematic}, s \rangle\!\rangle)$,
 $z : (s_{utt} \models \langle\!\langle \text{third}, z \rangle\!\rangle) \cap (s \models \langle\!\langle \text{neuter}, z \rangle\!\rangle \wedge \langle\!\langle \text{sg}, x \rangle\!\rangle)$,
 $y : (s_{utt} \models \langle\!\langle \text{third}, y \rangle\!\rangle) \cap (s \models \langle\!\langle \text{male}, y \rangle\!\rangle \wedge \langle\!\langle \text{sg}, y \rangle\!\rangle \wedge$
  $\langle\!\langle \text{be-many-potatowise}, \text{concerning}{:}z, \text{concerned}{:}y \rangle\!\rangle)$,

$$x : (s_{utt} \models \langle\!\langle \text{speaker}(s_{utt}), x \rangle\!\rangle) \cap (s \models \langle\!\langle \text{sg}, x \rangle\!\rangle)|$$
$$(s \models \langle\!\langle \text{little-younger-sibling}, \text{possessum} : y, \text{possessor} : x \rangle\!\rangle)$$

(2') expresses a parametric proposition whose situation is restricted by the requirement that it is thematic in the utterance situation, and whose infon is the relation of "little-younger-sibling-of" holding between some male not involved in the discourse who is concerned by some large quantity of potatoes, and the speaker: Talking about a situation where a man has many potatoes, my little brother is such a man.

We now can see that the restriction of Cayuga complements to prefixed pronouns does not entail a restriction in expressive power, since the lexical specification of the arguments can be done by ana- or cataphoric coreference. So the answer to the question asked above: How do the Cayugas express the content of sentences like 'Your mother has prepared the meal' if the verb allows only pronominal complements as in 'She has prepared it'?—the answer is simply: by linking the three predications into a cata- and anaphoric chain: 'You have her as a mother, she has prepared it, it is the meal'.

But this answer to the first question raises immediately a second one. If virtually every word form has inherently two-place person prefixes, then the expressive power of Cayuga must be seriously restricted in another respect, since it can only express two-place relations. But this restriction can also be overcome. One way of encoding three-place relations is the incorporation of roots into complex stems mentioned above. In order to express the infon "I prepare food for you" we take the root 'prepare', premodify it by the root 'food', prefix this stem by the 'I-you' morpheme and modify the result by a dative suffix, which changes the undergoer in a benefactive role. Another imaginable way of overcoming the same restriction would be the splitting of sentences like "I do it for you" into something like "I do it, it is for you."

But how about lower arities? The problem is exactly analogous to the problem a subject-predicate language like English faces in the case of zero-place predicates like raining. The solution in English is the use of a dummy subject 'it': 'it is raining', although semantically still zero-place (location does not count here, since it is not an argument, but a specifier), is syntactically one-place, as required. The Cayuga solution to the less-than-minimal arity problem is basically the same, but due to its inherent binarity it has two possibilities for the encoding of semantically unary predicates: Either the undergoer or the actor role can be filled by a dummy. The first case, person prefixes with the feature structure $\langle \ldots, \langle \text{undergoer, third, singular, neuter} \rangle \rangle$ is called the 'subject-intransitive paradigm', the second case, person prefixes with feature structure $\langle \langle \text{undergoer, third, singular, neuter} \rangle, \ldots \rangle$ is called the 'object-intransitive paradigm'. Therefore the 'it-it'-case opens two possibilities: ka- is chosen for semantically empty undergoers, o- for semantically empty actors. An example of the former case is ka-nyáhtę:

with the root -nyahtę: 'turtle', yielding 'it turtles (it)' or 'it turtles'. An example of the second case is o-né:nǫ' containing the root ne:nǫ' 'warm', literally '(it) warms it' or 'it is warmed', meaning 'it is warm weather'.

Another example with semantically empty actor is given by the forms built from the stem -ǫkweh' 'be a person'. Prefixing it by h-, ak-, and k a:k- with feature structures $\langle\langle$actor, third, singular, male$\rangle$, $\langle$undergoer, third, singular, neuter$\rangle\rangle$, $\langle\langle$actor, third, singular, female$\rangle$, $\langle$undergoer, third, singular, neuter$\rangle\rangle$, and $\langle\langle$actor, third, plural, female$\rangle$, $\langle$undergoer, third, singular, neuter$\rangle\rangle$, results in clause-words meaning 'he is a man', 'she is a woman', and 'they are women', respectively. The translations suggest that there is informational redundancy where there is none. 'It is a male person', 'it is a female person', 'they are female persons' would be better, but it would not be free of wrong implicatures either. (4') is a Situation Semantic representation of (4), the Cayuga translation of (3):

(3)   He is a man.

(4)   h-ǫkweh'

(4U) $s : (s_{utt} \models \langle\langle\text{thematic}, s\rangle\rangle),$
         $x : (s_{utt} \models \langle\langle\text{third}, x\rangle\rangle) \cap (s \models \langle\langle\text{male}, x\rangle\rangle \wedge \langle\langle\text{sg}, x\rangle\rangle)|$
         $(s \models \langle\langle\text{person}, x\rangle\rangle)$

5   Looking for Appropriate Supporters

So far, so good. We see now how it is possible to get along without nouns and noun phrases, and how everything can be expressed by two-place predicates, and we understand thus the structure of the forms of Cayuga paradigms. But as we saw right at the beginning of our field work, when we looked at the structure of the Cayuga lexicon, there are, alongside with the paradigms, particles in Cayuga, particles like nę́:kyęh, "this," a demonstrative.

(5)   nę́:kyęh

Here, we have no person prefix, hence no motivation to represent this expression in a way similar to the representation of word forms, which wouldn't make sense anyway, since a use of 'this' does clearly not constitute a speech act with a propositional content at all. What it does is rather introduce a new parameter which can only be anchored to an entity pointed at by the speaker in the utterance situation:

(5') $x : (s_{utt} \models \langle\langle\text{point-at}, \text{pointer:speaker}(s_{utt}), \text{pointed:}x\rangle\rangle)$

Therefore a use of such a deictic element constitutes always an incomplete utterance, which needs company, as in (6):

(6)   nę́:kyęh h-ǫkweh'

This can be translated, in an appropriate context, as "this man," but we know that literally it means "this one, he is a person." We could of course stick the contribution of the deictic element directly into the restriction of the relevant parameter, as in (6'), but this would be cheating, since it would conceal the anaphoric pick-up of the person prefix, mimicking the structure of the loose translation, not of the literal one:

(6') $s : (s_{utt} \models \langle\!\langle \text{thematic}, s \rangle\!\rangle)$,
  $x : (s_{utt} \models \langle\!\langle \text{point-at}, \text{pointer:speaker}(s_{utt}), \text{pointed:}x \rangle\!\rangle \wedge \langle\!\langle \text{third}, x \rangle\!\rangle)$
   $\cap (s \models \langle\!\langle \text{male}, x \rangle\!\rangle \wedge \langle\!\langle \text{sg}, x \rangle\!\rangle)|(s \models \langle\!\langle \text{person}, x \rangle\!\rangle)$

The following representation (6'') certainly gives a more precise picture of the way the meaning is composed, introducing first a parameter for a deictically identified object and then a parameter for a singular male who is neither speaking nor addressed:

(6'') $s : (s_{utt} \models \langle\!\langle \text{thematic}, s \rangle\!\rangle)$,
  $x : (s_{utt} \models \langle\!\langle \text{point-at}, \text{pointer:speaker}(s_{utt}), \text{pointed:}x \rangle\!\rangle)$,
  $y : (s_{utt} \models \langle\!\langle \text{third}, y \rangle\!\rangle) \cap (s \models \langle\!\langle \text{male}, y \rangle\!\rangle \wedge \langle\!\langle \text{sg}, y \rangle\!\rangle)|(s \models \langle\!\langle \text{person}, y \rangle\!\rangle)$

(6'') shows that the deictic speech-act constituted by the utterance of nę:kyęh introduces as a new thematic entity the object pointed at by the speaker, and that the following utterance of h-, the person prefix of h-ǫkweh', introduces a second parameter. Then, by anaphor resolution, the two are identified. But now another question arises: What is the role of the thematic situation s in such a proposition? It seems to be needed for the support of the features maleness and singularity at most. Whatever the thematic situation was before the utterance of nę:kyęh, the utterance itself introduces a new theme into the discourse, namely the object pointed at, and therefore this very object suggests itself as the supporting part of the new proposition. This is what the representation (6''') encodes:

(6''') $s : (s_{utt} \models \langle\!\langle \text{thematic}, s \rangle\!\rangle)$,
  $x : (s_{utt} \models \langle\!\langle \text{point-at}, \text{pointer:speaker}(s_{utt}), \text{pointed:}x \rangle\!\rangle)$,
  $y : (s_{utt} \models \langle\!\langle \text{third}, y \rangle\!\rangle) \cap (s \models \langle\!\langle \text{male}, y \rangle\!\rangle \wedge \langle\!\langle \text{sg}, y \rangle\!\rangle)|(x \models \langle\!\langle \text{person}, y \rangle\!\rangle)$

But now we have a problem if we stick with alternative 9.2, admitting of objects that are not situations, and don't want to give up the assumption that only situations can support infons. (6''') contains a proposition-like form where an object supports an infon, and the whole thing would only be well-formed if the object pointed at happened to be a situation. But we can turn this risky business into a safe one (and one that conforms more with the intuitions, at least those of the author) if we choose alternative 9.1 and subsume all objects under the situations (or cases). Then the thematic slot of a proposition can be filled equally well by a situation and an object. And this seems to be exactly what is required for a natural account of deixis, since the entities referred to by pointing gestures are at least equally well objects as situations.

Another unfamiliar phenomenon becomes visible once the intended anaphor resolution is carried out: the proposition takes the form

$$(x \models \langle\!\langle \text{person}, x \rangle\!\rangle)$$

Does this make sense at all? Can an object possibly support an infon with that very object in the argument role of the infon's relation? I think it can, and it is even an obvious candidate for playing both roles, that of the supporter and that of an argument in the supporting infon, in cases like the one above, where the seeming argument role turns out to be no argument role at all, at least not in the standard sense of something that belongs to the arity of the relation under consideration, if we look closer at the kind of role this could be. To see this we have to ascertain first the arity of 'person'. I think it is zero-place, like 'raining', and not one-place, like 'sleeping', because every case of sleeping involves a sleeper, but cases of raining as well as cases of persons are self-sufficient: We have to bear in mind that there is a difference between playing the subject role in an instantiation of a relation and being such an instantiation itself. (The latter is sometimes referred to as 'the Davidsonian argument', misleadingly, as I would claim.) So a better notation would seem to be $(x \models \langle\!\langle \text{person} \rangle\!\rangle)$ and $(s \models \langle\!\langle \textit{rain} \rangle\!\rangle)$. But then there are cases where one wants to be able to keep track of both the instantiation r of a relation R that minimally supports the corresponding infon and other, larger situations s that still support it, so it is helpful to have a notation like $(s \models \langle\!\langle R, \text{i:}r \rangle\!\rangle)$, where the 'i:' marks the pseudo-argument role of instantiation.

Now all languages have a device for turning the instantiation role into an argument role, which is called copula, if it is a word, and zero-copula, if it is simple concatenation. Semantically, this is nothing else than putting the instantiation relation into the infon. So the following are equivalent:

(a) $\langle\!\langle \text{person}, \text{i:}x \rangle\!\rangle$

(b) $\langle\!\langle \text{be-a-person}, \text{subject:}x \rangle\!\rangle$

(c) $\langle\!\langle \text{be}, \text{subject:}x, \text{predicate:person} \rangle\!\rangle$

(d) $\langle\!\langle \text{instantiate}, \text{instantiation:}x, \text{instantiated:person} \rangle\!\rangle$

Cayuga, as we have seen, is a language with zero-copula, since it encodes instantiation by concatenation of the person prefix with the word stem. Therefore, in examples like

$$(s \models \langle\!\langle \text{little-younger-sibling}, \text{possessum:}y, \text{possessor:}x \rangle\!\rangle)$$

above, we should replace the argument role label 'possessum:' by the instantiation role label 'i:'. And we should modify the notation convention about role labels: They are omitted with one-place relations for the argument role (there is only one), and with zero-place relations (there is only the instantiation role around).

I will close this section with the analysis of a complex Cayuga sentence, hoping that it will reveal more about objects as possible supporters in propositions:

(7)   a-   hó-   htǫ:'   ho-   tkwę't-   a'   nę:kyę́   h-   ǫkweh'
       Past-   it:him-   lose   it:him   wallet-   Nom   this:one   he-   person

As one can read off the morphematic gloss, (7) means literally something like (and here I quote Sasse's (1991) wording): "It was lost to him, it is his wallet, this one, he is a man," or, simply, "This man lost his wallet." But unlike this English translation, (7) encodes not one, but potentially three different propositions. This is expressed by the representation (7′) (disregarding tense and other subtleties):

(7′) a. $s : (s_{utt} \models \langle\!\langle \text{thematic}, s \rangle\!\rangle)$,
 $x : (s_{utt} \models \langle\!\langle \text{third}, x \rangle\!\rangle) \cap (s \models \langle\!\langle \text{neuter}, x \rangle\!\rangle \wedge \langle\!\langle \text{sg}, x \rangle\!\rangle)$,
 $y : (s_{utt} \models \langle\!\langle \text{third}, y \rangle\!\rangle) \cap (s \models \langle\!\langle \text{male}, y \rangle\!\rangle \wedge \langle\!\langle \text{sg}, y \rangle\!\rangle)|$
  $(s \models \langle\!\langle \text{lose}, \text{possessum}{:}x, \text{possessor}{:}y \rangle\!\rangle)$

 b. $s' : (s_{utt} \models \langle\!\langle \text{thematic}, s' \rangle\!\rangle)$,
 $z : (s_{utt} \models \langle\!\langle \text{third}, z \rangle\!\rangle) \cap (s' \models \langle\!\langle \text{neuter}, z \rangle\!\rangle \wedge \langle\!\langle \text{sg}, z \rangle\!\rangle)$,
 $u : (s_{utt} \models \langle\!\langle \text{third}, u \rangle\!\rangle) \cap (s' \models \langle\!\langle \text{male}, u \rangle\!\rangle \wedge \langle\!\langle \text{sg}, u \rangle\!\rangle)|$
  $(s' \models \langle\!\langle \text{wallet}, \text{i}{:}z, \text{possessor}{:}u \rangle\!\rangle)$

 c. $s'' : (s_{utt} \models \langle\!\langle \text{thematic}, s'' \rangle\!\rangle)$,
 $v : (s_{utt} \models \langle\!\langle \text{point-at}, \text{pointer}{:}\text{speaker}(s_{utt}), \text{pointed}{:}v \rangle\!\rangle)$,
 $w : (s_{utt} \models \langle\!\langle \text{third}, w \rangle\!\rangle) \cap (s'' \models \langle\!\langle \text{male}, w \rangle\!\rangle \wedge \langle\!\langle \text{sg}, w \rangle\!\rangle)|$
  $(v \models \langle\!\langle \text{person}, w \rangle\!\rangle)$

The truth conditions for (7′) are the following: (a) There is a situation s that is thematic in the utterance situation and in s a third person male y who lost some singular object x; (b) there is a thematic situation s' and in s' some singular wallet z belonging to a third person male u; (c) there is a thematic situation s'' and some v pointed at by the speaker and in s'' some singular male w such that v supports the infon that w is a (male) person, i.e., a man. If we reduce (7′) to its maximally coherent form, identifying all compatible parameters and thereby resolving the anaphora, and if we pack non-focused propositions into the restrictions on the parameters of the focused one, as we did above in (2′), the result is (7″):

(7″) $s : (s_{utt} \models \langle\!\langle \text{thematic}, s \rangle\!\rangle)$,
 $x : (s_{utt} \models \langle\!\langle \text{third}, x \rangle\!\rangle) \cap (s \models \langle\!\langle \text{neuter}, x \rangle\!\rangle \wedge \langle\!\langle \text{sg}, x \rangle\!\rangle)$,
 $y : (s_{utt} \models \langle\!\langle \text{third}, y \rangle\!\rangle \wedge$
  $\langle\!\langle \text{point-at}, \text{pointer}{:}\text{speaker}(s_{utt}), \text{pointed}{:}y \rangle\!\rangle) \cap$
  $(s \models \langle\!\langle \text{male}, y \rangle\!\rangle \wedge \langle\!\langle \text{sg}, y \rangle\!\rangle \wedge \langle\!\langle \text{wallet}, \text{i}{:}x, \text{possessor}{:}y \rangle\!\rangle) \cap$
  $(y \models \langle\!\langle \text{person}, y \rangle\!\rangle)|$
  $(s \models \langle\!\langle \text{lose}, \text{possessum}{:}x, \text{possessor}{:}y \rangle\!\rangle)$

(7″) is true if there is some thematic situation with some non-speaking, non-addressed singular thing and some non-speaking, non-addressed singular male pointed at by the speaker where the former is a wallet possessed by the latter who is a man, such that in that situation the former got lost to the la`ter. Conceivable paraphrases are 'Speaking about a wallet possessed by this man here, it got lost to him' or, keeping the postspecifying order, 'It got lost to him, where 'it' means a wallet owned by him and 'him' means this man here.'

A comparison with the English translation shows that the conveyed information is the same, whereas the way its organization is encoded differs. In both languages, the relations of getting lost, of being one's wallet, and of being a man are expressed, and the focal role of the first one is opposed to the background role of the latter ones. But the difference between focus and background information is encoded in Cayuga by the difference between first and non-first position in the sentence, whereas in English, it is expressed by the difference between verbal and nominal encoding.

A closer examination of (7″) shows that the propositions which play a role in restricting the three parameters in the main proposition fall into three categories according to what kind of entity supports the corresponding infon: The utterance situation, the thematic situation or a thematic object. The question is, if one wants to challenge Olson's choice, if we couldn't do equally well without the last type. I think we could do without the last type, but we couldn't do equally well. Suppose we replace the last restricting proposition by $(s \models \langle\!\langle person, y \rangle\!\rangle)$. Then we can conjoin its infon with the three infons of the preceding proposition and we are left with two kinds of information about y: Infons supported by the thematic situation and infons supported by the utterance situation. And now the difference between the Olsonian (7″) and its alternative becomes visible: The alternative would entail nothing about the personhood of y in other situations than s, not even in the possibly different s_{utt}, whereas (7″) entails that y is a person by virtue of its identity, independent of the situation in which y happens to be, and as a result also in s_{utt}. So Olson's choice seems to be especially welcome for those propositions that ascribe non-changing properties to objects.

But was it necessary in order to reach this conclusion to travel so far to the Cayuga Indians? Of course it was not, at least epistemologically, but it certainly was psychologically helpful to gain some distance from the well-known and to look at unfamiliar languages first before coming back to the familiar ones. Now we can see that we could have gained the same insight from a thorough investigation of English sentences like "This here, it is a blackboard" or "This is a blackboard." But that's the way it sometimes is with traveling: Its pay-off comes less from having seen the foreign country with your own eyes than from being able to see your own country with foreign eyes.

6 Summary

Now it is about time to return from Ontario and to ask ourselves whether and how our imaginary trip has fulfilled the three purposes stated at the beginning of the third section.

First, we wanted to find out whether Situation Semantics is flexible enough to deal equally well with Cayuga as with English, and I think we can say that the little evidence we could gather on the short field trip does not contradict this assumption. On the contrary, what we found supported the view that idealized languages of the Iroquoian type are even easier to handle, since the difference between verbal and nominal encoding of relations vanishes on the semantic level anyway. And this is true not just for Situation Semantics, but for most formal theories of meaning.[7]

Second, we wanted to know whether Iroquoian could better be analyzed with a theory incorporating Olson's choice, and what we found out seems to support this hypothesis. But again, our findings are not restricted to the special pairing of Situation Semantics with Cayuga. This time, we could replace Cayuga by any natural language, and argue that propositions of the form 'this is an x' are most naturally conceived of as containing a thematic case, which may at least equally well be an object as a situation, and which should be chosen according to the life-span of the validity of this property ascription.

Third, concerning the Humboldt-Sapir-Whorf hypothesis concerning the impact of linguistic structure on the ways humans carve up their world, our trip was rather inconclusive, but from the few examples we have looked at, it looks like even such a dramatic difference as the lack of lexical complements and noun phrases may force speakers to organize the information they want to convey in different ways, but it does not force or even induce them to see the world differently. As an exercise the reader may try to speak English the Cayuga way, replacing for instance 'Let us eat the pie which I have baked' by 'Let's eat it. I have baked it. It pies' and so on. My prediction is that he will develop, if he does this for a sufficiently long period, a different style of communicating, but not a different perspective on the world. This is a Gedankenexperiment, and as such, it may help to assess plausibilities, not more. But if the conjecture it suggests can be corroborated, then we have to conclude that at least that part of the Iroquoian perspective which is induced by its sentence structure differs from the European one only with respect to the style of linguistic communication, without any further far-reaching consequences.

References

Barwise, J. 1989. *The Situation in Logic.* CSLI Lecture Notes Number 17. Stanford: CSLI Publications.

Chomsky, N. 1970. Remarks on Nominalization. In *Readings in English Transformational Grammar*, ed. R. A. Jacobs and P. S. Rosenbaum, 184–222. Waltham: Ginn.

[7]Just as a reminder: Montague (1974) had to distinguish two categories, t/e (intransitive verb phrases) and $t//e$ (common noun phrases) as English counterparts of the semantic type $\langle\langle s,e\rangle,t\rangle$ of properties. For an idealized language of the Iroquoian type, this distinction could simply be dropped.

Givón, T. 1984. *Syntax: A Functional-Typological Introduction.* Amsterdam: John Benjamins.

Mithun, M., and R. Henry. 1982. *Watęwayę́stanih : A Cayuga Teaching Grammar.* Brantford, Ontario: Woodland Indian Cultural Educational Centre.

Montague, R. 1974. The Proper Treatment of Quantification in Ordinary English. In *Formal Philosophy: Selected Papers of Richard Montague,* ed. R. H. Thomason. New Haven: Yale University Press.

Sasse, H.-J. n.d. The Evolution of Person Prefixes in the Iroquoian Languages and Its Functional Background. University of Cologne.

Sasse, H.-J. 1988. Der Irokesische Sprachtyp. *Zeitschrift für Sprachwissenchaft* 7:173–213.

Sasse, H.-J. 1991. Predication and Sentence Constitution in Universal Perspective. In *Semantic Universals and Universal Semantics.* GRASS 12, ed. D. Zaefferer. Dordrecht: Foris.

Whorf, B. L. 1956. The Relation of Habitual Thought and Behavior to Language. In *Language, Thought, and Reality,* ed. J. B. Carroll. New York: Wiley and Sons.

Zaefferer, D. 1988. Following the Lead of Natural Language: Principles of a Case-Based Algebraic Speech-Act Semantics. Paper read at the Workshop on Situation Theory and Information Processing, Edinburgh University, September.

Zaefferer, D. 1989. Untersuchungen zur strukturellen Bedeutung deutscher Sätze—mit Hilfe einer fall-basierten algebraischen Sprechaktsemantik. Unpublished Habilitationsschrift, Institut für Deutsche Philologie der Ludwig-Maximilians-Universität, München.

Part IV

Visual Information

24

Visualization and Situations

C. MICHAEL LEWIS

1 Introduction

A metamorphosis is now occurring in our relation to computers, transforming them from tools of work into instruments of perception. This shift is most noticeable in the use of supercomputers where scientists are converting their machines from inferential engines into representational ones, but extends to graphical interfaces of all kinds. Three years ago at the height of their euphoria responsible scientists were making claims such as:

> The gigabit bandwidth of the eye/visual cortex system permits much faster perception of geometric and spatial relationships than any other mode, making the power of supercomputers more accessible.

> Visualization is a method of computing. It transforms the symbolic into the geometric, enabling researchers to observe their simulations and computations. Visualization offers a method for seeing the unseen. It enriches the process of scientific discovery and fosters profound and unexpected insights. In many fields it is already revolutionizing the way scientists do science.

> Immediate visual feedback can help researchers gain insight into scientific processes and anomalies and can help them discover computational errors. For example, one astrophysicist found an erroneous boundary condition in his code after examining an image of a jet stream with an obvious reflection not apparent in the numbers. (McCormick et al. 1987, ACM panel report to NSF, reprinted in *Computer Graphics*)

The cognitive performance they describe, apparently unlimited channel capacity, representation by objects rather than symbols, and effortless real-time interaction stands in stark contrast to the symbolic representation and limited capacity processing posed by a modal theory of cognitive psychology.

Situation Theory and Its Applications, vol. 2.
Jon Barwise, Jean Mark Gawron, Gordon Plotkin, and Syun Tutiya, eds.
Copyright © 1991, Stanford University.

$$\exists X_i, X_j \; b(X_i) \land p(X_i, X_j) \rightarrow \neg p(X_i, X_j)$$
$$\exists X_i, X_j \; p(X_i, X_j) \rightarrow b(X_i) \land \neg b(X_j) \lor \neg b(X_i) \land \neg b(X_j)$$
$$p(X_{14}, X_4) \land p(X_{14}, X_5) \land p(X_2, X_{18}) \land p(X_2, X_9) \land$$
$$p(X_5, X_8) \land p(X_5, X_{12}) \land p(X_4, X_3) \land p(X_8, X_{16}) \land$$
$$p(X_8, X_9) \land p(X_{12}, X_9) \land p(X_{18}, X_7) \land p(X_9, X_1) \land$$
$$p(X_{16}, X_{13}) \land p(X_3, X_{15}) \land p(X_{15}, X_{17}) \land p(X_{15}, X_{10}) \land$$
$$p(X_{16}, X_{13}) \land p(X_1, X_{11}) \land p(X_7, X_{11}) \land p(X_7, X_6)$$

Problem: Prove $b(X_1)$.

Figure 1 Logic Version of the Blocks Problem

X_{14} is on top of X_4 and X_5 and X_5 is on top of X_8 and X_{12} and
X_4 is on top of X_3 and X_2 is on top of X_9 and X_{18} and
X_{12} is on top of X_9 and X_8 is on top of X_9 and X_{16} and
X_3 is on top of X_{15} and X_{16} is on top of X_{13} and
X_9 is on top of X_1 and X_{18} is on top of X_7 and
X_{15} is on top of X_{17} and X_{10} and X_1 is on top of X_{11} and
X_7 is on top of X_{11} and X_6

Problem: Which blocks do you need to move before you can
move X_1 and in what order do you need to move them?

Figure 2 Natural Language Version of the Blocks Problem

In this paper we will accept as data these reports of "sudden and profound insight" and apprehension of unexpectedly large amounts of information and attempt to identify cognitive processes which could accommodate them.

Our thesis is that visual situations can be engineered to exploit intuition. The approach follows situation theory in focusing on situations as carriers of information rather than simple determiners of facts. We argue that working memory limitations apply only to the storage of facts and propose a general method for smuggling information past this barrier by constructing situations which do it for us. This is accomplished by identifying a new situation in which the structure of attuned constraints corresponds to that of relevant constraints in the situation to be visualized. A psychological theory which allows this to happen requires a form of mental representation resembling Johnson-Laird's (1983) mental models in which "the structures of mental models are identical to the structures of the states of affairs" and automatic processes which involve relational constancies. A rough sketch of such a theory and discussion of its relation to current theories of human information processing is provided in the second section.

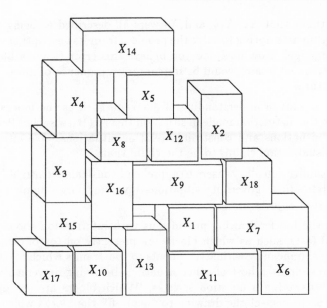

Figure 3 Move Block X_1

To illustrate the relation between visualization and attunement to constraints, consider the three representations of the entities $X_1, \ldots, X_{18}$ shown in Figures 1, 2, and 3. These representations are equivalent in expressing the constraints among the X_i's which must be satisfied in solving the problem. Try solving each of these problems in the form in which they are presented.

We suspect you will find the seven step solution trivially easy for the blocks version of the problem. It is, after all, merely a child's game of blocks. The natural language and logic versions of the *same* problem will prove *extremely* difficult. For most of us, they simply cannot be solved without a sheet of scratch paper and considerable effort.

Before leaving this example try two more experiments:

(1) Glance at the blocks, then turn away and try to solve the problem from memory. Can you solve it? If so, is it more difficult? Now, without looking answer the question, 'Which blocks need to be moved before moving X_2?'

(2) Conduct a gedanken experiment. How likely do you believe you might be to commit an error in planning a sequence of steps such as: $b(X_{14})$, $b(X_5)$, $b(X_8)$, $b(X_2)$, $b(X_9)$ which satisfies two of the constraints on $b(X_9)$ involving $p(X_8, X_9)$ and $p(X_2, X_9)$ but misses the third involving $p(X_{12}, X_9)$? How likely do you believe that error might be (not

noticing that X_8, X_{12}, and X_2 were all described as being on-top of X_9) in attempting to solve the problem from its description in natural language? How likely do you believe this error (leaving block, X_{12}, suspended in air) would be in planning a sequence of moves from the picture?

Our account of understanding of diagrams such as the blocks drawing draws on the distinction made in situation theory (Barwise and Perry 1983) between situations and constraints relating situations. We interpret the earlier visualization claims to be the claim that:

> Visualization allows users to apprehend constraints (insight/understanding) governing situations involving large numbers of related objects.

Viewing the blocks drawing provides us with information about both determined facts, such as which blocks are presently on top of other blocks, but more significantly with attunements to constraints which allow this situation to support a host of other situations involving movements of these blocks. Answering a question such as, 'Which blocks are on top of X_1', requires us to inspect the drawing to "read off" the blocks which stand in an on-top relation to X_1. This process of "fact finding" will be referred to as inspection. From a psychological perspective, inspection is significant because it is the simplest form of controlled processing. An act of inspection such as reading the blocks from the diagram is a goal directed and conscious effort but involves no processing beyond control of attention (requires no storage or encoding).

Inspection plays a key role in our theory of visualization because it makes information available to controlled processing with the minimum demand on processing resources. The 'which blocks are on-top' question cannot be answered by inspection for the linguistic or logic versions of the problem, because after inspecting the expression(s) containing X_1, the viewer must perform additional mental operations to identify symbols related to X_1 through transitivity. Accounts of visualization which rely solely on explicit portrayal of facts are theories of table-reading. By these accounts, Table 1, should be an adequate replacement for the blocks drawing in answering on-top questions. It does work well for questions about on-top relations in the actual table. For example, the question, 'Which Xs stand in relation p to X_1', can be answered by reading off the entries on the X_1 row. The planning task to clear X_1, is just as easily solved by reading X's off in descending order, but discovering this strategy requires a conscious effort not necessary in answering the same question from the blocks sketch. When confronted with more complex sequences involving re-positioning of multiple blocks such as, 'Which blocks are on top of X_1 if X_{14} is moved on top of X_7 and X_2 is moved on top of X_5 and X_4 is moved on top of X_2', the table rapidly deteriorates as a problem solving representation,

X_j	Intervening Blocks				
	0	1	2	3	4
X_1	X_9	X_2, X_8, X_{12}	X_5	X_{14}	
X_2					
X_3	X_4	X_{14}			
X_4	X_{14}				
X_5	X_{14}				
X_6	X_7	X_9, X_{18}	X_2, X_8, X_{12}	X_5	X_{14}
X_7	X_9, X_{18}	X_2, X_8, X_{12}	X_5	X_{14}	
X_8	X_5	X_{14}			
X_9	X_2, X_8, X_{12}	X_5	X_{14}		
X_{10}	X_{15}	X_3	X_4	X_{14}	
X_{11}	X_1, X_7	X_9, X_{18}	X_2, X_8, X_{12}	X_5	X_{14}
X_{12}	X_5	X_{14}			
X_{13}	X_{16}	X_8	X_5	X_{14}	
X_{14}					
X_{15}	X_3	X_4	X_{14}		
X_{16}	X_8	X_5	X_{14}		
X_{17}	X_{15}	X_3	X_4	X_{14}	
X_{18}	X_2				

Table 1 $p(X_i, X_j)$

while the drawing degrades only slowly. Introspectively, the difference is between "imagining blocks being moved" and "trying to remember whether or not you have marked a table entry and what you should do if you have." This distinction between remembering states and applying rules and imagining the movement of blocks is precisely where our account differs from the modal theory. We claim that because of our long exposure to situations involving objects such as blocks, we have developed automatic[1] attunements to the constraints governing these situations. As a result, an imagined movement automatically yields the resultant mental state for inspection without recourse to memory, other than noting the move.

This view of attunement is similar to that proposed by Barwise (1989) in which attuned constraints link mental states in much the same way that actual constraints link the actual situations to which the mental states correspond. Mental states are then linked with actual situations through an additional "process," $\#s \Rightarrow s$. We identify the classification of a mental state, $\#S$, needed to discriminate a situation of type S with the process of inspection introduced earlier. We concur with the view that mental

---

[1] The distinction between automatic and controlled processes is discussed in the next section. Gibson's use of the term, attunement, strongly suggests that he would have considered attunements and affordances to involve automatic processes.

states with their attuned constraints and external situations with actual constraints are distinct and not necessarily isomorphic. The psychological problem lies in identifying these differences and reconciling the cognitive effects associated with attunement with the limitations that characterize human information processing.

Our examination focuses on the simplest case, attunements to constraints linking situations of the same type. We make the additional assumption that, as an active agent, an organism's attunements must also allow for the origination of action. Our ability to imagine the effects of our actions such as moving blocks supports this extension. To describe this condition we introduce the notation:

$$\#s \Rightarrow_a \#s'$$

which is interpreted as, the mental state, $\#s'$, is made mentally factual by the originated action, a, in the mental state, $\#s$. The arrow with a subscripted letter indicates the joint effect of a constraint (the arrow) and an originated action (the letter). Envision is defined as a special class of this relation for which $\#s'$ is a completely determined. In the blocks example, for instance, attuned constraints would be envisionable for $a =$ 'move' but not for $a =$ 'knock down'. This view of cognition is similar to that proposed by Johnson-Laird (1983) with the additional stipulations that: (1) attuned constraints provide the "laws" which govern the behavior of mental models and (2) attunement to constraints results from automatic processing. These additions are significant because they suggest that it may be possible to minimize the cognitive difficulty (controlled processing) associated with tasks by re-representing them as situations which require only inspection to process.

Attuned constraints may enter into cognition in a number of ways:

$$
\begin{array}{ccc}
s & \Rightarrow & s' \\
\Uparrow & & \Uparrow \\
\#s & \Rightarrow & \#s'
\end{array}
$$

The form described in Barwise 1989, in which the mental state $\#s'$ is supported by both the actual situation s' and the mental state $\#s$ through a mental constraint, can describe normal interactions with the environment.

$$
\begin{array}{ccc}
s & & s \\
\Uparrow & & \Uparrow_{\Delta} \\
\#s & \Rightarrow_a & \#s'
\end{array}
$$

A form in which the actual state of affairs remains static but a mentally originated action is imagined to produce a new mental state. This can describe planning and corresponds to the mode of processing involved in imagining movements of blocks. The mental state, $\#s'$, continues to be supported by the actual state, s, to the extent that it is anchored with respect to the action $\#s \Rightarrow_a \#s'$, a form in which an originated action is applied to a mental state to produce a new mental state. This would correspond to use of a mental model in a situation in which it is not externally supported such as the tableaus hypothesized by Johnson-Laird (1983) to explain subjects' performance in solving syllogisms. In the absence of an external soa to inspect, this requires storing a mental state in working memory and therefore should be more strongly affected by resource limitations.

Returning to the gedanken experiments, the act of inspecting a visual scene to read off relations is an example which relies on the correspondence between s and $\#s$. The example involving the movement of multiple blocks corresponds to the second case in which $\#s'$ is supported by s through remembered differences. We attribute the difference in difficulty between table and block representations of this situation to the absence of attunements to such actions for situation types involving tables. This distinction can be thought of as a psychological version of the frame problem. Where attunements involving a set of actions are present the mental state is updated correctly and automatically. Where attunements are not present, the mental state must be updated explicitly and errors are likely. (The earlier introspection on the relative likelihood of particular types of errors when using different representations also illustrates this point.) The attempt to solve the blocks problem from memory provides an example of the third case. We expect that difficulties you encountered involved trying to remember blocks and labels, not in deciding which blocks to move if they were remembered.

2 The Modal Model

The three memory structural model of human information processing organizes data in ways generally accepted within psychology.[2] According to this model, stimuli initially reside in a register in which they are represented in a form analogous to sensation. Sensory representations of stimuli are presumed to be *encoded* into some non-sensory mental form and entered into short term memory (STM) which in communication with long term memory (LTM) gives rise to cognitive phenomena.

The capacity of working memory is commonly expressed in *chunks* which are defined as unitary encodings. The word, 'dog' for example could be variously encoded and retrieved as a single chunk, 'dog' or the three chunks 'd', 'o', 'g'. A consensus in the field holds that working memory has some limited capacity within an order of magnitude ranging from 2 chunks for running memory (Moray 1980) to twenty chunks (Anderson 1983) for computer simulations, with a median estimate falling between 4

---

[2] The primary memory (STM)-secondary memory (LTM) distinction, which is its central feature, was proposed by William James who also stressed the significance of what is currently termed automatic processing. While there is disagreement over the literal existence of such structures, the organization of experimental data they provide is generally accepted.

and 6. The structural model presumes that the contents of working memory are encodings of data from the sensory registers memories from LTM, or intermediate results of processing and that it is the number of such encodings which is limited. So, for instance, if we have encoded 'dog' there is an upper bound of 6 or so more words we might encode, yet this would leave us unable to answer a question such as "Was there a word with a 'g' in it?" without forgetting other words on the list.

Some forms of human information processing termed *automatic processing* by Shiffrin and Schneider (1977) appear to function outside the restrictions of this structural model and are immune to its 4 bit ceiling. Automatic processes are developed under conditions in which mappings between stimuli and response remain constant over large numbers of trials. Automatic processes are characterized by little or no demand on processing resources, cognitive impenetrability, and insensitivity to conscious control.

The nature of mental representation is psychologically undecidable because hypothesized representations cannot be experimentally separated from hypothesized processes which operate on them (Anderson 1977). Although there is less consensus on the nature of mental representation/operations than there is for the structural model, the dominant view is that mental representation/operations are in some way propositional. In the most popular variant, mental representations are classified as *declarative* or *procedural* knowledge. Declarative knowledge describes static data structures containing information and is usually portrayed as being organized into a network in which members of structures may be either values or pointers to other structures. Procedural knowledge refers to processes which operate on this declarative knowledge and is usually modeled as a production system.

This representational model is mated to the structural model by presuming some control process in working memory which maintains goals, which, along with encoded stimuli and declarative knowledge, are matched within a production system to return new values or pointers to declarative knowledge for storage within working memory. Working memory is presumed to hold either values ('d' 'o' 'g') or pointers (chunks) to values ('dog' → 'd','o','g') but must encode and store information in the form it is used in processing. The use of this controllable rule-set and access mechanism are presumed necessary for flexible use of declarative knowledge in novel situations. Automatic processing is presumed to rely upon an alternative and more efficient condition matching scheme in which encoded stimuli and/or working memory contents are inflexibly matched to "compiled" production rules. The automatization of procedural knowledge is portrayed as a process of specialization which substitutes constants and eliminates intermediate computations present in more general procedural and declarative knowledge, much as an optimizing compiler might unfold loops and merge instructions.

The challenge visualization poses to the modal model lies in the declarative interpretation it places on terms such as 'understanding' or 'insight'. If visualization depended on controlled processing of visual information then it must abide by the limitations of working memory and cannot employ more than 4 or 5 chunks of encoded stimuli. But, in many instances, the understanding/insight derived from visualization would have required a larger number of encodings exceeding this capacity (for instance the blocks drawing).

A minor modification which resolves some of these problems is to presume that visual information enjoys a privileged status which allows visually available objects to be processed without storage or encoding limitations. This modification appears to be intended by psychologists who refer to visually available information as an "external memory" (Larkin and Simon 1987, Kotovsky, Hayes, and Simon 1985) without specifying anything more about its nature or status.

Larkin and Simon (1987) provide an account of visualization from this modal perspective by distinguishing between sentential and diagrammatic representations. Diagrammatic representations are presumed to explicitly preserve "information about the topological and geometric relations among the components of the problem" while sentential representations do not. Larkin and Simon subscribe to the external memory view of visual information and define diagrammatic representation as "a data structure in which information is indexed by two-dimensional location." Their theory is described using two examples.

In the first example, a problem involving a pulley system, they contrast the number of elements searched (sentential = 138) with indexed locations accessed (diagrammatic < 23) in solving the problem. This comparison relies on what we referred to earlier as the table-reading account because its effects depend on the correspondence between spatial location and the sequence in which values and relations are processed. A corresponding contrast in the blocks problem would compare performance on the 'Which blocks are on top of X_1?' task for the table of relations and a misordered list of those relations.

Their second example is a geometry proof (Figure 4) of the congruence of triangles formed by two parallel lines and two transversals, where the transversals intersect between the parallel lines and one bisects the other. For this problem, Larkin and Simon claim that diagrammatic representation leads to a "perceptually enhanced data structure" in which relations which must be inferred in the sentential representation are enhanced by "easier recognition of conditions for geometry rules in the diagram." In their discussion they point out that "we are asked to prove congruent two triangles that have not been mentioned" as one evidence of this perceptual enhancement. This is a disguised version of the table-reading account because the advantages of the diagrammatic representation depend only on

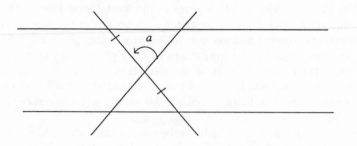

Figure 4 Prove the Triangles Congruent

the explicit representation of objects and relations which are missing from the sentential one. This example corresponds to our comparison between the logic or linguistic versions of the blocks problem in which transitive relations were not represented explicitly and the table of relations in which they were.

The crucial difference between the modal account and the one we are proposing lies in the answers to other questions such as: 'What would happen if angle *a* were increased?' We suspect that a person asked this question, would imagine the lines pivoting like a pair of scissors and provide an account of a sequence of events from the elimination of the triangles when the transversals no longer intersect the parallel lines, to the eventual merging of the transversals into a single line. Although none of these states or events are explicitly represented in the drawing, imagining this behavior is at least as easy as the geometry proof. The processing that would be required for Larkin and Simon's production system to perform this task, however, would be far greater than that needed for either the pulley or geometry problems. Such discrepancies suggest that although a table-reading explanation describes some advantages of visualization, it cannot provide a full account.

3 An Ecological Alternative

Gibson's ecological psychology is commonly portrayed as inconsistent with the structural model (Ullman 1980) because constructs such as direct perception appear to circumvent the structural model's requirements for the encoding of stimuli and the mental processing of these encodings. We argue that, as a functional theory, ecological psychology is not about structure, but instead presents an alternative to the modal theory of mental representation. The ecological constructs of direct perception, attunement, and affordances are inconsistent with the distinctions made between declarative and procedural knowledge and the presumption that automatization leads to higher specificity in independent productions, not the structural model.

If we consider perception to be the most accessible instance of automatic processing rather than an ad hoc exception, a different picture of mental representation emerges. Our ability to individuate objects and apprehend their relations through perception meets all the conditions the structural model places on automatic processes. It imposes light demand on resources, it is not subject to conscious control, it is cognitively impenetrable, and it involves a task at which we have had extended practice under constant (at the level of Gibson's invariants) mapping conditions. If we equate the immediacy of perceptions with the automaticity with which they arise, *direct perception* results. To say that individuated objects spring automatically to attention without effort or apparent impact on mental resources seems functionally equivalent to the claim that they are perceived directly.

By this view the structural model plus "external memory" exception could more accurately be described by an ecological/structural model in which the objects of cognition are the union of the contents of working memory and information which is directly (automatically) available through perception. But if the prototypical automatic process mediates inferences of this flexibility and complexity then the account of automatization as a compilation process in which general productions are specialized into many restricted productions is violated.

Arguments for the specificity of automatic processes are of two sorts. The first interprets the relative inflexibility and specificity of automatic responding developed in the laboratory to be evidence that more flexible responses involving constant mappings (such as Gibson's perceptual invariants) are not possible. Experiments (Shiffrin and Schneider 1977, Eberts and Schneider 1985), however, consistently find that the level of abstraction at which automatic responding can be developed is not fixed but depends on the level at which mappings are held constant and the number of trials. For attunements to nomic constraints where mappings are held constant by natural law and trials extend an entire life, it would not be unreasonable to expect automatic processes to be much more general. The second argument depends on a computer analogy with optimizing compilation. Because more efficient encodings of procedures on digital computers involve strategies such as replacing variables with constants and merging instructions, which lead to greater specificity, it is concluded that automatization of processes in human information processing must do the same.

The opposite conclusion is reached by assuming that the distinguishing characteristic of human cognition is its flexibility. Under this assumption, the most efficient information processing architecture will be one which allows for the flexible use of "compiled" knowledge. Substituting an object oriented programming analogy for the optimizing compilation one leads to the conclusion that an architecture allowing data abstraction (attunement) would be more efficient than one which narrowly optimizes compilation.

In this section we have attempted to reconcile cognition incorporating attunements to constraints with accumulated psychological data requiring distinctions between forms of processing and their relation to working memory. The ecological theory is shown to disagree with the representational/processing assumptions of the modal theory but not the empirically supported distinctions made by the structural theory. Our objective of identifying cognitive mechanisms compatible with visualization claims has been met by the inspect and envision operations and the contention that objects of perception are inspectable without encoding or storage in working memory. Our characterization of these processes is prescriptive because it identifies the conditions under which effortless cognition is possible:

(1) A situation is inspectable if the relevant discrimination among mental states depends only on observable facts.

(2) A situation is envisionable if imagined actions result in an inspectable mental state.

4 Why Problems are Hard

To illustrate this approach we will re-examine the Tower of Hanoi (TOH) and Monster Globe (MG) problems which differ in difficulty by a factor of 16, despite formal equivalence.

The classic approach to problem description (and Simon 1972) characterizes a problem as a pair of states (initial and goal), a set of operators for transforming states, and a set of rules governing the application of these operators. The problem solving task is depicted as a problem space in which states are the vertices and edges are (legally applied) operators. Problem solving is modeled as a search of this graph to identify some sequence of operators (edges) which transforms the initial state into the goal state. Why these models are often successful in predicting difficulty is easy to see. They predict that subjects will find problems with larger spaces to search, more distant goals, or more choices to make, more difficult. In our initial blocks example a problem space formulation would predict that problems involving more blocks, taller stacks, or targets near the bottom of stacks would prove more difficult. What it fails to account for are the substantially greater differences in difficulty associated with solving a formally equivalent problem using blocks, logic, or language.

If problems are considered as situations the description is quite different. A problem, is presented to subjects through a cover story, which defines a situation involving the sorts of objects, relations, and actions which are involved. The mental problem is, therefore, defined by the described situation, attunements to constraints affecting actions in this type of situation plus any additional constraints imposed by the problem's rules. Under these conditions the problem space is usually a limiting best case description of the problem being solved. Problem rules which exclude states of affairs or actions allowed by the situation's envisionment will result in the

Figure 5 Tower of Hanoi and Monster-Globe

search of an effectively larger space. Problems in which actions relate states of affairs in ways which are not envisionable cannot rely on automatic processing to transform mental states and are effectively a much more difficult class of problem.

In the three disk Tower-of-Hanoi problem (shown in Figure 5), disks of three sizes are moved between three posts. A problem rule specifies that a larger disk cannot be moved on top of a smaller one. Subjects are presented with the task of reaching a goal state from an initial state by determining a sequence of moves.

In the Monster-Globe (move) version posts are replaced by small, medium and large monsters and the disks by globes. The goal is to have each monster holding its own sized globe. Problem rules specify that a larger globe cannot be passed to a monster holding a smaller globe and that if a monster is holding multiple globes, only the smallest globe can be passed.

In the Monster-Globe (change) version (shown in Figure 5), disks are replaced by monsters and posts by globes. The goal is again having each monster holding its own sized globe. Monsters are allowed to change the sizes of their globes according to rules of etiquette which require that if two monsters have the same sized globe only the larger monster is allowed to change (only the disk at the top of a stack can be moved) and a smaller monster cannot change its globe to a size held by a larger monster (a larger disk cannot be placed on a smaller one).

Subjects find the Monster-Globe problems much more difficult. Hayes and Simon (1977), for example, report differences in average solution times of less than two minutes for the three disk Tower of Hanoi problem, and half an hour for the corresponding Monster-Globe (change) problem. The Monster-Globe (move) problem is of intermediate difficulty.

The envisionment of the Tower of Hanoi involves a substantially larger problem space than either of the other problems because it distinguishes the ordering of disks on posts which is irrelevant to the formal description. This results in an unconstrained space of 60 states and 468 transitions. The unconstrained MG spaces, by contrast, have only 27 states and 81 transitions. The Tower of Hanoi envisionment, however, aids problem solving in two ways. Our attunements to situations involving the movement of physical objects prevents us from imagining that disks might dematerialize from their pegs to reappear at arbitrary locations but instead automatically constrains us to "see" only movements between positions at the top of the pegs. This sort of unimaginability is what we have meant by envisioned constraints. The coincidence of a problem rule with an envisioned constraint simplifies the space to 108 transitions and 60 states. Because posts are observable objects in the problem's soa, problem states in which larger disks are on top of smaller ones can be discriminated through inspection without additional controlled processing. This reduces the problem to a controlled search of a space of 50 states and 75 transitions in which all other processing is automatic. Although this is substantially more complex than the official 27 state, 39 transition problem space each of the 36 prohibited moves are immediately ruled out through inspection. To contrast this with a problem which is completely constrained by its envisionment, consider a block un-stacking task, in which the goal is to move a block which is six blocks deep in a stack. The number of steps required is the same as the most difficult 3-disk TOH problem and the aggregate complexity of constraints to be satisfied is greater, yet most would agree that it is an easier task.

The Monster-Globe (move) problem has a 27 state 81 transition envisionment. Unlike the Tower of Hanoi in which the initiation of moves is restricted by envisioned constraints, the MG problem requires inspection and a controlled comparison with the rule restricting globes which may be moved for each move considered. The state resulting from the move requires an additional inspection and a controlled comparison because the state alone, is insufficient to determine legality. The controlled processing required by these comparisons makes this problem more difficult despite a problem space of comparable complexity.

The Monster-Globe (change) problem has objectively the same problem space as the move version but is much more difficult. We attribute this difficulty to the absence of an envisionment for the situation described in the cover story. We assume that situation-types involving tangible objects have available some very general attunements which apply to physical situations including such things as:

- object constancy: physical objects and their properties remain constant
- movement: an object can be moved from one spatial location to another. Unless it is moved it will not change location.
- extension: two objects cannot occupy the same space at the same time

Change problems are not envisionable because they violate object constancy, a basic attunement which plays a primary role in theories of psychology ranging from cognitive development to perception. Which is not to say that we could not imagine objects changing *normally* constant properties, or perceive such changes but rather that imagining events which do

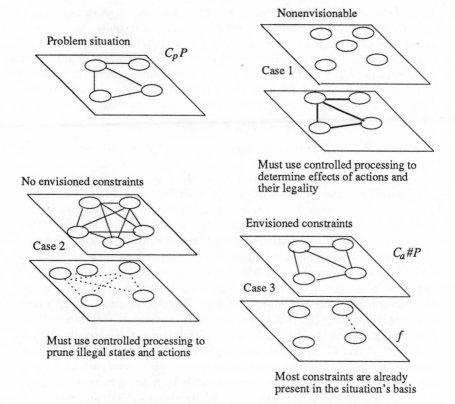

Figure 6 Interactive Situations

not follow our attunements requires controlled processing. The movement of disks, by contrast, can be envisioned because its situation anchors object properties (object constancy) and obeys our attunements to movement for this type of situation. As a consequence, we can imagine moving a disk from one peg to another and inspect the state which results. This claim can be tested by introspection on the way you solve the TOH problem in Figure 5 (goal is to arrange disks large to small from left to right). Now examine the MG version. Imagine two of the globes to be of different sizes then "change" the size of the third. Even this simple exercise is relatively difficult because automatic processes are not available to reorder the problem state.

5 Making Hard Problems Easy

In problems such as the Tower of Hanoi isomorphs or interaction with a computer the actual situation and its constraints are completely specified. We will call situations of this sort, *interactive situations*. The correspondence between an interactive situation and its mental counterpart can be described as an equivalence between constrained situations. Let P be an interactive situation with constraints C_p and and $\#P$ be a mental situation with exactly the same constituents (objects and relations) as P but having as constraints C_a, a user's attunements to constraints governing situations of this type. Now define f (the constraints which must be actively supplied by the user) to be a set of additional constraints such that:

$$C_p P \cong f \cdot C_a \#P.$$

But since P and $\#P$ have exactly the same constituents we can write $C_p P = f \cdot C_a P$.

This f has various interpretations as the cognitive effort required by the interaction, the instructions which must be provided to the user, or the difference between actual constraints and attunements to constraints governing the situation. Figure 6 depicts this relationship showing states as nodes and their associations through constraints as edges. The solid lines in Case 1 correspond to unenvisionable situations such as the Monster Globe Change problem in which states resulting from actions must be explicitly constructed in memory. The dotted lines in Case 2 correspond to situations such as the Monster Globe Move problem in which events are envisionable but the problem solver must consciously supply additional constraints (delete the dotted lines) to match the problem constraints. In Case 3 $C_p P$ and $C_a \#P$ differ only slightly. This corresponds to problems such as Tower of Hanoi in which constraints which were part of f in the other problems have been made envisionable by moving them into C_a.

The relation between a situation and its visualization can be similarly described as a correspondence between interactive situations.

$$F : C_s S \Rightarrow C_s' S'$$

and their accompanying mental situations:

$$f \cdot C_a \#S \Rightarrow f' \cdot C_{a'} \#S'$$

A visualization of an interactive situation can be found by substituting relations which preserve the discrimination of states and allow the substitution of attuned constraints in C_a' for the user supplied constraints in f. The ability to instruct the problem solver to supply the constraints in f makes this approach quite general. It amounts to constructing metaphors incrementally with an error term.

If F just happens to be decomposable into one-to-one mappings between constituents, then other benefits accrue. Additional constraints involving S which were not considered in deriving the visualization are induced and mental translations between states of the situation and its visualization are determined by inspectable facts.

Visualizations can be constructed by grouping mutually anchored relations into potential "objects." Problem constraints can then be merged in an aggregate expression incorporating their interactions to provide a template for substitutions into f'. This "situation" can then rewritten by substituting relations which make events and constraints envisionable or reduce the number of "objects" which must be inspected to determine the applicability of the remaining constraints. In this notation "objects" are written as groups of mutually anchored relations with dots indicating those which are unanchored, integers used to indicate anchored orderings, and Δ used to indicate originated actions. Two substitution rules are used:

(1) Free substitution: Any relation type can be substituted for any other relation type as long as it allows the same discriminability of states.

(2) Overlay substitution: Relations grouped within a single "object" may be "overlayed" by a substitution which preserves the original discrimination but uses the same relation to make an additional discrimination.

Attunements to Property Anchorings			
Type	Class	Instance	Attunement
spatial	extension	object-length	anchored
spatial	extension	object-size	anchored
spatial	location	object-location	unanchored
visual	appearance	object-color	anchored

Attuned Constraints
$same(\dot{l}, \dot{l}')$: $on\text{-}top(\dot{l}, \dot{l}') \Rightarrow \neg\Delta\dot{l}'$
$stack(\dot{l}, \dot{l}') \Rightarrow on\text{-}top(\Delta\dot{l}, \dot{l}')$

In this notation the MGC problem could be written as:

- S = monster size, s = globe size, where S and s are relations of type *size*, and l is an anchoring relation between them of type *location*:

$$\langle S_1 l\dot{s}, S_2 l\dot{s}, S_3 l\dot{s}\rangle$$

with constraints:

  o If two monsters are holding globes of the same size, the smaller monster cannot change the size of its globe: $same(\dot{s}, \dot{s}') \wedge S < S' \Rightarrow \neg\Delta\dot{s}$

  o A smaller monster cannot change the size of its globe to the same size as a globe held by a larger monster: $\neg same(\dot{s}, \dot{s}') \wedge S < S' \Rightarrow \neg same(\Delta\dot{s}, \dot{s}')$

  o Substitution template: $S < S' \Rightarrow \neg\Delta\dot{s} \vee \neg same(\Delta\dot{s}, \dot{s}')$

Location is the only property tabled as unanchored, so rewrite $\dot{s}$ as $\dot{l}$ and l as s. This produces the move version of the problem in which objects of three sizes are moved between objects at three locations. By making events envisionable, problem difficulty has already been cut in half.

- For S, s, l as above:

$$\langle S_1 \dot{l}s_1, S_2 \dot{l}s_2, S_3 \dot{l}s_3 \rangle$$

- Rewrite s as an ordinal location and overlay on $\dot{l}$ (nominal) to simplify:

$$\langle S1\dot{l}, S2\dot{l}, S3\dot{l} \rangle$$

  with constraints:
  - $S < S' \wedge same(\dot{l}, \dot{l}') \Rightarrow \neg \Delta \dot{l}$
  - $S < S' \wedge \neg same(\dot{l}, \dot{l}') \Rightarrow \neg same(\Delta \dot{l}, \dot{l}')$
  - Template: $S < S' \Rightarrow \neg \Delta \dot{l} \vee \neg same(\Delta \dot{l}, \dot{l}')$

- Consulting the table of attunements, *on-top*, a relation of type *location* and connotation *same*, is found which matches the first constraint and has a related action stack which matches $same(\Delta \dot{l}, \dot{l}')$ allowing a consistent substitution into the template which becomes:
  - $S < S' \Rightarrow \neg stack(\Delta \dot{l}, \dot{l}')$

- No further rewriting is possible so the instruction 'A smaller S cannot be stacked on a larger S' must be provided to the problem solver to supply the missing constraint. This visualization provides a block stacking version of Tower of Hanoi which is more than an order of magnitude easier than the original problem.

The same method of rewriting can be used to derive visualizations for two familiar scheduling problems. Job-Shop scheduling problems involve scheduling n jobs on m machines in such a way that total production time or some other criterion is minimized. The Flow-Shop problem differs from the general Job-Shop problem in that its technological constraints (the order in which fixed duration operations must be performed) are the same for all jobs. In the general Job-Shop problem the order of operations is independently fixed for each job. In both problems it is assumed that only one job can be processed on a machine at one time and that a job cannot be simultaneously processed on more than one machine. Both problems are intrinsically hard, being NP-complete for machines > 2.

The technological constraint and fixed operation times anchor the problem. The activity of scheduling consists of filling in indeterminate starting times for jobs on machines. Starting times can be rewritten as spatial locations to make the problem envisionable and the machine relation along another spatial dimension to preserve its ordering. In the Flow Shop problem the nominal ordering on jobs can be rewritten as a nominal ordering on the final spatial dimension to obtain matches with the attunement to extension for both the single machine and single job constraints. A relation "abut" which associates object extension with spatial location can then be matched to associate process times with scheduled times. In this visualization a newly scheduled operation "abuts" in the dimension assigned to time with either the location of the last job on the same machine plus the extension associated with its processing time or the location of the last machine for the same job plus the extension associated with its processing time. This visualization is realizable because it does not violate nomic constraints or their attunements. Because the rewriting anchors object location for machines and jobs and the anchoring attunement for object location is indeterminate, instructions that objects cannot be moved in dimensions 'machine' or 'job' must be generated. Although the technological constraint was needed for the rewrites it was not itself matched to attunements so the instruction "Objects must be stacked from left to right with those for the same machine kept in order."

The "Chinese puzzle" shown in Figure 7 is an instance of this visualization which maps the Flow-Shop problem to a situation involving a set of blocks. Problem constraints are all conveyed through attunements and object properties follow anchoring attunements except as noted in the generated instructions. The job associated "keys" ($l_j \neq l_{j-1}$) cause blocks to rest on either the previous "same-job" block or the top "same-machine" block, satisfying the single machine, single job, and technological constraints. The instructions require that blocks be stacked in the row in which they are found (the location anchored by the technological and single machine constraints) and in the same orientation (the location anchored by the single job constraint).

Any solution to this Chinese puzzle is also a feasible Flow-Shop schedule. The puzzle solution which results in the lowest stack of blocks is the shortest production time solution. The stacking arrangement which is lowest for blocks bearing a particular "key" corresponds to the schedule which expedites that job. The assemblies which eliminate large gaps in the puzzle are those which avoid long waits for in-process inventory.

The Flow-Shop problem is a special case of the more general Job-Shop problem and is of interest because in many industrial processes operations must be performed in single fixed order. The Job-Shop problem differs from the Flow-Shop problem in having a technological constraint which allows each job have its own fixed order of operations. A machine shop in which parts are manufactured on different sequences of general purpose machines such as lathes, drills, and milling machines would be an example of a job shop. Difficulty arises in rewriting the Job-Shop problem because machines can no longer be ordered on a single spatial dimension. Even though start times, durations, machines, and jobs remain mutually anchored they cannot be consistently assigned to locations and extensions as they were in the Flow-Shop. This is not a major obstacle because the rewrite method is incremental and generates instructions when attunements cannot be matched. Time and processing duration are again rewritten as a spatial location and extension to obtain envisionability and access to attunements involving extension and abutting objects. Machines and jobs, however, impose conflicting orderings on the extensions of these

Instructions:

Blocks should be stacked in the row and orientation in which they are found.
Blocks for the same job should not be stacked out of order.

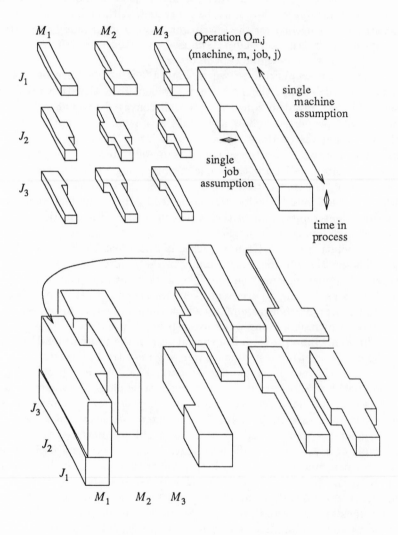

Figure 7 Flow-Shop Scheduling with Blocks

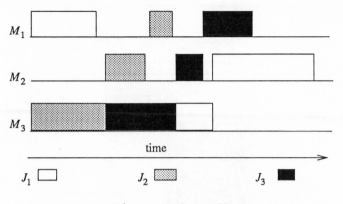

Figure 8 Gantt Chart

objects so they cannot be guaranteed to coincide at a single spatial location. One of these relations must therefore be assigned to a nonspatial property and portrayed relative to time independently of the other. The instructions that processing objects can be moved in the dimension labeled time but objects of the same color are not allowed to overlap in the dimension labeled machines is generated from the unmatched constraints.

This partial visualization produces the familiar Gantt chart shown in Figure 8. Despite its failure to completely convey constraints through attunement the Gantt chart has proved an invaluable tool in helping human schedulers understand and solve scheduling problems. It is reassuring that the preferred visualization of a well known operations research problem is identified by the same methods which transform the difficult Monster-Globe (change) problem into the easy Tower of Hanoi problem.

These examples demonstrate that even very weak relation substitution methods may be sufficient to construct visualizations of simple problems. Constructing diagrams from attunements in this fashion produces problem situations which support both envisionment and inspection. Envisionment is supported because the situations respect attunements to constraints and anchorings which were used in their construction. Inspection is supported because the situation is organized around objects or, in case of impasse, groupings corresponding to objects. As a result, changes in problem state are reflected as changes in particular objects or groupings making changes in state inspectable.

6   A Steam Plant Can Be a Seesaw

The visualization and control of processes is another application for which engineered situations are well suited. Displays having equivalent perceptual resolution are equivalent in conveying a process state making the ability to

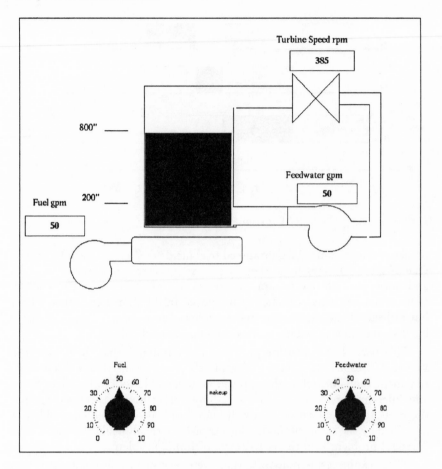

Figure 9 Mimic Display

convey relations among parameters and constraints governing the process the features distinguishing good displays from poor ones.

The most direct solution to this problem is to relate process parameters through a single display. Although there is a consensus in the human factors and design communities that displays should be integrated, there is little agreement on how to do it. The leading contenders are mimic displays and object displays. Mimic displays portray parameters in the context of simplified piping and instrumentation diagrams or schematics. Object displays portray parameters as features of geometric objects such as line lengths. Mimic displays (Figure 9) obey many of the principles we have been advocating by providing a context which makes some constraints visible. However, it is the control of states as well as pipes that is essential

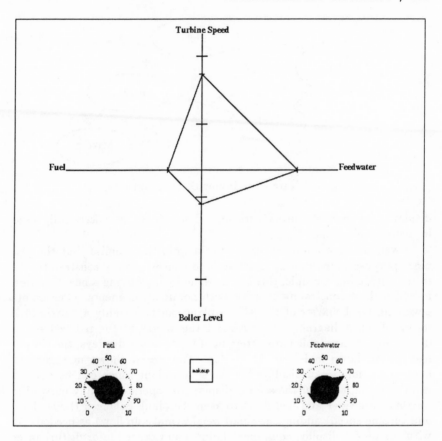

Figure 10 Object Display

to managing a process. This is the primary disadvantage of mimics. The operator is thrown back on his own resources to mentally model how parameters which do not have visible expressions (such as turbine speed in a steam plant) fit with the plant behavior he can "see." This problem of invisible parameters is encountered frequently enough to be a major obstacle to the use of mimics.

Object displays (such as Figure 10) resolve this problem by shifting monitoring to a new situation in which all parameters are visible. In doing so, however, object displays sacrifice the ability to convey constraints which we maintain is the primary purpose of process displays. Object displays are the integration strategy of choice for the position associating visualization effects with table-reading and explicit representation of state. A geometric object can convey any measurable set of parameters in a form allowing immediate relational comparison. Despite such imposing features, object

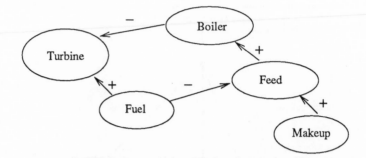

Figure 11 Influence Diagram

displays remain a laboratory curiosity while mimics are successfully used in many applications.

A visualization approach would begin from the premise that the primary purpose of integrating displays is to convey process constraints. As in the scheduling example, this can be done by identifying a new situation in which these constraints coincide with nomic attunements. Constraints governing the behavior of this steam plant can be roughly approximated in an influence diagram. If we restrict this model to the reduced set of displayable/controllable parameters used in the other displays, the simplified model shown in Figure 11 results. The seesaw shown in Figure 12 is one of a number of displays for the steam plant which can be derived from this diagram. For the seesaw display, the operator simply moves the weights (feedwater and fuel flow) to keep the plank balanced (boiler level and turbine speed) adding the small weight (make up flow) as needed. As with the object display, equipment failures and other major disturbances are made apparent by anomalies in the display such as a severe warping of the 'plank'.

7 Discussion

The examples presented in this paper illustrate the sorts of contributions a robust theory of situations might make to applied problems. Despite twenty years of research, cognitive science has done little to help us design cognitively compatible artifacts. The absence of results is not for lack of effort but rather because a solipsistic psychology offers no way to assist cognition from the outside. Each of our examples involved problems which were very difficult when presented in some forms and very easy in others. In each instance the size of the search space had very little impact while the context of the problem had a very major one.

The basic datum psychology brings to the study of cognition is that, in humans, information is processed by a very peculiar architecture. The psychologist's dilemma lies in explaining how the complexity of thought can

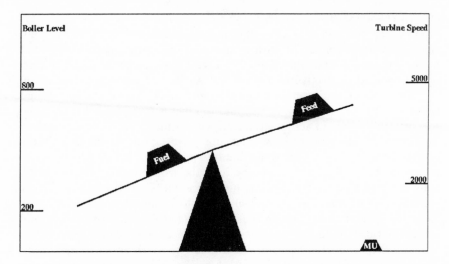

Figure 12 Visualization of Steam Plant

be coaxed from a device with a 3-bit bus. In the balance, our speculations respect architectural necessity more closely than the modal theory because they relegate most complex cognitive processing to resource free automatic processes.

Two questions, however, are raised:

(1) How can attunements fail if they are general rather than highly specific? (How to explain naive physics?)

(2) How are attunements accessed and used outside of their native situations? (A theory of metaphor and analogy?)

8   When Attunements Fail

A psychological theory which posits attunements to regularities which endow people with mental constraints causing their mental states to "follow" those of the environment, should at least predict that people will be accurate in "following" the most pervasive of these regularities (e.g., nomic constraints). There are widely replicated findings in psychology, however, which suggest people simply do not have an accurate model of simple physical events. Populations ranging from high school to advanced college physics students, repeatedly and in substantial numbers, provide inaccurate accounts.

These experiments in naive physics typically employ line drawings and ask subjects to sketch events such as trajectories of falling objects. Experimenters usually find that a third or more of their subjects will exhibit misconceptions such as drawing bombs which fall straight to the ground

60% (McCloskey 1983) or water spraying in a spiral from a coiled hose, 34% (Kaiser, Jonides, and Alexander 1986). These data are disturbing both because they are inconsistent with a theory of monolithic attunements and because the individual differences they reveal could make the manipulation of attunements ineffective as a general strategy for conveying information.

Our account relies on the characterization of mental states reached through attunement as qualitative and the distinctions made between the role of attunements in actual situations/animations, diagrams, and mental models. If an attunement to a constraint exists, it cannot involve a more precise classification of situations than is available for actual events or animations. Naive physics data can be re-examined from this perspective by comparing anomaly judgments for animations with line drawings of the sort collected in earlier studies. If subjects cannot distinguish anomalous events then they cannot be attuned to the constraints governing those events, and misconceptions found in drawings cannot reflect a failure of attunement.

We have conducted such an experiment in which subjects viewed an elevated car dropping a ball which fell behind, straight down, or followed a Newtonian trajectory. Subjects were given data sheets prior to viewing the animations and instructed to rate each animation as appearing: artificial, somewhat artificial, or realistic. They were additionally asked to sketch what they had seen. After ratings and sketches were completed, subjects were asked to rank the animations they had viewed from most natural to least natural in appearance. Our results agreed with McCloskey's (1983) finding that a substantial number of subjects drew the ball falling straight to the ground (under all conditions). The sketches, however, were not related to the ratings of realism, which in turn were only weakly ($tau = .20$) related to the rankings. All but one of the 41 subject's, however, rated the animation in which the ball fell behind the point of release as either artificial or somewhat artificial. The range of disagreement among subjects about how such events should appear is illustrated by their rankings in which 51% ranked the forward trajectory as most realistic, 34% ranked the downward trajectory most realistic while 39% ranked the forward trajectory least realistic. Other recent experiments employing anomaly judgments such as Kaiser and Proffitt's (1987) study of elastic collisions in which subjects accepted deflections within a 40° envelope find similar latitude in assessing realism. These results suggest that naive misconceptions probably do not reflect attunements, but instead involve attribution about weakly (mentally) constrained events. Our animation apparently carried little more information than the statement 'the car dropped the ball.'

Although these anomaly experiments salvage a psychological theory of attunement, they do so by demonstrating that even under the best circumstances an identity between actual constraints and attunements to them cannot be presumed. These differences emphasize the need for a more complete psychological theory of attunement.

9   The Siamese Room

An implicit assumption throughout this paper has been that visualization can help us interact with difficult situations by re-representing them as easy ones. In the discussion of Tower-of-Hanoi isomorphs we argued that despite formal equivalence, subjects were solving very different problems. It remains to be explained how understanding a different problem could help understand the one which is presented. A situational account of analogy, metaphor and re-use of attunements is beyond the scope of this paper but the special case of using visualization to solve problems, can be addressed. Refer back to Figure 5 showing the Tower-of-Hanoi and Monster-Globe (change size) problems and try to "translate" between them. Although the problems have isomorphic problem spaces, the Monster-Globe (change) problem remains difficult, even with an easy visualization. If you imagine solving the Monster-Globe (move) problem instead, the translation becomes very easy and problem solving might be expected to benefit. We believe that this difference lies in the mapping between the problems. The mapping between Tower of Hanoi and Monster-Globe move is decomposable into mappings between constituents, the mapping to the change problem is not. Two disks on a peg, for example, corresponds to two monsters holding two globes of the same size. We are presently conducting a study testing this and related hypotheses in which we hope to demonstrate that small shifts in representation can produce large performance differences when using a visualization to aid problem solving. The Monster-Globe (change) problem, for example, can be made congruent with Tower-of-Hanoi without altering the nonenvisionability of its constraints by the simple expedient of having monsters change color rather than globe-size. Although it is difficult to solve the Monster-Globe (change) problem by referencing the Tower-of-Hanoi, Tic-Tac-Toh, an isomorph which represents the problem using markers in a 3×3 matrix, can make events envisionable and states inspectable while providing a mapping between constituents. The addition of engineerable translations completes the approach, making it possible to re-represent situations either to simplify problems or to aid in understanding them.

In this paper we have outlined an approach to designing graphics which manipulates context to convey information. Instead of using embedding circumstances to identify infons which are supported, we are suggesting that a specification of information to be carried can be used to embed circumstances supporting the desired infons. With or without a cognitive (or semantic) theory the shift to meaning through computer graphics is as inevitable as the graphical interfaces on our desks. Although the simple expedient of displaying inspectable states of affairs offers substantial benefits, we believe that the real potential of computer mediated representation lies in treating graphics as carriers of information rather than facts. This alternative requires us to treat computer graphics as we do radio signals. Instead of considering them informative in their own right (telegraphy) we should treat them as carriers to be carefully modulated to smuggle information. The examples in this paper demonstrate that even a very sketchy description of nomic attunements and unsophisticated methods for identifying carrier situations may be relatively effective at this task.

References

Anderson, J. R. 1978. Arguments Concerning Representations for Mental Imagery. *Psychological Review* 85(4):249–277.

Anderson, J. R. 1983. *The Architecture of Cognition.* Cambridge, MA: Harvard University Press.

Barwise, J. 1989. *The Situation in Logic.* CSLI Lecture Notes Number 17. Stanford: CSLI Publications.

Barwise, J., and J. Perry. 1983. *Situations and Attitudes.* Cambridge, MA: MIT Press.

Eberts, R., and W. Schneider. 1985. Internalizing the System Dynamics for a Second Order System. *Human Factors* 27:371–393.

Hayes, J. R., and H. A. Simon. 1977. Psychological Differences Among Problem Isomorphs. In *Cognitive Theory*, ed. N. J. Castellan, D. B. Pisoni, and G. R. Potts. Hillsdale, NJ: Erlbaum.

Johnson-Laird, P. N. 1983. *Mental Models: Towards a Cognitive Science of Language, Inference, and Consciousness.* Cambridge, MA: Harvard University Press.

Kaiser, M. K., J. Jonides, and J. Alexander. 1986. Intuitive Reasoning About Abstract and Familiar Physics Problems. *Memory and Cognition* 14(4):308–312.

Kaiser, M. K., and D. R. Proffitt. 1987. Observers' Sensitivity to Dynamic Anomalies in Collisions. *Perception and Psychophysics* 43(2):275–280.

Kotovsky, K., J. R. Hayes, and H. A. Simon. 1985. Why are Some Problems Hard? Evidence from Tower of Hanoi. *Cognitive Psychology* 17:248–294.

Larkin, J. H., and H. A. Simon. 1987. Why a Diagram is (Sometimes) Worth Ten Thousand Words. *Cognitive Science* 11:65–100.

McClosky, M. 1983. Intuitive Physics. *Scientific American* 122–130.

McCormick, B. H., T. A. DeFanti, and M. D. Brown. 1987. Visualization in Scientific Computing. *Computer Graphics* 21(6).

Moray, N. 1980. *Human Information Processing and Supervisory Control.* Cambridge, MA: MIT, Man-machine System Laboratory.

Newell, A., and H. A. Simon. 1972. *Human Problem Solving.* New Jersey: Prentice-Hall.

Shiffrin, R., and W. Schneider. 1977. Controlled and Automatic Human Information Processing, II. *Psychological Review* 84:127–190.

Ullman, S. 1980. Against Direct Perception. *The Behavioral and Brain Sciences* 3:373–415.

25

A Situation-Theoretic Account of
Valid Reasoning with Venn Diagrams

SUN-JOO SHIN

Venn diagrams are widely used to solve problems in set theory and to test the validity of syllogisms in logic. Since elementary school we have been taught how to draw Venn diagrams for a problem, how to manipulate them, how to interpret the resulting diagrams and so on. However, it is a fact that Venn diagrams are not considered valid proofs, but heuristic tools for finding valid formal proofs. This is just a reflection of a general prejudice against visualization which resides in the mathematical tradition. With this bias for linguistic representation systems, little attempt has been made to analyze any nonlinguistic representation system, despite the fact that many forms of visualization are used to help our reasoning.

The purpose of this paper is to give a semantic analysis for *a* visual representation system—the Venn diagram representation system.[1] I was mainly motivated to undertake this project by the discussion of multiple forms of representation presented in "Visual Information and Valid Reasoning" by Barwise and Etchemendy (1990). More specifically, I will clarify the following passage in the same paper, by presenting Venn diagrams as a formal system of representations equipped with its own syntax and semantics:

> As the preceding demonstration illustrated, Venn diagrams provide us with a formalism that consists of a standardized system of representations, together with rules of manipulating them. ... We think it should be possible to give an information-theoretic analysis of this system, ...

In the following I name the formal system of Venn diagrams VENN. The analysis of VENN will lead to interesting issues which have their analogues in other deductive systems. An interesting point is that VENN, whose

---

[1] In this paper I limit myself to the use of Venn diagrams to test the validity of syllogisms from traditional logic.

Situation Theory and Its Applications, vol. 2.
Jon Barwise, Jean Mark Gawron, Gordon Plotkin, and Syun Tutiya, eds.

primitive objects are diagrammatic, not linguistic, casts these issues in a different light from linguistic representation systems. Accordingly, this VENN system helps us to realize what we take for granted in other more familiar deductive systems. Through comparison with symbolic logic, I hope my presentation of VENN contributes some support to the idea that valid reasoning should be thought of in terms of manipulation of information, not just in terms of manipulation of linguistic symbols.

To support my claim that this use of Venn diagrams is a standard representation system, I aim to develop the syntax and the semantics of this formal system in the following way:

In Section 1, I clarify what the primitive objects are for this system and which diagrams are well-formed. In this section, several interesting issues arise from the fact that the primitive objects of VENN are diagrammatic. For example, unlike with linguistic representation systems, we need an extra relation among tokens of the same type. Also, we need to specify a relation among diagrams which look very similar to each other.

In Section 2, the semantics of this system is developed with the help of situation-theoretic tools. First, I formalize a homomorphic relationship between Venn diagrams drawn, say, on a piece of a paper, and information conveyed in syllogisms. It is this relation which allows us to represent certain facts (about which we aim to reason) in terms of certain diagrams and to tell what a diagram conveys. What it is for one one diagram to follow from other diagram(s) is definable by the relation of the contents of the diagrams.

In Section 3, I define what it is to obtain one diagram from other diagrams in this system and introduce five ways of manipulating diagrams. This establishes the syntax of this system.

The soundness of this system is proved in Section 4. Namely, whenever diagram D is obtainable (as defined in Section 3) from a set of diagrams Δ, diagram D follows (as defined in Section 2) from Δ.

In the last section, Section 5, I prove that this system is complete. That is, this system, along with its own transformation rules, allows us to obtain any diagram D from a set of diagrams Δ, if D follows from Δ.

1 Syntax

1.1 Preliminary Remarks

Let us assume that any representation system aims to represent information about the situation about which we want to reason. VENN, which we are about to examine, adopts diagrams as its medium to effect this representation. We aim to examine the formalism with which Venn diagrams provide us in the following respects:

1. What are the formation rules of meaningful units in this system?
2. What are the meaningful units of this system about?

These two questions help us to answer whether this Venn diagram system is a standard formal representation system or not. If this system is deductive (which we want to claim), then one more question should be answered:

3. What are the rules for manipulating the objects of this system?

These questions will be discussed in Sections 1, 2, and 3, respectively. In order to address the first point, i.e., what are the formation rules, we need to specify the set of primitive objects of which a meaningful unit in this system consists. Before this syntactic discussion begins, let us consider some of the features we want to incorporate into this representation system.

Let us think of the information which this system aims to convey. The following are examples:

> All unicorns are red.
> No unicorns are red.
> Some unicorns are red.
> Some unicorns are not red.

These four pieces of information have something in common. That is, all of these are about some relation between the following sets—the set of unicorns and the set of red things. Each piece of information shows a different relation between these two sets. Therefore, the Venn diagram system needs to represent the following: sets and relations between sets.

A set is represented by a differentiable closed curve which does not self-intersect, as follows:

However, a main question is whether we want to have an infinite number of different closed-curve-types *or* only one closed-curve-type. An analogy with sentential logic might be helpful in this matter. In sentential logic we are given an infinite sequence of sentence symbols, $A_1, A_2, \ldots$. An atomic sentence of English is translated into a sentence symbol. When we translate different atomic sentences of English into the language of sentential logic, we choose different sentence symbols. It does not matter which sentence symbols we use, as long as we use different symbol-types for different English sentence-types. Another important point is that after choosing a sentence symbol (type), say A_{17}, for a certain English sentence (type), we have to keep using this sentence symbol, the 17th sentence symbol, for the translation of this English sentence-type.

Therefore, if the first alternative—to have different closed-curve-types—is chosen for this system, then we can say, just as in the language of sentential logic, that tokens of the same closed-curve-type represent the same set. However, in this system we would have to accept the following counterintuitive aspect: Very similar looking (or even identical looking) closed-curve-tokens might belong to different closed-curve-types. Even though I think it is theoretically possible to have such a system, I decide to choose the other alternative, that is, to have only one closed-curve-type.

Now one question is how to represent different sets by closed curves. Of course, we want to say that in VENN different sets are represented by different closed curves. However, these different closed curves are tokens of the same type—the closed-curve-type, since we have only one closed-curve-type. In the case of sentential logic, we have an infinite number of sentence symbol-types to represent an infinite number of English sentence-types. Therefore, different English sentence-types are represented by different sentence symbol-types. In VENN we have only one closed-curve-type to represent an infinite number of sets. A main problem is how to tell whether given closed curves represent different sets or not. Of course, we cannot rely on how these tokens look, since every token of a closed curve belongs to one and the same type. It seems obvious that we need an extra mechanism to keep straight the relation among tokens of a closed curve, unlike in the case of sentential logic. This point will be discussed after the primitive objects are introduced.

Suppose that the following closed curve represents the set of unicorns:

Accordingly, this closed curve makes a distinction between the set of unicorns and anything else. Strictly speaking, the area enclosed by the closed curve, not the closed curve itself, represents the set of unicorns. It will be good if we can treat anything else as a set as well. However, there is no such set as the set of non-unicorns, unless there is a background set. Therefore, we want to introduce a way to represent the background set in each case. Whatever sets we want to represent by closed curves, we can always come up with a background set which is large enough to include all the members of the sets represented by the drawn closed curves. A background set is represented by a rectangle, as follows:

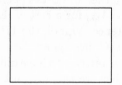

As in the case of closed curves, we also need some mechanism in order to make sure whether tokens of a rectangle represent the same background set or not.

For the given example, we will draw two closed curves within a rectangle to represent three sets: the set of unicorns, the set of red things and the background set. However, in order to represent the four pieces of information mentioned above, we should be able to represent the following sets: the set of non-red unicorns and the set of red unicorns.[2] We might need to represent the set of red non-unicorns and the set of non-red non-unicorns as well, depending upon the information we want to convey. The moral is to draw closed curves in such a way that we should be able to represent all of these sets in one diagram:

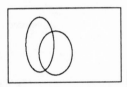

In addition to the background set, the set of unicorns and the set of red things, the overlapping closed curves make a distinction among the set of red unicorns, the set of non-red unicorns, the set of red non-unicorns and the set of non-red non-unicorns. This feature should be incorporated not only into the syntax of this system, that is, into the formation rules, but into the semantics of this system in the following way: Two sets represented by two disjoint areas do not share any element. And a background set, which a rectangle represents, is divided exhaustively by the sets represented by the enclosed areas which are included in the rectangle.[3]

So far, we discussed how this system represents sets. Now what we need is a way to represent relations between sets. For example, the information that all unicorns are red conveys information about a certain relation between the set of unicorns and the set of red things. That is, every member of the former set is also a member of the latter set. However, this relation can be expressed in terms of the set of non-red unicorns. That is, the set of non-red unicorns is empty. In the previous paragraph, we suggested that this system should represent the set of non-red unicorns. Therefore the problem of representing relations between sets reduces to the problem of representing the emptiness or non-emptiness of sets. For the emptiness of a set, we shade the whole area which represents the set. In order to represent

---

[2] "All unicorns are red" conveys the information that the set of non-red unicorns is empty, while "Some unicorns are not red" conveys the opposite information, that is, the set of non-red unicorns is not empty. "No unicorn is red" says that the set of red unicorns is empty, while "Some unicorns are red" says the opposite.

[3] After establishing the semantics, we can prove that these two desired features are expressed in this semantics. For more detail, see Shin 1990.

that a set is not empty, we put down $\otimes$ in the area representing the set. If the set is represented by more than one area, we draw $\otimes$ in each area and connect the $\otimes$'s by lines. For this, we adopt the expression $\otimes^n$ ($n \geq 1$) and call it an X-sequence. Each X-sequence consists of a finite number of X's and (possibly) lines. The formation rules, which will be discussed in Section 2.3, deal with each object in detail.

1.2 Primitive Objects

We assume we are given the following sequence of distinct diagrammatic objects to which we give names as follows:

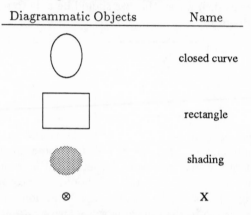

Diagrammatic Objects	Name
	closed curve
	rectangle
	shading
$\otimes$	X

How can we talk about diagrams or parts of diagrams of this system? In the case of linguistic representation systems, we adopt the convention to use quotation marks. For this visual representation system, I suggest that we write down a letter for the name of each diagram or each closed curve or each rectangle. Introducing letters as names (not as part of the language but as a convention for our convenience) solves our problem of how to mention diagrams, rectangles or closed curves. But, how do we mention the rest of our system, i.e., shadings and X's?

First, let me introduce three terms for our further discussion—region, basic region and minimal region. By *region*, I mean any enclosed area in a diagram. By *basic region*, I mean a region enclosed by a rectangle or by a closed curve. By *minimal region*, I mean a region within which no other region is included. The set of regions of a diagram D (let us name it $RG(D)$) is the smallest set satisfying the following clauses:

1. Any basic region of diagram D is in $RG(D)$.
2. If R_1 and R_2 are in set $RG(D)$, then so are the intersection of R_1 and R_2, the union of R_1 and R_2, and the difference between R_1 and R_2.

For reasons that we will see soon, we need to refer to the regions of a diagram. We can name the regions which are made up of rectangles or closed curves by using the names of the rectangles and closed curves. For example, in the following diagram,

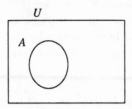

there are three regions—a part enclosed by a rectangle, U, a part enclosed by a closed curve, A, and a part enclosed by U and not by A. As said above, let us name a region after the name of the closed curve or the rectangle which encloses it. So, the first region is region U and the second is region A. Since the third region is the difference between region U and region A, I name it region $U - A$. Let us think of the case in which some closed curves overlap with each other, as in the following example:

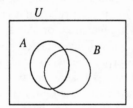

We refer to the region intersected by both region A and region B as region *A-and-B*, and refer to the region which is the union of region A and region B as region $A + B$.

To implement these ideas, we get the following conventions for naming the regions:

1. A basic region enclosed by a closed curve, say closed curve A, or enclosed by a rectangle, say rectangle U, is named region A or region U.

Let R_1 and R_2 be regions. Then,

2. A region which is the intersection of R_1 and R_2 is named R_1-*and*-R_2.
3. A region which is the union of R_1 and R_2 is named $R_1 + R_2$.
4. A region which is the difference between R_1 and R_2 is named $R_1 - R_2$.

Recalling the definition of set $\mathrm{RG}(D)$ (the set of regions of diagram D) given above, we know that this convention of naming the regions exhausts the cases.

Let us go back to the question of how to talk about shadings and X's. As we will see soon, any shading or any X of any diagram (at least any interesting diagram) is in some region. Now, in order to mention these constituents of our language we can refer to them in terms of the names of the smallest regions. For example, we can refer to a shading or an X which is in region A (where A is the smallest region with these constituents) as the shading in region A or the X in region A.

Before moving to the formation rules of this system, we need to discuss one more point mentioned in the preliminary remarks: a relation among closed-curve-tokens and a relation among rectangle-tokens. Suppose that the following are given to us:

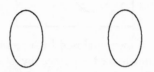

How can we tell whether these two closed curves represent different sets or not? It depends on whether a user of the Venn diagrams intends to represent the same set or different sets by these two tokens of the closed curve. Accordingly, the relation in which we are interested is the relation that holds among closed-curve-tokens or among rectangle-tokens which represent the same set. Let us name this relation a counterpart relation. Then, we can think of the following features for this special relation: First of all, this relation should be an equivalence relation among basic regions of given diagrams. Second, a counterpart relation holds only among tokens of the same type—among closed curves-tokens or among rectangle-tokens. Third, since a user would not draw two closed curves within one diagram to represent the same set, we want to say that within one diagram a counterpart relation does not hold among distinct basic regions.

Given diagrams $D_1, \ldots, D_n$, let a counterpart relation (let us call it set cp) be an equivalence relation on the set of basic regions of $D_1, \ldots, D_n$, satisfying the following:

1. If $\langle A, B \rangle \in cp$, then both A and B are either closed curves or rectangles.
2. If $\langle A, B \rangle \in cp$, then <u>either</u> A is identical to B <u>or</u> A and B are in different diagrams.

Within one diagram, every basic region enclosed by a closed curve or a rectangle has only one counterpart, that is, itself. Therefore, we have only one cp set. However, when more than one diagram is given, there would not be a unique set cp. For example, with regard to the following diagrams,

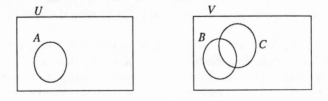

each of the following sets satisfies the conditions of set cp:

1. $\{\langle U, U \rangle, \langle V, V \rangle, \langle A, A \rangle, \langle B, B \rangle, \langle C, C \rangle\}$
2. $\{\langle U, U \rangle, \langle V, V \rangle, \langle A, A \rangle, \langle B, B \rangle, \langle C, C \rangle, \langle U, V \rangle, \langle V, U \rangle\}$
3. $\{\langle U, U \rangle, \langle V, V \rangle, \langle A, A \rangle, \langle B, B \rangle, \langle C, C \rangle, \langle A, B \rangle, \langle B, A \rangle\}$
4. $\{\langle U, U \rangle, \langle V, V \rangle, \langle A, A \rangle, \langle B, B \rangle, \langle C, C \rangle, \langle A, C \rangle, \langle C, A \rangle\}$
5. $\{\langle U, U \rangle, \langle V, V \rangle, \langle A, A \rangle, \langle B, B \rangle, \langle C, C \rangle, \langle U, V \rangle, \langle V, U \rangle, \langle A, B \rangle, \langle B, A \rangle\}$
6. $\{\langle U, U \rangle, \langle V, V \rangle, \langle A, A \rangle, \langle B, B \rangle, \langle C, C \rangle, \langle U, V \rangle, \langle V, U \rangle, \langle A, C \rangle, \langle C, A \rangle\}$

Among these equivalence relations, a user chooses set cp for each occasion. For example, if a user intends to represent the same set with A and C and the same set with U and V, then this user chooses the sixth equivalence relation as set cp. Some user might intend to represent the same set by A and B and the same set by U and V. In this case, the fifth relation above will be the set cp the user chooses. Or, some user might intend to represent different sets by each closed curve and by each rectangle. In this case, the user chooses set cp such that all of its elements consist of a basic region and itself—the first relation above.

1.3   Well-Formed Diagrams

We assumed that any finite combination of diagrammatic objects is a diagram. However, not all of the diagrams are well-formed diagrams, just as not all of the expressions are well-formed formulas in sentential logic or first-order logic. The set of well-formed diagrams, say $\mathcal{D}$, is the smallest set satisfying the following rules:

1. Any rectangle drawn in the plane is in set $\mathcal{D}$.
2. If D is in the set $\mathcal{D}$, then if D' results by adding a closed curve interior to the rectangle of D by the partial-overlapping rule (described below), then D' is in set $\mathcal{D}$.

   Partial-overlapping rule: A new closed curve should overlap *every* existent minimal region, but *only* once and *only* part of each minimal region.
3. If D is in the set $\mathcal{D}$, and if D' results by shading some entire region of D, then D' is in set $\mathcal{D}$.
4. If D is in the set $\mathcal{D}$, and if D' results by adding an X to a minimal region of D, then D' is in set $\mathcal{D}$.
5. If D is in the set $\mathcal{D}$, and if D' results by connecting existing X's by lines (where each X is in different regions), then D' is in set $\mathcal{D}$.

According to this recursive definition, every well-formed diagram should have one and only one rectangle. It also tells us that if there is any closed curve on a diagram, it should be in the rectangle. Therefore, this definition rules out all the following diagrams as ill-formed:

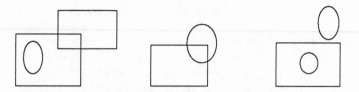

Let me illustrate through examples how the partial-overlapping rule in clause 2 works. By the first clause, for any well-formed diagram there should be a rectangle in it. Let us name it U as follows:

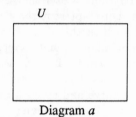

Diagram a

First, let us try to draw a new closed curve, A. How does this partial-overlapping rule work? In Diagram a, there is only one minimal region—the region U. The new closed curve A should be drawn to overlap a part of this existent region. Therefore,

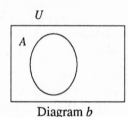

Diagram b

Next, I am going to draw another new closed curve, B, on this sheet of paper. In Diagram b, there are two minimal regions—region A and region $U - A$. According to this partial-overlapping rule, the new closed curve B should overlap each of these two regions, but only partially and only once. That is,

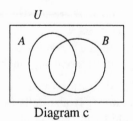

Diagram c

Therefore, the following diagrams are ruled out:

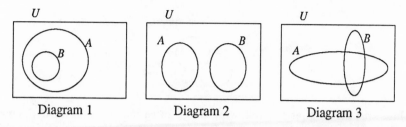

Diagram 1	Diagram 2	Diagram 3

In Diagram 1, one minimal region—region $U - A$—is not overlapped by the new closed curve B. In Diagram 2, one minimal region—region A—is not overlapped by B at all. In Diagram 3, minimal region $U - A$ is overlapped by the new closed curve B twice.

Next, we want to draw one more closed curve, C. All the following diagrams are eliminated:

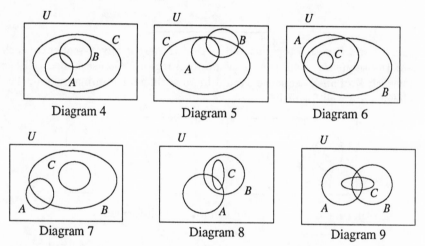

Diagram 4	Diagram 5	Diagram 6
Diagram 7	Diagram 8	Diagram 9

Diagram c on page 590 has four minimal regions—region $U - (A + B)$, region $A - B$, region A-and-B and region $B - A$. We have to make sure that the third closed curve, C, should overlap every part of these four minimal regions. That is,

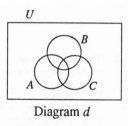

Diagram d

Clause 3 says that, a shading, if there is any, should fill up region(s). Therefore, the following is not well-formed:

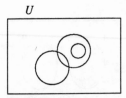

Clause 4 tells us that the following diagram cannot be well-formed, since an X is not in a minimal region. It is in region B. However, region B is not a minimal region:

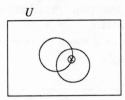

Clause 4 and Clause 5 together tell us that if there is any X-sequence, each X of the sequence should be in a minimal region. Clause 5 also tells us that each X of an X-sequence should be in a different minimal region. The following are well-formed:

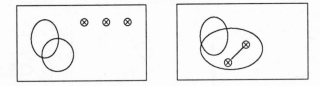

On the other hand, the following cannot be well-formed:

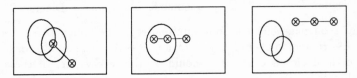

From now on, let us abbreviate a "well-formed diagram" by a "*wfd*."

2 Semantics

As discussed in the preliminary remarks, this representation system aims to represent sets and certain relations among those sets. I think that two kinds of homomorphisms are needed for this representation system, one for the representation of sets and the other for the representation of relations among sets. Based on these two homomorphisms (which are defined in Section 2.1 and Section 2.2 respectively), we will formalize what it is for one diagram to follow from other diagrams in Section 2.3.

2.1 From Regions to Sets

Each basic region, which is made by a closed curve or a rectangle, represents a set. Since we are concerned with well-formed diagrams, let us define the set BRG to be the set of all basic regions of well-formed diagrams. Let $\mathcal{D}$ be a set of well-formed diagrams. That is,

$$\text{BRG} = \{\text{a basic region of } D \mid D \in \mathcal{D} \}.$$

Let U be a non-empty domain. Then, for any function f such that

$$f \colon \text{BRG} \to \mathcal{P}(U), \text{ where if } \langle A, B \rangle \in cp, \text{ then } f(A) = f(B),$$

we can extend this function to get the mapping from set RG—the set of all regions of diagrams in set $\mathcal{D}$—to $\mathcal{P}(U)$. This extended relation is a homomorphism between regions and sets. That is,

$\overline{f} \colon \text{RG} \to \mathcal{P}(U)$, where

1. $\overline{f}(A) = f(A)$ if $A \in \text{BRG}$.
2. $\overline{f}(A) = \overline{f}(A_1) - \overline{f}(A_2)$ if $A = A_1 - A_2$.
3. $\overline{f}(A) = \overline{f}(A_1) \cap \overline{f}(A_2)$ if $A = A_1\text{-}and\text{-}A_2$.
4. $\overline{f}(A) = \overline{f}(A_1) \cup \overline{f}(A_2)$ if $A = A_1 + A_2$.

2.2 From Facts to Facts

Among the primitive objects of this system listed in Section 1.1, rectangle-tokens and closed-curve-tokens make up regions, and these regions represent sets as seen above. The other objects—a shading and an X—represent certain facts about the sets represented by the regions in which these constituents are drawn. The following are important representational relations in this system:

- A shaded region represents the empty set.
- A region with an X-sequence represents a non-empty set.

How do we define this representational relation? We want to define a function between facts about regions of a diagram and facts about sets of a situation. There are many facts about regions of a diagram. However, as said before, not all of them are representing facts. The function we have in mind is concerned only with the representing facts in diagrams. What are the representing facts in this system? The two kinds of representational relations listed above show us what the representing facts are:

1. A region, say A, is shaded.
2. An X-sequence is in a region, say A.

There is something to note about the second statement. This statement can be ambiguous in the following sense: If an X-sequence is in region A, then we can say that the X-sequence is also in region B if region A is a part of region B. For example, it is true that the X-sequence, $\otimes^2$, is in region A in the following diagram:

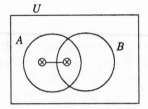

However, it is also true that the X-sequence is in region $A + B$, or in region U. In this case, we are concerned with the smallest region with the X-sequence. Since each $\otimes$ of the X-sequence is in a minimal region in a *wfd*, the union of the minimal regions with $\otimes$ is the smallest region with the X-sequence. Now, we can express the representing facts (listed above) by means of situation-theoretic terminology—infons—as follows:

(1)　$\langle\!\langle$ shaded, $A; 1 \rangle\!\rangle$.

(2)　$\langle\!\langle$ In, $\otimes^n, A; 1 \rangle\!\rangle$, where $A = A_1 + \cdots + A_n$, and for every $1 \le i \le n$, A_i is a minimal region with $\otimes$.

What are the facts that these representing facts represent? Based upon the homomorphism $\overline{f}$ defined above, let us express these represented facts by means of situation-theoretic terminology:

(1′)　$\langle\!\langle$ Empty, $\overline{f}(A); 1 \rangle\!\rangle$

(2′)　$\langle\!\langle$ Empty, $\overline{f}(A); 0 \rangle\!\rangle$

If these were all representing facts, then we would have to say that the following two diagrams contain the same representing facts:

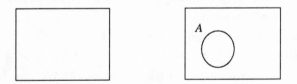

However, we want to say that these two diagrams represent different facts. Intuitively, we want to say that the diagram on the right hand represents the set A along with the background set, while the left diagram does not represent any set, except the background set. Therefore, I want to add one more representing fact:

(3)　$\langle\!\langle$ Region, $A; 1 \rangle\!\rangle$

The following fact is represented by this representing fact:

(3′)　$\langle\!\langle$ Set, $\overline{f}(A); 1 \rangle\!\rangle$

Let $\mathcal{D}$ be a set of well-formed diagrams. Let $\mathcal{D}$-*Facts* be the set of the facts about diagrams in $\mathcal{D}$. That is,

$$\mathcal{D}\text{-}Facts = \{\alpha \mid D \models \alpha \text{ and } D \in \mathcal{D}\}, \text{ where}$$
$$D \models \alpha \text{ iff } \alpha \text{ is true of the diagram } D.$$

Let S-$Facts$ be as follows: (Suppose that U is a non-empty domain.)

$$S\text{-}Facts = \{\alpha \mid \alpha = \langle\!\langle \text{Empty}, a; i\rangle\!\rangle \text{ or } \langle\!\langle \text{Set}, a; 1\rangle\!\rangle\}, \text{ where}$$
$$i \in \{0,1\} \text{ and } a \in \mathcal{P}(U).$$

Since not all of the facts about diagrams are representing facts, the homomorphism between $\mathcal{D}$-$Facts$ and S-$Facts$ must be partial. Define a homomorphism h from facts about diagrams to facts about sets as follows:

$$h(\langle\!\langle \text{Shaded}, A; 1\rangle\!\rangle) = \langle\!\langle \text{Empty}, \overline{f}(A); 1\rangle\!\rangle,$$
$$h(\langle\!\langle \text{In}, \otimes^n, A; 1\rangle\!\rangle) = \langle\!\langle \text{Empty}, \overline{f}(A); 0\rangle\!\rangle.$$
$$h(\langle\!\langle \text{Region}, A; 1\rangle\!\rangle) = \langle\!\langle \text{Set}, \overline{f}(A); 1\rangle\!\rangle.$$

2.3 Content of a Diagram

In a deductive system, the semantics of the system allows one to define what it is for a sentence (of the language) to follow from a set of other sentences (of the language). In the case of sentential logic, *wff* α follows from a set Γ of *wff*s if and only if every truth assignment which satisfies every member of Γ also satisfies α. In the case of first-order logic, sentence α follows from a set Γ of sentences if and only if every model of Γ is also a model of α. In either case, a definition for a logical consequence seems to fit our intuition that a conclusion follows from the premises if the truth of the premises guarantees the truth of the conclusion.

What we want is for the semantics of VENN to define a similar kind of inference between a *wfd* and a set of *wfd*s. What is it for one *wfd* to follow from a set of other *wfd*s, using the analogy of deductive systems? I think that in this representation system, the content of a *wfd* is a counterpart of truth assignment (in sentential logic) or of structure (in first-order logic). As a logical consequence relation between *wff*s is defined in terms of the truth values of *wff*s, we can expect a similar consequence relation between *wfd*s to be defined in terms of the contents of *wfd*s, as follows:

(1) *Wfd* D follows from a set Δ of *wfd*s (written $\Delta \models D$) iff the content of the diagrams in Δ involves the content of the diagram D.

Therefore, we need to formalize the content of a diagram and the involvement relation between the contents of diagrams.

What is the content of a diagram? By the two homomorphisms defined in Section 2.1 and Section 2.2, we can draw a diagram to represent certain facts of the situations about which we aim to reason. Also, we can talk about what a diagram represents—the content of a diagram. Therefore, the content of a well-formed diagram D, $Cont(D)$, is defined as the set of the represented facts:

$$Cont(D) = \{h(\alpha) \mid D \models \alpha \text{ and } D \in \mathcal{D}\},$$

where h is the homomorphism defined above.

Suppose Δ is a set of *wfds*. Then, the content of the diagrams in this set (say, $Cont(\Delta)$) is the union of the contents of every diagram in Δ. So,

$$Cont(\Delta) = \bigcup_{D \in \Delta} Cont(D)$$

What does it mean that the content of *wfds* in Δ involves the content of *wfd* D? Let us express this as $Cont(\Delta) \Rightarrow Cont(D)$. Here, I use Barwise's and Etchemendy's infon algebra scheme (1990) to define the relation between the contents of diagrams.

Let U be a set such that it is a universe of objects. Let Sit be a subset of $\mathcal{P}(\mathcal{P}(U))$ such that it is closed under $\cup$ and $-$. I define a situation s to be $s \in Sit$—a set of subsets of U closed under $\cup$, and $-$. Let σ be a basic infon such that $\sigma = \langle\langle R, a; i \rangle\rangle$, where $R \in \{$Empty, Set$\}$, a is a set and $i \in \{0, 1\}$. I define what it means for a basic infon σ to be supported by one of these situations s, as follows:

$$s \models \langle\langle \text{Empty}, x; 1 \rangle\rangle \quad \text{iff} \quad x \in s \text{ and } x = \emptyset.$$
$$s \models \langle\langle \text{Empty}, x; 0 \rangle\rangle \quad \text{iff} \quad x \in s \text{ and } x \neq \emptyset.$$
$$s \models \langle\langle \text{Set}, x; 1 \rangle\rangle \quad \text{iff} \quad x \in s.$$

Let Σ_1 and Σ_2 be sets of infons. I define the involvement relation as follows:

(2) $\quad \Sigma_1 \Rightarrow \Sigma_2 \quad$ iff $\quad \forall_{s \in Sit}(\forall_{\alpha \in \Sigma_1} s \models \alpha \rightarrow \forall_{\beta \in \Sigma_2} s \models \beta)$

This formal scheme, expressed in (2), reshapes our intuitive idea on the inference of a *wfd* from a set of *wfds*, expressed in (1), as follows:

Definition 1 *Wfd* D *follows* from a set of *wfds* Δ ($\Delta \models D$) iff every situation which supports every member of $Cont(\Delta)$ also supports every member of $Cont(D)$ ($Cont(\Delta) \Rightarrow Cont(D)$).

Recall that our definition of the content of a *wfd* tells us the information that the diagram conveys. Then, the content of the diagrams in Δ involves the content of the diagram D if and only if the information of diagram D is extractable from the information of the diagrams in Δ. Therefore, the above definition for $\Delta \models D$ reflects our intuition that a valid inference is a process of extracting certain information from given information.

3 Rules of Transformation

In this section, I aim to define what it is to obtain a diagram from some other diagrams.

Definition 2 Let Δ be a set of *wfds* and D be a *wfd*. *Wfd* D is *obtainable* from a set Δ of *wfds* ($\Delta \vdash D$) iff there is a sequence of *wfds* $\langle D_1, \ldots, D_n \rangle$ such that $D_n \equiv D$[4] and for each $1 \leq k \leq n$ <u>either</u>

---

[4] D_1 is equivalent to D_2 if and only if (i) every basic region of D_1 has a counterpart region in D_2 and vice versa, (ii) every shading of D_1 has a counterpart shading in D_2 and vice versa, (iii) every X-sequence of D_1 has a counterpart X-sequence in D_2 and vice versa. For more rigorous definition, refer to Section 2.3.2 of Shin 1990.

(a) there is some D' such that $D' \in \Delta$ and $D' \equiv D_k$, <u>or</u>

(b) there is some D' such that for some $i, j < k$, a rule of transformation allows us to get D' from either D_i or D_j (or both) and $D' \equiv D_k$.

We are concerned with transformations only from well-formed diagrams to well-formed diagrams. Therefore, let us assume that given diagrams are always well-formed. Also, it is assumed that we should not get an ill-formed diagram and should apply each rule within this limit so as to get only well-formed diagrams.[5]

R1: *The rule of erasure of a diagrammatic object*

We may copy[6] a *wfd* omitting a diagrammatic object, that is, a closed curve or a shading or a whole X-sequence. Let us go through examples for erasing each object.

(i) When we erase a closed curve, certain regions disappear. Shadings drawn in these regions are erased as well so that the resulting diagram is a *wfd*. In the following cases, the transformation from the left figure into the right one is done by the application of this rule.

(Case 1)

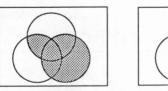

(Case 2)

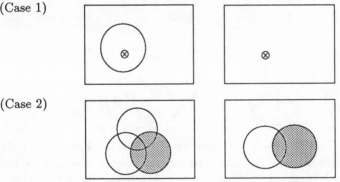

(ii) When we omit the shading in some region, we should erase the entire shading in a minimal region. Otherwise, we would get an ill-formed diagram. In the following case, this rule allows us to transform the diagrams on the left to the diagrams on the right.

(Case 3)

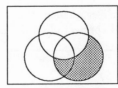

---

[5] Another alternative: We could formulate each rule in such a way as to prevent us from getting any ill-formed diagrams.

[6] If diagram D_1 is a *copy* of diagram D_2, then two diagrams are equivalent to each other. For more detail, see Shin 1990.

(iii) The erasure of a whole X-sequence allows the transformation from the left figure to the right one.

(Case 4)

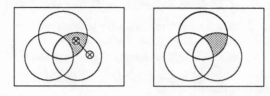

R2: *The rule of erasure of the part of an X-sequence*

We may copy a *wfd* omitting any part of an X-sequence only if that part is in a shaded region. That is, we may erase ⊗- or -⊗, only if the ⊗ in ⊗- or -⊗ is in a shaded region. Let's compare the following two cases:

(Case 5)

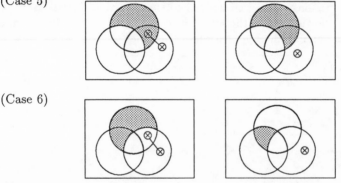

(Case 6)

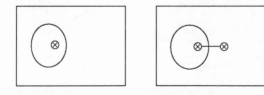

The transformation in case 5 is legitimate by this rule. However, we do not have any rule to allow the transformation in case 6. The part of the X-sequence which is erased in the diagram on the right, that is, -⊗, is not in the shaded part of the diagram on the left. Therefore, rule 2 does not allow this partial erasure. Rule 1 is concerned only with the erasure of a whole X-sequence, not with a proper sub-part of an X-sequence.

R3: *The rule of spreading X's*

If *wfd* D has an X-sequence, then we may copy D with ⊗ drawn in some other region and connected to the existing X-sequence. For example,

(Case 7)

(Case 8)

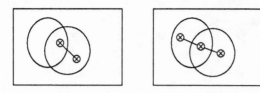

R4: *The rule of conflicting information*

If a diagram has a region with both a shading and an X-sequence, then we may transform this diagram to any diagram. This rule allows us to transform the diagram on the left to the diagram on the right.

(Case 9)

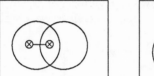 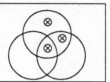

R5: *The rule of unification of diagrams*

We may unify two diagrams, D_1 and D_2, into one diagram, call it D, if the given cp relation contains the ordered pair of the rectangle of D_1 and the rectangle of D_2.

D is the *unification* of D_1 and D_2 if the following conditions are satisfied:

1. The rectangle and the closed curves of D_1 are copied[7] in D.
2. The closed curves of D_2 which do not stand in the given cp relation to any of the closed curves of D_1 are copied in D. (Note: Since D is a *wfd*, the partial overlapping rule should be observed.)
3. For any region A shaded in D_1 or D_2, the $\overline{cp}$-related region[8] to A of D should be shaded.
4. For any region A with an X-sequence in D_1 or D_2, an X-sequence should be drawn in the $\overline{cp}$-related regions to A of D.

Let me illustrate this rule through several examples.

(Case 10) Two diagrams D_1, D_2 are given, where $\langle U_1, U_2 \rangle, \langle A_1, A_2 \rangle \in cp$:

---

[7] Let A and B be closed curves. If A is a *copy* of B, then $\langle regionA, region \rangle \in cp$.

[8] Given set cp, set $\overline{cp}$ is a binary relation on RG such that $\overline{cp}$ is the smallest set satisfying the following:

    1. If $\langle A, B \rangle \in cp$, then $\langle A, B \rangle \in \overline{cp}$.

Suppose that $\langle A, B \rangle \in \overline{cp}$ and $\langle C, D \rangle \in \overline{cp}$.

    2. If $A + C \in$ RG and $B + D \in$ RG, then $\langle A + C, B + D \rangle \in \overline{cp}$, $\langle A\text{-and-}C, B\text{-and-}D \rangle \in \overline{cp}$, $\langle A - C, B - D \rangle \in \overline{cp}$ and $\langle C - A, D - B \rangle \in \overline{cp}$.

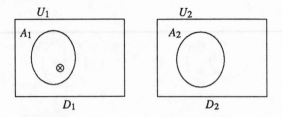

$$D_1 \qquad D_2$$

Since the given *cp* relation holds between the rectangle of D_1 and the rectangle of D_2, we can unify two diagrams. First, we copy the rectangle and the closed curve of D_1 and name them U_3 and A_3 respectively. Accordingly, $\langle U_1, U_3 \rangle$, $\langle A_1, A_3 \rangle \in cp$. Since the closed curve of D_2, i.e., A_2, is *cp*-related to the closed curve of D_1, i.e., A_1, we do not add any closed curve. An X in region A_1 of D_1 should be drawn in region A_3 of D, since A_1 and A_3 are $\overline{cp}$-related and A_3 is a minimal region. Therefore, we obtain diagram D:

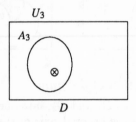

$$D$$

(Case 11) Let $\langle U_1, U_2 \rangle \in cp$, and $\langle A_1, A_2 \rangle \notin cp$. Since A_2 is not *cp*-related to any closed curve in D_1, we draw the *cp*-related closed curve, i.e., A_4, in D, to get diagram D as follows (notice that the partial overlapping rule is observed):

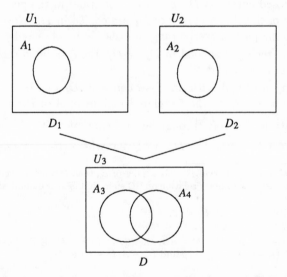

$$D$$

(Case 12) Let $\langle U_1, U_2 \rangle \in cp$, $\langle A_1, A_4 \rangle \in cp$, $\langle A_2, A_3 \rangle \notin cp$. By definition of set cp, $\langle A_1, A_2 \rangle \notin cp$, $\langle A_3, A_4 \rangle \notin cp$. Accordingly, $\langle A_1, A_3 \rangle \notin cp$ (since cp is an equivalence relation). After copying the rectangle and the closed curves of D_1, we need to copy closed curve A_3. Therefore, the following holds: $\langle U_1, U_3 \rangle$, $\langle U_2, U_3 \rangle$, $\langle A_1, A_5 \rangle$, $\langle A_4, A_5 \rangle$, $\langle A_2, A_6 \rangle$, $\langle A_3, A_7 \rangle \in cp$.

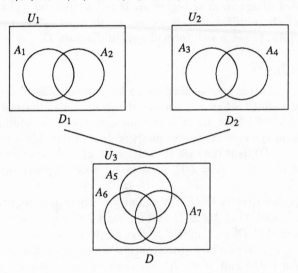

Now, we will see how this rule transforms diagrams with shadings or X-sequences into one diagram:

(Case 13) Let $\langle U_1, U_2 \rangle \in cp$ and $\langle A_1, A_3 \rangle$, $\langle A_2, A_3 \rangle \notin cp$.

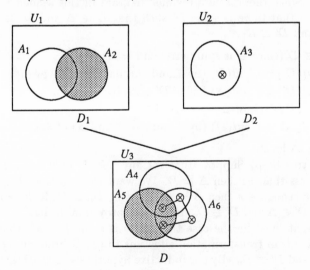

Suppose that closed curve A_4 is the copy of A_1, A_5 is of A_2 and A_6 is of A_3. Accordingly, $\langle A_1, A_4 \rangle$, $\langle A_2, A_5 \rangle$, $\langle A_3, A_6 \rangle \in cp$. Clause 3 of the unification rule tells us that the shading in region A_2 of D_1 should be copied in the $\overline{cp}$-related region, i.e., region A_5, in diagram D. Our syntactic rule prevents us from copying the X in region A_3 into the $\overline{cp}$-related region, i.e., region A_6, in the unified diagram, since region A_6 is not a minimal region any more. Clause 4 of the unification rule guides us to draw $\otimes^4$ in the $\overline{cp}$-related region, i.e., A_6, to get a well-formed unified diagram D.

4   Soundness

We defined what it is for one diagram to follow from other diagrams. ($\Delta \models D$) We also defined what it is for one diagram to be obtained from other diagrams. ($\Delta \vdash D$) Now, we raise the question about the soundness of this representation system. Whenever one *wfd* D is obtainable from a set Δ of *wfds* (i.e., $\Delta \vdash D$), is it the case that the content of diagrams in Δ involves the content of D (i.e., $\Delta \models D$)? That is, we want to prove that if $\Delta \vdash D$, then $\Delta \models D$.

Proof. Suppose that $\Delta \vdash D$. By definition, there is a sequence of *wfds* $\langle D_1, \ldots, D_n \rangle$ such that $D_n \equiv D$ and for each $1 \leq k \leq n$ *either* (a)there is some D' such that $D' \in \Delta$ and $D' \equiv D_k$, *or* (b) there is some D' such that for some $i, j < k$, a rule of transformation allows us to get D' from either D_1 or D_2 (or both) and $D' \equiv D_k$. We show by induction on the length of a sequence of *wfds* that for any diagram D obtainable from Δ, the content of the diagrams in Δ involves the content of D.

(Basis Case) This is when the length of the sequence is 1. That is, $D_1 \equiv D$. Since there is no previous diagram in this sequence, it should be the case that there is some D' such that $D' \in \Delta$ and $D' \equiv D_1$. Since $D_1 \equiv D$ and $D' \equiv D_1$,

1. $D' \equiv D$ (since $\equiv$ is symmetric and transitive)
2. $Cont(D') = Cont(D)$ (by 1 and corollary 8.2 of Appendix B)
3. $Cont(D') \subseteq Cont(\Delta)$ (since $D' \in \Delta$, by the definition of $Cont(\Delta)$)
4. $Cont(D) \subseteq Cont(\Delta)$ (by 2 and 3)
5. $Cont(\Delta) \Rightarrow Cont(D)$ (by 4 and the definition of $\Rightarrow$)

Therefore, $\Delta \models D$.

(Inductive Step) Suppose that for any *wfd* D if D has a length of a sequence less than n, then $\Delta \models D$. We want to show that if *wfd* D has a length of a sequence n then $\Delta \models D$. That is, $D_n \equiv D$. If there is some D' such that $D' \in \Delta$ and $D' \equiv D_n$, then as we proved in the basis case, $\Delta \models D$. Otherwise, it must be the case that there is some D' such that for some $i, j < n$, a rule of transformation allows us to get D' from either D_1 or D_2 (or both) and $D' \equiv D_n$. By our inductive hypothesis, $\Delta \models D_i$ and $\Delta \models D_j$. That is, $Cont(\Delta) \Rightarrow Cont(D_i)$ and $Cont(\Delta) \Rightarrow Cont(D_j)$. Therefore,

$Cont(\Delta) \Rightarrow (Cont(D_i) \cup Cont(D_j))$. Since each rule of transformation is valid,[9] if D' is obtained by either D_i or D_j, then $(Cont(D_i) \cup Cont(D_j)) \Rightarrow Cont(D')$. By the transitivity of the involvement relation, it is the case that $Cont(\Delta) \Rightarrow Cont(D')$. Since $D' \equiv D_n$ and $D_n \equiv D$, $D' \equiv D$. Hence, $Cont(D') = Cont(D)$. Accordingly, $Cont(\Delta) \Rightarrow Cont(D)$. Therefore, $\Delta \models D$. $\qquad\square$

5 Completeness

In this section, we raise the question about the completeness of this representation system. Whenever the content of diagrams in Δ involves the content of D (i.e., $\Delta \models D$), is it the case that one *wfd* D is obtainable from a set Δ of *wfds* (i.e., $\Delta \vdash D$) in this system?

5.1 Closure Content

According to the definition of the content of a diagram in Section 2.3, given a homomorphism, the representing facts of a diagram determine the content of the diagram. However, according to the definition of the involvement in Section 2.3, the content of a diagram might involve more than its content itself. For example, the following diagram supports only two infons—$\langle\!\langle In, \otimes^2, A; 1 \rangle\!\rangle$ and $\langle\!\langle Shaded, A\text{-}and\text{-}B; 1 \rangle\!\rangle$:

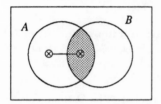

Hence, $Cont(D) = \{\langle\!\langle Empty, \overline{f}(A); 0 \rangle\!\rangle, \langle\!\langle Empty, \overline{f}(A\text{-}and\text{-}B); 1 \rangle\!\rangle\}$. However, the content of this diagram involves other sets of infons as well. For example, $\{\langle\!\langle Empty, \overline{f}(A - B); 0 \rangle\!\rangle, \langle\!\langle Empty, \overline{f}(A + B); 0 \rangle\!\rangle\}$ is involved by the content of this diagram. That is, the content of the diagram above involves the content of the following diagram:

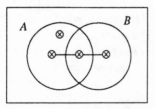

If we unify these two diagrams by the unification rule, then the content of the unified diagram is involved in the content of these two diagrams.

---

[9]For the proof, refer to Shin 1990.

Here, we are interested in the maximal content involved by the content of a given diagram. Let $Closure\text{-}Cont(D)$ be a set such that it is the maximal content involved by the content of diagram D. That is,

$$Closure\text{-}Cont(D) = \{\alpha \mid Cont(D) \Rightarrow \{\alpha\}\}.$$

By the definition of $Closure\text{-}Cont(D)$, we know that $Cont(D) \Rightarrow Closure\text{-}Cont(D)$. We also know that $Cont(D)$ is a subset of $Closure\text{-}Cont(D)$. Therefore, by the definition of involvement relation, $Closure\text{-}Cont(D) \Rightarrow Cont(D)$. We can prove[10] that for any diagram D which does not convey conflicting information[11] VENN allows us to obtain a diagram whose content is the maximal content of D.

5.2 Maximal Representation

Let us extend this idea to a set of diagrams. In Section 2.3 we defined the content of diagrams in Δ (i.e., $Cont(\Delta)$) as the union of the contents of diagrams in Δ. Here we define the closure content of diagrams in Δ as the set of the maximal content involved by $Cont(\Delta)$. That is,

$$Closure\text{-}Cont(\Delta) = \{\alpha \mid Cont(\Delta) \Rightarrow \{\alpha\}\}$$

We know that $Cont(\Delta) \Rightarrow Closure\text{-}Cont(\Delta)$ and $Closure\text{-}Cont(\Delta) \Rightarrow Cont(\Delta)$. By the induction of the cardinality of set $Cont(\Delta)$, we can prove the following interesting theorem[12]:

Maximal Representation Theorem. *Given set Δ of diagrams, there is a diagram D such that $\Delta \vdash D$, where $Cont(D) = Closure\text{-}Cont(\Delta)$.*

5.3 Completeness

Now, we want to prove that if $\Delta \models D$ then $\Delta \vdash D$.

Proof. Suppose that $\Delta \models D$. That is, $Cont(D)$ is involved by $Cont(\Delta)$. Hence, $Cont(D) \subseteq (Closure\text{-}Cont(\Delta))$. Maximal Representation theorem tells us that diagram D' whose content is $Closure\text{-}Cont(\Delta)$ is obtainable from Δ. Therefore, $Cont(D) \subseteq Cont(D')$. It suffices to show that $\{D'\} \vdash D$.

If $Cont(D) = Cont(D')$, then D' is what we want.

If $Cont(D) \subset Cont(D')$, check what $Cont(D') - Cont(D)$ is. What could be a difference in the content among two diagrams? In other words, what kind of different representing facts can two diagrams support? We can think of three kinds of representing facts which can make a difference in the content between two diagrams: Whether one region is shaded or

---

[10]Refer to Theorem 9 of Appendix C of Shin 1990.

[11]That is, D does not have a region both with a shading and an X-sequence. If D has a region both with a shading and an X-sequence, then by rule of conflicting information we can get any diagram. It is also uninteresting.

[12]For the proof, refer to Appendix C of Shin 1990.

not, whether one region has an X-sequence or not, and whether one closed curve exists or not.[13] In each case, we apply the following procedure:

(i) If $\langle\!\langle$Empty, $a; 1\rangle\!\rangle \in (Cont(D') - Cont(D))$, then apply the rule of erasure of a primitive object to D' to erase a shading.

(ii) If $\langle\!\langle$Empty, $a; 0\rangle\!\rangle \in (Cont(D') - Cont(D))$, then apply the rule of erasure of a primitive object to D' and erase an X-sequence.

(iii) If $\langle\!\langle$Set, $a; 1\rangle\!\rangle \in (Cont(D') - Cont(D))$(where there is a basic region A such that $f(A) = a$), then apply the rule of erasure of a primitive object to erase closed curve A from D'.

We removed (from diagram D') the representing facts which make a difference in these two sets. Hence, we get diagram D such that $\{D'\} \vdash D$ where $Cont(D') - Cont(D)$, that is, $Cont(D) \subseteq (Closure\text{-}Cont(\Delta))$. $\square$

References

Barwise, J., and J. Etchemendy. 1990. Visual Information and Valid Reasoning. In *Visualization in Mathematics*, ed. W. Zimmerman. Washington, DC: Mathematical Association of America.

Gardner, M. 1982 (1958). *Logic Machines and Diagrams*, 2nd ed. Chicago: Univeristy of Chicago Press.

Shin, S. J. 1990. An Analysis of Inference Involving Venn Diagrams. Stanford University.

Venn, J. 1886. *Symbolic Logic*. New York (1971): Burt Franklin.

---

[13]Since both diagrams are well-formed, it is impossible that two diagrams have the equivalent basic regions but not the equivalent regions.

26

Reasoning with Words, Pictures, and Calculi: Computation Versus Justification

KEITH STENNING AND JON OBERLANDER

1 Introduction

This paper takes as its starting point the work on the Hyperproof system, reported in Barwise and Etchemendy 1990a,b. The authors of that paper argued that reasoning with and about graphical objects has certain properties that distinguish it from reasoning with and about sentences of a logical language. They further argued that graphical reasoning need not be simply 'heuristic': within a situation-theoretic framework, it can be treated just as formally as any more traditional variety of reasoning; and that it is perfectly sound. We applaud their motivation in attempting to rehabilitate graphical reasoning methods; but in this paper, we argue that a full account of the differences between graphical and language-based reasoning will require a psychological characterization; given the prevailing paradigm in the cognitive sciences, this means a *computational* characterization. The question then arises: what constraints does our choice of foundational account place upon possible implementational accounts?

We first sketch the features of Hyperproof that will be relevant to our discussion, and then introduce a distinction between the justification and performance of inference. This raises the issue of the distance between foundational and implementational accounts of reasoning. We urge that what makes graphical reasoning interesting must be given an implementational account. To this end, we then outline a cognitive theory of graphical, as compared to linguistic, representations. The central features of our account are that graphical representations are one sort of representation which exhibit a property we call 'specificity'; that this property brings with it ease of processing; and that processing considerations make natural language

Situation Theory and Its Applications, vol. 2.
Jon Barwise, Jean Mark Gawron, Gordon Plotkin, and Syun Tutiya, eds.
Copyright © 1991, Stanford University.

discourse conventions stay closer to graphics in this respect than do fully abstractive logical languages. Furthermore, we propose an explanation of why graphical techniques such as Euler's Circles and Venn diagrams for teaching abstract reasoning are so didactically effective; the explanation trades on the fact that the internal working memory representations we use in some reasoning tasks share with graphical representations the property of specificity.

2   Starting Point: Hyperproof

Barwise and Etchemendy's Hyperproof is a tutorial program designed to teach students of logic how to establish proofs using logical formulae. Students start out with little knowledge of logic, and learn how to construct proofs by comparing and contrasting the information presented in the formal language they are learning with visual representations of the same information. To this end, proofs can involve manipulating both symbols and graphical representations.

As well as its intended tutorial use, Hyperproof also serves theoretical ends. Part of its purpose is to illustrate the fact that proofs can be carried out using mixes of linguistic rules (as in natural deduction systems) and rules about possible graphical transformations; or even using purely graphical rules. These proofs are every bit as rigorous as the standard variety framed in traditional logical calculi.

The student is confronted with an interface like the one illustrated in Figure 1. In the example Barwise and Etchemendy (B&E) give in their paper, reasoning starts with the presentation of a diagrammatic world. This corresponds to the provision of a set of premises in a conventional calculus. Some additional information is then given in the form of several calculus statements (corresponding to additional premises). Problems of various sorts can then be posed: yes/no questions and proofs of the answers (corresponding to the posing of a target theorem and a request for proof or disproof); identifications (corresponding to uniqueness proofs); and more complex tasks, such as saying everything about an object that follows from the diagram and calculus statements.

The example B&E pursue is one of identification. The reasoning uses both information from the calculus premises and the diagrammatic 'premises' to draw a conclusion about a correspondence between a constant in the linguistic premises and an object represented in the diagram. The reasoning employs inference steps, such as splitting and merging cases, which specially 'exploit the power of visual representations in reasoning' (Barwise and Etchemendy 1990b). The calculus equivalent of these steps is the reduction of premises into disjunctive normal form. B&E observe that an equivalent proof in the calculus alone would take many more lines and they suggest that the proof, long and torturous, would be around 200–300

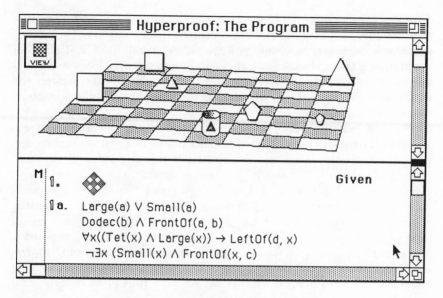

Figure 1 The Hyperproof Interface

lines long. Certainly, some proofs which involve relatively few graphical transformations may be more economical than others involving many sentential transformations.

The work on Hyperproof both illustrates and helps test a situation-theoretic account of mixed graphical-logical reasoning. Providing a uniform account of these diverse forms of reasoning is an essential component in a full account of graphical reasoning; but in indicating the formal grounding of graphical reasoning, it is easy to lose sight of another component in the full account. That is: we would like to know what it is about graphical reasoning that establishes its distinctive difficulty profile. A frequent, if informal observation, is that some pieces of information are 'free' in visual representations, but require explicit inference to locate in logical representations. For example, if A is to the left of B, and B is to the left of C, then we can transitively infer that A is to the left of C. There is a strong intuition that in a visual presentation of the same information, the conclusion (that A is to the left of C) is somehow 'already there'; it doesn't need to be computed from visual premises; it just needs to be read off the situation as it stands. A full account of graphical reasoning must show why it's *different* from logical reasoning, as well as how it's similar.

3   Inference: Justification and Performance

It is by now a common-place in the cognitive sciences that a competence theory of some of aspect of human behavior may not always be conveniently converted into a performance theory of the same behavior (see for instance Dennett 1987 or Clark 1990). A competence theory offers an explicit account of a behavior, in terms, perhaps, of representations and rules for transforming them. In the case of language use, we may focus our attention on the information resources required by the ideal speaker-hearer, and formulate a theory that will account for the grammaticality judgments of that ideal language user.

It might sometimes be deemed useful to proceed from this competence model to the construction of a performance model of a real speaker-hearer, using the same theoretical entities and relationships posited in the competence theory, now framed in processing terms. This happened with transformational grammar, it being be proposed that humans actually carry out transformations in processing a piece of language, converting a surface syntactic form into a deep structure, and thence into a logical form of some sort. This allowed particular empirical hypotheses about human performance to be framed, in the Derivational Theory of Complexity (Fodor, Bever, and Garret 1974, p. 320–8). For example, the more transformations required, the slower the reaction time of an experimental subject.

This piece of history exemplifies the yawning gap between competence and performance: the data indicated, to use Dennett's words, that the phases/steps or whatever of the competence theory had no correspondence in the actual phases and steps of the language users. Following Marr 1977, most cognitive scientists are now happy to hold that the computational level of explanation ($\approx$ competence theory), where what a function computes is described, is quite separable from the algorithmic level, where how a function is computed is specified. Doubts about the separability of levels notwithstanding (Foster 1990), we can maintain that if an account of two behaviors indicates that they are *at that level of explanation* equivalent in specifiable ways, then we must look to another level of explanation to account for the differences between those two behaviors.

This is the position with respect to a unified situation-theoretic account of graphical and logical reasoning. The framework accommodates these two modes of reasoning by (i) concentrating not on what users actually *do* when using Hyperproof, but on what they *could do* and (ii) showing that everything that can be done in one mode can ultimately be done in the other. One might wish to claim, with Barwise and Etchemendy, that there are some inferences which are valid in only one mode, or only when both are employed. However, our current discussion proceeds only from the weaker claim, that some inferences in Hyperproof require radically fewer operations when they are carried out within a graphical mode rather than a logical one.

According to the account we have just sketched, we now have to look to the algorithmic level performance theory to find out what makes the graphical mode *different* from the logical mode. And bearing in mind Dennett's warning, we should not automatically expect that the possession of a competence theory, however good, will make the specification of the performance theory any easier.

Another way of expressing this point is to observe (following Harman 1986) that logical proofs provide *justifications* for inference patterns; but they don't constitute *performances* of inference. Even on the most simple-minded view, in which we bring justification as close to performance as possible, to actually *execute* an inference, we must augment a logic with a theorem-prover. An account of human (or mechanical) inference must provide both formal foundations *and* computational implementations. And if we have a formal foundation that encompasses both logical and graphical reasoning, so much the better. But, to the extent that performance of inferences in these two modes diverges, the burden of explanation lies in locating the right implementations to lay upon the formal foundations.

Cognitive psychology is full of confusions which stem from the failure to realize that logics have to be implemented before they embody reasoning processes. It turns out that different implementations give very different 'difficulty profiles'. In particular, the data indicate that human memory does not lend itself to the obvious 'pencil-and-paper' implementation of natural deduction systems (see Johnson-Laird 1983; but also Braine 1978).

Thus, we agree with Barwise and Etchemendy that classical logical accounts of inference patterns neglect the importance of graphical reasoning. But we wish to emphasize that an explanation of the relative ease of various inferences in the two modes will require appeal to an implementational account. Indeed, a foundational account which captured the validity of a graphical inference in some way *inexpressible* in a logical language would still need a complementary implementational account. That's where we can explain the ease with which the putative graphical inference is computed.

4 A Cognitive Theory of Graphical Reasoning

Having emphasized the need for an implementational picture of the relation between graphics and logics, we need to demonstrate that an implementational account is at least possible. This section therefore elaborates one such account. First, we explore a particular property of graphical representations, and indicate which representation systems seem to possess this property. Then, we adduce certain observations about the architecture of human working memory. Finally, we put the theoretical characterization of graphical representations to work, by indicating how the proposed property can be used in conjunction with facts about working memory to explain human inferential performance in syllogism solving, and can explain the effectiveness of certain graphical reasoning devices.

4.1   Representations

First, then, let us sketch a rough outline of what is distinctive about graphical representations. In what follows, it is important to bear in mind that what we are calling graphical representations need not be visual, and that reasoning with them is not confined to agents with fully functional visual systems. In fact, although it is true that standard graphical devices (like line drawings or Venn Diagrams) possess various particular visual properties (such as size and position), we wish to concentrate on their more general computational properties. To see that the two are at extensionally separable, consider that Euler's Circles (to which we return below) could be embossed on paper, and used by blind reasoners. Although we know of no such studies, it is just as plausible that such embossed circles would be helpful to blind reasoners in similar ways.

It should also be observed that reasoning with an external visual aid is very different from reasoning without it, not least in terms of the additional memory load imposed on a reasoner with no external reminder of the problem statement. The fact that such aids can sometimes be 'internalized' should serve to remind us that an external visual aid is part of the overall reasoning system. But the same fact should not be taken to imply that assisted reasoning is reducible to unassisted reasoning.

The kernel of the theory is just this: what is special about graphical representations is that they (i) limit abstraction and that (ii) this has desirable computational consequences. In particular, (iii) human working memory is adapted to holding mappings with computational properties similar to graphical representations, and (iv) natural language (as opposed to artificial logical calculi) is also used under conventions which limit the use of available abstractive mechanisms.

In what ways, then, do graphics limit abstraction? In Hyperproof's graphical representation of a situation, certain facts about the situation are, so to speak, transparent. Given that different objects are constrained to occupy different regions of space-time, Hyperproof's representation faithfully places distinct objects at distinct locations. If I see two cubes in the picture, I know that these are *different* cubes, even if I do not know their names. By contrast, the expression of this distinctness information is less transparent in a logical formula: $\exists x \exists y \ Cube(x) \wedge Cube(y)$ is not the whole story: to say what the graphic says, we must add $x \neq y$. One way of expressing this is to say loosely that the graphical representation is more 'searchable' than the logical one, since all non-equalities are pre-computed. If we insisted that the constants of our logical representation accorded with a unique names hypothesis (different constant, different object), then we would endow the logic with the same searchability; but even under this assumption, distinctness information must still be explicitly stated in constant-free formulae encoding the same information.

This characteristic exemplifies a special property of graphical representation systems. We call this property 'specificity', and contrast it with 'abstraction'. Specificity is a property of representational *systems*, not of particular representations. Systems that demand the specification of information are said to be 'specific'. There are degrees of specificity and there are different types of information with regard to which a system may be specific. Such an observation is by no means new: Bishop Berkeley noted that geometry diagrams had this property: a triangle must be irregular, isosceles, or equilateral but the word 'triangle' can denote these three types indifferently.

The example above illustrated, in the context of the specification of identity information, that a logical language *can* specify (either by stating non-identities explicitly, or by using constants with a unique naming hypothesis). But such a representation system does not *have to* specify. By contrast, a graphical representation system must specify. As we will see below, it is, however possible to cancel some specifications.

To see what this intuitive characterization of specificity is meant to capture, consider the two extremes of highly-specific and highly-abstractive representation systems. At the specific extreme, we can find model enumeration algorithms which produce one representation per model; this is close to a truth-table like approach, where we provide a separate representation for each line of the truth table. At the abstractive extreme, there are languages in which we can find a propositional function for any partitioning of models. Note that although graphical systems are specific, systems can easily be specific without being graphical, as in a restricted language with no variables and obligatory unique names.

Between these extremes, we can discern a continuum of representation systems, starting with pictures and permitting greater and greater degrees of abstraction. We can explore this continuum by taking a piece of information, expressing it an extreme style of representation, and then refining it until we eventually reach the other end of the continuum. If we start at the abstract 'logical' end, we can gradually regiment the representation of the information until we reach the specific 'graphical' end.

Some stages along this dimension of 'regimentation' are illustrated by: a quantified abstraction; a disorderly text; an orderly text; and a sequence of successively more graphical tables. These latter are: an alphabetized table of intercity distances; the same table with cities ordered by longitude in the column labels and latitude in the row labels; and finally, a map.

First, then, consider a quantified abstraction. The elliptical example below doesn't contain as much information as the subsequent examples;

but it illustrates that the type of purely quantifier-variable description we have discussed can be extremely opaque.

> Something is to the north of something that is to the south of something that is the northernmost city ...

In particular, comparison with the final map will indicate that there are two ways of making the description true, depending on whether the 'something to the north ...' is taken to be the 'northernmost city' or not. The conventions for producing expository texts in natural language (and for resolving anaphors in them) are designed to help the reader to construct a unique model (Stenning 1978). Logically, the statement 'There is a cube and an object 5 squares back' is satisfied in models in which a single individual has both properties, but in an expository text, the statement introduces two distinct individuals.[1] The convention that logically independent indefinite descriptions will not be used to introduce the same individual licenses this inference.

Consider next the disorderly text, which uses names for the cities, and redundantly provides all the distance information that is relevant.

> A is four miles from C. B is two miles from A. C is four miles from A. C is five miles from B. A is two miles from B. B is five miles from C.

The relational information is presented in an order which, intuitively speaking, makes it hard to keep track of the overall situation. Compare this with the same textual information re-organized into a particular order, generating three pairs of sentences.

> A is two miles from B. A is four miles from C.
> B is two miles from A. B is five miles from C.
> C is four miles from A. C is five miles from B.

It's a relatively small step from this orderly text to a simple, alphabetically ordered table, encoding the same information once more. Here the column and row headings together with the cells' contents mutually define linguistically expressed propositions, but their arrangement in a table can allow search of the same type as that offered by a diagram.

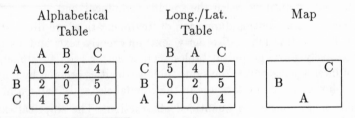

Alphabetical Table				Long./Lat. Table				Map

	A	B	C
A	0	2	4
B	2	0	5
C	4	5	0

	B	A	C
C	5	4	0
B	0	2	5
A	2	0	4

---

[1] We maintain that this is not a matter of logical form, but do not argue that here.

The degree to which the table facilitates inference depends on the congruence between the spatial relations it offers and the semantics of the statements it contains. The switch from the alphabetical city ordering to the geographical ordering brings the table into a closer congruence with the map, since the spatial relations between cells of the table now represent themselves. Finally, in the last version, the zeros in the earlier tables become the cities on the map.

Tables lie between words and pictures on the dimension of regimentation. Unless they are supplemented by quasi-verbal conventions, diagrams demand the determination of all spatial relations: you can't draw a picture without determining all spatial relations. Tables apparently demand more specificity than texts but less than diagrams. The minimal demands of tables are, in fact, very close to the conventions of ideal expository texts.

The last paragraph offers a reminder that actual graphical systems aren't in fact at the specific extreme. Quite apart from the possibility of their containing linguistic expressions as parts, ordinary diagrams frequently achieve some degree of abstraction by making one graphic stand for several models. Recall that the extreme of specificity lies where we use one graphic for every model. As soon as we allow a graphic to represent more than one model, it is abstracting information. An interpretative convention for the diagram may be either explicit, or understood.

For example, consider degenerate 2×2 tic-tac-toe diagrams. There are two possible symbols, O (nought) and X (cross), and so there are 16 possible diagrams. In the first instance, a particular diagram will stand for itself; it will partition the space of models into two parts, the first containing the diagram; the second containing all other diagrams. By introducing an interpretative convention, we can make a diagram partition the space of models in a different way; for example, we can fix it so that two models fall into the first partition. One such natural convention introduces a new symbol, the Blank, and glosses its meaning: 'Blanks mean unknown values'.

A table such as the left hand one, then means *either* the middle *or* the right.

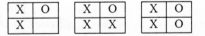

But it is not easy to fill in the single indeterminate left-hand table below to mean *either* the middle *or* the right-hand table,

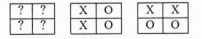

without also covering

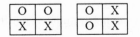

An 'indifference to rotation' convention does not partition the space in this way: it picks out the latter two diagrams as well. The example indicates that some abstractions are relatively easy to pick out using a single diagram augmented with an interpretative convention. Hence, representational systems using such diagrams escape from the extreme of specificity, but cannot achieve all abstractions. How to characterize 'natural' and 'unnatural' interpretative conventions remains for us an open question.

4.2 The Architecture of Working Memory: The Implementation of Binding

We have outlined the idea of specificity, and indicated the extent to which it can be found in graphical representations. To explain why graphical reasoning is sometimes easy, we need to put the property to work in a processing account. Basically, our view is that we can explain the role of specificity in processing by placing it within the context of a theory of the representations underlying human working memory. On this account, specificity makes for ease of processing (under some circumstances) because it enables the construction of determinate models of premises.

In more detail, on this theory of memory, the natural unit is the model: bindings between individuals and properties. Furthermore, only one model can be entertained at a time, unless by abstraction of interpretation. The representational system for memory thus exhibits specificity.

Diagrams and natural NL expositions of premises both impose a smaller memory load than unordered sets of calculus premises. However, there are substantial differences between them. Even when we compare performance with a continually present diagram and a continually present text (where we might naïvely expect no memory load), we can see that the diagram is easier to operate with. Our visual apparatus at least gives the illusion of 'immediate' access to information in a diagram to resolve a question posed. A text, by contrast, still has to be overtly scanned and inferences performed. But notice how part of the improved comprehensibility of our 'orderly text' above was gained via formatting decisions.

It is of course notorious that once the diagram (or the text, for that matter) disappears, memory load becomes apparent. Unless we have committed the information to memory, we lose it: I have picture of the Hyperproof example to hand as I type for that very reason. Nevertheless, the picture appears to provide this information in a form rather close to that in which it is stored in the working memory in which inferences are made. Similarly, the well ordered expository text approaches that form much more closely than randomized sentences (see, for example, Stenning 1986 Experiment 2, or Mani & Johnson-Laird 1982). An *explanation* of phenomena in visual and verbal reasoning demands an account of the computational properties of this memory.

Elsewhere, Stenning, Shepherd, and Levy (1988) presented experimen-

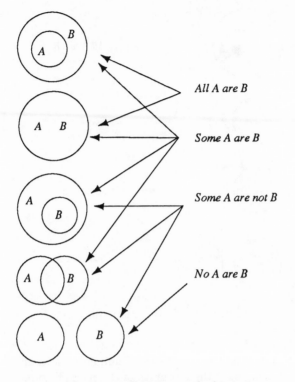

Figure 2 Gergonne relations

tal observations of performance on memory for mappings; Stenning and Levy (1988) proposed that the important characteristic of this memory is that it represents the binding of properties and relations to individuals in a distributed fashion; and that constraint satisfaction must be performed to retrieve information for use in reasoning processes. The constraint satisfaction device generally returns a model which satisfies the greatest subset of premises (the whole set may be inconsistent). The nature of the device means that it can return only one total model; not two, and not one partial model. A model is precisely a total mapping of properties onto individuals: it is in this sense that it requires *specificity*. These properties of working memory explain why the representational system in working memory exhibits the specificity it does.

4.3 Solving Syllogisms Using Graphical Representations

With this model of memory in place, we can sketch a theory of a reasoning system based on this memory system, thus providing an example of this approach to relations between graphics and language.

In particular, we can consider human performance in solving syllogisms,

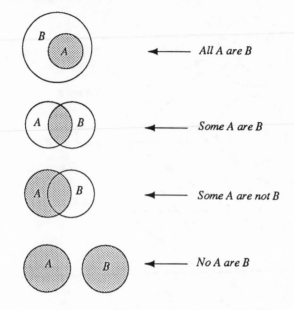

All A are B

Some A are B

Some A are not B

No A are B

Figure 3 Characteristic diagrams

as an example domain where graphics are historically important as didactic aids, and also in psychological theories of human performance. Syllogisms are expressible using only the resources of the monadic predicate calculus, and the search for counterexamples to conclusions can thus be carried out in finite domains. Although they are logically rather simple, some are also notoriously hard for humans to solve.

Despite Johnson-Laird's protestations to the contrary, mental models notation is provably equivalent to a standard interpretation of the more traditional Euler's Circles system (see Stenning and Oberlander in preparation). Here, we indicate how to move from a rather specific system of Euler Circles, which requires one diagram for each model, to a system which is more economical with diagrams, by abstracting over them and permitting the employment of strategies. The move involves the construction of a language by adding annotations and interpretative conventions to diagrams.

In the basic system, there are five diagram-types each relating two sets pictured as circles, as shown in Figure 2.

If we use a totally specific graphical approach to reasoning, using as many diagrams as are required for each sentence, then combining two premises leads to a combinatorial explosion, e.g., *Some A are B* and *Some B are C* leads to sixteen diagram pairs to amalgamate, each in several possible ways.

But we can enrich the graphical representation system with additional

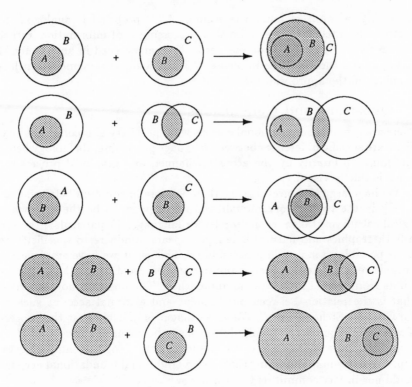

Figure 4 Registration

interpretative conventions. With the introduction of shading, to mean 'non-empty', there are unique 'characteristic' diagrams for each premiss, as in Figure 3. A novice reasoner will learn to choose the right diagram and to combine diagrams for two premises, making minimal assumptions.

Syllogism-solving then consists in unifying diagram pairs by 'registering' the B circles from each diagram (as shown in Figure 4). This then enables the subject to reason about the relevant cases in terms of movements of the C circle, relative to A. The graphics naturally focuses on the range of cases which must be considered.

We have indicated, then, how it is that a highly specific representation system can be given enough abstractive power to be a useful external tool in reasoning. We have also indicated that there is in place a theory of human working memory which explains the need to be able to compute with the smallest number of total determinate mappings from properties to objects. Hence, an implementational theory of graphical reasoning can be provided. We have done little more than sketch that theory here. But it is interesting to note that mental models notation has been put forward as a 'semantic processing' account of human reasoning. This proposal is analogous to Barwise and Etchemendy's claim that processing is of information, rather than of form. By contrast, on our account, what we need in an account of reasoning is a theory of the implementation of logic on a memory which is 'graphic', in the appropriate sense.

5   Questions and Conclusions

There are general computational reasons why specificity aids computability. There are specific differences between language processing, its biology being determined primarily by the acoustic channel, and graphical processing, which is chiefly visual.

We have argued, however, that there is more in common between processing in the two sensory modalities than appears to be the case when logical calculi are taken as the model for language. In particular, the use of both graphics and natural language appears to adhere to specificity as far as possible to maintain processibility. This is, as we have emphasized, a cognitive implementational account. Early on, we distinguished such accounts from formal foundational approaches. The question now emerges: what is the relation between our account and a formal account such as Barwise and Etchemendy's? We agree that it is unlikely that the process of reasoning requires the manipulation of symbols; and we agree that their formal account avoids commitment to such a view of cognitive implementation. We differ in maintaining that even a traditional foundational account would not in fact commit us to such a view.

References

Barwise, J., and J. Etchemendy. 1990a. Information, Infons, and Inference. In Cooper et al. 1990.

Barwise, J., and J. Etchemendy. 1990b. Visual Information and Valid Reasoning. In *Visualization in Mathematics*, ed. W. Zimmerman. Washington, DC: Mathematical Association of America.

Braine, M. D. S. 1978. On the Relationship Between the Natural Logic of Reasoning and Standard Logic. *Psychological Review* 85:1–21.

Clark, A. 1990. Connectionism, Competence, and Explanation. *British Journal of the Philosophy of Science* 41:195–222.

Cooper, R., K. Mukai, and J. Perry (ed.). 1990. *Situation Theory and Its Applications,* vol. 1. CSLI Lecture Notes Number 22. Stanford: CSLI Publications.

Dennett, D. C. 1987. *The Intentional Stance.* Cambridge, MA: MIT Press.

Fodor, J. A., T. G. Bever, and M. F. Garrett. 1974. *The Psychology of Language.* New York: McGraw Hill.

Foster, C. L. 1990. *Algorithms, Abstraction and Implementation: a Massively Multilevel Theory of Strong Equivalence of Complex Systems.* PhD thesis, University of Edinburgh.

Harman, G. 1986. *Change in View.* Cambridge: MIT Press.

Johnson-Laird, P. N. 1983. *Mental Models: Towards a Cognitive Science of Language, Inference, and Consciousness.* Cambridge, MA: Harvard University Press.

Mani, K., and P. N. Johnson-Laird. 1982. The Mental Representation of Spatial Descriptions. *Memory and Cognition* 10:81–87.

Marr, D. 1977. Artificial Intelligence - A Personal View. *Artificial Intelligence* 9:37–48.

Stenning, K. 1978. Anaphora as an Approach to Pragmatics. In *Linguistic Theory and Psychological Reality*, ed. M. Halle, J. Bresnan, and G. A. Miller. Cambridge, MA: MIT Press.

Stenning, K. 1986. On Making Models: A Study of Constructive Memory. In *Reasoning and Discourse Processes*, ed. T. Myers, K. Brown, and B. McGonigle, chapter 7, 165–185. London: Academic Press.

Stenning, K., and J. Levy. 1988. Knowledge-Rich Solutions to the Binding Problem: A Simulation of Some Human Computational Mechanisms. *Knowledge Based Systems* 1:143–152.

Stenning, K., and J. Oberlander. n.d. Logic and Implementation in a Cognitive Theory of Heterogeneous Reasoning. In preparation.

Stenning, K., M. Shepherd, and J. Levy. 1988. On the Construction of Representations for Individuals from Descriptions in Text. *Language and Cognitive Processes* 2:129–164.

Name Index

Aczel, P., 3–8, 16, 52–60, 67, 78,
   180, 230, 236
Alexander, J., 578
Allen, J., 478
Almeder, R., 117, 118
Alshawi, H., 470, 478, 495
Anderson, J. R., 559, 560
Appelt, D. E., 408, 437, 470
Ayer, A. J., 118

Baker, C. L., 372, 390
Bancilhon, F., 230
Barwise, J., 25, 32, 36, 69, 81, 82,
   89, 94–97, 99–102, 104, 105,
   115, 118, 129, 130, 132,
   133, 140–142, 162, 164, 181,
   192, 216, 219, 221, 223,
   231, 235, 247, 258, 295,
   296, 298, 300, 301, 303,
   311, 317, 332, 363–365, 368,
   409, 410, 434, 437, 471,
   534–537, 539, 556–558, 581,
   596, 607, 608
Belnap, N., 376
Berman, S., 376, 386, 388, 389
Bever, T. G., 610
Bolinger, D., 368
Braine, M. D. S., 611
Bresnan, J., 406
Bridgman, P. W., 121
Buneman, P., 230, 231, 237
Bunt, H., 471, 496
Burge, T., 162, 169
Burke, T., 128

Carter, D. M., 470
Castañeda, H.-N., 83, 440
Chellas, B. F., 141
Chen, W., 230
Chierchia, G., 327
Chomsky, N., 405, 534
Clark, A., 610
Clark, R., 393
Codd, E. F., 229
Cohen, P. J., 26
Cohen, P. R., 437
Comorowski, I., 368, 376, 389, 391,
   399
Cooper, R., 300, 307, 312, 314, 322–
   326, 329, 406, 415
Cooper, R. P., 323
Cormack, A., 470, 473
Crimmins, M., 364

Dalrymple, M., 511
Davidson, S., 230
Dennett, D. C., 610
Devlin, K. J., 25, 33, 41, 303, 366
Dewey, J., 118, 119, 126–128, 135
Dörre, J., 194, 250
Doyle, J., 421
Dretske, F., 154, 155, 284

Eberts, R., 563
Engdahl, E., 364, 370, 392–394, 398,
   399
Etchemendy, J., 32, 69, 115, 118,
   162, 164, 221, 223, 231,
   317, 409, 410, 581, 596,
   607, 608

Evans, G., 323, 339, 340, 347, 349–352, 357–360

Fainsilber, L., 449
Falkenhainer, B., 449
Fauconnier, G., 456
Fenstad, J. E., 312
Fernando, T., 55, 56, 65, 69
Fischer, P. C., 230
Fodor, J. A., 610
Foster, C. L., 610
Foulis, D., 135

Gaifman, H., 161, 162
Garret, M. F., 610
Gawron, J. M., 302–304, 312, 323, 335–363, 364–368, 392–396, 421, 495, 499, 510
Gazdar, G., 406
Geach, P., 348
Gentner, D., 449
Ginzburg, J., 372, 374, 386, 393, 399, 401
Givón, T., 535
Goguen, J. A., 233
Grinder, J., 337
Groenendijk, J. A., 364, 376, 386, 388, 392, 393, 399, 472
Grosz, B., 470
Gunji, T., 406, 427
Gödel, K., 164

Hale, S., 105
Halvorsen, P.-K., 218, 230, 312
Hamblin, C. L., 364, 382, 383
Hanks, S., 223, 225
Harman, G., 611
Hasida, K., 407, 415
Hayes, J. R., 561, 565
Hayes, P. J., 222, 224, 225
Haïk, I., 514
Heim, I., 327, 340, 343–348, 392, 491, 510
Hellan, L., 514, 516
Henry, R., 540
Higginbotham, J., 364, 399
Hintikka, J., 376
Hobbs, J., 408, 415, 420, 470, 474

Höhfeld, M., 231, 249, 251, 252
Holyoak, H. J., 449
Hurum, S., 470

Iida, M., 338, 353, 425, 430, 431
Indurkhya, B., 449, 466
Ishizaki, S., 407
Israel, D., 131, 147–149, 159
Iwayama, M., 449, 466

Jackendoff, R., 379, 426
Jaffar, J., 180, 181, 191, 249
James, W., 121, 559
Jespersen, O., 363
Johnson, M., 407, 449, 456, 457, 495
Johnson-Laird, P. N., 554, 558, 559, 611, 616
Jonides, J., 578

Kadmon, N., 327, 340, 342, 343, 346
Kaiser, M. K., 578
Kameyama, M., 425, 428, 431
Kamp, H., 311–313, 320, 324, 330, 345, 409, 472, 478, 481, 512
Kanazawa, M., 343
Kaplan, D., 129
Kaplan, R., 370
Karttunen, L., 364, 376, 382, 385, 386, 399, 512
Kasper, R., 238, 245
Katagiri, Y., 435
Keenan, E. L., 393
Keller, W. R., 415
Kempson, R., 470, 473
Khoshafian, S. N., 230
Kifer, M., 230
Kleene, S., 320
Klein, E., 406, 495, 512
Kotovsky, K., 561
Kratzer, A., 319, 320
Kripke, S. A., 99, 132, 136
Kuno, S., 425–428, 431, 435, 440, 445
Kurtzman, H. S., 494
Kyburg, H., 163

Ladusaw, W., 338, 353, 388

Lakoff, G., 449, 456, 457
Langholm, T., 312
Larkin, J. H., 561, 562
Lassez, J., 180, 191, 249
Lerner, J., 512
Levy, J., 616, 617
Lewis, D. K., 103, 105, 440
Link, G., 352, 360, 481, 533
Lloyd, J. W., 181
Lunnon, R., 4, 7–10, 52, 54, 60, 78

Maier, D., 230, 233
Mally, E., 83
Mani, K., 616
Marr, D., 610
Martin, P., 408, 470
Martin-Löf, P., 212
May, R., 364, 398, 399, 494
McCarthy, J., 222–225, 421
McCloskey, M., 578
McDermott, D., 216, 222–225, 421
McDonald, M. C., 494
Mendler, N., 16, 55, 67
Meseguer, J., 233
Michaylov, S., 181
Mithun, M., 540
Momoi, K., 445
Montague, R., 163, 509, 548
Moore, R. C., 470
Moran, D. B., 470
Moray, N., 559
Moschovakis, Y., 26
Moss, L. S., 181
Mukai, K., 183, 230, 249
Munsat, S., 386, 388

Nagel, T., 534
Nakashima, H., 218, 226, 230
Nariaki, F., 532
Neale, S., 327
Nerbonne, J., 338, 353, 510
Newell, A., 564
Noringa, M., 531
Nunberg, G., 449

Oberlander, J., 618
Ohori, A., 230, 249
Olin, D., 163

Olson, K., 535
Ortony, A., 449

Paige, R., 183, 209
Panevová, J., 411
Parsons, C., 162
Partee, B., 341, 471
Peirce, C. S., 115–144
Pelletier, F. J., 341, 345, 470, 472,
    478–480
Pereira, F., 470, 511
Perrault, C. R., 437
Perry, J., 25, 36, 82, 101–104, 115,
    129–131, 139, 147–149, 159,
    219, 258, 332, 363–365, 368,
    409, 434, 437, 471, 556
Peters, S., 218, 230, 302–304, 312,
    323, 335–341, 353–356, 363–
    368, 392–393, 396, 399, 421,
    495, 499, 510
Piaget, J., 535
Piron, C., 135
Plantinga, E., 449
Poesio, M., 480, 481
Pollard, C., 248, 303, 370, 406, 426
Postal, P., 337
Proffitt, D. R., 578
Pullum, G. K., 406
Putnam, H., 26, 27, 143, 534

Quine, W. V., 88, 117, 339, 384

Randall, C. H., 135
Rapaport, W., 83
Reinhart, R., 485
Reyle, U., 312, 313, 324, 330
Roberts, C., 480
Rooth, M., 345, 346, 379, 471, 479,
    491
Rosenschein, S., 258–265, 271, 273,
    276, 277, 282, 290–292
Ross, J. R., 378, 391
Rounds, W., 181, 194, 238, 245, 249,
    250
Russell, B., 117, 118, 144

Saarinen, E., 348
Sag, I., 248, 303, 370, 406, 426

Sapir, E., 535
Sasse, H.-J., 533, 535, 538–541, 546
Schatz, U., 512
Schmandt-Besserat, D., 37
Schneider, W., 560, 563
Schubert, L., 341, 345
Schubert, L. K., 470, 472, 478–480
Seligman, J., 132, 141, 258, 287,
    290, 291
Sells, P., 425, 430, 431
Sem, H. F., 312, 336
Sgall, P., 411
Shakespeare, W., 236
Shepherd, M., 616
Shieber, S., 234, 238, 415, 420, 470,
    511
Shiffrin, R., 560, 563
Shin, S. J., 585, 596–597, 603–604
Shoham, Y., 216, 222
Simon, H. A., 561, 562, 564, 565
Sirai, H., 407
Skorstad, J., 449
Smith, A. G., 470
Smolka, G., 231, 245, 249–252
Steen, L. A., 27
Stenning, K., 614, 616–618
Stickel, M., 408
Stokhof, M. J. B., 364, 376, 386,
    388, 392, 393, 399, 472
Stuckey, S., 184, 191
Suzuki, H., 218, 230, 415
Sæbø, K. J., 336

Tanaka, H., 449, 466, 519

Tarjan, R. E., 183, 209
Tarski, A., 122, 161, 162
Thayer, H. S., 117, 118, 126
Thomason, R. H., 163
Tokieda, M., 531
Tokunaga, T., 449, 466
Tutiya, S., 415

Ullman, S., 562

Van Benthem, J., 312
van Eijck, J., 478, 495
van Gucht, D., 230
Vendler, Z., 386
Venn, J., 581
Verne, G. B., 336
Vestre, E. J., 336
Vickers, S., 118

Warren, D., 230
Watters, A., 230
Webber, B. L., 349, 360, 470
Westerståhl, D., 51, 52, 78, 238, 322,
    373
Whorf, B. L., 533
Williams, J. G., 4
Winskel, G., 246
Wu, J., 230

Zaefferer, D., 538
Zaenen, A., 370
Zalta, E., 81, 83, 84, 86, 88, 92, 96,
    102, 110
Zucchi, S., 480, 481

Subject Index

Abduction, 407
absorption, 338, 348, 349, 500, 509
    principle, 304, 335–340, 350, 353–
        356, 393, 421, 502, 512
abstract, 349
    object, 25
    situation, 217
abstraction, 335, 336, 338, 349–351,
        360, 612, 613
abstractive
    logical languages, 608
    representation system, 613
acceptability, 477
accessibility
    conditions, 489
    of concepts, asymmetry in 438
action, 120, 133
actual
    situation, 95, 98
    world, 98–100
adjunction, 414
adnominal determinacy, 529
adverbial determinacy, 525
af, 10
agent awareness default, 438
algorithmic level, 610, 611
α-set, 233
α-bisimulation, 16, 21
α-equivalence, 16
anaphora, 336–338, 341, 343, 347,
        353, 389, 499, 504, 509,
        614
    E-type, 339–361
    Ñ, 338, 352, 353

parameter-reusing, 338
plural, 480
Q-type, 339, 353, 354, 356
anchoring, 342–344, 349, 360
    set, 485
answer, 377
anti-founded
    S-sorted universe, 67
    $\mathcal{U}, \lambda$-universe, 10
    universe, 7, 54
appears in, 184
appropriateness conditions, 304
arbitrary individual, 164, 165
architectural
    coincident content, 158
    connecting facts, 150
    connection, 158
    constraint, 150
    content, 148
    information, 157
    relations, 150
architecturally
    connected carrier, 150
    coordinated information, 154
    grounded relation, 150
    mediated information, 154
architectures
    coincident, 149, 151
    combinative, 149, 151, 153
    coordinated, 158
    flow, 149, 154, 158
areru, 526
argument role, 500
assertoric speech acts, 372

associated paths, 478
ASTR, 486
atom, 232
ATOM, 481
atomic formula, 407
attunement, 555–578
Austinian proposition, 166, 168, 537
automatic processing, 554, 557–560,
        563, 565–567, 577
automaton, situated, 265

B-bounded form system, 6
Bach-Peters structure, 513
background
        condition, 218, 285
        knowledge, 453
        situation, 30
belief, justifiability of 163
binding
        lemma, 193
        principle, 506, 516
bisimulation, 16, 21, 185
bound parameter, 11, 188
bounded quantification, 178
branch points, 82

C-command, 514
canonical
        clause, 188
        compactness theorem, 197
        support theorem, 198
causatives, 518, 524
Cayuga, 534, 538–548
        paradigm, 543
channel, 258, 277, 279
        activity, 277, 280, 284
        closure of sets of, 282
        conditional, 283, 286, 289
        conditions, 283
choice, 201
circular proposition, 168
circumstances, 502, 503
clause, 186, 407
        adnominal, 518
        adverbial, 518
closed class, 7
CLOSER$_{p\acute{o}v}$, 438

co-parametric analysis of pronouns,
        503, 505, 508
cognitive processes, 554, 577
coincident
        architectural content, 158
        architectures, 149, 151
coinductive
        definition, 231
        semantics, 203
collections, 409
combinative architecture, 149, 151,
        153
combinatorial complexity, 412
common sense, 454
communication system, 277
compact constraint language, 185
compatibility, 73
competence, 422
        theory, 609, 611
complementation, 414
completeness, 603
        satisfaction, 192
                theorem, 199
        theorem, 208
complex object, 230, 233
complexity
        combinatorial, 412
        derivational theory of, 610
components, 5
compositionality, 325, 326
computation, 259, 264, 607, 610, 612
        control, 421
        state, 201
        tree, 202
concept, 122, 123, 134, 135, 138
        of self, 434
        hierarchy, 454
conditional information, 148
conditions, 475
connective DRS, 488–9
consequence, 120
        logical, 595
constituency, 530
constituency-based grammar, 411
constraint, 100, 131–133, 139, 186,
        258, 299–300, 405, 451
        architectural, 150

compact, 185
definable, 181
isomorphism, 460
language, 185
logic programming, 231, 251
  scheme, 191
ordering, 478, 489
positive, 186
rules, 187
satisfaction, 617
structural, on perspectivity, 437
content, 502, 503
  descriptive, 30
context, 140
convergence, 152
coordinated architecture, 158
coreference rule for 'zibun', 439
correspond, 192
cost, 408
counterpart relation, 588
covering a role, 501

Davidsonian argument, 545
de, 521
de se reading, 440
deduction, 407
deductive representation system, 583
default interpretation, 419
defeating agent awareness default, 441
defined
  formula, 408
  predicate, 408
definition clauses, 408
dependency
  functions, 474
  grammars, 411
dependent parameter, 501, 502, 507, 509, 512
derivational theory of complexity, 610
described proposition, 437
descriptive content, 30
determinacy
  adnominal, 529
  adverbial, 525
diagram, 581
  unification, 599
  well-formed, 589

difference, 586
disambiguation
  information, 482
  schema, 496
discourse
  conventions, 608
  role for perspectivity, 432
  situation, 437
discrimination, 33
disjointness condition, 485, 489
DIST, 491
distancing, 481, 491
domain knowledge, 453
donkey
  pronoun, 323, 327
  sentence, 338, 339, 345, 347, 352, 508
double-pro-drop language, 539
DRS, discourse representation structure, 311–315, 317–319, 321, 322, 324–327, 330, 331, 475
  connective, 488-9
  quantifier, 488
  referential, 480, 489–490
DRT, discourse representation theory, 311, 312, 322, 323, 325–328, 330, 340, 345, 472, 475
DRT_0, 475, 488
DRT_1, 488
DSE, 490
dynamic bindings, 268, 271

E-type
  anaphora, 339–341, 343–350, 352–354, 356–361, 510
  pronoun, 323, 340–341
efficiency, 219
elementary universe, 3, 5, 53
elliptical VP, 336
embedding
  DRS-satsifying, 490
  functions, 476
  question, 386
empathy, 435
encoding, 83, 86, 92, 96, 105
entailment, 476
environment, 286

epistemic logic, 163
equivalent regions, 588
Euler circles, 608, 612, 618
exemplification, 83, 84, 86, 92, 105
extended prediction problem, 223
external property, 82, 83, 85, 98
extraction procedure, 492

Fact, 93, 137
factoring, 407
factual soa, 93
feature, 232, 407
    specification, 407
    structure, 247
field, 186
    of view, 289
file, 152
    labeled, 153
file change semantics, 323
finitary hyperset, 184
finite shape, 61
fixed point, 171, 177
floating quantifier, 416
flow
    architecture, 149, 154, 158
    information, 154–157, 257–258,
        279, 405
form system W, 56
formalism, 25, 26
formula, 475, 490
    atomic, 407
    defined, 408
    free, 408
    Σ_n, 41
foundational account of reasoning,
    607, 611, 620
frame
    of reference, 271
    problem, 216, 222
    theory, 222
free formula, 408
full algebra, 53

Game of life, 260
Γ-infon, 42
Γ-oracle, 42
general metaphor, 457

generalized quantifier, 323, 329, 330,
    538
generated universe, 8
German, 537
glider, 267, 270
graphical rules, 608
GROUP, 481

Habit, 120
Hamblin-set, 364, 385
head, 408
    category, 412
heuristics, 458
Holmesian proposition, 537
homogeneity, 263, 264, 266, 275
homomorphism, 582, 592
HPSG, 303, 307
human
    information processing, 554, 558–
        560, 563
    working memory, 611, 612, 616,
        619
Humboldt-Sapir-Whorf hypothesis, 534,
    538, 548
Hungarian, 539
hyperequation, solvable, 212
Hyperproof, 607–609, 612, 616
hyperterm, 211
hypothesis, 407

Identification, 608
implementation, 611
implementational account of reason-
    ing, 607, 611, 620
incremental information, 147, 157,
    517
indefinite NPs, 479
indefinites as variables, 313, 323, 326,
    327, 330, 332
index, 132–135, 489
    set, 9
indexical perspectivity, 426, 434
    priority of self, 438
    uniqueness, 438
individual, 120, 409
    arbitrary, 164, 165
individuation, 32, 33
    scheme, 115, 132, 137

inference
  about situations, 216
  in a situation, 216
  performance, 476
  rules, 476
  of DRT$_1$, 493
inferential perspectivity, 426, 436
infon, 27, 28, 42, 138, 257, 594
  algebra, 307, 317, 325, 596
  basic, 296, 298
  compound, 299
  conjunctive, 307
  disjunctive, 307
  negative, 307
  parametric, 364
  quantified, 298, 303
information, 131, 138, 257, 297, 306
  carried, 258, 261, 289
  channel, 258, 277, 279
  complete, 302, 305
  conditional, 148
  content, 258, 261, 264–266, 270,
    276
  flow, 154, 155, 157, 257, 258,
    279, 405
  incremental, 147, 157, 517
  locality of, 258
  reflexive, 148, 158
  system, 148
injective sum, 73
interaction theory of metaphor, 449
intermediate
  stages of computation, 406, 411
  structures, 405
internal property, 82, 83, 85, 86, 98
interpretation, 172, 174, 202
  minimal, 418
  of a token, 171
  of thought-tokens, 174
  preferences, 494
interpretative conventions, 616, 619
interrogative speech acts, 374
intersection, 586
intractability, 421
intuition, 554
investigation scheme, 122, 133–135
involvement, 277

is-a, 217
isomorphism of constraints, 460
issue, 296
  general, 134, 138
  set of, 42
  singular, 134, 138
Italian, 538

Japanese, 539
Japanese reflexive 'zibun', 425
justification, 607, 611
  of belief, 163

Korean, 539
kureru, 429

Labeled
  argument role, 500–501
  file, 153
λ-universe, 9
  pre-, 9
  well-founded, 10
large $(\mathcal{U}, X)$-soe, 22
liar paradox, 161, 178
life, game of, 261, 267, 270
literal, 186, 408
  defined, 408
  free, 408
location, 259, 271, 287
  dynamic aggregate, 261–267, 270–
    271
  by channel, 289
logic, 297, 306
  classical, 318
  LP, 481
  of relations, 87
  sentential, 583
  strong Kleene, 318
logical
  consequence, 595
  form, 470

Make-factual, 93
marker, 475
  introducers, 475
mathematical
  objects, 84, 92
  reasoning, 28

mathematics, 25
maximal
    representation, 604
    X_0-parametric extension, 9
metaphor, 449
    general, 457
    interaction theory of, 449
    understanding, 449
metonymy, 457
minimal
    interpretation, 418
    X_0-parametric extension, 9
missing
    antecedent, 337–339
    arguments, 432
mixed-founded S-sorted universe, 69
mode of presentation, 149, 153, 159
model, 166, 202, 616
modus ponens, 477
monotonicity
    downward, 308
    upward, 308
mother category, 406, 411, 412

Naive physics, 577, 578
name-like expressions, 368
natural deduction, 608, 611
natural language understanding systems, 517
necessity, 139
negation, 312, 313, 317–319, 321, 322, 326, 330, 479
    as failure, 209
    external, 307, 308
    Kleene, 323
ni, 525
non-parametric
    core, 3, 8
    object, 8
non-well-founded situation, 99
Nootka, 535
normal clause, 188
Norwegian, 503, 507
noun phrase, referential, 301
number, 37

Object, 134–139
    abstract, 349
    complex, 230, 233
    mathematical, 84, 92
    non-parametric, 8
    theory of, 81, 83, 91
    type, 306
object-intransitive paradigm, 542
occurrence, 8, 20
    bound, 20
    free, 20
Olson's choice, 535, 536, 538, 547, 548
ontology, 5, 6, 53
    S-sorted, 66
operation, 133
operationalism, 115, 120, 123
operator, 486
optional quantification, 412
oracle, 41, 42
$\mathrm{Oracle}_\Gamma(a)$, 42
ordering constraint, 478, 489

P$_A$, 486
pair-list reading, 393
paradigm, 538, 543
    Cayuga, 543
    object-intransitive, 542
    subject-intransitive, 542
parallel context, 452
parameter, 7, 9, 232, 335–342, 347–351, 355–360
    absorption, 335, 350
    anchoring, 360, 486
    bound, 11, 188
    dependence and absorption, 499
    dependent, 355, 501, 502, 507, 509, 512
    function for cA, 9
    map, 8
    pronoun, 341, 342, 348, 350
    restricted, 322, 335–336, 344, 355–358
    utilizing, 501
parametric
    infon, 364
    soa, 500
parsing, 518
    bottom-up, 517
part-of, 94, 217, 272, 296, 298, 308

partial-overlapping rule, 589
partiality, 117, 128
particle, 538, 543
partition refinement algorithm, 209
passive, 518, 524
    adversative, 526
path, 204
    associated to SF 493
performance, 422, 611
    of inference, 607
    theory, 610
persistence, 94, 130, 295–307, 313,
        319–322, 330
persistent soa, 95
perspectival
    relativity, 129, 132
    representation of the environ-
        ment, 432
perspective, 132–134, 258, 287, 290
    indexical, 135, 438
        priority of self, 438
    visual, 287
perspectivity, 425
    discourse role for, 432
    indexical 426, 434, 438
    inferential 426, 436
    sensitive expressions, 428
    structural constraints on, 437
phrase-structure, 406
physical world, 258
Platonism, 25, 26
plural, 347
    anaphora, 480
point of view, 276, 287
positive constraint, 186
possibility, 139
possible
    situation, 97, 174
    world, 96, 99, 103, 129, 140
potential energy, 406
pragmatic maxim, 121
pragmatics, 346, 358
preclusion, 283
predicate
    calculus, 312, 330
    defined, 408
presupport, 189

presuppositions of questions, 376
principle of integrity, 519, 521
priority of self as the indexical per-
        spective, 438
pro-drop language, 538, 539
    double, 539
procedures, 405
processing
    loads, 415
    order, 405
program, 200
    clause, 200
projection, 218, 481, 483, 501, 506,
        510, 516
    and persistence, 220
pronoun, 335–359
    binding, 304
    co-parametric 503, 505, 508
    donkey, 323, 327
    E-type, 323, 340–348
    parameter, 350
    role linking, 503, 505
property, 120, 123, 135, 137, 138
    external, 82–85, 98
    internal, 82–85, 86, 98
    soa, 85–86, 90–96
    uniqueness, 275, 279
proportion problem, 491
proposition, 30, 117, 129–130, 134,
        140, 173, 178, 295–297, 305–
        307, 519
    Austinian, 166, 168, 537
    circular, 168
    described, 437
    Holmesian, 537
PROSIT, 218

Q-type
    anaphora, 339, 353, 354, 356
QORG, 483
qualification problem, 222
quantification, 341–349, 356–359, 511
    bounded, 178
    expressions, 368
    into-wh, 364
    natural language, 296, 299–307
    optional, 412
quantified, 358

DRS, 480
    infon, 298, 303
    soa, 418
quantifier, 338, 339, 345, 353, 355
    DRS, 488–490
    floating, 416
    generalized, 323, 329, 330, 538
    scope, 336, 410
    storage, 406, 415
quantity, 410
queried type, 379
question
    embedding, type of, 386
    presuppositions of, 376
    wh-, 363

Range of significance, 165
RAOQ, 482
realism, 122, 127
reasoning
    foundational account of, 607, 611, 620
    implementational account, 607, 611, 620
    mathematical, 28
    graphical, 553, 581, 607
records, 409
referential DRS, 480, 489, 490
reflexive information, 148, 158
region, 586
    basic, 586
    equivalent, 588
    minimal, 586
relation, 88–90, 101, 120, 123, 135, 137, 138
    complex, 297
relational
    reading, 393
    semantic framework, 471
    theory of meaning, 437
representation, 257
    maximal, 604
    system, 583
        deductive, 583
        visual, 586
    theorem, 53
representative ontology for the universe cA, 6

resource situation, 301–303, 305, 325, 326, 329, 330, 450, 453
restriction, 421
right branching grammar, 530, 531
robotics, 258, 259, 264, 290
role, 410, 500
    covering, 501
    discourse, for perspectivity, 432
    labeled, 500–501
    linking, 503, 507, 508, 516
        analysis of pronouns, 503, 505
ROR, 482
rule of inference, 476

S-sorted
    ontology, 66
    universe, 66
        anti-founded, 67
        mixed-founded, 69
        well-founded, 67
    X-form system, 66
SAE language, 533, 534
satisfaction completeness, 180, 192
    theorem, 199
saturated soa, 500
scope forest, 477, 489, 492
sentential logic, 583
set of issues, 42
SFE, 483
shape, 60
Σ_n formula, 41
Σ_n-skolem hull, 41
sign, 124, 125
signal structure, 148
similarity, 458
simile, 457
simulation, 207, 236
sinu, 526
situation, 25, 28, 31, 92, 94, 96, 129, 134, 140, 257, 271, 409
    absolute, 296, 301
    actual, 95, 98, 273, 280
    and numbers, 25
    C-closed, 281, 284
    C-coherent, 283
    closure conditions, 301, 307
    condition, 276, 281, 288
    described, 300–302, 304

dynamic, 273
external characterization, 298
identity of, 273
indistinguishability of, 274, 275,
    278, 288
internal characterization, 298
invariant, 274, 279, 286
non-well-founded, 99
physical, 257, 287
possible, 97, 174, 273
relative, 296, 301
resource, 301–303, 305, 325, 326,
    329, 450, 453
semantics, 311–314, 317–319, 325,
    330, 409
state, 275
static, 273
theory, 29, 71, 81, 92, 101, 257,
    312–314, 321–324, 409, 582
type, 275, 276, 288
    background, 285
sloppy
    ambiguity, 503
    reading, 507, 511, 514
soa (state of affairs), 86, 87, 89, 90,
    105, 409, 434, 500, 519
    conditioning, 519
    factual, 93
    parametric, 500, 519
    persistent, 95
    property, 85–86, 90–96
    quantified, 418
    saturated, 500
    unsaturated, 500, 503
soe, 6, 10
solution, 6, 54, 187, 203
    compact structure, 180, 191
    compactness theorem, 198
    lemma, 184, 235
    of an soe, 10
    to induced conjunctive type, 521
    tree, 204
solvable hyperequation, 212
soundness, 477, 602
    theorem, 208
source domain, 449
space, physical, 262, 263

Spanish, 537, 538
spatial invariant, 263, 274
speaker priority requirement, 429
specificity, 607, 608, 613, 615–617,
    620
srd, 55
    uniform, 57
standard average European language,
    533
standard substitution, 7
state, 259, 270
    distribution, 262
    for aggregates, 263
    of affairs, see infon, soa
stream, 204
strict
    ambiguity, 503
    reading, 514
structural constraints on perspectiv-
    ity, 437
structural determination, 295, 296,
    299–301, 303–305, 307
subcat, 406, 414
subcat feature principle, 414
subject binding rule for 'zibun', 427
subject-intransitive paradigm, 542
subsequent, 377
substitution, 7
    lemma, 184
    operation, 7
    standard, 7
subsumption, 186, 237, 238
    problem, 194
subuniverse, 7
success conditions, 158
support, 7, 189
surprise quiz paradox, 163
syllogism, 582, 612, 617
syntactic dependence, 412
system, 185
    of equations (soe), 6, 184
    X-form, 5

Table, 613, 614
target domain, 449
τ-set, 233
te–ni–o–wa, 530
temporal

behavior, 265–266, 270
  invariant, 266, 274
theory of objects, 81, 83, 91
θ-criterion, 415
thought-token, 167, 169
threads running through beads, 532
time, 259, 287
  behavior over, 265, 266, 270
  period, 265, 270, 271
token, 584, 585
Toposa, 535
Tower of Hanoi, 564–568, 570, 573, 579
transferability, 432
transformation
  intermediate structures, 405
  rule, 597
transformational linguistics, 405
transition, 201
transitive class, 7
truth, 115, 142, 143, 297, 476
  table, 613
type, 231, 297, 308, 335, 336, 341, 342, 409, 500, 512, 519
  complex, 297
  extensional, 308
  hierarchy, 454
  infon based, 297, 307
  object, 306
  of embedding questions, 386
  parametric, 335
  queried, 379
  situation, 275, 276, 288, 297, 298, 306, 307
  supports, 297

U, λ-universe, 10
U-system of equations, 6, 54
U-universe, 6, 53
U-X-form system, 6
(U, X)-system of equations, 10
unification, 212, 234, 407
  diagrams, 599
  over hyperterms, 211
  theorem, 192
uniform srd, 57
union, 586
unique name, 612, 613

uniqueness
  of the indexical perspective, 438
  property, 275, 279
universe, 5
  anti-founded, 7, 54, 67
  elementary, 3, 5, 53
  generated, 8
  map, 73
  mixed-founded, 69
  representative ontology for, 6
  S-sorted, 66
  well-founded, 6, 10, 67
  with parameters, 3, 8
unsaturated soa, 500, 503

Vagueness, 473
variables, indefinites as, 313, 323, 326, 327, 330, 332
Venn diagram, 581, 608, 612
visual representation, 586
VP ellipsis, 338–339, 351, 354, 510–511

Waka, 531
Wakasha family, 535
watasi, 429
way, 129, 134, 139
weak universal instantiation, 485
well-formed diagram (wfd), 589
well-founded
  λ-universe, 10
  S-sorted universe, 67
  universe, 6, 54
  with respect to restricted components, 69
wf, 6, 10
wh-movement, 369
wh-question, 363
word order, 414
working memory, 608, 611, 616
world, 97, 259, 273
  actual, 98–100, 280
  condition, 258, 260, 266, 276, 281
  physical, 258
  possible, 96, 99, 103, 129, 140, 258, 273, 280
  system, 260, 271

theory, 97, 100
WUI (weak universal instantiation),
485

X_0-parametric extension
maximal, 9

minimal, 9
of cA_0, 9
X_0-generated extension of A_0, 9
X-form system, 5, 53
Xerox principle, 154, 157

CSLI Publications

Lecture Notes

The titles in this series are distributed by the University of Chicago Press and may be purchased in academic or university bookstores or ordered directly from the distributor at 5801 Ellis Avenue, Chicago, Illinois 60637.

A Manual of Intensional Logic Johan van Benthem, second edition, revised and expanded. Lecture Notes No. 1. ISBN 0-937073-29-6 (paper), 0-937073-30-X (cloth)

Emotion and Focus Helen Fay Nissenbaum. Lecture Notes No. 2. ISBN 0-937073-20-2 (paper)

Lectures on Contemporary Syntactic Theories Peter Sells. Lecture Notes No. 3. ISBN 0-937073-14-8 (paper), 0-937073-13-X (cloth)

An Introduction to Unification-Based Approaches to Grammar Stuart M. Shieber. Lecture Notes No. 4. ISBN 0-937073-00-8 (paper), 0-937073-01-6 (cloth)

The Semantics of Destructive Lisp Ian A. Mason. Lecture Notes No. 5. ISBN 0-937073-06-7 (paper), 0-937073-05-9 (cloth)

An Essay on Facts Ken Olson. Lecture Notes No. 6. ISBN 0-937073-08-3 (paper), 0-937073-05-9 (cloth)

Logics of Time and Computation Robert Goldblatt. Lecture Notes No. 7. ISBN 0-937073-12-1 (paper), 0-937073-11-3 (cloth)

Word Order and Constituent Structure in German Hans Uszkoreit. Lecture Notes No. 8. ISBN 0-937073-10=5 (paper), 0-937073-09-1 (cloth)

Color and Color Perception: A Study in Anthropocentric Realism David Russel Hilbert. Lecture Notes No. 9. ISBN 0-937073-16-4 (paper), 0-937073-15-6 (cloth)

Prolog and Natural-Language Analysis Fernando C. N. Pereira and Stuart M. Shieber. Lecture Notes No. 10. ISBN 0-937073-18-0 (paper), 0-937073-17-2 (cloth)

Working Papers in Grammatical Theory and Discourse Structure: Interactions of Morphology, Syntax, and Discourse M. Iida, S. Wechsler, and D. Zec (Eds.) with an Introduction by Joan Bresnan. Lecture Notes No. 11. ISBN 0-937073-04-0 (paper), 0-937073-25-3 (cloth)

Natural Language Processing in the 1980s: A Bibliography Gerald Gazdar, Alex Franz, Karen Osborne, and Roger Evans. Lecture Notes No. 12. ISBN 0-937073-28-8 (paper), 0-937073-26-1 (cloth)

Information-Based Syntax and Semantics Carl Pollard and Ivan Sag. Lecture Notes No. 13. ISBN 0-937073-24-5 (paper), 0-937073-23-7 (cloth)

Non-Well-Founded Sets Peter Aczel. Lecture Notes No. 14. ISBN 0-937073-22-9 (paper), 0-937073-21-0 (cloth)

Partiality, Truth and Persistence Tore Langholm. Lecture Notes No. 15. ISBN 0-937073-34-2 (paper), 0-937073-35-0 (cloth)

Attribute-Value Logic and the Theory of Grammar Mark Johnson. Lecture Notes No. 16. ISBN 0-937073-36-9 (paper), 0-937073-37-7 (cloth)

The Situation in Logic Jon Barwise. Lecture Notes No. 17. ISBN 0-937073-32-6 (paper), 0-937073-33-4 (cloth)

The Linguistics of Punctuation Geoff Nunberg. Lecture Notes No. 18. ISBN 0-937073-46-6 (paper), 0-937073-47-4 (cloth)

Anaphora and Quantification in Situation Semantics Jean Mark Gawron and Stanley Peters. Lecture Notes No. 19. ISBN 0-937073-48-4 (paper), 0-937073-49-0 (cloth)

Propositional Attitudes: The Role of Content in Logic, Language, and Mind C. Anthony Anderson and Joseph Owens. Lecture Notes No. 20. ISBN 0-937073-50-4 (paper), 0-937073-51-2 (cloth)

Literature and Cognition Jerry R. Hobbs. Lecture Notes No. 21. ISBN 0-937073-52-0 (paper), 0-937073-53-9 (cloth)

Situation Theory and Its Applications, vol. 1 Robin Cooper, Kuniaki Mukai, and John Perry (Eds.). Lecture Notes No. 22. ISBN 0-937073-54-7 (paper), 0-937073-55-5 (cloth)

The Language of First-Order Logic (including the Macintosh program, Tarski's World) Jon Barwise and John Etchemendy. Lecture Notes No. 23. ISBN 0-937073-58-X (paper)

Tarski's World Jon Barwise and John Etchemendy. Lecture Notes No. 25. ISBN 0-937073-67-9 (paper)

Other CSLI Titles Distributed by UCP

Agreement in Natural Language: Approaches, Theories, Descriptions Michael Barlow and Charles A. Ferguson (Eds.) ISBN 0-937073-02-4 (cloth)

Papers from the Second International Workshop on Japanese Syntax William J. Poser (Ed.) ISBN 0-937073-38-5 (paper), 0-937073-39-3 (cloth)

The Proceedings of the Seventh West Coast Conference on Formal Linguistics (WCCFL 7) ISBN 0-937073-40-7 (paper)

The Proceedings of the Eighth West Coast Conference on Formal Linguistics (WCCFL 8) ISBN 0-937073-45-8 (paper)

The Phonology-Syntax Connection Sharon Inkelas and Draga Zec (Eds.) (co-published with The University of Chicago Press) ISBN 0-226-38100-5 (paper), 0-226-38101-3 (cloth)

The Proceedings of the Ninth West Coast Conference on Formal Linguistics (WCCFL 9) ISBN 0-937073-64-4 (paper)

Japanese/Korean Linguistics Hajime Hoji (Ed.) ISBN 0-937073-57-1 (paper), 0-937073-56-3 (cloth)

Experiencer Subjects in South Asian Languages Manindra K. Verma and K. P. Mohanan (Eds.) ISBN 0-937073-60-1 (paper), 0-937073-61-X (cloth)

Grammatical Relations: A Cross-Theoretical Perspective Katarzyna Dziwirek, Patrick Farrell, Errapel Mejías Bikandi (Eds.) ISBN 0-937073-63-6 (paper), 0-937073-62-8 (cloth)

Books Distributed by CSLI

The Proceedings of the Third West Coast Conference on Formal Linguistics (WCCFL 3) ($10.95) ISBN 0-937073-45-8 (paper)

The Proceedings of the Fourth West Coast Conference on Formal Linguistics (WCCFL 4) ($11.95) ISBN 0-937073-45-8 (paper)

The Proceedings of the Fifth West Coast Conference on Formal Linguistics (WCCFL 5) ($10.95) ISBN 0-937073-45-8 (paper)

The Proceedings of the Sixth West Coast Conference on Formal Linguistics (WCCFL 6) ($13.95) ISBN 0-937073-45-8 (paper)

Hausar Yau Da Kullum: Intermediate and Advanced Lessons in Hausa Language and Culture William R. Leben, Ahmadu Bello Zaria, Shekarau B. Maikafi, and Lawan Danladi Yalwa ($19.95) ISBN 0-937073-68-7 (paper)

Hausar Da Kullum Workbook William R. Leben, Ahmadu Bello Zaria, Shekarau B. Maikafi, and Lawan Danladi Yalwa ($7.50) ISBN 0-93703-69-5 (paper)

Ordering Titles Distributed by CSLI

Titles distributed by CSLI may be ordered directly from CSLI Publications, Ventura Hall, Stanford University, Stanford, California 94305-4115 or by phone (415)723-1712 or (415)723-1839. Orders can also be placed by e-mail (pubs@csli.stanford.edu) or FAX (415)723-0758.

All orders must be prepaid by check, VISA, or MasterCard (include card name, number, expiration date). For shipping and handling add $2.50 for first book and $0.75 for each addi-tional book; $1.75 for the first report and $0.25 for each additional report. California residents add 7% sales tax.

For overseas shipping, add $4.50 for first book and $2.25 for each additional book; $2.25 for first report and $0.75 for each additional report. All payments must be made in US currency.